THE OXFORD HISTORY OF PROTESTANT DISSENTING TRADITIONS
VOLUME II

THE OXFORD HISTORY OF PROTESTANT DISSENTING TRADITIONS

General Editors:
Timothy Larsen and Mark A. Noll

The Oxford History of Protestant Dissenting Traditions, Volume I
The Post-Reformation Era, c.1559–c.1689
Edited by John Coffey

The Oxford History of Protestant Dissenting Traditions, Volume II
The Long Eighteenth Century, c.1689–c.1828
Edited by Andrew C. Thompson

The Oxford History of Protestant Dissenting Traditions, Volume III
The Nineteenth Century
Edited by Timothy Larsen and Michael Ledger-Lomas

The Oxford History of Protestant Dissenting Traditions, Volume IV
The Twentieth Century: Traditions in a Global Context
Edited by Jehu J. Hanciles

The Oxford History of Protestant Dissenting Traditions, Volume V
The Twentieth Century: Themes and Variations in a Global Context
Edited by Mark A. Hutchinson

The Oxford History of Protestant Dissenting Traditions
Volume II

The Long Eighteenth Century, c.1689–c.1828

Edited By
ANDREW C. THOMPSON

Great Clarendon Street, Oxford, OX2 6DP,
United Kingdom

Oxford University Press is a department of the University of Oxford.
It furthers the University's objective of excellence in research, scholarship,
and education by publishing worldwide. Oxford is a registered trade mark of
Oxford University Press in the UK and in certain other countries

© Oxford University Press 2018

The moral rights of the authors have been asserted

First Edition published in 2018

Impression: 1

All rights reserved. No part of this publication may be reproduced, stored in
a retrieval system, or transmitted, in any form or by any means, without the
prior permission in writing of Oxford University Press, or as expressly permitted
by law, by licence or under terms agreed with the appropriate reprographics
rights organization. Enquiries concerning reproduction outside the scope of the
above should be sent to the Rights Department, Oxford University Press, at the
address above

You must not circulate this work in any other form
and you must impose this same condition on any acquirer

Published in the United States of America by Oxford University Press
198 Madison Avenue, New York, NY 10016, United States of America

British Library Cataloguing in Publication Data

Data available

Library of Congress Control Number: 2017964309

ISBN 978-0-19-870224-5

Printed and bound by
CPI Group (UK) Ltd, Croydon, CR0 4YY

Links to third party websites are provided by Oxford in good faith and
for information only. Oxford disclaims any responsibility for the materials
contained in any third party website referenced in this work.

Acknowledgements

I am grateful to Tim Larsen and Mark Noll for the original invitation to edit this volume. Both provided wise advice at the initial stages of shaping what this volume, and the series as a whole, would look like. The editors of the other volumes in the series have also provided support and guidance, as well as encouragement, along the way. All of the contributors have displayed both patience and generosity of spirit with the uneven pace of progress that inevitably accompanies a volume of this kind. At OUP, Tom Perridge and Karen Raith have eased considerably the process of editing. The volume as a whole has benefitted considerably from the care and attention it has received from Brian North and Saranya Jayakumar and the team at SPi Global. David Wykes from Dr Williams's Library has followed the progress of the project with interest and helped with providing some of the illustrations. Many of the contributors to this volume owe much, both directly and indirectly, to DWL. Kristen McDonald from the Lewis Walpole Library provided images with almost unbelievable speed and efficiency and reminded me what a scholarly treasure that institution is. Closer to home, my research students Nicholas Dixon and Dan Waterfield continue to help me think about eighteenth-century religious history, and Margaret Thompson has provided archival advice and pamphlet suggestions, whilst also casting a critical eye over my prose.

Andrew C. Thompson

Cambridge
November 2017

Contents

List of Figures	ix
List of Contributors	xi
Series Introduction by Timothy Larsen and Mark A. Noll	xv
Introduction *Andrew C. Thompson*	1

PART I: TRADITIONS WITHIN ENGLAND

1. Presbyterians *Alasdair Raffe*	11
2. Congregationalists *Stephen Orchard*	30
3. Baptists *Karen E. Smith*	54
4. Quakers *Richard C. Allen*	77
5. Methodists *Richard P. Heitzenrater*	99

PART II: TRADITIONS OUTSIDE ENGLAND

6. Protestant Dissent in Ireland *Andrew R. Holmes*	119
7. Protestant Dissent in Scotland *Stewart J. Brown*	139
8. Protestant Dissent in Wales *Eryn White*	160
9. Dissent in the American Colonies before the First Amendment *Catherine A. Brekus*	183
10. Dissent in the Atlantic World, 1787–1830 *Katherine Carté Engel*	200

PART III: AWAKENING

11. Revival — Michael J. McClymond … 225
12. Missionary Societies — Brian Stanley … 243

PART IV: CONTEXT

13. Toleration, Dissent, and the State in Britain — Andrew C. Thompson … 263
14. Abolitionism and the Social Conscience — G. M. Ditchfield … 284

PART V: CONGREGATIONS AND LIVING

15. Theology and the Bible — David M. Thompson … 305
16. Sermons — Françoise Deconinck-Brossard … 332
17. Dissenting Hymnody — J. R. Watson … 358
18. Dissent and Education — Mark Burden … 386
19. The Material Culture of Dissent: Meeting Houses, Chapels, and Churches in England and America, 1600–1830 — Carl Lounsbury … 411
20. Dissenting Print Culture — Tessa Whitehouse … 438

Index … 457

List of Figures

16.1 'The Substance of Several Sermons Preached By ye Revd Robt Bragg^<e> Minister of ye Gospel In Lime-Street London'.
© Trustees of Dr Williams's Library, London. 353

17.1 'The Sleeping Congregation' (1736) William Hogarth.
Courtesy of the Lewis Walpole Library, Yale University. 361

17.2 'Credulity, Superstition and Fanaticism' (1762) William Hogarth.
Courtesy of the Lewis Walpole Library, Yale University. 376

19.1 Rocky Hill meeting house, Amesbury, Massachusetts, 1785: exterior.
© Carl Lounsbury. 420

19.2 Rocky Hill meeting house, Amesbury, Massachusetts, 1785: plan.
© Carl Lounsbury. 420

19.3 Annesley's meeting house, Little St Helen's, Bishopsgate Street, London, 1672.
© Carl Lounsbury. 422

19.4 Stepney meeting house, London, 1674.
© Trustees of Dr Williams's Library, London. 423

19.5 Presbyterian meeting house, Bury St Edmunds, Suffolk, 1711: exterior.
© Carl Lounsbury. 424

19.6 Presbyterian meeting house, Bury St Edmunds, Suffolk, 1711: plan.
© Carl Lounsbury. 425

19.7 Presbyterian meeting house, Bury St Edmunds, Suffolk, 1711: pulpit.
© Carl Lounsbury. 426

19.8 Rocky Spring Presbyterian meeting house, Franklin Co., Pennsylvania, 1794: plan.
© Carl Lounsbury. 432

19.9 Buckingham Friends meeting house, Buckingham Co., Pennsylvania, 1768: exterior.
© Carl Lounsbury. 433

19.10 Buckingham Friends meeting house, Buckingham Co., Pennsylvania, 1768: plan.
© Carl Lounsbury. 434

19.11 George's Presbyterian meeting house, Exeter, Devon, 1760.
© Carl Lounsbury. 435

List of Contributors

Richard C. Allen is a Visiting Fellow in History at Newcastle University and former Reader in Early Modern Cultural History at the University of South Wales. He has published widely, particularly on migration and identity. His major publications include *Quaker Communities in Early Modern Wales: From Resistance to Respectability* (2007); and three co-edited volumes: (with Stephen Regan) *Irelands of the Mind: Memory and Identity in Modern Irish Culture* (2008), (with Joan Allen) *Faith of our Fathers: Popular Culture and Belief in Post-Reformation England, Ireland and Wales* (2009); and (with David Ceri Jones), *The Religious History of Wales: A Survey of Religious Life and Practice from the Seventeenth Century to the Present Day* (2014). He has recently completed (with Rosemary Moore and specialist contributors) *The Quakers, 1656–1723: The Evolution of an Alternative Community* (2018).

Catherine A. Brekus is Charles Warren Professor of the History of Religion in America at Harvard Divinity School. Her publications include *Strangers and Pilgrims: Female Preaching in America, 1740–1845* (1998); *Sarah Osborn's World: The Rise of Evangelicalism in Early America* (2013); and three edited volumes: *The Religious History of American Women: Reimagining the Past* (2007); (with W. Clark Gilpin) *American Christianities: A History of Dominance and Diversity* (2011) and *Sarah Osborn's Collected Writings* (2017).

Stewart J. Brown is Professor of Ecclesiastical History at the University of Edinburgh. His publications include *Thomas Chalmers and the Godly Commonwealth in Scotland* (1982); (with Timothy Tackett) *The Cambridge History of Christianity, Vol. VII: Enlightenment, Reawakening and Revolution, 1660–1815* (2006), and *Providence and Empire: Religion, Politics and Society in the United Kingdom, 1815–1914* (2008).

Mark Burden is Postdoctoral Research Associate on the Cambridge Platonists Project at the University of Bristol. His publications include *A Biographical Dictionary of Tutors at the Dissenters' Private Academies* (2013) and articles on the Puritan poet Lucy Hutchinson, the Episcopalian historian John Walker, and seventeenth-century church books.

Françoise Deconinck-Brossard is Emeritus Professor of eighteenth-century British studies at the Université Paris Nanterre, France. Since the publication of *Vie politique, sociale et religieuse d'après les sermons prêchés ou publiés dans le Nord de l'Angleterre, 1738–1760*, 2 vols. (1984), she has written extensively about eighteenth-century English sermons and hymns. She is preparing a critical edition of *The Sermons of John Sharp 1723–1792* (Boydell & Brewer for the Church of England Record Society).

G. M. Ditchfield is Emeritus Professor of History at the University of Kent. He is author of *George III. An Essay in Monarchy* (2002), together with many journal articles and contributed chapters on the religious and political history of eighteenth-century Britain. His edition of *The Letters of Theophilus Lindsey* was published in two volumes by the Church of England Record Society 2007–12. Among his current projects is an edition of the correspondence of Francis Blackburne (1705–87), archdeacon of Cleveland and ecclesiastical controversialist.

Katherine Carté Engel is Associate Professor of History at Southern Methodist University. She researches and teaches about religion in the eighteenth-century Atlantic world. Her publications include *Religion and Profit: Moravians in Early America* (2009), as well as numerous articles on early American religion. She is currently working on the impact of the American Revolution on the transnational Protestant community.

Richard P. Heitzenrater is William Kellon Quick Professor Emeritus of Church History and Wesley Studies at The Divinity School of Duke University. He has spoken and published widely in the area of Wesley studies, having been General Editor of the Wesley Works Editorial Project for twenty-five years. His most recent book is *An Exact Likeness: The Portraits of John Wesley* (2016).

Andrew R. Holmes is Lecturer in Modern Irish History at Queen's University, Belfast. He has published extensively on the history of Presbyterianism in Ireland, including *The Shaping of Ulster Presbyterian Belief and Practice, 1770–1840* (2006); (with Robert Armstrong, R. Scott Spurlock, and Patrick Walsh) *Presbyterian History in Ireland: Two Seventeenth-Century Narratives by Patrick Adair and Andrew Stewart* (2016) and *The Irish Presbyterian Mind 1830–1930* (forthcoming).

Carl Lounsbury is Adjunct Associate Professor of History at the College of William and Mary and retired Senior Architectural Historian at the Colonial Williamsburg Foundation. Among his publications are *An Illustrated Glossary of Early Southern Architecture and Landscape* (1994); *The Courthouses of Early Virginia* (2005); *Essays in Early American Architectural History* (2011); and (with Cary Carson) *The Chesapeake House* (2013). He has written extensively on British and early American churches and meeting houses.

Michael J. McClymond is Professor of Modern Christianity at Saint Louis University. Previously he held appointments at Wheaton College, Westmont College, the University of California–San Diego, Emory University, Yale University, and the University of Birmingham (UK). He edited the *Encyclopedia of*

Religious Revivals in America, 2 vols. (2007); co-authored (with Gerald R. McDermott) *The Theology of Jonathan Edwards* (2012); co-edited (with Lamin Sanneh) the *Wiley-Blackwell Companion to World Christianity* (2016); and authored *The Devil's Redemption: A New History and Interpretation of Christian Universalism*, 2 vols. (2018). He served as Co-Chair of the Evangelical Studies Group and the Pentecostal-Charismatic Movements Group in the American Academy of Religion (AAR).

Stephen Orchard is the former Principal of Westminster College, Cambridge and was President of the Cambridge Theological Federation. His recent publications include *The Sunday School Movement* (2007), co-edited with John Briggs and contributor; and *Nonconformity in Derbyshire* (2009). He has also contributed to *Religion and Change in Modern Britain* (2012), edited by Linda Woodhead and Rebecca Catto; and *The T&T Clark Companion to Nonconformity* (2013), edited by Robert Pope. He is a regular contributor to the *Journal of the United Reformed Church History Society* and has lectured for Gresham College.

Alasdair Raffe is a Chancellor's Fellow in History at the University of Edinburgh. His publications include *The Culture of Controversy: Religious Arguments in Scotland, 1660–1714* (2012) and *Scotland in Revolution, 1685–1690* (2018).

Karen E. Smith is a Tutor in Church History and Christian Spirituality at South Wales Baptist College, Cardiff and an Honorary Lecturer at Cardiff University. She teaches and writes in the area of Baptist History and Spirituality, with a special interest in the contribution of women. She is co-editor of the *Baptist Quarterly*, the Journal of the British Baptist Historical Society.

Brian Stanley is Professor of World Christianity at the University of Edinburgh. He has published widely on the history of the Protestant missionary movement. His latest book is *Christianity in the Twentieth Century: A World History* (2018).

Andrew C. Thompson is an Official Fellow and Senior College Lecturer in History at Queens' College, Cambridge. His publications include *Britain, Hanover, and the Protestant Interest 1688–1756* (2006) and *George II: King and Elector* (2011) as well as a number of articles on eighteenth-century religion, politics, and diplomacy.

David M. Thompson is Emeritus Professor of Modern Church History at the University of Cambridge, and a Life Fellow of Fitzwilliam College. His publications include *Nonconformity in the Nineteenth Century* (1972; 2nd edn 2016), *Cambridge Theology in the Nineteenth Century* (2008), and many articles on Nonconformity since 1662.

J. R. (John Richard) Watson is Emeritus Professor of English at the University of Durham. He is the author of books and articles on the Romantic and Victorian periods, and of *The English Hymn* (1997) and *An Annotated Anthology of Hymns* (2002). *Awake My Soul: Reflections on Thirty Hymns* appeared in 2005. He is a Life Vice-President of the Hymn Society of Great Britain and Ireland, a Fellow of the Royal School of Church Music, and a Fellow of the Hymn Society in the United States and Canada. He is currently co-editor of an ongoing project to replace John Julian's *A Dictionary of Hymnology* (1892, 1907), published online in 2013.

Eryn White is a Reader in History at the University of Aberystwyth. She has broad interests in the history of religion, culture, and society in early modern Wales and has published extensively on eighteenth-century Wales, print culture, and the history of early Welsh Nonconformity. Her publications include *The Welsh Bible* (2007) and (with David C. Jones and Boyd S. Schlenther) *The Elect Methodists* (2012).

Tessa Whitehouse is Senior Lecturer in Eighteenth-Century Literature at Queen Mary University of London. Her publications include *The Textual Culture of English Protestant Dissent 1720–1800* (2015) and articles about various aspects of religious publishing and manuscript culture in the eighteenth century.

Series Introduction

Timothy Larsen and Mark A. Noll

There is something distinctive, if not strange, about how Christianity has been expressed and embodied in English churches and traditions from the Reformation era onwards. Things developed differently elsewhere in Europe. Some European countries such as Spain and Italy remained Roman Catholic. The countries or regions that became Protestant chose between two exportable and replicable possibilities for a state church—Lutheran or Reformed. Denmark and Sweden, for example, both became Lutheran, while the Dutch Republic and Scotland became Reformed. The Peace of Westphalia (1648) established the right of sovereigns to choose a state church for their territories among those three options: Roman Catholic, Lutheran, or Calvinist. A variety of states adopted a 'multi-confessional' policy, allowing different faiths to coexist side-by-side. The most important alternative expression of Protestantism on the Continent was one that rejected state churches in principle: Anabaptists.

England was powerfully influenced by the Continental Reformers, but both the course and outcome of its Reformation were idiosyncratic. The initial break with Rome was provoked by Henry VIII's marital problems; the king rejected the Reformation doctrine of justification by faith and retained the Latin mass, but swept away monasteries and shrines, promoted the vernacular Scriptures, and had himself proclaimed Supreme Head of the Church of England. Each of his three children (by three different wives) was to pull the church in sharply different directions. The boy king Edward VI, guided by Archbishop Cranmer and Continental theologians like Martin Bucer and Peter Martyr Vermigli, set it on a firmly Reformed trajectory, notably through Cranmer's second Prayer Book (1552) and the Forty-Two Articles (1553). Mary I reunited England with Rome, instigating both a Catholic reformation and a repression of Protestants that resulted in almost three hundred executions. Finally, Elizabeth I restored the Edwardian settlement (with minor revisions), while sternly opposing moves for further reformation of the kind favoured by some of her bishops who had spent the 1550s in exile in Reformed cities on the Continent. In contrast to many Reformed churches abroad, the Church of England retained an episcopal hierarchy, choral worship in cathedrals, and clerical vestments like the surplice.

The 'half-reformed' character of the Elizabethan church was a source of deep frustration to earnest Protestants who wanted to complete England's reformation, to 'purify' the church of 'popish' survivals. From the mid-1560s, these reformers were called 'Puritans' (though the term was also applied indiscriminately to many godly conformists). They represented a spectrum of opinion. Some were simply 'Nonconformists', objecting to the enforcement of certain ceremonies, like the sign of the cross, kneeling at communion, or the wearing of the surplice. Others looked for 'root and branch' reform of the church's government. (All Dissenting movements would remain expert at employing biblical images in their public appeals, as with 'root and branch', taken in this sense from the Old Testament's book of Ezekiel, chapter 17.) They wished to create a Reformed, Presbyterian state church; that is, to make over the Church of England into the pattern that ultimately prevailed north of the border as the Church of Scotland. Still others gave up on the established church altogether, establishing illegal separatist churches. Eventually, England would see a proliferation of home-grown sects: Congregationalists (or Independents), General Baptists, Particular Baptists, Quakers (or Friends), Fifth Monarchists, Ranters, Muggletonians, and more.

These reforming movements flourished during the tumultuous mid-century years of civil war and Interregnum, when the towering figure of Oliver Cromwell presided over a kingless state and acted as protector of the godly. But when the throne and the established church were 'restored' in 1660, reforming movements of all sorts came under tremendous pressure. The term 'Dissent' came to serve as the generic designation for those who did not agree that the established Church of England should enjoy a monopoly over English religious life. Some of the sects—such as the Ranters, Muggletonians, and Fifth Monarchists—soon faded away. Others, especially Independents/Congregationalists, Baptists, and Quakers, survived. Crucially, they were now joined outside the established Church by the Presbyterians ejected from their livings in 1660–2. Although Presbyterians continued to attend parish worship and work for comprehension within the national church, they were (as Richard Baxter noted) forced into a separating shape, meeting in illegal conventicles. In 1689, Parliament confirmed the separation between Church and 'Dissent' by rejecting a comprehension bill and passing the so-called Act of Toleration. The denominations of what became known as 'Old Dissent'—Presbyterians, Congregationalists, Baptists, and Quakers—now enjoyed legally protected freedom of worship, even as their members remained second-class citizens, excluded from public office unless they received Anglican communion.

Over the course of the seventeenth century, all of these Dissenting movements had established a presence in the British colonies of North America. (They became 'British' and not just 'English' colonies in 1707, after the Union of England and Scotland that created 'Great Britain'.) In the New World began what has become a continuous history of English Dissent adapting to conditions outside of England. In this instance, Congregationalists in New England set up a system that looked an awful lot like a church establishment, even as they continued to dissent from the Anglicanism that in theory prevailed wherever British settlement extended.

Complexity in the history of Dissent only expanded in the eighteenth century with the emergence of Methodism. This reforming movement within the Church of England became 'New Dissent' at the end of the century when it separated from Anglican organizational jurisdiction. In America, that separation took place earlier than in England when the American War of Independence ruled out any kind of official authority from the established church across the sea in the new nation.

In the great expansion of the British Empire during the late eighteenth and throughout the nineteenth century, Anglophone Dissent moved out even farther and evolved even further. Canada, Australia, New Zealand, South Africa, and other imperial outposts in Africa and Asia usually enjoyed the service of Anglican missionaries and local supporters. But everywhere that Empire went, so also went Dissenting Protestants. The creation of the Baptist Missionary Society (1792) and the London Missionary Society (1795) (which was dominated by Congregationalists) inaugurated a dramatic surge of overseas missions. Nowhere in the Empire did the Church of England enjoy the same range of privileges that it retained in the mother country.

Meanwhile, back in England, still more new movements added to the Protestant panoply linked to Dissent. Liberalizing trends in both Anglican and Presbyterian theology in the later eighteenth century saw the emergence of the Unitarians as a separate denomination. Conservative trends produced the (so-called Plymouth) Brethren who replicated the earlier Dissenting pattern by originating as a protest against the nineteenth-century Church of England—as well as lamenting the divisions in Christianity and longing to restore the purity of the New Testament church. The Salvation Army (with roots in the Methodist and Holiness movements) was established in response to the challenges of urban mission.

Even further complexity appeared during the twentieth and twenty-first centuries when Pentecostal movements arose, usually with an obvious Methodist lineage, especially as developed by the Holiness tradition within Methodism, but also sometimes with a lineage traceable to representatives of 'Old Dissent' as well. Historically considered, Pentecostals are grandchildren of Dissent via a Methodist–Holiness parentage.

Whether 'New' or 'Old'—or descended from 'New' or 'Old'—all of these traditions have now become global. Some are even dominant in various countries or regions in their parts of the globe. To take United States history as an example, in the eighteenth century Congregationalism dominated Massachusetts. By the early nineteenth century, Methodism was the largest Christian tradition in America. Today, the largest Protestant denomination in the United States is the Southern Baptist Convention. Or with Canada as another example, Anglicans remained stronger than did Episcopalians in the United States, but Methodists and Presbyterians often took on establishment-like characteristics in regions where their numbers equalled or exceeded the Anglicans. In different ways and through different patterns of descent, these North American traditions trace their roots to English Dissent. The same is true in parallel fashion and with different results in many parts of Africa, Asia, Latin America, and elsewhere, where Pentecostalism is usually the dominant style of Protestantism.

THE FIVE VOLUMES OF THIS SERIES

The five-volume *Oxford History of Dissenting Protestant Traditions* is governed by a motif of migration ('out-of-England', as it were), but in two senses of the term. It first traces organized church traditions that arose in England as Dissenters distanced themselves from a state church defined by diocesan episcopacy, the Book of Common Prayer, the Thirty-Nine Articles, and royal supremacy, but then follows those traditions as they spread beyond England—and also traces newer traditions that emerged downstream in other parts of the world from earlier forms of Dissent. Second, it does the same for the doctrines, church practices, stances towards state and society, attitudes towards Scripture, and characteristic patterns of organization that also originated in earlier English Dissent, but that have often defined a trajectory of influence independent of ecclesiastical organizations. Perhaps the most notable occasion when a major world figure pointed to such an influence came in 1775 when Edmund Burke addressed the British Parliament in the early days of the American revolt. While opposing independence for the colonies, Burke yet called for sensitivity because, he asserted, the colonists were 'protestants; and of that kind, which is the most averse to all submission of mind and opinion'. Then Burke went on to say that 'this averseness in the dissenting churches from all that looks like absolute government' was a basic reality of colonial history. Other claims have been almost as strong in associating Dissenters with the practice of free trade, the mediating structures of non-state organization, creativity in scientific research, and more.

This series was commissioned to complement the five-volume *Oxford History of Anglicanism*. In the introduction to that series, the General Editor, Rowan Strong, engaged in considerable handwringing about the difficulties of making coherent, defensible editorial decisions, beginning with the question of how fitting the term 'Anglicanism' was for the series title. If such angst is needed for Anglicanism, those whose minds crave tidiness should abandon all hope before entering here. Beginning again with just the title, 'Dissenting' is a term that obviously varies widely in terms of its connotations and applicability, depending on the particular time, place, and tradition. In some cases, it has been used as a self-identifier. In many other cases, groups whom historians might legitimately regard as descendants of Dissent find it irrelevant, incoherent, or just plain wrong. An example mentioned earlier suggests some of the complexity. In colonial Massachusetts, 'Dissenting' Congregationalists in effect set up an established church supported by taxes and exercising substantial control over public life. In that circumstance, 'Dissent' obviously meant something different from what it did for their fellow Independents left behind in England. Nevertheless, Massachusetts Congregationalism is still one of the traditions out-of-England that we have decided to track wherever it went—even into the courthouse and the capitol building. Much later and far, far away, Methodism in the Pacific Island of Fiji would also take on some establishmentarian features, which again suggests that 'Dissent' points to a history or affinities shared to a greater or lesser extent, but not to an unchanging essence. Indeed, because Dissent is defined in relation to Establishment, it is a relative term.

Another particularly anomalous case is Presbyterianism, which has been a Dissenting tradition in England but a state church (and a Dissenting tradition) in Scotland and elsewhere. When one examines it in other parts of the world, a sophisticated analysis is required—for example, in the United States and Canada (where Presbyterianism was once a force to be reckoned with) and in South Korea (where it still is). In these countries, one encounters a tradition originally fostered by missionaries and emigrants with both Dissenting and establishmentarian roots. By including Presbyterians in these volumes, we communicate an intention to consider 'Dissent' broadly construed.

Other terms might have been chosen for the title, such as 'Nonconformist' or 'Free Churches'. Yet they suffer from the same difficulty—that all groups that might in historical view be linked under any one term will include many who never used the term for themselves or who do not acknowledge the historical connection. Yet 'Dissenting Studies' is a recognized and flourishing field of academic studies, focused on the history of those Protestant movements that coalesced as Dissenting denominations in the seventeenth century and on the New Dissent that arose outside the established church in the eighteenth and nineteenth centuries.

Still, the problem of fitting terminology to historical reality remains. The farther in geographical space that one moves from England and the nearer in time that one comes to the present, the less relevant any of the possible terms becomes for the individuals and Protestant traditions under consideration. Protestants in China or India, for example, generally do not think of their faith as 'Dissenting' at all—at least not in any way that directly relates to how that word functioned for Unitarians in nineteenth-century England. Even in the West, a strong sense of denominational identity or heritage has been waning, due to increasing individualism and hybridization. Such difficulties are inevitable for a genealogy where trunks and branches outline a common history of protest against church establishment, but very little else besides broadly Protestant convictions.

The five volumes in this series, as well as the individual chapters treating different regions, periods, and emphases, admittedly brave intellectual anomalies and historical inconsistencies. One defence is simply to plead that untidiness in the volumes reflects reality itself rather than editorial confusion. Church and Dissent, Anglicanism and Nonconformity were defined by their relationship, and the wall between them was a porous one; while it can be helpful to think in terms of tightly defined ecclesiastical blocs, the reality of lived religion often defied neat lines of demarcation. Many eighteenth and nineteenth-century Anglicans read Puritan works, while many Dissenters imbibed the works of great Anglicans. Besides, an editorial plan that put a premium on tidiness would impoverish readers by leaving out exciting and important events, traditions, personalities, and organizations that do fall, however remotely or obscurely, into the broader history of English Protestant Dissent.

Which brings us to the second, more significant justification for this five-volume series. On offer is nothing less than a feast. Not the least of Britain's contributions to world history has been its multifaceted impact on religious life, thought, and practice. In particular, this one corner of Christendom has proven unusually fertile for the germination of new forms of Christianity. Those forms have enriched British history, while doing even more to enrich all of world history in the last four centuries. By concentrating only on the history of Dissent, these volumes nonetheless illuminate the extraordinary contributions of some of the greatest preachers, missionaries, theologians, pastors, organizations, writers, and self-sacrificing altruists, and (yes, also) some of the most scandalous, self-defeating, and egotistical episodes in the entire history of Christianity. Taken in its broadest dimensions, this series opens the story of large themes and new ways of thinking that have profoundly shaped our globe—on the relationships between church and state, on the successes and failures of voluntary organization, on faith and social action, on toleration and religious and civil freedom, on innovations in worship, hymnody, literature, the arts, and much else. It is a story of traditions that have significantly influenced Europe, North America, Latin America, Africa, Asia, the Pacific Islands, and even the Middle East (for example, the founding of what is now the American University of Beirut). Especially the two volumes on the twentieth century offer treatments of vibrant, growing forms of Christianity in various parts of the world that often have not yet received the scholarly attention they deserve. All five volumes present the work of accomplished scholars with widely recognized expertise in their chosen subjects. In specifically thematic chapters, authors address issues of great current interest, including gender, preaching, missions, social action, politics, literary culture, theology, the Bible, worship, congregational life, ministerial training, new technologies, and much more. The geographical, chronological, and ecclesiastical reach is broad: from the Elizabethan era to the dawn of the twenty-first century, from Congregationalists to Pentecostals, from Cape Cod to Cape Town, from China to Chile, from Irvingite apostles in nineteenth-century London to African apostles in twenty-first century Nigeria. Just as expansive is the roster of Dissenters or descendants of Dissent: from John Bunyan to Martin Luther King, Jr, from prison reformer Elizabeth Fry to mega-mega-church pastor Yonggi Cho, from princes of the pulpit to educational innovators, from poets to politicians, from liturgical reformers to social reformers. However imprecise the category of 'Dissent' must remain, the volumes in this series are guaranteed to delight readers with the wealth of their insight into British history in the seventeenth and eighteenth centuries, with what they reveal about the surprising reach of Dissent around the world in later periods, and with the extraordinary range of positive effects and influences flowing from a family of Christian believers that began with a negative protest.

Introduction

Andrew C. Thompson

Between the late seventeenth and early nineteenth centuries Dissenters both within and without Britain experienced considerable change. One of the most graphic ways in which these changes manifested themselves was in the public acknowledgement and status of Dissent. Joseph Hussey (1660–1726) grew up in a world in which the legal position of Dissent within the British Isles was complex, to say the least. Despite the persecution Dissenters were subjected to during the Restoration, Hussey was keen to find practical ways in which to profess his faith. He was educated at Morton's Academy in Newington Green and he preached his first sermon in August 1681.[1] His 'Church Book', now preserved in Cambridgeshire County Archives, gives details of the more than 3,600 sermons that he preached between then and his death in 1726.[2] Hussey's initial ministerial path was typical of many Dissenters in the febrile days of the 1680s—he entered into the service of Sir Jonathan Keate as a domestic chaplain. Keate, a sugar merchant, was clearly sufficiently sympathetic towards Dissent to have someone like Hussey within his household but he maintained a veneer of outward conformity and had served briefly as MP for Hertfordshire. Hussey eventually felt that he needed to pursue his ministerial vocation elsewhere and, in the autumn of 1688, he sought ordination. This involved a series of examinations from other ministers and Hussey also undertook fasting and prayer, alongside confession of his sins. Ultimately, he was ordained, with the laying on of hands by members of the Presbytery at Dr Samuel Annesley's house 'in the Spittle Fields of London, and in an upper chamber, Octob. 26th 1688 even while the Prince of Orange, afterwards King

---

[1] For brief details of the Academy see 'Charles Morton's Academy, Newington Green (c.1666–1685)', *Dissenting Academies Online*, http://dissacad.english.qmul.ac.uk/sample1.php?parameter=academyretrieve&alpha=114 (last accessed 4 April 2017).
[2] Joseph Hussey's 'Church Book', Cambridgeshire County Archives (N/C R107/109). For details of Hussey's early life, see A. G. Matthews, *Diary of a Cambridge Minister* (Cambridge, 1937).

William, was under sail for England'.³ Six ministers were involved, although Hussey noted that one of them 'was shie because of the cloudiness of the Times and would neither subscribe, nor be known to me'.⁴ While the other five were prepared to reveal their names to Hussey, even they were cautious. Instead of issuing him with a certificate to confirm their participation in Hussey's ordination, they were simply prepared to sign a document stating they knew him to be ordained.

The comments about the Prince of Orange reveal that Hussey must have written up the account of his ordination retrospectively. Concerns about whether the improvements to Dissenters' position and status would be permanent remained long after 1688. As several chapters in the current volume reveal, many Dissenters continued to separate from each other because of disputes about theological orthodoxy or even due to personality clashes (the Cambridge congregation whose minister Hussey became in 1691 had originally been inclined towards Presbyterianism; Hussey led it in a Congregational direction and so the more Presbyterian elements of his flock left to form their own church in 1696). Very often ownership of church buildings became an important issue within these splits.

Looking at buildings themselves opens a window, as Carl Lounsbury's chapter shows, into the shifting position of Dissent. Early meeting houses differed little from the houses around them, blending into the surrounding environment. By the early nineteenth century, in both position and architectural style, a greater degree of self-confidence was discernible. It was even becoming difficult to determine which group occupied a religious building, simply from its exterior. Yet, the legacy of earlier Dissenting uncertainty about the future was profound. Meeting houses were frequently owned by trustees, rather than congregations directly. Consequently, when divisions emerged, determining who had the right to claim that they represented the congregation could be problematic. Moreover, the question as to whether it was the congregation, the trustees, other lay patrons, or a local synod who had the right to appoint the minister could also be a cause of disagreement. Stewart J. Brown's chapter traces the impact of patronage disputes on Scottish Dissent but the problems were more general. That some of these issues emerged was, in itself, a sign that some of the existential concerns about Dissent's position had dissipated. Yet, anxieties about the future continued to manifest themselves in subtle ways and with unintended consequences.

Anxiety was central to other areas of Dissenting experience. This is not simply to reduce religious experience to the outworkings of inner psychological dramas, as some classic accounts suggest.⁵ Rather, it is to be aware that,

---

³ Hussey 'Church Book', p. 11.
⁴ Ibid.
⁵ E. P. Thompson, *The Making of the English Working Class* (London, 1963), ch. 12.

in an uncertain world where mortality rates were high, the risks of disease serious, and harvest failure a very real risk, then the search for meaning and purpose was important. The impact on eighteenth-century protestant Christianity of revivalist movements was also profound. As David Hempton, in a recent excellent general history of Christianity in this period, puts it, Pietism was partly a response to the failures of state churches (an observation that has currency beyond central Europe) and its close cousin, revival, 'thrived on anxiety'.[6] While Michael McClymond's chapter is devoted entirely to the topic of revival, the ripple effects of it can be felt throughout the volume. McClymond traces the links between those inside and outside state churches, as well as noting the expansive geographical sweep of revivalist movements. While this is a story that cannot be told simply from a Dissenting perspective, nor is it one that can be adequately explained without it.

Revival was closely connected to a renewed emphasis on vital religion, the centrality of the Scripture, and the importance of mission. All three of these themes find their place within the volume. Brian Stanley explores the impulses behind the formation of missionary societies. While he acknowledges the importance of earlier European precedents and contemporary Anglican efforts, Dissenters' missionary activities were groundbreaking in two important respects. First, their mission field was not restricted by previous colonial connection and second, by eschewing state sponsorship entirely, they were instrumental in developing a voluntarist approach to mission. David Thompson's chapter touches on different traditions of biblical interpretation, although he emphasizes the importance of 'plain readings' and literalist views for many. Yet the importance of Scripture was broader. It could be seen in Dissenting hymnody which J. R. Watson explores. Psalms were clearly important as a basis for hymnody but Watson also shows how hymns were used both to open up Scripture and, in the case of Watts, to provide justifications for wider Dissenting principles. Françoise Deconinck-Brossard elucidates the specifics of Dissenting sermon culture with a detailed discussion of both printed and manuscript sermons. Grayson Ditchfield illustrates the ways in which vital religion could have practical impact, with his discussion of abolitionism and the social practice of Dissent. While a variety of motivations have been noted in the movement to eliminate the slave trade, the importance of a shift in public attitudes and a broader evangelical milieu, to which Dissenters contributed fully, cannot be ignored.

The wider context for religious change is important to remember as well. David Bebbington's claim that religious revival was a product of enlightenment thought has proved persuasive.[7] This was a period in which print culture

---

[6] David Hempton, *The Church in the Long Eighteenth Century* (London, 2011), p. 142.
[7] D. W. Bebbington, *Evangelicalism in Modern Britain* (London, 1989), pp. 50–69. See also Dorinda Outram, *The Enlightenment*, 3rd edn (Cambridge, 2013), pp. 117–18.

was expanding rapidly. While the proportion of religious titles published was decreasing, given the huge growth in the number of books being published, religious works were still selling in considerable numbers. Tessa Whitehouse's chapter, complementing the work on hymns and sermons, takes a broader look at the emergence of print culture. She indicates the diversity of both readers and material that Dissenters consumed in the period. While doctrinal and controversial works have often attracted attention in the past, the importance of works of practical divinity for both clergy and laity alike needs to be remembered. Dissenting contributions to the development of education have traditionally attracted considerable interest, not least because of some of the claims made about the importance of Dissenting academies for the rise of rationalism.[8] A major (and long overdue) reassessment of the academies is now in train.[9] In his chapter on education in this volume, Mark Burden considers the academies but also notes the important contributions made by Dissenters in other areas of education. While the Dissenting interest in the Sunday School movement is reasonably well established, the role played by Dissenters in the encouragement of charity schools and educating the poor needs to be acknowledged too. Indeed, churches across Europe and beyond remained central to educational provision for much of this period.

This volume seeks to explore Dissent in ways that recognize the changes that have taken place within historical study more generally in recent years. There is a strong emphasis on placing the Dissenting experience within a broad, global context. This manifests itself in a variety of ways. Politically, it means ensuring that perspectives from the history of empire and the Atlantic world find their place. It also means being alive to the differences between Dissent inside and outside England and to the problematic nature of 'establishment'.[10] To give just two examples of the tensions, the Glorious Revolution moved the Scottish ecclesiastical establishment from an Episcopalian to a Presbyterian form which was reinforced and reconfirmed by the 1707 Act of Union whereas in Massachusetts, Congregationalism benefitted from being the official religion of most towns and from support through the tax system. Despite these caveats, the terminology adopted throughout the volume tends to be one of 'Dissent' (although references to 'Nonconformity' make occasional appearances). Both terms imply a degree of difference and diversity.

---

[8] Herbert McLachlan, *English Education under the Test Acts* (Manchester, 1931) for a classic articulation.

[9] Isabel Rivers with Mark Burden, eds, *The History of the Dissenting Academies in the British Isles, 1660–1860*, 4 vols. (Cambridge, forthcoming).

[10] On the importance of 'establishment' more generally, see Stewart J. Brown, *The National Churches of England, Scotland, and Ireland 1801–46* (Oxford, 2001) and James E. Bradley, 'The Religious Origins of Radical Politics in England, Scotland, and Ireland, 1662–1800', in James E. Bradley and Dale K. Van Kley, eds, *Religion and Politics in Enlightenment Europe* (Notre Dame, 2001), pp. 187–253.

Catherine Brekus is anxious to avoid whiggish teleologies by suggesting that Dissenters' ideological disagreements with establishment inevitably ensured the triumph of liberty of conscience in early America. She also shows that Dissenters were just as capable of arguing with each other as with their Anglican opponents. Nevertheless, despite the suspicion of religious pluralism which characterized many of the early settlers, the practicalities of diversity meant that enforcing uniformity proved difficult and it had been abandoned in most places before the first amendment enshrined it in law. Indeed, as Katherine Carté Engel shows, Dissenters cemented their position at the heart of American religious life in the aftermath of the passing of the first amendment. The trend towards religious disestablishment continued apace and, while the denominations of Old Dissent lost some ground numerically, the growth of Methodism meant that by the middle of the nineteenth century some three-quarters of Americans were members of one of the major Dissenting denominations. Groups that had started out as minorities and outsiders increasingly found themselves enjoying influence and status.

Across the Atlantic, a similar story could be traced, albeit on a smaller scale, in relation to religious believers in Wales. Eryn White notes the importance of revivalism for laying the foundations of Dissenting strength. Yet she also points to the wider context in which revival took place and echoes themes encountered elsewhere in the volume. The passing of the Toleration Act had removed some of the immediate barriers to Dissenting consolidation but fears that the religious situation was still in flux remained. Consequently, Dissenting leaders in Wales saw the value of education—both at the level of academies and in promoting education and literacy more generally. Language mattered here. While the SPCK saw religion and education as going hand in hand in Wales (as elsewhere), the willingness of Dissenters to contribute to a nascent Welsh-language print culture and Welsh-medium education was important.

Yet the situation in Wales also highlights one of the other problems that any history of Dissent in this period encounters. Many of the supporters of revival within Wales began their journey within Anglicanism, even if they ended up as Methodists. As Richard Heitzenrater notes, the Wesleys themselves would have resisted the connection of Methodism and Dissent. Yet, both theologically and organizationally Methodism was not simply reducible to Charles and John and their public utterances. In terms of their practice, Methodist emphasis on lay preaching, the importance of local organization, and a lack of emphasis on traditional parish boundaries displayed structural similarities with 'Old Dissent' which, as time went on, also found expression in more formalized separation from the Established Church. Consequently, this volume adopts a relatively catholic approach to what constituted Dissent and includes Methodists alongside Presbyterians, Congregationalists, Baptists, and Quakers.

Although the present volume begins with separate chapters on each of the major denominations of Dissent, it seeks to avoid a narrow 'genealogical' approach which Patrick Collinson identified as being one of the dangers of Dissenting historiographies built around the idea of denomination.[11] Indeed, as Alasdair Raffe points out, there is considerably more to the story of English Presbyterianism in this period than the descent (or ascent, depending on one's perspective) into Unitarianism. Yet, as he also acknowledges, and Stewart J. Brown and Andrew Holmes also affirm in their discussions of Scotland and Ireland respectively, the extent to which requiring subscription to human (as opposed to scriptural) formularies remained an important issue of contention.

Arguments about the importance of authority and status also feature in Stephen Orchard's contribution on Congregationalism. Yet Orchard also reminds us that the denominational lens can be unhelpful in assessing the experience of eighteenth-century Dissenters. The quest by subsequent generations to trace lineage, and often legitimacy, masked the messiness and unevenness of lived experience. While Presbyterians and Congregationalists increasingly developed separate structures, particularly when it came to the training and funding of candidates for ordained ministry, in other ways the boundaries between the two groups remained porous, both personally and intellectually.

In a similar way, Karen Smith is keen to question aspects of early nineteenth-century Baptist self-fashioning. There is a need to move attention beyond urban congregations and (an almost exclusively) male leadership in order to appreciate the familial context of covenant life. Other chapters in the volume also seek to echo this general approach. Moreover, the notion that Baptist decline was a product of arcane theological controversy that needs to be set against the vitality of revivalism is a narrative with wider significance. While it may have suited later revivalists to paint their forebears in the blackest possible light, the reality was more complicated. Indeed, this sort of move extended beyond Dissent—it suited both Evangelicals and Tractarians to portray the eighteenth-century Church of England as torpid and disengaged, not least because it helped to justify their reformist programmes.

Quakers or Friends, as Richard Allen shows, were initially interested in pressing the limits of the Toleration Act. Questions about tithes, financial support for the military (particularly the militia), and the continuing importance of oaths for demonstrating loyalty all created points of tension where Quakers found themselves at odds with many of their fellow subjects. Was their previous radical heritage something that should be cherished and preserved, with a distinctiveness from wider society maintained by not

---

[11] Patrick Collinson, 'Towards a Broader Understanding of the Early Dissenting Tradition', in his *Godly People: Essays on English Protestantism and Puritanism* (London, 1983), pp. 527–62.

'marrying out', or something that needed to be overcome in a quest for broader respectability and acceptance? Again, these themes have wider resonance and importance for all the Dissenting groups discussed within the volume.

Joseph Hussey lived in a world that was alive to the ever-present workings of providence. While he might have been surprised that it took so long for the Test and Corporation Acts to be repealed after the passing of the Toleration Act in 1689, he might also have wondered that the celebrations to mark their final repeal were attended by the king's brother. This volume charts some of the manifold ways in which Dissent moved from the fringes to a position of significance and centrality within the anglophone world. Whether the yoke had been easy and the burden light remains an open question.

Part I

Traditions within England

1

Presbyterians

Alasdair Raffe

What became of English and Welsh Presbyterians in the long eighteenth century? For many of their historians, the answer has been clear: Presbyterianism declined and its character changed beyond recognition. Or, to put it another way, Presbyterianism as it was known at the start of the period disappeared in much of the country, to be replaced by Unitarianism. Statements of these views abound in nineteenth-century denominational histories, notably the works of Thomas M'Crie and A.H. Drysdale, members of Churches affiliated to Scottish Presbyterianism. According to M'Crie, the 'eighteenth century ushered in a religious declension'. Though this affected all churches, among Presbyterians the decline was particularly pronounced. In theological terms, the Calvinist 'orthodoxy' that generally prevailed in 1689 was abandoned. In its place, ministers developed Arminian understandings of salvation, in which human free will had a central role, and Arian definitions of God, according to which Christ was subordinate to God the Father. As the century advanced, '[s]tep by step the descent was made from the highest Arianism to the lowest Socinianism', entailing a more complete denial of the Trinity. Without adequate church courts, Presbyterians were unable rigorously to scrutinize candidates for ordination, and the ministry was filled with men of increasingly heterodox opinions.[1] Compounding the problem, in Drysdale's account, was the control that chapel trustees and ministers exercised over the choice of new ministers. Whereas among the Independents, the congregation as a whole chose its minister, Presbyterians vested the nomination in a small, unrepresentative elite, often more liberal in their beliefs than were rank-and-file worshippers. The result was a pattern of unpopular clerical appointments, leading to divided chapels and the secession of conservative lay people to

---

[1] Thomas M'Crie, *Annals of English Presbytery: From the Earliest Period to the Present Time* (London, 1872), esp. pp. 297–306, quotations at pp. 297, 298. M'Crie was an emeritus professor of the English Presbyterian College, an institution linked to the Free Church of Scotland.

Congregational meeting houses or Methodism.[2] Pockets of Presbyterian orthodoxy persisted in northern England and London, however. In the nineteenth century, it was these Presbyterians, in alliance with evangelicals of Scottish origin, who raised the denomination from its lowest ebb.[3]

Not all nineteenth- and early twentieth-century historians used such negative vocabulary about English Presbyterianism. Some writers praised the intellectual achievements of Presbyterianism's liberal theologians.[4] Unitarian historians sympathized with the appearance in Presbyterian pulpits of the 'rational' belief that Christ was not divine, but simply a human messenger, and that only God the Father was to be worshipped.[5] But in the mid twentieth century, historians focusing on Presbyterianism itself continued to employ the language of 'collapse' and 'demise'.[6] Only since the 1960s have more critical, and less denominational, perspectives on the changing nature of Presbyterianism emerged.[7]

When we consider the size of the Presbyterian community in eighteenth-century England and Wales, of course, it is difficult to avoid talk of decline. That there were large falls in the number of chapels and in the total Presbyterian population is clear from a comparison between the list compiled by John Evans for the Committee of the Three Denominations in 1715–18 and the next detailed and reliable survey, the religious census of 1851. Evans recorded 637 English Presbyterian congregations and 25 in Wales. In 1851, 202 of England's chapels were Unitarian, the label used by many Presbyterians after statutory toleration of Unitarianism was granted in 1813. There were also 142 congregations of the Presbyterian Church in England and the United Presbyterian Church (the main bodies connected to Scottish Presbyterianism) and 27 Unitarian meetings in Wales. Drawing on the Evans list, Michael Watts estimates that there were 179,350 English Presbyterians in 1715–18, making

---

[2] A. H. Drysdale, *History of the Presbyterians in England: Their Rise, Decline, and Revival* (London, 1889), pp. 509–14, 526–32. Drysdale was a member of the Presbyterian Church of England, formed in 1876 from a union of English and Scottish United Presbyterian congregations.

[3] John Black, *Presbyterianism in England in the Eighteenth and Nineteenth Centuries* (London, 1887), esp. pp. 10–11, 17, 21–5.

[4] e.g. Fred. J. Powicke, 'An Apology for the Nonconformist Arians of the Eighteenth Century', *Transactions of the Unitarian Historical Society* [hereafter *TUHS*], 1, 2 (1916).

[5] e.g. Henry Solly, *Our English Presbyterian Forefathers; A Sketch of their History and Principles, from the Time of the Reformation to the Present Day* (London, 1859); Alexander Gordon, *Heads of English Unitarian History* (London, 1895). See, most recently, Leonard Smith, *The Unitarians: A Short History* (Arnside, 2006).

[6] Basil Hall, 'From Dissent to Free Churchmanship', *Journal of the Presbyterian Historical Society of England*, 10, 2 (1953), p. 75; James C. Spalding, 'The Demise of English Presbyterianism, 1660–1760', *Church History*, 28, 1 (1959).

[7] Particularly significant are Jeremy Goring, 'The Break-up of the Old Dissent', in C. G. Bolam and others, *The English Presbyterians: From Elizabethan Puritanism to Modern Unitarianism* (London, 1968); and Russell E. Richey, 'Did the English Presbyterians become Unitarian?', *Church History*, 42, 1 (1973), which develops some of the points made in this chapter.

them the largest Dissenting denomination, with around 3.3 per cent of the national population. In 1851, there were 34,110 English Unitarians (roughly 0.2 per cent of the population), and the two other Presbyterian Churches accounted for 50,080 worshippers (0.3 per cent of the population). By 1851, English Presbyterians were dwarfed by an Independent population of over 650,000 and Methodist bodies amounting to more than 1.5 million churchgoers. In Wales, where Congregationalists began the period in the strongest position, and for which Evans's figures are less reliable, the Presbyterian population was around 6,080 in 1715–18 (1.96 per cent of the national total). The Unitarians numbered a mere 2,901 (0.29 per cent) in 1851.[8] It is difficult to establish reliable figures for Presbyterian populations between 1718 and 1851, but some have inferred from John Thompson's lists of 1772–3 that there were around 300 meeting houses at that time.[9]

Numbers aside, however, the narrative of decline is tendentious and distorting. Presbyterians ceded numerical dominance, and made no claim to lead evangelical Nonconformity. But as the principal 'rational Dissenters' in the final third of the eighteenth century, and thereafter as Unitarians, they retained a position of social and political prominence within Old Dissent. Owing to the support of Joseph Priestley and others for the French Revolution, their authority was under attack in the 1790s. But it was only in the 1830s that their leading roles in the Committee of Three Denominations and the Dissenting Deputies came to an end.[10] Thus historians who chart Presbyterian decline allow one contemporary judgement to crowd out another. Whereas the evangelicals David Bogue and James Bennett, in 1808, diagnosed the long-term 'effects of Arianism' as 'desolation and death', the Unitarian Samuel Heywood, writing the previous year, asserted that the Unitarians were 'increasing much'. Whatever the truth of this, Heywood's claim that Unitarianism drew in 'men of great Learning & Talents' from other denominations, especially General Baptists and Anglicans, identifies a crucial reconfiguration of Dissent.[11] Of the meeting houses called 'Presbyterian' at the start of the eighteenth century, most that survived to its end had ceased to uphold Calvinist doctrine; their organization had become essentially congregational.

---

[8] Michael R. Watts, *The Dissenters: Volume II: The Expansion of Evangelical Nonconformity* (Oxford, 1995), pp. 22–9.

[9] Drysdale, *History of the Presbyterians*, p. 532; Alan P.F. Sell, 'Presbyterianism in Eighteenth-Century England: The Doctrinal Dimension', in Sell, *Dissenting Thought and the Life of the Churches: Studies in an English Tradition* (San Francisco, 1990), p. 151.

[10] See e.g. John Seed, '"A set of men powerful enough in many things": Rational Dissent and Political Opposition in England, 1770–1790', in Knud Haakonssen, ed., *Enlightenment and Religion: Rational Dissent in Eighteenth-Century Britain* (Cambridge, 1996); H. L. Short, 'Presbyterians under a New Name', in Bolam and others, *English Presbyterians*, pp. 229–52.

[11] James Bogue and David Bennett, *The History of Dissenters, from the Revolution to the Year 1808*, 2nd edn, 2 vols. (London, 1833), II, p. 197; G. M. Ditchfield, 'A Unitarian View of English Dissent in 1807', *TUHS*, 18, 2 (1984), p. 12.

English and Welsh Presbyterians were not what they had been in the seventeenth century, nor what they would be later in the nineteenth. But only the tunnel vision of vertical, denominational history could perceive these transformations as 'decline' followed by 'revival'.

To think more critically about eighteenth-century Presbyterianism, we should emphasize two points. First, we must recognize that, for much of the period, the boundaries of English Presbyterianism were ill-defined. In the few decades after 1689, there was much cooperation between Presbyterians and Independents; in some localities, there was no such distinction to be made among the Dissenting population. Even later in the period, former Presbyterians became Congregationalists, and Congregationalists including Joseph Priestley and Thomas Belsham redesignated themselves Presbyterians. Significantly, both men had taught in Dissenting academies, institutions catering to young men of diverse religious origins. In the late eighteenth and early nineteenth centuries, renegade Anglicans such as Gilbert Wakefield and John Disney, and the former Baptists Robert Aspland and Thomas Southwood Smith, were important Unitarians. The second point is that Presbyterianism's theological evolution did not follow some predetermined liberalizing trajectory set by the debates at Salters' Hall in 1719, when a majority of Presbyterians voted against requiring ministers to subscribe to any man-made confession of faith as a test of doctrinal orthodoxy. A small number of Presbyterians at that date doubted that Christ was equal to God the Father, as specified by Trinitarian creeds. But it is unhelpful to imply that this made the Presbyterians' retreat from Calvinism, or their adoption of Unitarianism, inevitable. Priestley and Belsham were attracted to Presbyterianism by its liberal theological culture. But the Unitarianism they and others forged was not a 'decayed' remnant of an old denomination, but rather a new strand of Dissent, formed not only of Presbyterians, but also of other Nonconformists and erstwhile Anglicans. The emergence of Unitarianism in chapels founded by Presbyterians, or financed by the London-based Presbyterian Fund or other Presbyterian charities, was a contingent result of the commitment of most Congregationalists to doctrinal orthodoxy, and of the failure of attempts to reform the Church of England's Articles and terms of communion. In what follows, we shall consider these two themes at greater length, beginning with the position of Presbyterians among other Dissenters in the period after 1689.

PRESBYTERIANS AFTER THE TOLERATION ACT

The Toleration Act made way for the settling of fixed congregations, with the sort of ecclesiastical infrastructure impossible in the Restoration period. At first, the patronage of gentry families and other wealthy supporters remained important, as it had been before the revolution, especially in rural areas. At Elland, West Yorkshire, Presbyterian meetings took place at the home of John Brooksbank, probably a cloth merchant, until 1697, when a chapel was provided on his land. This meeting place was later endowed thanks to Brooksbank's will. When a chapel gained settled funds, an administration based on trustees was usually instituted, making it more likely that the meeting house would survive.[12] The building of permanent meeting houses was a significant step, but where a congregation was small or impoverished, worship took place in temporary accommodation for some years. Carlisle's first purpose-built meeting house was constructed in 1707; the Presbyterian congregation at Morpeth built a chapel for John Horsley, the eminent antiquarian and Newtonian, in 1721, at least twelve years after his arrival as their minister.[13]

Horsley also served as a schoolmaster, a common combination of offices among low-paid Presbyterian ministers.[14] In 1690, a fund was established at London with the aim of supplementing the stipends of Presbyterian (and, at first, Congregational) clergy. The fund's survey of English and Welsh ministers and their provision revealed the great variety of financial maintenance on offer. Archibald Hamilton, a Scottish Presbyterian preaching at High Wycombe, was promised £26 per year, but this 'now falls Short'. The congregation at Threlkeld or Penruddock in Cumberland raised a mere £15 or £20 for its minister, and received a further £10 from Dissenters in Newcastle.[15] Like the underpaid curates of the Church of England, a large number of Presbyterian clergy faced the consequences of genteel poverty. Thomas James, Presbyterian minister of Ashford in Kent, struggled to find a wife prepared to share his small income.[16] One beneficiary of the Presbyterian Fund, James Clegg of Chapel-en-le-Frith, Derbyshire, earned from his ministry little more than £20 per year. To support his family, he leased a farm and practised as a physician, without the necessary episcopal licence, procuring a

---

[12] John Goodchild, 'Christ's Chapel, the Origins and Development of the English Presbyterian and later Unitarian Congregation at Elland, c.1685–c.1917', *Transactions of the Halifax Antiquarian Society*, new ser., 11 (2003), p. 71; David L. Wykes, '"The settling of meetings and the preaching of the gospel": The Development of the Dissenting Interest, 1690–1715', *Journal of the United Reformed Church History Society* [hereafter *JURCHS*], 5, 3 (1993), pp. 127–45.

[13] Ian Moonie, 'Presbyterians and Independents or Congregationalists in Carlisle, 1648–1736', *Transactions of the Cumberland & Westmorland Antiquarian & Archæological Society*, 3rd ser., 9 (2009), p. 124; Leslie W. Hepple, 'John Horsley and the Presbyterian Chapel in Morpeth', *Archaeologia Aeliana*, 5th ser., 35 (2006), pp. 105–7.

[14] David Boyd Haycock, 'Horsley, John (1685/6–1732)', *Oxford Dictionary of National Biography*, Oxford University Press, 2004 [http://www.oxforddnb.com/view/article/13819, accessed 16 Sept. 2015].

[15] Alexander Gordon, ed., *Freedom after Ejection: A Review (1690–1692) of Presbyterian and Congregational Nonconformity in England and Wales* (Manchester, 1917), pp. 9, 22.

[16] David Wykes, '"A minister's case is different from all other men": Thomas James's Early Ministry', *JURCHS*, 7, 2 (2003), pp. 65–7.

degree from King's College, Aberdeen to protect himself from prosecution. Clegg declined invitations to transfer to more remunerative meeting houses.[17]

The formation of district associations and classes was a sign both of the growing institutionalization of Dissent, and of the cooperation of Presbyterians and Independents in the years after 1689. A Somerset association was initiated in 1689, and others including the better documented Cheshire classis and Exeter Assembly began meeting in 1691.[18] Unlike Scottish presbyteries, which included lay elders, these bodies consisted of ministers only. Assemblies existed mostly in areas of Presbyterian strength, and were not formed in counties such as Cambridgeshire and Northamptonshire where Independents were the dominant Dissenters. Nevertheless, Congregational ministers took part with Presbyterians at Exeter and elsewhere.[19] The associations oversaw ordination, assisted with cases of discipline, and administered funds to support students preparing for the ministry. In these weighty matters, Presbyterian ministers expected to act collectively. This is evident from the exhortation by John Rastrick, made at the ordination of Samuel Savage in Suffolk in 1714, a source that also reveals the tendency of ministers to operate independently when their numbers were few. Rastrick counselled Savage not to excommunicate

> by *your self alone*, but by and with the Advice and Consent of a compleat Number of Presbyters; or, at least, with the Concurrence of the Majority of the most Knowing, and most Pious of the Congregation, where no *Classes* are form'd, and Ministers are so thin, and so distant from each other, that their advice cannot readily and jointly be had.[20]

As this suggests, classical associations aimed to harmonize practice in formerly autonomous or newly established congregations. The ministers of the Exeter Assembly considered it 'very expedient that we frequently hold meetings for mutual advice touching things pertaining to our Office, the right ordering of our Congregations, & the promoting of purity & unity in the Churches of Christ'.[21] To this end, the associations in Exeter and Cheshire provided a channel of communication to the influential ministers of London. The

---

[17] *The Diary of James Clegg of Chapel en le Frith, 1708-1755*, ed. Vanessa S. Doe, 3 vols. (Derbyshire Record Society, 1978-81), I, pp. xii-xiii, xliii, III, pp. 917, 919, 943.

[18] See esp. Geoffrey F. Nuttall, 'Assembly and Association in Dissent, 1689-1831', in G. J. Cumming and Derek Baker, eds, *Councils and Assemblies* (Cambridge, 1971); Geoffrey F. Nuttall, '"The Sun-shine of liberty": The Toleration Act and the Ministry', *JURCHS*, 4, 4 (1989).

[19] David L. Wykes, 'After the Happy Union: Presbyterians and Independents in the Provinces', in R. N. Swanson, ed., *Unity and Diversity in the Church* (Oxford, 1996), pp. 284-5.

[20] John Rastrick, *A Sermon preach'd at the Ordination of Mr Samuel Savage* (London, 1714), p. 59.

[21] *The Exeter Assembly: The Minutes of the Assemblies of the United Brethren of Devon and Cornwall, 1691-1717*, ed. Allan Brockett (Torquay, 1963), p. 1.

capital's Presbyterians and Independents came together in a short-lived 'Happy Union', based around the Common Fund and the *Heads of Agreement* adopted in 1691.[22] That year, the London Presbyterian minister John Howe sent advice about the Lord's Supper to the Cheshire classis in the name of the now 'United Brethren'.[23] In 1694, the Exeter Assembly resolved that it was 'very necessary for the advancement of the interest of Religion that there be a General Correspondency betwixt all the United Ministers throughout the Kingdom', to be led from London.[24]

The Happy Union broke down in London in 1694–5, amid a theological controversy between Presbyterians and Congregationalists to which we shall return later in the chapter. In the south-west, Independents chafed at the Exeter Assembly's attempt to control ordination, believing that it was within the jurisdiction of individual congregations. In 1696, Stephen Towgood and John Ashwood ordained a minister without the Assembly's permission at Bridport in Dorset. Though he was reluctant to accept the Assembly's ruling that it should oversee all ordinations, Towgood (but not Ashwood) continued to participate in its meetings.[25] Thus attitudes towards ordination were a key point distinguishing Presbyterians and Independents, at least in areas where Dissenters of both persuasions were present. Whereas Independents understood ordination as establishing a relationship between the pastor and his church alone, Presbyterians ordained ministers to the universal Church. The *Heads of Agreement* reflected the Presbyterian view, asserting that '*Ordination is only intended for such as never before had been ordained to the Ministerial Office*'. But the *Heads* allowed for a 'Solemn' ceremony resembling ordination when a minister transferred to a new congregation.[26] Notwithstanding the compromise in the *Heads*, when the young Edmund Calamy sought ordination in 1694, his request was controversial for several reasons. His was to be the first ordination in public in London since 1662, an indication that Dissenters remained cautious in the few years after the Toleration Act. He and Thomas Reynolds 'insisted upon being ordained ministers of the Catholic Church, without any confinement to particular flocks, or any one denomination'. Despite this statement of Presbyterian principle, Calamy hoped to involve Congregational ministers in the ceremony, even as the Happy Union was unravelling. As it happened, the ministers who ordained Calamy were all Presbyterians.[27]

---

[22] *Heads of Agreement assented to by the United Ministers in and about London* (London, 1691).
[23] *Cheshire Classis Minutes, 1691–1745*, ed. Alexander Gordon (London, 1919), pp. 3–4.
[24] *Exeter Assembly*, p. 19.
[25] Ibid., pp. xi–xiii, 29–30, 37–8.
[26] *Heads of Agreement*, p. 7.
[27] Edmund Calamy, *An Historical Account of My Own Life*, ed. John Towill Rutt, 2 vols. (London, 1829), I, pp. 339–49, quotation at p. 341.

As is discussed elsewhere in this volume, various forms of discrimination against Dissenters persisted after 1689.[28] The veteran Presbyterian minister Philip Henry was grateful for toleration, but he wrote that until 'the Sacramental Test bee taken off, our Business is not done'.[29] Conforming occasionally to the Church of England was a solution for office-holding Presbyterians, and for those who wished to retain some link with the national establishment. James Clegg's Derbyshire congregation included many of the area's wealthiest inhabitants, some of whom kept pews in the parish church.[30] Despite the failure of the comprehension bill in 1689, and the opposition of the Church of England's convocation, the Exeter Assembly declared in 1691 that 'if an Act of Comprehension should be pass'd we shall be ready to close in with it, so far as we are persuaded in our consciences we may do'.[31] There was little prospect of reunion with the Church of England, but some Presbyterians and low churchmen remained hopeful long after 1689.[32]

If the boundaries between moderate Dissent and the Church of England were sometimes indistinct, there was also widespread cooperation between Nonconformists of different views. Early in the period, the deeds to new chapels often did not state whether the buildings were for Presbyterian or Independent use.[33] Across England, there were numerous places where Presbyterians and Independents worshipped together, or where there was considerable collaboration between congregations of differing ecclesiological principles.[34] Particularly in London, Northumberland, and Cumberland, congregations affiliated to Scottish Presbyterianism, and 'English' chapels served by Scottish ministers, formed part of the diverse Dissenting religious provision.[35] Moreover, where there were few Dissenters, or poor congregations, cooperation was a necessary expedient. Brighton's meeting house heard sermons from both Presbyterians and Congregationalists, until the first settled minister, a Presbyterian, arrived in 1698.[36] At Carlisle, the congregation was likewise mixed in the early years after 1689. In John Menzies, the minister for about a decade after 1693, Carlisle's Dissenters employed an unusually flexible Scot who had conformed to episcopacy and Presbyterianism in his native

---

[28] See ch. 13 in this volume, Andrew C. Thompson, 'Toleration, Dissent, and the State in Britain'.

[29] *Diaries and Letters of Philip Henry*, ed. Matthew Henry Lee (London, 1882), p. 362.

[30] *Diary of James Clegg*, I, pp. xxix–xxx, xxxvi.

[31] *Exeter Assembly*, p. 1.

[32] See e.g. Geoffrey F. Nuttall, 'Chandler, Doddridge and the Archbishop: A Study in Eighteenth-Century Ecumenism', *JURCHS*, 1, 2 (1973).

[33] Richey, 'Did the English Presbyterians become Unitarian?', pp. 67–8.

[34] Wykes, 'After the Happy Union'.

[35] Kenneth Macleod Black, *The Scots Churches in England* (Edinburgh, 1906), esp. appendix II; George G. Cameron, *The Scots Kirk in London* (Oxford, 1979).

[36] Michael J. Burchall, 'Introduction', in *Brighton Presbyterian Registers, 1700–1837*, ed. Michael J. Burchall (Brighton, 1979), pp. i–iii.

country, and received support from both the Presbyterian and Congregational Funds in London.[37]

By the second quarter of the eighteenth century, however, the Congregational Fund restricted its support to ministers of proven orthodoxy. The failure of the Presbyterian Fund to apply a similar policy was one factor encouraging theological divergence between the denominations.[38] The Dissenting academies of the mid eighteenth century remained places in which students of different Dissenting backgrounds were educated.[39] But new entrants to the ministry were increasingly required to choose a denomination on the basis of their doctrinal views, and their attitudes towards confessions of faith and free enquiry. It is to developments in theology that we now turn.

THEOLOGICAL CHANGE

At the start of our period, most English Presbyterians could be located on a theological spectrum ranging from the orthodox Calvinism of the Westminster confession of faith (1646) to the teachings of Richard Baxter. Baxter and his admirers accepted that a Christian's salvation depended on divine assistance, but they did not believe that God had predestined some for damnation, or that the salvation of all was impossible. In this way, the Baxterians modified the Westminster confession's doctrines of predestination and the atonement, without giving human free will the role in salvation envisaged by Arminians. Baxter's theology was thus intended as a peaceable, catholic 'middle way' between Calvinism and Arminianism. Writing in 1714, John Rastrick, a proponent of the middle way, argued that both the Calvinist emphasis on free grace and the Arminian assertion of free will were true, mutually compatible, and taught by the Westminster Assembly's catechisms.[40]

For all their pacific intent, Baxterians did not fight shy of controversy. Baxter and his ally Daniel Williams entered a heated exchange with extreme Calvinists after the sermons of the antinomian Tobias Crisp were republished in 1690. Williams's major contribution to the debate, *Gospel-Truth Stated* (1692), undermined the Happy Union, not only because some Independents

---

[37] Moonie, 'Presbyterians and Independents', pp. 121–3; Hew Scott, *Fasti Ecclesiae Scoticanae: The Succession of Ministers in the Church of Scotland from the Reformation*, rev. edn, 8 vols. (Edinburgh, 1915–50), I, p. 246.

[38] Roger Thomas, 'Presbyterians in Transition', in Bolam and others, *English Presbyterians*, pp. 165–6.

[39] See ch. 18 in this volume, Mark Burden, 'Dissent and Education'.

[40] Rastrick, *Sermon preach'd at the Ordination of Savage*, pp. 64–9. See Geoffrey F. Nuttall, *Richard Baxter and Philip Doddridge: A Study in Tradition* (London, 1951), pp. 2–4, 22–3; N.H. Keeble, *Richard Baxter: Puritan Man of Letters* (Oxford, 1982), pp. 69–73.

espoused the doctrines of Crisp that Williams attacked, but also because the book's imprimatur was signed, in the second edition, by forty-nine Presbyterian ministers. It seemed an antagonistic and partisan statement. In the work, Williams reacted against Crisp's teaching that the covenant of grace was entirely unconditional, requiring no performance on the part of believers. Williams asserted that the Westminster Assembly saw the covenant as conditional, though he underlined the point that the conditions—faith and repentance—are 'performed by Grace, and not by Natural Power'.[41] According to Williams, Crisp was wrong to believe that the benefits of justification are possessed by a member of the elect before her effectual calling, and even before her birth. Williams therefore rejected the antinomian conclusion that 'the worst Sinners, if elect, have as much interest in Christ, as the greatest Saint'. After effectual calling, the elect would persevere on the path to salvation, but these justified Christians were nonetheless to be counted guilty of whatever sins they committed.[42] The controversy provoked by *Gospel-Truth Stated* alienated Congregationalists, some of whom criticized Williams for promoting a legalistic understanding of salvation. But perhaps in the longer term, the significance of Williams's book was to raise the profile of 'middle way' theology in English Presbyterianism.[43]

The Baxterian system had powerful support among Dissenters at the start of the eighteenth century. Orthodox Calvinists, by contrast, wished for a more uncompromising bulwark against the rationalizing tendencies of Arminians, Socinians, and deists. In 1697, the Independent Stephen Lobb complained that though Baxterians 'set up for Men of a *middle way*' between Calvinists and Arminians, 'yet, on the turn from the former, they fall in so far with the latter' that they 'at last, fall in entirely with them, and run their length'. Arminians, Lobb suggested, would likewise tend to become Socinians.[44] Indeed, some Arminians saw the middle way as an unstable compromise, whose exponents would tend to magnify the contribution of human free will to salvation, and would thus be led to a fully Arminian position. According to Edmund Calamy, Bishop Gilbert Burnet took this view; consequently, Burnet failed to explain the 'middle way' when discussing predestination in his widely read *Exposition of the Thirty-Nine Articles* (1699).[45]

---

[41] Daniel Williams, *Gospel-Truth Stated and Vindicated: Wherein some of Dr Crisp's Opinions are Considered, and the Opposite Truths are Plainly Stated and Confirmed*, 2nd edn (London, 1692), pp. 44, 45 (quotation), 49–50, 86–101.

[42] Ibid., pp. 1–2, 75 (quotation), 102, 146.

[43] For the controversy, see Roger Thomas, *Daniel Williams, 'Presbyterian Bishop'* (London, 1964); Thomas, 'Presbyterians in Transition', pp. 117–25.

[44] Stephen Lobb, *The Growth of Error: Being an Exercitation concerning the Progress of Arminianism, and more especially Socinianism* (London, 1697), pp. 2–3.

[45] Calamy, *Historical Account*, I, pp. 468–71.

While some Baxterians did change their theological stance, we should be wary of assuming that there was an inevitable drift to Arminianism among Presbyterians. The idea of a slippery slope towards heterodoxy was, as we have seen, part of the evangelical reading of Presbyterian history. It was frequently expounded in the eighteenth century, for example in the well-known manuscript 'View of the Dissenting Interest in London' (1731). The Calvinist author attributed some blame for the modest decline in the capital's nonconformist population since the 1690s to 'the manifest growth of error'. Arminianism led to Arianism and Socinianism, he argued, and likewise to deism and 'Infidelity':

> when person[s] that have had a religious education, or have made a perticular profession of Christianity, begin to apostatise it is very often first manifested in their atacking the divine decrees, by aplauding the doctrine of universal redemption, as a sentiment that is full of benevolence, from thence they appear fond of pleading the cause of the heathens, and of the possibillity of salvation merely by the light of nature In a sincere improvement of the powers and faculties of men, and by degrees these charitable sentiments produce a small opinion of revelation and of the necessity of it in order to salvation, they will be often attempting to prove it Inconsistent or contradictory, & no wonder they become hereupon scepticks, and amongst other truths the doctrine of the Trinity is with them matter of Jest and ridicule[.][46]

This narrative of an irresistible lapse into heresy ignores the specific influences contributing to any individual's theological development. The memoirs and biographies of eighteenth-century ministers make it clear that there were numerous possible routes to heterodoxy. Life stories show that Presbyterians read extensively and critically in a spirit of free enquiry as early as the 1690s. Some young men perused directly the classics of rationalizing theology: works from which earlier students might have been shielded. James Clegg read Socinus and his followers in the late 1690s. He was generally unimpressed, though he 'could never after be entirely reconcild to the common doctrine of the Trinity but then begun to incline to that Scheme' later promoted by the Anglican Samuel Clarke in *The Scripture-Doctrine of the Trinity* (1712). Clegg's contemporaneous reading of the Dutch Remonstrant Episcopius ensured that he 'could never well relish the doctrines of Rigid Calvinism'.[47] Biographical sources also reveal the contribution of the wide-ranging education in theology provided in the Dissenting academies, as well as the domestic factors in a Presbyterian's intellectual formation. As a young man, the rational Dissenter Richard Price learned from modern theologians such as Clarke, but

---

[46] 'A View of the Dissenting Interest in London of the Presbyterian & Independent Denominations from the year 1665 to the 25 of December 1731', Dr Williams's Library, MS. 38.18, fos. [41]v.–[42]r.

[47] *Diary of James Clegg*, III, p. 913.

Price also reacted against the strict Calvinism of his father.⁴⁸ In the era of politeness, Presbyterians were keen to shake off any association between Christian doctrines and austere manners. According to Price's biographer William Morgan, writing in 1815, the opinions of the father were 'narrow, selfish and gloomy', those of the son contrastingly 'candid, liberal and benevolent'.⁴⁹ Joseph Priestley felt it necessary to deny that Dissenters were 'all canting hypocrites, the farthest in the world from any thing of a liberal taste or disposition, that we never laughed from generation to generation'.⁵⁰

Samuel Clarke was an important inspiration, but his influence on Presbyterianism should not be misstated. In the *Scripture-Doctrine*, he argued, against Arianism, that Christ was both co-eternal with God and begotten—not created—by him. Controversially, however, Clarke emphasized the supremacy of God the Father, and cast doubt on the biblical evidence for standard Trinitarian definitions.⁵¹ Relatively few Presbyterians seem to have been impelled by reading Clarke's work to depart from orthodox Trinitarianism, though the book led Hubert Stogdon of Exeter to pronounce himself an Arian.⁵² But Clarke's hermeneutical approach, based on the analysis of all scriptural references to the persons of the Trinity, certainly won Presbyterian admirers. Under Clarke's influence, mid eighteenth-century theologians produced a series of deliberately revisionist tracts written against orthodox dogmas they considered to be ill-founded in Scripture. In *The Scripture-Doctrine of Original Sin* (1740), John Taylor assessed all biblical texts relating to the transgression in the Garden of Eden and its consequences. Adam's sin, Taylor maintained, brought death into the world, but did not entail that all subsequent humans were by nature sinful. Taylor's work was condemned by theologians as illustrious as John Wesley and Jonathan Edwards.⁵³ In *The Scripture-Doctrine of Atonement Examined* (1751), Taylor accepted that Christ's sacrifice on the cross made atonement for humans' sins, but controversially denied that those sins were imputed to, or borne vicariously by, Christ.⁵⁴ Joseph Priestley's *Scripture-Doctrine of Remission* (1761) took a

---

⁴⁸ D. O. Thomas, *The Honest Mind: The Thought and Work of Richard Price* (Oxford, 1977), pp. 1–11.

⁴⁹ William Morgan, *Memoirs of the Life of the Rev. Richard Price*, ed. D. O. Thomas, in *Enlightenment and Dissent*, 22 (2003), p. 3.

⁵⁰ Joseph Priestley, *A View of the Principles and Conduct of the Protestant Dissenters, with Respect to the Civil and Ecclesiastical Constitution of England*, 2nd edn (London, 1769), p. 3.

⁵¹ Samuel Clarke, *The Scripture-Doctrine of the Trinity* (London, 1712). For a brief discussion, see Thomas C. Pfizenmaier, 'Why the Third Fell Out: Trinitarian Dissent', in Robert D. Cornwall and William Gibson, eds, *Religion, Politics and Dissent, 1660–1832: Essays in Honour of James E. Bradley* (Farnham, 2010).

⁵² Allan Brockett, *Nonconformity in Exeter, 1650–1875* (Manchester, 1962), pp. 80–2.

⁵³ John Taylor, *The Scripture-Doctrine of Original Sin proposed to Free and Candid Examination* (London, 1740), esp. pp. 63, 161; G. T. Eddy, *Dr Taylor of Norwich: Wesley's Arch-heretic* (Peterborough, 2003), esp. chs 9–11.

⁵⁴ John Taylor, *The Scripture-Doctrine of Atonement Examined* (London, 1751), esp. pp. 91–2, 100.

further step away from orthodoxy in contending that 'the Death of CHRIST is no proper Sacrifice nor Satisfaction for Sin: but that pardon is dispensed solely on account of repentance, or a personal reformation of the Sinner'. Arguably, however, Priestley exposed the limitations of the 'scripture-doctrine' project, asserting that individual biblical passages were vague and figurative, tending to distract from the 'plain general tenor of scripture'.[55]

Clarke's *Scripture-Doctrine* reinforced the most important trend in early eighteenth-century English Presbyterianism. This was the increasing acceptance of the view that religious tests, aside from acceptance of the Bible as the rule of faith, were unwarranted and objectionable. The Toleration Act required nonconformist ministers seeking protection for their worship to subscribe to the Thirty-Nine Articles of the Church of England. Excluded were the first clause of article 20 (asserting the Church's authority to impose ceremonies), articles 34 (concerning Church traditions), 35 (specifying the Anglican homilies), and 36 (on ordination and consecration).[56] It is unclear how widely Presbyterians complied with this provision, which remained in force until 1779. Edmund Calamy established his ministerial career without subscribing; in 1713, he advised the young John Fox in Devon to do the same.[57] On the other hand, the *Heads of Agreement* of 1691 stated that churches should 'acknowledge the *Scriptures to be the word of God*, the *perfect and only Rule of Faith and Practice*; and own either the Doctrinal part' of the Thirty-Nine Articles, the Westminster confession or catechisms, or the Savoy declaration (1658), 'to be agreeable to the said Rule'.[58] Though the Exeter Assembly and Cheshire classis investigated the views of candidates for the ministry, elsewhere the undertakings expected of preachers prior to ordination varied. In Westmorland, Samuel Bourn, who became minister of Crook in 1711, controversially refused to subscribe to the shorter catechism at his ordination. John Taylor, ordained by Derbyshire ministers in 1716, was not expected to subscribe to any confession.[59]

Opposition to human formulas was particularly contentious when it seemed to arise from heterodox views, especially with regard to the Trinity. In 1718, Martin Tomkins preached a sermon in his meeting house at Stoke Newington, Middlesex, which resulted in his expulsion by the congregation. Tomkins argued that no doctrines could be considered crucial unless clearly specified in the New Testament. The Trinity, he alleged, was scarcely mentioned there. Thus it was not a fundamental article of faith, whatever creeds

---

[55] [Joseph Priestley], *The Scripture Doctrine of Remission* (London, 1761), title-page, p. 17.
[56] 1 Wm. & Mary c.18.
[57] 'Memoirs of Himself, by Mr John Fox, of Plymouth', *Monthly Repository*, XVI, no. 183 (1821), p. 135.
[58] *Heads of Agreement*, pp. 14–15.
[59] Alan P. F. Sell, 'A Little Friendly Light: The Candour of Bourn, Taylor and Towgood', in Sell, *Dissenting Thought*, p. 221; Eddy, *Dr Taylor of Norwich*, pp. 13–15.

and confessions said. Tomkins denied that his sermon promoted an Arian understanding of God. But he objected to the imposition of the orthodox doctrine.[60] By the time of Tomkins's provocative sermon, the dissatisfaction of the minister James Peirce and his associates with orthodox Trinitarianism had sparked a local controversy in Exeter. The dispute was referred to the Dissenting ministers in London. The resulting debate at Salters' Hall, on 24 February 1719, centred on whether to include an assertion of Trinitarian belief in a paper of advice to be sent to Exeter. The meeting's decision, by a majority of 57 to 53, not to do so exposed a division between those ministers who favoured subscription (the minority), and those opposed to it. The vote split all the Dissenting denominations, but whereas most Independents supported the principle of subscription, the majority of Presbyterians, especially the younger ministers, saw the Bible as the only measure of faith.[61] Though the non-subscribing position would give succour to Arians, only a few of the non-subscribers at Salters' Hall inclined to heterodoxy.[62] Moreover, liberal-minded Presbyterians would continue to feel more welcome in some parts of the country than in others. In Exeter, Peirce was ejected from his pulpit, and the Exeter Assembly continued to examine candidates for ordination until 1753.[63]

Opposition to subscription is usually interpreted as a development of Richard Baxter's credal minimalism and hostility to human imposition in religion. At the restoration of the Church of England in 1661–2, Baxter and his brethren opposed the Anglicans' claim that liturgical practices could be decreed by human authority, limiting the freedom of worship apparently granted by God. For Edmund Calamy, writing in 1704, the Nonconformists' objection to the Established Church remained its insistence on uniformity in matters such as worship, where Scripture was indifferent. Calamy could find no reason to believe that bishops, church councils, or the magistrate had a right to ordain ceremonies or articles of belief.[64] But if Baxter and Calamy saw the question of human imposition as one separating Anglicans from moderate Nonconformists, after 1719 there was also a dividing line among Dissenters. By the mid eighteenth century, refusal to subscribe to the confessions of faith was a standard position among English Presbyterians. The London minister Samuel Chandler included a discussion of subscription in his *History of Persecution* (1736), writing that 'Subscriptions have ever been a Grievance in

---

[60] Martin Tomkins, *The Case of Mr Martin Tomkins* (London, 1719), pp. 18, 23–35.

[61] Of the many accounts, see esp. Thomas, 'Presbyterians in Transition', pp. 151–74; Brockett, *Nonconformity in Exeter*, pp. 74–95; Roger Thomas, 'The Non-Subscription Controversy amongst Dissenters in 1719: The Salters' Hall Debate', *Journal of Ecclesiastical History*, 4, 2 (1953).

[62] Thomas, 'Non-Subscription Controversy', p. 175, n. 4.

[63] *Exeter Assembly*, p. vii.

[64] Edmund Calamy, *A Defence of Moderate Nonconformity... Part II* (London, 1704), 'Introduction', pp. 1–94.

the Church of God'.[65] Samuel Bourn thought that 'Subscriptions to human Articles of Faith' have 'been the Plague and Shame of the Church'. Significantly, given Bourn's Arianism, he described subscription as 'an Engine of Division and Contention ever since the Council of *Nice*'.[66] For Micaiah Towgood, a minister at Exeter, adherence to the Bible alone was fundamental to Presbyterianism. Dissent, Towgood wrote, was a 'protest which we publicly make against *A new Edition of* CHRISTIANITY, *with Corrections and Amendments*', in favour of 'the old, the primitive, plan of doctrines and rites which CHRIST and his *Apostles* established in the Church'.[67]

In the case of Joseph Priestley, we can see how rational Dissent and Unitarianism were in continuity with mid eighteenth-century Presbyterianism and at the same time innovative.[68] Priestley's *View of the Principles and Conduct of the Protestant Dissenters* (1769) was written to defend the opinions and loyalty of Nonconformists from the aspersions of the MP and lawyer William Blackstone. Priestley outlined a series of Dissenting principles, most of which would have been recognizable to earlier Presbyterians such as Calamy. Thus Priestley argued that human authority had no claim to impose in religion; that the Anglican hierarchy was unwarranted; that ministers could not be required to use vestments and specific rites; that the Book of Common Prayer of 1662, and uniform national liturgy more generally, were objectionable. He also echoed Calamy's more secular argument for the toleration of Dissent: that pluralism and freedom of discussion helped to preserve religious and civil liberties. Whereas some Anglicans wished that Nonconformity would disappear, Priestley claimed, 'We think it is greatly for the advantage, both of religion, and the society, that no obstruction be thrown in the way, either of *forming* new sects, or of *continuing* the old ones.'[69] Considering the role that Priestley would play over the following decades in the emergence of Unitarianism, this was a revealing statement.

Where Priestley differed from earlier Presbyterian apologists was in his emphasis on continuous theological development. He admitted that most Dissenters accepted the doctrines of the Thirty-Nine Articles. But a growing number of Nonconformists, 'the most distinguished for learning and freedom of inquiry', were participating in a progressive emancipation from the

---

[65] Samuel Chandler, *The History of Persecution* (London, 1736), pp. 424–37, quotation at p. 428.

[66] Samuel Bourn, *A Vindication of the Principles and Practice of Protestant Dissenters* (London, 1748), p. 25.

[67] Micaiah Towgood, *A Dissent from the Church of England, fully Justified* (London, 1753), p.v.

[68] See David L. Wykes and Isabel Rivers, eds, *Joseph Priestley: Scientist, Philosopher, and Theologian* (Oxford, 2008).

[69] Priestley, *View of the Principles*, pp. 7–16, 79, 80 (quotation); Calamy, *Historical Account*, I, p. 263.

attitudes of the sixteenth century, a trend in continuity with the Reformation itself. In Priestley's view, this entailed abandoning such dogmas as original sin and predestination, and rejecting the Trinity as unreasonable and unscriptural.[70] The Trinity was 'an opinion which, as I conceive, denies the maker of all things the honour and worship that are due to him alone'.[71] It was not a doctrine that could survive the process of intellectual and moral improvement characteristic of Priestley's sort of Dissenters. Among Unitarians of a later generation, Robert Aspland experienced a particularly rapid intellectual journey from orthodoxy, through Arianism to Unitarianism. In 1805, Aspland preached that the 'notion of Jesus being God Almighty is utterly irreconcileable [sic] with the whole tenor of the Bible'. He called the Arian belief in Christ's 'pre-existence' as a spirit before his birth to Mary 'harmless', but Aspland nevertheless considered this idea an ill-founded 'error'.[72] Other leading figures, notably Thomas Belsham, were more combative in their rejection of Arianism.

Unitarianism gained its own denominational accoutrements in the early nineteenth century. A Unitarian Fund was established in 1800, and a series of societies followed, including the British and Foreign Unitarian Association in 1825. In 1806, Aspland founded the *Monthly Repository* as a forum for Unitarian news, history, and criticism. Directed by Belsham, the Unitarian Society for the Promotion of Christian Knowledge published an 'improved' version of the New Testament in 1808. Richard Wright, George Harris, and the less well-known William Allard of Bury, Lancashire, conducted missionary tours; Allard planted preaching stations served by lay people.[73] If these were unusual tactics, they showed that Unitarianism was not moribund or complacent, even by the evangelicals' standards.

PRESBYTERIAN THEOLOGY AND THE LAITY

We can conclude by considering how Presbyterianism's theological developments affected rank-and-file worshippers. New doctrinal views and especially the appointment of heterodox ministers frequently sparked local disputes and secessions. At Wrexham in 1691, supporters of Daniel Williams, a native of

[70] Priestley, *View of the Principles*, pp. 16 (quotation), 17–19.
[71] Ibid., p. 6.
[72] R. Brook Aspland, *Memoir of the Life, Works and Correspondence of the Rev. Robert Aspland* (London, 1850), p. 157.
[73] Short, 'Presbyterians under a New Name', pp. 237–40; H. L. Short, 'The Founding of the British and Foreign Unitarian Association', *TUHS*, 16, 1, supplement (1975); Deryck W. Lovegrove, *Established Church, Sectarian People: Itinerancy and the Transformation of English Dissent, 1780–1830* (Cambridge, 1988), p. 108.

the town, left the mixed Presbyterian and Independent congregation to found a new meeting house willing to accept Baxterian preaching.[74] If the reputation of Williams won followers for Baxter's system in Wrexham, many other lay people preferred more thoroughgoing Calvinism. Around 1692, Dissenters in Andover, Hampshire, asked Edmund Calamy to settle there as a minister. When he counselled the congregation to pay for weekly sermons from the existing Presbyterian, Mr Sprint, Calamy was told that '"Alas, he [Sprint] is a Baxterian! he is a middle way man! he is an occasional Conformist! he is neither fish nor flesh, nor good red herring!".'[75] In the early 1720s, Southport experienced its own antinomian controversy, after the congregation made a call to Samuel de la Rose. His extreme Calvinism prompted other nearby ministers to investigate and condemn his teaching, helping to divide the congregation.[76]

In various other cases, doctrinal disputes fractured meeting-house communities. After the death of its minister Matthew Henry in 1714, the Presbyterian congregation at Hackney split in two. One party favoured John Barker, a Calvinist minister, while the other group built a new chapel and employed Arminian preachers.[77] In Derby, theological differences may have been a factor behind the establishment of a new Independent congregation in 1778; the existing Presbyterian chapel was Unitarian by 1799.[78] The appointment in 1748 of a heterodox minister at the Mill Hill Presbyterian meeting house in Leeds led one worshipper to complain of the new man's sermons. 'To hear the doctrines which our pious forefathers suffered for, but not only so, such doctrines as the Scriptures, in my apprehension of things, appear clearly to hold forth – in a manner confuted – it gives me great concern.'[79] Surveying the religious landscape in the mid eighteenth century, the widely travelled layman Joseph Williams of Kidderminster lamented the rise of heterodoxy among Presbyterians. Of the period's leading ministers, Williams especially disliked Samuel Bourn and John Taylor. After the death of his own minister in 1742, Williams was involved in the fractious search for a replacement, quizzing candidates on the Trinity, original sin, and justification before the appointment of Benjamin Fawcett in 1745. Fawcett disguised his own heterodox

---

[74] Michael R. Watts, *The Dissenters: Volume I: From the Reformation to the French Revolution* (Oxford, 1978), p. 296.
[75] Calamy, *Historical Account*, I, pp. 303–9, quotation at p. 308.
[76] *Cheshire Classis Minutes*, pp. 60–6, 167; *Diary of James Clegg*, III, pp. 919–20.
[77] Alan R. Ruston, *Unitarianism and Early Presbyterianism in Hackney* (Oxhey, 1980), pp. 7–10.
[78] K. M. Eagers, 'A Short History of the Central United Reformed Church, Derby', *Derbyshire Miscellany*, 15, 6 (2000), p. 161.
[79] Quoted in R.K. Webb, 'The Emergence of Rational Dissent', in Haakonssen, ed., *Enlightenment and Religion*, p. 28.

opinions, and his theologically diverse congregation remained intact, dividing only after his death in 1780.[80]

Frequently, then, unpopular ministerial appointments led to local secessions and haemorrhaging congregations. These reinforced the orthodoxy of the Independent and evangelical chapels that received new members, while ensuring that, in the particular localities, Presbyterianism represented a narrower range of more liberal opinion. But the pattern was by no means universal. In parts of northern England, many congregations (some of Scottish affiliation) remained committed to traditional beliefs, and provided a receptacle for worshippers seceding from heterodox Presbyterian chapels.[81] Rational Dissenters were aware that theirs was not a particularly popular religion. Looking back from 1807, Samuel Heywood recognized that eighteenth-century Presbyterian ministers' Arianism had alienated lay people, to the benefit of other denominations.[82] Yet the urban congregations of the leading rational Dissenters contained influential and wealthy members.[83]

Between the 1690s and the early nineteenth century, Presbyterians took a leading role in explaining—and expanding—the reasons to dissent from the Church of England. Not only did they reject the imposition of ceremonial uniformity by bishops and civil governors, figures whose ecclesiastical authority they questioned. Most Presbyterians also came to oppose compulsory subscription to man-made creeds, and to assert a right to free theological enquiry. Those most committed to this principle repudiated orthodox doctrines, notably original sin, the atonement, and the Trinity. Yet theological diversity remained at the end of our period, and Calvinist doctrines continued to be heard in the chapels of Scottish congregations. The century's theological changes, like the reconfiguration of relations between Presbyterians and Independents, were not foreseeable at the collapse of the Happy Union, or at Salters' Hall in 1719. A century later, it was possible to view Unitarianism as a new denomination, drawing together theological liberals from various protestant traditions. Nevertheless, Presbyterians were at the heart of its development. Theologically, the Presbyterian spectrum had shifted; numerically, Presbyterians were fewer. But Presbyterianism retained its pivotal position among the Protestant Dissenting traditions of England and Wales.

---

[80] Isabel Rivers, 'Joseph Williams of Kidderminster (1692–1755) and his Journal', *JURCHS*, 7, 6 (2005); Goring, 'Break-up of the Old Dissent', p. 203.

[81] Sell, 'Presbyterianism in Eighteenth-Century England', pp. 145, 148; Black, *Scots Churches in England*, esp. pp. 293–5.

[82] Ditchfield, 'Unitarian View of English Dissent', p. 10.

[83] John Seed, 'Gentlemen Dissenters: The Social and Political Meanings of Rational Dissent in the 1770s and 1780s', *Historical Journal*, 28, 2 (1985).

SELECT BIBLIOGRAPHY

Bolam, C. G., and others, *The English Presbyterians: From Elizabethan Puritanism to Modern Unitarianism* (London, 1968).

Drysdale, A. H., *History of the Presbyterians in England: Their Rise, Decline, and Revival* (London, 1889).

Eddy, G. T., *Dr Taylor of Norwich: Wesley's Arch-heretic* (Peterborough, 2003).

Haakonssen, Knud, ed., *Enlightenment and Religion: Rational Dissent in Eighteenth-Century Britain* (Cambridge, 1996).

Nuttall, Geoffrey F., 'Assembly and Association in Dissent, 1689–1831', in G. J. Cumming and Derek Baker, eds, *Councils and Assemblies* (Cambridge, 1971), pp. 289–310.

Nuttall, Geoffrey F., *Richard Baxter and Philip Doddridge: A Study in Tradition* (London, 1951).

Richey, Russell E., 'Did the English Presbyterians become Unitarian?', *Church History*, 42, 1 (1973), pp. 58–72.

Sell, Alan P. F., *Dissenting Thought and the Life of the Churches: Studies in an English Tradition* (San Francisco, 1990).

Thomas, Roger, 'The Non-Subscription Controversy amongst Dissenters in 1719: The Salters' Hall Debate', *Journal of Ecclesiastical History*, 4, 2 (1953), pp. 162–86.

Wykes, David L., 'After the Happy Union: Presbyterians and Independents in the Provinces', in R. N. Swanson, ed., *Unity and Diversity in the Church* (Oxford, 1996), pp. 283–95.

Wykes, David L., '"The settling of meetings and the preaching of the gospel": The Development of the Dissenting Interest, 1690–1715', *Journal of the United Reformed Church History Society*, 5, 3 (1993), pp. 127–45.

Wykes, David L. and Isabel Rivers, eds, *Joseph Priestley: Scientist, Philosopher, and Theologian* (Oxford, 2008).

2

Congregationalists

Stephen Orchard

The years of nonconformist repression were ended in 1689 by the Toleration Act. Though celebrated then and since as enlightened legislation, it did not actually abolish the penal laws, but licensed the dissent of Baptists, Congregationalists, and Presbyterians. By declaring their general agreement with the doctrines of the Church of England and their abhorrence of Roman Catholicism before a court of law, these Dissenters were allowed to license meeting houses for public worship and claim exemption from the legislation requiring conformity to the Church of England. They were tolerated, but not expected to flourish. Roman Catholics were allowed no such clemency; those who were now termed Protestant Dissenters claimed credit for their loyal abhorrence of popery. By 1828, when the Test and Corporation Acts were repealed, removing the major obstacle to Dissenters taking part in civic life, the politics of the situation had changed radically. The tolerance then being extended to Roman Catholics required similar action on behalf of Dissenters, though there still remained barriers to their full participation in society. By now Congregationalists had formed societies for home and foreign mission in most English counties and were on the verge of drawing them together in the Congregational Union of England and Wales, founded in 1831. This union is what we can recognize as a religious denomination in the modern sense.

THE EMERGENCE OF CONGREGATIONALISM

In 1689 the ties which bound Congregationalists together were much more informal; indeed, it becomes a matter of conjecture whether a particular Dissenter was Presbyterian, Congregational, or Baptist in their convictions. Early Dissenting congregations often mixed the three denominations together, sometimes holding separate worship, sometimes declaring for one or the other label according to their minister's preferences. Moreover, many Dissenters attended their parish church as well as their separate meetings and, doubtless, parishioners not counted as Dissenters might have attended their meeting houses from time to time. All this was against a background of speculation about whether a comprehensive settlement could be reached with the Church of England which would enable Dissenters to conform. This speculation continued for decades. It is tempting to argue that the twenty-first century Church of England, with its various options for liturgy and ministry and its inability to enforce its rules on the uncooperative, is what would have accommodated eighteenth-century Congregationalists in their search for 'comprehension'. However, any kind of reading of a denominational consciousness, as the contemporary world knows it, back into this period is to misunderstand the past history of churches in England.

The broad Calvinistic doctrines of the Westminster Confession of Faith were accepted by both Presbyterians and Congregationalists. The Congregationalists had their nuanced version in the Savoy Declaration of 1658. Although they had set out to prepare a new statement of faith, so many of them were veterans of the Westminster Assembly of the previous decade that its Confession is echoed throughout. The chief difference then and in 1658 was over Erastianism and the power of presbytery over the local congregation. Congregationalists were not necessarily Separatists but they did believe that the local church meeting, under the guidance of the Holy Spirit, was able to determine matters of order and doctrine. They were prepared to consult with and take guidance from other Congregationalists but not to yield the power of command to presbyteries any more than to prelates. In particular, they distinguished between temporal and spiritual authority. Civil powers had a duty to provide for religion to flourish but not to control it. In this Congregationalists were persuaded more by the pre-Constantinian church structures of the New Testament than the positions adopted by Reformers such as Luther and Calvin. Here the Savoy Declaration trod a narrow line between excluding the magistrate from determining matters of religion, and expecting the state to censure those who used religious freedom as a licence to promote perversions of faith. Congregationalists always had a weak flank on which they could be attacked for abandoning restraint in matters of religion to the point of allowing fanaticism to flourish. The debates on antinomianism at the Westminster Assembly were not abstract discussions but fundamental to public policy in a time when people were taking the law into their own hands. All Nonconformists who took the necessary oath in 1689 to free them from the penal laws declared their broad acceptance of the Thirty-Nine Articles, subjecting their beliefs to the state to that extent at least.

Toleration came, therefore, with conditions. Partly, it was regularizing the position of those local magistrates who had turned a blind eye to nonconformist activity in their locality so long as it was low profile and uncontentious.

The generation who had known active repression was in evidence for at least another twenty years. There were still over a hundred ejected ministers living in 1700 and a handful survived into the following decade. Something under a half of these were active in nonconformist meetings. They formed a small part of Alexander Gordon's index to ministers mentioned in the records of the Common Fund, which supported Nonconformists in the 1690s.[1] Overall he lists approximately 300 ministers active in 1700, of whom about seventy he designates Congregationalists. Many of these 300 who were not themselves ejected ministers were their direct descendants. Add to that the children who had grown up in nonconformist households before 1689, and who lived well into the next century as lay members of meetings, and the makings of a kind of tribal identity are evident. Two notable eighteenth-century Dissenters, Isaac Watts and Philip Doddridge, were grandchildren of those who suffered in the penal years and so, whatever intellectual objections they might raise when tempted to conform, there was family loyalty to consider.

For these reasons it is difficult to apply the modern concept of a religious denomination in this period. What we identify as Congregationalism in such figures is an ethos or philosophy, which Congregationalists wished to see adopted by the Church of England. People put a premium on ideas in the eighteenth century. In religion they pursued doctrinal differences, including the emergence of what we would now term Unitarianism, with an unspoken assumption that the Church of England would somehow coalesce once more, once the right negotiating positions had been secured. What is more, not all those who were sympathetic to a puritan position left the Church of England in 1662. Of the 2,000 or so who did leave, or were deprived between 1660 and 1662, many hundreds retired to their own property and sat at the back of the church, literally and metaphorically. Later legend turned them all into heroic resisters, holding clandestine meetings, paying fines, and languishing under arrest. In fact, the Nonconformists were matched by a kind of puritan fifth column remaining in the Church of England and sympathetic to the idea of welcoming back the prodigals.

SIZE AND DEVELOPMENT

Just how many were the former Nonconformists, now better described as Dissenters? Counting the number of meetings in the 1690s is not an exact science, since they opened and closed all the time and for a variety of reasons. However, around 600 at any one time is a reasonable estimate. These meetings

---

[1] Alexander Gordon, ed., *Freedom After Ejection* (London, 1917).

were the legacy of the resistance before 1689. Although subject to qualification, one indication of nonconformist numbers at this time is given in the Compton Census of 1676.² This is reckoned to show a total of 108,000 in England and Wales, of which about 68,000 were in England. This represents a very small proportion of the population. If we assume that a minority of Dissenters identified themselves with the Congregational or Independent standpoint, then they are an even rarer species. Add to this the fact that they were not evenly distributed around the country and you will find them very poorly represented in, say, North Yorkshire, but comparatively more prominent in London and the West Country. The most widely accepted statistics suggest that, following the Toleration Act, there were 338,120 Dissenters in England in the early eighteenth century, comprising about 6 per cent of the population. Within this total were about 60,000 Congregationalists or Independents.³ The Congregational historian, Albert Peel, reckoned that in 1716 'there were probably 380 Independent congregations in England and Wales, not more than one-sixth of whom had meeting-houses'. By 1811 the Independents had 799 congregations and by 1829 possibly as many as 1,665.⁴

Numbers are not everything and the average was usually exceeded in urban areas. Dissenters were prominent in local government, usually making a token gesture of conformity to their parish church in order to qualify for election.⁵ Dissenters were married and buried in the Church of England. They began to open their own burial grounds when incumbents refused to bury children baptized in Dissenting Meetings. Some children of Dissenters were baptized twice, first by their own minister and then in the parish church, the first ceremony being religious and the second for legal purposes. The porous boundaries between Church and Dissent make statistics inexact and suggest that Dissenting ideas were influential out of all proportion to the assumed size of their community. On one extreme lay High Church Anglicans and on the other the High Calvinists; the spectrum of opinion between the extremes included many overlaps. Fear that Dissenters were a kind of fifth column in the state was used to raise mobs against meeting houses at the beginning of the eighteenth century and to sack Joseph Priestley's house at the end.

Two notable pieces of fiction explore the nature of society in the early eighteenth century. One is Jonathan Swift's *Gulliver's Travels*. Swift was a High Church Tory. His Lemuel Gulliver is the vehicle for uncovering Swift's dark view of humanity. What passes for wisdom is folly; wars are fought over trivial

---

² Anne Whiteman, ed., *The Compton Census of 1676* (Oxford, 1986).
³ Michael Watts, *The Dissenters: From the Reformation to the French Revolution* (Oxford, 1978). These statistics originate there and have been widely accepted.
⁴ Albert Peel, *These Hundred Years 1831–1931* (London, 1931), pp. 19–20.
⁵ John Coffey, 'Church and State, 1550–1750: The Emergence of Dissent', in Robert Pope, ed., *T & T Clark Companion to Nonconformity* (London, 2013), p. 65.

causes; people exploit one another mercilessly. The other traveller is Daniel Defoe's *Robinson Crusoe*. Defoe was a Whig, though often in Tory employ, and a Dissenter. Robinson Crusoe recognizes that his thirst for adventure usually lands him in difficult situations but his ingenuity always saves him in the end. On his island he develops a prosperous community, where people of different beliefs live together harmoniously. In *The Further Adventures of Robinson Crusoe* he depicts a French catholic priest who brings about the religious conversion and moral regeneration of villainous mutineers. It is true that he represents some of the locals as warring cannibals who may justifiably be killed and that he takes a gloomy view of the Spanish Inquisition, but he otherwise describes a world in which a creative human response to the justice and mercy of God brings about a happy life. Just as we must take responsibility for our own mistakes, rather than blame a malignant deity, so we must make our own good life, rather than pray for a particular providence to transform our situation. Above all, Crusoe finds satisfaction in creating a world where people of different religions and nationality can live together in harmony. It embodies the ideas of the influential Czech Reformer, Jan Comenius. What Defoe shows to us above all, both in the character of Robinson Crusoe and in another of his original creations, Moll Flanders, is the inner struggles of conscience which are characteristic of a Puritan.

Defoe's own life is only partly represented in that of Crusoe. Defoe was not a world traveller but a good listener to those who were. He did prosper in business but was reduced to his previous state of poverty. His poem, *The True-Born Englishman*, poured scorn on narrow patriotism, for Dissenters saw themselves as part of protestant Europe, freed from popery. He took a purist view of Nonconformity in his *An Inquiry into Occasional Conformity* (1698). Prominent Nonconformists who wished to take a part in public life had developed the practice of taking communion in the Church of England on an occasional basis in order to give lip service to the legal requirement. Defoe saw this as a betrayal of principle. The Lord Mayor of London, Sir Humphrey Edwin, had attended St Paul's in the morning and Pinners' Hall Meeting in the afternoon, wearing his official robes and with his sword of office. Defoe characterized this as 'playing Bo-peep with God Almighty'. Defoe stoked up the controversy when the next Lord Mayor, Sir Thomas Abney, repeated the act, by attending John Howe's meeting house in Silver Street. This episode suggests that Defoe's Dissent, generally described as Presbyterian, veered more towards Congregationalism. He was Presbyterian insofar as he favoured the monarchy and had little enthusiasm for Cromwell. More controversy was to follow. His ironic pamphlet of 1702, *The Shortest-Way With Dissenters*, was misread and landed him in trouble. After being found guilty of sedition he faced three days in the pillory and imprisonment in Newgate. From there he was rescued by the Tory politician Robert Harley, later earl of Oxford, and worked for him as long as he was in government. After Queen Anne's death Defoe transferred his services to the Whigs who formed the new government.[6]

Defoe is most remembered for his writing and his time as a government agent. In the first part of his life he had been a merchant. Dissent was heavily dependent on the merchant class for its survival. As we have seen, Sir Thomas Abney, who is generally described as a Presbyterian, supported the Silver Street Meeting in the City of London, whose minister was the Presbyterian, John Howe. His first wife, Sarah Caryl, was the daughter of Joseph Caryl, a prominent Congregational minister. The Abney family came from Derbyshire but Thomas made his money in London and took a leading part in Whig politics and Dissent. His second wife, Mary Gunston, inherited a property at Stoke Newington, subsequently known as Abney House, where Abney lived in the latter part of his life, though spending his summers at his other house at Theobalds in Hertfordshire. Although Abney withdrew from an active part in the Nonconformist community in his later life he and his widow supported Isaac Watts, the celebrated Congregationalist, who lived with them at Stoke Newington and Theobalds from 1712 after ending his active ministry on the grounds of ill health. The patronage of merchants like Abney was critical for the survival of Dissent.

It is no surprise, therefore, to find Abney as one of the original trustees of the Common Fund, set up to underwrite the costs of Presbyterian and Congregational ministry. Briefly it seemed that these two schools of Dissenting thought would make common cause. After the Common Fund of 1690 London ministers of both parties formed an association known as the Happy Union in 1691, which was followed by similar associations in the provinces. By definition a Dissenting community contains people with strong ideological convictions and assertive, even combative, personalities. The best efforts of the irenic may not be sufficient to prevent breaches. By 1693 cracks were appearing in the Common Fund and the establishment of a new, Presbyterian Fund, took place.[7] Abney is found on the new board, over which presided his minister, John Howe. In spite of its name the new fund continued to support some Congregational ministers and students. The overall purpose was to encourage the continuation of local meetings of Dissenters and the training of a new generation of ministers. Another City merchant was George Boddington (1646–1719), who made his fortune in the Levant trade. He gave support to the new regime of William and Mary and was one of the first directors of the Bank of England. He served

---

[6] Paula R. Backscheider, 'Defoe, Daniel (1660?–1731)', *Oxford Dictionary of National Biography*, Oxford University Press, 2004; online edn, Jan. 2008 [http://www.oxforddnb.com/view.article/7421, accessed 24 July 2015].

[7] Extracts from the minutes and an analysis of the rift are to be found in Gordon, *Freedom After Ejection*, p. 183.

alongside Abney in the Common Fund but was one of those who, as part of its break-up, established the Congregational Fund in 1695.[8]

These funds are critical sources of information on early Dissent. From their records we can map out where individual meetings and ministers were and who acted as correspondents. The term 'meeting' is used advisedly. When we read of sixty or a hundred hearers in one parish that rarely means they are all resident there. A congregation would be gathered in small groups from a wide area and not necessarily every week. It sometimes suited Dissenters to meet in remote rural spots, where they would outnumber potential opponents. In London, meetings were held in hired halls more often than in dedicated buildings. Ministers travelled between these meetings and around the homes of members to baptize their children, to catechize, or to bring the sacrament to the sick. From the fund minutes and the surviving records of individual congregations a picture emerges of local ministerial associations, the mutual recognition of ministers, and the commendation of members from one congregation to another. This was all done on a basis of trust rather than legal commitment. Although we speak of Presbyterians there is little evidence of a formal structure of presbyteries such as we associate with modern Presbyterian churches. When the Congregationalist John Milton wrote that the new presbyter was but the old priest writ large he was indicating the hierarchical ethos of Presbyterianism at a time when Parliament was trying to impose it on the Church of England. Presbyterian meetings of the early eighteenth century operated as Independents for all practical purposes, but still with the assumption that they were a shadow national church. Congregationalists were more wary of establishment, even though they found ways of accommodating it in New England. In the absence of a formal superstructure for either Presbyterians or Congregationalists, the funds provided support and also validation for local initiatives.

DEBATE AND DOCTRINE

This absence of formal structures, indeed, the debate about whether they were necessary, lay at the heart of what is known as the Salters' Hall controversy. Historically this has been seen as a key doctrinal controversy, marking the beginning of the growth of what was to become Unitarianism. More recent scholarship has drawn attention to the sub-text, which was the question of who determines what is orthodox and enforces it. For Dissenters, this was an integral part of any doctrinal question. The details of the controversy are to be

---

[8] John H. Taylor, 'The Congregational Fund Board' (1995), supplement to *Journal of the United Reformed Church History Society* (hereafter *JURCHS*).

found elsewhere in this volume. For Congregationalists, the ecclesial questions were bound up with the doctrinal ones. London ministers were asked to subscribe to a paper of formal advice to ministers meeting in Exeter. This advice maintained an orthodox Trinitarian position. Analysis has shown that almost half the subscribers were Congregationalists and most of the non-subscribers Presbyterian. It was also the older ministers who subscribed and the younger who did not.[9] In Exeter the assembled ministers, including the Congregationalists, required the subscription which the subscribers at Salters' Hall had recommended and drove out those who resisted it. This neither resolved the debate on the nature of authority amongst Dissenters nor halted the rising tide of heterodoxy.

Academic enquiry, by its very nature, led to exploration of doctrinal topics. The Dissenting academies came under scrutiny by their potential supporters, as was the case in Exeter. Academies were individual enterprises by ministers. Once Joseph Hallet was driven out of Exeter for unorthodoxy the academy there ceased. The uncertainties of relying on individuals to set up appropriate places had led the Congregational Fund Board to establish its own academy at Moorfields, under Isaac Chauncy, who died in 1712. Some Congregationalists were not content with his successors, Thomas Ridgley and John Eames, with complaints made that there was too much education and not enough piety. In the 1720s the doubters formed the King's Head Society, named after the inn in Sweeting's Alley where they met. In 1731 they opened their own academy at Clerkenwell Green under the tutorship of Samuel Parsons. This moved to Deptford under the care of Abraham Taylor in 1735. The rules of the Society included a provision that:

> The students under the care of this Society shall be examined at least twice in a year as to their proficiency in learning, and conversed with also twice a year as to their experimental sense of religion by a committee of ministers and other gentlemen members of the Society which shall be appointed for those purposes.[10]

In its determination to balance piety and education the Society eventually deserted Taylor and its academy went through several more migrations before eventually settling at Homerton in 1769, where it continued to the end of the century with a succession of impeccably orthodox and evangelical tutors.

The Coward Trust, like the King's Head Society, established a public lectureship in London and supported ministerial education, though across several academies. It was established under the will of the merchant, William Coward, who died in 1738.[11] A similar concern had been shown by Sir John

---

[9] The declarations by the subscribers and non-subscribers are given in Alan P.F. Sell, David J. Hall, and Ian Sellars, eds, *Protestant Nonconformist Texts*, vol. 2 (Aldershot, 2006), pp. 67–70.
[10] John Waddington, *Congregational History 1700–1800* (London, 1876), p. 265.
[11] John H. Thompson, *The Coward Trust* (1998), supplement to *JURCHS*.

Hartopp, third baronet (1637–1722), who was a politician and convinced Independent. He was a friend of both John Owen and Isaac Watts, who served Hartopp's son as a tutor before becoming assistant minister to Isaac Chauncy at Mark Lane. The friendship continued and Watts visited Hartopp at his houses in Epsom and Freeby, near Melton Mowbray, both of which claim to be places where Watts once preached. Hartopp was a neighbour of the Abneys at Stoke Newington. His attempt in his will to leave £10,000 for the education of Dissenting ministers was contested by his family and eventually only part of it went to that purpose and was administered by the Coward Trust. This lay patronage of ministerial education through a range of trusts and funds secured Congregationalism from clericalism. Abney, Boddington, Hartopp, and Coward were weighty lay people whose patronage was important to ministers. This was not just a London phenomenon. Henry Bright (1715–1777), a merchant in Bristol, was an active supporter of Congregationalists. He made his money in the sugar and slave trades, which now seems repellent, but was a common route to riches for many a Bristol merchant at that time. Across England, in provincial towns, there were merchants and bankers who supported Dissent. Thomas Whitty, who was baptized in the Independent Meeting in Axminster in 1713, moved from weaving into the manufacture of hand-knotted carpets which became synonymous with the town. By the end of the eighteenth century his business was nationally celebrated. His own account of his life centred on his religious beliefs and two of his daughters married ministers.[12] A similar example from the middle of the century would be the Simonds family, brewers and bankers in Reading.

To the merchants and manufacturers might be added Whig politicians and local land owners who kept a foot in both camps, Church and Dissent, and used their influence to protect Dissenters, employed Dissenting ministers as chaplains and tutors, and opened their buildings for meetings. John Thompson MP (1648–1710) was a Dissenter by conviction and was vigorous in his opposition to James II and support for William and Mary. His loyalty to the new regime earned him his peerage as Baron Haversham. Grey Neville MP (1681–1723) was another politician sympathetic to Dissenters. He left money to Jeremiah Hunt, minister at Pinners Hall Meeting, to preach a sermon. Dissenters needed all the political friends they could get. They were politically threatened by the Tory government under Queen Anne. Legislation had already been enacted against Occasional Conformity and, in the closing weeks of the queen's life, a Schism Act, which would have effectively closed the academies, went through Parliament. The queen's death on 1 August 1714 and the consequent change of regime put the Act into suspense. So a new

---

[12] Wendy Hefford, 'Whitty, Thomas (*bap.* 1713, *d.* 1792)', *Oxford Dictionary of National Biography*, Oxford University Press, 2004; online edn, Jan. 2008 [http://www.oxforddnb.com/view/article/57827, accessed 24 July 2015].

marvellous providence was added to the list which began with the wind which scattered the Armada and passed via the defeat of the Gunpowder Plot to the Glorious Revolution of 1688. God's support of Protestantism could now be particularized to Dissenters. In a sermon in St Albans on 22 August 1714 Samuel Clarke said:

> Particularly let us Dissenters gratefully improve those liberties and privileges, which though lately attacked and invaded, we may now hope will, by the favour of the Government, be continued and secured to us. It is our part to use them for the most valuable ends and purposes, for the advancement of the kingdom of Christ, and the spreading of religion in its power and beauty, and let the danger we have been in, and our deliverance from it, stir us up to the greatest seriousness, diligence, and holy zeal, so that God may delight to bless us, and dwell among us and do us good.[13]

What we see in Clarke is not Dissent for Dissent's sake, or a purely political agenda based on religious liberty, but a sense that these are the precursors to effective evangelism and a rich Christian life.

DODDRIDGE AND WATTS

Clarke's sense of that wider mission for Dissent is even more evident in his protégé, Philip Doddridge. Subsequent generations have reckoned Doddridge and Isaac Watts as the outstanding Congregational ministers of the eighteenth century. Clarke and Doddridge met in St Albans in 1715 after the death of Philip's father, who was the son of an ejected minister, John Doddridge. Philip's mother was the daughter of a Czech Lutheran pastor who had found refuge in Kingston upon Thames, after the Thirty Years War. This background of religious persecution in his family was heightened by the further circumstance that the newly born Philip had been set aside as a stillborn child but then showed signs of life and was revived. It was in this personal history that Doddridge located his own religious identity.[14] On moving from Kingston, where he had been at school, to St Albans, Doddridge naturally gravitated to the Independent Meeting and Clarke soon recognized his promise. The move had been organized by his guardian, a man called Downes, who was declared bankrupt in 1718, rendering his ward virtually penniless. Forced to leave his school in St Albans, Doddridge took refuge with his sister, who was

---

[13] Waddington, *Congregational History*, p. 167.
[14] G.F. Nuttall, ed., *Philip Doddridge 1702-1751: His Contribution to English Religion* (London, 1951); G.F. Nuttall, ed., *Calendar of the Correspondence of Philip Doddridge, D.D. 1702-1751* (London, 1979); Malcolm Deacon, *Philip Doddridge of Northampton* (Northampton, 1980); Alan C. Clifford, *The Good Doctor* (Norwich, 2002).

married to the Revd John Nettleton, and living on Hampstead Heath. He was considering how to make a living when Clarke made the generous offer to support him and to look for a place at an academy. In 1719 Doddridge was received into the academy of John Jennings at Kibworth in Leicestershire. Congregationalism had, as it were, folded protective arms around the young man and drawn him into the path towards a famous ministry. Doddridge was a good scholar and could have restricted himself to the life of one, especially when he moved to Northampton from his first ministry, at Market Harborough, in 1729 and set up his academy, but he had a broader vision. His Northampton lectures were published after his death and remained influential. His academy drew support both in Northampton and further afield. Amongst those who provided books for its library were John Channing (c.1703–1775), a London apothecary and pioneer Arabist, Thomas Cotton (1701–1749), from the family of iron-founders, and Hugh Farmer (1714/15–1787), a former pupil who went on to be chaplain to the philanthropist William Coward at Walthamstow and a celebrated preacher.[15]

Doddridge believed his academic gifts were for teaching congregations as well as ministers. The two instruments he used for this were *The Family Expositor*, a six-volume expository commentary on the Bible designed for use in the home, and his hymns, based on Scripture, which were published after his death. In addition, he took a leading part in the civic life of Northampton, supporting all kinds of philanthropic enterprises. Clarke's aspiration, 'the spreading of religion in its power and beauty', was admirably fulfilled in Doddridge. In Doddridge we also find the first signs of the opening of Old Dissent to New Methodism. He corresponded with George Whitefield and, although sometimes critical of him, defended him against Dissenting critics. In Doddridge we find the spiritual fervour which naturally allied itself to the Methodist movement. The continuance of this fervour amongst the Independents in the first half of the eighteenth century has been little documented and the impact of Methodism thereafter much explored. The consequence is that the swelling of Congregationalism in the late eighteenth century by the entry of Calvinistic Methodists might be seen as a change of direction, rather than the renewed dominance of an old strand of piety, which was more widespread than is sometimes allowed.[16] This is well illustrated in the journal of Joseph Williams (1692–1755), who had a weaving business in Kidderminster. He made conscious efforts to link the old puritan zeal and the new Methodist enthusiasm.[17]

---

[15] I am grateful to Dr Kyle B. Roberts for his list of donors of books to Doddridge's academy.
[16] See G.F. Nuttall, 'Methodism and the Older Dissent: Some Perspectives', *JURCHS*, 2, 8 (1981), p. 259f.
[17] See Isabel Rivers, 'Joseph Williams of Kidderminster (1692–1755) and his Journal', *JURCHS*, 7, 6 (2005), p. 359f.

No one could accuse the other dominant ministerial figure amongst eighteenth-century Congregationalists as lacking in spiritual fervour. Once to have sung Isaac Watts' hymn, 'When I survey the wondrous Cross', is to have encountered his spiritual intensity. Watts was primarily an academic theologian, who communicated with the wider Christian public through his hymns. The early influence of John Owen and Isaac Chauncy was acknowledged by Watts in the letter he sent to the Mark Lane Meeting on accepting the pastorate in 1702.[18] In this letter he sets out the delicate balance between the necessary calling of a minister by a congregation and the recognition that this is ultimately the call of Christ. The minister has the authority of Christ in him recognized by the congregation. However, he acknowledges that:

> they are not bound to submit blindly to the government of the pastor, unless he approves himself therein to act according to the mind and will of Christ in his Word; and it is the neglect of this consideration that has brought in that unbounded authority and usurped dominion of the priest, and that implicit faith and blind obedience of the people in the anti-Christian Church.[19]

This is Congregationalism's answer to the charge that if ministers are not approved by bishops they are sectarians and likely to fall into the errors of sectarianism. In both this letter and his subsequent one in 1712, when he began his long period of absence, Watts sets out what his Congregational contemporaries regarded as their convictions and practices in the matter of ministry.[20] These included the principle that a congregation might have more than one minister but that an ordained minister was needed to preside at the Lord's Table. It was also a Congregational aspiration to avoid party feeling and raised voices in a church meeting and to conduct affairs quietly and with prayer. Like Doddridge, Watts had an eye to the education of the laity, perhaps best expressed by his collection of hymns for children. His friendship with Elizabeth Rowe, née Singer (1674–1737), though he found her writing almost too fervent, further illustrates the continuing strand of evangelical piety in Congregationalism. Rowe's verse remained popular into the nineteenth century.

Watts, again like Doddridge, felt the need to relate his Christian convictions to contemporary developments in philosophy and science. The primary influence here was John Locke, who not only raised new philosophical possibilities but also argued for religious toleration. Respect for Locke was qualified; his religious views overall were heterodox. For Watts the balance between reason and revelation should always come out on the side of revelation. There comes a point, wrote Watts, in one of his hymns, where Reason, with all her powers

---

[18] Waddington, *Congregational History*, p. 15f. [19] Ibid., p. 17.
[20] Sell, Hall, and Sellars, *Protestant Nonconformist Texts*, p. 393f.

fails; at this point we need Faith, which prevails, and Love, which simply adores God.[21] Take, for instance, the question of the resurrection of the body, discussed by both Doddridge and Watts. If it were true, as science proposed, that our bodies consisted of minute particles, known as atoms, which were constantly renewing themselves, what were the logical consequences for personal resurrection? Such dilemmas are constantly thrown up by scientific theory and have only multiplied over the centuries. Watts believed that a reconciliation of faith and reason was possible because faith was not dogma. In the matter of personal resurrection, for instance, it might be possible to suppose that some few atoms of our original body stayed with us throughout our lives and that God could preserve these for union with our everlasting souls.[22] Neurology had not developed to the stage when it could question the very idea of a soul.

INTELLECTUAL AND SOCIAL IMPACT

Congregationalists in the eighteenth century were favourably disposed towards science. Science challenged superstition and opened up a larger view of the providence of God, both developments favouring Protestantism as they saw it. Leading scientists such as Robert Boyle, Isaac Newton, and Joseph Priestley all took this view. Amongst Congregationalists come some of the lesser scientific lights, but noted contributors to their field of study. Joseph Warder (1654/5–1724) was a physician and member of the Independent Meeting at Croydon in Cambridgeshire, of which his son-in-law, Richard Conder, was the minister. His 1712 book, *The True Amazons*, was based on the minute observations he had made of bees, using the new microscopic technology. His recommendations in this book established the principles of modern bee-keeping. Henry Smeathman was baptized in the Old Independent Meeting House in Scarborough in 1742. Although he studied theology and elocution before taking a place as tutor in a private family this was not the route to ministry. He was drawn into the circle which formed the second Aurelian Society (1762–6). This gave him a lifelong interest in entomology. From 1771 to 1775 he was based in the Banana Islands off the coast of what is now Sierra Leone, sponsored to study the plants and insects. It was here he began his lifelong studies of termites, for which he became famous. He also took a great interest in the slave trade, which dominated the local economy, and was one of the original sponsors of the plan to create a colony of freed slaves in Sierra Leone. He died of fever in 1786 in London before it came into effect.

[21] 'Join all the glorious names'.
[22] Sell, Hall, and Sellars, *Protestant Nonconformist Texts*, p. 19.

Humphrey Gainsborough (1718-1776) was born in a Congregational family at Sudbury, in Suffolk, and was brother to the artist Thomas Gainsborough. He studied at the Moorfields Academy under John Eames, a friend of Isaac Newton. This gave Humphrey a taste for mechanics which remained throughout his life. It became a part of his ministry to extend the benefits mechanical invention could bring to the wider community. Around 1748 he became minister in Henley, which was to enjoy the greatest benefits of his ingenuity. Amongst other projects he devised a system of locks on the Thames, downstream from Reading, to ensure that Henley was not bypassed by a proposed Reading to Maidenhead canal. At the time of his death he was working on developments to the steam engine to improve the working of the locks. It is argued that the credit given to James Watt ought to be extended to Gainsborough as well. Henry Field (1755-1837) was a key figure in the development of the Society of Apothecaries and the regulation of the profession. He was a direct descendant of Thomas Cromwell, and his children were all baptized at Haberdashers Hall Independent Meeting. He was known for his sense of the tradition in which he stood and his philanthropy. Dissent also had its share of enthusiasts in the margins of knowledge. James Conder (1761-1823), youngest son of the minister John Conder, had a business as a haberdasher and snuff seller in Ipswich but gave up a large part of his time to coin collecting and local history. He collected materials for a history of Nonconformity in Suffolk, which was never written, although he gave access to it to other historians. He did publish a work on trade tokens. He was a member of Tacket Street Independent Chapel, Ipswich.[23] Thomas Fisher (1772-1836), artist and antiquary, recorded many important antiquities, especially in Bedfordshire, but was also active in Congregational circles.

SPIRITUALITY AND REVIVAL

Thus far Congregationalists as a group were not socially and intellectually distinguishable from other Dissenters. Field, after all, had a brother who was a Unitarian minister. What moved these groups further apart as the eighteenth century progressed was the spirituality we have seen in Doddridge and Watts.

---

[23] See Karl Showler, 'Warder, Joseph (1654/5-1724)', *Oxford Dictionary of National Biography*, Oxford University Press, 2004; online edn, Jan. 2008 [http://www.oxforddnb.com/view/article/28720, accessed 24 July 2015]; Starr Douglas, 'Smeathman, Henry (1742-1786)', *Oxford Dictionary of National Biography*, Oxford University Press, Oct. 2005; online edn, Sept. 2013 [http://www.oxforddnb.com/view/article/93969, accessed 24 July 2015]; and David Tyler, 'Gainsborough, Humphrey (bap. 1718, d. 1776)', *Oxford Dictionary of National Biography*, Oxford University Press, Oct. 2006; online edn, Sept. 2013 [http://www.oxforddnb.com/view/article/77225, accessed 24 July 2015].

Even some of Doddridge's friends and allies worried about his contacts with George Whitefield. The Evangelical Revival is first located in the Church of England, with the Wesleys and Whitefield as chief standard bearers. A small group of incumbents welcomed their preaching and gave them pulpit hospitality. The majority resisted and the Methodists were driven into field preaching. They soon recognized this as advantageous in reaching people who would not come into a church. To advance their cause with the middle classes and aristocracy field preaching was not enough. Their aristocratic supporters, such as the countess of Huntingdon, provided salons and chapels for meeting. They borrowed Dissenting meeting houses where the proprietors were sympathetic. These tended to be Congregational rather than Presbyterian. They also created meeting places of their own, famously Whitefield's Tabernacle in Moorfields, London. To stay within the law such places needed to be registered for protestant Dissenting worship. The Methodists, however much they protested that they wished to remain within the Church of England, began to find themselves in the same position as the original Nonconformists. They may not have been prosecuted with the same vigour as a hundred years before, but they were subject to mob violence and legal challenge. Like their predecessors they took the view that the Church of England should change to accommodate them. Conservative forces within the Church of England resisted such change and branded the Methodists as a danger to the social order.

From the beginning the Methodists who leaned towards Calvinism, such as Whitefield and the countess of Huntingdon, found friends and allies among Dissenters. That support was not confined to ministers, but included the merchants who funded Dissent. One of Doddridge's friends was the London merchant Robert Cruttenden, descended from an old Nonconformist family. In 1743 Cruttenden joined the Congregational Church meeting in Lime Street, near Leadenhall Market. This required him to offer a personal testimony as to his faith. Cruttenden's testimony survives because it was printed as a tract and issued by George Whitefield. The two remained in contact and it was Cruttenden who acted as the channel for donations from the countess of Huntingdon and other Church of England friends to reach Doddridge to fund his voyage to Lisbon in 1751, in search of a cure for his tuberculosis, a search which ended in his death there.[24]

Cruttenden died in 1763, just as Thomas Wilson (1731–1794) was beginning his time as a London merchant. He was a member of the Haberdashers Hall Meeting and friend of Whitefield and the countess of Huntingdon. Wilson came from a family of yeomen farmers in Derbyshire and had made a modest fortune by his own efforts and his marriage with Mary Remington,

---

[24] G.F. Nuttall, 'George Whitefield and his Nonconformist Friends', *JURCHS*, 7, 2 (2003), p. 103.

daughter of a family of Dissenters and merchants in Coventry. He had heard Whitefield at the Tabernacle and from that point spread his religious life between Congregationalism and the evangelical associates of Whitefield. A process began which, in time, bolted together the founding myths of Congregationalism and the independent evangelical churches associated with Whitefield and his friends. First of all, evangelical religious sentiment united people who were divided ecclesiologically. The fruit of this cooperation was found in religious societies, such as the Bible Society. Then people of an evangelical sentiment who were impatient with the restraints imposed by the existing parish system formed their own congregations. Needing to support one another, and to join together in evangelism, some of those of a Calvinist nature coalesced around the principles of Congregationalism. This is most evident in the life of Thomas Wilson and his family. Thomas Wilson's son continued his philanthropy, directed towards the creation of Congregational churches throughout England, and his grandson, Joshua Wilson, completed the work by driving forward the Congregational Union of England and Wales when it was formed and placing it in grand offices at Memorial Hall, complete with library, to mark the bi-centenary of the Great Ejectment in 1862.[25] On the other hand, a Wilson cousin of similar evangelical temper, Daniel Wilson, stayed within the Church of England and became a celebrated Bishop of Calcutta.

As the eighteenth century progressed and Methodism prospered, neither the Arminian nor the Calvinist enthusiasts would admit that their efforts would lead to separate denominations. John Wesley held himself to be an Anglican to his dying day, even in the face of non-episcopal ordinations in America. Whitefield died in 1771 before the issue became acute, although the expulsion of six Methodist students from Oxford in 1768 was a sign of the coming crisis. His various followers, including those associated with the countess of Huntingdon, were left with the dilemma of how to perpetuate their societies, especially those amongst working people alienated from the Church of England, if the bishops would not ordain popular preachers. On the one hand, Dissenters were useful allies of the Methodist movement, as the countess of Huntingdon recognized.

> Next, I think we ought to have great respect to the dissenters, first, as they have been originally the protectors of our Civil and Religious Liberties, and next as they have been great friends in our late reformation and their peace and order of Government ought to be sacred to us. We still owe them much and, tho the balance of power is in the Established Church, yet they have alike saved us from the blind pride and arrogance of the priesthood, which has ever been as foolish as

---

[25] S.C. Orchard, 'The Wilson Family and Derbyshire', *JURCHS*, 6, 8 (2001), p. 570.

it is wicked, and in this view they are a refuge in this land from imposition and are yet the thorns (from the toleration allowed them) in High Churchmen's sides.[26]

On the other hand, the countess of Huntingdon, like John Wesley, regarded ordination among the Dissenters as irregular. She regretted the haemorrhaging to Dissenting meetings of preachers she had trained. On the one hand she wanted a corps of travelling evangelists, episcopally sanctioned, to bring about spiritual revival; on the other hand the young men she prepared at Trefeca settled in Dissenting congregations and were ordained by them because they were turned down by the bishops. The situation was further complicated by what she regarded as Wesley's misinterpretation of the Thirty-Nine Articles which, for her, were immutably Calvinistic. She summed up the situation in a paper prepared for the bishops.

> My present observations I will confine for your Lordships' better information under these three distinct points on which they now severally stand in England, Wales &c. viz.
>
> 1st. Those which are the real Church professors, Clergy and People. 2nd. Mr Wesley's people. And 3rd. the Dissenters.
>
> Those in the Church as honest Clergymen and as subscribing and maintaining the grammatical sense of her Articles according to the royal declaration, attending strictly to their obligations of Ordination and labouring for the salvation of souls upon their own faithful and attached principles and engagements so to act.
>
> Mr Wesley from a real desire of useful labour, and in which many good people with him are engaged, has from his writings, preachings &c departed from the sense and meaning &c that avowedly of the Church Articles, and it is not his evasions that can make an honest Man of commonsense but smile at any pretensions for him to say one word in their defence. Those fundamentals he so warmly defends are diametrically in opposition to every one of them.
>
> The Dissenters exclude themselves uprightly by wanting the protection they from Modes of Worship in the Church, and other principles, cannot agree to, and these are retained purely by the Act of Toleration and are of course subjected to by their own choice and consent.[27]

She foresaw exactly what was to happen, although her argument proved wrong.

> Tho difficulties can arise from Mr Wesley and his people as they will make a sect of themselves, tolerated as not belonging to the principles of the Church and, holding the Doctrine of Perfection as denied by our Church,...[28]

When action was taken against her liberal interpretation of church law, which she construed as allowing her to have any number of domestic chaplains, she

---

[26] Countess of Huntingdon to William Piercy, n.d., Westminster College, Cambridge, Cheshunt Archives (hereafter WCC, CA), A4/3/5.
[27] Countess of Huntingdon to bishops, n.d., WCC, CA, E3/2/17.
[28] Ibid.

was forced to register her chapels under the Toleration Act. When the bishops refused to ordain her candidates for ministry she settled for presbyterial ordination, albeit by priests in the Church of England. She possibly regarded all this as a temporary expedient, until such time as the Church of England saw sense, but she termed herself 'a Seceder'. Like the Wesleyans, and like the Nonconformists of a century earlier, she had set her foot on the road to separation. Independent Calvinistic congregations, all fruit of the Evangelical Revival, sprang up in the late eighteenth century and registered as Dissenting meetings, some in the Countess of Huntingdon's Connexion, but many outside it. Those who formed the leadership of the Revival were forced to make choices. John Newton havered between Church and Dissent, finally deciding for the Church. John Clayton (1754–1843), trained at Trefeca, chose Dissent and fathered a Congregational dynasty.

REVIVAL AND REVOLUTION

A further complication was political. Congregationalists were not exempt from the general history of the period. The Jacobite threat alarmed them along with most other people. The wars, especially with France, affected their trade and travel as much as that of anyone else. Perhaps, above all, the growth of colonial trade and the rise of industrialism which generated wealth and changed social relationships made the rise of religious dissent more possible. That very rise was seen as a threat by the conservative establishment. At the outbreak of the French Revolution, Dissenters of all shades, including Congregationalists, were optimistic that in the end of an old regime they were seeing some equivalence with the Glorious Revolution of 1688. A protestant and parliamentary France beckoned. Joseph Cottle (1770–1853), a Bristol bookseller, is remembered as the publisher of Wordsworth and Coleridge. Without his assistance Coleridge, in particular, would have lived in poverty. Cottle was an evangelical Calvinist, who eventually belonged to Broadmead Baptist Church and then Zion Congregational Church in Bristol. At this point in his life Coleridge was still considering a life as a Dissenting minister. The young William Hazlitt was much influenced by him. For a brief moment the energy of the Romantic movement and Dissent merged in welcoming the French Revolution. When Wordsworth remembered that, 'Bliss was it in that dawn to be alive, but to be young was very heaven', he could be describing a religious experience.[29] As the horrors of the Terror began in France, Dissenters found themselves on the wrong side of public opinion. The

---

[29] William Wordsworth, *The Prelude*, XI France, lines 108–9.

old prejudices against them were reinforced and they retreated into political conservatism. In this they were no different from Wordsworth and Coleridge, who made their peace with the establishment, much to Hazlitt's disgust. Hazlitt retained his political radicalism and moved away from religion. For people like Cottle, a diversion of energy into purely pious activities was the way forward.[30]

The trustees of Cheshunt College, newly removed from Trefeca to replace the countess of Huntingdon's college there, tried to steer a course between 'the rocks of Bigotry on either hand, the Church on the one, and the stiff Dissenters on the other', by concentrating on the spread of the Gospel.[31] But politics would not go away. Reports reached the trustees that there were plans to burn down the college soon after it opened in 1792 and they arranged to increase the insurance and set the students to keep watch.[32] They were probably more alarmed when reports circulated that the students were against the government and they made every effort to suppress them.[33] Steering this course was a testing business. Another part of this same evangelical constituency sponsored an academy at Newport Pagnell, under the care of the Congregational minister there, William Bull, friend of John Newton and the poet, William Cowper.[34] It seemed possible to cooperate with sympathetic Dissenters to undermine the High Church opposition in the Church of England. Many Congregationalists were prepared to join in. 'Stiff Dissent' included some Congregationalists and Baptists but was mainly old Presbyterianism, moving towards Unitarianism. One of the subscribers to both Cheshunt and Newport Pagnell was the older Thomas Wilson (1731–1794), who was also treasurer of the New English Academy, founded in 1778, which had an establishment at Hoxton. In this he was associated with Robert Keen and Daniel West, agents of the countess of Huntingdon. The students in all these colleges might suspect that any anti-government sentiment on their part could also be found in their governing bodies, largely comprised of merchants and Whigs. Having steered between the High Church and Dissent the sponsors had also to plot a course between patriotism and opposition to government policies, which were bad for trade.[35]

---

[30] For Cottle's involvement with Coleridge, Southey, and Wordsworth, see Ralph A. Manogue, 'Cottle, Joseph (1770–1853)', *Oxford Dictionary of National Biography*, Oxford University Press, 2004; online edn, Oct. 2007 [http://www.oxforddnb.com/view/article/6407, accessed 24 July 2015].

[31] Edwin Welch, ed., *Cheshunt College, the Early Years* (Ware, 1990), p. 53.

[32] Ibid., p. 50.   [33] Ibid., p.77.

[34] F.W. Bull, 'The Newport Pagnell Academy', *Transactions of the Congregational Historical Society*, 4, 5 (May 1910), pp. 305–22 (also published separately); Marilyn Lewis, 'The Newport Pagnell Academy 1782–1850', *JURCHS*, 5, 5 (1994), pp. 273–82.

[35] Joshua Wilson, *A Memoir of the Life and Character of Thomas Wilson, Esq.* (London, 1845).

The most significant product of the alliance of Calvinistic Methodists and Congregationalists was the formation of the Missionary Society in 1795, later known as the London Missionary Society. The two generous donations which enabled the society to get under way came from the Revd Thomas Haweis, an Anglican ally of the countess of Huntingdon, and the Revd Samuel Greatheed, tutor at the Newport Pagnell Academy and a convert to Congregationalism.[36] Haweis was carrying forward the missionary enthusiasm of the countess herself, who had tried to promote missions in America and Sumatra. Thomas Wilson was one of the merchants who subscribed to the new society. The chief London merchant involved was Joseph Hardcastle (1752–1819), who combined his Congregational ancestry with the new Evangelicalism. He was associated with the anti-slavery cause and the Sierra Leone project. He was the first treasurer of the London Missionary Society and one of the promoters of the Bible Society. Less remembered is his enthusiasm for village itinerancy, equally a fruit of the Evangelical Revival. He made his home, at Hatcham House, Deptford, available for meetings of the societies he supported. All this served to promote Congregationalism. Some Evangelicals fought their corner in the Church of England; others relished the freedom that Congregationalism gave them to take on new challenges in mission and devise new means of tackling them.

The porous boundaries between Congregationalism and Presbyterianism meant that some Old Presbyterian causes were taken over by the new evangelical Congregationalists. In other towns across the country meetings split as those fired with the new enthusiasm set up rival meetings. For instance, Thomas Wilson co-sponsored with the Countess of Huntingdon's Connexion a new meeting in Brookside Derby to rival the old Friar Gate one.[37] Thomas Wilson's son, also Thomas (1764–1863), retired from business in 1798 and gave himself entirely to developing Hoxton Academy and sponsoring new chapels around the country, as well as reviving old ones. He lived well within his income and his fortune was boosted by a bequest from his mother's brother in 1813. Preaching ability and evangelical sentiments were his requirements for Hoxton students; he contributed to chapels in which such students might prosper. He made a particular point of seeking out old meeting houses where only a few members were left and offering them an evangelical ministry. His son, Joshua Wilson, writing his father's biography, listed a great many of his father's benefactions, including three large church buildings in London, but confessed that he was unable to catalogue all the small donations to chapel building in the provinces.

---

[36] This is evident from a manuscript note in Greatheed's copy of *Sermons preached at the formation of the Missionary Society* (London, 1795), now in the library of Westminster College, Cambridge.

[37] S.C. Orchard, 'The Wilson Family and Derbyshire', *JURCHS*, 6, 8 (2001), p. 570.

TRADITION AND ASSOCIATION

Joshua cultivated the idea that the new evangelical Congregational churches were the true successors to historic Dissent, even in its Presbyterian forms, and sought to exclude Unitarians from representative bodies for Dissenters. This distancing from what he regarded as heterodox was political as well as religious. With growth came a new self-confidence among Dissenters and an increased sense of civil grievance. Joshua Wilson wrote of his father's commitment to 'the cause of evangelical nonconformity which he regarded as identified with the cause of political freedom, for he considered the liberty of religious worship as the best bulwark and surest safeguard of the civil rights and political immunities of Britons'.[38] Thomas Wilson had opposed the war with France as 'murder abroad and corruption at home'.[39] He had seen the Peterloo massacre and regarded it as a mistake by the government. He was committed to political reform and the abolition of tariffs. He wanted to see the repeal of the Test and Corporation Acts which discriminated against Congregationalists. It is therefore unsurprising that he wished to marshal like-minded people in a Congregational Union, rather than see evangelical Congregationalism dismissed as 'a disjointed, disorganised aggregation'.[40] An attempt was made in 1806 to form such a union, but this initiative, taken by the London Congregational Board, and supported by the Hampshire Association, came to nothing.[41] It was not until 1830 that another, and partly successful, attempt was made, although adherence to the Congregational Union of England and Wales formed in 1831 was patchy. At the inaugural meeting twenty-two county associations were represented, principally from southern England. There was no one representing Yorkshire; Lancashire and Cambridgeshire sent letters questioning the whole enterprise. Union suggests structure when, in fact, what was created was a voluntary membership organization, only one step up from a disorganized aggregation.[42]

The associations which made up the Congregational Union were themselves a development of the Evangelical Revival. Previously such associations had been meetings of ministers for preaching and prayer with a view to maintaining Congregationalism in their area. The new Congregationalists of the 1790s saw such meetings as springboards for mission at home and abroad. The meeting was still largely a time for sermons but also for sharing news of the London Missionary Society and home missions. This naturally

---

[38] Wilson, *Life of Wilson*, p. 260.
[39] Ibid., p. 184. [40] Ibid., p.181.
[41] Hampshire support came through David Bogue, Wilson's ally in Gosport.
[42] For details of the formation of the Congregational Union of England and Wales, see Peel, *These Hundred Years*.

led to fundraising, not only from the traditional sources of merchants and landowners, but from congregations. One such association embraced Derbyshire, Nottinghamshire, and the West Riding of Yorkshire. In a small publication called *Family Instruction*, published in 1799, we learn a little about its meetings.[43] In an appendix are to be found the minutes of their association for 1798 and 1799. The founding brothers, as they termed themselves, who met in the vestry of the Nether Chapel, Sheffield on 19 April 1798, were Burgess of Chesterfield, Boden and Reece of Sheffield, Ellis of Barnsley, Phillips of Rotherham, Kirkpatrick of Sutton in Ashfield, Alliot of Nottingham, Thorpe of Penistone, Sugden of Moor Green, on the Nottinghamshire–Derbyshire border, and Bincliffe of Alfreton. They agreed that there would be three meetings a year, a permanent Secretary, and minutes and a membership list would be kept. Their expenses were to be met personally, admission was by vote, members would keep their own minutes, and there would be a 5s. fine for non-attendance. On the positive side, they would dine together, but only one joint of meat and no wine or spirits, or tobacco, were allowed. Three sermons were required at each meeting and a moderator would be appointed, to sit with a Bible and the Rules before him. Members were expected to come prepared for edifying conversation. It was this body, led by Boden and Alliott in concert with the Rotherham Academy, which was committed to the revival and establishment of Congregational churches in its area.

Round about 1811 a new association of churches in the counties of Leicester, Nottingham, and Derby began to be canvassed and it came into being in 1814, under the leadership of Alliot, with James Gawthorn of Derby as secretary.[44] From 1815 it was called 'The District Union and Itinerancy Society of the Counties of Nottingham, Leicester, & Derby'. Its printed reports concentrate on promoting the London Missionary Society, with briefer reports on the missionary activity in the three counties. Presumably because he was in possession of the minute book we find it records a Derbyshire body, with Gawthorn as secretary, from 1824 onwards, though a report of the old association was published for 1825. Gawthorn was to remain an advocate for the London Missionary Society for the rest of his life, serving as Derbyshire representative. In his time the printed reports of the Derbyshire Congregational Union always began with the LMS report. Gawthorn no doubt encouraged the drawing up of formal rules for the Derbyshire Union. In other respects it continued the traditions of the 1798 Association—promoting new churches, organizing representation at ordinations, inductions, and chapel

---

[43] *Family Instruction. A circular letter from an Association of Ministers in the counties of Derby & Nottingham & in the West Riding of the county of York, addressed to the Congregations under their Pastoral Care* (Doncaster, 1799), Derby Local Studies Library, 3786/4.

[44] R. Tudur Jones, *Congregationalism in England, 1662–1962* (London, 1962), p. 175, n. 2, lists Derbyshire as an early county union of 1815 without mentioning the other two counties.

openings, and celebrating the Lord's Supper when it met. Meetings were held over several days and consisted largely of worship with substantial sermons, often from visiting ministers. Business, while taken seriously, was secondary to encouragement and exhortation.[45] This pattern of development in the East Midlands can be seen elsewhere. The London Missionary Society features as a common factor, along with reports from the Home Missionary Society. The early meetings of the Congregational Union of England and Wales were to give substantial time to LMS reports.

By the time of the repeal of the Test and Corporation Acts the country was on the verge of the railway age, having already moved greater tonnages of goods on canals than had ever been possible by road. The port of Bristol grew in prosperity, Liverpool emerged as a significant focus of trade and the financial systems of London grew ever more complex. With urbanization, the parish system of the Church of England proved slow to adjust in the new centres of population. Dissenters had much more flexibility when it came to opening new church buildings. They also had supporters with disposable income derived from the new commerce. Congregationalists had their due proportion of the new merchants and manufacturers, ready to fund evangelism and the training of ministers. The scene was set for the nineteenth-century heyday of Congregationalism. Its strength came, not from a determined effort to promote a national institution, but from local enthusiasm and initiative. Instruments were created to pool resources for mission, education, church extension, ministerial training, and political lobbying, but these were always subject to local control and fuelled by local energy. The Britain of light regulation and vigorous entrepreneurs was one in which the old Congregational ideals could be reinterpreted and flourish.

SELECT BIBLIOGRAPHY

Deacon, Malcolm, *Philip Doddridge of Northampton 1702–1751* (Northampton, 1980).
Gordon, Alexander, ed., *Freedom After Ejection* (London, 1917).
Harding, Alan, *The Countess of Huntingdon's Connexion* (Oxford, 2003).
Jones, R. Tudur, *Congregationalism in England, 1662–1962* (London, 1962).
Kay, Elaine, *For the Work of Ministry: Northern College and its Predecessors* (Edinburgh, 1999).
Manning, Bernard Lord, *The Protestant Dissenting Deputies* (Cambridge, 1952).
Mullett, Michael, *Sources for the History of English Nonconformity 1660–1830* (London, 1991).

---

[45] S. C. Orchard, 'James Gawthorn and Derbyshire Congregationalism', *JURCHS*, 9, 1 (2012), p. 6.

Nuttall, G. F., ed., *Philip Doddridge 1702-1751: His Contribution to English Religion* (London, 1951).
Nuttall, G. F. and Chadwick, Owen, eds, *From Nonconformity to Unity 1662-1962* (London, 1962).
Pope, Robert, ed., *T & T Clark Companion to Nonconformity* (London, 2013).
Sell, Alan P. F., Hall, David J., and Sellars, Ian, eds, *Protestant Nonconformist Texts* (Aldershot, 2006).
Waddington, John, *Congregational History* (London, 1876).
Ward, W. R., *Early Evangelicalism: A Global Intellectual History, 1670-1789* (Cambridge, 2006).
Watts, Michael, *The Dissenters: From the Reformation to the French Revolution* (Oxford, 1978).
Welch, Edwin, *Spiritual Pilgrim. A Reassessment of the Life of the Countess of Huntingdon* (Cardiff, 1995).
Wilson, Joshua, *A Memoir of the Life and Character of Thomas Wilson, Esq.* (London, 1845).
Wilson, Walter, *The History and Antiquities of Dissenting Churches*, 4 vols. (London, 1808-14).

3

Baptists

Karen E. Smith

A print of an etching of fifteen men, found in Underwood's *History of the English Baptists*, says a good deal about the Baptists at the end of the long eighteenth century.[1] The etching is of a group of formally dressed men, who are portrayed as leaders of the denomination. Barely visible in the background are the faint portraits of others, which appear to represent seventeenth-century forebears who paved the way for Nonconformity.

The etching, of unknown provenance, ideally depicts the public face of Baptists at the beginning of the nineteenth century: male, middle class, and respectable. In fact, for those who were unaware, the etching could easily be mistaken for a scene from a men's club, a boardroom, or bank.

A depiction of such sophistication and propriety demonstrates how the image of the two main groups of Baptists—General and Particular—had changed since their separate seventeenth-century beginnings.[2] No longer did they find themselves defiantly taking a stand against magistrates who enforced penal codes that restricted their ability to gather for worship. Nor was there a need to meet secretly as they had in the previous century; the Toleration Act (1689) had ensured that they were no longer persecuted for being dangerous 'sectaries' to whom 'youths and wenches flock thither' as one opponent had so disdainfully put it.[3] Of course, while they had freedom to worship, they were not given civil equality and remained, in effect, second-class citizens until the Test and Corporation Acts were repealed in 1828.

---

[1] A. C. Underwood, *A History of English Baptists* (London, 1947), p. 168.

[2] There were two main groups of Baptists in the seventeenth century. General Baptists believed in 'general atonement', or that Christ died for all people. Particular or Calvinistic Baptists believed that Christ died only for the elect. There is also evidence of a much smaller group of Sabbatarian or Seventh-Day Baptists in London in the seventeenth century.

[3] Thomas Edwards, *Gangraena* (1646) as cited in B. R. White, *The English Baptists of the Seventeenth Century* (London, 1983), p. 32.

Although the legal status of Dissent put them at some cultural and political disadvantage, the eighteenth century brought spiritual renewal, too. Unlike General Baptists, English Calvinistic Baptist congregations were not open to the Arminian views of salvation proclaimed by Wesleyan preachers. Yet, they did go to hear the Calvinistic Methodist, George Whitefield, and exchanged letters with other evangelical figures. As time went on, Baptists in England and Wales gained members who had first been 'awakened to faith' by Methodist preachers before being persuaded of the rightness of Baptist principles, especially believer's baptism by immersion.

In addition to contributing members to Baptist congregations, the Evangelical Revival also encouraged closer cooperation with other Nonconformists, as well as members of the Established Church. By 1792 when the Particular Baptist Society for the Propagation of the Gospel Amongst the Heathen, known later as the Baptist Missionary Society (BMS), was founded, it drew support from Anglicans and Dissenters. Cooperation with others for the purpose of evangelism and mission convinced some Baptists of the benefit of working together and by 1813 there was a call (though not wholeheartedly accepted by all) for greater organization and denominational unity.

In the eighteenth century, however, many Baptists remained wary of any encroachment on their congregational independence. While they cooperated with other Baptists in regional associations that met for fellowship and advice on various matters, these General meetings, as they were first called, had no authority over the churches. Baptist ecclesiology was firmly rooted in the concept of the 'gathered church'.[4] This emphasis on the Church was not simply an organizing principle; Baptists believed they were bound together 'in Christ'. This did not mean that they saw themselves in an insular way, simply as 'a garden wall'd around' as they have sometimes been described. Nor did it mean that they had no concern to proclaim the Gospel to others. However, their faith was nurtured within community life as they promised in making their covenants to build one another up, look after one another, and care for the needs of one another, spiritual and material.

In spite of the fact that covenant community was central to their understanding of Christian faith, the Baptist story has sometimes been told by drawing information from the records of prosperous urban churches, positively highlighting the development of social and political influence, as well as tracing the growth of denominational structures dominated by men. It is important, however, to recall other narratives as well. These, of course, are the stories of the people who would not have been included in a formal etching of Baptist leaders: women, children, and those who were identified

---

[4] See, E. A. Payne, *The Fellowship of Believers*, 2nd edn (London, 1952), and Paul Fiddes, *Tracks and Traces: Baptist Identity in Church and Theology* (Milton Keynes, 2003).

at the time as part of a serving class. Yet, these men and women, many of whom were illiterate, were a vital part of local 'gathered' congregations. Their piety was rooted in a Puritan devotion which emphasized 'mind and heart'—doctrine and experience. This heart-felt faith nurtured in covenant communities served them well as they faced the challenges of the long eighteenth century.

COVENANT LIFE TOGETHER

Unlike those who identified the Church with a state church, Baptists (like other Dissenters) believed that Church was best represented as a community 'gathered' by God to be the visible Church. They claimed that the Church was made up of those who believe that they have been called together by God to walk in the ways of Christ 'revealed or yet to be made known'. The 1689 London Confession of Faith, a document which provided the framework for belief for Calvinistic Baptists throughout the eighteenth century, described the members of local churches as:

> Saints by calling, visibly manifesting and evidencing (in and by their professing and walking) their obedience unto the call of Christ; and do willingly consent to walk together according to the appointment of Christ, giving up themselves, to the Lord and to one another by the will of God, in professed subjection to the Ordinances of the Gospel.[5]

As a means of expressing their life together, congregations drew up covenant agreements. Although the wording differed, the purpose of covenant documents was to emphasize that the members had been brought together by God to be a visible community of faith and by joining together they were pledging themselves to embrace both the duties and privileges of church membership, including worship, prayer for one another, attendance at the ordinances, and participation in the discipline and government of the congregation. These were not simply rules to be adhered to, but were seen as a means to help individuals spiritually and practically, too.

The idea of being gathered by God to be a Church meant that Baptists did not equate the Church with an institutional structure. In fact they shied away from any group or person appearing ready to seize ecclesial control. They met

---

[5] 'Second London Confession of Faith put forth by the Elders and Brethren of many congregations of Christians (baptized upon Profession of their Faith) in London and the Country' (London, 1677, 1689), in W. L. Lumpkin, *Baptist Confessions of Faith* (Valley Forge, PA, 1959, revised 1969), p. 286.

regularly in general meetings or Associations; yet, each local gathered community of faith was independent and free to come together in order to worship and to seek the mind of Christ for themselves. While at times Associations approved the sending out of messengers or preachers to proclaim the Gospel in new areas, they mainly came together to encourage one another in their local church relationships.

The importance of congregational life among Calvinistic Baptists was highlighted in a book published by Benjamin Keach (1640-1704) entitled *The Glory of a True Church and its Discipline display'd* (1697). Keach had been in a General Baptist congregation in Tooley Street, Southwark before moving only a short distance to serve as pastor of a Calvinistic congregation in Horsleydown in London.[6] He had been one of the signatories of the Second London Confession (1689) and wrote forty-three works for which, on at least one occasion, he was fined, pilloried, and imprisoned. Keach was also at the centre of the controversy over hymn singing among Baptists at the end of the seventeenth century. *The Glory of a True Church*, written late in his life as a church manual and guide for order and discipline in the Church, claimed that those who were part of the Church,

> do by mutual agreement and consent give themselves up to the Lord, and one to another, according to the Will of God; and do ordinarily meet together in one Place, for the Publick Service and Worship of God; among whom the Word of God and Sacraments are duly administered, according to Christ's Institution.[7]

Significantly appended to his book on the Church was a sample church covenant which provided a pattern which was widely followed among many eighteenth-century Baptists both in Britain and in the American colonies. Not all churches used Keach's covenant, of course, but for those that did the covenant, along with the 1689 Confession of Faith, helped shape their life together. Keach claimed he had written the work at the request of others because 'ignorance of the rules of Discipline, causes no small trouble and disorders in our Churches'.[8] Published eight years after the Toleration Act, perhaps signs of indifference and disorder among Baptist churches were already beginning to show.

---

[6] Austin Walker, 'Benjamin Keach (1640-1704) Tailor Turned Preacher', in J. H. Y. Briggs (ed.), *Pulpit and People: Studies in Eighteenth-Century Baptist Life and Thought* (Milton Keynes 2009), pp. 25-42.

[7] Benjamin Keach, *The Glory of a True Church and its Discipline display'd* (London, 1697) p. 5.

[8] Keach, *The Glory of a True Church*, p. iv.

BAPTIST IDENTITY IN A NEW ERA: THE IMPORTANCE OF ORDER AND ARDOUR

When the Toleration Act was passed in 1689, Nonconformists must have breathed a collective sigh of relief. Joshua Thomas, a Welsh Baptist historian, perhaps expressed the general feeling of all Baptists when he wrote: 'With this, peace at last prevailed through out the kingdom.'[9] Peace and religious toleration there might have been, but not civil equality. The restrictions the Test and Corporation Acts put on Baptists, as well as other Dissenters, meant that they were not allowed to hold public office and were barred from attending the universities.[10] Moreover, Lord Hardwicke's Marriage Act (1753) stipulated that only weddings celebrated in an Anglican Church were legal. Baptism outside the Anglican Church was also not recognized which meant that many Dissenters were denied burial in the graveyards of Established Churches.

Since this circumscriptive legislation imposed on Dissenters was not repealed until the nineteenth century, in 1732 Baptists joined with Presbyterians and Independents in London to form the Protestant Dissenting Deputies, a committee of laymen seeking to protect the civil rights of Dissenters and to work to repeal the Test and Corporation Acts.[11] Baptists cooperated with Presbyterians and Congregationalists in other ways, too. Concerned about the growing tide of Arianism and Socinianism (seen as two threats to Trinitarian belief), both General and Particular Baptists were represented at a meeting of Nonconformist ministers in Salters' Hall in London in 1719 where a discussion of the doctrine of the Trinity concluded with the publication of a statement of what was considered to be an orthodox view. All but two of the Calvinistic Baptists were happy to subscribe to the statement, but only one General Baptist would sign. While it appears that later some General Baptists drifted into Unitarian churches, non-subscription at Salters' Hall should not be interpreted as the first step on 'a slippery slope' to doctrinal deviation. At the time some Baptists who refused to sign the Salters' Hall statement did so on the grounds that Scripture alone must be adhered to and not human statements of faith.[12]

Baptists and other Dissenters also worked together in practical ways. In 1733, for instance, they formed The Society for the Relief of the Necessitous

---

[9] Joshua Thomas, *Hanes y Bedyddwyr Ymhlith y Cymry* (1778), p. 39, as cited by D. Densil Morgan, 'Nonconformity in Wales', in *T & T Clark Companion to Nonconformity*, ed. Robert Pope (London, 2013), p. 32.

[10] David Bebbington has noted three eighteenth-century Baptist MPs. See D. W. Bebbington, 'Baptist MPs in the Seventeenth and Eighteenth Centuries', *Baptist Quarterly*, 28, 6 (1980), pp. 261–2 and D. W. Bebbington, 'Baptist MPs: A Supplemental Note', *Baptist Quarterly*, 42, 2 (part 2) (2007), p. 153.

[11] B. L. Manning, *The Protestant Dissenting Deputies* (Cambridge, 1952).

[12] Roger Hayden, *English Baptist History and Heritage* (Didcot, 2005), p. 47.

Widows and Children of Protestant Dissenting Ministers (popularly known as The Widows Fund).[13] Through the years Baptists maintained an active role in that society, with many ministers being asked to preach the annual sermon and thereby retaining life membership in the society.[14] As the number of ministers increased throughout the eighteenth and nineteenth centuries the demand on the Widows Fund grew as well. By 1801, it was reported in the *Baptist Annual Register* that each English widow received £10 10s. and the Welsh received £8 8s. The number of widows listed as receiving help for that year was 154 with fifty being English Baptists and twenty-three being Welsh from one of the three participating denominations.[15]

In spite of legal and social limitations and struggles still faced by Dissenters at the beginning of the eighteenth century, it must have seemed like a door of opportunity was opening up for Baptists. Yet, it signalled the end of an age too. John Bunyan, author of *Pilgrim's Progress*, had died in 1688, a year before the Toleration Act was passed. Hanserd Knollys, an Anglican clergyman turned Baptist, died in 1691 and his good friend William Kiffin who had been instrumental in leading Calvinistic Baptists in a time of persecution died in 1701. Thomas Collier who had taken the Calvinistic Baptist witness to the west of England died in 1691, while the General Baptist Thomas Grantham who had taught Arminian views of the atonement of Christ to congregations in the north-east of England died in Norwich in 1692.

The deaths of these leaders who had been so shaped by the Puritan spirit did not immediately mark the end of what some have called the golden age of Dissent. There were still those who were reading devotional works such as *The Practice of Piety* by Lewis Bayley (which John Bunyan had found so influential), and many still organized their sermons according to the pattern laid out by the Puritan divine, William Perkins (1558–1602). They also continued to emphasize self-examination as an important part of devotion. However, in a very real sense, it appears that early in the eighteenth century the Puritan emphasis on both 'heart and mind' which had been so apparent in Baptist life in the seventeenth century was in danger of being put to one side. Was the ardour of Puritan piety to be replaced with an emphasis on mere theological order and reason? For a time in the early part of the century in England and

---

[13] John Rippon, *The Baptist Annual Register for 1798, 1799, 1800 and Part of 1801* (London, 1801), pp. 426–8. See my article, 'What about the Widows? An Appeal to Nineteenth-Century Baptist Women', in J. H. Y. Briggs (ed.), *Baptists and the World: Renewing the Vision* (Milton Keynes, 2010).

[14] Among the many Baptists who participated in the society were Samuel Stennett, John Fawcett, James Dore, John Rippon, Robert Hall, Andrew Fuller, F. A. Cox, Isaiah Birt, Eustace Carey, and John Howard Hinton. *The Annual Account of and list of subscribers to, the Society for the Relief of the Necessitous Widows and Children of Protestant Dissenting Ministers Instituted 1733* (London, 1839), pp. 11–14.

[15] Rippon, *The Baptist Annual Register for 1798, 1799, 1800 and Part of 1801*, p. 427.

Wales, it appeared so when Baptists, along with other Dissenters, complained of the loss of 'vital religion'.[16]

DECLINE AND GROWTH: STRUGGLES IN CHURCH LIFE

While no one single cause may be given for periods of decline in Dissent, doctrinal error and disputes have often been blamed for what was seen as a sort of spiritual decay in the early part of the eighteenth century. Baptists certainly had theological differences. Raymond Brown has noted that because of their 'literal interpretation of biblical passages', General Baptists sometimes divided over what might be 'quite marginal issues'.[17] However, they also lost members over greater doctrinal matters, particularly an understanding of the Trinity as may be seen in the case of Matthew Caffyn (1628–1714) whose Christological views caused more than a little consternation.[18]

For Calvinistic Baptists one of the main theological debates was on what became known as High or Hyper-Calvinism. The main proponents of these ideas were the London Baptist pastors: John Skepp (1675–1721), John Brine (1703–1765), and John Gill (1697–1771). Gill, in particular, became known for his *A Body of Practical Divinity* (1770). He believed that since not everyone responded to the Gospel message, it must be that God did not intend all to respond. Hence if a person was destined to salvation or excluded from it, the most important thing was that a person should submit to God's will for the greater glory of God. High Calvinism was promoted out in the provinces as well as in London. Anne Dutton, though not considered to be as astute or theologically well-trained, nor as influential as her male counterparts, nevertheless reflected the views of many when she wrote against the Moravians and declared:

> Whereas our Lord saith, That he laid down his life for his sheep, John X. 15. For the Elect of God, appointed to Salvation thro' Jesus Christ, before the World began. For these, given by God the Father to Christ, to be his sheep, did HE as the Good Shepherd lay down his Life. And not for the Goats, who shall stand at the last Day on his Left-Hand and be sent away from him, as cursed into everlasting Fire prepar'd for the Devil and his angels, Mat.XXV.33, 41.[19]

[16] See the discussion by Michael R. Watts, *The Dissenters: From the Reformation to the French Revolution*, vol. I (Oxford, 1978), pp. 382–93.
[17] Raymond Brown, *English Baptists of the Eighteenth Century* (Didcot, 1986), p. 18.
[18] Alan P. F. Sell, 'Doctrine, Polity, Liberty: What do Baptists Stand For?', in W. H. Brackney and Paul Fiddes (eds), *Pilgrim Pathways: Essays in Honour of B.R. White* (Macon, GA, 1999), pp. 5–9.
[19] Anne Dutton, 'Some Mistakes of the Moravian Brethren', in *Selected Spiritual Writings of Anne Dutton: Eighteenth-Century British-Baptist, Woman Theologian*, vol. 6, *Various Works*, compiled by Joann Ford Watson (Macon, GA, 2010), p. xv.

How much of the spiritual lethargy among Calvinistic Baptists may be laid at the door of High Calvinism is difficult to judge. It has been argued that Gill's theology dominated Calvinistic Baptist pulpits and was only firmly countered when Andrew Fuller (1754-1815) of Kettering published his work *The Gospel Worthy of All Acceptation, or the duty of sinners to believe in Jesus Christ* (1785). Others would argue that evangelical Calvinism expressed by Fuller and others in the latter part of the eighteenth century merely characterized the overall mood among Baptists in Bristol and the West Country in the seventeenth and early eighteenth centuries.[20] So much so, that the work of Andrew Fuller and others is important 'not because they initiated the evangelical form of Calvinism but because they formulated more precisely, and perceived the implications more clearly, of doctrines which had been held by some ministers and churches before them'.[21]

Whether Moderate Calvinism, or Fullerism, as it became known, was a new expression of evangelical doctrine or simply a reinterpretation of the warm heartfelt faith of Old Dissent, the effect of it was the same. Fullerism suggested that it was the duty of people who hear the Gospel to have faith. If that were so, it was the responsibility of Christians to proclaim the gospel message far and wide.[22] This emphasis on proclamation of the Gospel would find expression in a concern for missions, especially in the latter part of the century, when societies for the support of home and foreign missions were founded, Sunday Schools were established, and members of different denominations cooperated together in the publication of religious periodicals.[23] Most importantly, village preaching became a task which engaged the settled pastor as well as the itinerant preacher.

Apart from generally acknowledging the influence of the Evangelical Revival, the way this new evangelical impetus developed among Old Dissent in the mid eighteenth century has never been satisfactorily explained. While there were numerous social, political, and economic factors affecting religious life, at the very least it may be understood as an effort to moderate an inherited Calvinist theology and church polity while at the same time taking account of

---

[20] L. G. Champion, 'Evangelical Calvinism and the Structures of Baptist Church Life'. *Baptist Quarterly*, 28, 5 (1980), pp. 196-208. See also Roger Hayden, *English Baptist History and Heritage* (Didcot, 1990, 2005), p. 112.

[21] Champion, 'Evangelical Calvinism', p. 203.

[22] P. J. Morden, 'Andrew Fuller and the Gospel Worthy of All Acceptation', in Briggs (ed.), *Pulpit and People*, pp. 128-51.

[23] One of the earliest periodicals to be published was *The Evangelical Magazine* which was established by Independents in 1793. It was followed by *The Protestant Dissenters Magazine* in 1794. While neither of these were strictly Baptist publications, many Baptists contributed to them until they began to print their own *Baptist Magazine* in 1809. See Rosemary Taylor, 'English Baptist Periodicals, 1790-1865: A Bibliography and Survey' (M.Phil. thesis, University of London, 1974). A bibliography which formed the first part of her thesis was printed as an article, 'English Baptist Periodicals, 1790-1865', *Baptist Quarterly*, 27, 2 (1977), pp. 50-82.

Revival experience. However, what Bernard L. Manning argued of Congregationalism in the eighteenth century may be applied more widely to the 'revival' of Dissent, and that is that it cannot be adequately described in terms of 'a story of depression after the Toleration Act, an inglorious sleep, and then a waking to the trumpet of Wesley and Whitefield'. Nor, it might be added, among Baptists was it due simply to the missionary call of Andrew Fuller.[24] However, 'a renewed theology' did lead to a rediscovery of mission and eventually the creation of new organizations to fulfil that mission.[25]

Fuller, of course, engaged in other theological debates which occupied the attention of Baptists, including a discussion over the issue of 'closed' or 'strict communion'. Along with other notable ministers such as Abraham Booth (1734–1806) of London and Joseph Kinghorn (1766–1832) of Norwich, Fuller felt that the Lord's Table should be strictly guarded and only those who had been baptized as believers should be allowed to share in the Lord's Supper. Others like John Ryland Snr and his son John Ryland Jnr favoured open communion. Both father and son served the College Lane congregation in Northampton which, like some other Baptist churches, had decided to welcome in membership both those who had been baptized as infants as well as those who had been baptized as believers by immersion and felt quite strongly that the table should be open to all.[26] The issue did not seem to trouble Welsh Baptists who on the whole favoured strict or closed communion. Yet for some Baptists the notion that believers who had not been baptized by immersion might be accepted into membership of a congregation was a renunciation of the Baptist view of the Church. For others, such as Daniel Turner, it was important to embrace a more universal view of the Church. Turner's reasoning was that all human opinions are fallible and while they may hold to their particular interpretations of Scripture with passionate conviction, they must leave the final judgement to Christ.[27]

Robert Robinson (1735–1790), minister in Cambridge for more than thirty years, held similar views and was caught up in controversy for most of his ministry. A fine preacher, he published books and treatises and spoke out on a number of social and political issues, including slavery. He also believed strongly in religious freedom and stood against demanding a subscription to any kind of credal formula. For him, forced subscription to any creed was

---

[24] B. L. Manning, 'Congregationalism in the Eighteenth Century', *Essays in Orthodox Dissent* (London, 1939), p. 189.

[25] Champion, 'Evangelical Calvinism', p. 197.

[26] John Taylor, *Bi-centenary Edition, History of College Street Church, Northampton: with biographies of Pastors, Missionaries and Preachers and notes of Sunday Schools, Branch Churches and Workers* (Northampton, 1897), p. 12.

[27] Paul S. Fiddes, 'Daniel Turner and Theology of the Church Universal', in Briggs (ed.), *Pulpit and People*, p. 124.

a way of usurping 'the rights of Christ'.[28] While he remained in contact with many well-known Baptists, his friendship with Theophilus Lindsey (1723–1808), a Unitarian, and perhaps the fact that Robinson was one of few Calvinistic Baptists to preach at a General Baptist Assembly (1789), made many people doubt the orthodoxy of his teaching.[29]

How much of the growth or decline among Baptists in the eighteenth century was related to theological controversy is difficult to discern. At times doctrinal differences were quickly resolved as in the case of the College Lane Church in Northampton when they called John Moore (d.1726) of Lancashire to be pastor.[30] Apparently the congregation had always been a 'mixed' communion church, having grown out of the Congregational Church known as the Castle Hill Meeting (later associated with Philip Doddridge). The church covenant at the time the Baptist Church was formed is dated 1697 and states clearly that both believers in baptism by immersion and infant baptism would be recognized for membership in the congregation. With the arrival of Moore, who practised believer's baptism, the congregation took the opportunity to add a few lines to their church covenant promising that 'our difference in Judgment shall not cause a Breach of Union or affection'.[31]

In spite of the church's struggle to pay his salary, Moore stayed in the church for twenty-five years and during his time in ministry it is reported that he admitted 264 members to the church: 80 men and 184 women.[32] Among them would have been his daughter Anne, who married the High Calvinist John Brine, pastor of the Baptist congregation at Curriers' Hall, Cripplegate, in London for thirty-five years. Anne Dutton, who was born in Northamptonshire to Congregationalist parents, but baptized as a believer by Moore, also became a member of the church. She claimed later that 'the special Advantage I receiv'd under his Ministry was the Establishment of my Judgment in the doctrines of the Gospel'.[33] Significantly, after her first marriage, Dutton joined Skepp's congregation in London where she would exclaim that 'there she found the same doctrines of the gospel maintained and vindicated in the ministry of Mr. Skepp, as I was wont to hear under Mr. Moore, with abundance of glory, life and power'.[34]

---

[28] Karen E. Smith, 'The Liberty Not to be a Christian: Robert Robinson (1735–1790) of Cambridge and Freedom of Conscience', in Marc A. Jolley with John D. Pierce (eds), *Distinctively Baptist: Essays on Baptist History* (Macon, GA, 2005), p. 167.
[29] Smith, 'The Liberty Not to be a Christian', p. 168.
[30] John Taylor, *History of College Street Church*, p. 6.
[31] John Taylor, *History of College Street Church*, p. 5.
[32] John Taylor, *History of College Street Church*, p. 13.
[33] Anne Dutton, in *Selected Spiritual Writings of Anne Dutton: Eighteenth-Century British Baptist, Woman Theologian*, vol. 3, *Autobiography*, compiled by Joann Ford Watson (Macon GA, 2006), p. 50.
[34] Anne Dutton, in *Selected Spiritual Writings of Anne Dutton: Eighteenth-Century British Baptist, Woman Theologian*, vol. 2, *Discourse, Poetry, Hymns and Memoir* (Macon, GA, 2004), p. 88

During the first twenty years under Moore's leadership the church grew, though in the last five years of his ministry, the congregation experienced decline.[35] The church records mention that there was great dissatisfaction among the members which may have been linked to theological differences. Certainly, there was consternation among church members that, in spite of the covenant agreement, Moore preached a sermon on believer's baptism and began to insist that members must be baptized by immersion. He died in 1726, but by this time the church had declined in numbers considerably. The church underwent a period of division and turmoil, including a decision by a few members gathered at a church meeting to cease being a church which was shortly after reversed, but struggled on for a few years until it was served by John Ryland Snr (1723–1792) and his son John Ryland Jnr (1753–1825).

In addition to his ministry in the church at Northampton, John Ryland Snr had a school. He eventually moved to Enfield, near London and left his son, who had served as co-pastor, in sole charge of the church. John Ryland Jnr became active in the Northamptonshire Baptist Association and was good friends with many of the pastors, including John Sutcliff, Andrew Fuller, and William Carey. John Ryland Jnr eventually moved with his second wife, Frances, to Bristol where he became pastor of the Broadmead Church and head of the Bristol Academy.[36]

Although theological differences may have played some part in the decline among churches, it was by no means responsible for large losses among all Baptist churches. Indeed, like the College Lane Church, it appears that in the first half of the century other congregations reported periods of both growth and decline in membership. For instance, in 1743 the Baptist congregation in Broughton in Hampshire, reported eighty-eight members in the congregation. Two years later, in 1745, there were ninety-one members.[37] Between 1745 and 1756, however, there were no baptisms. And one woman wrote in her diary in March 1749 that the church 'have set apart each Wednesday before church meeting to set apart some time for prayer on account of our low estate'.[38]

Many different reasons were given at the time for uneven periods of growth and decline. Some loss of members was of course due to the very high mortality rate. Smaller churches in rural areas sometimes fell prey to illness as was lamented by a visitor to the Baptist congregation at Haycombe near Bath in 1750: 'this ancient church have [sic] little by little drop'd away by death and no increase and now looks Likely that God will soon remove his candlestick out of this place'.[39] Lack of ministers was another difficulty. In the

---

[35] John Taylor, *History of College Street Church*, p. 13.
[36] Grant Gordon, 'The Call of Dr John Ryland Jr', *Baptist Quarterly*, 34, 5 (1992), pp. 214–27.
[37] Broughton Church Book, 1730–1756, The Angus Library, Regent's Park College, Oxford.
[38] Diary of Anne C. Steele, 22 March 1749, Steele family papers, The Angus Library, Regent's Park College, Oxford.
[39] Diary of Anne C. Steele, 2 September 1750.

provinces especially, it seems that churches sometimes went several years without a minister. When John Voicey, the pastor at Lymington, died in 1764 the church was said to be in a 'destitute condition' for three years before a minister could be found. Noting the decline in this period the church records stated:

> No one went in and out before us to break the Bread of Life unto us. At length some grew careless and others were disheartened. We kept the House of God open Lords Days by reading and prayer. Endeavours were used to get a Gospel minister, but to no purpose.[40]

Churches who were able to find ministers could not always support them. The Particular Baptist Fund (1717) and the Bristol Fund (1717) had been formed for the support of ministry and churches. Yet, as was certainly the case in Wales, many ministers in England taught or had another job as well as serving as minister of the Church. James Fanch (1704–1767) helped his brother-in-law Daniel Turner (1710–1798) run a school and then later when Turner moved to Abingdon, Fanch went to preach at Romsey and Lockerley where, helped by support by the Particular Baptist Fund and money from the congregation, he was able to continue preaching in villages in and around Hampshire and Wiltshire.[41]

While it is difficult to ascertain the exact number of Baptist congregations or to estimate the gains and losses in them, W. T. Whitley suggested that there were about 220 congregations in England and Wales around 1715 to 1718. By the 1750s it seems that the number may have dropped to around 150 churches.[42] The decline appears to have been due to a combination of factors, including mortality rates, lack of ministers, or the inability to support a minister. Deryck Lovegrove, who credits the later revival in Dissent with the work of itinerant preachers, has suggested that the real problem was 'isolation'.[43] 'The very strength of independency, the internal cohesion of the gathered church, became its weakness as geographical remoteness conspired with autonomy and lack of common purpose to foster decline.'[44] While there can be no doubt that the work of itinerant preachers assisted in the growth of congregational life towards the end of the century, Lovegrove's bold claim seems to overlook the more positive features of congregational life.

---

[40] Records of the Lymington Baptist Church 1768–1831, 1832 [HRO56M84/1] Hampshire Record Office.

[41] Karen E. Smith, 'James Fanch (1704–1767): The Spiritual Counsel of an Eighteenth-Century Baptist Pastor', in Briggs (ed.), *Pulpit and People*, pp. 61–8.

[42] W. T. Whitley, 'Baptist Ministers in England about 1750 A.D.', *Transactions of the Baptist Historical Society* 6 (1918–19), pp. 138–57.

[43] Deryck W. Lovegrove, *Established Church, Sectarian People: Itinerancy and the Transformation of English Dissent, 1780–1830* (Cambridge, 1988), p. 7.

[44] Lovegrove, *Established Church*, p. 7.

In truth, the cause of spiritual lethargy is never easily discerned. At the time, naturally, the state of religion was judged on the increase or decrease in the size of congregations. Blame was laid squarely on ministers who demonstrated 'unsuitable gaiety', 'levity of conduct', and 'a lack of interest in serving anything but prestigious congregations'.[45] Others suggested that ministers were preaching 'odd notions' and individuals were 'imbibing error'. One writer put the blame squarely on 'two monsters: Methodists and the Glasites'.[46] Later historians not only measured decline by decrease in numbers, but they also explained the loss as related to the apparent crisis of orthodoxy, and an initial failure by Old Dissent to accept the Evangelical Revival.

ENGAGING WITH THE ENTHUSIASM OF THE EVANGELICAL REVIVAL

In the past, there has often been a rather too simplistic explanation for the revival of Dissent in the latter part of the eighteenth century: simply crediting the work of the Evangelical Revival with the renewal of Dissent. Yet, Calvinistic Baptists in Wales and England did not readily embrace Wesleyan Methodism. In Wales, both General and Particular Baptists were more cautious in their acceptance of the Methodists due to: (1) a suspicion of established religion, (2) fear of emotionalism, and (3) theological differences, particularly over the nature of saving faith.[47] 'The Welsh Baptist movement', as Densil Morgan puts it, 'had drunk deeply by this time of the sobriety of Old Dissent.'[48]

Since their forebears had struggled for the freedom to meet for worship, it is unsurprising that early eighteenth-century Baptists held firmly to their Dissenting heritage. However, there can be no doubt that some of the growth they experienced was due to the growing 'enthusiasm' of the revival preachers. There are numerous examples of Baptists in contact with Methodist leaders. Anne Dutton, for example, corresponded with Howel Harris (1714–1773),

---

[45] [Anon.], *Some Observations Upon the Present State of Dissenting Interest* (London, 1730).

[46] [Anon.], *The Causes and reasons of the Present declension Among the Congregational Churches in London and the Country in a letter addressed to Pastors, deacons, and members of those Churches by one of that denomination interspersed with reflections on Methodism and Sandemanianism* (London, 1766).

[47] D. Densil Morgan, 'Smoke, Fire and Light: Baptists and the Revitalisation of Welsh Dissent', *Baptist Quarterly*, 32, 5 (1988), p. 226.

[48] Morgan, 'Smoke, Fire and Light', p. 226.

Selina Hastings, the countess of Huntingdon (1707–1791), and William Seward (1711–1740), as well as George Whitefield.[49]

Moreover, there are a number of examples of ministers who claimed that they had first come to faith under the ministry of a Methodist preacher: notably, Robert Robinson said he had been converted while hearing George Whitefield preach. Likewise, John Fawcett (1739–1817) joined with the Methodists in Yorkshire in 1762 and remained with them until 1764 when he became pastor of Wainsgate Baptist Church in Hebden Bridge. He served the congregation at Hebden Bridge for fifty-two years from 1764 until 1816 during which time it was said 'His talents emitted a steady and glorious lustre in the house of God'.[50] A hymn writer, he also opened an academy in Yorkshire and was influential in organizing the Yorkshire Auxiliary Society for the support of the Baptist Missionary Society.

Dan Taylor joined the Methodists before becoming a General Baptist in 1763.[51] By 1770 he had formed the New Connexion General Baptists who would be influential across the Midlands and the North of England. Wales also seems to have benefitted from the Methodist preachers and throughout the 1750s a number of Methodists came into the Baptist fold.[52]

Whitefield was, of course, the primary influence among Calvinistic Baptists. One Baptist woman in Hampshire recorded in her diary in 1752 that she and her husband attended a service at which Whitefield was preaching. She commented: 'God have [sic] been pleased to make him wonderfull usefull [sic] in the world as an instrument in his hand for the conversion of sinners', and she described his preaching in this way:

> He proposed a method and in some measure kept to it but made frequent and large digressions. He was very active and loud and endeavoured to strike the passions... as I had long wanted to hear him preach I attended with diligence.[53]

Whitefield's influence on Calvinistic Baptists, as on Dissent as a whole, is notable.[54] Writing in his *A History of the English Baptists* at the end of

---

[49] See, for example, a letter from Dutton to Whitefield with an accompanying note to Mrs Whitefield, 20 June 1752 in Timothy Whelan (transcribed and ed.), *Baptist Autographs in the John Rylands University Library of Manchester 1741–1845* (Macon, GA, 2009), pp. 5–7.
[50] I. Mann, *Memoirs of the late Rev. William Crabtree* (1815) as cited in Ian Sellers, 'Other Times, Other Ministries: John Fawcett and Alexander McClaren', *Baptist Quarterly*, 32, 4 (1987), p. 181.
[51] Adam Taylor, *Memoirs of the Rev. Dan Taylor* (London, 1820), pp. 9–12, 25.
[52] T. M. Bassett, *The Welsh Baptists* (Swansea, 1977), p. 95.
[53] Diary of Anne C. Steele, 22 June 1752.
[54] John Walsh said of Whitefield: 'If any single man deserves the credit for the resurgence of Dissent, it is he.' 'Methodism at the End of the Eighteenth Century', in Rupert E. Davies, George A Raymond, and E. Gordon Rupp (eds), *A History of the Methodist Church in Great Britain* 4 vols. (London, 1965–88), I, p. 293.

the eighteenth century, Joseph Ivimey suggested that an increase in the congregation at Portsmouth was the result of the fact that John Lacey invited George Whitefield to preach in the chapel.[55] Lacey was apparently criticized by some of the 'neighbouring ministers and others' for encouraging the Methodists and he replied: 'Would to God that Jesus Christ was preached at the corner of every street, I would not care by whom.'[56] While this explanation does not fully explain the growth there and in other places, it does underscore the impact of Whitefield's preaching. The spread of the Revival, naturally, did not rest entirely with him or indeed with any of the other evangelical leaders. In fact, its success depended upon the itinerant preachers, who went week by week around the countryside.[57]

While there can be no doubt that Baptists in England and Wales were challenged by the Methodist movement, care should be taken not to simply equate the Evangelical Revival with Wesleyan Methodism.[58] As Ian Sellers has pointed out, the work of the Anglican vicar and evangelist, William Grimshaw, was 'seminal for Baptists'.[59] John Fawcett was among Grimshaw's converts (though he also owed something to Whitefield). Likewise, there were other Yorkshire Baptist ministers who were indebted to Grimshaw's evangelistic preaching.

The slave-trader turned pastor and hymn writer, John Newton, was also friends with many Baptist pastors and in 1789 even received a letter of appreciation from the small congregation in Whitchurch in Hampshire. They wrote to express their appreciation for his sermons which, they claimed, had been read 'publickly' in 'assemblies, at our weekly meetings, as well as on the sabbath day when we had no preaching and we trust we can say, to our no small edification and comfort'.[60] They noted his ability to distinguish between 'the wild raptures and reveries of enthusiasm' and 'the work of God's Spirit', and they said they were sending him 'a mite towards encouraging your heart and strength(en)ing your hands in God's service'.[61] They closed the letter with

---

[55] He says the congregation doubled in size after Whitefield preached there and by 1777 the church consisted of 150 members and about 200 hearers. Joseph Ivimey, *A History of the English Baptists*, vol. IV (London, 1830), p. 487. Whitefield often went to Portsmouth. For example, in 1749 he preached there for more than a week. John Gillies, *Memoirs of Rev. George Whitefield* (Middletown, 1841), pp. 12-130.

[56] Ivimey, *A History of the English Baptists*, vol. IV, p. 487.

[57] Thomas Jackson, ed., *The Lives of Early Methodist Preachers Chiefly Written by Themselves*, 6 vols. (London, 1865).

[58] John Walsh, 'Methodism at the End of the Eighteenth Century', in *A History of the Methodist Church*, I, p. 289.

[59] Sellers, 'Other Times, Other Ministries', p. 182.

[60] Letter to John Newton from the Congregation at Whitchurch, Hampshire, 18 October 1789. Angus Library, Regent's Park College.

[61] Letter to John Newton, Angus Library.

a cordial invitation to him that included, nevertheless, a reminder of the division which existed between them, by saying:

> Should you ever come our way, we should be glad to entertain you as a christian Friend and fellow traveller Zion ward; and we lament that your connection with the establishment, forbids us to hope for a sermon from you.[62]

Although John Newton was widely respected as rector of St Mary Woolnoth in London, it may at first seem surprising that a Baptist congregation would take the time to send him a formal letter. Yet, his approach to piety had been shaped by his upbringing in 'orthodox Dissent and his reading of the Puritans'.[63] As Hindmarsh reminds us:

> To these roots can be traced, for example, his biblicism, his intense moral seriousness and preoccupation with indwelling sin, his tendency to stress words over symbols as instruments of devotion; and his emphases upon introspection, discursive meditation, and the importance of the affections.[64]

In fact, Newton had close links with many Baptists, among them his good friend, John Ryland Jnr who (as already noted) became the minister at Broadmead Church in Bristol and the President of the Bristol Academy in 1794.

THE RENEWAL OF 'HEART AND MIND'

The Academy at Bristol was of paramount importance for renewal among Baptists in the eighteenth century. The oldest Baptist Academy (now Bristol Baptist College) was started in 1679 with money bequeathed by a member of the Broadmead Church in Bristol and by 1720 it was effectively at work. From 1720 until 1758 Bernard Foskett (1685–1758) served as tutor and under his leadership the reputation of the Academy was established.[65] At his death, he was succeeded by a Welshman, Hugh Evans (1712–1781), who had trained under Foskett some years before. John Rippon, who had been a student under Hugh Evans, said of him: 'His gift in prayer was uncommon—his students thought it unequalled... nor did any preacher know better what it was to reign

---

[62] The letter was signed by minister Charles Cole, deacons Joseph Saunders, John Brackstone, and John Cook, and six male members of the congregation.

[63] D. Bruce Hindmarsh, *John Newton and the English Evangelical Tradition* (Grand Rapids, MI, 1996, 2001), p. 236.

[64] Hindmarsh, *John Newton and the English Evangelical Tradition*, p. 237.

[65] John Rippon, 'A Brief Essay Towards the History of the Baptist Academy at Bristol read before the Bristol Education Society at their annual meeting in Broadmead, 26th August, 1795', *The Baptist Annual Register, 1794, 1795, 1796–7*, II (London, 1797), p. 440ff.

over his audience, enlightening their understanding, convincing their judgment, and then kindling all their passions in a blaze of devotion.'[66]

Evans was later joined in the work of the Academy by his son, Caleb Evans, who assisted him until his death in 1781. Under their leadership students were encouraged to bring together their enthusiasm for the Christian faith with critical and sound scholarship. Students attended the academy for three years and their programme of study included logic, English grammar, languages, oratory, geography, astronomy, natural and moral philosophy, Jewish antiquities, ecclesiastical history, and a system of divinity.[67] Students were also sent out to preach in the churches in order to give them practical training. As the need for more ministers in the churches became apparent, Caleb Evans increased the size of the Academy in Bristol and in 1770 the Bristol Education Society was formed whose primary purpose was to gain financial support for the Academy in order to provide 'destitute churches' with 'a succession of able and evangelical ministers'.[68] Roger Hayden has argued that there was a warm heartfelt evangelistic strain of Old Dissent—seen particularly in the work of those who were associated with Bristol Academy—which has sometimes been ignored by those who want to see moderate Calvinism as a direct result of the prodding of the Evangelical Revival.

Although Bristol was the first Academy to be formed, others in England and Wales would follow. Dan Taylor, the leader of the New Connexion General Baptists, began an academy at Mile End in 1798. In 1804, John Fawcett started the Northern Education Society. In Wales, the churches had depended almost exclusively on the Academy at Bristol until 1807 when Micah Thomas of Pontypool established an Academy at Abergavenny which would later move to Pontypool and then to Cardiff at the end of the nineteenth century.[69]

Since all of the aforementioned academies were for the training of ministers, Baptist women had limited opportunities for formal education. While there were a number of boarding or day schools in London and in the provincial towns in the eighteenth century, the level of education in these varied greatly depending on the ability of the teacher. Many focused heavily on sewing and embroidery, and besides reading and writing many did not venture beyond basic arithmetic, though some schools included French, music, and dancing as part of their programme.[70] One highly rated school for girls was run by a

---

[66] Norman S. Moon, 'Caleb Evans, Founder of the Bristol Education Society', *Baptist Quarterly*, 24, 4 (1971), pp. 175-6.

[67] H. Wheeler Robinson, 'A Student's programme in 1744', *Baptist Quarterly* (1924-5), pp. 249-52. 'Catalogue of a Few useful Books for a young minister drawn up by Caleb Evans in 1773', *Baptist Annual Register*, 1790, 1791, 1792, and part of 1793, vol. I (London, 1793), p. 353.

[68] *An Account of the Bristol Education Society 1770-1784* (Bristol, 1784), p. 9.

[69] W. T. Whitley, *A History of British Baptists* (London, 1923), pp. 235-40.

[70] Marjorie Reeves, *Female Education and Nonconformist Culture, 1700-1900* (Leicester, 1997), p. 18.

Baptist woman, Martha Trinder (d.1794) of Northampton.[71] Significantly, when John Newton visited Northampton to see his friend John Ryland, he visited Martha Trinder's school and conducted a service for the students. In September 1774, he said this of one of his visits to Northampton:

> Indeed the Lord's work seems to flourish there, and Mr. Ryland, amidst the many particularities which give him an Originality of Character beyond most men I ever knew, appears to new and greater advantage every time I see him. The Lord is pleased always to own me to the comfort of the serious young persons in Mrs. Trinders school, of whom I conversed with about 12 this time, who seem very promising.[72]

The developing opportunities for religious education among Baptists in many ways mark a continuation of their Puritan heritage. Faith was a matter of mind and heart. So meeting together for Scripture reading, prayer, and preaching was always important. This continuing Puritan influence on devotional life can be seen throughout the eighteenth century. In 1795, Frances Barrett Ryland, second wife of John Ryland Jnr, wrote in her diary:

> I have lately been reading Dr. Owens evidences of the faith of Gods Elect. So far as my judgement goes he appears to enter deep into experimental religion, devotedness of the soul to God, and what are the most decisive marks of being a partaker of true faith.[73]

The continuing emphasis on Puritan devotion may be seen in preaching and worship as well. The approach to preaching throughout the eighteenth century was grounded in the pattern laid down by William Perkins in his work *The Art of Prophecying or a Treatise Concerning the Sacred and Onely True Manner and Methode of Preaching* (1617) which favoured a head to heart acquisition of knowledge. Sermons began with an exposition of doctrine, but moved toward an application which ended with an appeal for self-examination. The theme of self-examination continued to be an important one in the eighteenth century and shaped Baptist congregational approaches to baptism and the Lord's Supper, as well as preparation for death.[74]

---

[71] She was Martha Smith and married Thomas Trinder. See, 'Some Account of Mrs Martha Trinder, of Northampton', in *The Baptist Annual Register I, for 1790, 1791, 1792, and part of 1793*, ed. John Rippon (London: Dilly, Button, and Thomas, 1793), pp. 135–42.
[72] Diary of John Newton (1773–1805), 11 September 1774, as cited in Hindmarsh, *John Newton and the English Evangelical Tradition*, p. 143.
[73] 'Diary of Frances Barrett Ryland', Lords day 25 [Oct. 1795] in *Nonconformist Women Writers, 1720–1840*, ed. Timothy Whelan (London, 2011), p. 357.
[74] Karen E. Smith, 'Preparation as a Discipline of Devotion in Eighteenth Century England: A Lost Facet of Baptist Identity?', in Ian M. Randall, Toivo Pilli, and Anthony R. Cross (eds) *Baptist Identities: International Studies from the Seventeenth to the Twentieth Centuries* (Milton Keynes, 2006), pp. 22–144.

Sermons were important for public and private devotions. Many pastors would have agreed with William Steadman of Broughton that they 'wrote little and delivered sermons without notes'.[75] Yet there were many eighteenth-century pastors who copied their sermons and published them, particularly funeral sermons which became an important evangelistic tool. In Wales the most famous preacher towards the end of the century was Christmas Evans (1766–1838), who was influenced early on by Calvinistic Methodists and then later joined with the Baptists.[76] Considered a masterful preacher, it is said that he brought a formidable memory, imagination, and drama to the art of preaching.[77] There were many others, of course, who began in the eighteenth century to develop the art of preaching. James Fanch of Romsey, though not as well known as his brother-in-law Daniel Turner, published a book of sermons which stressed the need to make a 'close and home application' throughout the sermon.[78]

Hymn singing became an important means of teaching and reflecting on doctrine. Many ministers wrote hymns to be used as a doctrinal summary at the end of the service. While some of these were little more than doggerel, there were a number of notable Baptist hymn writers who contributed to the renewal of Baptist life through their presentation of rich theological themes. Benjamin Beddome (1717–1795), the minister at Bourton-on-the-Water for fifty-five years, wrote a number of hymns which sought to engage the mind and the heart. There were women hymn writers, too. Anne Steele (1717–1778) of Broughton was perhaps the best known. Her work was not originally written for publication, but rather for use in the church at Broughton in Hampshire where her father was pastor. However, she was part of a wider circle of friends that included Caleb Evans of Bristol and John Ash of Pershore who would include many of her hymns in their *A Collection of Hymns Adapted to Public Worship* (1769).

A sometimes neglected aspect of eighteenth-century Baptist life, but one which fostered the values of the spirituality of Old Dissent, centred on the home and family. While the actual practice of family devotions is difficult to evaluate, it was certainly very much a part of the Puritan tradition which was so central to Dissent.[79] While the practice seems to have waned during the eighteenth century, there were Baptists who continued to emphasize the importance of household worship. Samuel Stennett (1727–1795), Baptist

---

[75] Thomas Steadman, *Memoirs of William Steadman* (London, 1838), p. 93.

[76] 'Christmas Evans on his Ministry', in Document III.17 in Alan P. F. Sell (ed.) with David J. Hall and Ian Sellers, *Protestant Nonconformist Texts: The Eighteenth Century*, vol. II (Aldershot, 2006), p. 172.

[77] John Thomas Jones, 'Christmas Evans', in the *Dictionary of Welsh Biography*, http://yba.llgc.org.uk/en/s-EVAN-CHR-1766.html.

[78] James Fanch, *Ten Sermons on Practical Subjects* (London, 1768).

[79] Karen E. Smith, 'Nonconformists, the Home and Family Life', in Pope (ed.), *T & T Clark Companion to Nonconformity*, pp. 285–304.

minister and hymn writer, wrote a treatise entitled *Discourses on Domestic Duties* in which he stressed that the 'orderly management of the business of the day' was helped by having at least two fixed times a day for family worship. The New Connexion General Baptist leader, Dan Taylor, wrote to a friend in 1789 of the joys and benefits of family worship and claimed: 'it is a wonder to me how any who take pleasure in devotion can live in neglect of it'.[80] Family worship was to include Bible readings, prayer, and a hymn. A collection of Benjamin Beddome's hymns was printed under the title, *Hymns adapted to Public Worship or Family Devotion.*[81]

BAPTISTS AT THE CLOSE OF THE CENTURY

Baptists at the end of the eighteenth century had experienced considerable change. Having emerged out of the political and social struggles of the seventeenth century, they brought to the eighteenth century an emphasis on covenant life and a piety shaped by their Puritan heritage. While church life had on the whole been focused on the local body of believers, they had continued to meet in regional Associations. In London as well as in the provinces of England and Wales, Baptists had bemoaned the lack of growth and complained of spiritual malaise. There had been doctrinal controversy and the differences over open or closed communion. Likewise, they had benefitted from the Evangelical Revival, which had prompted them to renew a warm evangelical piety that had its roots in Puritan devotion with its emphasis on Scripture and prayer.

By the end of the century, Baptists were beginning to think about the duty of Christians to preach the Gospel to all people. While some people have seen this impetus as the result of the development of a more moderate Calvinism under Andrew Fuller's leadership, others would claim that Baptists, like the rest of Old Dissent, shared with the new Evangelicals a common heritage in Puritanism which was grounded in personal faith informed by the spoken Word and improved by constant self-examination. For Baptists, this very rich evangelical devotion which one might associate with the older Dissenting tradition had always been nurtured at the Bristol Academy.

Bristol connections may be identified again in two other important events: the prayer call of 1784 and the formation of the Particular Baptist Society for the Propagation of the Gospel Amongst the Heathen in 1792. The prayer call

---

[80] Adam Taylor, *Memoirs of the Rev. Dan Taylor*, p. 260.
[81] B. Beddome, *Hymns adapted to Public Worship or Family Devotion* (London, 1818). This collection was left in manuscript form by Beddome for his family to use in family worship, but was reprinted for wider use with a recommendatory preface by Baptist minister Robert Hall (1764–1831).

was initiated by John Sutcliff (1752–1814), a Yorkshire man who had come to faith and been baptized by John Fawcett, and became a member of Wainsgate Baptist Church, near Hebden Bridge. He was later commended by the church and went to Bristol Baptist Academy in 1772.[82]

In 1775, Sutcliff went to Olney in North Buckinghamshire as pastor and remained there until his death in 1814. The church at Olney was part of the Northamptonshire Baptist Association and it was here that he came in contact with John Ryland Jnr, Andrew Fuller, Robert Hall, and William Carey. In 1784, Sutcliff issued a *Call to Prayer* which insisted that all Christians should be praying for revival and the spread of the Gospel of Christ. The argument for this call was based on the writings of Jonathan Edwards, the American revivalist and theologian, which he had discovered as a student at Bristol. Sutcliff had also read the *Life and Diary of David Brainerd* who had proclaimed the Gospel to Native Americans. Sutcliff firmly believed that it was the duty of all to tell others of Christ.

Sutcliff was not alone in these views. In 1781, Robert Hall Snr had published a work entitled *Help for Zion's Travellers*, which expressed a warm evangelical faith. By 1785, William Carey was a member of Sutcliff's church and deeply committed to reaching out to all people with the Gospel. It was, of course, also in 1785 that Fuller published his *Gospel Worthy of All Acceptation*. In 1791, John Sutcliff preached a sermon at a meeting of the Northamptonshire Baptist ministers in which he insisted that the Church should be 'very jealous for the Lord of hosts'. Brian Stanley notes that this 'characteristically Puritan sentiment was matched by an humanitarian emphasis typical of the age of enlightenment' in which he argued that they must reach out to the whole human race. His sermon was followed by one given by Fuller who warned of the danger of delay in doing the work of God.[83] In 1792, Carey, by this time the pastor of the congregation at Leicester, stood at a meeting of the Northamptonshire association and called for the proclamation of the Gospel to all people. His address was later published under the title, *An Enquiry into the Obligations of Christians to use Means for the Conversion of the Heathens*. He wrote:

> As our blessed Lord has required us to pray that his kingdom may come, and his will be done on earth as it is in heaven, it becomes us not only to express our desires of that event by words, but to use every lawful method to spread the knowledge of his name.[84]

---

[82] Michael A. G. Haykin, '"A Habitation of God, Through the Spirit": John Sutcliff (1752–1814) and the Revitalization of the Calvinistic Baptists in the Late Eighteenth Century', *Baptist Quarterly*, 34, 7 (1992), pp. 304–19.

[83] Brian Stanley, *The History of the Baptist Missionary Society, 1792–1992* (Edinburgh, 1992), pp. 9–10.

[84] William Carey, *An Enquiry into the Obligations of Christians to use Means for the Conversion of the Heathens* (Leicester, 1792), p. 1.

Out of this meeting and the efforts of the Association in Northamptonshire, the Society for the Propagation of the Gospel Amongst the Heathen was formed. William Carey and John Thomas, the first missionaries, travelled to India in 1793. Almost immediately, the work of the society began with smaller auxiliary societies being formed in Hampshire, Birmingham, and Yorkshire. By 1797, a society for the encouragement and support of itinerant preaching was formed. Men like William Steadman and John Saffrey were making journeys to Cornwall to preach the Gospel and others were taking up the call to reach out to preach in villages and hamlets. In Wales, too, the work of the mission society advanced.

The work of the mission society served as a catalyst to unite Baptists and other evangelicals and served to draw British Baptists closer to a larger worldwide Baptist family. Yet, responding to a call to reach out to all people with the Gospel of Christ would also bring other challenges to their church life and devotion. In the next century, Baptists would find themselves faced squarely with issues of social justice and equality, not least the abolition of slavery and the role of women in the Church and society. Moreover, in the nineteenth century there would be a move in England and Wales toward a more centralized pattern of organization. Both English and Welsh Baptists, in their own ways, at first tried to resist the move. Many feared that greater denominationalism signalled a step towards centralized power reminiscent of a boardroom and not just greater co-operation between the Churches. Yet, at the close of the eighteenth century the perspective on church life was already changing. Writing of the great Welsh preacher, Christmas Evans, Densil Morgan described the changes in this way:

> Just as he [Christmas Evans] spanned the country geographically, he also spanned two cultures and two separate centuries. Despite his obvious early disadvantages, he had nonetheless inherited the traditions of the Older Dissent. That was a minority movement, sober, fairly cerebral and marginal to Welsh religious life. By 1815 the Older Dissent had vanished. It had been replaced, by the new evangelicalism, zealous, popular and extrovert.[85]

What was true in Wales was also true to some extent among Baptists in England. While the emphasis on evangelism would bring steady numerical growth in the next century, the understanding of covenant life together in a local church, while not lost, would never be quite the same.

---

[85] D. Densil Morgan, 'Christmas Evans (1766–1838) and the Birth of Nonconformist Wales', *Baptist Quarterly*, 34, 3 (1991), p. 122.

SELECT BIBLIOGRAPHY

Bassett, T. M., *The Welsh Baptists* (Swansea, 1977).
Brackney, W. H. and Fiddes, Paul, eds, *Pilgrim Pathways: Essays in Honour of B. R. White* (Macon, GA, 1999).
Briggs, J. H. Y., ed., *Pulpit and People: Studies in Eighteenth-Century Baptist Life and Thought* (Milton Keynes, 2009).
Brown, Raymond, *The English Baptists of the Eighteenth Century* (Didcot, 1986).
Copson, Stephen and Morden, Peter, eds, *Challenge and Change: English Baptist Life in the Eighteenth Century* (Didcot, 2017).
Dutton, Anne, *Selected Spiritual Writings of Anne Dutton: Eighteenth-Century British-Baptist, Woman Theologian*, vol. 6, *Various Works*, compiled by Joann Ford Watson (Macon, GA, 2010).
Fiddes, Paul, *Tracks and Traces: Baptist Identity in Church and Theology* (Milton Keynes, 2003).
Hayden, Roger, *English Baptist History and Heritage* (Didcot, 2005).
Ivimey, Joseph, *A History of the English Baptists*, vol. IV (London, 1830).
Lumpkin, W. L., *Baptist Confessions of Faith* (Chicago, 1969).
Payne, E. A., *The Fellowship of Believers*, 2nd edn (London, 1952).
Pope, Robert, ed., *T & T Clark Companion to Nonconformity* (London, 2013).
Reeves, Marjorie, *Female Education and Nonconformist Culture, 1700–1900* (Leicester, 1997).
Sell, Alan P. F., Hall, David J., and Sellers, Ian, eds, *Protestant Nonconformist Texts: The Eighteenth Century*, vol. II (Aldershot, 2006).
Smith, Karen E., 'The Liberty Not to be a Christian: Robert Robinson (1735–1790) of Cambridge and Freedom of Conscience', in Jolley, Marc A. and Pierce, John D., eds, *Distinctively Baptist, Essays on Baptist History* (Macon, GA, 2005), pp. 151–70.
Smith, Karen E., 'Preparation as a Discipline of Devotion in Eighteenth-Century England: A Lost Facet of Baptist Identity?' in Randall, Ian M., Pilli, Toivo, and Cross, Anthony R., eds, *Baptist Identities: International Studies from the Seventeenth to the Twentieth Centuries* (Milton Keynes, 2006), pp. 22–144.
Stanley, Brian, *The History of the Baptist Missionary Society, 1792–1992* (Edinburgh, 1992).
Underwood, A. C., *A History of English Baptists* (London, 1947).
Whelan, Timothy, ed., *Baptist Autographs in the John Rylands University Library of Manchester 1741–1845*, transcribed and ed. Timothy Whelan (Macon, GA, 2009).
Whelan, Timothy, *Nonconformist Women Writers, 1720–1840*, 8 vols. (London, 2011).
White, B. R., *The English Baptists of the Seventeenth Century* (London, 1983).
Whitley, W. T., *A History of British Baptists* (London, 1923).

4

Quakers

Richard C. Allen

The passing of the Toleration Act on 24 May 1689 was a major turning point in the history of religious dissent in Britain. For the first time protestant Dissenters, except Socinians, were recognized as legal citizens and there was an acceptance that the enforcement of the penal code had not led to conformity of worship and the liturgy of the Established Church. After many years of persecution, for members of the Religious Society of Friends (Quakers) this was a welcome, if tokenistic, measure of relief.[1] In theory, they were now entitled to gather for worship and practise their faith without fear of reprisals, and yet the Act contained a number of significant limitations. Meetings for worship, held in either Friends' houses (conventicles) or specific meeting houses, had to be licensed and during such gatherings the doors had to remain unlocked. Furthermore, allegiance to the monarchy had to be clearly demonstrated which, for Friends, meant an affirmation of loyalty rather than the swearing of an oath.[2] This was nevertheless a cause of internal friction and it took until 1722 for the affirmation question to be resolved.[3] In other ways, too, Friends felt that toleration was only partially delivered as they were required to pay tithes and church rates, while other parochial obligations still remained. In the wider community they were still regarded as outsiders, being denied entry to political or civil offices, unable to access university education, and forced to provide substitutes and financial support for the militia. As pacifists, of course, they could do neither.[4]

---

[1] See Library Society of Friends (hereafter LSF), *Great Book of Sufferings* (hereafter *GBS*), a multi-volume account of the persecution of Quakers, and J. Miller, '"A Suffering People": English Quakers and their Neighbours, *c*.1650–*c*.1700', *Past and Present*, 188, 1 (2005), pp. 71–103.

[2] For a wider assessment of the Toleration Act, see S. Sowerby, *Making Toleration: The Repealers and the Glorious Revolution* (Cambridge, MA, 2013).

[3] N. Morgan, *Lancashire Quakers and the Establishment, 1660–1730* (Halifax, 1993), pp. 141–70.

[4] See J. Besse, *Brief Account of many of the Prosecutions...* (London, 1736).

Three examples illustrate the level of anxiety felt by Anglicans over the granting of toleration. In 1692 the Revd Edward Bowerman of Caddington, Bedfordshire, wrote to Bishop Thomas Tension of Lincoln that Quakers and other 'sectaries' were 'poor deluded People... pouffed up with pride, & possessed with an assurance of their holiness & Election'. They had been 'freed by the Laws [and were now] deaf to the clearest Testimonies of reason & scripture, & deride the fairest means of conviction'.[5] Four years later a damning attack was launched by Charles Leslie, an Anglican non-juror. He argued that the Friends were deviant in their behaviour and misled by their own befuddled theology. He called them false prophets and conjurers, and believed that they were possessed men and women who would damn 'all the World but themselves'.[6] *The Quakers Bookes*, an anonymous single-sided engraved broadside published c.1700, indicates that there were others who did not agree with their theological position. As the polemic insists, Quaker publications were no match for the Bible and 'whole Heaps of such poor superficiall Toys; All Faith and Doctrine not Deriv'd from thence Is but a specious Vain Impertinence'.[7] In the years immediately following the passing of the Toleration Act there was clearly still friction between the Quakers and the authorities. The intention here is to trace the activities of Friends and their changing relationship with the Church and state, and wider community, from this limited measure of toleration to their newfound respectable status thereafter.

THE LIMITS OF TOLERATION

Prior to the Toleration Act, the Quakers were still viewed as dangerous subversives. Indeed, as graphically illustrated in the tearing down of the Sunderland meeting house in 1688, they were the targets of popular hostility.[8]

---

[5] Lambeth Palace Library, Ms.933, no. 9. Bowerman to Tenison, 17 December 1692, and quoted in C. Rose, *England in the 1690s* (Oxford, 1999), p. 174.

[6] C. Leslie, *The Snake in the Grass, or Satan transform'd into an Angel of Light* (London, 1696), pp. xvi–xix, 21–8.

[7] Anon., *The Quakers Bookes* (London, 1700). See also R. I. Clark, 'The Quakers and the Church of England, 1670–1720', University of Lancaster, PhD thesis, 1988; J. A. I. Champion, *The Pillars of Priestcraft Shaken: The Church of England and its Enemies 1660–1730* (Cambridge, 1992); A. Walsham, *Charitable Hatred: Tolerance and Intolerance in England 1500–1700* (Manchester, 2006); D. Manning, 'Accusations of Blasphemy in English Anti-Quaker Polemic, c.1660–1701', *Quaker Studies* (hereafter *QS*), 14, 1 (2009), pp. 27–56. For a discussion of Quaker publications post-toleration, see R. T. Vann, 'Friends' Sufferings—Collected and Re-collected', *Quaker History*, 61, 1 (1972), pp. 24–35.

[8] LSF, *GBS*, V, pt. 1, pp. 195–6. Friends had briefly enjoyed periods when Declarations of Indulgence had been issued (1672, 1687, and reissued in 1688), but these Declarations for Liberty

This continued after 1689 whereby Friends were instructed by the London Yearly Meeting to be compliant and to give 'no offence nor occasions to these in outward government, nor way to any controversies, heats, or distractions of this world'.[9] Their refusal to close shops on feast days nevertheless provoked acts of petty malice, including property destruction, the despoiling of goods, the ransacking of meeting houses, and proclamations to make Quakers 'comply with the people of the world... in the keeping [of] their shop windows on feast days and holy days shut up'.[10] John Miller highlights an appeal in 1713 to London magistrates to ensure that the law was upheld. In 1715 Oxford Friends were subjected to sporadic attacks, while twenty years later Exeter Quakers were roughly abused by a mob on their way to meeting.[11] Even as late as 1794 York Friends encountered popular opposition when they refused to put lights in their windows to celebrate royal events, despite having already professed their loyalty to the monarchy.[12]

Quaker missionaries who were still intent on proselytizing pushed the limits of toleration beyond what the state deemed acceptable. In a number of provocative encounters, Christopher Meidel, a Norwegian missionary (1659–c.1715), adopted a confrontational position. Even though he was imprisoned for disrupting the service of Ivor Bruich, a Lutheran Pastor, in London he continued to provoke the authorities.[13] On 24 February 1701 at Green's coffee house in Cornhill, London, Meidel, along with Richard Claridge (1649–1723), criticized the Baptist preacher and controversialist writer Benjamin Keach (1640–1704) for accepting state maintenance as a minister.[14] A few years later, Meidel delivered an appraisal of religious practices and popular customs. On 16 September 1705, the two Quakers challenged the decision of a non-member to bury his Quaker mother in Barking parish churchyard. Before being ejected, Meidel 'exhorted the people to repentance', and accused the minister's son of being 'a vain young fellow' and the churchwarden as 'a man of a loose conversation'. They followed this up with a speech outside the Anchor and Crown and called on the townspeople to avoid 'false teachers, who make merchandize of their souls, divining for money, and preaching for hire, and from all false ways and

---

of Conscience were often short-lived as Anglicans opposed them on moral and constitutional grounds. See Sowerby, *Making Toleration*, pp. 32–5, 153–92.

[9] London Yearly Meeting (hereafter LYM), *Epistles from the Yearly Meeting of Friends in London* (hereafter *Epistles*) (New York, 1821), p. 36.

[10] LSF, *Meeting for Suffering*, 8, p. 52 (Stourbridge, Worcestershire, 25 December 1691), and cited in Miller, 'A Suffering People', p. 102.

[11] Miller, 'A Suffering People', pp. 101–2.

[12] S. Allott, *Friends in York* (York, 1978), p. 41.

[13] Haverford College Library, PA, Special Collections (hereafter HCSC), 1121. Box 59, Henry J. Cadbury papers. This is an undated encounter.

[14] J. Besse, ed., *The Life and Posthumous Works of Richard Claridge*, 3rd edn (London, 1836), pp. 92–105.

worships'. They attracted a large but peaceable crowd, and suggested that this was a result of their preaching rather than the unusual spectacle of two men fervently challenging the religious convictions of the wider community.[15]

Equally significant was Meidel's disruptive behaviour at the parish church in Liskeard, Cornwall. After his arrest he was brought before the magistrates at Truro and fined £20 for contravening Clause XVIII of the Toleration Act:

> if any person...shall willingly and of purpose, maliciously or contemptuously come into any cathedral or parish church, chapel, or other congregation permitted by this act, and disquiet or disturb the same, or misuse any preacher or teacher, such person or persons, upon proof thereof before any justice of peace, by two or more sufficient witnesses, shall find two sureties to be bound by recognizance.[16]

Meidel and the magistrates were clearly at odds in their interpretation of the law. While the Quaker considered that he was entitled to question the vicar after the sermon had been read ('the priest had in appearance ended [his sermon])', the magistrates insisted that the law unambiguously prohibited any disputation on church property, particularly during the church service.[17] This example was replicated by others and is in stark contrast with the view that all Quakers had become quietists.[18]

OATHS AND THE AFFIRMATION CRISIS

The ambiguities associated with the Quakers' refusal to swear, and thereby their unwillingness to tender the oath of allegiance, led to accusations that they were disloyal subjects or, in some quarters, that they were Jesuits in disguise despite protestations to the contrary.[19] Leading Friends were eager to accommodate the wishes of the post-Revolution authorities. They distanced themselves from the radical posturing of the mid seventeenth century and presented the Society as a respectable religious community.[20] By 1691 the

---

[15] Besse, *Richard Claridge*, pp. 159–64. See also LSF, Portfolio, 14.25, p. 5. This is fully discussed in R. C. Allen, '"Turning hearts to break off the yoke of oppression": The Travels and Sufferings of Christopher Meidel, c.1659–c.1715', *QS*, 12, 1 (2007), pp. 54–72.

[16] See A. Browning, *English Historical Documents, 1660–1714* (London, 1953), pp. 400–3.

[17] LSF, Case 19 (n.d.). The case of Christopher Meidel—prisoner at Launceston Castle.

[18] For Quaker quietism, see R. Rogers Healey, 'Quietest Quakerism, 1692–c.1805', in S. W. Angell and P. Dandelion, eds, *The Oxford Handbook of Quaker Studies* (Oxford, 2013), pp. 47–8, 50–1.

[19] B. Reay, *The Quakers and the English Revolution* (London, 1985), pp. 59–60; Morgan, *Lancashire Quakers and the Establishment*, pp. 113–40. In one particular case, Christopher Meidel acknowledged Queen Anne's 'Right of Government'. See LSF, Case 19.

[20] These changes are discussed in E. Isichei, 'From Sect to Denomination among English Quakers', in B. R. Wilson, ed., *Patterns of Sectarianism: Organisation and Ideology in Social and*

first generation of leading Friends, including George Fox and Robert Barclay, were dead, and William Penn's influence was diluted because of his intimate attachment to the Stuart court.²¹ George Whitehead was now the man spokesperson and his 'creed' of 1693 was in keeping with early statements of the Friends. He nevertheless observed that this was not a credal statement for Quakers, but rather a declaration of faith intended for others.²² These transitions had significant consequences for the Society. The rapprochement with the wider community tended to water down the tenacity of proselytizing, increasingly ushering in a period of quietist introspection whereby Quakers used 'various insulating measures to survive in a hostile world', and ultimately occasioned a decline in membership.²³

In some regional meetings, however, the transformation was not fully accomplished. Indeed, the prevailing attitudes of Friends in Lancashire continued to reflect the characteristics of a sect, while the reservations of other members in England over the exact wording of an affirmation in place of an oath demonstrated the deep anxieties that prevailed.²⁴ From 1692 onwards the London-based Meeting for Sufferings canvassed for change. Moreover, opposition from Anglican clergymen and MPs only gradually led to a further measure of reform. In 1696, John Taylor of York was requested to join a small deputation of leading Friends in Nottingham who had been tasked by London Quakers to petition the king about several prosecutions in the Exchequer and Ecclesiastical courts for not swearing the oath of allegiance. William III granted an audience, listened to their concerns, and agreed to look into the

---

Religious Movements (London, 1967), pp. 161–81; R. T. Vann, *The Social Development of English Quakerism, 1655–1755* (Cambridge, MA, 1969); M. Mullett, 'From Sect to Denomination? Social Developments in Eighteenth Century Quakerism', *Journal of Religious History*, 13, 2 (1984) pp. 168–91; C. L. Leachman, 'From an "Unruly Sect" to a Society of "Strict Unity": The Development of Quakerism in England, c.1650–89', University of London, PhD thesis, 1997 D. A. Scott, *Quakerism in York, 1650–1720*. Borthwick Papers, No. 80 (York, 1991).

²¹ M. K. Geiter, *William Penn* (Harlow, 2000), pp. 56–7.
²² For examples, see E. Burrough, *Declaration to all the World of Our Faith* (London, 1657) and G. Fox, *Something in answer to all such as falsly say, the Quakers are no Christians* (London, 1682).
²³ Catherine Wilcox has argued that this was a 'fading of the early vision' where the intensity of early Quaker proselytizing had given way to a more formalized mode of behaviour and worship. See C. M. Wilcox, *Theology and Women's Ministry in Seventeenth-Century English Quakerism* (Lewiston, NY and Lampeter, 1991), pp. 95, 120–1; R. C. Allen, 'An Alarm Sounded to the Sinners in Sion: John Kelsall, Quakers and Popular Culture in Eighteenth-Century Wales', in J. Allen and R. C. Allen, eds, *Faith of Our Fathers: Popular Culture and Belief in Post-Reformation England, Ireland and Wales* (Newcastle, 2009), particularly pp 73–4; N. C. Tousley, 'The Experience of Regeneration and Erosion of Certainty in the Theology of Second-Generation Quakers: No Place for Doubt?', *QS*, 13, 1 (2008), pp. 6–27; P. Collins, 'Discipline: The Codification of Quakerism as Orthopraxy, 1650–1738', *History and Anthropology*, 13, 2 (2002), pp. 17–32.
²⁴ See J. W. Frost, 'The Affirmation Controversy and Religious Liberty', in R. S. Dunn and M. Maples Dunn, eds, *World of William Penn* (Philadelphia, PA, 1996), pp. 303–22.

matter.²⁵ Consequently, the affirmation statement was reworded, but it did not appeal to all Friends. This was especially true of Friends in the northern counties, although most Quarterly Meetings accepted the changes as an interim step. A further affirmation was drawn up in 1705, but the wording still proved to be difficult to reconcile with Friends' consciences. This was only resolved in 1722, when Parliament decreed that the reference to God in the affirmation could be removed.²⁶

It is evident that Quakerism remained regionally distinctive and there were various reactions to the shifting position of the Society in the post-Revolution years. The role of English female Friends in this period is certainly a case in point. As Robynne Rogers Healey stresses, women 'provided an alternative to the models of submission and domesticity'. They continued to preach in public and to mixed gatherings, and thereby 'retained an independent spiritual identity and spiritual authority' which differed sharply from the accepted eighteenth-century stereotype.²⁷ It should nevertheless be noted that increasingly they were subject to the exacting strictures of the London Morning Meeting.²⁸

CODE OF BEHAVIOUR AND POPULAR CULTURE

From the mid-1660s leading Friends had helped to establish an organizational structure that would secure their future. They gradually moved away from the radicalism of the past and developed an internal framework which regulated the behaviour of members.²⁹ This codification of Quaker discipline acted as a moral guide for Friends and strengthened their fellowship.³⁰ In this context, alongside ministers and elders, Quarterly and Monthly Meetings appointed

---

[25] Allott, *Friends in York*, p. 18.

[26] This is fully discussed in Morgan, *Lancashire Quakers and the Establishment*, pp. 141–70.

[27] Healey, 'Quietest Quakerism', p. 48.

[28] S. Wright, '"Gaining a Voice": An Interpretation of Quaker Women's Writing 1740–1850', *QS*, 8, 1 (2003), pp. 36–50. For a wider discussion on the changing role of female Friends, see P. Mack, *Visionary Women: Ecstatic Prophecy in Seventeenth-Century England* (Berkeley, CA and Oxford, 1992); G. Shaw '"The Inferior Parts of the Body": The Development and Role of Women's Meetings in the Early Quaker Movement', *QS*, 9, 2 (2005), pp. 191–203.

[29] Richard C. Allen, 'Restoration Quakerism', in Angell and Dandelion, eds, *Oxford Handbook of Quaker Studies*, pp. 35–6.

[30] *The Christian and Brotherly Advices...* (*Book of Extracts*), provided by the LYM in 1738, helped to crystallize this code, but the nature of the 'queries' over time increasingly became rather prescribed. For details, see C. F. Carter, 'Unsettled Friends: Church Government and the Origins of Membership', *Journal of the Friends' Historical Society* (hereafter *JFHS*), 51, 3 (1967), pp. 143–53; M. A. Mullett, '"The Assembly of the People of God": The Social Organization of Lancashire Friends', in Mullett, ed., *Early Lancaster Friends* (Lancaster, 1978), pp. 12–21, and Mullett, 'From Sect to Denomination? Social Developments in Eighteenth Century Quakerism'.

overseers to police their religious community, regulate conduct, visit recalcitrant members and, all the while, insisted on compliance with this code of behaviour. Members could be censured for petty failings, including falling asleep in silent meetings or speaking too excessively in others,[31] to the more serious breaches of Quaker practice, such as their failure to withhold military taxes or tithes,[32] involvement in the 'worldly' affairs of the wider community or enjoying their pastimes, or an unwillingness to accept the judgement of the meeting when internal disputes between members occurred. Those who rejected the advice of their meetings, or did not recant, were regularly disowned.[33] Thus, in July 1696, the Quarterly Meeting of Wiltshire Friends cooperated with Purton Friends over a lengthy dispute between two members. When the two Friends repeatedly refused to accept their joint counsel they were disowned.[34]

In their adoption of this code, Friends excluded themselves from a wide variety of traditional customs, while they were still prepared to vehemently condemn the baneful effects of popular culture, such as dancing, music, theatrical performances, and sporting events, and this naturally set them apart from the wider community.[35] This is best illustrated in John Kelsall's (1650–1684) tract of 1682 entitled *A Testimony against Gaming, Musick, Dancing, Singing, Swearing... Drinking to Excess, Whoring, Lying and Cheating*,[36] while on May Day 1706 in Stratford in Essex, 500 copies of a broadside

---

[31] In York, Friends were told to avoid 'unsettled behaviour' in Meetings for Worship and 'tuning the body and the eye on those concerned to speak', while others were censured for failing to accept the advice of the Quarterly or Monthly Meetings. See Allott, *Friends in York*, pp. 26–8.

[32] Evidence for England and Wales (including individual data for Lancashire, Lincolnshire, Somersetshire, and Staffordshire) is provided in Morgan, *Lancashire Quakers and the Establishment*, ch. 6, particularly the tables provided on pp. 196 (Table 3), 199 (Table 5), and 290–1 (Appendix 5). For tithe demands and militia taxes in the post-Revolution years, changes in the law for Small and Great Tithes (c.1699), and opposition to as well as payment by various Friends, see E. J. Evans, '"Our Faithful Testimony": The Society of Friends and Tithe Payments, 1690–1730', *JFHS*, 52, 2 (1969), pp. 106–21, and Evans, 'Tithing Customs and Disputes: The Evidence of Glebe Terriers, 1698–1850', *Agricultural History Review*, 18, 1 (1970), pp. 17–35; Vann, 'Friends' Sufferings', pp. 25–7; H. Forde, 'Friends and Authority: A Consideration of Attitudes and Expedients with Particular Reference to Derbyshire', *JFHS*, 54, 3 (1978), pp. 115–25.

[33] For details, see P. Dandelion, *An Introduction to Quakerism* (Cambridge, 2007), pp. 68–73.

[34] Wiltshire and Swindon Record Office, 1699/38. Quarterly Meetings... Wilts, 1678–1708, 6 July 1696, and cited in K. S. Taylor, 'Society, Schism and Sufferings: The First 70 years of Quakerism in Wiltshire', University of the West of England, PhD thesis, 2006, p. 123.

[35] For Quaker relations with their neighbours, see A. Davies, *The Quakers in English Society 1655–1725* (Oxford, 2000), pp. 201–4.

[36] J. Kelsall, *A Testimony against Gaming, Musick, Dancing, Singing, Swearing...* (London 1682). For other examples, see R. C. Allen, 'Establishing an Alternative Community in the North-East: Quakers, Morals and Popular Culture in the Long Eighteenth Century', in H. Berry and J. Gregory, eds, *Creating and Consuming Culture in North-East England, 1660–1832* (Aldershot, 2004), pp. 98–119; E. Bell, '"Vain unsettled fashions": The Early Durham Friends and Popular Culture, c.1660–1725', *QS*, 8, 1 (2003), pp. 23–35.

entitled 'Assembled to Dance' were distributed which openly criticized the customary festivities:

> To whom do you keep your *May-Days*, and set up *May-Poles*, and *Garlands*, and play your *May-Games*, and Sing your *May-Songs*, and Dress your Houses and Places of Worship with *May*? Was it not in former times to the Goddess *Maia*, or the Strumpet *Flora*? And did not the Heathens *Dance*, and keep their *Floralia*, or Feasts of Flowers and Blossoms to Worship her, and in acknowledgment of this their *Bountiful Goddess*, like the Milk-Folks now with the Pails, Garlands, Silver and Gold upon their Heads.[37]

This was constantly reiterated throughout the eighteenth century. In 1739 the London Yearly Meeting wrote to Friends condemning involvement in 'Balls, Gaming-Places, Horse-Races, and Playhouses' which were denounced as 'nurseries of debauchery and wickedness'.[38]

Alehouse culture, with its excessive drinking, was condemned as demoralizing, provoking

> *Vain Mirth*, *Foolish Jesting*, *Wanton Singing* and *Dancing*, *Gaming* and *Playing*; Nurseth up *Lewdness*, *Whoredom*, and *Debauchery*; Provokes to *Cursing*, and *Swearing*; Occasions *Quarrelling*, *Fighting* and *Murther*; Renders People *Brutish*, *Sottish*, *Idle*, *Unfit for Business*, and *Contemptible* in the sight of God and Sober Men; and such often turn to *Robbing* and *Stealing*, and so come at last to the *Gallows*.[39]

Furthermore, Friends continued to address social superiors by the informal 'thee' and 'thou', refused to hat honour or respect titles, and wore plain clothing which tended to undermine the prevailing cultural norms. Naturally, some members were unable, or unwilling, to accept the exacting demands of the Society, and their behaviour contravened the rules of conduct. This included gambling or bringing the Society into disrepute by rowdy behaviour. Thus, in August 1732, two Gloucestershire Friends monitored the behaviour of members to ensure that they were not frequenting taverns.[40] Clearly, any improper relationship or sexual misconduct was not tolerated. In August 1699 the Monyash Meeting in Derbyshire condemned the behaviour of Hannah Buxton and Daniel Clarke, and read a paper against their fornication, while in the early eighteenth century the Breach Monthly Meeting in the same county testified against the behaviour of Job Lacy 'for having a childe babe gott'. As

---

[37] LSF, Morning Meeting, III, pp. 226, 232 (29.2.1706, 3.4.1706); LSF, Broadsides 'A', p. 146. '[Christopher Meidel] To my neighbours and others... Assembled to Dance on the 1st of the 3[r]d month, called May-Day, 1706'.

[38] LYM, *Epistles*, p. 186.

[39] LSF, Broadsides 'A', p. 146.

[40] Gloucestershire Record Office, D 134. A/M1. Gloucestershire Quarterly Meeting, 1670–1733 (August 1732). See also Richard Lacock, 'Quakers in Gloucestershire, 1655–1737', University of Birmingham, M.Phil thesis, 2001, p. 65.

Helen Forde observed, this was not a regular concern in the county as there were only four recorded cases of such behaviour between 1699 and 1761.[41] Examples from York between 1765 and 1824 also show the determination of the Friends to censure others who had committed sexual offences. Unmarried mothers were disowned, and a father and his daughter who shared a bed were cast out of the Society in 1772, even though this may have had a perfectly innocent explanation. An additional case in 1824 was less ambiguous as Elizabeth Nellist had her membership rescinded when she informed the meeting that she did not intend to marry her partner despite cohabiting with him.[42]

The rules on marriage, particularly with non-members, were increasingly enforced from the late seventeenth century onwards, and revealed the Society's anxiety that marriages to outsiders ('walking disorderly') could undermine unity, but the large number of disownments indicates that many members were unable to comply. Michael Watts observes that after the publication of the 1754 rules on marriage were printed disownments accelerated. In the six London Monthly Meetings there were 1,025 disownments between 1750 and 1794. Of these, 425 were marital transgressions.[43] This obviously had a significant impact on membership as it deprived the Society of younger members and new converts.

Friends were required to act fairly in all business engagements, and the Society sought to ensure that members were responsible for their actions and avoided reproach. The lure of fashionable society or the simple enjoyment of community activities nevertheless proved irresistible, and some faced censure and potential disownment. Friends disapproved of extravagance and wastefulness, and increasingly insisted upon plain attire, criticizing members who dressed immoderately. This is demonstrated in the efforts of Henry Lombe, a Quaker cloth manufacturer in Norfolk, to avoid '*making any Figured and Gaudy Stuffs*, whose end and Service was chiefly to satisfy the Vain and Proud Minds of Men and Women'.[44] In July 1709 Durham women Friends were warned that they should

> keep out of all needless and superfluous Fashions, as that of cutting and powdering the hair and having too much compass in the browes of quoifes or setting our

---

[41] Helen Forde, 'Derbyshire Quakers 1650–1761', Leicester University, PhD thesis, 1977, p. 141, and citing Nottinghamshire County Record Office, Q86. Monyash Monthly Meeting, 1672–1735 (3 August 1699), Q59. Breach Monthly Meeting, 1701–62 (8 December 1703).

[42] For these and other examples, see Allott, *Friends in York*, p. 60.

[43] J. Tual, 'Sexual Equality and Conjugal Harmony... A View of Early Quaker Matrimony', *JFHS*, 55, 6 (1988), pp. 161–73; M. Watts, *The Dissenters: From the Reformation to the French Revolution* (Oxford, 1978), pp. 329–31.

[44] H. Lombe, *An Exhortation... To all that have been in any measure turned unto truth* (London, 1696), p. 5; S. Stevens, *Quakers in North East Norfolk... 1690–1800* (Lewiston, NY and Lampeter, 2012), p. 294.

hoods over high and making mantoes with over wide sleeves, short lapps, and too much to pin upp behind and making them soe farr distant on the Breast and wearing great handkerchiefs to be puffed out.[45]

In October 1716 female Friends were instructed to avoid the 'foolish and indecent fashion of wearing hoppt pettycoats'.[46] Plainness increasingly became an essential 'badge of membership' and, in an effort to retain membership levels in the 1690s, some leaders over-identified 'to an extraordinary degree adherence to these testimonies as tantamount to real commitment'. Paradoxically, such impositions, which had formerly marked Quakers out as 'a peculiar people', progressively provoked an internal reaction to these 'symbols of purity'. For some members these traits had become 'too rigidly identified as the measure of allegiance and thus ignored what they saw as inward and genuine spiritual growth'. Some contemporaries, on the other hand, considered Friends' attitudes to community attire and customs as 'rude', 'arrogant', 'conceited', and 'clownish'.[47] In contrast, Michael Mullett and Nicholas Morgan, in their investigations into the testy relationship that Lancashire Friends had with the Church and state, express doubts about the Society's behavioural code as fostering an unhelpful insularity and a more passive outlook. Consequently, the change from early radicalism to respectable denominational status was far from complete by the eighteenth century as Hanoverian Quakers still exhibited the characteristics of a sect.[48]

By the beginning of the nineteenth century the Religious Society of Friends was a more diverse group. There were those who retained the simple attire, but other members (gay or fast Friends) did not adhere to these traditional requirements or modes of behaviour.[49] In the early months of 1798 the seventeen-year-old Elizabeth Fry visited London so that she could 'become acquainted for herself with those amusements and fascinations that the world offers... That she might have the opportunity of "trying all things"', and choosing for herself that which appeared to her 'to be good'.[50] Perhaps, this

---

[45] Durham County Record Office (hereafter DCRO), SF/Du/QM/3/1, Durham Quarterly Meeting minutes 1679-1751, 28 July 1709.

[46] DCRO, SF/Du/QM/3/1, 2 October 1716.

[47] Davies, *Quakers in English Society*, p. 46. See also J. Rowntree, *Quakerism Past and Present* (London, 1859), pp. 55-65, 77-88, 92-6, 167-86, and T. Hancock, *The Peculium... the causes of the decline of the Society of Friends* (London, 1859), pp. 166-7; W. C. Braithwaite, *The Beginnings of Quakerism*, 2nd edn (London, 1912, repr. York, 1981), p. 309, and Braithwaite, *The Second Period of Quakerism*, 2nd edn (London, 1919, repr. York, 1979), pp. 630-47; R. M. Jones, *The Later Periods of Quakerism*, 2 vols. (London, 1921); Morgan, *Lancashire Quakers*, pp. 244-78.

[48] Mullett, 'From Sect to Denomination', pp. 190-1.

[49] For further details, see J. Kendall, 'The Development of a Distinctive Form of Quaker Dress', *Costume*, 19 (1985), pp. 58-74; D. J. Hall, 'Plainness of Speech, Behaviour and Apparel in Eighteenth-Century English Quakerism', in W. J. Shiels, ed., *Monks, Hermits and the Ascetic Tradition* (Oxford, 1985), pp. 307-18.

[50] *Memoir of the Life of Elizabeth Fry*, 2 vols. (London, 1847), I, p. 38.

is characteristic of a generational shift in Quakerism, and/or linked to the reflective mode that some scholars associate with *fin de siècle* transitions.[51] Fry's alternative approach to worldliness might be viewed in this way. Her visit to London included Drury Lane and Covent Garden, but she was nevertheless disappointed with the plays, opera, and other entertainments, as a diary entry on 1 March records:

> I own I enter into the gay world reluctantly. I do not like plays. I think them so artificial that they are to me not interesting... To-night I saw Hamlet and Bluebeard; I suppose that nothing on the stage can exceed it. There is acting, music, scenery to perfection, but I was glad when it was over; my hair was dressed and I felt like a monkey.

Despite publicly disparaging late eighteenth-century high society gossip and tattletales, Elizabeth confessed her 'love' of scandal, but thirty years later in 1828 she believed that these experiences had taught her a good lesson. She thought that such indulgences were wrong, particularly the impact they had on young, impressionable men and women. Consequently, she felt it easy to pull back from such worldly pleasures believing that 'all public places of amusement... [tended] to promote evil... [and] led many from the path of rectitude and chastity, and brought them into much sin'. The so-called 'pleasures of this life', were to her, 'vanity and folly... which the tendency is not to satisfy, but eventually to enervate and injure the heart and mind'.[52]

SCHISM

The organizational foundations of the Society were enhanced by Foxian centralization in the decades after 1660. These changes, however, occasioned a fervent response from apostate Quakers, while outsiders believed that Friends were insufficiently Trinitarian and thereby ineligible to benefit from

---

[51] Most of the reflections concerning the *fin de siècle* are dominated by nineteenth-century scholars, and yet the same momentum for change can be determined in the previous century. For details of nineteenth-century changes, see S. Ledger and S. McCracken, *Cultural Politics at the fin de siècle* (Cambridge, 1995); P. McGuinness, ed., *Symbolism, Decadence and the fin de siècle French and European Perspectives* (Exeter, 2000); and Gail Marshall, ed., *The Cambridge Companion to the fin de siècle* (Cambridge, 2012). For a comparative discussion of cultural changes and patterns of taste throughout the eighteenth century, see L. Weatherill, *Consumer Behaviour and Material Culture in Britain, 1660–1760* (London, 1988); J. Brewer, *The Pleasures of the Imagination: English Culture in the Eighteenth Century* (London, 1997); M. Berg, *Luxury and Pleasure in Eighteenth-Century Britain* (Oxford, 2005).

[52] *Memoir of the Life of Elizabeth Fry*, I, pp. 38–40. For a wider discussion, see M. A. Mullett 'Catholic and Quaker Attitudes to Work, Rest and Play in Seventeenth- and Eighteenth-Century England', in R. N. Swanson, ed., *The Use and Abuse of Time in Christian History* (Woodbridge, 2002), pp. 185–209 (particularly pp. 207–9).

the terms of the Toleration Act. The development of the Society from a sect to denominational status produced three theological responses (quietism, rationalism, and evangelicalism), but their mutual coexistence could only last while the Society held together. Once the differences were exposed this led to internal divisions and ultimately schism. Francis Bugg, an apostate Quaker who championed religious liberty, scrutinized the attitudes of Fox and Penn, particularly their centralizing activities, and from the 1680s until his death in 1724 was a stern opponent both publicly and in print.[53] On the other side of the Atlantic, George Keith, surveyor-general of Pennsylvania, questioned whether Friends had lost their way and maintained that there was a discernible lack of Christian knowledge in the colonies and elsewhere. In 1698 he concluded that Friends were insufficiently Christian and led a breakaway group, leaving considerable chaos in his wake. The divisions were only slowly healed by leading Quakers, such as George Whitehead,[54] before being reopened by Hannah Barnard and the Irish Separation at the end of the eighteenth century.[55]

In the post-Revolution years, leading Friends attempted to stress the peaceful nature of the Society and sought to 'rewrite' their history to demonstrate this. Indeed, in Whitehead's 1716 edition of James Nayler's works many of his more 'controversial' pieces were deliberately excluded.[56] And, as Healey observes, 'under Whitehead's pen, Nayler was reinvented in the Quaker mould from a convicted blasphemer to an "Everyman" figure of the suffering Quaker'.[57] The impact of the Enlightenment can also be seen in the development of rationalism (moderate Quakerism), but the writings of some eighteenth-century Friends demonstrate that many clung to older ideas, including the importance of silence in their meetings.[58] The final component of Quaker theology was evangelicalism and its reach was transatlantic. The 'Great Awakening' sparked an evangelical fervour for religious observance,

---

[53] For example, see F. Bugg, *The Pilgrim's Progress, from Quakerism to Christianity* (London, 1698).

[54] The influence of George Whitehead in the years after the death of George Fox and Robert Barclay, particularly the development of Quaker theology, is discussed in Healey, 'Quietist Quakerism', pp. 48–52.

[55] The Keithian schism and other internal disputes are discussed in J. W. Frost, *The Keithian Controversy in Early Pennsylvania* (Norwood, PA, 1980), and C. J. L. Martin, 'Controversy and Division in Post-Restoration Quakerism...', Open University, PhD thesis (2003), pp. 173–275.

[56] E. Bell, 'Eighteenth-Century Quakerism and the Rehabilitation of James Nayler, Seventeenth-Century Radical', *Journal of Ecclesiastical History*, 59, 3 (2008), pp. 432, 437–9. Nayler was one of the leading Quaker theologians of the 1650s. He nevertheless courted controversy, particularly in 1656 when he was convicted of blasphemy after re-enacting Christ's entry into Jerusalem while visiting Bristol. See L. Damrosch, *The Sorrows of the Quaker Jesus: James Nayler and the Puritan Crackdown on the Free Spirit* (Cambridge, MA, 1996).

[57] Healey, 'Quietist Quakerism', p. 50. She, like Bell, also stresses the intrusive censorship of the Morning Meeting concerning Quaker publications in the eighteenth century.

[58] This is discussed in Healey, 'Quietist Quakerism', p. 51 who observes that 'avoidance of extremes was a key component of Quaker rationalism'.

and members were not immune from the spread of this revivalist movement. And yet, despite their origins as an ecstatic movement, the Society advocated that 'the process of salvation was gradual, not sudden'.[59] The revivalist movement nevertheless sharpened divisions among Friends in the late eighteenth and nineteenth centuries.[60]

BUSINESS AND RESPECTABILITY

After 1750 Friends became increasingly distanced from their radical origins and held respectable roles in eighteenth-century society, representing 'a curious paradox', whereby they had to accommodate the challenge of consumerism and adopt a pragmatic approach to the wider community and its affairs. They had to 'distance themselves from the world and reject temptations, its transient and material pleasures, yet they also set out to prepare themselves and their offspring to make the most of its economic potential'.[61] The distinct business and mercantile networks they created became a defining feature of Friends in this period. Arthur Raistrick and other historians have thrown considerable light on the careers of many members and the realities of creating and preserving successful businesses, especially industrial entrepreneurs.[62] These include the Fell–Rawlinson group, the Champion and Lloyd families, and the Darbys of Coalbrookdale, whose 'experimental work... resulted in the conversion of the iron industry from a small domestic craft to one of the basic industries of the country'.[63] Mining companies were also analysed, particularly the copper industry and the Quaker Lead Company, both of which had their roots in the seventeenth century before they expanded in the following century.[64] Friends were also identified as successful manufacturers (including confectioners such as the Cadbury, Tukes, and later Fry and Rowntree

[59] Healey, 'Quietist Quakerism', p. 52. See also J. W. Frost, *The Quaker Family in Colonial America* (New York, 1973); M. L. Tarter, 'Reading a Quaker's Book: Elizabeth Ashbridge's Testimony of Quaker Literary Theory', QS, 9, 2 (2005), pp. 176–90.

[60] For the deeper divisions, see Thomas D. Hamm, 'Hicksite, Orthodox, and Evangelical Quakerism, 1805–1887', in Angell and Dandelion, eds, *Oxford Handbook of Quaker Studies*, pp. 63–71.

[61] J. Walvin, *The Quakers: Money and Morals* (London, 1997), p. 50. He also notes their 'uneasiness' about such commercial activity, observing that there was 'a distaste... about material success'.

[62] A. Raistrick, *Quakers in Science and Industry* (Newton Abbot, 1950).

[63] Raistrick, *Quakers in Science and Industry*, pp. 89–160 (p. 89). See also A. Raistrick, *Dynasty of Ironfounders: The Darbys of Coalbrookdale* (London, 1953); H. Lloyd, *The Quaker Lloyds in the Industrial Revolution* (London, 1975); A. Prior, 'Friends in Business... 1700–1830', University of Lancaster, PhD thesis, 1997; H. Roberts, 'Friends in Business: Researching the History of Quaker Involvement in Industry and Commerce', QS, 8, 2 (2004), pp. 172–93.

[64] Raistrick, *Quakers in Science and Industry*, pp. 161–88. See also A. Raistrick, *Two Centuries of Industrial Welfare: The London (Quaker) Lead Company, 1692–1905* (London, 1938).

families),[65] scientists and bankers,[66] or more generally as 'sedate, thoughtful, sober, diligent' honest traders and merchants.[67]

Extensive Quaker business records reveal their remarkable success,[68] and these include the daily activities of Quaker apprentices and traders.[69] Yet these networks were often under considerable pressure towards the end of the eighteenth century. As James Walvin points out, the growth of nationalist fervour and colonial wars 'transformed Britain, primarily in that a great deal of the nation's economic activities were diverted, directly or indirectly, towards the war effort'. Friends who were ironmasters were caught between their business interests and pacifism, while a further moral dilemma was faced by those who prospered from the material gains arising from the slave trade. As he notes, 'so ubiquitous and complex were the commercial benefits of this produce that it became desirable to sidestep the issues surrounding such profit-making'.[70]

The respectability of Friends became paramount. Quaker businessmen/women were cautioned against the dangers of excess and were given a lesson in cost effectiveness. The Quaker community helped those members who became bankrupt if they had paid attention to Friends' warnings but fallen into debt. For other members, their mismanagement was censured by their meetings. Thus, in 1703 Newcastle Friends were asked to examine the financial mismanagement of John Airey, a soap-boiler, who was accused by members of 'fraudulent dealings with divers persons'. His refusal to take the meeting's advice led the Society to testify against him.[71] Sunderland Friends also disowned Joseph and Sarah Maude in November 1710 for breaking their agreement with Andrew Jopling. The alleged fraud, which the Maudes flatly denied, had 'become the greatest discourse of the town', and raised questions about the reputation of Friends.[72]

---

[65] Walvin, *Quakers: Money and Morals*, pp. 155–77; S. Diaper, 'J. S. Fry & Sons: Growth and Decline in the Chocolate Industry, 1753–1918', in C. E. Harvey and J. Press, eds, *Studies in the Business History of Bristol* (Bristol, 1988), pp. 33–54.

[66] For examples, see E. C. Cripps, *Plough Court... a Notable Pharmacy, 1715–1927* (London, 1927); M. Ackrill and H. Leslie, *Barclays: The Business of Banking, 1690–1996* (Cambridge, 2001).

[67] T. Clarkson, *A Portraiture of Quakerism*, 3 vols. (London, 1806), III, p. 217.

[68] Raistrick, *Quakers in Science and Industry*, pp. 61–82 provides information on the number of Quaker businessmen. For networks, see Walvin, *Quakers: Money and Morals*, pp. 81–90; Jordan Landes, *London Quakers in the Trans-Atlantic World* (Basingstoke, 2015).

[69] See Anon., 'Account of an early business journey of John Hill Lovell', *JFHS*, 10, 2 (1913), pp. 98–9 for a brief insight into Hill's travels for the London firm of George Crosfield and Company.

[70] Walvin, *Quakers: Money and Morals*, p. 89.

[71] Tyne and Wear Archives and Museums (hereafter TWAM), Ms. 3744/3, 15 March 1703, 11 April 1703.

[72] TWAM, 3744/233 (Mf. 188), fol. 3.

ASSOCIATIONAL ACTIVITY AND CAMPAIGNING

As part of their bid to secure a respectable position, Friends also frequently acted as agents of political, social, and economic change in industrial Britain and in its relationship with its colonies. There were, however, some constraints. When William Tuke of York wrote in 1800 about voting in elections, it was suggested that eligible Friends should do this quietly 'without endeavouring to influence others'.[73] In many other areas of social policy they were not quiet. The drive towards reform was in direct opposition to the quietism of the Society and raises questions about whether Friends were detached from the world, or if they played a significant part in improving it. They acquired a notable reputation as peacemakers, initially expressed as an unwillingness to bear arms, but later pacifism became a principled position.

The pacifism of Friends in the years after 1660 was sorely tested, particularly in the conflicts that engulfed Britain and her colonies in the centuries that followed. At the local level, Quaker meetings were asked to ensure that members continued to uphold their pacifist commitments by refusing to bear arms, provide substitutes, or pay for the county militia. Consequently, when constables and bailiffs came to arrest them or distrain their goods, Friends did not protest or resist. Even as late as 1831 James Backhouse of York had a clock worth £6 7s. 6d. seized after he refused to serve in the militia. In his letter to the authorities he explained that he could not 'become a soldier, neither can I engage anyone to become one in my stead, as I cannot conscientiously do that by proxy what I cannot for conscience' sake do in person'.[74] There were some members who nevertheless, inadvertently or deliberately, transgressed the pacifism of the Society. Quaker industrialists, such as the Darbys of Coalbrookdale, trod a fine line in the production of goods that could be used for armed conflict.[75] Additionally, Quaker merchants, constantly threatened by privateers, faced losing their cargoes or arming their ships and having to explain their actions to the Monthly or Quarterly Meeting. In 1706, Yorkshire Friends considered the legitimacy of carrying guns on ships, while in 1714 Joseph Linskill of Whitby offered a 'sorrowful confession' that 'in heat and passion' he had used guns to defend his ship.[76] This seems to have been a recurrent theme for many Quaker shipowners/masters. In April 1756 Scarborough Friends reported that they were dismayed by the behaviour of those members who had armed themselves for 'their defence contrary to our professed principles'.[77] The question of conflict continued to cause distress

---

[73] Allott, *Friends in York*, p. 34.
[74] Allott, *Friends in York*, p. 60.
[75] Raistrick, *Dynasty of Ironfounders*, pp. 66–8.
[76] T. H. Woodwark, *The Quakers of Whitby* (Whitby, 1926), p. 10.
[77] Hull University Archives, DQR. 11/4, 6 June 1756. See also DQR. 11/4, 1 June 1760.

and in 1781 their Quarterly Meeting informed members that they had compiled a list of Friends who owned ships in which guns were carried. Subsequently, Thomas Scarth was disowned and the subscriptions of Abel Chapman were refused until he sold his ship. Later testimonies were given against fourteen Friends for arming their vessels, but the Whitby meeting refused to publicly admonish them.[78] It is notable that upon his death in 1785 the Quarterly Meeting classified John Walker, the former mentor of James Cook, as a non-member, presumably because of his refusal to disarm his ships.[79] That this was not just an issue for Yorkshire Friends is clear in the response of other meetings in England towards Quaker shipowners who were prepared to defend their ships or those members who were acting as privateers.[80]

For the most part, however, Friends stood at the forefront of the campaign for an end to armed conflict. The revolutionary wars of the eighteenth century, and especially the Napoleonic Wars (1793–1815), certainly galvanized them. Over time, attitudes to change, whereby the process of fatalism was 'replaced by a variegated peace-or-war debate in which an articulate minority went as far as to argue for the achievability of positive and lasting peace'.[81] On 7 June 1814 William Allen, a London-based chemist, alongside Joseph Tregelles Price, an ironmaster from Neath in Wales, and other like-minded individuals met together at Plough Court Pharmacy in Lombard Street, London, to discuss the formation of a Peace Society. This transition was important for the way in which Quakers offered a moral compass for British people, particularly as the Society of Friends was, at the same time, redefining itself as a reformist body rather than an introversionist community of believers.[82]

It was not until after the Peace of Paris that a more formal structure was put in place at a meeting of peace activists on 14 June 1816. Thereafter the London-based Society for the Promotion of Permanent and Universal Peace (and a number of auxiliary societies) was established.[83] The original London-based group consisted of ten participants, including the prominent reformers Thomas Clarkson and Joseph Hall, and argued that war was 'inconsistent with the spirit of Christianity and the true interests of mankind' and were 'desirous

---

[78] Woodwark, *Quakers of Whitby*, pp. 10–11.

[79] LSF, Unpublished 'Dictionary of Quaker Biography' (John Walker). See also P. Brock, *The Quaker Peace Testimony 1660 to 1914* (York, 1990); M. Ceadel, *The Origins of War Prevention: The British Peace Movement and International Relations, 1730–1854* (Oxford, 1996); M. B. Weddle, *Walking in the Way of Peace: Quaker Pacifism in the Seventeenth Century* (Oxford, 2001).

[80] For examples, see P. Griffith, 'Early Quakers in Cornwall, 1656–1750', University of Exeter, PhD thesis, 2004, pp. 213–14.

[81] Ceadel, *Origins of War Prevention*, p. 2.

[82] E. Isichei, *Victorian Quakers* (London, 1970), p. 150ff.

[83] Minutes of the Peace Society Committee, 7 December 1816, and cited in Ceadel, *Origins of War Prevention*, p. 216.

of the promotion of peace on earth and good-will towards men'. Despite intense opposition, the members of the Peace Society produced a programme that advocated arbitration to prevent war, a reduction in armaments manufacturing, and an international court for the settlement of disputes.[84] Throughout the remainder of the century they campaigned for peaceful resolution to conflict, particularly in peace rallies and in the pages of their journal, *The Herald of Peace*, which was first published in 1819.

The humanitarian strand of Quaker pacifism was also expressed in their determination to abolish slavery. The opposition of Friends to the pernicious slave trade can be traced back to the seventeenth century and the centrality of leading Quakers in abolition is well documented.[85] With the establishment of meetings in the Caribbean, particularly Barbados, Friends were, in terms of slave-holding, scarcely distinguishable from other plantation owners. Gradually from the mid-seventeenth century onwards these attitudes were challenged and modified, particularly in 1671 when, following a visit to the island, George Fox wrote to the Governor of Barbados in response to the accusation that Friends were deviant in their religious practices, social malcontents, and were inciting a slave rebellion.[86] He sought to defend their religious community, while also outlining their wider social responsibilities. Yet, even this pre-eminent Quaker evangelist was reluctant to denounce the practice of slaveholding among the faithful. While his intervention had an ameliorating impact, it fell far short of the egalitarian ideals espoused by the Society. Moreover, this lost opportunity was to have long-term consequences for Barbados as well as American Quakerism and the question of slavery.[87] Friends were thereby compromised because the economic rewards of slaveholding undermined their efforts to secure abolition. Nevertheless, some did challenge the practice.

John Farmer of Saffron Walden, who visited America on two occasions between 1711 and 1720, denounced slave-holding, but he and other critics were either censured or disowned for speaking without permission of the Society.[88] In 1738, Benjamin Lay criticized those ministers and elders (the

---

[84] M. E. Hirst, *The Quakers in Peace and War* (London, 1923), p. 244.

[85] See J. W. Frost, ed., *The Quaker Origins of Antislavery* (Norwood, PA, 1980); J. R. Soderlund, *Quakers and Slavery* (Princeton, NJ, 1985); B. Carey, *British Abolitionism and the Rhetoric of Sensibility: Writing, Sentiment, and Slavery, 1760-1870* (Basingstoke, 2005); B. Carey and G. Plank, eds, *Quakers and Abolition* (Urbana, IL, 2014).

[86] G. Fox, *For the Governor of Barbados... 1671*, and cited in J. L. Nickalls, ed., *The Journal of George Fox* (pb edn, Philadelphia, PA, 1997), pp. 602-6.

[87] See also L. Gragg, *The Quaker Community on Barbados* (Jefferson City, MO, 2009); Kristen Block, 'Quaker Evangelisation in Early Barbados: Forging a Path toward the Unknowable', in Carey and Plank, eds, *Quakers and Abolition*, pp. 89-105.

[88] H. J. Cadbury, ed., 'John Farmer's First American Journey, 1711-1714', *American Antiquarian Society*, 53, 1 (1943), pp. 80-1.

'old rusty candlesticks') who kept slaves,[89] while, in 1741, another anti-slavery campaigner was John Bell. And yet, like Fox, he did not advocate manumission but rather the 'kind treatment' of slaves.[90] This was followed in 1754 by the publication of John Woolman's *Some Considerations on the Keeping of Negroes*. This produced a significant reaction among Friends who had gradually begun to accept that the trade, despite the economic benefits, was immoral and based on human suffering.[91] Others, such as Anthony Benezet, were also promoting an end to the trafficking of slaves, and in 1757 the London Yearly Meeting strongly condemned the 'Filthy Lucre... in Dealing with Negroes'. The following year they were equally vociferous in the comments they made concerning the 'iniquitous Practice of *dealing in Negroes and other Slaves*'.[92] The Philadelphia Yearly Meeting promptly endorsed Benezet's position, but it was not until 1776 that the same meeting censured Friends who held slaves.[93] The London Yearly Meeting decided that those who participated in the slave trade should face disownment, but this was not followed through. For, as Elizabeth Cazden points out, this was believed to be a peculiarly 'American problem'.[94]

Influenced by Benezet's writings, Friends and other liberal thinkers began to articulate the case for the end of this transatlantic 'trade'. In 1783 a petition, signed by 273 people, was delivered to the House of Commons demanding the cessation of the British slave trade, but to little avail. The publication of numerous pamphlets on anti-slavery informed the public debate, and in 1787, along with other religious groups, Friends helped establish the Committee for the Abolition of the Slave Trade which helped orchestrate campaigns, petitions, and the boycotting of slave products.[95] By the nineteenth century, many Friends were vocal in their support for the Anglican evangelist, William Wilberforce and his reform campaign. In 1807, in York, members of the Murray, Priestman, and Tuke families called on Friends to assist Wilberforce's candidacy as an MP, while others raised funds to help pay the costs of those eligible to vote,[96] leading to the passing of the Act for the Abolition of the

---

[89] J. Marietta, *The Reformation of American Quakerism, 1748–1783* (Philadelphia, PA, 1984), p. 113.

[90] E. Cazden, 'Quakers, Slavery, Anti-Slavery, and Race', in Angell and Dandelion, eds, *Oxford Handbook of Quaker Studies*, pp. 347–62 (p. 350).

[91] Marietta, *Reformation of American Quakerism*, pp. 113–16. See also G. Plank, *John Woolman's Path to the Peaceable Kingdom* (Philadelphia, PA, 2012).

[92] LSF, London Yearly Meeting, 1757–8, and cited in Cazden, 'Quakers, Slavery, Anti-Slavery, and Race', p. 351.

[93] Marietta, *Reformation of American Quakerism*, pp. 121–7. For Benezet, see M. Jackson, *Let this Voice be Heard: Anthony Benezet. Father of Atlantic Abolitionism* (Philadelphia, PA, 2009).

[94] C. L. Brown, *Moral Capital: Foundations of British Abolitionism* (Chapel Hill, NC, 2006), p. 100; Cazden, 'Quakers, Slavery, Anti-Slavery, and Race', p. 352.

[95] Brown, *Moral Capital*, pp. 413–14.

[96] Allott, *Friends in York*, p. 34.

Slave Trade later in the year. Despite this legislation many Quaker merchants remained wedded to the economic benefits derived from slave labour in the British Empire and gradual emancipation was only accepted after the Slavery Abolition Act of 1833.[97]

Alongside such campaigns, Friends were in the vanguard of wider philanthropic activity. In their responses to Quarterly Meeting enquiries, members were called on to ensure that poorer members were looked after. A meeting 'stock' was organized to pay for the relief of those members who were elderly, infirm, sick, widowed, or orphaned, while a system of settlement and removal that mirrored parish poor relief was increasingly adopted. To assess the rights to membership registers were kept and meetings throughout England (and elsewhere) offered assistance to the poor as they believed it was their duty to help their fellow Quakers. This was strengthened when, in 1737, the Rules of Settlement ensured that poorer members were the responsibility of their original meeting. This had been the accepted practice, but it was now formalized. There were, of course, cases when Friends challenged their meeting's interpretation of the right to settlement and thereby the prospect of relief.[98] It was also their belief that they had to be as generous to the poor as, or more generous than, the local parish. If the meeting was unable to provide relief for their own poor members, who were then forced to turn to the parish overseer for help, this would undermine their role as a religious and beneficent Society. Moreover, there was a fear that impoverished members might turn to crime if they could not support themselves. In 1698 the Bristol Yearly Meeting stated that members should 'take no notice of any person that shall at any time pretend to come begging or procureing of money... since noe Honest ffriends are Ever Exposed after that manner'.[99] Adrian Davies draws attention to the provision of clothing, including burial attire, staple foodstuffs, household linen, and cooking utensils, as well as assistance with rents and apprenticeships for the children of indigent Quakers. He also notes that of Essex Friends who made wills, nearly one-fifth bequeathed money for the relief of the meeting's poor.[100] Elsewhere, providing for a wide-ranging relief programme could, over time, undermine the ability to cope with the numbers of recipients. In the case of Cornish Friends, the more prosperous Monthly Meeting at Falmouth and Liskeard provided the majority of the poor funds for the Quarterly Meeting, but small meetings were unable to offer such support and their members had to appeal directly to the Quarterly Meeting for any assistance.[101] Other meetings had alternative solutions. Bristol Friends

---

[97] See S. Farrell, M. Unwin, and J. Walvin, eds, *The British Slave Trade* (Edinburgh, 2007).
[98] Allott, *Friends in York*, pp. 42–3.
[99] R. S. Mortimer, 'Quakerism in Seventeenth-Century Bristol', University of Bristol, MA thesis, 1946, p. 229.
[100] Davies, *Quakers in English Society*, pp. 64, 82–4, 203.
[101] Griffith, 'Early Quakers in Cornwall', pp. 65, 95.

established a workhouse (c.1696) and, in 1702, this was replicated in Clerkenwell in London. These institutions provided a modicum of relief, while poor children could receive a basic education or training, but they also drew criticism from recipients. In the case of Bristol, poor members were concerned that their children were being treated like slaves. Such criticism forced Friends to review the situation and provide better conditions for the poor.[102]

Education for Friends' children was a high priority and there is evidence throughout the English meetings of basic provision where parents would encourage their children to adopt Quaker principles, and tutors would develop literacy skills in the young often while risking imprisonment for not licensing their activities and affirming that they had done so.[103] From c.1691 the Society established 'schools' in many meetings based on spiritual and moral principles where the children were instructed in 'habits of regularity, of decency, and respectful subordination to their superiors, of forbearance, affection, and kindness towards each other; and of religious reverence towards their maker'.[104]

Highly regarded Quaker schools were founded in the course of the eighteenth and nineteenth centuries, including Ackworth in Yorkshire (c.1779), Sidcot in Somersetshire (c.1808), and Wigton in Cumbria (c.1815).[105] The emphasis placed on reading the Bible and their own publications, coupled with the growth of literacy within meetings, cannot be overstated.[106] Significantly, in the eighteenth and nineteenth centuries, Friends throughout England had access to well-stocked libraries in their meeting houses.[107]

---

[102] R. S. Mortimer, ed., *Minute Book of the Men's Meeting...Bristol, 1686–1704* (Bristol, 1973), 26 July 1696. See also Mortimer, 'Quakerism in Seventeenth Century Bristol', pp. 241–8; T. Hitchcock, *Richard Hutton's Complaints Book...of the Quaker Workhouse at Clerkenwell, 1711–1737* (London, 1987).

[103] For details, see D. G. B. Hubbard, 'Early Quaker Education, 1650–1780', University of London, MA thesis, 1940; L. J. Stroud, 'The History of Quaker Education in England, 1647–1903', University of Leeds, MEd thesis, 1944; G. Mason, 'Quaker Women and Education 1642–1840', University of Lancaster, MA thesis, 1987; D. L. Wykes, 'Quaker Schoolmasters, Toleration and the Law, 1689–1714', *Journal of Religious History*, 21, 2 (1997), 178–92; G. N. Cantor, *Quakers, Jews, and Science: Religious Responses to Modernity and the Sciences in Britain, 1650–1900* (Oxford, 2005); C. Leach, 'Religion and Rationality: Quaker Women and Science Education 1790–1850', *History of Education*, 35, 1 (2006), pp. 69–90.

[104] J. C. Lettersom, *Memoirs of John Fothergill M.D.*, 4th edn (London, 1786), p. 137. See also Hubbard, 'Early Quaker Education', pp. 180–240; Stroud, 'History of Quaker Education in England', ch. 8.

[105] V. Foulds, *Ackworth School, From its Foundation in 1779 to...1946* (London, 1959); Hubbard, 'Early Quaker Education', pp. 284–302; F. A. Knight, *A History of Sidcot School...1808–1908* (London, 1908); Cumberland Record Office, Carlisle, DFCF 7/1, Wigton School Admission Book, 1815–74; DCRO, SF/Su/116/1/2. Report and Accounts of Wigton School, 1822.

[106] L. Wright, *The Literary Life of the Early Friends, 1650–1725* (New York, 1932).

[107] For Quaker libraries in the north-East of England see TWAM, Mf. 211–12; DCRO, SF/Su/2, Sunderland Preparative Meeting minutes 1706–37, 11 December 1710, 10 November 1724.

A final component of Friends' associational work was their attempt to provide a more humane judicial society. It is a truism that they cannot assert that they 'invented the concept of "penal reform", [but] they might legitimately claim to have institutionalized it'.[108] English Friends were certainly at the forefront of the movement against corporal and capital punishment, improvement of prisons, and the reform of prisoners. Towards the end of the seventeenth century John Bellers, a London Quaker merchant, advocated a root and branch reform programme, but to little avail. Other Quakers, notably Thomas Fothergill, took up the challenge in the eighteenth century, but it was Elizabeth Fry, William Allen, and Peter Bedford in the nineteenth century who provided insights into the depravity of English prison life and offered reasoned arguments for reform. Fry helped to create educational provision for imprisoned children. She was also critical of the mixed prison population and promoted separation of the sexes as well as better conditions for prisoners. Allen (along with Bedford and Fry) championed the abolition of the death penalty from 1808, established the Prison Discipline Society (c.1817), and sought to eradicate juvenile delinquency.

In the years immediately after the passing of the Toleration Act, whatever its limitations for Dissenters, the presence of itinerant Quaker preachers could still provoke widespread reaction. These Friends were likened to their mid-seventeenth-century counterparts who were prepared to suffer deprivations and other indignities, fines, and imprisonment for their beliefs. It is debatable whether some of their spokespeople perceived their actions to be in direct contravention of the Act, while it is certainly questionable whether the measure was workable given how easy it was to circumvent. Earlier limited measures of toleration under the Stuart regime had come and gone, and this new measure of relief was again hedged with various clauses. Thereby members interpreted the law according to the dictates of their conscience, while others pushed it to its very limits, not only going against the spirit of the law but its very wording. Post-Revolution and the desire for greater accommodation with the state authorities, the Quaker code of conduct increasingly regulated Friends' behaviour and with it a renegotiation of the Society's position from radical fringe sect to part of the respectable heterogeneous religious community of eighteenth-century England. There were nevertheless challenges that they had to overcome as a religious body and individually in their interactions with each other and with their neighbours. Their presence as a pressure group prior to the repeal of the Test Acts demonstrates their tenacity to promote reform as well as the diversity of their religious community. There may have been quietist Quakers, but they were far from passive in

---

[108] M. Nellis and M. Waugh, 'Quakers and Penal Reform', in Angell and Dandelion, eds, *Oxford Handbook of Quaker Studies*, p. 377.

their pursuit of a better life in post-Revolution England and this mirrored their long-held convictions for a more tolerant and humane society.

SELECT BIBLIOGRAPHY

Angell, Stephen. W. and Dandelion, Pink, eds, *The Oxford Handbook of Quaker Studies* (Oxford, 2013).
Braithwaite, William C., *The Second Period of Quakerism*, 2nd edn (London, 1919, repr., York, 1979).
Brock, Peter, *The Quaker Peace Testimony 1660 to 1914* (York, 1990).
Cantor, Geoffrey N., *Quakers, Jews, and Science: Religious Responses to Modernity and the Sciences in Britain, 1650–1900* (Oxford, 2005).
Carey, Brycchan, and Plank, Geoffrey, eds, *Quakers and Abolition* (Urbana, IL, 2014).
Ceadel, Martin, *The Origins of War Prevention: The British Peace Movement and International Relations, 1730–1854* (Oxford, 1996).
Davies, Adrian, *The Quakers in English Society, 1655–1725* (Oxford, 2000).
Frost, Jerry W., ed., *The Quaker Origins of Antislavery* (Norwood, PA, 1980).
Isichei, Elizabeth, *Victorian Quakers* (London, 1970).
Landes, Jordan, *London Quakers in the Trans-Atlantic World* (Basingstoke, 2015).
Morgan, Nicholas, *Lancashire Quakers and the Establishment, 1660–1730* (Halifax, 1993).
Raistrick, Arthur, *Quakers in Science and Industry* (Newton Abbot, 1950).
Soderlund, Jean R. *Quakers and Slavery* (Princeton, NJ, 1985).
Vann, Richard T., *The Social Development of English Quakerism, 1655–1755* (Cambridge, MA, 1969).
Vann, Richard T. and Eversley, David, *Friends in Life and Death: The British and Irish Quakers in the Demographic Tradition* (Cambridge, 1992).
Walvin, James, *The Quakers: Money and Morals* (London, 1997).
Weddle, Meredith B., *Walking in the Way of Peace: Quaker Pacifism in the Seventeenth Century* (Oxford, 2001).
Wright, Sheila, *Friends in York: The Dynamics of a Quaker Revival, 1780–1860* (Keele, 1995).

5

Methodists

Richard P. Heitzenrater

The relationship between Methodism and Dissent is somewhat tangled from the beginning. The Wesley brothers, especially in their mature years, would shudder at the presence of the two terms in the same sentence. But in spite of the Wesleys' personal opinions on the matter, there is a viable connection between any two movements (such as these) that shared a tendency to distance themselves from the public impressions of Established Church thought and practice during the eighteenth century.

Certain touch points can be seen from the earliest days of the Wesleyan movement. At Oxford, John Wesley became convinced that a holy life was the main mark of a Christian—that if he were to be ordained as priest of the Church of England, his life should exemplify the best application of the teachings of Christ. He did not learn this position from the examples of priests around him, but from his upbringing at Epworth by his parents, both raised as Dissenters with a puritan moralistic bent, and from reading of the Pietist and puritan authors who comprised his devotional reading list at Oxford.[1] True religion was not so much a manner of believing as it was a method of living. He understood that there was an inherent and necessary connection between thought and action, between being and doing, between belief and life.

The early compatriots of Wesley at Oxford were known by several names that reflected their public persona—the activities that they performed in keeping with their approach to being a good Christian. So they were called

---

[1] Three authors and their writings are often given credit for his change of heart and mind in the 1720s: Thomas à Kempis, *Imitatione Christi*; Jeremy Taylor, *Holy Living and Holy Dying*; and William Law, *A Serious Call to a Devout and Holy Life*. However, his readings during his last ten years at Oxford numbered nearly a thousand books, many of which influenced the development of his own life and are thought to include his own selections from High Church and puritan positions; Lutheran and Calvinistic Protestantism; medieval, English, and German Pietism; early Church, Eastern, and contemporary theology; and mystical, Moravian, and holy living traditions.

the 'Holy Club' for about six months in 1730-1 because they performed acts of holiness, both personal and social: gathering together for devotion, study, and reading of works of divinity as well as initiating a programme of teaching orphans, visiting the sick, feeding the poor, and giving clothes to the needy. For their regular attendance at the table of the Lord's Supper they were also known as 'Sacramentarians'; for their frequent study of the Scriptures they were known for a while as 'Bible Moths'; for their many works of kindness and mercy around town they became known as 'Supererogation Men'. The term that eventually stuck to them starting in late 1732 was 'Methodist', since most of what they did was characterized by the title of a well-known book of the time, *The Way of Living in a Method and by Rule* (1722). John Wesley's acknowledged leadership within the movement came from his ability to fit these various pursuits together with a sense of religious purpose, which gave direction and spiritual impulse to their search for salvation. To catch the essence of Methodism at Oxford is to recognize this religious impulse as well as the developing lifestyle that it elicited.

The name 'Methodist' is often associated with this manner of living which became obvious very early in their history. But it may be equally possible that the title derived from their pattern of religious thinking, which fell into the cracks between puritan/Calvinist and Church of England theology. Their approach to Christian thinking could be generally categorized as Arminian, following the thinking of Jacobus (or James) Arminius on several key matters. This method of theological reflection was not in keeping with either the orthodox Calvinism of the seventeenth century or the common approach of the non-High Church thinking of the English of that time. Wesley's approach was very much in keeping with that of John Owen, John Goodwin, and Richard Baxter, who were not only known as 'Dissenters' from the Church of England, but were seen as 'New Methodists' by those who favoured the 'old method' of traditional Calvinism, characterized by the decisions of the Synod of Dort (1619).[2] In this sense, Wesley, as early as his life at Oxford (like Arminius), challenged the five orthodox Calvinist principles of Dort: total depravity ('tea-total' original sin), unconditional election (God's arbitrary choice of the elect), limited atonement (Christ died only for the elect), irresistible grace (those who are chosen cannot resist God's grace), and perseverance of the saints (once saved, always saved). Wesley himself tells us that the first person to name his movement as such said, 'Here is a new set of *Methodists* sprung up'. To the average ear, John Bingham's comment (naming them as 'a new set of Methodists') would be the same as referring to them as

---

[2] *A War among the Angels of the Churches* (London, 1693), pp. 6-7. See also Richard Heitzenrater, 'What's in a Name? The Meaning of "Methodist"', in his *Mirror and Memory: Reflections on Early Methodism* (Nashville, 1989), pp. 18-25.

'a set of New Methodists',[3] since the Wesleyans also did not rely in such a single manner on *sola fide* and did have a place for good works in their scheme of salvation.

As the Wesleyans grew from a small group of students at Oxford University to a larger connection of primarily working-class people that covered the British Isles, they developed a distinctive set of practices that differentiated them both from the Church of England and from most other religious sects or factions of the time. Methodism has often been classified among the Dissenters in English ecclesiastical history, largely because of their separation from the Church of England four years after Wesley's death in 1791. But there were activities before the end of the century that made that distinction come to mind.

To be a Dissenter was not just a matter of nomenclature. Since the Toleration Act, those who could not or would not consent to (literally 'subscribe') the Thirty-Nine Articles were treated as second-class citizens, disenfranchised from much of the public life of the nation. They could not hold public office nor attend the universities. Dissenters had limitations on their sacred meetings, on their teaching, and on their exercise of religious freedoms in many ways. John Wesley especially did not want to limit the exercise of first-class citizenship among his followers.

Wesley tried always to influence the Methodist movement to conform to the thought and practice of the Established Church in every way that he could, while trying at the same time to transform the lives of its members, its leaders, and the Church itself by aligning their practices more with scriptural and traditional guidelines. The Wesleyans were like the Puritans within the Church of England in that they were a self-conscious reform movement, generally evangelical, and against separation from the Church (so said John constantly). While they shared a strong moral sense, which the Wesleys had learned from their parents, who had both grown up as Dissenters before becoming Church of England members, they did not have the strong Calvinist bent to reform the organization of the Church along scriptural lines, as the Puritans (English Calvinists) often did. They also did not share all of the theological Calvinism of many Puritans, especially concerning the absolute decrees that were at the heart of double predestination. Wesley had a lifetime aversion to the Calvinism of George Whitefield on this very theological point (as well as some possible personality differences). Whitefield

---

[3] In the preface to 'The Character of a Methodist', Wesley says, 'This is not a name which they take to themselves, but one fixt upon them... It was first given to three or four young men at Oxford, by Mr. John Bingham, then Student of Christ-Church.' 'To the Reader', §3, in *The Character of a Methodist* (Bristol, 1742), [3]. Twenty-three years later, Wesley remembered the context and comment as follows: 'The exact regularity of their lives, as well as studies, occasioned a young gentleman of Christ Church to say, "Here is a new set of *Methodists* sprung up".' *A Short History of Methodism* (London, 1765), p. 5.

had associated himself with the Methodists in Oxford and in Georgia, but had a severe falling-out with Wesley on the matter of predestination in the late 1730s. Whitefield, who became known as a 'Calvinist Methodist', became an antagonist of Wesley and associated himself with the Dissenting movement of Selina Hastings, the countess of Huntingdon. Wesleyan Methodists were Dissenters of a sort but not official or legal Dissenters, at least according to JW's method of thought and action.[4]

At the same time, it must be said that every action that Wesley took to reform the Church through implementing particular actions or institutions within Methodism, resulted in a stronger self-consciousness among his people called Methodists. Every major feature of the Methodist movement, from lay preaching to annual conferences to special offerings to a publication programme, originated as attempts to revitalize the Church, but in the end led to, and became hallmarks of, a separate religious organization known by the end of the century (after Wesley's death) as the Wesleyan Methodist Church.

How Wesley himself could consistently say 'we do not separate' and 'we are not Dissenters' (while appearing in many ways to fall into both categories) is one of the great tensions that moves the history of Methodism along in the eighteenth century. Let us just look at a few main points in the mission, theology, and structure of the eighteenth-century Wesleyan movement that might have led the Church of England and its leaders, the bishops, to call the Methodists a separate body characterized by Dissent: lay preaching (across parish boundaries); a theological emphasis on Christian perfection (the reality of holiness); separate doctrinal standards and worship materials (part of the publications programme); and a network of societies tied together in annual conferences (with a method of deployment, annual funds, and published rules of practice).[5]

MISSION

Very few reformations in Christianity have been based upon a new or different view of the mission of the Church. The consensus among various groups is

---

[4] From the early 1740s, a central registry for births, deaths, and marriages for Independents, Baptists, and Presbyterians was kept at Dr Williams' Library. It was later expanded to include materials concerning other sects. The old catalogue at Dr Williams' library was contained in four books—one was entitled 'Methodists', which included groups that were neither Church of England nor technically 'Dissenters' (i.e. fanatical but hard to classify).

[5] Wesley's position on religion can be divided into several parts: his attitude toward church government (polity), his attitude toward religious thought (theology), his attitude toward personal activity (ethics), his attitude toward other religions (ecumenism), and his attitude toward organized religious activities (mission).

that the Christian religion focuses on helping persons to understand what it means, in life and thought, to be a disciple of Christ. Their 'mission statements' (if such things exist or could be constructed) would sound like variations on this common theme. The differences would occur primarily in the implementation of their positions in the ways in which their view would become manifest in the life and thought of adherents.

The Methodists viewed their existence as a manifestation of the divine purpose in the world. God chose the Methodist preachers, as Wesley specified in their *Minutes*, 'to reform the nation, and in particular the Church, to spread scriptural holiness over the land'.[6] This purpose for their existence is so general as to be somewhat superfluous as a foundation upon which to build a separate denomination, which is exactly what Wesley had in mind. There were no requirements listed for joining their societies—the only condition mentioned in the *Nature and General Rules of the United Societies* was that persons wanting admission to their efforts should demonstrate 'a desire to flee from the wrath to come, to be saved from their sins'.[7]

The classic avoidance of the typical differentiations of Christian sects can be found in Wesley's discussion of the 'distinguishing marks' of a Methodist.[8] That which sets apart the Methodist is not an opinion about Scripture—a special interpretation of its inspiration or sufficiency or focus: Methodists agree with other Christians on its fundamental nature and role, which speak to its fundamental nature at the root of Christianity. Methodists do not put a special emphasis on certain words or phrases, any quaint mode of speaking or uncommon form of expression. Methodists are not distinguished by special usages or customs of an indifferent nature: how they dress, what they eat, whether they marry, or how they posture themselves. Nor do Methodists stress part of their message as if it were the whole, such as law or gospel, faith or good works, evangelism or sacraments. Rather, a Methodist, says Wesley, is one who loves God with all his heart, soul, mind, and strength, and while he thus exercises his love to God, he knows that such a person also 'loves his neighbour as himself', doing the will of God to his glory. Wesley says that these are 'the principles and practices of our sect; these are the marks of a true Methodist'.[9]

The discerning reader/listener will say, but these are only the common basic principles of Christianity. Wesley agrees, saying, 'So I mean. That is the very truth. [I] do vehemently refuse to be distinguished from other men by any but

---

[6] 'Large' *Minutes*, A & B (§4), in *The Works of John Wesley* (Nashville, 1978-), 10, p. 845.
[7] *General Rules*, 4, in Wesley, *Works*, IX, p. 70. Wesley reiterated this principle many times throughout his lifetime, including his description of Methodism in *Thoughts upon a Late Phenomenon* (1788); in *Works*, IX, p. 536.
[8] This pamphlet was similar to the letter to Dr Middleton, in which Wesley outlined the distinguishing marks of a genuine Christian. See Wesley, *Works*, XI, pp. 527-38.
[9] Wesley, 'The Character of a Methodist', in *Works*, IX, pp. 32-46.

the common principles of Christianity – the plain, old Christianity that I teach, renouncing and detesting all other marks of distinction.' The difference between Methodists and all others who claim such is that Methodists not only preach this truth but embody it 'in heart and life'. The Methodist has 'the mind that was in Christ, [and] so walks as [he] walked'.[10] To make his point absolutely clear, he reiterates his main point: 'From real Christians, of whatsoever denominations they be, we...earnestly desire not to be distinguished at all, nor from any who sincerely follow after what they know they have not yet attained'.[11]

Wesley enunciates this idea throughout his works, at times using slightly different words or emphases, depending upon his audience: Methodists are not a group that requires its members to believe a particular opinion to be true, but asks that its members live (with the assistance of divine power/presence/ energy through the divine Spirit) according to the fundamental principles of Christianity outlined in Scripture and summarized by Jesus Christ as the Great Commandment: love God (faith/piety) and love neighbour (works/ mercy).[12]

THEOLOGY

In the Wesleyan scheme of things, right actions were based upon correct thinking. Wrong ideas never produced right actions. This principle is probably the main reason why the Methodists differed from some of the other schools of religious thought that were prevalent among Christians of the day. Wesley could not see rigid predeterminism producing moral responsibility, and as a result he differed from many Dissenters who were Calvinists or leaned in that direction in their theological arguments and ethical conclusions. He did not think that the Anabaptist and Baptist position of adult baptism (and at times re-baptism) exhibited a firm trust in the real justifying action of God's Spirit in the act of infant baptism by which the person was freed from the taint and punishment of original sin. He did not think that the Lutherans took the idea of sanctification seriously, instead collapsing it into Christ's justifying activity, which detracted from the subsequent empowering and sustaining and comforting and guiding and convicting work of God's Spirit in the lives and minds of Christians.

---

[10] Ibid., 41.   [11] Ibid., 42.
[12] Wesley's distinction between different opinions (which are to be tolerated) and essentials of the faith (which are to be held firm) is best unfolded in his sermon 39, 'Catholic Spirit', in *Works*, II, pp. 81–95.

Wesley therefore opposed solifidianism, antinomianism, gospel preaching, and many theological emphases that resulted in 'single issue' Christianity, whether they appeared in mainline or borderline groups. His stress on 'Christian perfection' (a term that he borrowed directly from William Law's *A Practical Treatise on Christian Perfection* (1729)) was seen by many as a schismatic tendency that over-emphasized an ascetic view of Christian living. Wesley himself saw it as the basic scriptural principle that underlies the Christian life, seen in the life and ministry of Jesus Christ (Be ye perfect, even as your father in heaven is perfect) and the teachings of the Pauline epistles (press on toward perfection). Anything that was a positive command of Christ would bring with it the divine power to fulfil the command—otherwise, the command was fallacious and the commander devious. Wesley felt that his choice of terminology was unfortunate in that it suggested 'perfectionism', a longtime heresy that plagued the medieval Cathari, the Anabaptists of the sixteenth and seventeenth centuries, the French prophets of his day, and others.

What Wesley tried to stress was the possibility of the believer being totally infused with the love of God: being completely overcome by the presence and power of God to the point of not being able to do anything but love God and neighbour. He saw this as nothing heretical, nothing extreme, nothing enthusiastic. It was simply the focal point of the Christian gospel and the life that the Scriptures expected—'having the mind of Christ and walking as he walked'.[13] He saw the problem as being one of terminology—if he had only used the term 'perfect love' instead of the more controversial 'Christian perfection'. And although his position was controversial in part because he saw this perfection as *possible* within one's span of life (since it was a divine command), he was practical enough at first, at least, to realize that it was not *probable* in this lifetime, except perhaps just before death. He was later enamoured of the actual possibility and wanted for it to be an actual manifestation of perfect love in the lives of those who claimed it. This one point, the possibility of Christian perfection, of having perfect love in this lifetime, probably kept the evangelical Church of England priests (and many others) from joining with him more fully in his ministry to the Methodists and the people of England.

Nevertheless, the theology of the Church of England provided the foundation for Methodist religious thinking from the beginning. From that basic starting point, however, John Wesley began to build his own expanded vision of Christian thought. John and Charles were raised by parents who themselves bore the mark of their own parents' puritan moralism. But the Wesley brothers were also influenced by the strictness of their parents' conversion to the Church of England and its doctrine. One who is a convert generally has a

---

[13] Wesley's paraphrase of Philippians 2:5–8 that he reiterated over fifty times in his sermons and mentioned often in much of his other writing and speaking.

strong attachment to the new faith, and that was the case with Susanna and Samuel Wesley. Although son John came under the influence of many theological positions during his lifetime, he was never fully converted from the familial Church of England theology to any one of them permanently. While at school at Charterhouse, he came under the influence of Calvinist and Lutheran writers, and although his horizons were broadened by this contact, he subsequently discarded much of what he considered to be weak in these 'wrong-headed Germans'.[14] At Oxford, he was moved by the medieval and English Pietists, and drank deeply from the Early Church influence that was prevalent in the High Church of England views there, through Thomas à Kempis and Jeremy Taylor.

Although the ideas prevalent in the university provided many good suggestion for his own growing position, he moved beyond them and the Arminian views of the 'New Method-ists' into the realms of medieval mysticism and William Law. He read the works of William Beveridge[15] and felt the pull of the Early Church through William Wake and Cave.[16] But he soon came in contact with the Moravians, and in Georgia he saw another form of German Pietist thought that seemed as pristine as any since the New Testament times. He was cured of this enamourment by his controversy with William Molther and the Quietist version of English Moravianism, which he found to be different from that of Count von Zinzendorf and German Moravianism. Through the whole of his meandering through the varieties of Christian thought and practice, he was never 'converted' wholly by any of them. Instead, he was putting together his own eclectic theology by picking and choosing scriptural, consistent, practical points from each of the various positions that impinged upon his mind and experience and was generally consistent with his Anglican upbringing. This process continued throughout most of his long life, during which he was always willing to hear new ideas or be corrected in his own way of thinking, as long as the challenge was rational, scriptural, traditional, and practical. So for his early group at Oxford to be variously called Sacramentarians, Bible-Moths, Holy Club, Enthusiasts, Supererogation Men, and

---

[14] Although Wesley himself uses this phrase, Calvin could never be considered a German.

[15] Beveridge was bishop of Asaph in the early eighteenth century and was known as a great restorer of the primitive piety of the early Christians, largely through his writings and the instigation of religious societies in England.

[16] Wake, archbishop of Canterbury during Wesley's time at Oxford, produced many translations of the early writers of the church and became a proponent of early Christianity within the Church of England. William Cave, DD, author of many works, including *Primitive Christianity*, was also influential during this period through his careful research and many published writings on the Early Church. See Thomas Buchan, 'John Wesley and the Constantinian Fall of the Church: Historiographical Indications of Pietist Influences', in Christian T. Collins Winn, Christian Gehrz, G. William Carlson, and Eric Holst, eds, *The Pietist Impulse in Christianity* (Cambridge, 2012), p. 157.

Methodists was not out of keeping with his deeply felt and serious, but widely thrown, perimeter of religious thought and action.

During the first fifty years of his life, Wesley was positively influenced by a number of different views of Christianity, from which he picked and chose points that fitted into his developing method of thinking and acting. His position is generally within the holy living tradition, which includes some Roman Catholics, some Calvinists and Lutherans, some Presbyterians, some Quakers, some Anglicans, and several other cousins in the faith. But his view is his own construct, balanced between the reforming practicality of the Early Church's view of holiness as seen in Monsieur de Renty and Thomas à Kempis on the one hand and his loyalty to the established structures of his setting as seen in the monarchy and the Church of England on the other.

This middle way, and Wesley's attempt to draw people from the extremes toward the centre, put him in a position to be criticized by leaders from all parts of the theological spectrum. Among those who positively influenced him were several Dissenters, who held positions not far removed from continental Protestants. In trying to defend his own position that stressed the necessity of good works (even before justification), Wesley found himself attacking antinomianism and solifidianism to the point of being accused of works-righteousness (a term used only to accuse an opponent of having a heretical reliance on good works for salvation).[17] At the same time, Wesley would try to show those who viewed the Christian life mainly in terms of living a good life that they also needed to have a living faith in Christ: that good works and faith in Christ were both made possible by the grace of God—the divine presence, power, energy. For this, he was accused of being an enthusiast, for leaning too far toward the present work of God in the lives of people through the work of the divine Spirit.

ORGANIZATION

In later life, Wesley liked to say to his internal detractors that they had no complaint against his leadership—that they had come to him for direction in the beginning and he was still wont to give it to them. In fact, the movement grew largely as a result of people, often leaders of local revivals, wanting to become a part of his movement. He has been accused recently of 'cannibalizing the revival movement in England.[18] Perhaps one might say more accurately

---

[17] Wesley had trouble with the deterministic Calvinism of Whitefield that might lead to antinomianism, even though Whitefield often stressed holy living, which Wesley thought was inconsistent with Whitefield's Calvinism, especially the stress on the Absolute Decrees.

[18] Henry Rack, *Reasonable Enthusiast*, 2nd edn (Nashville, 1992), p. 214.

that he was able to provide leadership for a variety of people who did not have the breadth of vision that marked the Methodist movement. The fact that many Dissenting types—Baptists, Presbyterians, Independents, Quakers, nonconformists of all sorts—felt a kinship with his movement speaks to the wideness of his developing brand of evangelical traditionalism. He bordered on radicalism in his social outreach; he seemed staunchly traditional in his stress on the sacraments; he tried hard to balance the desire to reform and the need to be loyal; he incorporated persons with a variety of theological positions so long as they were open to leading a new life under the direction of the Holy Spirit.

People who led institutions that were threatened by such thinking and acting were quick to brand him as a Dissenter, an enthusiast, a reformer, a papist, a revolutionary, a heretic—anything that indicated that his position was dangerous, threatening, or wrong. The fact that he encouraged lay preaching, field preaching, and hymn singing placed him in a category that included the usual Dissenting groups. Field preaching was not unheard of in England, though not practised widely in the Established Church. Lay preaching, though not technically illegal, was a mark of bodies that saw themselves as separate from the Church of England. Hymn singing, using tunes and words other than the traditional Psalter, was a mark of 'newness' that many traditionalists saw simply as novelty.

These groups were naturally drawn to each other, and many of them came under the wings of Wesley and his movement. Anyone familiar with organizational stability, however, would recognize that in the long run, such divergences of thought and action would result in the fragmentation of any movement. With the amalgamation of his movement, therefore, Wesley saw the need for bringing the main leaders together on the same page, so to speak. He tried to gather together his brother, John Nelson, George Whitefield, and August Gottlieb Spangenberg in 1743 to talk about this problem. The latter two did not show up and the conference approach to unifying their thoughts and actions did not take place. The following year, however, the event did take place, with four priests and six lay preachers in attendance. Even a year after that, Wesley invited some of the leaders that had emerged in his movement to a conference to sort out their differences and move carefully within the general parameters of the Church of England, of which the Wesley brothers were both priests (as were some of his compatriots).

The annual Conference, largely consisting of lay preachers, developed into a body that not only provided focus for the Methodists but represented a location, an event, at which Wesley exercised his authority over the movement. True, he was a good listener; true he was able to bend his vision to the needs of the people; true he was the main connection between Methodism and the official Church of England. But the Conference gave the impression of an ecclesiastical organization that was indeed separate from the Church. Wesley himself spoke in terms that sounded at times like a radical reformer, telling his people to expect change in themselves and a new day in the Church. But at the same time, he held that the Methodists proclaimed nothing but what was in the Thirty-Nine Articles, the Book of Common Prayer, and the Book of Homilies (both books). While continuing to claim this adherence to the Church, he instigated a Model Deed upon which the property of Methodist preaching houses should be legally settled, in which the local leadership pledged to preach nothing from the pulpits of such preaching houses that was contrary to the doctrines outlined in Wesley's own four volumes of *Sermons* (1746–60) or his biblical commentary, *Explanatory Notes upon the New Testament* (1755).

Such manoeuvres, necessary to the solidity of the movement, were often seen as subversive to his claim of not separating from the Church. Why were such strictures needed if the Methodists were simply following the Articles, the Homilies, and the Book of Common Prayer? Why were they organized into societies that met separately from the Church service and had membership tickets that were renewed quarterly? Why were many of the preachers laity (unordained) and gathered into a Conference annually with Wesley to go over the rules and regulations that governed their communal thought and action? In a class-conscious society, why did the Wesleyans seem to attract many working-class people by aiming their message and benevolence toward them? The Establishment (be it political or religious or social) consisted largely of a well-heeled leadership that tried to keep the country under their control, and the modern ideas of democracy (alive and developing in America) seemed to threaten their power.

Wesley himself started publishing booklets as early as 1733, when he was an Oxford tutor. This means of summarizing important works, classifying rules and procedures, and promoting important ideas, however, became a lifetime enterprise. The Wesleyan publication process soon grew into a rather large business that used the lay preachers as book sellers, entailed setting up an independent printing operation, and published over four hundred items (many in multiple editions) in Wesley's lifetime.[19] The documents that became standard guidelines for Methodist thought, organization, and practice rolled off these presses: Wesley's *Sermons on Several Occasions* and *Explanatory Notes upon the New Testament* (the boundaries of Methodist preaching); the *Minutes of Conversations* (the principles passed by Annual Conferences); the 'Large' *Minutes* (connexional regulations for thought and action); the *Sunday Service* and many hymn pamphlets and books (materials for worship

---

[19] Although Wesley was often accused of profiting from a lucrative printing operation, he was wise enough to separate himself at an early stage from the enterprise and make sure that the profits were donated to the connexion for the use of 'tired and worn out preachers, their wives and children'.

and devotion); and dozens of other writings by the Wesleys and others that contributed to the life and thought of the Methodists.

Not only were the Methodists a publishing people, they also felt the impact of many anti-Methodist books, pamphlets, newspapers, and prints that were produced widely in the country. The name 'Methodist' itself caught on as a result of early letters and pamphlets in 1732 and 1733 that were printed against the Wesleyans.[20] The boundaries of propriety were very low when it came to attacks on people and movements in that day, whether the objects of scorn were seen as dangerous papists, ranting Dissenters, boring High Churchmen, crooked politicians, drunken working-class dolts, or general miscreants in society. Wesley himself was portrayed in print as a sly fox, a papist in disguise, a Dissenter at heart, a sexual deviant, a raving enthusiast, a weak-brained plagiarist, and most of the other decrepit types that could be imagined by the public.[21] Although many such portrayals go beyond the limits of believability, one must admit that many of the critical views were loosely based on a popular image of the man and his movement that made the criticism somewhat believable (and therefore saleable).

As the Wesleyan movement grew in the last half of the eighteenth century to numbers that reached over 75,000 largely lower-class people, the movement was seen as a possible threat to both Church and monarchy. But Wesley's ability to keep his people largely under his control—not by harsh authoritarian means but by flexibly broad interpretations of human needs—combined with his penchant for loyalism to the established monarchy kept his movement from moving in the direction of the more radical revolutionaries in other countries. The Methodists, while small in number (less than 1 per cent of the population), were a disciplined force that could follow their leader in powerful ways that belied their size.[22] That is partly why W. E. H. Lecky and Elie Halévy have said that Wesley was a primary mover in keeping England from having a revolution like France or America, a view that has generally not stood up well under the continuing criticism of later historians.

Another major reason for such a development is that Wesley started to turn away from the American revolutionary cause and began to support the monarchy's opposition to the rebel cause, even using military means. He had in mid-1775 tentatively supported much of the American position, writing to the Secretary of State for the Colonies (William Legge, the earl of Dartmouth)

---

[20] See *Fog's Weekly Journal*, 9 Dec. 1732, and *The Oxford Methodists* (London, 1733).

[21] See many specific examples in Albert M. Lyles, *Methodism Mocked: The Satirical Reaction to Methodism in the Eighteenth Century* (London, 1960) and Helen Pierce, *Unseemly Pictures: Graphic Satire and Politics in Early Modern England* (New Haven, 2008).

[22] This tendency became evident in the next century when Methodism (still a small percentage of the population) became one of the major forces that helped bring labour unions into existence and the Labour Party into a more powerful position. See W. Reginald Ward, *Religion and Society in Nineteenth-Century England: 1790–1850* (London, 1972).

and the First Lord of the Treasury (Frederick, Lord North) that the colonists seemed to be asking for 'nothing more than their legal rights, and that in the most modest and inoffensive manner that the nature of the thing would allow'.[23] In this political view, Wesley was in league with many Calvinists and Dissenters in opposing British royal actions against the Americans. However, in 1774 he had put together a treatise, *Thoughts upon Slavery*, that depended heavily on the work of a Philadelphia Quaker, Anthony Benezet, pointing out that the existence in America of bondage for African slaves negated all their talk about 'unalienable rights ... of life, liberty, and the pursuit of happiness'.

John then switched his views, publishing an abridgement of Samuel Johnson's *Taxation no Tyranny* as *A Calm Address to our American Colonies* (1775). Wesley's anti-American position was further solidified by his publication of *Observations on Liberty* (1776), which was aimed directly at the Unitarian Richard Price, who had joined forces with many British Calvinists to support the American cause.[24] Wesley continued to break with the Calvinist and Dissenting opposition to the monarchy on this matter of war and money. He published a letter answering the criticism of Caleb Evans (who published under the pseudonym 'Americanus'), a British Calvinist Baptist minister who had long criticized the government for opposing the American cause. He specifically criticized Wesley for publishing his *Calm Address*, which Evans saw not only as blatant plagiarism, but also shameful and malicious in intent.[25] Charles finally in 1779 wrote a long poem denigrating the disloyal American colonists and criticizing the ineptness of the British general, William Howe, for not following royal orders to crush the Americans when he had the opportunity.[26]

This break with the Calvinists, which happened during the controversies following the death of George Whitefield in 1770,[27] was followed by a strange incident in which John found himself at odds with his brother Charles and in league with the Protestant Association, an organization led by the Calvinist, Lord Gordon. An attempt to modify the restrictive laws against Catholics in 1780 led to a series of demonstrations, the 'Gordon Riots', which incensed parties on all sides. Charles published his striking criticism of the riots, while

---

[23] Wesley, *The Letters of the Rev. John Wesley*, ed. John Telford (London, 1931), 6, pp. 155–64.
[24] Richard Heitzenrater, *Wesley in America* (Dallas, 2003), pp. 31–5.
[25] Evans' piece brought John Fletcher, Wesley's friend, into the fray, causing him to publish a strong defence of Wesley and attack on Evans' published letter that attacked Wesley's position
[26] S. T. Kimbrough, *Unpublished Poetry of Charles Wesley* (Nashville, 1988), pp. 141–59.
[27] These controversies, which heightened the thirty years of tension between Wesleyans and Calvinists, were brought on in part by Wesley's downplaying his longstanding differences with Whitefield (in his funeral discourse at the Whitefield Tabernacle) and by the 'Calvinist Minute' at Conference, which said that the Wesleyans differed by only a 'hair's breadth' from the Calvinist point of view. See Wesley, 1770 Minutes, *Works*, X, pp. 302–4.

John sent a letter to the editor of the *Public Advertiser* defending the Protestant Association and its leaders in their attempts to curb the expansion of liberties of the traitorous 'papists'. In spite of his own irenic views expressed in the sermon 'Catholic Spirit' and his 'Letter to a Roman Catholic', he now warned people of the dangerous intent of these people who owed their allegiance to a foreign power (the Pope) and he sympathized with the innocent citizens who saw 'the purple power of Rome advancing by hasty strides to overspread this once happy land'. Whether these words were actually written by Wesley or simply attributed to him, the damage had already been done by Father O'Leary's clever title page construction in his response to John's attacks,[28] and he was viewed by many as a strong supporter, if not spokesman, for the Protestant Association.

SEPARATION

Throughout his life, John Wesley developed various means to fulfil his goal to reform the Church. He characterized his people as simply exhibiting the basic qualities of Christian living, but their thought and organization were marked by methods that were distinctively Wesleyan in tone and structure. Every major characteristic of Methodism that Wesley implemented can be seen as an attempt to renew or revitalize or reform the Church, and yet in almost every instance, these measures resulted in an increased Methodist self-identity that seemed to contribute to an inevitable separation from the Church of England. But Wesley always insisted that his intention was never to separate. Even though many Dissenters joined his ranks and their tendency to favour separation infected the body of Methodism, he resisted. To separate, he said in 1758, 'would be to act in direct opposition to that very end for which we believe God has raised us up'.[29]

Many of the lay preachers wanted to become 'full-service' ministers to their people. As Methodist lay preachers, they were unordained and therefore could not administer the sacrament. In many cases, they were not allowed to baptize or even to marry. If they registered as Dissenters, they could be ordained by their local congregation and provide all these services to their people. The pressure on John Wesley grew in such areas as Norfolk to move in this direction. Charles Wesley, always more of a supporter of the Methodist

---

[28] David Hempton, *Methodism and Politics in British Society; 1750–1850* (London, 2004), pp. 41–2. Wesley apparently did write letters to the *Public Advertiser* and *Freeman's Journal*, but the authorship of the *Defence of the Protestant Association* (which contains the quoted rhetoric) did not come from his pen.

[29] He refers obviously to the reason why God raised up the Methodist Ministers. *Reasons against a Separation from the Church of England*, [I] 12, in *Works*, IX, p. 336.

connection to the Church than his brother John, was appalled that such a move would even be considered. John himself came very close to caving in to this pressure. In some instances, local Methodist preaching houses were registered, but John always asked that they be registered as Methodist preaching houses, not as Dissenting meeting houses—a fine distinction, perhaps, but legally quite a different thing. In the Methodist instance, the preacher and the people were not legally considered to be Nonconformists according to the Toleration Act, which was one of Wesley's main concerns.

In the early 1770s, two Methodist leaders tried to convince John of a way to bridge the gap between the Established Church and official Dissent. They proposed that the Wesleyan organization become technically a 'daughter church' of the Church of England. John Fletcher and Joseph Benson thought that by means of this more or less legal method, Methodism could develop reformed Articles of Religion (rectified according to the Gospel) and appropriate the liturgy (Book of Common Prayer) and homilies with some 'needful alterations'. This Methodist Church of England could then, among other things, defend the Mother Church against 'all the unjust attacks of the Dissenters'. The bishops of the Church of England would ordain the Methodist preachers so that they would then be full ministers and able to fulfil the total duties expected by their people, including the administration of the sacraments. Wesley, cognizant that such a proposal would never be accepted by the Church, did not approve its implementation within British Methodism, although what he proposed to the American branch of the movement a decade later, after the Rebellion of the Colonies had resulted in a political and ecclesiastical separation from England, generally resembled this earlier proposal.

There were only two ways that Wesley saw such an organizational severance as taking place in England: (1) if the Church of England threw them out; or (2) if they consciously left its organization. He was clever enough to avoid the first, and was firm enough never to allow the second. Wesley managed to keep Methodism within the Church as long as he lived, although he was also realistic enough to realize that something drastic would happen at his death. He predicted as early as 1769 that, once he was gone, the members of his movement would subsequently go three ways: (1) a quarter of the preachers would become more closely attached to the Church of England and secure preferment; (2) some would turn fully fledged Independents and Dissenters and get separate congregations; and (3) the rest would remain together in Conference as Methodists.[30] In this prediction, he was in part a prophet. What Wesley did not envision was the 'Plan of Pacification' in the *Deed of Declaration* that provided for actual separation from the Church, and the divisions

---

[30] *Works*, X, p. 377; see Wesley letter 'To the Travelling Preachers', 3, in *Letters*, ed. Telford, V, p. 144.

within Methodism itself that resulted in the rise of Church Methodists, Conference Methodists, New Connexion Methodists, Bible Christians, and other subsequent divisions.[31]

Methodism after Wesley never declared itself officially a Dissenting or nonconformist body, and two generations later, Richard Watson went to great lengths in making this point in his observations on remarks in Robert Southey's *Life of Wesley*.[32] But the natural inclination of the body of Methodists in the British Isles, in spite of its attachment to (and occasional use of) the Book of Common Prayer well into the nineteenth century, was to find its place eventually among the non-established (if not nonconformist) denominations of the country.

SUMMARY

The leader of the Wesleyan revival in the eighteenth century, John Wesley (an ordained priest of the Church), exhibited a constant desire that his followers, 'the people called Methodists', remain within the Church of England and hold fast to its basic doctrine and polity. At the same time, he spent his life trying to reform that Church and implement a developing view of holy living as the crux of Christian life and thought. In this endeavour, he could be seen as following in the Dissenting tradition in which his parents matured. Methodists of that period, and Wesley himself, are often seen as fitting into the Dissenter mould because their thought and practice often pushed the edges of their understanding of the Church beyond the limits that were prevalent in that day. Wesley's constant claim that he would 'live and die a Church of England man' was his way of saying that. Although the Church of England was the best example of New Testament Christianity among the national churches in the world, Methodism in fact represented for him what the Church of England should be able to do for its people, in thought and deed.

Although Methodism did not technically separate from the Church of England until after Wesley's death, the eventual development of a separate denomination was a foregone conclusion long before Wesley died. Later in life, his brother Charles claimed that Methodism had, in fact, separated. Many of the Methodist lay preachers wanted to be registered as Dissenters so they could become ordained ministers and administer the sacraments among their people. Although Methodism had its own separate mission to the poor, a strong organization that spread beyond the political boundaries of the three

---

[31] See John Walsh, 'Methodism at the End of the Eighteenth Century', in Rupert Davies, A. Raymond George, and E. Gordon Rupp, eds, *A History of the Methodist Church in Great Britain*, 4 vols. (London, 1965–88), I, pp. 277–315.

[32] Richard Watson, *The Life of the Rev. John Wesley* (London, 1835), pp. 457–73.

kingdoms, a spiritual mission that traversed the ecclesiastical boundaries within the nation, and a sense of internal discipline that was stronger than any religious society, their leader (the centre of their union) constantly said that they would stay within the Church of England. Many of the Methodist people exhibited the enthusiasm of the Moravians, the devotional seriousness of Roman Catholics, the organizational savvy of the Anglicans, the moral imperative of the Puritans, the scriptural knowledge of the Dissenters, and the social conscience of the Radical Reformers. That was fine; that was the way believers should manifest their Christianity. But for Wesley, the inherent threats of the Toleration Act to make people essentially second-class citizens if they should ever become Nonconformists, was enough to claim always that his movement was within the Established Church and would remain such as long as he lived. So it was.

SELECT BIBLIOGRAPHY

Buchan, Thomas, 'John Wesley and the Constantinian Fall of the Church: Historiographical Indications of Pietist Influences', in Collins Winn, Christian T., Gehrz, Christian, Carlson, G. William, and Holst, Eric, eds, *The Pietist Impulse in Christianity* (Cambridge, 2012).
Heitzenrater, Richard, 'What's in a Name? The Meaning of "Methodist"', in Heitzenrater, *Mirror and Memory: Reflections on Early Methodism* (Nashville, 1989), pp. 13–32.
Heitzenrater, Richard, *Wesley in America* (Dallas, 2003).
Hempton, David, *Methodism and Politics in British Society: 1750–1850* (London, 2004).
Kimbrough, S. T., *Unpublished Poetry of Charles Wesley* (Nashville, 1988).
Lyles, Albert M., *Methodism Mocked: The Satirical Reaction to Methodism in the Eighteenth Century* (London, 1960).
Pierce, Helen, *Unseemly Pictures: Graphic Satire and Politics in Early Modern England* (New Haven, 2008).
Walsh, John, 'Methodism at the End of the Eighteenth Century', in Davies, Rupert and Rupp, Gordon, eds, *A History of the Methodist Church in Great Britain*, 4 vols. (London, 1965–88), I, pp. 217–315.
Ward, W. Reginald, *Religion and Society in Nineteenth-Century England: 1790–1850* (London, 1972).
Watson, Richard, *The Life of the Rev. John Wesley* (London, 1835).
Wesley, John, *The Letters of the Rev. John Wesley*, ed. Telford, John, 8 vols. (London, 1931).
Wesley, John, *The Works of John Wesley*, 34 vols. (Nashville, 1976–). [Especially *The Character of a Methodist*; *The Nature, Design, and General Rules*; *Reasons against a Separation from the Church of England*; *A Short History of Methodism*; sermon on 'Catholic Spirit'; *Thoughts upon a Late Phenomenon*; 'Large' *Minutes*; and 'To the Travelling Preachers'.]
Whitefield, George, *Works* (Edinburgh, 1977).

Part II

Traditions outside England

6

Protestant Dissent in Ireland

Andrew R. Holmes

Protestant Dissent in Ireland was not indigenous but appeared in the wake of various population movements throughout the seventeenth century. Presbyterianism came with settlers from Scotland whose presence was reinforced by sporadic immigration, especially in the 1690s. They were by far the most numerically and politically important branch of Irish Dissent, and one of the reasons was their regional dominance in the north-eastern counties of Antrim, Down, and Londonderry. Independents, Baptists, Quakers, and other groups that emerged during the wars of the three kingdoms came to Ireland with Cromwellian forces, though in terms of numbers and political influence they were largely insignificant by the middle of the eighteenth century. Yet numbers only tell part of the story and Raymond Gillespie notes that the variety of groups meant that protestant Dissent in late seventeenth-century Ireland was a contested phenomenon. Dissenters themselves held a variety of positions: Presbyterians supported the idea of an established church but did not conform to the type established in Ireland; amongst the small minority of Dissenting Protestants in the south of Ireland there were those who wanted a comprehensive protestant state church; Quakers and Baptists dissented from the theory of an established church in principle. Unsurprisingly, those belonging to the established Church of Ireland resented the fact that this sizeable group of Protestants was not included under episcopal oversight nor subject to legal restraint. Nonconformist meetings were not proscribed by law and there was no Irish equivalent of the English Conventicle Acts or the Test Act of 1673.[1]

Yet the fact that all Protestants made up, at best, a quarter of the Irish population often created a marriage of convenience against the substantial catholic majority. During the reign of James II, the shared fear of catholic

---

[1] Raymond Gillespie, 'Dissenters and Nonconformists, 1661–1700', in Kevin Herlihy, ed., *The Irish Dissenting Tradition, 1650–1750* (Dublin, 1995), pp. 11–28.

Jacobitism fostered unity amongst the protestant minority. Intra-protestant defiance was best organized in Ulster and symbolized during the siege of Derry, which ended on 28 July 1689 after 105 days. After Williamite forces had defeated the Jacobites at the battles of the Boyne and Aughrim, a re-energized Irish Parliament now dominated by Church of Ireland Protestants set about erecting a system of penal laws against Catholics. This consolidated episcopal protestant control of Ireland and effectively neutralized the natural clerical and landed leadership of catholic Ireland. Conforming to the pattern throughout Europe, Ireland was a confessional state. Of course, what made Ireland unique was that Catholics were not dominant; instead, the minority episcopal Church of Ireland was the Church as by law established. Therefore, protestant Dissenters in Ireland found themselves in the difficult position of opposition to the form—even principle—of the protestant state church yet also fearful of the catholic majority. As a consequence, rather than a simple two-fold confessional division of Irish society, relations between churchmen, Dissenters, and Catholics remained politically significant and would contribute to attempted rebellion in the 1790s.

The chapter begins with an overview of the numbers and organization of the principal groups of Dissenters in Ireland. As Presbyterians comprised the largest and most important group, they will be the main focus of the essay. The second section examines dissent and politics from the Revolution to the 1730s, while the third discusses the impact of the Enlightenment and evangelicalism on the religion and politics of dissent. The final section considers the politicization and radicalization of Presbyterians in the second half of the century that culminated in the formation in 1791 of the Society of United Irishmen and the rebellion of 1798.

NUMBERS AND STRUCTURES

By the early eighteenth century there were in Ireland about 6,000 Quakers, 2,000-odd Baptists, and a small number of other protestant Dissenters, including refugees from catholic Europe. Over the course of the century, these forms of protestant Dissent stagnated or declined—Quakers had about 5,000 members in 1750, but Baptist numbers had collapsed to 500 by 1800. By contrast, a well-placed Presbyterian clergyman in the 1780s estimated the total population of Presbyterians at 514,800, despite the emigration of thousands to the American colonies.[2] The scale of the decline of Irish Dissent excluding

---

[2] These figures are taken from Toby Barnard, 'Identities, Ethnicity and Tradition among Irish Dissenters, c.1650–1750', in Herlihy, ed., *The Irish Dissenting Tradition*, p. 33n; S. J. Connolly,

Presbyterians was much sharper than in England and owed much to the pressure for protestant unity, an overdependence on English troops in Ireland, and the lack of towns and manufacturing. That said, Sean Connolly rightly observes that numbers express only a part of the Irish Dissenting experience. The creation and perpetuation of a self-contained and largely self-regulating Presbyterian society in Ulster was a matter of considerable importance for the subsequent history of the island. In Dublin, a lively religious subculture developed during the first half of the eighteenth century with at least twenty-five Dissenting places of worship, some of which had only a fleeting existence.

By 1690 a powerful Presbyterian community had been established in Ulster. It was an offshoot of the Presbyterian Church of Scotland and saw itself as a potential Presbyterian Church of Ireland. It had a strong popular base; in many parts of Ulster, Presbyterians outnumbered Episcopalians and were in fact the largest single denomination. The largest Presbyterian body throughout this period was the General Synod of Ulster, the Irish equivalent of the General Assembly of the Church of Scotland. This body was formed in 1690 and provided a framework for the various Presbyterian structures that had emerged after 1660. Below the synod were regional presbyteries that had their origins in the 1650s and, amongst other things, regulated the education, supply, and maintenance of ministers. Each presbytery had jurisdiction over the local congregations in its area, which, in turn, were overseen by the Kirk session comprising an ordained minister and lay elders who had been chosen from the local church membership. Though concentrated in Ulster, congregations existed in the southern provinces and there was a sizeable Presbyterian presence in Dublin that was closer in outlook to English than to Scottish Presbyterianism. The position of Presbyterians in Ulster was consolidated in the 1690s by the immigration of between 40,000 and 70,000 people from Scotland, many of whom were refugees from famine during the 'lean years' of 1694–7.[3] Links with Scotland remained strong throughout the following century, not least because all ministers had to be university educated. Presbyterians were excluded from Trinity College, Dublin, and they instead attended Scottish universities, most notably the University of Glasgow.

The next numerically largest group of Dissenters after Presbyterians was the Society of Friends, or the Quakers. As Richard Harrison has shown, their continued presence owed much to the structures that had been assembled

---

Divided Kingdom: Ireland 1630–1800 (Oxford, 2008), pp. 283–4; I. R. McBride, *Scripture Politics: Ulster Presbyterians and Irish Radicalism in the Late Eighteenth Century* (Oxford, 1993), pp. 27–8.

[3] McBride, *Scripture Politics*, p. 27n.

in the early eighteenth century.[4] Weekly meetings had spawned monthly meetings, provincial meetings were held every six weeks, and national meetings every six months. Tried and trusted elders offered leadership, and women had their own meetings, though they were still subservient to male headship. Distinctive structures and piety did not make them immune to various pressures and their economic prosperity brought the threat of ill-discipline and worldliness. As with other Dissenters, they continued to suffer legal and social disabilities, including the payment of tithes and the legal consequences of their refusal to take oaths. A 'parliamentary committee' had been established in 1698 to address these issues as well as to draw up loyal addresses, monitor parliamentary proceedings, and correspond with the more powerful Quaker lobby in London. They were granted religious toleration in 1719 and in 1746 legislation was passed that permitted them to take affirmations rather than oaths. By 1750, however, there was a significant decline in numbers as intermarriage with other protestant communities increased and wealthier members conformed to the Established Church. There was also an increasing tendency towards spiritual introspection.

The pattern displayed by the Quakers was repeated by the Baptists and Independents. They were a scattered, numerically insignificant presence in Ireland and were heavily dependent on the presence of English troops. In the late seventeenth century, Baptists in Ireland had no formal creed owing to their weak legal position, eccentric personalities, and the fear of losing numbers from an already small group. An Irish Baptist Association was meeting biennially by 1725 and yearly by 1757, but around 1725 there were only three congregations in Dublin and eight elsewhere. Kevin Herlihy has noted that from 'boldness and optimism' in 1650, Baptists in Ireland had succumbed to 'misgiving and apprehension' by 1780.[5] The imperative to seek common cause with other Protestants against the overwhelming catholic majority militated against the maintenance of a distinct identity and they, like the Quakers, suffered the defection of wealthy members to the Church of Ireland. Those who remained became ever-more insular. 'By the late eighteenth century their piety and perception was so introspective that they were easily dismissed, marginalised and ill-defined by those outside their community.'[6]

---

[4] R. S. Harrison, '"As a garden enclosed": The Emergence of Irish Quakers, 1650–1750', in Herlihy, ed., *The Irish Dissenting Tradition*, pp. 81–95.

[5] Kevin Herlihy, 'Preface', in Kevin Herlihy, ed., *The Religion of Irish Dissent, 1650–1800* (Dublin, 1996), p. 7.

[6] Kevin Herlihy, '"A gay and flattering world": Irish Baptist Piety and Perspective, 1650–1780', in Herlihy, ed., *Religion of Irish Dissent*, p. 67.

DISSENT AND POLITICS AFTER THE REVOLUTION

Presbyterians were committed to the Williamite cause and outnumbered members of the Church of Ireland during the siege of Derry. Presbyterians expected that their loyalty would be rewarded and William personally increased the royal grant—the *regium donum*—to Presbyterian ministers during his stay in Ulster in 1690. English ministers in 1692 and again in 1695 suggested an Irish toleration act similar to the English act of 1689 but this was strenuously opposed by both houses of the Irish Parliament. The Presbyterian struggle for toleration during the reign of William failed because churchmen would not countenance such a move without the imposition of a sacramental test. As J. C. Beckett noted, Irish churchmen were obsessed by the threat posed by Presbyterians and their handling of other Dissenters by comparison was indulgent—French Protestants who did not conform were given toleration, and most subsequently joined the Established Church, while Quakers received favourable treatment. The principal reason, of course, was that there was a clear and obvious Presbyterian threat owing to their power base in the north-east. Moreover, the Presbyterian argument that toleration was essential to secure the unity and interest of Protestants in general was undermined by the fact that they equally distrusted Catholicism and would always support the protestant interest.

Between 1690 and 1714, a variety of issues exercised Presbyterian and Church of Ireland spokesmen. Debates occurred over differences in ecclesiology, doctrine, and liturgy, but more important was the competition for souls. The Church of Ireland had to face its own weaknesses—a membership that was geographically scattered, financial and material deficiencies, and pluralism and non-residence, especially in the south and west of the island. In Ulster, there was a fear of Presbyterian numerical dominance, which was reinforced by the surge of Scottish immigration in the 1690s and led to a significant increase in the number of congregations by 1716. Though over 90 per cent of Presbyterians lived in Ulster, there were unwelcome signs of Presbyterian expansion outside of the province with the formation of a congregation at Drogheda in 1708. This expansion raised the spectre of the Synod of Ulster as a would-be Established Church exercising the functions that ought to be the sole preserve of the Church of Ireland—marrying and burying, claiming a regular maintenance, exercising church discipline to a degree that made the established clergy both envious and bitter. What galled many churchmen even more was state recognition of Presbyterianism through the continued payment of the *regium donum* and the Anglo-Scottish union of 1707 that had confirmed the Established Church of Scotland as Presbyterian. Informing this fear of dominance were memories of the 1640s and the alleged disloyalty and republicanism of Presbyterians. How could such people be granted legal toleration never mind access to political power?

The campaign against Presbyterians between 1690 and 1714 took various forms. There was an extensive print war between advocates on both sides. Though doctrine, liturgy, and marriage were covered, in terms of public life, the various publications on Presbyterian rights and privileges are especially important. There were two elements involved—legal toleration to worship freely and to exercise spiritual jurisdiction, and a share in political power. The vicar of Belfast, William Tisdall, penned his *A Sample of Trew-Blue Presbyterian Loyalty* in 1709 and was responded to by John McBride in *A Sample of Jet-Black Prelatic Calumny* (1713) and by James Kirkpatrick's *An Historical Essay upon the Loyalty of Presbyterians* (1713). Tisdall's critique of Presbyterians ranged widely—'a state within a state', Presbyterians as a would-be establishment, disloyalty and republicanism—and this rhetoric would remain a staple of church polemic into the 1730s and beyond. Much of Tisdall's bile was created by his own experience of Presbyterian strength in Belfast and especially by his acrimonious relations with John McBride, a Scottish minister in the town and a leading spokesman of the Presbyterian community who, along with Alexander McCracken and John Riddell, refused the Oath of Abjuration in 1703 as it implied recognition of the existing episcopal establishment. The campaign against Presbyterians was also carried out through the legal system. Lay members were sometimes hauled before the courts on account of their refusal to take certain oaths or failure to pay tithes, while ministers were prosecuted in church courts for irregularly celebrating marriages. Sectarian violence occurred at parliamentary elections in County Antrim and its boroughs in 1713 and 1715, while mobs attacked Presbyterians and their meeting houses in the summer of 1714.

The campaign reached a climax in legislation. In 1704 a sacramental test was added to the Popery Act by English Tory interests and 'required all holders of civil and military office under the crown to receive Holy Communion once a year in the Established Church'.[7] This effectively excluded Presbyterians from national and local government office, and from corporate government in towns, though some southern Presbyterians practised occasional conformity. The legislative position of Presbyterians deteriorated further during the later years of the reign of Queen Anne when in 1714 payment of the *regium donum* was suspended and the provisions of the Schism Act against Nonconformist schools in England were extended to Ireland, though both actions were reversed after the accession of George I. Presbyterians were outraged, and there were various attempts to secure repeal of the test over the next thirty years. Great offence was taken at the

---

[7] D. W. Hayton, 'Exclusion, Conformity and Parliamentary Representation: The Impact of the Sacramental Test on Irish Dissenting Politics', in *Ruling Ireland, 1685–1742: Politics, Politicians and Parties* (Woodbridge, 2004), p. 186.

symbolism of the test as it had been attached to a major piece of penal legislation against Catholics—had their sacrifices for the Williamite cause against the Jacobites meant nothing? The case for repeal was pressed by Presbyterian gentry and merchants, Irish Whigs, and some political interests in England. Despite this coalition, repeal faced solid opposition within the Irish Parliament, predictably from High Church Tories but also from many Whigs. Attempts were made in 1707, 1709, 1714–15, and 1716, before in 1719 Presbyterians received a 'bare' toleration in the form of an Indemnity Act that softened the impact of the test and a long-awaited though practically meaningless Toleration Act. Two further attempts at repeal failed in the early 1730s.

As D. W. Hayton has noted, the impact of the test was milder than the rhetoric of both sides would imply. Unlike Catholics, it did not bar Presbyterians from sitting in parliament or from voting in county and some borough elections. Furthermore, indemnity acts from 1719 mitigated the impact of the test, particularly for commissioned officers in the militia, yet these did not provide continuous exemption and did not extend to posts in municipal corporations. Presbyterians lost direct parliamentary representation in Derry, Belfast, and, possibly, Coleraine—the number of identifiable Presbyterian MPs fell from nine in 1703 to five in 1727. The real impact occurred at local government, especially borough corporations in Ulster where Presbyterian numbers and wealth entitled them to representation. The same was also true in Dublin, though by the 1720s there was something of a revival there and the Dissenting interest clearly exercised Jonathan Swift. Though only a relatively small number of propertied Dissenters were affected, Hayton observes that the imposition of the test revealed a fundamental problem of Presbyterian representation and influence. There was a drift of Presbyterian commercial and landed families towards conformity, which meant that the natural leaders of Presbyterian politics, the gentry, were a negligible presence; in Ulster by 1720, there were twelve Church of Ireland landlords to every one Presbyterian. In addition, Presbyterians lacked a serious political figure to communicate their grievances. Sympathetic liberal Anglicans proved untrustworthy and the attitude of Whigs in both England and Ireland to Presbyterian claims was lukewarm and, on occasions, positively hostile. As a consequence, Presbyterians lacked the ability to have their interests articulated in parliament. Repeal of the test was a necessary first step to regaining influence in order then to address other grievances. Yet by the 1770s, repeal was not seen as the answer to the systemic problems militating against Presbyterian political influence. By that stage Presbyterians realized that only a restructuring of the political and electoral system itself would meet their needs. This was reinforced by the fact that traditional Church of Ireland hostility to Presbyterians 'continued and grew' and they remained committed to the principle of subordination expressed through the test. As a consequence, 'the attitudes of those who made and enforced religious policy in Hanoverian Ireland veered between forbearance and vindictiveness. And so it was that the Test Act lasted so long.'[8]

ENLIGHTENMENT AND EVANGELICALISM

The granting of toleration in 1719 came at an awkward time for Presbyterians. Toleration was predicated on the fact that the beliefs tolerated were orthodox and conformed to the various creeds adopted by mainstream Protestantism, including the Thirty-Nine Articles and the Westminster Confession of Faith. The problem was that a movement was emerging within the Synod of Ulster that questioned the necessity of subscribing to human-made statements of faith as it was an infringement on the rights of conscience of the individual. These nonsubscribers shared the more relaxed attitude of English Presbyterians who in 1719 had decided against requiring subscription at the Salter's Hall conference in London. This decision was part of a series of challenges to religious orthodoxy in the period, most notably the Bangorian Controversy in the Church of England, the early enlightenment emphasis on freedom, reason, and science, and radical Whig politics that stressed individual liberty. In 1703 Thomas Emlyn, an English Presbyterian in Dublin, was found guilty of denying the divinity of Christ, fined £1,000, and imprisoned for a year, while in Ulster, the Belfast Society was formed in 1705 to allow ministers to discuss the latest developments in theology and philosophy.

Since 1698 all who were licensed to preach by the Synod of Ulster had to subscribe to the Westminster Confession. This was strengthened in the wake of the Emlyn trial in 1705 when it was decided that all ministers must subscribe before ordination. Despite this legislation, John Abernethy, a leading member of the Belfast Society and a well-respected leader of the synod, published in 1719, *Religious Obedience Founded on Personal Persuasion*. The sermon was mildly Arminian rather than Calvinist in tone, but more important was Abernethy's assertion that individuals ought to follow their own persuasion of what was true rather than being required to subscribe to human-made statements of belief. Abernethy's sermon was the prelude to what has come to be known as the Subscription Controversy. Events moved quickly, and in 1720 Samuel Haliday was accused of heresy by his fellow minister Samuel Dunlop, both of whom had attended Salter's Hall. The synod passed the so-called Pacific Act that allowed ministers who would 'scruple any phrase or phrases' in the Westminster Confession to give their own wording for the doctrines, if

---

[8] Toby Barnard, 'The Government and Irish Dissent, 1704–1780', in Kevin Herlihy, ed., *The Politics of Irish Dissent 1650–1800* (Dublin, 1997), pp. 20, 27.

presbytery was convinced they were 'sound in faith'.⁹ Less than a month after this act had been passed, however, Haliday was installed in one of the Belfast congregations and refused to subscribe at all. At synod the following year, the great majority of those in attendance voluntarily subscribed to the Westminster Confession. The synod was now clearly divided between Old Light subscribers and New Light non-subscribers, and the ensuing controversy produced well over fifty publications. In 1725 the non-subscribers were all placed in a newly formed Presbytery of Antrim and the following year they were formally separated from ecclesiastical fellowship with the synod.

Throughout the controversy, there was a significant middle-ground who did not want the synod unnecessarily divided, but it is also clear that the laity were attached to subscription. The expulsion of the non-subscribers in 1726 was carried by lay elders as a majority of two ministers had actually voted to retain them. New Light ministers served congregations in east Ulster and Dublin, areas that had a more cosmopolitan outlook, a product of urban and commercial sociability; Old Light dominated rural Presbyterianism. Though an overture and resolution copper-fastening subscription were passed in 1734–5, moderation began to pervade the synod and it was clear that some presbyteries were not enforcing strict adherence to these rules. Congregations periodically disputed the settlement of New Light ministers. One such case in Ballykelly, County Londonderry, in 1766 produced a pamphlet debate and saw the emergence of Benjamin McDowell as a leading defender of subscription and Calvinist orthodoxy. What is significant is that McDowell's concerns were not shared by most of his colleagues. Such was the spread of non-subscription by 1774 that the Presbytery of Belfast was formed to accommodate subscribers. By the 1780s, only four of fourteen presbyteries kept up even a nominal subscription.

New Light Presbyterianism embodied the enlightenment attitudes of moderation and toleration that permeated its religious and political character. In terms of religious views, New Light Presbyterians held with conservatives that Christ alone was the sole head of the Church and the final authority of the Bible. However, they emphasized the right of private judgement in determining the meaning of the Bible and shifted the focus of practical morality from doctrine to conduct. There was also a domino effect in terms of how these principles affected doctrinal belief as individuals began to question and then reject doctrines such as original sin, imputed righteousness, and vicarious atonement. By late century a handful of individuals, most notably John Cameron, minister of Dunluce, had quietly rejected the divinity of Christ, though Arianism was not a significant cause of controversy until the 1820s. In terms of politics, New Light had a significant impact. Ian McBride has noted how Presbyterian political discourse between 1690 and 1730 proceeded upon a

---

⁹ Cited in J. S. Reid, *History of the Presbyterian Church in Ireland*, ed. W. D. Killen, 3 vols., 2nd edn (Belfast, 1867), III, pp. 127–8.

repudiation of the seventeenth-century Covenants and based the case for toleration on past loyalty and, increasingly, the language of rights.[10] Non-subscription proved an important stimulus in this transformation as it questioned the existence of religious establishments and redefined 'popery' as any infringement upon the rights of conscience. As a consequence, New Light Presbyterianism became associated with radical Whig politics, especially what is variously lumped together as classical republicanism, civic humanism, civic virtue, or the Commonwealth tradition.

A leading figure in this wider movement was an Irish Presbyterian. Francis Hutcheson (1694–1746) was the son of the manse and intended to become a minister, though his name is now associated with moral philosophy and he is widely credited as being the 'Father of the Scottish Enlightenment'.[11] His moral sense theory of benevolence over selfishness seemingly reconciled the kingdom of God with civic virtue. During his years as a tutor in Dublin in the 1720s, Hutcheson developed these ideas in dialogue with Robert, Viscount Molesworth, and several New Light Presbyterians, including the radical poet James Arbuckle, the publisher William Bruce, and the Revd Thomas Drennan. He was appointed professor of moral philosophy at Glasgow in 1730 and his teaching and example had a significant impact on a generation of students. They learnt that political authority was based on the consent of the people and that the principal means of opposing tyranny and corruption was by virtuous citizens who put the public good before their private interests and upheld natural rights, equality, and religious toleration. The powers of central government would be curbed by a mixed constitution and parliamentary control of the executive, and their principal role was to promote 'the greatest happiness for the greatest number'. He advocated the rights of women, servants, slaves, animals, and colonies, and defended the right of citizens to resist oppressive rulers.

Hutcheson's influence was widespread and profound. In Scotland he popularized the language of civic virtue and helped foster the emergence of the Moderate Party in the Church of Scotland. Hutcheson also had a significant influence in the New World. One of his followers, John Witherspoon, helped make the College of New Jersey into one of the principal seats of learning in the thirteen colonies. Witherspoon also succeeded in reconciling his evangelical principles with a commitment to natural rights, contract theory, and the right of resistance, and was the only clerical signatory of the Declaration of Independence. Another of Hutcheson's admirers, Francis Alison, played a

---

[10] I. R. McBride, 'Ulster Presbyterians and the Confessional State, c.1688–1733', in D. G. Boyce, Robert Eccleshall, and Vincent Geoghegan, eds, *Political Discourse in Seventeenth- and Eighteenth-Century Ireland* (Basingstoke, 2001), pp. 169–92.

[11] I. R. McBride, 'The School of Virtue: Francis Hutcheson, Irish Presbyterians and the Scottish Enlightenment', in D. G. Boyce, Robert Eccleshall, and Vincent Geoghegan, eds, *Political Thought in Ireland Since the Seventeenth Century* (London, 1993), pp. 71–99.

significant role as an educationalist. Of the careers of forty-six of his students that can been traced, five signed the Declaration of Independence and many more were deeply involved in the revolutionary cause; only five were loyalists.[12] In Ireland, Hutcheson's ideas were employed by New Light Presbyterians against the abuses and inequalities of the Irish confessional state, and as we shall see in what follows, the cause of virtue was a principal concern of political radicals in the last quarter of the century.

Nevertheless, the reign of New Light Presbyterianism was shallow and the influence of the Enlightenment was not limited to the self-styled 'thinking few' who adopted a less rigid attitude to doctrine. New Light was confined socially and geographically amongst the better-off sections of Presbyterian society. At Glasgow, both liberal and conservative students from Ulster received the same education and moral philosophy was the single most popular course taken by them. According to one conservative writer, to 'a lad of good principles, that class may be very useful but I assert, that to a lad of no principles, the Moral Philosophy class is a very dangerous one', because it talked of 'moral virtues' but did not tell students that 'the true root of morality is love to God and man, and union to Jesus'. Though some would object that this was to teach divinity, the author noted that the majority of students in the moral philosophy class at Glasgow were would-be ministers and, as a consequence, 'it is no wonder, that their sermons have a greater similitude to the writings of the heathen philosophers, than to the writings of the prophets and apostles'.[13]

The writer of these cautious words was John Rogers, the professor of theology for the Burgher Seceders in Ireland. Though conservative Presbyterianism suffered in the Synod of Ulster with the eclipse of the Old Light party, it was revived and considerably extended elsewhere by the arrival from the 1740s of Seceder Presbyterian preachers from Scotland. As outlined elsewhere in this volume, the causes of the Secession were a concern that Calvinist doctrine was being set aside in the Church of Scotland and the existence of lay patronage that minimized the right of church members to choose their own ministers. Those who protested against these developments left the Kirk and formed the Associate Presbytery in 1733 and an Associate Synod in 1745. Two years later, however, the movement split over the terms of a new oath in Scotland into Burgher and Anti-Burgher factions. The first congregation of Seceders in Ireland was formed at Lylehill, County Antrim, after a land dispute between the Revd William Livingstone of Templepatrick—an orthodox subscriber—and

---

[12] D. F. Norton, 'Francis Hutcheson in America', *Studies in Voltaire and the Eighteenth Century*, 154 (1976), pp. 1547–68.
[13] John Rogers, *Dialogues, Between Students at the College; Which Contain a Defence of the Leading Doctrines of Christianity: Also Shewing their Tendency to Promote Holiness; Interspersed with Philosophical Observations* (Monaghan, 1782), pp. 24–5.

Samuel Henderson. This resulted in Henderson leaving the congregation with a number of other members, and, on 8 July 1746, the Revd Isaac Patton from Scotland was ordained the first Seceder minister in Ireland.

The Secession spread rapidly, even though the 1747 split was replicated in Ireland for no reason. A Burgher synod was formed in 1779, an Anti-Burgher one in 1788, and in 1818 both united to form the 'Presbyterian Synod of Ireland, distinguished by the name Seceders', which comprised a total of 114 congregations, eighty-three Burgher and thirty-one Anti-Burgher. Seceders made most progress amongst recent Scottish immigrants in the south and west of the province where the Synod of Ulster was not as well represented. The early spread of the Secession owed much to problems in the Synod of Ulster, including concern about the spread of New Light and long-term vacant congregations. The latter had parallels with lay patronage in the Church of Scotland and owed its origins to a regulation of 1733 that gave the wealthy members of a congregation more of a say over the choice of minister. There was also significant tension between Old Light ministers and newly arrived Seceder itinerants. Old Light clergy looked to Seceders for support, but they were also under threat, and even though they used the same arguments, the Old Light party was compromised by remaining within the synod. There was an acrimonious pamphlet debate between both parties in which 'the Seceders justified their advent by exposing the unfaithfulness of the Synod in matters of doctrine, discipline, and worship, while the ministers of the Synod replied by accusing the Seceders of exaggeration, calumny, and schism'.[14] Apart from the commitment of the Seceders to Calvinism and Presbyterianism, their style of public worship attracted adherents. Open-air and enthusiastic preaching coupled with the communion season, so memorably satirized in Robert Burns' poem 'Holy Fairs', mixed religious seriousness with festivity and also offered a rigorous code of personal morality that appealed to those who wished to improve their earthly prospects.

Covenanters or Reformed Presbyterians offered an even-more true-blue form of Presbyterianism. This group believed in the perpetual obligation of the Scottish Covenant of 1638 and the Solemn League and Covenant of 1643. For them, the Revolution settlement was fatally compromised as it did not mention the binding obligation of the Covenants and recognized episcopacy. The small minority who supported this position organized themselves into societies in both Scotland and Ireland. The renewal of the covenants at Auchinsaugh in 1712 applied to Ireland and when the first presbytery of the Reformed Presbyterians was established in Scotland in 1743, two ministers were sent to Ireland, and in 1757 William Martin was ordained as the first Covenanter minister. A presbytery established in 1763 had collapsed by 1779 but was reconstituted in 1792 with six ministers and twelve congregations.

---

[14] David Stewart, *The Seceders in Ireland with Annals of their Congregations* (Belfast, 1950), p. 71.

Both the Seceders and the Covenanters were committed Presbyterians who opposed Catholicism, Erastianism, and episcopacy. Ian McBride notes that what distinguished them was their attitude to the Covenants and political obedience to the Hanoverian state. Covenanters made the perpetual obligation of the Covenants a term of communion while Seceders tried to treat civil and religious constitutions separately. However, the attempt to reconcile two kingdoms in a complex Erastian British state was difficult and led Seceders to focus more on religious concerns. Yet members of both groups remained committed to a form of Covenanter radicalism that offered to remodel society along biblical lines in preparation for the millennial reign of Christ.

These intra-Presbyterian tensions have led some scholars to argue that evangelicalism was alien to Irish Presbyterianism.[15] They point as evidence to the concern of Presbyterians with having the right answers to ecclesiological and theological questions, the lack of response to the Irish preaching tours of George Whitefield in the 1750s, and suspicions about the new birth. However, the burgeoning historiography of the identity and character of evangelicalism has demonstrated that it was not a homogeneous movement and interacted in specific ways with pre-existing denominational and religious cultures. In that regard, there existed a form of Presbyterian evangelicalism that remained committed to Presbyterian organization and discipline and which mobilized its own theological resources to spread the Gospel, including the necessity of divine grace, the person and work of Christ, personal conversion, and millennial eschatology. Though committed to a rigid form of Presbyterianism, the Seceders freely offered the Gospel to all who would listen and members of the Old Light party such as Benjamin McDowell were committed to evangelical activism and utilized the language of the Enlightenment.

Of course, it was not only Calvinist dissent that grew in Ireland during this period. More familiar were Moravians and Methodists who both owed their existence to the international and central European origins of the evangelical movement.[16] The Moravian itinerant preacher John Cennick arrived in Ireland in 1746 at the invitation of Baptists in Dublin. This itinerant preacher from Wiltshire formed religious societies, in which women played a conspicuous and significant role, to promote the new birth and discipleship amongst Protestants from all denominational backgrounds. As elsewhere, Moravian preachers experienced mob violence and opposition, but by the early 1750s there were thirty to forty Moravian preachers serving ten chapels and over 200 societies. Despite the commitment of individuals, Moravianism did not grow

---

[15] D. W. Miller, 'Presbyterianism and "Modernization" in Ulster', *Past & Present*, 80, 1 (1973), pp. 66–90.
[16] W. R. Ward, *The Protestant Evangelical Awakening* (Cambridge, 1992); David Hempton and Myrtle Hill, *Evangelical Protestantism in Ulster Society 1740–1890* (London, 1992), ch. 1

in Ireland and one of the reasons for this was disputes with Methodists. John Wesley first visited Ireland in 1747 and returned twenty-one times over the next forty years, visiting Ulster for the first time in 1756. Unlike in England, Wesley focused on the protestant gentry and garrison towns, though he was not an uncritical observer of Ascendancy Ireland. One of the principal reasons for this strategy was his opposition to Catholicism, though he disliked Calvinism almost in equal measure. Methodist preachers too faced opposition, especially in Cork in 1749 and 1751, and from the 1770s onwards the centre of Methodism moved northwards. Methodism had a significant impact on protestant minorities, including the Palatines, most of whom emigrated from Ireland in 1760. Two of their number, Philip Embury and Barbara Heck, formed the first Methodist society in America in New York in 1766. As with Moravianism, women played a conspicuous and essential part in the spread of Methodism, including as preachers.

POLITICIZATION AND REBELLION

As the eighteenth century developed, Ireland was deeply influenced by the growth of the Atlantic economy. An estimated 250,000 to 300,000 people emigrated from Ireland to North America after 1719, most of whom were Presbyterians from Ulster.[17] At the same time, between c.1750 and 1770, Ireland's economy grew significantly owing to the expansion of the linen industry in south Ulster.[18] This expansion led to greater wealth and social mobility amongst farmer-weavers and the urban middle classes, especially in Belfast, who became increasingly aware of broader political and cultural debates. Indeed, the well-established tradition of emigration facilitated the spread of ideas and news of political events, not least the growing tensions between the thirteen colonies and the British Crown. By that stage, however, economic expansion had slowed but price inflation continued, which led to sharp, short-term difficulties. Crop failures and food shortages in the early 1770s accelerated emigration to America and hit rural areas and small farmers hardest. As the population continued to increase, attempts were made by landlords, the church, and local government to squeeze more money from inhabitants of the countryside by increasing rents and altering the terms of leases. These economic factors produced widespread resentment in rural

---

[17] The classic study is R. J. Dickson, *Ulster Emigration to Colonial America, 1718–1775* (London, 1966).

[18] The following paragraph draws on W. H. Crawford, 'Change in Ulster in the Late Eighteenth Century', in Thomas Bartlett and D. W. Hayton, eds, *Penal Era and Golden Age: Essays in Irish History 1690–1800* (new edn, Belfast, 2005), pp. 186–203.

society that was expressed through agrarian agitation in which Presbyterians played a prominent role—the Hearts of Oak disturbances of 1763 were organized protests against tithes and other dues in south and west Ulster, while the Hearts of Steel (1770-2) were a secret society in east Ulster who engaged in nocturnal outrages as a consequence of new leasing arrangements on Lord Donegall's estate.

Despite the localized nature of these disturbances, Presbyterians were looking beyond their own sectional interests and were beginning to agitate for more substantial political changes that would affect all the inhabitants of Ireland. Since the early 1750s, patriotism had become an increasing irritant in Anglo-Irish relations. This involved opposing any challenge to Ireland's status as a 'sister kingdom', particularly the subordination of the Irish Parliament and restrictions on trade. From the 1760s, an identifiable 'patriot' opposition existed in the Dublin Parliament and an 'independent interest' expressed itself in defiance of landlord interests in county constituencies in 1768. In 1776 various grievances coalesced to return two independent MPs for Ulster—John Richardson in County Londonderry and James Wilson in Antrim—largely on the basis of Presbyterian voters. By addressing these broader issues, Presbyterians in Ireland were following the example of protestant Dissenters throughout the North Atlantic world who were advocating political reform. What united Dissenters in England, Scotland, and Ireland was their minority status, a common ideology of anti-popery and anti-clericalism, harassment by the establishment, an awareness that the catholic threat had declined, and the impact of the American Revolution.[19] The 'Imperial Crisis' that began in 1775 produced an economic recession that focused Irish criticism on trade restrictions, but the example of American self-assertion seemed especially relevant to Ireland as it raised issues of patriotism, political subordination, and civil and religious liberty.

Ireland was also left open to French invasion owing to the need to send regular troops to North America, and in 1778 the first companies of Volunteers were formed in Ulster. There had been a tradition of voluntary Presbyterian defence forces against the threat of Jacobite and French invasion earlier in the century; this time, Volunteering was described in the language of classical republicanism by many of the Presbyterian ministers who had become chaplains as a volunteer citizen militia defending liberty. In spring 1779, there were 12,000 Volunteers; by May 1782, there were 60,000. Formal leadership was provided by landlords, but pressure from the Presbyterian middling sort of Ulster was often irresistible. McBride notes that they had the leisure, disposable income, and political knowledge to transform the

---

[19] J. E. Bradley, 'The Religious Origins of Radical Politics in England, Scotland, and Ireland, 1662–1800', in J. E. Bradley and D. K. van Kley, eds, *Religion and Politics in Enlightenment Europe* (Notre Dame, 2001), pp. 187–253.

Volunteers from a home guard into an effective extra-parliamentary pressure group. The Volunteers scored some remarkable successes. Trade restrictions on Ireland were abolished in 1779 after a large-scale show of Volunteer strength in Dublin. More significantly, the Dungannon Convention of the Volunteers in February 1782 acted like a national parliament, declaring restrictions on legislative autonomy 'unconstitutional' and 'a grievance'. The threat of the Volunteers produced the so-called 'Constitution of 1782' that effectively gave the Irish Parliament legislative independence.

The American war also had a significant impact on religious policy. Many of the penal restrictions on Catholics were removed between 1778 and 1782 in order to encourage recruitment to the British army, and the sacramental test itself was quietly dropped in 1780. By that stage, Presbyterian politics had moved from a sole focus on their own grievances to a much broader political platform, which, in some cases, included support for the further political claims of Catholics. In that context, Volunteering was crucial for the politicization of Presbyterians. General economic trends helped to focus Presbyterian anxiety and resentment on their exclusion from local and national political power, while the language of civic virtue provided a critique of government and existing constitutional relationships. Presbyterians had embraced Irish patriotism and used the example of America to great effect. The Volunteers provided an example of what extra-parliamentary agitation, backed up by paramilitary organization, might achieve. 'It was a culture which was republican in the classical sense, founded on the active participation of the arms-bearing citizen. If radicalism had lost its momentum after 1785, the machinery for popular mobilization was still there.'[20]

After the heady days of 1782, the Volunteer movement declined in effectiveness owing to internal tensions and the regrouping of the Irish Episcopalian elite. During the late 1780s, Presbyterian radicals became increasingly frustrated at the lack of further political reform. The Irish Parliament remained unreformed and represented only the minority Church of Ireland. The frustration felt by Presbyterian radicals seemed to be relieved in July 1789 by the storming of the Bastille that signalled the beginning of the French Revolution. Indeed, events in France were greeted with enthusiasm, a millennial moment that seemed to herald the decline and fall of the papacy. Radical Presbyterians eagerly read Thomas Paine's *The Rights of Man* and were enthralled with the language of liberty, equality, and fraternity. This was especially the case for William Drennan, a New Light Presbyterian whose father Thomas had been a close friend of Francis Hutcheson. Drennan had studied medicine in Scotland and had returned to practise in Ireland in 1778. A freemason who had radical ideas in religion, Drennan was inspired by Irish patriots, but like many other

---

[20] McBride, *Scripture Politics*, p. 161.

radicals in the Volunteers, he wished to include Catholics in a new definition of patriotism. In his correspondence he talked of establishing a secret society a 'benevolent conspiracy', that would unite all Irishmen in order to attain full political rights for all.[21] As a consequence of his efforts and those of others, the Society of United Irishmen was formed in Belfast on 18 October 1791 and a Dublin society on 9 November. All but one of the founding members of the Belfast society were middle-class Presbyterians, including Samuel Neilson, William and Robert Simms, Henry Haslett, William Tennent, and Samuel McTier; the only non-Presbyterian was the Episcopalian, Wolfe Tone. Despite the militancy of some, the Society focused on political education and recruitment, especially through their newspaper, the *Northern Star*. They also sought to influence public debate, and at a Belfast town meeting in January 1792, they orchestrated the passing of a resolution calling for immediate Catholic emancipation.

Owing to war with France and frustration at the lack of political reform in Ireland, the society in 1795 transformed itself from a political movement into a revolutionary republican conspiracy. Direct contact was made with the republican regime in France, which produced an ill-starred invasion of Ireland in December 1796. They also sought to expand their membership by forging an alliance with the Defenders, a catholic secret society established to protect its community from protestant aggression and which exhibited a mixture of sectarian and enlightenment elements. Between 1796 and 1798, Presbyterian radicals from east Ulster helped to create this mass revolutionary movement and by February 1798 an estimated 280,000 individuals throughout Ireland had taken the oath of the society. This growth inevitably brought about a simplification of ideology, and tensions developed between leaders and followers, northern and southern radicals. Was the United Irish movement committed to political principle and enlightenment values? Did it seek to promote social change? Was it to be a vehicle for catholic Defenders and sectarian Presbyterians to bring about their conflicting visions of a theocratic society?

Whatever the tensions, the government response was uncompromising. The militia was reconfigured in 1793, a protestant yeomanry emerged in late 1796, and an extensive network of spies and informers was established. Drennan was tried for sedition in 1794 and subsequently retreated from public political life. The Insurrection Act of 1796 introduced the death penalty for the administration of oaths and gave new powers to magistrates. One victim of this new legislation was a Presbyterian farmer from County Antrim, William Orr, whose dying confession in October 1797 gave expression to how sectional and national interests had now been combined: 'I am no traitor. I die for a

---

[21] A. T. Q. Stewart, *A Deeper Silence: The Hidden Roots of the United Irish Movement* (London, 1993).

persecuted country. Great Jehovah receive my soul. I die in the true faith of a Presbyterian.'[22] Martial law was proclaimed in Ulster and by spring 1798 the United Irishmen were in disarray. When the rebellion broke out in the summer, it was uncoordinated and bloody. The most successful of the regional uprisings occurred in County Wexford in May–June, but it quickly degenerated into chaos and sectarian killings. The rebellion in Ulster was largely a Presbyterian affair, but the skirmishes at Antrim and Ballynahinch in early July were one-sided and Catholic–Protestant unity quickly evaporated.

Though Presbyterians were at the forefront of radicalism and rebellion, this does not mean that most Presbyterians were radicals, and 1798 found Presbyterians on both sides of the political divide for a variety of reasons. All the Presbyterian churches asserted their loyalty to the state, though Ian McBride has shown that around a fifth of Presbyterian ministers were implicated in the rebellion. The Presbytery of Bangor was particularly affected—three of its members were executed and others left for America. The motives that encouraged Presbyterian clergy and the laity to rebel were many, and there is debate over the precise balance between Enlightenment and Covenanter radicalism, differences between ministers and the laity, and the relative importance of material circumstances and political developments. 'The '98 was a rebellion of New Lights against the priestcraft and superstition perpetuated by Church and State, of Old Lights against an erastian, idolatrous, and unscriptural establishment, and of all Presbyterians against a government which had allied itself with the forces of civil and religious tyranny.'[23]

Significantly more Presbyterians were not interested in revolution and, again, the reasons were varied. The majority of the clergy were not involved, and implication was not guilt. Generally speaking, Presbyterians remained political reformers rather than revolutionaries. It is also clear that anti-Catholicism played a significant role; Presbyterians were more likely to be radical in east Ulster where Protestants had a secure majority than in the south and west where fear of the catholic majority was greater.

More generally, the dislocation of the 1790s prompted reform and revival within Western Christianity. Amongst Irish Protestants, this manifested itself in evangelical religion. According to David Hempton, the 'events of the last decades of the century... focused attention on the potential of its moral creed and its anti-Catholicism to act as compelling antidotes to civil and political unrest'.[24] Heart religion seemed to offer a means of pacifying and improving Ireland. Ireland became a mission field and was visited by preachers such as

---

[22] A. T. Q. Stewart, *The Summer Soldiers: The 1798 Rebellion in Antrim and Down* (Belfast, 1995), p. 50.

[23] McBride, *Scripture Politics*, p. 13.

[24] David Hempton, *Religion and Political Culture in Great Britain and Ireland from the Glorious Revolution to the Decline of Empire* (Cambridge, 1996), p. 95.

Rowland Hill and Lorenzo Dow. Methodism in south Ulster experienced a remarkable religious revival in the wake of the rebellion. Membership doubled in the region, though this growth was volatile and erratic. High prices, food shortages, and religious tensions certainly played their part, but the commitment of itinerant preachers should not be dismissed. Gideon Ousley covered 4,000 miles per year and preached over twenty times a week. Five Seceder ministers in County Armagh formed the Evangelical Society of Ulster in October 1798 to promote itinerant preaching. They saw themselves as part of an international and interdenominational movement. Its first meeting was attended by thirteen ministers from four different Presbyterian denominations as well as Episcopalians and Independents. One of the ministers involved was the Revd Thomas Campbell who left Ireland in 1807 and in the United States helped form the Disciples of Christ.

The importance of these developments in the 1790s cannot be overemphasized. The growth of evangelicalism transformed Presbyterians and Irish Protestants more generally. From a concern with maintaining their own communities, they were swept along with the desire of evangelicals elsewhere to convert the world to Christianity. The heirs of the non-subscribers were forced out of the Synod of Ulster in 1829 by Henry Cooke who combined to great effect support for the Act of Union (1800) with evangelical religion and political conservatism. Yet the clear majority of his fellow ministers remained political liberals and were opposed to the continued ascendancy of the Church of Ireland. The rise of Irish catholic nationalism in the nineteenth century may have created protestant unity against the threat of 'Rome Rule', but it did not submerge the distinctive position of Presbyterians in Irish life that had been so obvious and important during the previous century.

SELECT BIBLIOGRAPHY

Beckett, J. C., *Protestant Dissent in Ireland 1687–1780* (London, 1948).
Connolly, S. J., *Divided Kingdom: Ireland 1630–1800* (Oxford, 2008).
Hayton, D. W., *Ruling Ireland, 1685–1742: Politics, Politicians and Parties* (Woodbridge, 2004).
Hempton, David and Hill, Myrtle, *Evangelical Protestantism in Ulster Society 1740–1890* (London, 1992).
Herlihy, Kevin, ed., *The Irish Dissenting Tradition 1650–1750* (Blackrock, 1995).
Herlihy, Kevin, ed., *The Religion of Irish Dissent 1650–1800* (Blackrock, 1996).
Herlihy, Kevin, ed., *The Politics of Irish Dissent, 1650–1800* (Dublin, 1997).
Herlihy, Kevin, ed., *Propagating the Word of Irish Dissent, 1650–1800* (Dublin, 1998).
Holmes, A. R., *The Shaping of Ulster Presbyterian Belief and Practice 1770–1840* (Oxford, 2006).
Holmes, R. F. G., *Our Irish Presbyterian Heritage* (Belfast, 1985).

McBride, I. R., *Scripture Politics: Ulster Presbyterians and Irish Radicalism in the Late Eighteenth Century* (Oxford, 1998).

Miller, D. W., 'Presbyterianism and "Modernization" in Ulster', *Past & Present*, 80, 1 (1978), pp. 66–90.

Stewart, A. T. Q., *The Narrow Ground: Aspects of Ulster, 1609–1969* (London, 1977).

Stewart, A. T. Q., *A Deeper Silence: The Hidden Roots of the United Irish Movement* (London, 1993).

Whan, Robert, *The Presbyterians of Ulster, 1680–1730* (Woodbridge, 2013).

7

Protestant Dissent in Scotland

Stewart J. Brown

The Revolution of 1688–9 brought the re-establishment of Presbyterianism within the national Established Church of Scotland. For Presbyterians, it ended decades of persecution and suffering, and opened the prospect of making Scotland a godly nation. From 1662 to 1689, the established national Church of Scotland had been an Episcopal Church, governed by bishops and recognizing the king as the supreme governor of the Church. The Stuart monarchs had conducted a brutal campaign to suppress Presbyterianism. The state had harried the Presbyterians, especially those Scots who remained loyal to the Covenants of 1638 and 1643, by which members of the Scottish national Church had pledged themselves before God to maintain the Presbyterian and Reformed religion as the purest form of the Christian faith. Under persecution, the Covenanters had formed conventicles for clandestine worship, meeting on hillsides or in secluded glens. There had been two armed Presbyterian risings, in 1666 and 1679, both of them crushed by superior military force. During the 'killing times' of the early and mid 1680s, dragoons summarily executed Presbyterians suspected of participating in illegal worship in the hills. The numbers executed had probably been fewer than 200, but they had included some barbaric incidents, such as that of John Brown of Priesthill, shot in 1684 by dragoons at his home in front of his wife and children, or the alleged judicial killing of two women in 1685 in Wigtown (the facts are disputed), believed by many to have been staked and drowned in the incoming tide. Stories of the martyred Covenanters became part of Scottish folk culture.

The persecution of Presbyterians eased after 1687, as most Presbyterians accepted the Stuart monarch's declaration of indulgence of that year and received considerable freedom of worship and practice within their churches. Nonetheless, when news that the Stuart monarch had fled from London to France reached Scotland in late December 1688, Presbyterians viewed it as an act of God. Presbyterian crowds, some of them made up predominantly of women, in different parts of the country sought revenge for three decades of persecution by 'rabbling' or forcing the Episcopal clergy out of their churches and manses.[1] In March 1689, a Convention of Estates met in Edinburgh and in April it offered the Scottish Crown to William and Mary. The Estates, which declared itself a Parliament in June 1689, also promised to establish in Scotland the form of church government that would be 'most agreeable to the inclinations of the people'. It is unclear whether the majority of the Scottish people in 1689 supported Presbyterianism or Episcopacy.[2] The new king William, a Dutch Calvinist but also a pragmatist, was largely uninformed about the religious situation in Scotland. He would have been content for the Church of Scotland to remain Episcopalian, so that all three of his kingdoms— England, Ireland, and Scotland—would have Established Churches with a similar ecclesiastical structure. However, the Scottish Bishops were openly hostile to the new regime, and many Episcopalians supported Viscount Dundee's ill-fated military campaign in the summer of 1689 to restore James to the Scottish throne. So in 1690, the Scottish Parliament established Presbyterianism as the government of Scotland's national Church and the Calvinist Westminster Confession as the standard of faith.[3] Scotland was now to be Presbyterian, and some 60 'Antediluvians', elderly Presbyterian ministers driven from their churches in 1662, were restored to their parishes. But significantly Parliament did not revive the Covenants, and William instructed the Presbyterian Church establishment to show 'moderation' in its policies. 'Moderation', he wrote to the General Assembly of the Church of Scotland in October 1690, 'is what religion enjoins, neighbouring churches expect from you, and we recommend to you.'[4] The seventeenth century had been for Scotland a time of religious strife and religiously motivated civil war, and the new king now wanted peace in his northern kingdom. Although William was unsuccessful in 1692 in securing for the Episcopalian ministers a share in the government of the Established Church, a sense of toleration nonetheless emerged in Scotland, largely because the monarchical state, in its commitment to political stability, was now less committed to enforcing religious uniformity.[5] This in turn allowed the growth and diversification of protestant Dissent.

---

[1] Alasdair Raffe, *The Culture of Controversy: Religious Arguments in Scotland, 1660–1714* (Woodbridge, 2012), pp. 218–33.
[2] A. C. Cheyne, *Studies in Scottish Church History* (Edinburgh, 1999), p. 61.
[3] L. K. J. Glassey, 'William II and the Settlement of Religion in Scotland, 1688–1690', *Records of the Scottish Church History Society* [hereafter *RSCHS*], 23, 3 (1989), pp. 317–29.
[4] A. L. Drummond and J. Bulloch, *The Scottish Church 1688–1843: The Age of the Moderates* (Edinburgh, 1973), p. 10.
[5] R. Buick Knox, 'Establishment and Toleration during the Reigns of William, Mary and Anne', *RSCHS*, 23, 3 (1989), pp. 330–60.

THE CAMERONIANS OR SOCIETIES

One of the first Dissenting bodies to emerge in Scotland following the Revolution of 1688–9 was made up of uncompromising Covenanters. They were sometimes referred to as Cameronians—after the Covenanting field-preacher, Richard Cameron, killed by dragoons in 1680—or sometimes simply as the 'Societies' or the 'hillmen'.[6] The Society people refused to acknowledge the legitimacy of the Revolution settlement, in part because there had not been a renewal of the Covenants and in part because the post-1690 political and ecclesiastical order included many who had been among their persecutors during the 'killing times'. They had suffered too much for the Covenants for them now to accept the compromises being made for the sake of peace. The uncovenanted Scottish state, they believed, was an offence before God. Their most influential field preacher, the kind-hearted James Renwick, had been captured and executed by the Stuart state in February 1688. The three surviving ministers of the Societies, William Boyd, Alexander Shields, and Thomas Lining, joined the re-Established Church of Scotland in 1690. But many of the Society people, who were spread across much of the Lowlands, continued after 1690 to meet regularly in their conventicles on remote hillsides or in the glens for prayer, Bible reading, Psalm singing, and emotional support, and to honour the memories of the Covenanting martyrs. Lay activism was crucial to their survival. Refusing to recognize the uncovenanted state, they would not pay taxes, take oaths of loyalty, make use of the law courts, or be married in, or have their children baptized in, parish churches.

In 1706, eighteen years after Renwick's execution, the Society people finally found a minister when James Macmillan (1669–1753), Church of Scotland minister of Balmaghie, embraced their cause and accepted their call. Over the following decades, Macmillan travelled through the Lowlands, preaching, catechizing, and baptizing among the scattered groups of Society people— whose adherents ebbed and flowed but could at times number as many as 10,000. In 1712, the Societies held a gathering in the moorlands of Upper Clydesdale, to swear anew their allegiance to the Covenants. Macmillan administered communion in the field, the Societies' first celebration of the sacrament since their refusal to recognize the Revolution settlement. After some thirty-seven years as the Societies' sole minister, Macmillan was joined in 1743 by Thomas Nairn, who had been ordained in the Church of Scotland. Nairn's arrival was vital because the Societies, as strict Presbyterians, had not believed that it was permissible to form a presbytery with only one minister. Macmillan and Nairn now formed a Reformed Presbytery, and as a presbytery they ordained some other ministers, including Macmillan's son. Nairn soon

---

[6] Matthew Hutchison, *The Reformed Presbyterian Church in Scotland: Its Origin and History 1680–1876* (Paisley, 1893), pp. 48–183; Raffe, *Culture of Controversy*, pp. 196–207.

returned to the ministry of the Established Church, but the Reformed Presbytery was secure. The Reformed Presbyterian outdoor communion celebration in 1761 at Sandhills in Galloway was said to have been attended by some 10,000.[7] Throughout the eighteenth century, Reformed Presbyterians remained strict Calvinists, oath-bound to the Covenants, viewing religious toleration as sinful, refusing to pay taxes, use the law courts, serve as magistrates or soldiers, take oaths of allegiance, or to recognize in any way the uncovenanted state.

THE EPISCOPALIANS

A second, and very different, protestant Dissenting denomination developed among the Episcopalians who were unable to accept the re-established Presbyterian order in the Established Church. The situation for the Episcopalians in Scotland was fluid and uncertain in the years after the Revolution. While many Episcopal clergy were 'rabbled' out of their churches and manses in 1688–9, others were allowed to remain in their parish churches and retain their incomes, provided that they took no part in church government and did not attempt to subvert the new Presbyterian system. This was in part because of a shortage of ministers. Also many parish communities, especially in the north-east, forcibly resisted attempts to remove well-loved Episcopalian ministers and replace them with Presbyterian ministers. As late as 1707, there were still 165 Episcopalian parish ministers, out of a total of about 930 parish ministers, in the Church of Scotland.[8] As Alasdair Raffe has shown, from the later seventeenth century Scottish Episcopalians were increasingly influenced by Anglican worship and theology, and they grew more and more distinct from the Presbyterians. By the early eighteenth century, Episcopalians were shifting towards Arminian attitudes (at a time when Presbyterians were insisting with greater rigour on subscription to the Calvinist Westminster Confession), growing critical of what they perceived as a Presbyterian piety emphasizing conversion, and embracing more liturgical forms of worship.[9] Episcopalian congregations began building their own meeting houses, in which they conducted services according to either the Scottish or English Prayer Book. The Presbyterian establishment called on the magistrates to

---

[7] Hutchison, *Reformed Presbyterian Church*, p. 228.
[8] Frederick Goldie, *A Short History of the Episcopal Church in Scotland* (Edinburgh, 1976), p. 35.
[9] Alasdair Raffe, 'Presbyterians and Episcopalians: The Formation of Confessional Cultures in Scotland, 1660–1715', *English Historical Review*, 125, 514 (2010), pp. 570–98.

suppress such illegal Episcopalian meeting houses, and Episcopal clergy were sometimes fined or imprisoned for conducting worship.

The sporadic persecution of Scottish Episcopalians was viewed with discomfort by many in the Established Church of England. This was especially the case after the Act of Union of 1707. Was it right in the new United Kingdom, asked many Anglicans, for Episcopalian clergy to be fined and imprisoned in Scotland for worshipping according to the English Prayer Book, or for English residents in Scotland to be deprived of Episcopal services and sacraments? Was it right that members of the Established Church in England could be persecuted for their beliefs in another part of the United Kingdom? Matters were brought to a head in 1709 when an Episcopal curate, James Greenshields, was imprisoned for four months for conducting worship in Edinburgh according to the English Prayer Book. Greenshields appealed against his sentence to the House of Lords, which in 1711 found in his favour. Parliament then proceeded in 1712 to pass a Toleration Act for Scotland, which allowed Episcopalians to conduct worship according to the English Prayer Book, provided that they abjured the Jacobite claimant to the throne, left the chapel doors unlocked, and prayed for Queen Anne and the Hanoverian succession. Those who accepted these conditions included many English residents in Scotland; they became known as the 'Qualifying' Episcopalians. Those who did not—and the majority of Scottish Episcopalians could not in conscience accept the conditions—were the 'non-jurors', and they continued to be harried by the law.

Leaders of the Presbyterian Established Church, meanwhile, were outraged by the Toleration Act. For them it was an infringement of guarantees given when the Act of Union was passed that the British Parliament would not interfere with the religious settlement in Scotland. Most Presbyterians viewed toleration of the 'prelatists' and their errors as a sin. Nor had they forgotten the persecution of the Presbyterians between 1662 and 1688; indeed, many feared that the Toleration Act was a step towards the re-establishment of Episcopacy in Scotland. Such a prospect, however, was remote, unless there were to be a Jacobite restoration. The majority of Scottish Episcopalians did remain Jacobite in sympathy, and opposed to the Hanoverian succession. Jacobites embraced a doctrine of sacred kingship, and believed that the Stuart 'king over the water' represented God's anointed sovereign. They further believed that God's favour had been withdrawn from a corrupt and sinful Scottish people for their disloyalty to His righteous order, and that divine favour would not return until the Stuarts were restored to the throne.[10] Scottish Episcopalian loyalties were demonstrated at the Jacobite rising of 1715, when large numbers of Episcopalian clergy, especially in the north, openly supported the Jacobite

---

[10] M. G. H. Pittock, *The Invention of Scotland: The Stuart Myth and the Scottish Identity, 1638 to the Present* (London, 1991), pp. 7–72.

cause with prayers, sermons, and petitions. The rising was quickly suppressed, and the non-juring Episcopalians were subjected to intensified harassment, including the shutting of meeting houses and fines and imprisonment for the clergy.

After 1715, the Scottish Episcopal Church began to develop forms of independent synodical church government. Episcopalians continued to hope for the return of the Stuart monarchs and their restoration as supreme governors of the Scottish national Church. But it was not clear when 'the king over the water' would return. There were, meanwhile, pressing needs within the Episcopal Church that had to be addressed. These included disagreements over liturgy, difficulties with providing priests and meeting houses for the faithful, and diocesan supervision of the approximately 150 remaining clergy. In 1727, and again in 1743, the bishops met quietly as a synod in Edinburgh, and amid considerable debate adopted a set of canons for their Church, which included the revival of diocesan bishoprics, rules for the election of bishops, definitions of episcopal authority, and perhaps most significantly, government through regular synods. The bishops were clear that they regarded this development of independent synodical government in their church as a temporary expedient, until they were restored as Scotland's national Established Church. But in the process they were creating the constitution for an independent Protestant Episcopal Church.

During the Jacobite rebellion of 1745–6, most Scottish Episcopalians, viewing the prospects of success as slim, avoided open support. Nonetheless, Episcopalians were branded as traitors and they suffered a new wave of persecution. It made little difference whether or not clergy and congregations had 'qualified' under the terms of the Toleration Act. In its march north in pursuit of the retreating Jacobites, the duke of Cumberland's Hanoverian army destroyed all the Episcopalian chapels it could find, and the policy of destroying Episcopal chapels continued after the destruction of the Jacobite army at Culloden. In 1746 and 1748, Parliament passed new penal laws, with yet harsher punishments for Episcopalian clergy who failed to take oaths of loyalty or pray for the Hanoverian monarch at all worship services. The acts, moreover, provided that only Episcopalian clergymen ordained by Church of England or Church of Ireland bishops could officiate at services attended by more than five persons in Scotland. Episcopal clergy were forced to conduct worship quietly in private houses or back-street meeting houses, under continual threat of imprisonment, and congregations dwindled in numbers. However, what Sir Walter Scott described as the 'poor and suffering Episcopal Church' abided. Under persecution, Episcopalians became more deeply attached to their forms of worship, especially the Scottish Communion Office, a liturgy based on the Scottish Prayer Book of 1637 and formally agreed by the Scottish Episcopal Synod in 1764.

As fears of another Jacobite rising waned, the persecution of the Scottish Episcopalians eased. By the 1780s, they had been, in Sir Walter Scott's phrase, 'reduced to a mere shadow of a shade', with four bishops and about forty clergy.[11] In 1784, the Scottish Episcopal Church performed a memorable service for the Anglican Communion when three of its bishops consecrated Samuel Seabury as bishop of Connecticut, following the American War of Independence. As a citizen of the new American republic, Seabury had been unable to take the oath of loyalty to the British monarch, and thus could not be consecrated by bishops of the Church of England. Seabury's consecration by Scottish non-juring bishops ensured the apostolic succession for the American Protestant Episcopal Church. In 1792, Parliament repealed the penal acts imposed on Scottish Episcopalians, which led to a new era of security and confidence. Leading members of the Scottish gentry and aristocracy, and many urban professionals—especially those with English family connections —began attending the Episcopal Church. It remained, however, a small denomination, representing only about 3 per cent of Scottish churchgoers in 1851.[12]

THE SECESSION CHURCHES

The most significant event for eighteenth-century Scottish protestant Dissent occurred in 1733, with the secession of several Presbyterian ministers from the Church of Scotland, including the influential brothers, Ebenezer and Ralph Erskine. The Secession of 1733 would, over the course of a few decades, swell the numbers of Scottish protestant Dissenters and gravely weaken the influence and authority of the national Church of Scotland. The Seceders were staunch Presbyterians, strongly committed to the doctrinal standards of the Westminster Confession of Faith. But they were convinced that the established Presbyterian Church had become corrupted by worldly interests.

There were two main sets of factors leading to the Secession. First, there was a growing concern among some Presbyterians over what they perceived as a moderate or half-hearted adherence to the standards of the Reformed faith taking hold in the universities and among church leaders. This laxness was demonstrated, many believed, in the lenient treatment of the heterodox John Simson, professor of Divinity at Glasgow University, who was only suspended from his chair after lengthy proceedings between 1714 and 1729, and even then was allowed to retain his full salary for life. It was also demonstrated in the General Assembly's condemnation, for doctrinal errors, of a work of

---

[11] George Grub, *An Ecclesiastical History of Scotland*, 4 vols. (Edinburgh, 1861), IV, p. 91.
[12] Callum G. Brown, *Religion and Society in Scotland since 1707* (Edinburgh, 1997), p. 45.

emotive seventeenth-century puritan devotion, the *Marrow of Modern Divinity*, which was republished in 1718 by Church of Scotland evangelicals who valued its message of salvation by divine grace alone. When a group of evangelical ministers protested against the condemnation, and defended the *Marrow* before the Assembly, they were in 1722 formally rebuked and admonished.[13] For many conservative Reformed ministers, the 'prevailing party' in the Church courts seemed intent on suppressing gospel preaching while winking at heresy in the universities.

This suspicion was strengthened by a second set of factors, related to the re-imposition in 1712 of lay patronage in the appointment of Church of Scotland ministers. Patronage had first emerged in the medieval church; it allowed the original founder of a parish church, and the founder's descendants, to present the clergyman to that church. Patronage had a tempestuous history in the Reformed Church, with the Crown and landed classes, who held nearly all patronage rights, supporting patronage, and zealous Presbyterians— with their emphasis on the spiritual independence of the Church and the rights of congregations to have a voice in choosing their ministers—strongly opposing it. The Scottish Parliament abolished patronage in 1690, replacing it with a system of election by kirk-sessions and heritors (the principal landholders in a parish). Its re-imposition by the new British Parliament in 1712 was felt as a blow against Presbyterianism. Most lay patrons were cautious and declined to exercise their rights during the next two decades; kirk-sessions and heritors continued to choose ministers in consultation with the congregations. However, by the late 1720s, patrons began presenting ministers to the churches in their gift—recognizing the value of church patronage in settling younger sons into livings, rewarding political supporters, or ensuring the appointment of moderate men who would support property rights and the subordination of ranks from the pulpits. Lay patrons tended to present 'moderate' ministers, who were less committed to 'gospel preaching'. For zealous Presbyterians, the intrusion of such 'worldly' ministers into parishes was undermining Scotland's Reformation heritage, and there was occasional popular violence in parishes aimed at blocking the induction of patrons' candidates. In response, the governing classes insisted that the Church courts must rigorously enforce patronage rights as a matter of public order. The 'prevailing party' in the Church courts showed that it was prepared to do this.

In October 1732, a Church of Scotland parish minister and moderator of the Synod of Perth and Stirling, Ebenezer Erskine, gave a sermon to the Synod in which he strongly criticized the Church's failure to resist the reintroduction of patronage or defend the rights of congregations to choose their ministers. Christ, he insisted, 'is rejected in His poor members, and the rich of this world

---

[13] D. C. Lachman, *The Marrow Controversy 1718–1723* (Edinburgh, 1988), pp. 409–75.

are put in their room'. The Church, he added, must 'beware of being swayed in the matters of Christ with the favour of great men'.[14] For this sermon, he was summoned before the bar of the General Assembly in May 1733, rebuked, and admonished. But Erskine, the son of a Covenanting field preacher, a supporter of the *Marrow of Modern Divinity*, and a minister of considerable influence, was not a man to back down. Rather, with the support of three other ministers, he submitted a formal protest to the Assembly against his rebuke. When the four ministers refused to withdraw their protest, the Commission of the General Assembly, meeting in November 1733, deposed them from the ministry. It was a crude demonstration of power, intended to silence opposition to patronage among the clergy. But instead of being silenced, Erskine and his three colleagues met in the village of Gairney Bridge in central Fife, where they were joined by two other ministers, including Erskine's brother, Ralph, a gifted poet and popular preacher. They announced their secession from the Church of Scotland, and they formed themselves into an 'Associate Presbytery'. Their congregations on the whole remained loyal to them and they invited others in the Established Church to join them.

And others did come. Reflecting dissatisfaction with patronage and the behaviour of the Church courts, a growing number of Church of Scotland adherents, sometimes whole congregations, asked to join the Associate Presbytery, or 'Secession Church', as it was popularly known. It was a difficult decision for people to step out of the parish structures of the national Church, with all the time-honoured associations. The Seceders were generally sturdy farmers, tradespeople, and skilled artisans—men and women of substance, uncompromising Reformed faith, and strict conscience, who were prepared to contribute to the support of their own churches and ministers, rather than have ministers imposed on them by upper-class patrons. The General Assembly soon recognized its error, rescinded its decision to depose Erskine and his fellow ministers, and asked them to return, but to no avail.

By 1740, there were eight ministers and some thirty Secession congregations; by 1746, there were forty-five congregations.[15] In 1737, the Secession Church set up a small divinity hall in Perth, in the manse of one of their ministers and initially with six students, for the training of ministers. In 1742, the hall moved to Abernethy, and the number of students increased to about thirty.[16] Their theology was firmly rooted in the Westminster Confession, they were Presbyterian in organization, and they believed in the unity of Church and state, even if they separated themselves from what they viewed as the corrupt Church of Scotland. Beginning in 1744, Secession congregations

---

[14] A. R. MacEwen, *The Erskines* (Edinburgh, 1900), p. 72.
[15] Drummond and Bulloch, *The Scottish Church 1688–1843*, p. 51.
[16] Jack C. Whytock, *'An Educated Clergy': Scottish Theological Education and Training in the Kirk and Secession, 1560–1850* (Milton Keynes, 2007), pp. 172–83.

adopted a practice of renewing the Covenants, identifying themselves as Scotland's true national Church. Renewal of the Covenants generally took place on the fast day before the celebration of communion (a biannual event in most congregations) and it involved the people standing and swearing allegiance to the Covenants of 1638 and 1643.[17] The Seceders made swearing allegiance to the Covenants a term of communion.[18] At the same time, the Secession Church affirmed the duty to obey the civil rulers, even though those rulers did not maintain the Covenants.[19] This meant that the Seceders rejected any connection with what they called the 'anti-government' hillmen or Society people. For the Seceders, they alone were God's true covenanted people in Scotland.

Their strict consciences and uncompromising attitudes soon led to a division in the Secession Church. While all Scottish towns required their citizens to demonstrate loyalty to the regime by taking a Burgess Oath, three towns, Edinburgh, Glasgow, and Perth, required a Burgess Oath with a religious clause, expressing allegiance to the 'true religion presently professed with this realm'. Refusal to take the oath could entail a heavy fine. Some Seceders interpreted the phrase 'true religion' to refer to the 'corrupt' Established Church of Scotland, and they insisted that no genuine Christian could take the oath. Other Seceders, including Ebenezer and Ralph Erskine, interpreted 'true religion' to refer more generally to Protestantism and believed that it was possible for Seceders to take the oath and participate in municipal government. Debates over the Burgess Oath in 1745 and 1746 grew heated, positions became entrenched, relations soured, and in 1747 the Secession Church split—with nineteen ministers opposed to the Burgess Oath breaking away to form the General Associate Synod, and severing all communion with the remaining twelve ministers in the Associate Synod.[20] In popular parlance, the two Churches were known simply as the 'Anti-Burgher Church' and the 'Burgher Church', and the division proved deep, bitter, and prolonged. The Anti-Burghers were the more militant and uncompromising of the two; indeed their Synod solemnly excommunicated Ebenezer and Ralph Erskine and declared them to be among the heathens. For all its acrimony, the 'breach', as it was called, did not halt the growth of the Secession Churches. By 1773, the Anti-Burghers had ninety-seven congregations with ministers, and another sixteen congregations seeking ministers, while the Burghers had forty-two

---

[17] John McKerrow, *History of the Secession Church* (Edinburgh, 1854), pp. 192–5.

[18] David Woodside, *The Soul of a Scottish Church: The Contribution of the United Presbyterian Church to Scottish Life and Religion* (Edinburgh, [1918]), p. 55.

[19] Grub, *Ecclesiastical History of Scotland*, IV, p. 74.

[20] William Law Mathieson, *Scotland and the Union: A History of Scotland from 1695 to 1747* (Glasgow, 1905), p. 273.

congregations with ministers and seventeen congregations seeking ministers.[21] Some claimed that the Seceders now had around 100,000 adherents, or about 7 per cent of the Scottish population. Both Churches maintained divinity halls for the training of ministers, and they sent ministers to the North American colonies.

WHITEFIELD, WESLEY, AND THE METHODIST MOVEMENT

Until about 1740, Protestant Dissenters in Scotland were nearly all committed to the ideal of Scotland as a uniform Christian commonwealth, with an alliance of Church and state, and a single Established Church. The different sects believed themselves to be the only true Church in Scotland, and they waited on God to restore the righteous order in Church and state. However, from about 1740, new attitudes began influencing Scottish Dissent. These attitudes were connected to the Protestant Awakening movement occurring throughout the North Atlantic world, a movement that had less to do with national churches and more with personal conversion and voluntary associations of the faithful. The Protestant Awakening included the movement known as Methodism, under the leadership of the evangelical Anglicans, John Wesley and George Whitefield.

George Whitefield made his first visit to Scotland in the summer of 1741 shortly after returning from his second preaching tour in the American colonies. He had been preaching with compelling power on both sides of the Atlantic, and he was invited to Scotland by Ralph and Ebenezer Erskine, who hoped that his preaching would invigorate the new Secession movement. They made it clear to Whitefield that he should restrict his preaching to Secession congregations, for to preach to Church of Scotland congregations would be to countenance the corrupt national Church. It was not true, as Whitefield reported, that Ralph Erskine had told him to preach only to the Seceders because 'they were the Lord's people', though such expressions were used by other Secession leaders. The Seceders also hoped to educate the youthful Whitefield, an ordained Church of England clergyman, in the truths of the Presbyterian system. Whitefield, however, refused to restrict his preaching to the Seceders or to embrace Presbyterianism; rather he insisted on preaching in established churches, in churchyards or in the fields—wherever he could find hearers. He was in consequence disowned by the Seceders, but his three-month preaching tour in 1741 had an immense impact.[22]

---

[21] Gavin Struthers, *The History of the Rise, Progress, and Principles of the Relief Church* (Glasgow, 1843), pp. 224, 569–71.
[22] D. Butler, *John Wesley and George Whitefield in Scotland* (Edinburgh, 1898), pp. 11–34.

He returned to Scotland the following year. Now his impassioned preaching contributed significantly to the revival movement which had begun a few months earlier in the Church of Scotland parish of Cambuslang. Attending the communion celebration at Cambuslang in July 1742, Whitefield preached to an estimated 20,000 gathered in the fields. In August, he spent three weeks in Cambuslang and nearby Kilsyth, preaching to vast, highly emotional crowds. The revival movement spread across Scotland, claiming thousands of converts.[23] The Seceders were furious over this 'Cambuslang Wark'. The Associate Presbytery held a day of fasting and humiliation in all their congregations in response to the revival, which they denounced as 'the delusions of Satan'. 'It is obvious', they proclaimed, 'that bitter outcryings, faintings, severe bodily pains, convulsions, voices, visions and revelations, are the usual symptoms of a delusive spirit.'[24] But many others in Scotland were profoundly affected by these emotive expressions of a personal, conversionist piety, associated with the transatlantic Awakening movement. Whitefield went on to make fourteen preaching visits to Scotland, with the last in 1768, though his later Scottish tours did not arouse the enthusiasm of the visits of 1741 and 1742.

John Wesley also sought to contribute to the Awakening to Scotland. The English Methodist leader visited Scotland no fewer than twenty-two times and sent a number of itinerant preachers. His first visit was in 1751. The Calvinist Whitefield had discouraged him, observing that 'you have no business there'.[25] Whitefield would have known that Wesley's Arminian theology and especially his doctrine of perfection would find little favour in Scotland. But Wesley persevered. By the early 1760s his preaching and organizational powers were beginning to gain Scottish supporters, and a number of Methodist societies were formed. Methodist hymns were proving especially popular among the Scots. Then came a Presbyterian backlash. In 1765, Wesley had published a revised version of James Hervey's *Theron and Aspasia*, a popular evangelical tract that challenged Calvinist teachings on election. The respected Edinburgh Church of Scotland evangelical minister, and strict Calvinist, John Erskine, responded to this with a fierce attack on Wesley's doctrine and the whole Methodist movement. Neither, Erskine insisted, was welcome in Calvinist Presbyterian Scotland. Erskine's denunciation of Wesley had an element of personal rancour; he denounced Wesley as an English intruder, a prelatist with Anglican ordination. Other Presbyterian polemicists joined in the assault, and Wesley and his itinerant preachers were thrown on the defensive across Scotland.[26] At the time of Wesley's death in 1791, there were in Scotland

---

[23] Ibid., pp. 34–43.
[24] McKerrow, *History of the Secession Church*, pp. 166–7.
[25] Margaret Batty, *Scotland's Methodists 1750–2000* (Edinburgh, 2010), p. 4.
[26] Ibid., pp. 14–19; Jonathan M. Yeager, *Enlightened Evangelicalism: The Life and Thought of John Erskine* (New York, 2011), pp. 113–26.

only sixteen Methodist preachers and about 1,200 members, divided among several meeting houses.²⁷ Yet while eighteenth-century Scottish Methodist numbers remained small, Whitefield and Wesley had contributed to the growth of more emotional, personal, conversionist forms of piety in Scotland, as expressed in part through the new popularity of hymns.

THE RELIEF CHURCH

There was another reason for the weakness of Methodism in Scotland from the 1760s. This was connected with a further secession from the Established Church of Scotland—a secession movement that was Presbyterian and Calvinist, but that did not look back to the Covenants, was more tolerant of other protestant beliefs, and shared many of the evangelical approaches of Whitefield and Wesley. The origins of this secession were to be found in the ongoing popular resistance to lay patronage within the parishes of the Church of Scotland. In 1751, the General Assembly instructed the Presbytery of Dunfermline to ordain a patron's candidate to the ministry of Inverkeithing, against the strong wishes of the parish community. When a majority of ministers in the Presbytery refused to ordain the patron's man, the General Assembly, under pressure from Scotland's governing elite, decided to make an example. It would depose one minister in the Presbytery, depriving him of his church, manse, income, and status. This example, the Assembly believed, would deter other ministers from any further resistance to the patronage law. For their victim, the Assembly chose Thomas Gillespie (1708–1774), the evangelical minister of Carnock, who had, unusually for a Scot at this time, been educated at the English Dissenting academy at Northampton and who had also been active in the Cambuslang Revival of 1742. Gillespie accepted his sentence with humility, although many viewed the proceedings as disgraceful. 'It is wonderful', wrote the American evangelical, Jonathan Edwards, from Massachusetts in November 1752 on learning the news, 'that a church which has itself suffered so much by persecution should be guilty of so much persecution.' Others predicted positive effects. 'I expect great good will come out of these confusions', observed Whitefield. 'Mr. Gillespie will do more good in one week now than before in a year.'²⁸ His supporters purchased a meeting house for him in nearby Dunfermline, where he continued to minister to a large congregation. Although driven out of the Established Church, he did not seek to join the Seceders, whose stern and rigid religion did not appeal to him. He retained his Presbyterian and Reformed convictions,

---

²⁷ Batty, *Scotland's Methodists*, p. 35.
²⁸ Struthers, *History of the Relief Church*, pp. 98–9, 111.

though with a refreshing liberality of spirit, which included inviting all Christians to join him in the sacrament of the Lord's Supper. 'I hold communion', he proclaimed as his motto, 'with all that visibly hold the Head [Christ].'[29]

Gillespie ministered to his Dunfermline congregation for several years without ministerial colleagues. But in time other Church of Scotland ministers and congregations, opposed to patronage but not sharing the rigid doctrines and attitudes of the Seceders, connected themselves with Gillespie's congregation. They included Thomas Boston, whose father had been a well-loved Church of Scotland minister and author of the influential devotional treatise, *Human Nature in its Fourfold State*. The younger Boston and his Jedburgh congregation had withdrawn from the Church of Scotland after a patronage dispute. In 1761, Gillespie, Boston, and another minister formed themselves into a presbytery 'for the relief of Christians oppressed in their Christian privileges' by patronage; this became the foundation of a new 'Relief Church'. Scotland now had a fourth Dissenting Presbyterian denomination, alongside the Reformed Presbyterian, the Burgher, and the Anti-Burgher Secession Churches. By the time of Gillespie's death in 1774, there were nineteen Relief Church congregations organized into two presbyteries.[30] The outlook of the Relief Church was liberal evangelical. The Relief Church officially adopted a policy of opposition to the slave trade in 1788, when its synod appointed a committee to coordinate anti-slavery activity.[31] It was active in home mission, especially among those outside any church connection, and it began sending itinerant evangelists to the Highlands in 1797. By 1800, their numbers had increased to sixty congregations and perhaps 36,000 adherents.[32]

QUAKERS, GLASSITES, OLD INDEPENDENTS, AND SCOTCH BAPTISTS

There had been Independents, Baptists, and Quakers in mid-seventeenth-century Scotland, connected with English soldiers and families in the Cromwellian army of occupation. Following the withdrawal of the Cromwellian army in the late 1650s, the Independents and Baptists had disappeared. The Quakers, however, abided in small meetings in some of the principal Scottish towns. They had experienced considerable persecution in later seventeenth-century Scotland, and a number had been imprisoned. When the British Parliament

---

[29] Ibid., p. 123.
[30] Kenneth B. E. Roxburgh, *Thomas Gillespie and the Origins of the Relief Church in 18th Century Scotland* (Bern, Switzerland, 1999), p. 173.
[31] Struthers, *History of the Relief Church*, p. 348.
[32] Roxburgh, *Thomas Gillespie*, p. 237.

passed an Affirmation Act for Scotland in 1714—allowing Quakers to affirm rather than take oaths in courts of law—conditions for Quakers improved. But the Society of Friends did not flourish in eighteenth-century Presbyterian Scotland, and their numbers remained small at about 1,500 adherents. Following a series of visits of the prominent English Quaker reformers, Elizabeth Fry and Joseph Gurney, from 1818, Scottish Quakers became increasingly active in prison reform.[33]

In the 1720s, a distinctively Scottish Independent or Congregational Church emerged, associated with John Glas (1695-1773), the Church of Scotland minister of Tealing, near Dundee. In the 1720s, Glas had come to reject the Presbyterian system and the alliance of Church and state, while arguing that there was no basis for the Covenants in the New Testament. A number of his parishioners accepted his views, and he formed in 1725 a small Congregational church, with about 100 members, within his parish (though he continued to claim his income and status as a minister of the Established Church). His congregation held monthly communion, instituted a fund for the poor, and had their own system of church discipline. When summoned before the Church of Scotland courts on charges of rejecting the Church's Presbyterian government and teachings, Glas appealed to Scripture, insisting that Congregationalism was the practice of the primitive church and should therefore be permissible in the Established Church. The General Assembly of the Established Church did not agree and deposed him from his ministerial charge in 1730.[34]

Soon after, Glas moved to Dundee where he established a second Independent congregation, while he also continued to preach regularly to the Tealing congregation. He became convinced that in primitive Christianity there had been several preaching elders in each congregation, while Scripture made no reference to university education or linguistic ability as qualifications for the eldership. So Glassite congregations appointed a plurality of preachers based solely on sound doctrine and ability to preach. Additional Glassite churches were formed in Perth in 1733, in Edinburgh in 1734, and then in several other towns. Each church was self-governing, and the preaching elders supported themselves as artisans or tradesmen. Glas exercised a general supervision, ensuring that the churches shared a common Calvinist theology, and similar practices in discipline and worship. By the mid 1760s, the Glassites had developed what for Scotland was an innovative liturgy, with weekly communion, the singing of hymns, and the kiss of charity (the subject of much ribaldry from critics), while lengthy sermons were replaced by shorter exhortations. Lists of the occupations of male members from the early 1770s show

---

[33] George B. Burnet, *The Story of Quakerism in Scotland 1650-1850* (London, 1952), pp. 13-173.

[34] J. T. Hornsby, 'The Case of Mr John Glas', *RSCHS*, 6, 2 (1938), pp. 115-37.

them to have been largely artisans—weavers, bleachers, tailors, shoemakers, tanners, blacksmiths, and printers—though with some small manufacturers and shopkeepers. Glas's son-in-law, Robert Sandeman (1718–1771), carried his congregational model to England, Wales, and New England, promoting the spread of what became known as Sandemanian churches. In Scotland, the Glassite movement was weakened by internal dissensions and a lack of evangelical fervour, and its membership remained very small.[35]

The later 1760s saw the emergence of another group of Scottish congregational churches, known as the Old Scottish Independents. It began with two Church of Scotland ministers, James Smith and Robert Ferrier, who had ministered to neighbouring parishes in Fife and had come under Glassite influence. Like the Glassites, they could find no Scriptural warrant for Presbyterianism, and in 1768 they left the Church of Scotland and founded a congregational church in the ancient Fife village of Balchristie, which tradition held had been the site of one of Scotland's first Christian churches. Their church resembled the Glassite churches, with a similar liturgy and organization, including a plurality of pastors, though they were less exclusive and did not accept Glas's leadership. A second Independent church was established in Glasgow in 1768; its chapel was built by a wealthy candlemaker and became known as the 'Candle Kirk'. Ferrier moved to Glasgow to become one of the elders, and David Dale (1739–1806), a successful textile merchant, was ordained as a second elder. Dale did much to win public acceptance in Glasgow for this small Independent church. A highly successful entrepreneur, he moved from importing textiles into producing cotton cloth, opening the New Lanark Mills in 1786. He developed a reputation as a benevolent master, providing decent housing and conditions for the workers, and establishing many of the programmes that would later be associated with his son-in-law, the early socialist, Robert Owen. Dale was also a partner in the establishment of the Blantyre cotton mills, where the Scottish Congregationalist and missionary, David Livingstone, worked as a child and benefitted from the educational opportunities. Dale became renowned as a philanthropist, donating large sums to charity, and importing grain to be sold cheaply to the poor during dearth years. And for over three decades he was an elder at the Candle Kirk, preaching regularly on Sundays and learning Greek and Hebrew to enrich his understanding of Scripture.[36] Several more Old Independent churches were formed by 1790. Another sect of Independents developed in central Scotland around the ministry of John Barclay (1734–1798), who left the Church of Scotland with his congregation over a patronage dispute

---

[35] J. T. Hornsby, 'John Glas: His Later Life and Work', *RSCHS*, 7, 2 (1941), pp. 94–113; Derek B. Murray, 'The Influence of John Glas', *RSCHS*, 22, 1 (1984), pp. 45–56.

[36] Harry Escott, *A History of Scottish Congregationalism* (Glasgow, 1960), pp. 24–36; Donald Beaton, 'The Old Scots Independents', *RSCHS*, 3, 2 (1929), pp, 135–45.

in 1773. Barclay helped to form several congregations in Scotland as well as in England. They took the name 'Bereans', after the early Christians at Berea who searched the Scriptures daily (Acts 17:11), and they sought to return to primitive Christian practices in all things. In 1823, the Bereans had congregations in Glasgow, Stirling, and Crieff.[37]

A small denomination known as Scotch Baptists developed in the 1760s, largely from former members of Glassite or Old Independent churches, who had become convinced of the doctrine of believer's baptism through English influences. A Scotch Baptist communion was formed in Edinburgh in 1765, when several members of the Old Independent church there were baptized by Robert Carmichael, an elder in the church, in the Water of Leith. Centres of Scotch Baptist worship emerged in Dundee in 1769, Montrose and Glasgow in 1770, and then in several other towns, where there were already Glassite or Old Independent churches. The Scotch Baptists, like the Quakers, Glassites, Old Independents, and Bereans, remained small in numbers and influence until the early nineteenth century.[38] All these churches were made up of people of independent minds, strong convictions, and often eccentric characters, who had taken a step not only out of the parish communities of the Established Church, but also out of the dominant Presbyterianism of Scotland, and who insisted on their right to do so.

RELIGION IN THE REVOLUTIONARY ERA

The social and political ferment of the 1790s, associated with the influences of the French Revolution and the social dislocations of early industrialization, contributed to the rapid growth of Dissent in Scotland. The democratic ideas associated with the French Revolution—including ideas of human equality, human rights and personal autonomy—strengthened the notion that individuals should be free to worship and express their beliefs in their own manner without deference to the authority of the Church by law established. These same democratic ideas encouraged new efforts to evangelize among the common people, to respect their human worth as beings with eternal possibilities, and to bring them to a genuine, life-changing Christian faith, as opposed to a nominal church adherence. The social impact of early industrialization, moreover, contributed to the growth of manufacturing districts with enlarged populations that were outside the influence of existing parish churches. The new industrial labouring classes, experiencing often

---

[37] Escott, *History of Scottish Congregationalism*, pp. 37–42.
[38] D. B. Murray, 'The Seventeenth and Eighteenth Centuries', in D. W. Bebbington, ed., *The Baptists in Scotland: A History* (Glasgow, 1988), pp. 9–25.

horrendous social conditions, could be deeply hostile to the established clergy, viewing them as too closely aligned with wealth and power in an unjust social order. For many working people, the Dissenting churches offered consolation, mutual support, independence, and hope for social betterment that were not to be found in the parish churches of the establishment.

The 1790s saw the birth of a vigorous new Scottish movement of evangelical Dissent associated with the Haldane brothers and the Congregational and Baptist churches. Robert (1764–1842) and James Haldane (1768–1851) were members of a Scottish landed family, and both had brief experience as naval officers. Robert was the eldest brother and inherited the large family estate near Stirling. Both brothers had experienced conversion in 1795 through the influence of the prominent English Independent minister, David Bogue. Robert had then wanted to lead a party of missionaries to India, but the East India Company discouraged missionary activity and the British government would not support him, as he was suspect for his liberal political views. So instead the Haldane brothers embraced the cause of home mission in Scotland. In 1797, James and two others, inspired by the work of English Dissenters, toured the Highlands and Islands, preaching in churches when open to them, or at market crosses, on roadsides, or in fields. James, who was handsome with a powerful voice and commanding personality, proved a popular lay preacher; his status as a gentleman attracted attention and his services gathered crowds of up to 4,000. He made a number of preaching tours of Scotland in the following years. In early 1798, he and his supporters formed the Society for Propagating the Gospel at Home, a non-denominational evangelical association which supported itinerant evangelists, promoted Sunday Schools, and distributed tracts. Robert sold a substantial part of the family estate and used the money to support home mission activity. In 1798, he purchased a former theatre in Edinburgh and turned it into a non-denominational preaching hall, or 'Tabernacle', with free sittings and a number of different preachers. Robert himself began lay preaching in the spring of 1798. The Edinburgh Tabernacle attracted large congregations, and Robert established similar Tabernacles in Glasgow, Dundee, Perth, Elgin, and Caithness.[39] Initially indifferent to denominational differences, the Haldanes and their close supporters, including the former Church of Scotland minister, Greville Ewing, became Congregationalists in late 1798, and their revival movement contributed to a major expansion of Scottish Congregationalism. Between 1800 and 1807, the number of Congregational churches in Scotland grew from 14 to 85.[40] Then in 1808, the Haldanes, ever restless and developing their theology as they went along, embraced a belief in adult baptism, and became Baptists. There

---

[39] A. Haldane, *The Lives of Robert Haldane of Airthey, and of his Brother, James Alexander Haldane* (Edinburgh, 1855), pp. 25–288.

[40] Escott, *History of Scottish Congregationalism*, p. 76.

was now a painful division in their revival movement, as the Haldanes forced Congregationalists out of the churches they supported financially. But at the same time, the Haldanes re-energized the Baptist movement in Scotland. There were forty-one Baptist churches in Scotland by 1810, twenty-three of them, over half, formed between 1808 and 1810. The Baptists became active in home mission, establishing the Baptist Home Missionary Society for Scotland in 1827.[41]

Within the Presbyterian Secession and Relief Churches, the revolutionary ferment, including the spread of liberal and egalitarian ideas, also contributed to growth and diversification. Many members of the Secession and Relief Churches initially welcomed the French Revolution (though they later turned from its violent excesses); in the early 1790s the Government regarded their loyalty as suspect.[42] The Secession and Relief Churches developed more evangelical attitudes and their numbers grew. By 1799, there were said to be 55,000 in the Burgher Secession Synod, 55,000 in the Anti-Burgher Secession Synod, and 36,000 in the Relief Church—in a Scottish population of about 1,526,000.[43] Within the Secession Churches, many developed new ideas—or as they put it, received 'new light'—concerning the teachings of the Westminster Confession of Faith on the civil magistrate and alliance of Church and state. Those receiving 'new light' became convinced, in part through the example of the new constitution in the United States, that the Covenants were outdated, that there should be a separation of Church and state, that toleration was a virtue, and that religious adherence should be 'voluntary', based on the decision of the believer. Their 'old light' opponents continued to believe in the Covenants and in the ideal of a close alliance of Church and state, even if they could not be part of the present 'corrupt' Established Church. But the new light party gained a majority in the Burgher Synod, which in 1799 embraced the 'voluntary' position. In consequence, the old light minority seceded—with the result that there was now a New Light Burgher Synod and an Old Light Burgher Synod. A similar new light movement gained dominance within the Anti-Burgher Synod, and the old light party seceded in 1806.[44]

The New Light Burgher Synod and New Light Anti-Burgher Synod united in 1820 to form the United Secession Church. The United Secession Church was Presbyterian and Calvinist, but also voluntary—believing that there should be a separation of Church and state, that church membership should be voluntary, that religion should be largely a matter of individual conscience,

---

[41] D. E. Meek and D. B. Murray, 'The Early Nineteenth Century', in Bebbington, ed., *Baptists in Scotland*, pp. 32, 37.

[42] Emma Vincent [Macleod], 'The Responses of Scottish Churchmen to the French Revolution, 1789–1802', *Scottish Historical Review*, 73, 2 (1994), pp. 206–7; Henry W. Meikle, *Scotland and the French Revolution* (Edinburgh, 1912), pp. 198–9.

[43] Struthers, *History of the Relief Church*, p. 408.

[44] McKerrow, *History of the Secession Church*, pp. 578–613.

and that all denominations should be equal under the law. This was a profound change from the position of the Secession fathers in 1733. The United Secession Church became increasingly liberal in its politics. In 1829, the Glasgow United Secession minister, Andrew Marshall, delivered and subsequently published an influential sermon, in which he openly denounced the principle of religious establishments and called for the disestablishment of the Church of Scotland. This was the opening salvo of what became known in Scotland as the 'Voluntary controversy' and the beginning of the prolonged nineteenth-century Scottish movement for disestablishment.

Scotland was a far more religiously diverse society in 1829 than it had been in 1690. At the end of the seventeenth century, virtually all Scots had been adherents of the national Church, the Church by law established. There had been little sense that Dissent should be permitted or that toleration was a virtue. With the gradual suppression of the Episcopalians, moreover, Scotland had become almost exclusively Presbyterian. Until about 1740, nearly all Scottish Dissenters had held to an ideal of a religiously uniform state, and had made subscription to the seventeenth-century Covenants a term of communion. By the end of the 1820s, however, the circumstances, composition, and attitudes of Scottish Dissent were very different. The social historian Callum Brown has determined that some 29 per cent of the entire Scottish population, and 32 per cent of the Scottish Lowland population, were now outside the Established Church. In some towns, levels of Dissent were much higher. In Jedburgh, for example, some 70 per cent of the population were Dissenters by the 1790s.[45]

While most Dissenters were Presbyterian, there was now a growing choice of Dissenting Presbyterian denominations—United Secession Church, Relief Church, Old Light Burghers, Old Light Anti-Burghers, and Reformed Presbyterians. There were also denominations of Congregationalists, Baptists, Methodists, Episcopalians, and Quakers. Adherence to the Covenants had waned and Scottish Dissent was increasingly voluntary. Men and women found that, if unhappy with their parish minister or the discipline of their parish church, they could step out of the parish community and join a Dissenting church without loss of social status or respectability. Indeed, to be outside the Established Church could show strength of character, courage of convictions, an unbending conscience, and an independent mind—traits highly respected in Scotland. The growth of eighteenth-century Dissent reflected the growing prosperity of Scotland, as more and more artisans, tradesmen, clerks, and small farmers could now afford to contribute to the maintenance of their own churches. The competition among the Churches, especially in the towns and cities, contributed to a dynamic in nineteenth-century Scottish

---

[45] Brown, *Religion and Society in Scotland since 1707*, p. 20.

religion. The established Church of Scotland continued to command considerable influence and authority, and it underwent a revival in its pastoral care and mission from about 1810. But even so it proved unable to revive the old idea of Scotland as a unified Christian commonwealth, or reverse the eighteenth-century growth and diversification of Dissent.[46]

SELECT BIBLIOGRAPHY

Batty, Margaret, *Scotland's Methodists 1750-2000* (Edinburgh, 2010).
Bebbington, D. W., ed., *The Baptists in Scotland: A History* (Glasgow, 1988).
Brown, Callum G., *Religion and Society in Scotland since 1707* (Edinburgh, 1997).
Burnet, George B., *The Story of Quakerism in Scotland 1650-1850* (London, 1952).
Butler, D., *John Wesley and George Whitefield in Scotland; or, The Influence of the Oxford Methodists on Scottish Religion* (Edinburgh, 1898).
Drummond, A. L. and Bulloch, J., *The Scottish Church 1688-1843: The Age of the Moderates* (Edinburgh, 1973).
Escott, Harry, *A History of Scottish Congregationalism* (Glasgow, 1960).
Goldie, Frederick, *A Short History of the Episcopal Church in Scotland* (Edinburgh, 1976).
Haldane, A., *The Lives of Robert Haldane of Airthey, and of his Brother, James Alexander Haldane* (Edinburgh, 1855).
Hutchison, Matthew, *The Reformed Presbyterian Church in Scotland: Its Origin and History 1680-1876* (Paisley, 1893).
MacEwen, A. R., *The Erskines* (Edinburgh, 1900).
MacKelvie, William, *Annals and Statistics of the United Presbyterian Church* (Edinburgh, 1873).
McKerrow, John, *History of the Secession Church* (Edinburgh, 1854).
Murray, Derek B., 'The Influence of John Glas', *Records of the Scottish Church History Society*, 22, 1 (1984), pp. 45-56.
Raffe, Alasdair, *The Culture of Controversy: Religious Arguments in Scotland 1660-1714* (Woodbridge, 2012).
Raffe, Alasdair, 'Presbyterians and Episcopalians: The Formation of Confessional Cultures in Scotland, 1660-1715', *English Historical Review*, 125, 514 (2010) pp. 570-98.
Roxburgh, Kenneth B. E., *Thomas Gillespie and the Origins of the Relief Church in 18th Century Scotland* (Bern, Switzerland, 1999).
Struthers, Gavin, *The History of the Rise, Progress, and Principles of the Relief Church* (Glasgow, 1843).

---

[46] The author wishes to thank Dr Alasdair Raffe for his very helpful suggestions on this chapter.

8

Protestant Dissent in Wales

Eryn White

The period between 1689 and 1828 witnessed a remarkable transformation in the religious affiliations of a large proportion of the people of Wales. Thomas Rees, the not precisely impartial historian of protestant Nonconformity in Wales, was able to declare in 1861 that 'the Welsh are now emphatically a nation of Nonconformists'.[1] This was in the wake of the 1851 Religious Census which demonstrated that the majority of worshippers in Wales attended nonconformist services rather than those of the established Anglican Church. That was a situation which had largely come about because of developments during the period in question. Welsh Nonconformists basked in their success by the second half of the nineteenth century because of some diligent efforts in the preceding centuries to maintain and to further protestant Dissent.

DISSENT IN 1689

With the passing of the Toleration Act in 1689, Dissenting congregations which had met secretly were able to register their meeting places and to worship without fear of persecution. Although the liberty granted fell far short of equality with the Anglican Church, never the less, life and worship were rendered considerably easier for most Dissenting groups. It may well have taken some time for the reality of their newfound freedom to sink in and for concerns that the situation might worsen again to abate. If Dissenting groups appear not to have been notably active in this period, it may well have been this trepidation and the need to adjust to their new circumstances which restricted them. During the years of persecution, arrangements had been

---

[1] Thomas Rees, *History of Protestant Nonconformity in Wales, from its Rise to the Present time* (London, 1861), p. 485.

difficult. Lines between denominations had become somewhat blurred, with Independents (or Congregationalists) and Presbyterians joining forces in some areas, and Independents and Baptists in others. The Llanigon Church in Breconshire and Radnorshire, led by Henry Maurice until his death in 1682, was one of those which included both Independents and Baptists, for instance, building on the itinerant mission of Vavasor Powell.[2] Rather than being distinct localized congregations, what were considered to be Dissenting 'churches' during the period of persecution had frequently consisted of a number of congregations, meeting at varying locations to avoid the attentions of the authorities, but with a single pastor in common. With the advent of toleration, as it became easier to sustain regular worship and to adhere to denominational principles about church organization, these loose federations of believers began to establish themselves as separate congregations allied to specific denominations with more permanent meeting houses.

Nevertheless, Dissenters in Wales comprised only a tiny minority of the population in the late seventeenth century. Evidence from the Compton Census, which may well have underestimated the strength of Dissenting support, suggests that the total number of Dissenters in 1676 was just over 4,200 compared to some 154,000 conformists, therefore around 1.15 per cent of the population.[3] The geographic distribution was quite uneven, with Swansea in the south and Wrexham in the north forming the two major centres of urban activity. Not surprisingly, the St David's diocese, as the largest in Wales, contained the highest total number of Dissenters, with some 2,400 listed, chiefly located in Breconshire and Carmarthenshire. However, large areas of the country experienced very little Dissenting activity, including the north-western counties. Some gradual growth was experienced in the years following the Toleration Act and by 1715 Dissenters may have amounted to an estimated 5.74 per cent of the population, largely based in the south of the country in Carmarthenshire, Glamorgan, and Monmouthshire, areas which were beginning to establish a tradition of religious and political radicalism.[4]

Of these Dissenters, the Independents boasted the highest level of support at the close of the seventeenth century and into the eighteenth century. They had benefitted greatly from some extremely energetic and dedicated ministers during the period of persecution, including Stephen Hughes, ejected from his living in Meidrim in 1661, who worked to maintain the churches in

---

[2] E. B. Underhill, ed., *The Records of a Church of Christ Meeting in Broadmead, Bristol* (Bristol, 1847), pp. 511–18; R. Tudur Jones, 'The Older Dissent of Swansea and Brecon', in Owain W. Jones and David Walker, eds, *Links with the Past: Swansea and Brecon Historical Essays* (Swansea, 1974), pp. 122–5.

[3] Thomas Richards, *The Religious Census of 1676* (London, 1927), p. 44; Geraint H. Jenkins, *Protestant Dissenters in Wales 1639–1689* (Cardiff, 1992), p. 58.

[4] Michael Watts, *The Dissenters: From the Reformation to the French Revolution* (Oxford, 1978), p. 510.

Carmarthenshire until his death in 1688 on the eve of toleration. The role of ministers ejected under the Act of Uniformity was often a crucial factor in maintaining some sort of Dissenting worship, even if illicit. Their efforts laid the foundation for a new generation of committed Independent ministers, such as Phylip Pugh, who led his congregations in north Cardiganshire for over fifty years between 1709 and 1760, apparently baptizing 680 children during that time.[5] The Presbyterians, who had quite often joined forces with the Independents during the period of persecution, did not prosper so well in the wake of toleration. Although a thread of Presbyterian influence continued to run through the Independent Church in Wales, by 1760 it was obvious that Independents and Presbyterians formed two separate camps, with the term 'Presbyterian' being increasingly attached to anti-Calvinist beliefs.

The Baptists in Wales, who had suffered rather more severe persecution than the Independents and Presbyterians during the pre-toleration period, were able to reforge their links with the London Association after 1689, with six churches remaining attached to that Association until the Western Association was formed in 1692. These included the church of Swansea, which comprised the remnants of the pioneering Ilston church established by John Miles, as well as the Rhydwilym church on the Pembrokeshire–Carmarthenshire border which had emerged during the period of persecution. By 1700 when the Welsh Association was formed, three new churches were added to the total, including Glandŵr, an offshoot of Rhydwilym.[6] In addition, Welsh Baptist authors embarked on a campaign to defend their principles against bitter criticism from Independents and Anglicans. This led to a public debate in 1692 between John Thomas, Llwyngrawys, on behalf of the Independents, and John Jenkins, Rhydwilym, for the Baptists.[7] The emphasis on adult baptism was one which caused considerable disquiet given the general consensus in favour of infant baptism and was an approach which Baptists upheld vigorously in print, in response to the publication of James Owen's *Bedydd Plant o'r Nefoedd* (*The Baptism of Children from Heaven*) in 1693.[8] The fact that Thomas Rees, who was an Independent minister, insisted on referring to them as 'the Anti-Pædobaptists' in his history of Nonconformity may be a sign of continued negativity.

Even so, it was without question the Quakers who had suffered most prior to 1689. Their lack of deference to their social superiors and the way their emphasis on the inner light seemed potentially to undermine biblical authority

---

[5] E. D. Jones, 'Phylip Pugh', *Diwinyddiaeth*, 15 (1964), pp. 62–9.

[6] T. M. Bassett, *The Welsh Baptists* (Swansea, 1977), pp. 48–52.

[7] Bassett, *The Welsh Baptists*, p. 73; R. Tudur Jones, *Congregationalism in Wales*, ed. Robert Pope (Cardiff, 2004), p. 88.

[8] Geraint H. Jenkins, *Literature, Religion and Society* (Cardiff, 1978), pp. 174–8; Geraint H. Jenkins, 'Goleuni Gwedi Torri Allan Ynghymry', in *Cadw Tŷ mewn Cwmwl Tystion* (Llandysul, 1990), pp. 88–101.

invariably aroused suspicion and resentment. Quakers were never very numerous in Wales, although there were pockets of influence in Merionethshire, Montgomeryshire, and Monmouthshire in particular. Their numbers were further reduced as many Quakers sought sanctuary on the other side of the Atlantic, drawn by the prospect of being able to worship freely in Pennsylvania. Between 1682 and 1700, some 2,000 left Wales for Pennsylvania, leaving the cause in Wales much depleted.[9] Half of the emigrants were drawn from the community of Merionethshire Quakers, leaving the cause there sadly reduced.[10] Strict rules regarding marriage to non-believers probably curtailed their numbers further during the eighteenth century. In general the story is one of decline during the eighteenth and early nineteenth centuries, as a result of the growth of the appeal of Methodism and of the many challenges presented by membership, including the emphasis on plainness and the disapproval of marrying outside of the community of Friends. Despite all these difficulties, they managed to retain a tenacious if minority presence.[11]

DEVELOPMENTS 1689–1737

From 1689 onwards, active recruitment seems to have been a slow process for the Dissenting groups in Wales, yet there were many important developments undertaken in this period which set the foundations for the future successes of Nonconformity in Wales. There was a trend in historical writing, set in train by Methodist writers in the eighteenth century, to decry the period prior to the Evangelical Revival in the 1730s as one of darkness and stagnation in the religious life of the Welsh people. More recent research has established beyond question that this period witnessed a good deal of activity, on behalf of both Anglicans and Dissenters, which helped contribute to the eventual outbreak of revival. These achievements centred on advances in publishing through the medium of Welsh and on improved standards of education.

One of the surely unforeseen consequences of the Act of Uniformity was the way it motivated ejected ministers to seek alternative ways of providing guidance for their former congregations. Several focused on the provision of education, either by acting as teachers themselves or by supplying instruction through devotional literature. As a result, Dissenters made a disproportionate contribution to Welsh print culture in the late seventeenth century, providing

---

[9] Jenkins, *Protestant Dissenters in Wales*, pp. 66–7.
[10] J. Gwynn Williams, 'The Quakers of Merioneth during the Seventeenth Century', *Journal of the Merioneth History and Record Society*, 8, 2 (1977–80), p. 122.
[11] Richard C. Allen, 'The Religious Society of Friends (Quakers)', in Richard C. Allen and David Ceri Jones, with Trystan O. Hughes, eds, *The Religious History of Wales* (Cardiff, 2014), pp. 61–4.

the impetus for an increase in the number of books published in Welsh in the 1670s and 1680s.[12] The work sponsored by the Welsh Trust, in particular, made a lasting contribution and was one of the most notable achievements of the pre-toleration period. The Trust was founded in 1674 by Thomas Gouge, the ejected minister of St Sepulchre in London, who was prompted by concern about what he heard of the state of religion and education in Wales.[13] Although some schools were set up under the auspices of the Trust, the chief contribution was the provision of religious literature through the medium of Welsh. By forging an alliance with Stephen Hughes, the ejected minister of Meidrim, Carmarthenshire, Gouge was able to implement a programme of publication, with Hughes identifying books which it would be beneficial to translate into Welsh, including works by Richard Baxter, Lewis Bayly, and William Perkins.[14] The greatest achievement of this printing initiative was undoubtedly the publication of a much needed new edition of the Welsh Bible in 1678, remarkable for having been edited and proofread by Stephen Hughes and Charles Edwards, two former ministers in the Anglican Church who were now Dissenters. Even more extraordinary was the fact that Hughes had actually been excommunicated previously for preaching at a conventicle and keeping school without a licence.[15] Edwards also produced his own, extremely influential, interpretation of Welsh religious history in the third edition of his *Y ffydd ddi-ffuant* (*The Unfeigned Faith*) which appeared in 1677.

The work of the Welsh Trust came to an end when Gouge died in 1681, although Hughes continued to fund publications in Welsh until his death in 1688. It would appear that some of the remaining funds from the Trust were transferred to the Society for Promoting Christian Knowledge (SPCK) when it was set up in 1699. The SPCK included Wales within its remit and shared common aims with the Trust, with a similar emphasis on the need to educate both through schools and printed works. Although it was a far more Anglican-orientated movement, Dissenters were also to benefit partially from the fruits of its philanthropy, particularly from its publishing campaign. As with the Welsh Trust, the SPCK schools had a limited impact because of the policy of teaching through the medium of English, possibly with an idea that this would be useful to the children in later life. It was, therefore, its publication campaign which also proved to be the most influential contribution to Welsh life. Despite choosing to establish schools in English, there seemed to be a tacit

---

[12] Jenkins, *Literature, Religion and Society*, p. 35.

[13] M. G. Jones, *The Charity School Movement: A Study of Eighteenth Century Puritanism in Action* (Cambridge, 1938), pp. 277–89.

[14] Geraint H. Jenkins, '"A lleufer dyn yw llyfr da": Stephen Hughes a'i Hoff Awduron', in J. Gwynfor Jones, ed., *Agweddau ar Dwf Piwritaniaeth yng Nghymru yn yr Ail Ganrif ar Bymtheg* (Lampeter, 1992), pp. 207–16.

[15] National Library of Wales (hereafter NLW), Records of the Church in Wales, SD/CCm/2; SD/CCB/6.

agreement that Welsh-medium literature should be produced in order to serve the needs of the large numbers of people with no knowledge of English. The SPCK was frequently responsive to the calls from its corresponding members in Wales for essential publications to be printed and distributed. In particular, it became the chief supplier of Bibles to the country, printing at least 80,000 copies by 1828.[16] The first edition it oversaw was the 1718 Bible, edited by Moses Williams, an Anglican clergyman, with 1,000 of the 10,000 printed copies distributed free to the poor. The year 1718 was notable for the history of printing in Wales in general, since it marked the launch of the first lawful printing press in the country. The licensing laws which limited the print industry to London, Oxford, and Cambridge finally lapsed in 1695, allowing Thomas Jones to establish his printing house in Shrewsbury soon after. Although that proved far more convenient for the printing and distribution of works in Welsh, it was the development of a print industry on Welsh soil which truly prompted the increase in publishing by the second half of the eighteenth century, which both encouraged, and in turn was boosted by the production of published materials aimed at raising levels of religious knowledge.

The unique contribution of Dissent in terms of education came in the form of the Dissenting academies. In Wales, these could be said to have been a particularly important development since the country had no university before Aberystwyth was founded in 1872. The academies thus offered the opportunity to acquire at least a measure of higher education without the added expense of having to journey to England or Scotland in order to achieve this. They undoubtedly also had a beneficial effect in raising standards of education more generally in the country, with several of the private schools which were set up by former students offering a rather better level of instruction than was available in many day schools before the further developments in elementary education during the nineteenth century. Despite the fact that the chief purpose of many of these academies was to prepare candidates for the Dissenting ministry in Wales, the Welsh language was never used as the medium of instruction.[17] It is difficult to know to what extent the language was used more informally as part of the instruction, given that some students may well have struggled with English, certainly initially. There would probably have been a greater awareness of the possible difficulties and it must have been easier in general for students to acclimatize to study in academies based in Wales.

---

[16] Eryn M. White, *The Welsh Bible* (Stroud, 2007), pp. 155–6.
[17] R. Tudur Jones, 'Nonconformity and the Welsh Language in the Nineteenth Century', in Geraint H. Jenkins, ed., *The Welsh Language and its Social Domains 1801–1911* (Cardiff, 2000), pp. 247–51.

The first Dissenting academy in Wales is believed to have been Brynllywarch, which was founded by the Presbyterian Samuel Jones at his home in Llangynwyd, near Bridgend, Glamorgan, by 1672, although an earlier date is possible. Jones had been removed as incumbent of the parish under the 1662 Act of Uniformity, so this was another example of how ejected ministers found alternative means of furthering the welfare of their former parishioners, leading to a far broader contribution to Welsh culture and society.[18] The earlier academies, like this one, tended to be located in Glamorgan and Monmouthshire, where Dissent was relatively well established. The first Baptist academy, for instance, was founded at Trosnant, near Pontypool, Monmouthshire in around 1730.[19] Academies were usually not sited in central locations, but were often to be found in rather more remote and rural areas. This was undoubtedly partly out of a desire to avoid any unwelcome attentions from the authorities, but also a consequence of the tendency to locate academies where it suited the individual tutor, with little regard for the convenience of students. Many tutors combined teaching with pastoral duties so required students to come to them. When Samuel Jones died in 1697, for instance, Roger Griffith took responsibility for his academy and moved it to Abergavenny.[20] Jones's academy can also be regarded as the precursor for the Carmarthen Presbyterian Academy, which was first established under William Evans c.1703 and received support from both the Presbyterian and Congregational Funds, but was often the subject of controversy and frequently regarded as a hotbed of radical ideas.[21] It was one of the earliest academies to settle within an urban environment, although Vavasor Griffiths as tutor insisted on moving the Academy to the more bucolic vicinity of Llwyn-llwyd in 1735 so as to remove students from the worldly temptations of Carmarthen town.[22] As a staunch Calvinist, Griffiths also hoped the move would dispel the growing Arminian atmosphere of the Carmarthen Academy. The Academy did return to the town for a time in 1743, but went through different incarnations before establishing itself permanently in Carmarthen from 1795.

[18] Thomas Richards, *Wales under the Indulgence 1672–1675* (London, 1928), 173–4; Geraint Dyfnallt Owen, *Ysgolion a Cholegau yr Annibynwyr* (Llandysul, 1939), pp. 3–5; D. R. L. Jones, 'Fame and Obscurity: Samuel Jones of Brynllywarch', *Journal of Welsh Religious History*, 1, 1 (1993), pp. 41–65.

[19] C. Mervyn Hinbury, *The South Wales Baptist College (1807–1957)* (Llandysul, 1957), pp. 11–14.

[20] H. P. Roberts, 'Nonconformist Academies in Wales (1662–1962)', *Transactions of the Cymmrodorion* (1928–9), pp. 14–15; Noel Gibbard, 'Roger Griffith's Academy, Abergavenny (1697–1702)', *Dissenting Academies Online: Database and Encyclopedia*, Dr Williams's Centre for Dissenting Studies, June 2011.

[21] Robert Pope, 'Defending the Faith: Theology in the Diocese of St Davids, c.1534–2000', in William Gibson and John Morgan-Guy, eds, *Religion and Society in the Diocese of St Davids 1485–2011* (Farnham, 2015), pp. 79–80.

[22] Dewi Eirug Davies, *Hoff Ddysgedig Nyth* (Swansea, 1976), pp. 40–1; Jones, *Congregationalism in Wales*, pp. 98–9.

As Nonconformity grew in support and confidence, it became far more common to find academies in more central locations, which often made it easier for students to find board and lodging nearby without having to be housed by their tutors. Burgeoning congregations also required a greater supply of ministers, so training colleges became even more essential to foster an informed ministry. The establishment of St David's College at Lampeter in 1827 to train Anglican clergy probably provoked a certain rivalry and a desire to ensure that Dissenting academies could continue to compete.[23] The academies were a significant element in improving educational standards and were of vital importance to the training of Dissenting ministers. Richard Price, who as a Dissenter was banned from attending university regardless of how intellectually capable he was, spent some time at Chancefield academy under Vavasor Griffiths in the 1730s, although he later moved to adopt a far more Arian theology than was taught there.[24] His father, Rees Price, of Ty'nton, was educated at Brynllywarch and inherited the care of the academy from Roger Griffith when the latter conformed in 1702. Since Price was a High Calvinist he was supported by the Congregational Fund Board rather than the Presbyterian Board.[25]

Despite the significance to the Dissenters of the academies, the major breakthrough in terms of popular literacy across Wales came with the circulating school system implemented by Griffith Jones, the rector of Llanddowror, Carmarthenshire, from around 1731 onwards. Jones was already a well-known figure as a result of his reputation as a highly influential preacher, capable of attracting large congregations in south-west Wales twenty years before the Evangelical Revival broke out. His reward was to be sternly rebuked by Bishop Adam Ottley for his temerity in crossing parish boundaries and transgressing against the conventions of the Church.[26] This did not deter him from launching an initiative to provide free basic instruction to all those who wished to learn to read the Bible, through the means of classes offered by peripatetic teachers who remained in a parish for a period of three months before moving on to another location. By concentrating on reading skills alone, at least in the first instance, it was possible to see impressive results within that short space of time. Such success would not have been feasible, however, were it not for Jones's decision to tutor pupils in their first language. In most regions of Wales, that meant conducting classes through the medium

---

[23] H. K. Archdale, *St David's College, Lampeter: Its Past, Present and Future* (Lampeter, 1952), pp. 10–12; D. T. W. Price, *A History of Saint David's University College, Lampeter*, vol. 1 (Cardiff, 1997).

[24] Davies, *Hoff Ddysgedig Nyth*, p. 101; D. O. Thomas, 'Price, Richard (1723–1791)', *Oxford Dictionary of National Biography*, Oxford University Press, 2004; online edn, May 2005 [http://www.cxforddnb.com/view/article/22761, accessed 4 Sept. 2015].

[25] Roberts, 'Nonconformist Academies', p. 15.

[26] NLW, Ottley Papers 100.

of Welsh, although English schools were also the norm in more anglicized areas such as Radnorshire and north Pembrokeshire. The teachers worked long hours, holding evening classes for those who were occupied during the day, as well as day classes for younger pupils. The aim was quite simply to ensure that people could read the Bible and thus come to a better understanding of the Christian faith. Since that was the sole consideration, it was immaterial which language was held to be the most useful for social and economic purposes. By the time of Jones's death in 1761, at least 200,000 pupils had been educated, out of an estimated population of some 450,000.[27] Despite this, the schools did not lack critics and there were those who accused Jones of nurturing Methodism and social revolution. To help defend against such allegations, Griffith Jones was persistent in seeking and publishing letters of approbation from parish clergy testifying to the beneficial effects of the schools on their parishioners. Yet, as it transpired, there was an underlying element of truth in the snide remarks of opponents who accused Jones of being a Methodist pope, since the increased levels of literacy brought about by the circulating schools did benefit the Methodist cause. Jones himself, although the source of sound and frequently blunt advice to the young Methodist leaders, never strayed from his loyalty to the Church and was often concerned that any association with the revival would damage the reputation of his schools, which relied on charitable donations for their survival.

THE IMPACT OF THE EVANGELICAL REVIVAL

The leaders of the Methodist revival were also all staunch members of the Anglican Church. William Williams had actually been raised in an Independent chapel before seeking deacon's orders in the Church following his conversion, abandoning his previous intention of a career in medicine at the same time.[28] The first permanent Methodist societies began to be established from 1737 onwards under the influence of Howel Harris in Breconshire and Daniel Rowland in Cardiganshire. The movement spread quite quickly to the counties of Carmarthenshire, Glamorgan, Radnorshire, Monmouthshire, and Pembrokeshire, although north Wales presented a greater challenge. Most of the early support for Methodism was to be found in rural areas, with societies often located in relatively remote farmhouses, close enough to other settlements to recruit members, but not too close to centres of authority to be the targets of persecution. Some magistrates were prepared to regard Methodist

---

[27] Geraint H. Jenkins, '"An Old and Much Honoured Soldier": Griffith Jones, Llanddowror', *Welsh History Review*, 11, 4 (1983), p. 465.

[28] Glyn Tegai Hughes, *Williams Pantycelyn* (Cardiff, 1983), pp. 2–3.

societies as contravening the terms of the Conventicles Act which still remained in force after the passing of the Toleration Act. As long as the societies were not registered as Dissenting meeting houses they were vulnerable to such attack, despite the leaders' arguments that Methodists were assembling as members of the Church and not providing alternative places of worship. Itinerant Methodist preachers might also find themselves arrested as vagrants or snatched by a press gang.

The new movement certainly awakened old memories of the religious and social upheaval of the previous century, with Methodist preachers in north Wales being abused as 'Roundheads'. Despite that, the level of persecution was by no means as fierce as that experienced by early Dissent, partly because of a lack of systematic response from either Church or secular authority in Wales and partly because the movement may well not have been perceived as a major threat in the 1730s and 1740s as it began to establish itself in the country. Support was limited and growth was gradual. The leaders insisted on adherence to the articles of the Church of England and urged members to continue to take communion and attend services in their parish churches. It hardly seemed likely at the outset that the end result of the revival would be the creation of a new nonconformist denomination. Indeed, it was by no means certain that the movement would survive to see the end of the century, given the bitter division which emerged by 1750. It was the new wave of revival in 1762 which really set the movement on the path to lasting success throughout Wales and set the pattern of revivalism which would continue at fairly regular intervals until the 1904–5 revival.

The Methodist influence was initially afforded a warm welcome by a number of Dissenters who had been hoping for some revitalization of religion. The wise and generous Independent minister, Phylip Pugh, offered Daniel Rowland valuable advice about how to tailor his message to his audience.[29] Howel Harris was contacted by several Dissenting ministers in the late 1730s, encouraging him to visit their areas to help spread the revival, including the Independents Rees Davies of Abergavenny, David Williams of Pwll-y-pant in Glamorgan, Edmund Jones of Pontypool, Henry Davies of Blaen-gwrach in Glamorgan, James Davies of Merthyr, and James Lewis of Pencader, Carmarthenshire.[30] Collaboration with Independents was perhaps easier than with the Baptists since there was no issue over baptism to be addressed. Indeed the Independents, Henry Palmer, Rees Davies, and John David, pleaded with Harris to visit Pembrokeshire to help counteract the preaching of the

---

[29] D. J. Odwyn Jones, *Daniel Rowland Llangeitho (1713–1790)* (Llandysul, 1938), p. 19.

[30] NLW, Calvinistic Methodist Archive (hereafter CMA), Trevecka MSS 100, Rees Davies to Howel Harris, 20 Aug. 1737; 112, David Williams to Howel Harris, 12 June 1738; 119, Edmund Jones to Howel Harris, 10 Aug. 1738; 122, Henry Davies to Howel Harris, 21 Sept. 1738; 138, James Davies to Howel Harris, 13 Jan. 1739; 218, James Lewis to Howel Harris, 8 Feb. 1740.

Baptist John Powell who 'daily pours out threatenings against that holy doctrine of Baptism of children'.[31] Even so, friendly overtures were received from Baptists such as Miles Harry of Pontypool and William Herbert of Trosgoed.[32]

However, there were some early indications of possible tensions, for example when Miles Harry reported in 1739 that Harris was suspected of not operating in the best interests of the Dissenters.[33] Despite their agreement over Calvinist theology, there were other issues which divided the Methodists from mainstream Dissenting opinion at that time. One of those was the doctrine of assurance, which the evangelicals maintained was an essential element of spiritual rebirth. As David Bebbington explains, 'Whereas the Puritans had held that assurance is rare, late and the fruit of struggle in the experience of believers, the Evangelicals believed it to be general, normally given at conversion and the result of simple acceptance of the gift of God.'[34] Phylip Pugh was moved to write to the Methodist Association stating his conviction that such assurance was not a necessary prerequisite for salvation.[35] Howel Harris was deeply concerned to hear that David Williams preached that one might be a good Christian and not know it.[36] The question of church order also inevitably caused difficulties as the Methodists clung to the structure of the Anglican Church, as Harris noted: 'I see I know nothing about Church Government but it seems that Independency to me is not right.'[37] The very presence of Dissenters in Methodist societies led to fears that they might draw members away from the Church. By the end of 1740, Harris was concerned that some of his 'spiritual Children' were turning to the Dissenters 'who I fear are dry'd up'.[38] There was some cause for these suspicions, given that some individuals and, indeed, entire societies turned to Dissent, such as the Groes-wen, Aberthin, and New Inn societies in 1745, 1749, and 1751. James William, who superintended a number of Carmarthenshire societies, reported in 1745 that there were far fewer tensions in societies from which the Dissenters had departed than in those where they remained.[39] By that point, the break with the Dissenters was quite clear, with some ill-feeling remaining. David Williams wrote to Harris in 1747 for the first time in seven years to

---

[31] NLW, CMA, Trevecka MS 231, Henry Palmer, Rees Davies, and John David to Howel Harris, 22 Mar. 1740.
[32] NLW, CMA, Trevecka MSS 187, Miles Harry to Howel Harris, 1 Sept. 1739; 92, William Herbert to Howel Harris, 8 Jan. 1737.
[33] NLW, CMA, Trevecka MS 165, Miles Harry to Howel Harris, 23 June 1739.
[34] David Bebbington, *Evangelicalism in Modern Britain: A History from the 1730s to the 1980s* (London, 1989), p. 43.
[35] NLW, CMA, Diaries of Howel Harris, 66, 19 Dec. 1740.
[36] NLW, CMA, Trevecka MS 303, David Williams to Howel Harris, c.25 Dec. 1740.
[37] NLW, CMA, Diaries of Howel Harris, 82, 2 Dec. 1741.
[38] NLW, CMA, Diaries of Howel Harris, 66, 16 Dec. 1740.
[39] NLW, CMA, Trevecka MS 3023, pp. 8–9.

accuse him of having taking advantage of the goodwill shown to him by Dissenters such as himself. He claimed that once Harris and the Methodists had gained a foothold in an area through the invitation of local Dissenters, he summarily discarded them as he had no further need of their help.[40]

Despite this parting of the ways, there was no doubt that the spirit of revival had infected many amongst the Dissenting groups. Some who sought ordination amongst the Dissenters had been inspired to turn to religion by Methodist preaching. The career of John Thomas of Rhayader, outlined in his spiritual autobiography, *Rhad Ras (Free Grace,* 1810), combines many of the major influences which went into the revitalization of Dissent in the mideighteenth century: he was converted under the influence of Harris, was taken on as a schoolmaster by Griffith Jones, and was encouraged to begin preaching by Daniel Rowland, before being ordained as an Independent. Some of the features of Methodist meetings became common amongst the Dissenters as well, including energetic preaching and fervent singing, as well as emotional responses to both.[41]

Although there seemed to be a closer interplay between the Methodists and the Independents, the Baptists were by no means unaffected. The denomination undoubtedly gained in confidence during the eighteenth century and produced some remarkably effective preachers, with Christmas Evans probably the most renowned of them. By 1777, the Baptists in south Wales felt sufficiently inspired to commence a missionary programme to north Wales, where it had previously experienced little success. Several preaching tours led to sufficient converts to have established nine churches in the north by 1790. At that point the Association divided itself into three: the south-eastern Association overseeing nineteen churches, the south-western caring for eighteen churches, and the considerably smaller northern Association left to fend for itself.[42] The Welsh Baptist Association seems previously to have exercised a rather distant oversight, with individual churches acting independently in most respects. Those churches were united in several aspects of doctrine which marked them as distinctive from other religious groups at that time, despite their conforming to the prevailing belief in Calvinist theology. Apart from the thorny issue of infant baptism, Baptists in Wales adhered to the practice of closed communion, which, although not always strictly enforced during the eighteenth century, seemed to have become the norm by the early nineteenth century. The question of the imposition of hands in addition to baptism also caused considerable debate throughout the eighteenth century and proved difficult to resolve. However, it was towards the end of the

---

[40] NLW, CMA, Trevecka MS 1268, undated, 1747.
[41] E. Wyn James, 'The Evolution of the Welsh Hymn', in Isabel Rivers and David Wykes, eds, *Dissenting Praise: Religious Dissent and the Hymn in England and Wales* (Oxford, 2011), pp. 239–68.
[42] Bassett, *The Welsh Baptists*, p. 107.

eighteenth century that the greatest controversies emerged over doctrinal differences and between those who accepted the evangelical influence and those like J. R. Jones who were unalterably opposed.[43] By the start of the nineteenth century, however, the Baptists seemed to manage to put these divisions behind them and to forge ahead with renewed confidence and sense of purpose.

TENSIONS AND DOCTRINAL DIFFERENCES

It was a sign of the tensions which could still arise in connection with Dissent that two Baptist ministers in Pembrokeshire, Henry Davies of Llangloffan and John Reynolds of Solfa, were suspected of having aided and abetted the French landing at Fishguard in 1797. No evidence could be found against either, but an effigy of Davies was burnt at Fishguard fair. Two Dissenting farmers from the area, Thomas John, a Baptist, and Samuel Griffith, an Independent, were held in Haverfordwest gaol for seven months before being found not guilty of treason at trial. William Richards, a Welshman who was a Baptist minister at King's Lynn, felt compelled to defend the honour of the Dissenters who had been thus falsely accused in his *Cŵyn y Cystuddiedig* (*Complaint of the Afflicted*, 1798).[44] The Methodists were also impelled to take up their pens to protest their loyalty to Crown and government, in contrast with some of the more radical Dissenting groups who espoused political reform as a means to gain greater freedom of conscience. Thomas Jones published *A Word in Season* in 1798 and Thomas Charles *Welsh Methodists Vindicated; In Answer to the Accusations against them* in 1801, two popular publications which demonstrated the conservative political attitude of the Methodists.[45]

Whatever differences there might be amongst the various groupings of Old Dissent and New Methodism when it came to their response to the affairs of this world, they were united in their defence of Calvinist doctrine and their opposition to the influence of Arminianism.[46] This had been a growing trend from the early eighteenth century, with concerns mounting over the Arminian atmosphere in the Carmarthen Academy. William Williams, Pantycelyn, had himself been brought up in the Independent Church of Cefnarthen which

---

[43] D. Densil Morgan, 'Christmas Evans and Nonconformist Wales', in *Wales and the Word: Historical Perspectives in Religion and Welsh Identity* (Cardiff, 2008), pp. 22–3.

[44] Bassett, *The Welsh Baptists*, p. 111; Geraint H. Jenkins, 'Glaniad y Ffrancod yn Abergwaun yn 1797', in *Cadw Tŷ mewn Cwmwl Tystion*, pp. 270–1.

[45] Marion Löffler, 'Thomas Charles a gwleidyddiaeth y Methodistiaid', in D. Densil Morgan, ed., *Thomas Charles o'r Bala* (Cardiff, 2014), pp. 99–104.

[46] Robert Pope, 'Defending the Faith', in Gibson and Morgan-Guy, eds, *Religion and Society in the Diocese of St Davids*, pp. 74–5.

developed a strong Arminian faction leading to a division in the church by 1740.[47] One development which, therefore, caused widespread concern was the emergence of Unitarianism. Anti-Trinitarians were viewed with suspicion by the authorities and were not granted the same rights as other protestant Dissenters under the terms of the Toleration Act. In Wales, their origins owed much to the establishment of Dissenting academies which could at times act as nurseries for more radical theological ideas. However, this radical, rational trend in theology never managed to mount a truly successful challenge to the prevailing Calvinism and failed to spread across the country as widely as other forms of Dissent. Its emphasis on independent thought presented difficulties in a poorly educated population and its attitude to the divinity of Christ may well have aroused fears of blasphemy. Unitarianism was largely confined to the south-west and to Glamorgan, where it established itself in towns such as Aberdare and Merthyr Tydfil. Even within the south-west, its spread was uneven, with the county of Cardiganshire forming the main focus.

The roots of the Unitarian cause in Cardiganshire can be traced back to Jenkin Jones, who had been a student at the Carmarthen Academy under Thomas Perrot, a former pupil of James Owen. Jones was forbidden to preach from the pulpit of the Independent church of which he was a member at Pantycreuddyn, near Llandysul in Cardiganshire, as a result of the disquiet caused by his Arminian tendencies. He went on to preach and conduct services in his home from 1726 before founding the first Arminian chapel in Wales in 1733 at Llwynrhydowen, near Lampeter, in Cardiganshire.[48] A remarkably tenacious stronghold was established in Cardiganshire in the form of a total of thirteen churches by the end of the nineteenth century in an area near the river Teifi between Llandysul and Lampeter along the Carmarthenshire–Cardiganshire border and heading westwards towards the coast. This close geographical grouping was largely created by the fact that many of the chapels were offshoots of the earliest causes at Llwynrhydowen and Alltyblaca. After Jones's death in 1742, his nephew, David Lloyd (or Llwyd), led the Arminian chapels further towards Arianism. In addition, some of Phylip Pugh's Independent chapels, located nearby, adopted Arminian principles after Pugh's death in 1760, including Caeronnen, Cilgwyn, and Ciliau Aeron. By 1802, two new, self-proclaimed Unitarian chapels were established at Pantydefaid and Capel-y-groes.[49] The result was a group of chapels by the early nineteenth century who were determined in their adherence to slightly differing shades of Arminian, Arian, and Unitarian beliefs. The

---

[47] Jones, *Congregationalism in Wales*, pp. 105–6.
[48] D. Elwyn Davies, *Y Smotiau Duon* (Llandysul, 1980), pp. 44–5.
[49] Geraint H. Jenkins, 'The Established Church and Dissent', in Geraint H. Jenkins and Ieuan Gwynedd Jones, eds, *Cardiganshire County History, Volume 3: Cardiganshire in Modern Times* (Cardiff, 1998), pp. 472–4.

area was dubbed the 'Black Spot' by the Calvinistic Methodists, who must have felt considerable chagrin at the existence of a seemingly impregnable outpost of rational Dissent located in an area a mere twenty miles or so from the major Methodist centre of Llangeitho.

The first Unitarian cause in Carmarthenshire, which was established in 1792 in Cwm Cothi, can be deemed in effect to be yet another offshoot of the Cardiganshire base, since its founder, Thomas Evans (Tomas Glyn Cothi), grew up not far from the chapels of Llwynrhydowen and Alltyblaca, which he attended as a boy. Unitarianism held its own in its stronghold in Cardiganshire for a number of reasons.[50] This close-knit, self-sufficient farming community remained very stable, with few of its inhabitants choosing to leave the area, so the chapels could usually count on the support of the next generation. In the absence of powerful landowners, farming families in these parishes perhaps had greater freedom to adopt a rather more independent attitude towards their choice of religion. In addition, the Carmarthen Academy was relatively close at hand to provide training for local candidates for the ministry who might then return to act as pastors in the area. As a result of all these factors, therefore, although the Unitarian cause did not spread extensively or grow very much numerically, it maintained a constant presence. It could also boast some leading political radicals among its members, including Iolo Morganwg (or Edward Williams) and Tomos Glyn Cothi (or Thomas Evans), who was pilloried and gaoled for sedition in 1801.[51]

The other religious cause which could be considered to be in direct competition with Calvinistic Methodism was Wesleyan Methodism. This brand of Methodism had not flourished in eighteenth-century Wales as its Calvinistic counterpart had done. Despite early hopes of cooperation between both sides, the doctrinal differences quickly proved too great a gulf to bridge. The Welsh Methodist leaders were led to a large extent by George Whitefield's response in 1741 to John Wesley's sermon 'Free Grace' (1739), which confirmed the fundamental difference in their approach to the question of salvation. When Howel Harris attended the Foundery Society in London as a guest of Charles Wesley in June 1741, he found himself shouted down by cries of 'Christ died for all'.[52] Although Harris referred to the Wesley brothers' opposition to the doctrine of election as 'a hellish infection', he continued to hope that by

---

[50] Euros Lloyd, 'Datblygiad Undodiaeth yn Ardal y Smotyn Du', *Ceredigion*, 15, 4 (2008), pp. 58–66; Euros Lloyd, 'Unitarianism', in Allen and Jones, eds, *The Religious History of Wales*, pp. 115–23.

[51] Geraint H. Jenkins, '"A Very Horrid Affair": Sedition and Unitarianism in the Age of Revolutions', in R. R. Davies and Geraint H. Jenkins, eds, *From Medieval to Modern Wales: Historical Essays in Honour of Kenneth O. Morgan and Ralph A. Griffiths* (Cardiff, 2004), pp. 175–96.

[52] S. T. Kimbrough and Kenneth F. C. Newport, eds, *The Manuscript Journal of Charles Wesley, MA* (Nashville, TN, 2008), pp. 315–17.

emphasizing the factors which united them and downplaying their differences, they could remain allies of sorts.[53] That proved extremely difficult to establish in practice and the two sides effectively parted ways from 1741. The Wesleys continued to visit Wales; in addition to passing through en route to or from Ireland, John Wesley visited on a total of thirty-five occasions after 1739.[54] However, his influence was inevitably restricted by his inability to communicate with a largely monoglot Welsh-speaking population. Wesley famously bemoaned the curse of the 'confusion of tongues' on one of his visits to the country and greeted English-speaking areas such as Gower with tangible relief: 'Here all the people talk English and are in general the most plain, loving people in Wales. It is therefore no wonder that they receive the word with all readiness of mind.'[55] Wesleyan Methodism was therefore chiefly confined to the more anglicized regions of the country and suffered from a lack of leaders and preachers who could communicate effectively through the medium of Welsh.

A significant development in the history of Nonconformity in Wales was the renewed missionary efforts of Wesleyan Methodism in the early nineteenth century. A more concerted effort to make use of the Welsh language and to establish new causes in Welsh-speaking areas began in the early nineteenth century, following a proposal to the Methodist Conference in London in 1800 by the Brecon-born Thomas Coke, who argued for the use of the Welsh language in order to recruit effectively.[56] As a result, Owen Davies and John Hughes were sent to Ruthin where the twenty-one-year-old Edward Jones of Bathafarn had already registered a Methodist meeting in a room in the town. Neither Davies nor Hughes were particularly fluent Welsh speakers, but were able to rely on the support of local preachers Edward Jones and John Bryan. By 1810, the Welsh-speaking mission had made considerable and rapid inroads in the north east, boasting sixty chapels with 5,549 members, whilst further circuits were established in mid and south Wales during the early nineteenth century. Building on these foundations enabled the Wesleyan cause to establish itself as the fourth of the leading nonconformist denominations in Wales by the mid nineteenth century.

---

[53] NLW, CMA, Trevecka MS 283, Howel Harris to George Whitefield, 27 Oct. 1740.
[54] A. H. Williams, *John Wesley in Wales, 1749–1790* (Cardiff, 1971), pp. 130–1.
[55] Williams, *John Wesley in Wales*, pp. 36, 71.
[56] Rees, *History of Protestant Nonconformity*, pp. 448–50; A. H. Williams, *Welsh Wesleyan Methodism 1800–1858* (Bangor, 1935), p. 45; Glyn Tegai Hughes, 'Welsh-Speaking Methodism', in Lionel Madden, ed., *Methodism in Wales: A Short History of the Welsh Tradition* (Llandudno, 2003), pp. 23–9.

THE CALVINIST METHODIST CHURCH AND THE GROWTH OF NONCONFORMITY

The rapid growth of a Welsh-speaking form of Arminian Methodism almost inevitably caused some disquiet to Calvinistic Methodism, which, at the time of these early Wesleyan incursions into north Wales, had yet to join the ranks of the Nonconformists. Thomas Rees noted that there were 171 nonconformist congregations in Wales in 1775 and 993 by 1816.[57] Whether or not his calculations are strictly accurate, the dramatic increase depicted by these statistics certainly took place during this period. This was largely the result of the secession of the Calvinistic Methodists from the Anglican Church, which occurred in 1811, and was one of the major factors in the swelling of the total numbers of Nonconformists in Wales by the religious census of 1851. The first generation of leaders remained adamantly opposed to separation, insisting on their adherence to the Thirty-Nine Articles of the Church. Yet, there were tensions almost from the outset, with some of the movement's lay preachers frequently chafing against the decision not to allow them to become ordained ministers and to register the societies as meeting houses. In some ways, departure from the Church may seem to have been virtually inevitable from the point in the 1740s when the movement first set up the Association as its governing body. This meant in effect that the structure for a separate denomination had already been in place for years by the time the movement finally decided to ordain its own ministers in the summer of 1811 and to establish itself in the Court of Chancery in 1826 as the Calvinistic Methodist Church of Wales. The decision to separate came as a result of the extreme difficulty in providing members of the Methodist movement with the sacraments of baptism and communion whilst having to continue to rely on sympathetic Anglican clergy. This predicament was particularly acute in north Wales, where only three ordained clergymen served the needs of all the Methodist causes. Lay preachers, who acted as careful pastors to their flocks in all other ways, were crying out for the opportunity to provide these additional, vitally important services. Thomas Charles, who had inherited the mantle of leadership after the deaths of Daniel Rowland and William Williams in 1790 and 1791, was finally persuaded of the need to ordain ministers by the arguments of several senior figures in the movement. There were a number of Methodist-orientated Anglican clergy who could not countenance this step and so parted company with the Methodist cause at this point, forming the basis for an evangelically inclined group within the Church.

The last of the major nonconformist groups to take shape, the Calvinistic Methodists were also slow to develop training for prospective ministers, partly

---

[57] Rees, *History of Protestant Nonconformity*, p. 485.

because of the emphasis they placed on the precedence of the work of the spirit. Despite this rather sceptical attitude, many prominent Methodists had benefitted from the education supplied by the academies. Both Howel Harris and William Williams attended the academy at Llwyn-llwyd, near Hay-on-Wye, although Williams may actually have attended the academy at its location at Chancefield, near Talgarth, which is where he heard Harris preach the sermon which led to his conversion.[58] Thomas Charles spent six years at Carmarthen Academy, during which time he was converted as a result of hearing a sermon preached by Daniel Rowland in 1773.[59] Lewis Edwards was famously reduced to tears in an association meeting in 1830 when he asked permission to attend London University and was cuttingly rebuked from the chair by Thomas Richard for displaying such pride.[60] Edwards would later go on to establish the first denominational training college for the Calvinistic Methodists at Bala in north Wales, demonstrating a growing awareness of the need for an educated, as well as an inspired, ministry.

It was also only in 1823 that the Calvinistic Methodist Church produced a Confession of Faith, a development which had been resisted for some time on the basis that the articles of the Church of England were quite sufficient. The forty-four articles of the Confession were decided upon by a committee at Aberystwyth working on drafts produced by two separate groups of representatives from south and north Wales. Although some articles, including that on redemption, proved somewhat contentious, there was widespread approval for the published *Confession* within the Connexion. According to Densil Morgan, it was 'more Christologically based than the Westminster symbol and a more balanced and satisfying treatment of the substance of the faith'.[61]

The *Confession of Faith* was but one example of the swelling stream of publications being produced by the various denominations with the intention both of informing their membership and of fostering in them a sense of an exclusive, united identity. The first religious journal was *Trysorfa Ysprydol*, edited by Thomas Charles and Thomas Jones, which appeared for the first time in 1799. It sought to replicate the success of the *Evangelical Magazine* in English and its format was in turn emulated by other denominational publications. The Wesleyan *Yr Eurgrawn* first appeared in 1809, the Baptist *Seren Gomer* in 1814, and the Independent *Y Dysgedydd* from 1832.[62] Most

---

[58] Davies, *Hoff Ddysgedig Nyth*, pp. 123–4.

[59] Thomas Jones, *Cofiant neu Hanes Bywyd a Marwolaeth Thomas Charles* (Bala, 1816), p. 161.

[60] Thomas Charles Edwards, *Bywyd a Llythyrau y Diweddar Barch. Lewis Edwards* (Liverpool, 1891), pp. 37–8.

[61] D. Densil Morgan, 'Theology among the Welsh Calvinistic Methodists, c.1811–1914', in John Gwynfor Jones, ed., *The History of Welsh Calvinistic Methodism, III: Growth and Consolidation (c.1813–1914)* (Cardiff, 2013), p. 76.

[62] Aled G. Jones, *Press, Politics and Society: A History of Journalism in Wales* (Cardiff, 1993), pp. 1–2.

were begun as the initiatives of individuals and were later adopted as official periodicals by the denominations, as was the case with *Seren Gomer*, edited by the Baptist minister Joseph Harris ('Gomer') and finally adopted as an official Baptist publication in 1880.[63] The launching of these periodicals in the early nineteenth century was the first sign of the substantial growth in denominational publishing through the medium of Welsh which would characterize the mid to late nineteenth century.

Why Wales should prove to be more fruitful ground for Nonconformity than England is difficult to determine with absolute certainty. The Anglican Thomas Phillips suggested in 1849 that two very different explanations were commonly proposed, neither of which he found satisfactory: 'one consists in attributing to the Welsh people more gross immorality and fanatical ignorance, joined to lofty spiritual pretensions, than is found in any other part of Europe; and the other, of claiming for them an amount of piety, good morals and religious information unequalled in any other country'.[64] Contemporary commentators—Joshua Thomas, Edmund Jones, Christmas Evans, and Robert Jones of Rhoslan—sought to identify the chief factors in its growth and invariably emphasized evangelical preaching. Its greatest proponents, such as Daniel Rowland, Christmas Evans, John Elias, and William Williams of Wern, became figures of renown who could attract audiences of several thousands, some of the largest mass meetings to assemble in Wales at that time. Such preaching was doubtless the means of attracting large numbers to the Methodists and Dissenters in the first instance and periodic outpourings of revival helped replenish the membership by attracting new converts, as well as renewing the commitment of existing members. The revivalist tradition with its vigorous preaching and heartfelt communal singing thus became a characteristic of Welsh Nonconformity from the second half of the eighteenth century onwards.[65] In addition, the whole network of prayer and fellowship meetings which grew up as part of chapel culture not only helped sustain individuals in their faith but also provided them with relatively rare social opportunities.

It was also frequently the nonconformist denominations which offered opportunities for education through the medium of Welsh. The Sunday Schools filled the vacuum left behind by the demise of the circulating schools after the deaths of both Griffith Jones in 1761 and his successor Bridget Bevan in 1777. Although inextricably linked in Wales with the name of Thomas Charles, it may have been the Baptist Morgan John Rhys or the Independent

---

[63] Huw Walters, 'The Periodical Press to 1914', in Philip Henry Jones and Eiluned Rees, eds, *A Nation and its Books: A History of the Book in Wales* (Aberystwyth, 1998), p. 199.

[64] Thomas Phillips, *Wales* (London, 1849), pp. vii–viii.

[65] Eryn M. White, 'Revivals in the Eighteenth, Nineteenth and Twentieth Centuries', in Gibson and Morgan-Guy, eds, *Religion and Society in the Diocese of St Davids*, pp. 129–56.

Edward Williams of Oswestry who was the first pioneer of the Sunday School in the country. Regardless of who should take the credit for being first in the field, there is no doubt that the schools helped teach generations of children to read and write in Welsh, whilst elementary education more generally concentrated on the English language.[66] It was an added element to the appeal and a way of fostering the next generation of adherents to the cause. The system ensured a strong foundation of biblical knowledge, which may at times have placed too much emphasis on learning verses by rote rather than analysing the message contained within. Nevertheless, the schools ensured that there was an informed and receptive audience for religious publications through the medium of Welsh and for the most intricate and detailed of nonconformist sermons.

Such natural use of the Welsh language must surely have played a part in the appeal and the ultimate success of Nonconformity. The Anglican Church by no means abandoned the Welsh language and evidence points to a continued awareness of the need to adhere to the principle laid down in the act for the translation of the Scriptures and divine service in 1563 that it should be the language of public worship in parishes where it was commonly used. The vast majority of bishops in Wales during this period were neither Welsh nor Welsh-speaking, although a few like Bishop Thomas Burgess appreciated the importance of the language. It was not uncommon for more valuable benefices to fall to non-resident clergy who had no knowledge of Welsh, but in such cases a Welsh-speaking curate was usually appointed to take on the duties. Yet the Church often had to wrestle with the problem of how to cater for an increasingly bilingual population, especially in the growing industrial communities. Since the parish church had a duty to provide opportunities for public worship for all those within its boundaries, it had to come up with solutions such as services in alternative languages or bilingual services, which could leave both language groups dissatisfied with the compromise.[57] The situation was far simpler for the nonconformist churches who recruited adherents of a particular language to a particular cause.

Many of these aspects of religious life perhaps appealed especially to the middle orders of society. It was the middling sorts in rural Wales who were the backbone of the Methodist and Dissenting causes during the period of growth in the eighteenth century. They were more likely to seek education in the charity schools and Sunday Schools and to involve themselves in leadership roles as elders and deacons, as well as ministers. Early eighteenth-century Dissent relied to a considerable extent on landowning ministers who had

---

[66] Jones, 'Nonconformity and the Welsh Language', pp. 251–2; Huw John Hughes, *Coleg y Werin: Hanes yr Ysgol Sul yng Nghymru rhwng 1780–1851* (Pwllheli, 2013), pp. 203–4.

[67] Eryn M. White, 'The Established Church, Dissent and the Welsh Language', in Geraint H. Jenkins, ed., *The Welsh Language before the Industrial Revolution* (Cardiff, 1997), pp. 249–51.

sufficient independent means to enable them to take on the pastoral care of churches who could not afford to pay them generously.[68] Many Methodist preachers also had private means to sustain them and those without such wherewithal often struggled to make a living whilst devoting time to itinerant preaching. Towards the end of the century, as both Dissent and Methodism commanded wider support in society, there emerged what Tudur Jones called 'a generation of proletarian ministers, not educated and not well provided for, whose dowry was their enthusiasm'.[69]

It was, therefore, undoubtedly the Evangelical Revival of the eighteenth century which provided the major spur to the growth of Nonconformity in Wales. Many adherents of Old Dissent felt uncomfortable when confronted with the heat of the Methodist Revival, preferring steadfast resolution to heady enthusiasm.[70] Before being exposed to the Methodist influence, Dissenters were frequently accused of being 'dry', as Harris suggested when he referred to them as 'dry'd up'. Their sermons were often solid and thoughtful, but perhaps also at times rather staid and plodding. John Thomas of Rhayader had been in two minds about joining the Dissenters because he feared that he would be infected by what he termed their 'lukewarmness'. Some of the Dissenters felt that he was too much of a Methodist for their liking, but 'when I was dry and deadly and discoursing through the power of reason, they said I was like a Dissenter'.[71] An injection of enthusiasm transformed the 'dry Dissenters' and it was those Dissenting groups which embraced the vibrant revivalist tradition that gained most ground from the eighteenth century onwards. The power of the message conveyed should not be forgotten either. Tudur Jones emphasizes how 'the extraordinary dynamic' of Calvinism when combined with evangelical zeal from the mid eighteenth century onwards made a lasting impact on the nation.[72] Densil Morgan suggests a change in the very nature of the Dissenting tradition as a result of the effects of the evangelical revival. Traditional Dissent, he argues, had been sober and cerebral, but marginal to the life of the nation, whilst the newer form of Dissent was an energetic and strangely exciting mass movement.[73] Welsh Nonconformity, as it emerged into the nineteenth century, in essence drew on both traditions, with an emphasis on a sober, informed study of the message of the Bible, combined with a fondness for enthusiastic preaching and revivalism.

By 1828, therefore, the four leading nonconformist denominations in Wales had established themselves, after a period of unprecedented growth. The

---

[68] Jenkins, *Literature, Religion and Society*, pp. 205–6, 282–3.
[69] Jones, *Congregationalism in Wales*, p. 118.
[70] Jones, *Congregationalism in Wales*, pp. 101–2.
[71] John Thomas, *Rhad Ras*, ed. J. Dyfnallt Owen (Cardiff, 1949), pp. 95–7.
[72] Jones, *Congregationalism in Wales*, p. 107.
[73] D. Densil Morgan, *Chrismas Evans a'r Ymneilltuaeth Newydd* (Llandysul, 1991), p. 159; Morgan, 'Christmas Evans and Nonconformist Wales', pp. 28–9.

Baptists, for instance, numbered around 1,600 in 1750, but grew to over 9,200 by the end of the eighteenth century, increasing further to the point that 76,865 attended Baptist services on the day of the religious census in 1851, amounting to 18 per cent of worshippers in Wales. The Independents had about eighty-seven congregations in Wales in 1742, around 100 in 1775 and 684 in 1851, with their membership comprising 23 per cent of the total worshippers, compared to the Wesleyan Methodists with 13 per cent, the Anglicans with 21 per cent, and the Calvinistic Methodists with 25 per cent.[74] Although claims that the Welsh were a nonconformist nation in some ways overstated the case, given the significant proportion of the population who did not attend any place of worship and seemed to have no religious affiliations, nevertheless, a radical transformation in the religious climate had taken place, which also had a considerable impact on society, culture, and politics.

The repeal of the Test Act, bone of contention as it had long been, did not resolve all issues for Welsh Nonconformists. The wounds inflicted under the Clarendon Code may have largely healed, but other grievances arose. The Nonconformists suspected that they represented the majority of worshipping Christians in Wales well before the 1851 religious census provided them with evidence to confirm their claim. That awareness of the breadth of their support made the privileges still enjoyed by the Established Church seem especially unjust in Wales. This meant that Welsh Nonconformity could find common ground in opposition to the Church's favoured position and in a concerted campaign for the remainder of the nineteenth century to seek disestablishment. It was an indication of how far Nonconformity had progressed from its position as a tiny minority, thankful for some small measure of liberty in 1689, that by the mid-nineteenth century it felt confident enough to mount a challenge to the pre-eminence of the Church within Wales.

SELECT BIBLIOGRAPHY

Bassett, T. M., *The Welsh Baptists* (Swansea, 1977).
Davies, D. Elwyn, *They Thought for Themselves* (Llandysul, 1982).
Davies, E. T., *A New History of Wales: Religion and Society in the Nineteenth Century* (Llandybïe, 1981).
Gibson, William and Morgan-Guy, John, eds, *Religion and Society in the Diocese of St Davids 1485–2011* (Farnham, 2015).
Jenkins, Geraint H., *Literature, Religion and Society* (Cardiff, 1978).

---

[74] E. T. Davies, *A New History of Wales: Religion and Society in the Nineteenth Century* (Llandybïe, 1981), p. 26; John Williams, *Digest of Welsh Historical Statistics*, 2 vols. (Cardiff, 1985), II, pp. 271, 352.

Jones, David Ceri, Schlenther, Boyd Stanley, and White, Eryn Mant, *The Elect Methodists: Calvinistic Methodism in England and Wales 1735–1811* (Cardiff, 2012).
Jones, Gareth Elwyn and Roderick, Gordon Wynne, *A History of Education in Wales* (Cardiff, 2003).
Jones, J. Gwynfor, ed., *The History of Welsh Calvinistic Methodism III: Growth and Consolidation (c.1813–1914)* (Cardiff, 2013).
Jones, M. G., *The Charity School Movement: A Study of Eighteenth-Century Puritanism in Action* (Cambridge, 1938).
Jones, R. Tudur, *Congregationalism in Wales*, ed. Robert Pope (Cardiff, 2004).
Madden, Lionel, ed., *Methodism in Wales: A Short History of the Welsh Tradition* (Llandudno, 2003).
Morgan, D. Densil, *Wales and the Word: Historical Perspectives in Religion and Welsh Identity* (Cardiff, 2008).
Morgan, Derec Llwyd, *The Great Awakening in Wales*, trans. Dyfnallt Morgan (London, 1988).
Williams, Glanmor, Jacob, William, Yates, Nigel, and Knight, Frances, *The Welsh Church from Reformation to Disestablishment, 1603–1920* (Cardiff, 2007).

9

Dissent in the American Colonies before the First Amendment

Catherine A. Brekus

Most of the colonists who came to the American colonies during the seventeenth and eighteenth centuries were from England, including significant numbers of protestant Dissenters. Three Dissenting groups in particular—the Presbyterians, the Quakers, and the Baptists—flourished in the New World. Of the many ways in which these Dissenting traditions shaped early American religion, perhaps the most momentous was in their defence of the liberty of conscience. Persecuted for their beliefs in England, they brought an ethos of resistance with them to America. From the founding of the first seventeenth-century colonial settlements until the creation of the United States in 1787, they refused to conform to the Established Churches.

When historians have sought to explain the rise of religious liberty in America, they have often portrayed it as a pragmatic response to the religious diversity of the original thirteen colonies. Since the colonies were settled by a wide variety of religious groups—including Anglicans, Congregationalists, Lutherans, Dutch Reformed, Presbyterians, and Baptists—no single group was able to enforce religious conformity. According to historian Perry Miller, 'By and large Protestants did not contribute to religious liberty, they stumbled into it, they were compelled into it, they accepted it at last because they had to, or because they saw its strategic value.'[1] In his view, an ethic of religious toleration was the only possible response to the sheer diversity of early American religion.

Other historians have emphasized the importance of the Enlightenment. Beginning in the seventeenth century, philosophers such as John Locke developed new, liberal ideas about individual freedom and natural rights.

---

[1] See Perry G. E. Miller, 'The Contribution of the Protestant Churches to Religious Liberty in Colonial America', *Church History*, 4, 1 (1935), pp. 65–6.

Rejecting the idea that belief could be coerced, Locke argued that true political and religious authority was based on voluntary consent. 'The care of souls cannot belong to the civil magistrate,' Locke explained, 'because his power consists only in outward force; but true and saving religion consists in the inward persuasion of the mind, without which nothing can be acceptable to God. And such is the nature of the understanding, that it cannot be compelled to the belief of anything by outward force.'[2] Enlightenment thinkers argued that no one should be asked to violate the dictates of their own conscience, and no one could be forced—only persuaded—to change their beliefs.

While recognizing the importance of both Enlightenment ideas and the pragmatic challenges posed by colonial religious diversity, this essay highlights a third issue: the role of British protestant Dissenters. Although there was no single cause of the rise of religious freedom in America, it is hard to imagine the passage of the First Amendment without the Presbyterians, Quakers, and Baptists who fought for liberty of conscience.[3] They laid the intellectual groundwork for the separation of Church and state after the American Revolution.

DISSENT IN EARLY AMERICA

Many of the seventeenth-century Dissenters who emigrated to the colonies had been harassed or persecuted in England by the Anglican Church. Dissenters were fined, imprisoned, and even executed, and the Church was closely linked to the state. Not only was the monarch the head of the Church, but Bishops were members of the House of Lords.

In 1607, when the Virginia Company declared the Church of England to be the Established Church of Virginia, this close relationship between Church and state was replicated in the colonies. Everyone in Virginia was legally required to pay taxes toward the Church of England's support, and only male, property-holding Anglicans could hold political office. Dissenters were not tolerated. The scattered Baptists and Presbyterians who settled in Virginia during the seventeenth century attracted little notice, but when Quaker missionaries began to arrive during the 1650s, they were persecuted for their beliefs. As Monica Najar explains:

> Quakers could be fined for missing Anglican services, for not having a child baptized, and for assembling in groups of five or more. At the same time, civil

---

[2] John Locke, *A Letter Concerning Toleration* (1689), available online: http://www.constitution.org/jl/tolerati.htm [accessed 17 January 2015].
[3] On the alliance between Deists and Pietists, see Sidney Mead, *The Lively Experiment: The Shaping of Christianity in America* (New York, 1963).

officials enacted penalties for those who facilitated the Friends' efforts, such as ship captains who brought Quakers into the colony, individuals who hosted Quaker preachers or distributed their literature, and even civil officials who did not prosecute them. Under these directives, local authorities disrupted Quaker meetings; fined, imprisoned, whipped, and banished Quakers; and fined offending ship captains and Quaker supporters.[4]

Following the British example, Anglicans in Virginia were determined to create a comprehensive state church that would enforce both religious orthodoxy and political order.

By the mid-eighteenth century, the Church of England was also established in parts of New York as well as in Maryland, South Carolina, North Carolina, and Georgia, which meant that it was the official church of six of the original thirteen colonies. (Maryland had originally been settled as a haven for Catholics, but in 1691, Anglicans seized control and required all freeholders to pay taxes to the Church of England.) Yet because America was settled by a variety of British proprietors and joint stock companies, each colony developed its own laws regarding church establishments, and Anglicans never attained the same hegemony that they had enjoyed in England. The number of Anglican priests in the colonies was small and, most important, there were no Anglican bishops in America. Men who wanted to become priests had to travel to England for ordination. Even in North Carolina, where the Church of England was nominally established, there was not a single Anglican minister in the colony during the seventeenth century. After 1708 there were rarely more than two in any given year.[5] The result was that the Quakers proved to be more religiously and politically influential in North Carolina than the Anglicans. Similarly, the Church of England was established in parts of New York, but particular towns sometimes flouted the law. In the town of Jamaica, for example, the inhabitants chose to support a Presbyterian minister rather than an Anglican one. According to an angry group of Anglicans, the Presbyterians 'call themselves the Established Church & us Dissenters'.[6]

With no single Established Church in the colonies, the boundaries between orthodoxy and Dissent were sometimes redrawn in surprising ways In a strange reversal of fortune, Anglicans found that the Congregationalists whom they had persecuted in England had become the religious establishment in New England. Since each town in Massachusetts and Connecticut had the right to choose its own minister, in theory any church (including the Church

---

[4] Monica Najar, 'Sectarians and Strategies of Dissent in Colonial Virginia', in Paul Rasor and Richard E. Bond, eds, *From Jamestown to Jefferson: The Evolution of Religious Freedom in Virginia* (Charlottesville, VA, 2011), p. 118.

[5] Thomas J. Curry, *The First Freedoms: Church and State in America to the Passage of the First Amendment* (New York, 1986), pp. 56, 61.

[6] Edmund B. O'Callaghan, ed., *The Documentary History of the State of New York*, 4 vols. (Albany, NY, 1849-51), III, p. 278, quoted in Curry, *First Freedoms*, p. 71.

of England) could have become the 'establishment', but in practice, the Congregationalists always dominated. There was no Anglican church in New England until 1686, when Edmund Andros, the royal governor, founded King's Chapel in Boston. (Andros was the governor of the Dominion of New England, which had been created in order to exert greater imperial control over trade, religion, and politics.) Regardless of personal conviction, all inhabitants were required to pay taxes towards the support of the Congregational Church. In Massachusetts Bay and in New Haven, all inhabitants were legally required to attend church, and the franchise was limited to male church members until 1664.[7]

Congregationalists complained bitterly about their persecution in England, but they were ruthless about eliminating dissent after their arrival in the New World. Even though they disagreed with Anglicans about *which* church should be established, they assumed that the state should enforce religious orthodoxy. As Mark Noll explains, 'Significantly, both Puritan Congregationalists and colonial Anglicans retained the European ideal of a comprehensive, established state church. Both sought the protection of government, assumed a right to influence the state, treated each other's missionaries as civil threats, and opposed efforts by other Christian groups to settle in their colonies.'[8] In 1636, the Puritans in Massachusetts Bay banished Roger Williams because of his objection to religious coercion and his insistence that the Congregationalists should officially separate from the Church of England. (The Puritans claimed that they wanted to reform the Church of England rather than secede from it.) A year later in 1637, they banished Anne Hutchinson for accusing Boston's ministers of preaching a doctrine of works rather than grace, a serious charge in a Calvinist religious culture that emphasized human helplessness and God's sovereignty.[9] The fact that Hutchinson was a woman made her criticism of the clergy seem especially offensive.

The Puritans also tried to suppress the Baptists and the Quakers. Although Baptists were part of the Reformed tradition, they disagreed with Puritans about infant baptism and the importance of a learned ministry. According to the Baptists, only adult believers could be baptized, and the only crucial qualification for ministry was a call from God, not a college education. In 1644, the General Court of Massachusetts passed a law sentencing Baptists to banishment on the grounds that they were 'the incendiaries of commonwealths, and the infectors of persons in maine matters of religion, and the

[7] Albert Edward McKinley, *The Suffrage Franchise in the Thirteen English Colonies in America* (Philadelphia, PA, 1905), pp. 404, 475.

[8] Mark A. Noll, *Old Religion in the New World: The History of North American Christianity* (Grand Rapids, MI, 2002), p. 31.

[9] On Williams, see Edmund S. Morgan, *Roger Williams: The Church and the State* (New York, 1987). On Hutchinson, see Timothy D. Hall, *Anne Hutchinson: Puritan Prophet* (Boston, MA, 2010).

troublers of churches in all places where they have bene'.[10] In cases where Baptists refused to leave, they were fined, whipped, and imprisoned.

Puritans affirmed their belief in the liberty of conscience, but they claimed that the conscience had to be disciplined if it were in error. As the Reverend John Cotton explained, the fundamental truths of Scripture were so clear that 'a man cannot but be convinced in Conscience of the Truth of them after two or three Admonitions'. If he remained obstinate, the state could punish him. 'He is not punished for his Conscience', Cotton insisted, 'but for sinning against his owne Conscience.'[11] In other words, people had the 'liberty' to believe only what the Puritans declared to be the truth.

The Puritan disliked the Baptists, but they especially loathed the Quakers, whom they subjected to fines, imprisonment, ear cropping, whipping, and banishment. Although many historians have depicted the Quakers as a radical branch of the Puritan movement, the Puritans did not see any family resemblance.[12] They found virtually all of the Quakers' ideas and practices abhorrent: their belief in direct revelation, their insistence that all people (including women) could preach, their rejection of a formal ministry, their elimination of the sacraments, their pacifism, and their denial of the doctrine of original sin. When zealous Quaker missionaries refused to leave the colony, the Puritan establishment sentenced them to death. Between 1659 and 1661, four Quakers were hanged on Boston Common.[13]

Congregationalists also tried to suppress Presbyterianism, but less zealously. Since the two groups shared the same Reformed theology, they had been close allies in England, but they differed in their models of church polity. Instead of vesting authority in local congregations, the Presbyterians advocated a more hierarchical church structure that was composed of presbyteries. They also rejected the Congregational practice of limiting full church membership to 'visible saints' (in other words, those who claimed to have experienced conversion). Like the Congregationalists, however, Presbyterians upheld the idea of a comprehensive church that would include the entire community. In Scotland, where the movement flourished, the Presbyterian Church was legally established.

In England, the political differences between Congregationalists and Presbyterians had seemed relatively unimportant, but as Puritans became the

---

[10] A. H. Newman, *A History of the Baptist Churches in the United States* (New York, 1898), p. 127.

[11] John Cotton, *The Bloudy Tenent Washed* ((London, 1647), quoted in Curry, *First Freedoms*, p. 6.

[12] On this theme, see Geoffrey F. Nuttall, *The Holy Spirit in Puritan Faith and Experience* (Oxford, 1946), and Carla Gardina Pestana, *Quakers and Baptists in Colonial Massachusetts* (New York, 2004).

[13] Jane Calvert, *Quaker Constitutionalism and the Political Thought of John Dickinson* (New York, 2009), p. 52.

establishment in New England, their disagreements loomed larger. In the Cambridge Platform of 1648, Congregationalists tried to suppress any leanings toward Presbyterianism by asserting that the church 'ought not to be of greater number than may ordinarily meet conveniently in one place'.[14] Congregationalists usually tolerated Presbyterians because of their shared theology, and in fact, many Puritans in Connecticut had strong Presbyterian leanings. But occasionally conflict erupted. In 1736 and 1737, for example, when a group of Scotch-Irish Presbyterians in Worcester, Massachusetts asked to be relieved of the obligation of paying taxes to the Congregational establishment, they were refused.[15]

Only four colonies in early America—Delaware, New Jersey, Pennsylvania, and Rhode Island—extended religious freedom to all Protestants and only Pennsylvania and Rhode Island allowed Catholics and Jews to worship freely as well. After being exiled from Massachusetts Bay, Roger Williams founded Rhode Island in 1636 to be 'a shelter for persons distressed for conscience'.[16] Rhode Island became renowned for the liberty that it gave to Baptists, Quakers, Jews, and small sects like the Sandemanians. William Penn, a Quaker, founded Pennsylvania as a 'Holy Experiment' that would offer refuge for all Dissenters who believed in God. According to Pennsylvania's 1682 Frame of Government:

> all persons living in this province, who confess and acknowledge the one Almighty and eternal God, to be the Creator, Upholder and Ruler of the world; and that hold themselves obliged in conscience to live peaceably and justly in civil society, shall, in no ways, be molested or prejudiced for their religious persuasion, or practice, in matters of faith and worship, nor shall they be compelled, at any time, to frequent or maintain any religious worship, place or ministry whatever.[17]

Even in Pennsylvania, however, Catholics and Jews were not allowed to vote or to hold political office.

The British protestant Dissenters who emigrated to America found that their ability to worship freely depended on the colony in which they lived. In Rhode Island, Pennsylvania, Delaware, and New Jersey, no Protestants were treated as Dissenters, but in the southern colonies of Virginia, South Carolina, North Carolina, and Maryland, Quakers, Presbyterians, and Baptists faced the

---

[14] *The Cambridge Platform*, ed. Peter Hughes (Boston, MA, 2008), p. 19.
[15] Alexander Blaikie, *A History of Presbyterianism in New England: Its Introduction, Growth, Decay, Revival and Present Mission* (Boston, MA, 1881), pp. 54–5.
[16] John Russell Bartlett, ed., *Records of the Colony of Rhode Island and Providence Plantations in New England*, 10 vols. (Providence, RI, 1856–64), I, p. 22, quoted in Andrew R. Murphy, *Conscience and Community: Revisiting Toleration and Religious Dissent in Early Modern England and America* (University Park, PA, 2001), p. 67.
[17] Frame of Government of Pennsylvania, 5 May 1682, available online: http://avalon.law.yale.edu/17th_century/pa04.asp [accessed 17 January 2015]. See also William Frost, *A Perfect Freedom: Religious Liberty in Pennsylvania* (Cambridge, 1990).

same legal penalties as they had in England. In New England, by contrast, Dissenters faced a new and powerful enemy in the Congregational Church.

Because of the diffusion of religious power in the colonies, Quakers and Baptists now had *two* Established Churches to oppose rather than simply one. (This was also true for Presbyterians in the seventeenth century, but less so in the eighteenth century as they joined forces with Congregationalists.) For example, even though Baptists in New England criticized the Anglican Church, they saved their greatest ire for the Congregationalists who taxed and imprisoned them. As a result, Dissenters gradually became less invested in criticizing the Church of England than in protesting against the general principle of religious establishment. As Christians since the fourth century had argued that the state should be based on religious principles, this was a momentous development. Although most Dissenters continued to affirm that religious beliefs and practices should influence public life, they increasingly questioned the wisdom of allowing any single group of Protestants to function as a state church.

TOLERATION AND ITS LIMITS

When the English Parliament passed the Toleration Act in 1689, protestant Dissenters in both England and the American colonies were relieved of some of the burdens that had impeded their ability to practise their faith. Under the law, Dissenters were allowed to worship freely if they were willing to swear their allegiance to the monarchy. The Act explicitly excluded Catholics as well as anyone who denied the doctrine of the Trinity (a category that encompassed both Unitarians and Jews), and it did not extend true religious freedom even to protestant Dissenters. Besides being required to register their meeting houses with the local Anglican authorities, Dissenters were required to pay tithes to the Anglican Church. They were also forbidden to hold public office. Although historians have often portrayed the Toleration Act as the product of early Enlightenment ideas about freedom of conscience, the immediate impetus behind the law seems to have been more pragmatic. When King James II was deposed during the Glorious Revolution of 1688, William and Mary hoped to win the support of protestant Dissenters by expanding their liberties. Yet despite the limitations of the Toleration Act, it laid the groundwork for future debates about the role of the state in enforcing religious orthodoxy. In the words of Thomas Curry, 'Toleration of dissenters from the dominant religion of a region or a country, which in the seventeenth century some groups resisted or only grudgingly accepted, came in the eighteenth century to be commonly embraced as a matter of principle.'[18]

[18] Curry, *First Freedoms*, p. 78.

In the first decades of the eighteenth century, both the Anglicans and the Congregationalists made provisions to accommodate Dissenters. In 1691, the revised Massachusetts Bay Charter extended liberty of conscience to all Christians except for Catholics, and in 1708, Connecticut guaranteed that all Protestants would be allowed to worship unmolested. These laws were expanded in 1727 and 1728 when each colony allowed Baptists, Quakers, and Anglicans to be excused from paying poll taxes to the Congregational establishment. To attain this privilege, Dissenting ministers and congregations were required to be officially licensed by the government. In Virginia, for example, Dissenters were still required to pay taxes to the Anglican Church, but Dissenting ministers could preach if they and their congregations applied for a licence from the General Court.[19] Since the General Court met only twice a year, this requirement was burdensome, but it symbolized the colony's growing recognition of Dissenters' rights.

The three largest groups of Dissenters in the colonies—the Presbyterians, the Quakers, and the Baptists—all advocated greater toleration, but they disagreed over how to define liberty of conscience. In principle, the Presbyterians were not opposed to church establishments, especially because of their privileged legal status in Scotland. But because of their minority status in America, they defended their right to practise their faith without interference from the state. When Francis Makemie, a Presbyterian missionary, was arrested in New York in 1707 for preaching without a licence, he defended himself on the grounds that he was protected under the Toleration Act. 'If our Liberty either depended on a License or a Certificate from the Bishops of England, or the Governours of America', Makemie objected, 'we should soon be deprived of our liberty of conscience, secured to us by Law, and repeated resolutions of our present Sovereign, and Gracious Queen [Elizabeth], inviolably to maintain the Toleration which she is pleased to signifie in Her Royal Instructions to all her Governours abroad.'[20] He also questioned whether the authority of the Church of England extended to the colonies. In 1707, after being acquitted by a jury, he published *A Narrative of a New and Unusual American Imprisonment of Two Presbyterian Ministers*, which emphasized that religious toleration had been decreed by the Crown. Notably, Makemie did not assert that liberty of conscience was a natural right, but he tried to guarantee that Presbyterians and other Dissenters would no longer be harassed or imprisoned.

---

[19] John A. Ragosta, *Wellspring of Liberty: How Virginia's Religious Dissenters Helped Win the American Revolution and Secured Religious Liberty* (New York, 2010), p. 18.

[20] Francis Makemie, *A Narrative of a New and Unusual American Imprisonment of Two Presbyterian Ministers: and Prosecution of Mr. Francis Makemie, One of Them, for Preaching One Sermon at the City of New-York* (Boston, MA, 1707), p. 38.

Unlike the Presbyterians, the Quakers and the Baptists made the more radical argument that church establishments were inherently corrupt because they were based on coercion. According to John Clarke, a Baptist and one of the founders of Rhode Island, religious purity was more important than power, and belief was not genuine unless it was freely chosen. True Christians chose to follow Jesus because they loved him, not because they wanted to gain political privileges. Forcing people to attend a particular church would lead only to violence, which was contrary to God's will. In *Ill News from New England, or a Narrative of New England's Persecution* (1652), Clarke complained, 'This outward forcing of men in matters of conscience towards God to believe as others believe and to practice and worship as others do cannot stand with the Peace, Liberty, Prosperity and Safety of a Place, Commonwealth or Nation. Therefore no servant of Christ can have any liberty, much less authority, to do so.'[21]

Most importantly, both Quakers and Baptists argued that any government that established a state church was guilty of trying to usurp God's power. As William Penn explained, 'Imposition, Restraint, and Persecution, for matters relating to conscience, directly invade the divine prerogative, and divest the Almighty of a due, proper to none besides himself.'[22] Only God, not the state, had the authority to determine an individual's religious beliefs. In the words of John Clarke, 'the great work of ordering the understanding and conscience' belonged to God alone. 'He hath reserved this great work in His own hand and in the hand of the Spirit and hath intended to manage it as part of His Kingdom, by His own Spirit.' Unlike the Presbyterians, the Quakers and the Baptists defended complete religious freedom, not simply toleration. No man, Clarke argued, 'should have dominion over another man's conscience'.[23]

Yet despite their radicalism, neither Quakers nor Baptists were religious pluralists before their time. Unlike modern-day religious liberals, who assert the validity of many different religions, Quakers and Baptists each insisted that they alone possessed the truth. In this way they resembled the Established Churches more than they would have liked to admit. Indeed, each claimed to be the one true church of Christ. Rather than defending liberty of conscience on pluralistic grounds, they argued that people would be able to recognize the truth once they were freed from coercion. As Jane Calvert explains about the Quakers, 'The hope that lay behind liberty of conscience was that individuals, once freed from the obligations of a state church, would eventually find

---

[21] John Clarke, *Ill News from New England, or a Narrative of New England's Persecution* (London, 1652), p. 59.
[22] William Penn, *The Great Case of Liberty of Conscience Once More Debated & Defended* (1670), in *Select Works of William Penn* (London, 1771), p. 187.
[23] Clarke, *Ill News from New England*, pp. 56–7.

their way to Quakerism.' At the Second Coming of Christ, there would not be many faiths, but only one.[24]

Although the Baptists and the Quakers feared that government-enforced worship would corrupt true religion, they did not advocate a strict separation of Church and state. Because of their assumption that religion was the foundation of morality, each envisioned a state based on shared protestant principles. In Quaker Pennsylvania, for example, all inhabitants were required to observe the Sabbath either by attending church or reading Scripture at home. Although the Frame of Government guaranteed freedom of worship, it also promised that 'offences against God' would be 'severely punished'. The list of 'offences' included 'swearing, cursing, lying, prophane talking, drunkenness, drinking of healths, obscene words', and 'stage-plays, cards, dice, May-games, gamesters, masques, revels, bull-baitings, cock-fightings, bear-baitings, and the like, which excite the people to rudeness, cruelty, looseness, and irreligion'.[25] Similarly, the Baptists of Rhode Island tolerated Catholics and Jews, but they also prohibited them from holding public office.[26] Instead of trying to exclude religion from public life, both the Baptists and the Quakers hoped that Protestantism would provide the foundation for a virtuous society.

No one in early America, including protestant Dissenters, portrayed religious pluralism as a positive good. All Protestants ultimately hoped for religious uniformity, but they disagreed over how best to achieve it. While Congregationalists and Anglicans were willing to use force, Presbyterians pleaded for toleration, and Quakers and Baptists insisted that Christian unity would emerge only when individuals had the religious freedom to follow their own consciences.

REVIVALISM, EVANGELICALISM, AND RELIGIOUS DISSENT

The 'Great Awakening', as it became known in the nineteenth century, had a profound effect on attitudes toward liberty of conscience. Dramatic religious revivals took place in New England and the Middle Colonies during the 1740s and 1750s and in the South from the late 1740s until the 1770s. These revivals were part of a larger religious movement that took place in Great Britain and in parts of Europe as well, and they should be understood as a response to

---

[24] Calvert, *Quaker Constitutionalism and the Political Thought of John Dickinson*, p. 145; Theodore Dwight Bozeman, 'John Clarke and the Complications of Liberty', *Church History*, 75, 1 (2006), pp. 69–93.

[25] Frame of Government of Pennsylvania; Curry, *First Freedoms*, pp. 80–1.

[26] Curry, *First Freedoms*, p. 90.

momentous changes that transformed the eighteenth-century transatlantic world, including technological innovations, religious toleration, the Enlightenment, and the rise of both merchant capitalism and a consumer revolution. As Protestants tried to adapt to these transformations, they gradually created a new kind of faith that they described as 'evangelical'. The Great Awakening marked the rise of the evangelical movement, a movement that valued personal experience as the most important source of religious authority.[27]

Few Quakers participated in the Great Awakening, which they saw as overly emotional and 'enthusiastic', but large numbers of Baptists and Presbyterians celebrated the revivals as an extraordinary outpouring of God's grace. As itinerant ministers warned sinners to repent and thousands of converts proclaimed that they had been 'born again', Dissenting churches grew rapidly. In 1740 there were fewer than 200 Presbyterian churches in the colonies, but by 1780 there were nearly 500. 'In 1774 alone', explains Edwin Gaustad, 'Presbyterians established 18 churches in Virginia.' Similarly, there were fewer than 100 Baptist churches in 1740, but more than 400 by 1780.[28]

The nascent evangelical movement undermined the principle of church establishment in two ways. First, the leaders of the revivals argued that only individuals could determine religious truth. Although evangelicals valued religious institutions (and they founded many of their own), they encouraged every person to encounter God alone, and they insisted that only those who had been 'born again' were true Christians. It was not enough to attend church, to read the Bible, or to obey the Ten Commandments. Only those who had personally experienced divine grace would be saved. Ultimately religious authority did not belong to churches or to the state, but only to converted individuals.

Second, the revivals led to denominational schisms that exposed deep divisions among Protestants. Although most Protestants continued to long for religious unity, it became increasingly apparent during the eighteenth century that they could not agree on which church, if any, should be established. For example, the Congregational establishment in New England split into 'Old Light' and 'New Light' factions, with many 'New Light' supporters of the revivals eventually founding their own churches. These 'Separate' congregations, as they were known, eventually turned Baptist. (In their quest for religious purity, they decided that the doctrine of infant baptism was unscriptural.) Similarly, Presbyterians were sharply divided over whether the revivals had been inspired by the Holy Spirit. After ministers broke into two parties, the 'New Side' and the 'Old Side', they attacked one another as ignorant and

---

[27] On this theme, see Catherine A. Brekus, *Sarah Osborn's World: The Rise of Evangelical Christianity in Early America* (New Haven, CT, 2013).

[28] Edwin Scott Gaustad and Philip L. Barlow, *New Historical Atlas of Religion in America* (New York, 2001), pp. 22, 38, 40.

deluded. In a scathing sermon delivered in 1742, the Reverend Gilbert Tennent argued that 'Old Side' ministers were unfit to preach because they had never been 'born again'. These 'unconverted ministers' were a disgrace to the Christian name, 'dead dogs that can't bark'. Unless ministers had experienced divine grace, they would never be able to lead others to Christ. 'Is a blind Man fit to be a Guide in a very dangerous Way?' Tennent thundered. 'Is a dead Man fit to bring others to Life?'[29]

Angered by this kind of invective, established Anglican and Congregationalist ministers denounced evangelicals as 'Enthusiasts—Bigots—Pedantic, illiterate impudent Hypocrites'.[30] They also encouraged colonial assemblies to pass laws against itinerant preaching and to prosecute Dissenters who failed to pay their church taxes. In 1742, Connecticut passed a law making it illegal for revivalists to preach without first receiving permission from the town's established minister, and in Massachusetts, many 'Separates' and Baptists were imprisoned for failing to pay their church assessments.[31] In Raynham, Massachusetts, for example, Esther White was imprisoned for more than a year after refusing to pay eight pence that she owed toward the support of the Congregational Church.[32] Even though the sum was paltry, she resisted on principle. 'It is not the PENCE but the power that alarms us', explained Isaac Backus, a leading Baptist minister.[33] Refusing to apply for preaching or to pay ministerial taxes, Baptists flaunted their disregard for the law. The result was that almost fifty Baptist ministers were imprisoned before the Revolution.[34]

Even though colonial governments had to obey British law by tolerating Dissenters, they burdened them with as many restrictions as possible. Toleration was not the same as religious freedom. Besides forcing all Dissenters to pay taxes to the Anglican Church, the Virginia legislature required Presbyterian and Baptist ministers to seek licences to preach as well as to swear an oath of loyalty to the king. The legislature also forbade them performing marriage ceremonies.

Fearful of angering the Anglican hierarchy, Presbyterians were cautious about how they responded to these legal restrictions. When the Reverend Samuel Davies began to preach in Virginia in 1747, he requested licences to

---

[29] Gilbert Tennent, *The Danger of an Unconverted Ministry* (Boston, MA, 1742) reprinted in Richard L. Bushman, ed., *The Great Awakening: Documents on the Revival of Religion, 1740–1745* (Chapel Hill, VA, 1969), p. 91.

[30] Richard J. Hooker, ed., *The Carolina Backcountry on the Eve of the Revolution: The Journal and Other Writings of Charles Woodmason, Anglican Itinerant* (Chapel Hill, VA, 1953), p. 42.

[31] *An Act for Regulating Abuses and Correcting Disorders in Ecclesiastical Affairs*, reprinted in Bushman, *Great Awakening*, pp. 58–60.

[32] Isaac Backus, *A History of New England with Particular Reference to the Baptists* (1871; rpt. New York, Arno Press, 1969), I, p. 97.

[33] Isaac Backus, *Government and Liberty Described*, in *Isaac Backus on Church, State, and Calvinism: Pamphlets, 1754–1789*, ed. William G. McLoughlin (Cambridge, MA, 1968), p. 359.

[34] Curry, *First Freedoms*, p. 135.

preach at three separate Presbyterian meeting houses, and as he gained more converts, he continued to seek new licences. Only in 1750, when the General Court of Virginia refused to give him permission to preach at an eighth meeting house, did he challenge the government's authority to regulate Dissenters. In a petition to the Bishop of London, he affirmed his respect for the Anglican Church while insisting that he was protected by the Toleration Act. 'I beg leave to declare, and I defy the world to confute me', Davies wrote, 'that in all the sermons I have preached in Virginia, I have not wasted one minute in exclaiming or reasoning against the peculiarities of the established church; nor so much as assigned the reasons for my own non-conformity.' Rather than attacking either the Anglican Church or the principle of church establishment, Davies argued that he and other Presbyterian ministers were 'properly professed dissenters' who should be allowed to preach freely.[35]

Even after the colonies proclaimed their independence from England, Presbyterians remained ambivalent about whether to demand full religious freedom or to settle for the fair enforcement of the Toleration Act. On one hand, many ministers were emboldened by the Revolutionary War, and in 1776, when a special political convention was called in Virginia, the Presbytery of Hanover submitted a petition demanding an end to preferential treatment for Anglicans. Religion needed no 'civil aid', they argued, and no church should receive state taxes. As they explained, 'When our blessed Saviour declares his *kingdom is not of this world*, he renounces all dependence upon state power.'[36] Yet on the other hand, many Presbyterian ministers remained adamant that the state should enforce Christian worship, and they were reluctant to support complete religious freedom. In 1784 the Hanover Presbytery reversed its earlier rhetoric by supporting Patrick Henry's proposal to levy a general assessment for the support of Christianity. Under this plan. Virginians would continue to pay religious taxes, but they would be permitted to designate which church would receive their money. Hoping to establish Christianity (though not any particular denomination) as the foundation of the state, the Presbytery voted that 'every Man as a good Citizen, be obliged to attach himself to some religious Community, publicly known to profess the belief of one God, his righteous providence, our accountableness to him, and a future State of rewards and punishments'.[37]

Only a year later, however, the Hanover Presbytery reversed itself again by deciding not to support Henry's 'Bill for Establishing a Provision for Teachers of the Christian Religion'. Not only were Presbyterians fearful that Anglicans

---

[35] Samuel Davies, 'Letter to the Bishop of London' (1752), quoted in Bushman, ed., *Great Awakening*, pp. 165–6.

[36] Ernest Trice Thompson, *Presbyterians in the South* (Richmond, VA, 1963), I, p. 100.

[37] Thomas E. Buckley, 'Church–State Settlement in Virginia: The Presbyterian Contribution', *Journal of Presbyterian History*, 54, 1 (1976), p. 113.

might regain their former power, but they were increasingly convinced that religious freedom was a universal human right. After Henry's bill was defeated, Presbyterians endorsed Jefferson's Virginia Statute for Religious Freedom (1786), which declared 'that no man shall be compelled to frequent or support any religious worship, place or ministry whatsoever, nor shall be enforced, restrained, molested, or burthened in his body or goods, nor shall otherwise suffer on account of his religious opinions or belief; but that all men shall be free to profess, and by argument to maintain, their opinions in matters of religion'.[38] Though it had taken decades of debate, Presbyterians now insisted that religious belief could not be coerced. Only God, not the state, had the right to determine religious truth.

Unlike the Presbyterians, whose commitment to religious freedom developed slowly, the Baptists never wavered in their radical insistence that church establishments were sinful. In 1786, when a group of Baptists in Virginia argued that the Anglican Church should not be given any special privileges, they echoed the arguments of John Clarke more than a century earlier. 'New Testament Churches, we humbly conceive, are, or should be established by the Legislature of Heaven, and not earthly power; by the Law of God and not the Law of the State; by the Acts of the Apostles, and not by the Acts of an Assembly.'[39] In New England, Isaac Backus insisted that God wanted Church and state to be separate. 'God has appointed two kinds of government in the world', he explained, 'which are distinct in their nature, and ought never to be confounded together; one of which is called civil, the other ecclesiastical government.'[40] No government had the authority to force an individual to worship against the light of his or her own conscience.

RELIGIOUS FREEDOM

The First Amendment to the Constitution represented a major victory for religious Dissenters. Passed in 1787, the Amendment declared that 'Congress shall make no law respecting an establishment of religion, or prohibiting the free exercise thereof'. The two separate clauses of the Amendment guaranteed that Congress would never establish a state church; nor would it prevent Americans from worshipping (or not worshipping) according to conscience.

---

[38] Thomas Jefferson, Virginia Statute for Religious Freedom, 1786, available online: http://www.digitalhistory.uh.edu/disp_textbook.cfm?smtID=3&psid=1357.

[39] H. J. Eckenrode, *Separation of Church and State in Virginia* (Richmond, VA, 1910), p. 119, quoted in *A Documentary History of Religion in America*, ed. Edwin S. Gaustad and Mark A. Noll, 2 vols., 3rd edn (Grand Rapids, MI, 2003), I, p. 244.

[40] Isaac Backus, *An Appeal to the Public for Religious Liberty against the Oppressions of the Present Day* (Boston, MA, 1773).

Until the passage of the Fourteenth Amendment in 1868, the First Amendment applied only to the national government, not to individual states, which meant that several state governments continued to require officeholders to declare their belief in God and 'a future state of rewards and punishments'.[41] Several states also continued to levy taxes for the support of Christian churches. Perhaps not surprisingly, Massachusetts, the original home of the Puritans, did not disestablish the Congregational Church until the late date of 1833. Nevertheless, the First Amendment guaranteed that the nation was committed not only to religious toleration, but to complete religious freedom.

The First Amendment would never have been passed without the support of Dissenting Protestants. While the Baptists were the most vocal supporters of religious freedom in early America, the Presbyterians gradually became more radical during the revivals, and the Quakers insisted that only God could judge the human conscience. Though the Quakers withdrew from the Pennsylvania Assembly in 1756 during the French and Indian War rather than compromise their pacifist principles, their commitment to religious liberty continued to be politically influential during the Revolutionary years. According to John Dickinson, a Quaker from Pennsylvania who served as a delegate to the First and Second Continental Congresses as well as to the Constitutional Convention,

> Religion and Government are certainly very different Things, instituted for different Ends; the design of one being to promote our temporal Happiness; the design of the other to procure the Favour of God, and thereby the Salvation of our Souls. While these are kept distinct and apart, the Peace and welfare of Society is preserved, and the Ends of both are answered. By mixing them together, feuds, animosities, and persecutions have been raised, which have deluged the World in blood, and disgraced human Nature.[42]

Influenced by his Quaker heritage, Dickinson insisted that government regulation of religion inevitably led to violence. Most importantly, he denounced church establishments as an affront to both humans and God.

Yet despite the important role of Dissenters in changing attitudes toward church establishments, it is important to recognize that they did not achieve this on their own. Joining their campaign were rationalists and Deists like Thomas Jefferson who defended religious freedom on different grounds.[43] Influenced by the Enlightenment, Jefferson argued that religious coercion led to 'priestcraft', superstition, and tyranny. In *Notes on the State of Virginia* (1786), he explained, 'Millions of innocent men, women, and children, since

---

[41] James Hutson, *Forgotten Features of the Founding: The Recovery of Religious Themes in the Early American Republic* (Lanham, MD, 2003), p. 17.
[42] Dickinson, quoted in James Hutson, ed., *The Founders on Religion: A Book of Quotations* (Princeton, NJ, 2005), p. 61.
[43] See Mead, *The Lively Experiment*.

the introduction of Christianity, have been burnt, tortured, fined, and imprisoned; yet we have not advanced one inch toward uniformity. What has been the effect of coercion? To make one-half the world fools and the other half hypocrites. To support roguery and error all over the earth.'[44] Unlike protestant Dissenters, who feared that state interference would contaminate the purity of Christianity, Jefferson feared the opposite: that church establishments would lead to the corruption of the state. He was willing to forge alliances with protestant Dissenters in order to ensure the passage of the Virginia Statute for Religious Freedom (1786) and the First Amendment (1787), but he remained suspicious of institutional religion, which he associated with violence and coercion.[45]

The fragile coalition that had linked Deists and rationalists to Baptists, Quakers, and Presbyterians splintered after the passage of the First Amendment. While Deists stood aloof from institutional religion, Baptists, Quakers, and Presbyterians increasingly competed with one another for converts in the new republic. Though they had worked together to legalize Dissent and to achieve religious freedom, each denomination continued to believe that their understanding of Christianity was the truth. The British protestant Dissenters who settled in the colonies in the seventeenth century not only contributed to the rise of religious freedom in the new nation, but they also fostered an ethic of competition that splintered American Protestantism into dozens of new denominations in the nineteenth and twentieth centuries. Contrary to their expectations, religious freedom did not lead to Protestant unity, but to the splintering of American Christianity.

Whatever their regrets about protestant pluralism, the Quaker, Baptist, and Presbyterian communities in early America celebrated their achievement in convincing other Protestants that religion could not be coerced. Intellectually, their defence of the liberty of conscience became the dominant way of thinking about religion in the new republic. Nineteenth- and twentieth-century Protestants would continue to argue over whose beliefs were true, but, like Isaac Backus, they argued that 'religion is ever a matter between God and individuals'.[46] Religious freedom—like life, liberty, and the pursuit of happiness—had become an unalienable right.

---

[44] Thomas Jefferson, *Notes on the State of Virginia*, ed. Frank Shuffelton (New York, 1989), p. 166.

[45] Peter S. Onuf, 'Jefferson's Religion: Priestcraft, Enlightenment, and the Republican Revolution', in his *The Mind of Thomas Jefferson* (Charlottesville, VA, 2012), pp. 139–68.

[46] Backus, *History of New England Baptists*, I, p. 336.

SELECT BIBLIOGRAPHY

Beneke, Chris, *Beyond Toleration: The Religious Origins of American Pluralism* (New York, 2006).

Buckley, Thomas E., 'Church–State Settlement in Virginia: The Presbyterian Contribution', *Journal of Presbyterian History*, 54, 1 (1976), pp. 105–19.

Buckley, Thomas E., *Church and State in Revolutionary Virginia, 1776–1787* (Charlottesville, VA, 1977).

Curry, Thomas, J., *The First Freedoms: Church and State in America to the Passage of the First Amendment* (New York, 1986).

Curry, Thomas J., *Farewell to Christendom: The Future of Church and State in America* (New York, 2001).

Frost, J. William, *A Perfect Freedom: Religious Liberty in Pennsylvania* (Cambridge, 1990).

McLoughlin, William G., *Isaac Backus and the American Pietistic Tradition* (Boston, MA, 1967).

McLoughlin, William G., *New England Dissent, 1630–1833: The Baptists and the Separation of Church and State*, 2 vols. (Cambridge, MA, 1971).

Mead, Sidney E., *The Lively Experiment: The Shaping of Christianity in America* (New York, 1963).

Miller, Nicholas P., *The Religious Roots of the First Amendment: Dissenting Protestants and the Separation of Church and State* (New York, 2012).

Murphy, Andrew R., *Conscience and Community: Revisiting Toleration and Religious Dissent in Early Modern England and America* (University Park, PA, 2001).

Najar, Monica, *Evangelizing the South: A Social History of Church and State in Early America* (New York, 2008).

Pestana, Carla Gardina, *Quakers and Baptists in Colonial Massachusetts* (New York, 2004).

Ragosta, John A., *Wellspring of Liberty: How Virginia's Religious Dissenters Helped Win the American Revolution and Secured Religious Liberty* (New York, 2010).

Stokes, Anson Phelps, *Church and State in the United States*, 3 vols. (New York, 1950)

Thompson, Ernest Trice, *Presbyterians in the South*, 3 vols. (Richmond, VA, 1963).

Trinterud, Leonard J., *The Forming of an American Tradition: A Re-Examination of Colonial Presbyterianism* (Philadelphia, PA, 1949).

Wilson, John F., *Church and State in America: A Bibliographical Guide*, vol. 1: *The Colonial and Early National Periods* (New York, 1986).

10

Dissent in the Atlantic World, 1787–1830

Katherine Carté Engel

Dissenters in the western Atlantic region faced a transformed world after 1787, one in which the very concept of 'Dissent' ceased to have the kind of meaning it had long carried. The end of the American Revolution saw a trend towards religious disestablishment in the new United States. Virginia's Statute for Religious Freedom (1786) and the First Amendment to the US Constitution (ratified 1791) were soon followed by the end of taxes to support churches in most states. None of the states admitted after 1792 created religious establishments, so as the United States rapidly conquered and absorbed territory to its west, denominations succeeded based on their abilities to confront new situations rather than their legal statuses. Meanwhile, in Canada, the Church of England was strengthened with the appointment of the first Anglican bishops on the western side of the Atlantic, even as the Dissenting denominations there also saw considerable growth.

This era of rapid legal change reconfigured the opportunities available to Dissenters in North America. In the United States, the denominations of Old Dissent saw a relative decline, though the combined numbers of Presbyterians, Congregationalists, Baptists, and Methodists began and ended the era as the majority of the new nation's population. In 1776, when the United States declared independence from Great Britain, the three denominations of Old Dissent accounted for more than 56 per cent of the new nation's religious adherents; in 1850, they accounted for just over a third. In addition, the New England states, the legal stronghold of Congregationalism, grappled with the ending of the Standing Order—the term for its establishment—and the increase of both denominational competition and theological diversity. Yet, looked at from another perspective, the early republic saw the heyday of Dissenting power in the United States. Methodism exploded on the national scene, growing from a tiny minority of the population before the war to 34 per cent of US religious adherents in 1850; combined with the numbers of Baptists, Congregationalists, and Presbyterians, those groups accounted for more than three-quarters of the United States' church-going population.[1]

Dissenters in the United States faced two different sets of challenges in this environment. The first can best be understood in terms of denomination, as each of the major groups grappled with distinctive organizational transformations. For Congregationalists, this was a regional, New England process. For Presbyterians, it was national in scope, and for Baptists, it was local in orientation. Methodists, the newest arrivals, expanded at a breathtaking pace, particularly in western and frontier areas, and they created dynamic national institutions as they went. The second set of challenges, issues such as building missionary efforts and grappling with the positions of women and African Americans within church communities, can better be understood as the collective effort to solidify a role for religion in a society that no longer had any legal religious establishment. As the political order stabilized, Dissenters looked beyond denominational boundaries, building new forms of interdenominational, and in some cases international, collaboration. In the areas of British North America that would later become a part of Canada, a different challenge emerged: whether Dissenters in those regions would primarily be oriented southwards towards the growing United States or across the Atlantic to Great Britain.

DENOMINATIONAL PERSPECTIVES

Congregationalists and Unitarians

Congregationalists in the United States were overwhelmingly centred in New England. For this reason, it is difficult to separate the history of Congregationalism in the era after the Revolution from the fate of New England's Standing Order, as well as the ideal it represented that each town should have a single church that united believers under a shared moral discipline and worked to soothe theological divisions. That vision had faced significant challenges during the eighteenth-century revivals led by George Whitefield and Jonathan Edwards, but had survived into the Revolutionary era nonetheless. As the decades passed, however, the percentage of the New England church-going population that was Congregationalist declined significantly, from 63 per cent of adherents in 1776 to 27 per cent in 1850.[2] Religious establishments endured into the nineteenth century throughout the region,

---

[1] Roger Finke and Rodney Stark, 'How the Upstart Sects Won America: 1776–1850', *Journal for the Scientific Study of Religion*, 28, 1 (1989), p. 31.
[2] Finke and Stark, 'How the Upstart Sects Won America', p. 30.

but increasing theological diversity meant that many towns either sported multiple congregations as a result of local schism or were home to many residents who followed a formal process to abstain from paying established ministers on the grounds of conscience. Legal struggles such as the 1782 Balkcom case, where some Dissenters in Massachusetts sought, ultimately without success, to avoid having to certify that they were not Congregationalists, point to the complex balancing act by which Congregationalists attempted to preserve their privileged position.[3] Throughout New England, legal disputes, often led by Baptists, pitted those who dissented from the Standing Order against local ministers and governmental authorities, who were generally Congregationalist. The corrosive and politicizing effect of this process made it impossible for religious leaders to imagine that they inhabited a unified Congregationalist society. In 1818, Connecticut's Baptists and Episcopalians together pushed for a revision to the state's 1662 colonial charter and ended the Congregational establishment. New Hampshire and Maine followed soon thereafter.[4]

New England's changing religious establishments resulted from fundamental shifts in the region's religious geography and culture. Both types of change made the town–church model that had characterized early New England increasingly difficult to sustain. Beginning shortly before the Revolution, large numbers of Yankees migrated out of southern and eastern New England and into the frontier regions to the north and west, as well as into Canada and Nova Scotia.[5] The migrants drew heavily from New England's evangelical communities, and a wave of revivals that swept through the region between 1778 and 1782 enhanced the further spread of evangelicalism. Stephen A. Marini and Shelby M. Balik have both emphasized the significance of rough frontier conditions in shaping the religious geography of the region, which Balik argues enhanced competition between 'itinerant' and 'town church' versions of religious organization. In the new settlements, dramatic mobility and population growth (Maine's population tripled between 1790 and 1820) meant that ministers often had many congregants move away, while newcomers frequently did not formally leave their old churches and join new ones. Moreover, as theological factions ranged from Edwardsian Calvinism to the occasional Unitarian, it was difficult for a town to settle on an individual minister.[6]

---

[3] Thomas J. Curry, *The First Freedoms: Church and State in America to the Passage of the First Amendment* (New York, 1986), pp. 171–2.

[4] William G. McLoughlin, *Soul Liberty: The Baptists' Struggle in New England, 1630–1833* (Hanover, NH, 1991), pp. 289–303.

[5] G. A. Rawlyk, *The Canada Fire: Radical Evangelicalism in British North America, 1775–1812* (Kingston and Montreal, 1994).

[6] Shelby M. Balik, *Rally the Scattered Believers: Northern New England's Religious Geography* (Bloomington, Indiana, 2014); Stephen A. Marini, *Radical Sects of Revolutionary New England* (Cambridge, MA, 1982).

The Unitarian threat to traditional Trinitarian Congregationalism was greatest, however, not on the frontier but in the heart of old Puritan New England. Unitarianism had deep native roots in the region, traceable to liberal theologians such as Charles Chauncy and Jonathan Mayhew, as well as to rationalist reaction against the resurgent Edwardsian Calvinism of ministers such as Samuel Hopkins, Jonathan Edwards, Junior, and Timothy Dwight.[7] Conrad Wright has argued that Calvinist-leaning clergy trained at Yale were increasing in influence in the 1790s, and liberals' positions within Massachusetts's Standing Order made the struggle between Calvinism and a growing Unitarianism a matter of ecclesiastical politics. In 1805, when both the presidency of Harvard and the prominent position of Hollis Professor of Divinity at the college were vacant, the competition became more focused. The election of liberal Henry Ware as the Hollis Professor set the Unitarian controversy in motion.[8]

Over the next two decades, liberals and Calvinists in Massachusetts began to build separate institutional structures and articulate more clearly their theological positions. Calvinists, having lost control of Harvard's theological voice, founded the Andover Theological Seminary in 1808 and the Park Street Church in Boston in 1809.[9] A decade later, William Ellery Channing's sermon, 'Unitarian Christianity', set the final division in motion. As churches and communities began to split, the controversy threatened the basis of the Standing Order: tax support for a town's primary church. In the 1820 Dedham decision, the state's courts held that schismatic groups had lost access to both church property and the claim of establishment. In 1825, Unitarian clergy under Channing's leadership founded the American Unitarian Association, though this was a union of individuals rather than a fully fledged denomination. In 1833, a state constitutional amendment eliminated tax support for churches altogether, completing the process of legal disestablishment in the United States.[10]

Ties between the growing American Unitarian movement and its English counterpart were weaker and more contentious than might be expected given the close relations between Boston and London in the years before American independence. King's Chapel in Boston, an Anglican congregation without a minister after the Revolution, began using a version of the liturgy influenced by Theophilus Lindsey in 1785, led by the church's Harvard-trained lay preacher, James Freeman. Two of North America's new Episcopal bishops, Samuel Seabury and Samuel Provoost, declined to get involved in Freeman's

---

[7] Conrad Wright, *The Beginnings of Unitarianism in America* (Hamden, CT, 1976).
[8] Ibid., pp. 252–80.
[9] Conrad Wright, 'Institutional Reconstruction in the Unitarian Controversy', in Conrad Wright, *American Unitarianism, 1805–1865* (Boston, MA, 1989), p. 5.
[10] J. William T. Youngs, *The Congregationalists* (New York, 1990), p. 128.

potentially controversial ordination in the midst of the significant transitions occurring in the Protestant Episcopal Church in America, so he was ordained by a lay committee from the church. In addition to the presence of Lindsey's work, significant figures from English Unitarianism travelled to the United States. William Hazlitt visited Boston at the same time as Freeman was leaving his Trinitarian beliefs behind, and Joseph Priestley settled permanently in Pennsylvania in 1794. Yet New England's religious liberals did not merge seamlessly with England's. Most of New England's Unitarians were Arian and largely rejected the Socinianism of English Unitarianism, and well into the nineteenth century competing interpretations of the relationship between the two groups continued.[11]

The history of Congregationalism in the United States between 1787 and 1830 is integrally linked to the regional evolution of New England from a post-Puritan society with strong church–state ties to a religiously pluralistic one. New pluralism came simultaneously in the form of increased revivalism and a growing liberal Unitarian movement. Congregationalism, which in the colonial period had been so linked to the Standing Order, saw the greatest declines of any of the Dissenting traditions in the early republic.

Presbyterians

Unlike Congregationalists, who were tightly centred in New England, late eighteenth-century Presbyterians stretched along the eastern seaboard from New York down to South Carolina and Georgia. While the Congregationalists to the north grappled with the failure of their church model, the Presbyterians revised their institutional structures to match the challenges of the new nation. The most extensive, non-political body in the Revolutionary United States was the Presbyterian Synod of New York and Philadelphia, which had been established in 1758 to heal the schism between Old Side, or orthodox, and New Side, or revivalist, factions that had resulted from the Great Awakening of the 1740s. It joined members over hundreds of miles and many jurisdictions into a single ecclesiastical body, and Presbyterians were conscious of their national perspective. The need to reform this large and unwieldy organization, however, was recognized even before independence, as attendance at annual synods was often poor because ministers and elders had to travel great distances to participate. The war exacerbated this problem, and that, along with the desire to create an American structure of church governance, led the Synod of 1785 to appoint a committee to that end. Over the next several years, a series of synods and committees discussed the future structure of American

---

[11] J. D. Bowers, *Joseph Priestley and English Unitarianism in America* (University Park, PA, 2007).

Presbyterianism, with perspectives that varied from adopting the model of the General Assembly of the Church of Scotland to a more Congregational approach. In the end, sixteen presbyteries were created, with a General Assembly at their head. Roughly equal numbers of congregations existed in the mid-Atlantic and South, and Hanover Presbytery in Virginia included congregations in Kentucky. As the federal government was still more of an idea than a reality in the 1790s, the Presbyterian Church in the United States of America was among the first truly national institutions.[12]

The Presbyterians' governing structure and documents reflected the United States' new political culture and apparatus. Although many were concerned about a wholesale importation of British (specifically Scottish) forms, the Westminster Confession was adopted with little comment and only a few revisions, as Mark Noll has noted, 'on the run'.[13] The changes made all dealt with the Presbyterians' view of civil government. For example, in chapter 20, on Christian liberty and liberty of conscience, a clause asserting that civil magistrates might take action against those who were 'destructive to the external peace and order which Christ hath established in the church', reserved that power to the church itself. A more dramatic shift came in chapter 23, where most of a lengthy paragraph was drafted. It replaced language that permitted civil magistrates to keep order in the church, handle heresies, and call synods, with one asserting that magistrates 'may not ... in the least, interfere in matters of faith', but could only 'protect the church of our common Lord, with out giving preference to any denomination of christians above the rest'.[14]

The new plan of government, approved by the last Synod of New York and Philadelphia in 1788, was preceded by an introduction, which was largely the work of John Witherspoon, the Scottish divine and president of Princeton who had signed the Declaration of Independence. Like the alterations to the Westminster Confession, the principles laid out in the plan's introduction asserted the importance of religious institutions' freedom from governmental interference and equality among denominations. Presbyterians, it asserted, 'do not even wish to see any religious constitution aided by the civil power, further than may be necessary for protection and security, and, at the same time, equal and common to all others'. The new governing structure possessed a centralized General Assembly that 'represent[ed] in one body, all the particular Churches of this denomination', but was composed of delegates from each

---

[12] Leonard J. Trinterud, *The Forming of an American Tradition: A Re-examination of Colonial Presbyterianism* (Philadelphia, PA, 1949), pp. 258–308.

[13] Mark Noll, 'What Has Been Distinctively American about American Presbyterians?' *Journal of Presbyterian History*, 84, 1 (2006), p. 9.

[14] *The Constitution of the Presbyterian Church in the United States of America* (Philadelphia, PA, 1789), pp. 29–35.

presbytery based on number of ministers.[15] The new form of church government, like the national government then in the process of being ratified, was designed to promote representative democracy in church matters. Although smaller bodies, like the Associate Reformed Presbyterian Church, peopled by Scottish Seceders and their descendants, remained outside of the new Presbyterian structure, the General Assembly nonetheless dominated American Presbyterianism for decades.[16]

Presbyterians began the early republic poised to take the leadership position among American denominations, but their conflicted response to the revivals that regularly spread through their own circles and the wider culture made it difficult for them to do so, at least in demographic terms. The greatest of these revivals, at Cane Ridge, Kentucky, in 1801, began as a Presbyterian communion fair led by minister Barton Stone. But as that revival and the ones that followed grew into a wider cultural phenomenon, Baptist and Methodist preachers, who were more comfortable with the camp-meeting style and the doctrinal looseness fostered by revivalism, tended to take the lead. Stone and others withdrew from the oversight of the Kentucky Synod to form the independent Springfield Presbytery in 1804, which then subsequently dissolved itself and became simply a 'Christian' church. Members of the Cumberland Presbytery also split off from the larger Presbyterian Church, limiting Presbyterian expansion in the Southwest.[17]

While Presbyterians lost the institutional advantage in one region, they gained it in another. Beginning in 1801, strong ties between Connecticut Congregationalists and mid-Atlantic Presbyterians flourished in the Plan of Union, which permitted congregations in the newly settled areas of western New York and the Ohio Valley to select clergy from either denomination. This partnership allowed migrating Yankees to come under the leadership of the (relatively) more nimble Presbyterians. The cultural match between Presbyterians and their Congregationalist followers, both of whom were acculturated to an educated and settled clergy, was much stronger than between Presbyterians and the more homespun revival culture that grew up after Cane Ridge. Thus, while Congregationalism did not expand significantly beyond New England, even though many New Englanders migrated to the Old Northwest, Presbyterianism did. According to Bradley J. Longfield, membership in the Presbyterian Church expanded from 18,000 to 248,000

---

[15] Jeffrey H. Morrison, *John Witherspoon and the Founding of the American Republic* (Notre Dame, IN, 2005), pp. 106–12; *The Constitution of the Presbyterian Church*, pp. cxxxiv, 147; Bradley J. Longfield, *Presbyterians and American Culture: A History* (Louisville, KY, 2013), pp. 46–51.

[16] Russell E. Hall, 'An Outline History of the Presbyterian Church in America', *Journal of the Presbyterian Historical Society*, 26, 4 (1948), pp. 227–50.

[17] Paul K. Conkin, *Cane Ridge: America's Pentecost* (Madison, WI, 1990).

between 1807 and 1834.¹⁸ As impressive as Presbyterian growth was, it still lagged behind the more expansive and populist Methodist and Baptist movements.

The Presbyterian commitment to an educated clergy and doctrinal consistency was also manifest in its educational projects. The College of New Jersey (Princeton) and Hampden-Sidney in Virginia were well established in their respective regions, but as Princeton in particular seemed to decline in its production of clerical candidates, the General Assembly chose to found Princeton Theological Seminary in 1812. The new school staked out a traditional Calvinist position. It provided intellectual leadership to a denomination and a society that was still trying to negotiate a new and unfamiliar relationship among church, state, and the ever-elusive hope of building a Christian republic.¹⁹

Baptists

Baptists enjoyed the same institutional flexibility as Congregationalists, but the tradition's history of being on the outside of state establishments in both New England and the Anglican-dominated southern states gave that group an advantage in the religious marketplace of the new United States. On the other hand, the Baptist tendency to group and regroup polities based on theological principles worked against the kind of national denominational organization the Presbyterians achieved. By the end of the 1780s, various Calvinist (Regular), Arminian (General), and Revivalist (Separate) Baptist groups claimed congregations throughout the country. As in other communities, the Revolutionary era saw old wounds heal and new divisions develop In 1787, for example, Separate and Regular Baptists in Virginia put aside their differences to form the United Baptist Churches. The joining did not eliminate all tensions, however, and controversy among strains of Baptists remained a creative, constructive, and defining force.²⁰ Still, everywhere the trajectory was towards dramatic growth. In 1776, 16.9 per cent of Americans who adhered to a religious group were Baptists; in 1850, that percentage had grown to just over 20 per cent. This increase also happened in an era of exploding population growth, as raw numbers of Baptists grew from 70,000 to 1.6 million. By contrast, Presbyterian numbers fell from 19 to 11.6 per cent of total adherents in this same period.²¹ In Maine, there were twelve Baptist congregations in 1790 and 154 in 1820.²²

---

[18] Longfield, *Presbyterians and American Culture*, pp. 57–9.
[19] Ibid., pp. 64–7.
[20] Philip N. Mulder, *A Controversial Spirit: Evangelical Awakenings in the South* (New York, 2002), pp. 41–4.
[21] Finke and Stark, 'How the Upstart Sects Won America', p. 31.
[22] Balik, *Rally the Scattered Believers*, p. 40.

Baptist revivals began even before the Revolution ended, and they contributed to an increasingly diverse religious tradition. In New England, the New Light Stir began in 1776, just as the war was beginning. Under the influence of individuals like Henry Alline in Nova Scotia and Benjamin Randel in New Hampshire, revivalism spread quickly. A further wave of revivals began in 1790, and many of the congregations involved ended up in the Baptist fold. Neither Alline nor Randel fitted within a traditional Calvinist model. Randel, for example, had started as a Congregationalist and then joined Calvinist Baptists in New Hampshire before he rejected traditional Calvinism and founded the Freewill Baptists in 1780. His followers spread throughout New England, and westward into Ohio and the Northwest Territories as well. Alline, who had also started his career within the Calvinist tradition, blended a range of theological and social perspectives, all with a primary focus on the New Birth.[23]

In the South, evangelical denominations saw rapid growth across the board, and the Baptists were no exception. In 1790, there were roughly 40,000 Baptists in the region, including about 4,000 African Americans. In 1813, total numbers had grown to 114,000, of whom nearly 23,000 were black (and generally enslaved). As both the territory of the US South and evangelicalism continued to swell, the total number of Baptists reached close to 300,000 (of whom 58,000 were black) by 1836. Although problems with measuring members and adherents make counting difficult, Baptist churches (and their Methodist and Presbyterian counterparts) were among the largest and strongest institutions in the antebellum South. Moreover, the majority of American Baptists were located there too.[24]

Baptists were theologically resistant to forming large organizations, yet the organizing forces present among Presbyterians could be found among Baptists as well. In Virginia, the centralizing efforts of the General Committee of Baptist Associations (founded 1784) and its successor organization, the General Meeting of Correspondence (1800–22), allowed for coordination, particularly with regard to political issues. Indeed, as Charles F. Irons has argued, Virginia's Baptists capitalized on their history and reputation of fighting for religious freedom to build their denominational presence. Other regional organizations likewise formed during the early republic. South Carolina's Baptists, for example, established a state-wide convention in 1821.[25] The largest Baptist organizations grew out of missionary projects. In the first years of the nineteenth century, Baptists began to organize regional missionary

---

[23] Ibid., pp. 50–2; Rawlyk, *The Canada Fire*, pp. 5–18.

[24] Christine Leigh Heyrman, *Southern Cross: The Beginnings of the Bible Belt* (Chapel Hill, NC, 1997), pp. 263–4.

[25] Charles F. Irons, 'The Spiritual Fruits of Revolution: Disestablishment and the Rise of the Virginia Baptists', *Virginia Magazine of History and Biography*, 109, 2 (2001), pp. 159–86.

societies, followed in 1814 by the launch of the Baptist General Convention for Foreign Missions. This umbrella organization brought Baptists from across the nation together, but missionary work—particularly when sponsored by a national body rather than a congregation—remained controversial among many Baptists.[26]

In the first decades of the nineteenth century, Baptists became a significant force in American religious culture. Their sheer numbers, particularly in the southern states, ensured that Baptists were major players in local and regional religious communities. At the same time, the group's resistance to forming binding national organizations muted its ability to speak as a single denomination, and its relatively smaller participation in the sorts of theological disputes embraced by Presbyterians meant that Baptist clergy were less frequently seen as spokesmen on national religious issues, despite the fact that Baptists were by far the most dominant and dynamic of the strands of Old Dissent in the new nation.

Methodists

The Methodists could only be called a nascent community in the United States during the American Revolution. The rapid eighteenth-century growth of evangelicalism that in Britain had occurred within Anglican circles found a comfortable home in the demographically dominant Dissenting denominations in America, so that Congregationalists, Presbyterians, and Baptists all included evangelical wings. Moreover, although John Wesley had sent a few missionaries to the colonies, his stance against the American political cause did not endear him to many Americans during the war years. The Methodist community recovered quickly thereafter, however, and Methodism became the dominant denomination in the antebellum United States. Only the Baptists could compete with them in sheer numbers. Led by Francis Asbury, Thomas Coke, and Richard Allen, and making use of a nimble clerical organization, Methodists transformed the religious culture of the United States.

Before the American Revolution, the numbers of Methodists in the British North American colonies were tiny, a combination of recent British and Irish immigrants who had been awakened to Methodism before crossing the Atlantic and the converts of a small handful of energetic Wesleyan envoys who worked in the wake of itinerant George Whitefield. Numbers were small but growth was notable, even during the difficult war years when most Wesleyan itinerants left the colonies and those who remained suffered under

[26] William H. Brackney, *Baptists in North America: An Historical Perspective* (Malden, MA, 2006), pp. 52–3.

suspicions of loyalism or pacifism or both. In 1773, Wesley's superintendent in America, Thomas Rankin, reported 1,160 members. In 1782, the number of members had swollen to almost 12,000.[27] Most of these lived in the mid-Atlantic states and the Upper South, but the movement spread widely and rapidly. In 1805, Francis Asbury placed membership around 100,000, but members were only a fraction of the total numbers who regularly heard Methodist preachers or attended Methodist services.[28]

The thorniest issues for Methodists in the years immediately after the American Revolution were closely related: the community's relationship to its English spiritual leader, John Wesley, and its relationship to the Anglican Church of which Wesley was a member, but which in the new United States was in a period of dramatic transformation. At the centre of these two questions was the pressing problem of providing the sacraments to Methodists. Most American Methodist preachers lacked the education or ordination necessary in Wesley's (or the Anglican Church's) eyes to administer the sacraments. To address this problem, Thomas Coke, Wesley, and another Anglican priest formed a 'Primitive presbytery' in the summer of 1784, setting in motion the process of ordaining clergy in North America. These actions provided the core for the creation of a separate Methodist denomination in America that would eventually be independent of both Wesley's close oversight and of the nascent Protestant Episcopal Church in North America. In Baltimore that winter, American Methodists—led by Wesley's appointed leaders, Coke and Francis Asbury, and probably moving beyond Wesley's vision at the time—reformed into the Methodist Episcopal Church at the Christmas Conference. Its leaders were elected by its clergy, making the new organization largely independent from Wesley's direct control.[29]

The new Methodist Church created a centre of gravity in North America from which Methodist growth reached outward. Coke, one of the key ties between Wesley and the American Methodist Church and a primary advocate of Methodist expansion in the western Atlantic world, inaugurated Wesleyan missionary work in the Caribbean in 1787.[30] Methodists in Nova Scotia requested clergy from the United States even as the Methodist Episcopal Church was being formed. The earliest Methodists in that region had come, like others further south, as part of economic migrations at mid-century. Their numbers swelled enormously after the war, when thousands

---

[27] Dee Andrews, *The Methodists and Revolutionary America, 1760–1800: The Shaping of an Evangelical Culture* (Princeton, NJ, 2000), pp. 47, 61.

[28] John H. Wigger, *Taking Heaven by Storm: Methodism and the Rise of Popular Christianity in America* (Urbana, IL, 2001), p. 4.

[29] Andrews, *The Methodists and Revolutionary America*, pp. 65–72.

[30] John W. Catron, 'Evangelical Networks in the Greater Caribbean and the Origins of the Black Church', *Church History*, 79, 1 (March 2010), pp. 77–144.

of refugee loyalists, both black and white, fled the United States for British soil to the north. Freeborn Garrettson, a Maryland Methodist preacher, was sent by the Christmas Conference in 1784 to Nova Scotia, where he joined William Black, a Yorkshire-born Methodist who corresponded with Wesley.[31] Freed slave Moses Wilkinson also preached in Nova Scotia, in the black community of Birchtown, and he eventually led his congregation, along with other black Methodists, such as Boston King, and Baptist ministers, including David George, to Sierra Leone in 1792. Black's and Garrettson's ties back (in Garrettson's case via Baltimore) to Wesley point to the importance of the Wesleyan connection in the Methodist movement, and also to its limitations, since both the black loyalists in Nova Scotia and Asbury in the United States ultimately interpreted Wesleyanism for their followers relatively independently of the movement's English founder and his successors.[32] Methodist missionaries from the United States worked in Upper Canada (Ontario) as well, so that ties between Methodists in British North America and the United States were often stronger than either were to Great Britain during the early years after US independence, though that began to change after 1815.[33]

The rapid expansion of the Methodist Episcopal Church in the United States in the two decades after its founding is most often attributed to the administrative acumen and pious zeal of Francis Asbury and the circuit rider system. Circuit riders, as Methodist itinerant preachers were known, travelled extensively in the American backcountry and frontier, able to follow migrating farmers from the more densely populated eastern regions, over the mountains and into new territories. These clergy were appointed by Asbury and supervised within a series of districts, a system that allowed strong centralized control over an enormous territory. Circuit riders often travelled into unknown regions where they organized local congregations and class meetings, which the riders would then visit every few weeks. The flexible and ever unpredictable nature of this system—congregations often met outdoors and in spaces not otherwise designed for worship, and itinerants could rarely arrive on Sundays or even on a reliable schedule—matched the rapidly changing American landscape well.[34]

The hierarchical tendencies of Methodism in the early republic, embodied in Asbury's own tight authority, were counterbalanced by a strong democratic impulse that gave Methodism the character of a popular evangelical movement. Circuit riders, the only paid Methodist clergy, came from the same

---

[31] David Hempton, *Methodism: Empire of the Spirit* (New Haven, CT, 2005), p. 151; Rawlyk, *The Canada Fire*, pp. 44–57; Neil Semple, *The Lord's Dominion: The History of Canadian Methodism* (Montreal, 1996), pp. 30–3.

[32] Cassandra Pybus, *Epic Journeys of Freedom: Runaway Slaves of the American Revolution and their Global Quest for Liberty* (Boston, MA, 2006), pp. 146–7.

[33] Semple, *The Lord's Dominion*, pp. 42–6.

[34] Wigger, *Taking Heaven by Storm*, pp. 25–36.

middling backgrounds as their hearers. As John H. Wigger has argued, 'In many instances the only real distinction between a Methodist preacher and the bulk of his audience was which side of the pulpit each was on.'[35] Even more important, the centrally directed itinerants worked in conjunction with a much larger number of unpaid preachers and lay exhorters who filled countless leadership roles in local Methodist communities. In 1809, there were some 597 circuit riders and 1,610 local preachers.[36] Thus, as circuit riders came into town and stirred up excitement, they were meeting with communities that would be sustained and nurtured by consistent leadership. Methodist expansion was a careful pairing of local democratic tendencies and centralized national organization. The system was not without conflict, however, as Christine Leigh Heyrman has argued. The young and uneducated Methodist itinerants often met with resistance and challenges to their authority, particularly in the hierarchical culture of the South.[37] Yet, on balance, the dramatically expanding numbers of Methodist members and hearers over the early republic suggest something of a successful formula.

Historians have generally balanced the dynamism of early Methodism with a more staid period beginning in the 1820s, when institution building and solidifying cultural gains became more significant issues for clergy and laity. Although early Methodist colleges had repeatedly suffered failures, including the short-lived Cokesbury College founded in 1787, between 1816 and 1830, the Methodists opened a wide range of schools. Publishing had a longer history in the denomination, and Wesley's writings had been circulating widely for decades, as had Whitefield's before him. The Methodist 'Book Concern' took off in the early nineteenth century and became a substantial vector for Methodist ideas; Methodist periodicals had some of the largest circulation numbers for any American publications in the era.[38] In short, a movement that started as peripheral and politically suspect at the beginning of the era represented the core of the American religious establishment by the end of it.

Society of Friends

The Society of Friends (Quakers) was by far the smallest of the Dissenting groups in North America, and it did not share in the growth that its fellow denominations experienced during the early republic. Excluded from the Protestant mainstream in the eighteenth century, Quakers saw themselves as a people apart, a 'nation of zion'.[39] Although they maintained much stronger

---

[35] Ibid., p. 49. [36] Ibid., p. 31. [37] Heyrman, *Southern Cross*, pp. 87–9.
[38] Wigger, *Taking Heaven by Storm*, pp. 179–80.
[39] Sarah Crabtree, *Holy Nation: The Transatlantic Quaker Ministry in an Age of Revolution* (Chicago, IL, 2015).

transatlantic links than other groups did, after the end of the war, Friends reconciled themselves to the American system. They also participated in larger national trends. Foremost among these was migration, as the group's strongholds in Pennsylvania, New York, New Jersey, and North Carolina were replaced by a broader national distribution. American Friends also found themselves struggling with theological issues, as the democratizing and rationalistic teachings of Elias Hicks divided Quaker communities after 1819. Hicks's opponents, termed Orthodox Friends, emphasized a Trinitarian conception of the divine, in contrast to Hicks's focus on the Quaker conception of the Spirit within.[40] The Hicksite split, which occurred in 1827, also revealed social divisions within Quakerism, as those with closer ties to the establishment resisted the Hicksite movement. Thomas D. Hamm estimates that about 40 per cent of Quakers joined this new movement.[41]

Compared with the more evangelical and numerous Methodists, Baptists, and Presbyterians, Quakers cut a lower profile in early nineteenth-century America. Smaller numbers and internal conflict (a phenomenon that was in no way unique to the Quakers) came on the heels of Quakers' experiences during the American Revolution, when they were persecuted for their pacifism. Friends were thus pushed to the fringes of the American religious establishment just as groups like the Baptists were moving to the centre through their advocacy of religious liberty. Although Quaker leadership in some reform movements, such as early prison reform and abolition, was notable, Quakers did not take centre stage in the effort to define the United States' religious culture in the new era.[42]

THE CHALLENGES OF BUILDING A CHRISTIAN REPUBLIC AND A CHRISTIAN SOCIETY

Historians of religion in the United States have traditionally viewed the era from 1790 to 1830 as dominated by the Second Great Awakening. An ambiguously dated epoch that stretches from the late Revolutionary era revivals of the 1780s to the almost institutionalized revivalism of Charles Grandison Finney in the 1820s and 1830s, the Second Great Awakening is associated with the triumphal rise of evangelical Methodists and Baptists, the spread and eventual institutionalization of camp meetings, and, through the

---

[40] H. Larry Ingle, *Quakers in Conflict: The Hicksite Reformation* (Knoxville, TN, 1986), p. 44.
[41] Thomas D. Hamm, *Quakers in America* (New York, 2006), p. 43.
[42] Bruce Dorsey, *Reforming Men and Women: Gender in the Antebellum City* (Ithaca, NY, 2002), p. 49; Jennifer Graber, *The Furnace of Affliction: Prisons and Religion in Antebellum America* (Chapel Hill, NC, 2011), p. 45.

enduringly significant work of Nathan O. Hatch, *The Democratization of American Christianity*, the process by which the United States' Protestant Christian culture came to embrace the same popular ethos that was then developing within its politics.[43] The tension inherent in these disparate narratives can be found in the space between the era's centripetal movement towards greater institutional organization, as Donald G. Mathews argued in 1969, and its centrifugal tendency towards greater popular control and democratic initiative.[44] Mark A. Noll, teasing out the shared theological trends of the time, notes that 'the key to understanding such broad developments is to realize that almost all of America's most prominent religious thinkers wanted to preserve the vocabulary of Christianity as an essential part of the language of America'.[45] Regardless of how the emphasis is laid, the Second Great Awakening, in the analysis of John L. Brooke, 'describes... a broadly Protestant ritual of national integration, where revival religion established a framework of popular virtue and organization across the new nation'.[46] The scope of these characterizations reflects the overwhelming power of once-Dissenting denominations within the American religious landscape, yet the inclination among historians in more recent years has been to see the era as one characterized by an anxious struggle between religious interests: between those promoting varied mechanisms for ensuring the morality of society; between those who controlled institutions and those who, like African Americans and women, tended to be on the outside; between different visions of how religion, politics, and the state should interact in the new nation.[47]

Congregationalists, Methodists, Baptists, and Presbyterians each faced specific challenges as denominations and as organizations in the new American environment, but, as various historians have noted, many of these challenges were shared. Each denomination moved from a world where the nature of imperial and colonial establishments set the terms of discussion to one where a marketplace of religious ideas dominated outcomes. As revivals spread through the Atlantic world, the rising tide of evangelicalism blunted the distinctions among denominations, particularly in the western United States where all institutional structures were new at best. In addition, shared challenges—such as those related to transnational ties, new missionary

---

[43] Nathan O. Hatch, *The Democratization of American Christianity* (New Haven, CT, 1989).

[44] Donald G. Mathews, 'The Second Great Awakening as an Organizing Process, 1780-1830: An Hypothesis', *American Quarterly*, 21, 1 (1969), pp. 23-43.

[45] Mark A. Noll, *America's God: From Jonathan Edwards to Abraham Lincoln* (New York, 2002), p. 229.

[46] John L. Brooke, 'Cultures of Nationalism, Movements of Reform, and the Composite-Federal Polity', *Journal of the Early Republic*, 29, 1 (Spring 2009), pp. 1-33, 15 (quotation).

[47] See, for example, David Sehat, *The Myth of American Religious Freedom* (New York, 2011); Eric R. Schlereth, *An Age of Infidels: The Politics of Religious Controversy in the Early United States* (Philadelphia, PA, 2013); and Amanda Porterfield, *Conceived in Doubt: Religion and Politics in the New American Nation* (Chicago, IL, 2012).

endeavours, the unstable place of women and African Americans within denominations, and setting of the course of a new and unsteady political system—united rather than divided most Dissenters.

The Canadian story, which was in some ways so linked to its southern neighbour, began to diverge from the United States' path by the War of 1812. Although the late eighteenth-century revivals led by figures like Baptist Henry Alline, Methodist Freeborn Garrettson, and African American preachers from both denominations left an imprint on the religious landscape of the region, the establishment of an Anglican bishop in Nova Scotia in 1787 solidified the Anglican position there, at least on a legal, if not a cultural, level. Moreover, the combined influence of ongoing Scottish immigration, growing Calvinism, and a focus on an educated clergy drew Baptists and Presbyterians in the Maritime Provinces away from their more populist southern neighbours and into the orbit of Great Britain. The increasingly tense relationship between the United States and Lower Canada had the same effect to the west.[48]

Some Dissenting leaders in the United States began seeking renewed ties to Britain soon after the Peace of Paris in 1783, though in a very different context from their neighbours to the north. The Revolution had ruptured many of the transatlantic ties between Dissenters. The New England Company, for example, which had been the Dissenting counterpart to the Anglican Society for the Propagation of the Gospel in Foreign Parts since the seventeenth century, withdrew from those areas that rebelled against royal authority and refocused its efforts in New Brunswick and Nova Scotia. As new religious leaders emerged in the United States, however, they sought out ties to their counterparts abroad. English Baptist John Rippon, for example, editor of the *Baptist Annual Register* between 1790 and 1802, received numerous letters from Americans seeking to describe Baptist revivals in North America.[49] The revivals and missionary movements that began in Britain in the 1790s had their American counterparts, as Baptists, Presbyterians, and Congregationalists all began to organize in various ways to missionize both to Indians and to European Americans (often in the rapidly settling West) who lacked religious services or commitments. Groups on both sides of the Atlantic were keenly aware of each other, seeing one another as sources of competition and inspiration. In its first issue of the *Connecticut Evangelical Magazine* (1800), the newly formed Missionary Society of Connecticut abstracted a recent report of the London Missionary Society and reprinted a letter from evangelical Anglican leader Thomas Haweis in London, declaiming, 'The children of God are all one household. The Atlantic flowing between prevents not our united hands and hearts from cordially meeting in this work of faith and labor

---

[48] Semple, *The Lord's Dominion*, p. 46.
[49] British Library, Letters of John Rippon, Add MS 25386–25389.

of love.'[50] Foreign mission efforts too looked to British partners, particularly after the founding of the American Board of Commissioners of Foreign Missions in 1810.[51]

Transatlantic ties between British religious communities and their American counterparts were strongest in the North. Interdenominational cooperation and voluntary societies marked many of the missionary efforts in the northern parts of the United States. Presbyterians and members of the Dutch Reformed, Reformed, and Baptist communities established the New York Missionary Society in 1796, and leaders explicitly urged their members and missionaries to avoid interdenominational squabbling and operate within broadly Calvinist lines. A few years later, the New York Missionary Society began a short-term partnership with the New York Baptist Association to further missionary goals, though these efforts were limited by the Baptist tendency to prefer congregational rather than organizational oversight of missions. The above-mentioned Missionary Society of Connecticut, one of the largest such state societies, was formed in 1797 with the goal of serving communities on the frontier and also building ties to 'dearly beloved brethren in Europe and North America'. As Brian Franklin has found, 'by 1810, mission societies had formed in every state north of Virginia' and Southern religious leaders pursued more local means of spreading the gospel. The mission movement was thus a reflection of religious leaders' desires throughout the nation to cooperate and build the strength of Protestant Christianity in regions beyond their own.[52]

Alongside missionary movements, American religious leaders founded a vast range of voluntary societies aimed at reforming and improving American society. These movements have come to be called the 'benevolent empire' by historians. They included the American Bible Society, founded in 1816; the American Sunday School Union, founded in 1817; and numerous temperance, Sabbatarian, and other moral societies that were self-consciously and sometimes actually national in scope.[53] John Brooke has argued that these efforts were a conservative attempt by the New England and mid-Atlantic 'Presbygationalist establishment' to build a national culture that transcended the various regional and state boundaries, and 'comprised a virtual proxy nation that counteracted the centrifugal forces of the market revolution and partisan politics'.[54] Indeed, though their overall numbers were substantially smaller

---

[50] *Connecticut Evangelical Magazine*, I (1800), p. 32. I would like to thank Brian Franklin for generously sharing this citation.

[51] Emily L. Conroy-Krutz, *Christian Imperialism: Converting the World in the Early American Republic* (Ithaca, NY, 2015).

[52] Brian Russell Franklin, 'American Missions: The Home Missions Movement and the Story of the Early Republic', PhD Dissertation, Texas A&M University, 2012, pp. 40, 53.

[53] Dorsey, *Reforming Men and Women*, pp. 76–80.

[54] Brooke, 'Cultures of Nationalism', pp. 17, 20.

than those of their Baptist and Methodist competitors, the influence of northeastern Presbyterians and Congregationalists extended broadly through these efforts. This moment of what might be termed a new Dissenting establishment for the United States lasted until about 1830, when the rise of abolitionism and the Southampton (Nat Turner's) Rebellion started the trend towards national religious and political disintegration.[55]

Southern Dissenters also participated in the national effort to build a strong religious culture, but they did it in ways that supported the institution of slavery. As Charles F. Irons has argued, the presence of substantial numbers of African American congregants, both enslaved and free, within the Southern Methodist, Baptist, and Presbyterian evangelical congregations and denominations played a profound role in the direction those organizations took. Working from the rich base of Virginia, Irons finds that outreach to slaves, as well as their incorporation into the fold, became a hallmark of evangelical religious culture in the South, justifying for whites the very institution of slavery. Simultaneously, the ability of African Americans to select among various ministers and denominations pushed those communities to provide space and even sometimes ordination to African American preachers. For many Southerners, both black and white, support for the American Colonization Society, an effort to settle freed slaves in Liberia, demonstrated the importance of spreading the Gospel throughout the world even within the context of slavery.[56]

In the North, many African Americans preferred to join separate denominations. The period before 1830 saw the emergence of major African American Dissenting leaders and denominations. Black Methodists established independent denominations with, initially, the blessing of white Methodists. Richard Allen had been born a slave in Delaware, and after being converted by Methodists, he had purchased his own freedom and become a lay preacher. Frustrated by his treatment by white Methodists, however, he formed Bethel Church in Philadelphia in 1793, an African American Methodist Church. Francis Asbury made Allen a deacon, but tensions persisted with the white Methodist Church, including over issues of property. In 1814, Allen formed an independent denomination, the African Methodist Episcopal Church, which he oversaw until his death in 1831. A similar history marked the formation of the African Methodist Episcopal Zion Church in New York, which also became an independent denomination. A separate African American Presbyterian church was formed in Philadelphia in 1807, although it remained within the purview of the broader Presbyterian denomination.[57]

The limitations of forming independent denominational structures in the slave-holding South did not prevent African Americans from building

---

[55] Sehat, *The Myth of American Religious Freedom*, pp. 51–69.
[56] Charles F. Irons, *The Origins of Proslavery Christianity* (Chapel Hill, NC, 2008).
[57] Wigger, *Taking Heaven by Storm*, p. 146.

networks of faith and leadership. John W. Catron has argued for the existence of an extensive system of Afro-Protestant churches throughout the Caribbean and US South during this period.⁵⁸ African American Baptist leaders, such as George Leile and David George, played a major role in spreading Christianity in the South and throughout the Atlantic world. Leile left Savannah with the British occupation and travelled to Jamaica, where he spent his career as a missionary, ultimately working with Baptists sent from London. George, who had himself been converted by Leile, went to Nova Scotia and then on to Sierra Leone with his congregation.⁵⁹

It is difficult to distil either 'Dissenting' or 'evangelical' teachings on slavery in the era between 1787 and 1830. While Baptists, Methodists, and sometimes Presbyterians spread the Gospel among enslaved and free African Americans, ordained black clergy, sent missionaries to slaves, and discussed the morality of slavery in their denominational meetings, they also shied away from dramatic statements that would have divided their religious polities in devastating ways. Several scholars have argued that Southern denominational leaders in particular treated slavery as a civil rather than a religious issue, thus shifting the discussion of the institution from outright abolition to managing an unpleasant situation.⁶⁰ In 1818, the General Assembly of the Presbyterian Church disciplined abolitionist George Bourne for his disruptive activities. It also issued a lengthy statement decrying the moral evil of slavery as 'inconsistent with the law of God', and calling it the 'duty of all christians... to correct the errors of former times, and as speedily as possible to efface this blot on our holy religion, and to obtain the complete abolition of slavery throughout christendom, and if possible throughout the world'. But the body stopped short of demanding immediate abolition in the South, where slavery, they argued, was an unfortunate system 'entailed' on their Southern co-religionists. The assembly *'exhort[ed] others* to forbear harsh censures, and uncharitable reflections' on those who lived in slave-holding areas. The denominational message was conflicted and ambiguous, as was the national political culture in 1830. Here, too, Dissenting denominations grappled with the mantle of national leadership.⁶¹

Women, like African Americans, found new space and also saw new options foreclosed within the Dissenting denominations in the early nineteenth century, a process historians have argued was linked to the denominations' changing positions within society. Susan Juster has suggested that as Baptists moved from

---

⁵⁸ Catron, 'Evangelical Networks in the Greater Caribbean'.

⁵⁹ Irons, *Origins of Proslavery Christianity*, p. 51; Pybus, *Epic Journeys of Freedom*, pp. 145–8, 210–11.

⁶⁰ Irons, *Origins of Proslavery Christianity*, p. 18; Monica Najar, *Evangelizing the South: A Social History of Church and State in Early America* (New York, 2008), pp. 160–1.

⁶¹ Extracts from the Minutes of the General Assembly of the Presbyterian Church (Philadelphia, PA, 1818), pp. 28–33, emphasis in the original.

the periphery to the centre of New England political culture in the late eighteenth century, they began to understand women's active and visible presence as 'disorderly'. In the era of disestablishment after the American Revolution, newly formalized church structures came to exclude women from roles they had exercised in a previous generation.[62] In the southern states, where evangelicalism arrived after the Revolution, Christine Heyrman has found a more complex picture, as Methodist and Baptist preachers, who were often themselves itinerants in newly settled areas, sought to work with white women they viewed as having special spiritual natures. Women's religious powers did not confer institutional or ministerial rights, however, so they remained on the peripheries of denominational structures. These contrasting findings point both to the uneven process by which denominational authority extended across the growing United States and to a general consensus by male clergy that women's roles would necessarily be limited.[63]

If the period following the Revolution was one of patriarchal retrenchment, women found new forms of authority and leadership nonetheless. Catherine Brekus has uncovered more than a hundred women who preached publicly during the era, particularly among the Freewill Baptists, Christian Connection, northern white Methodists, and African-American Methodists. These groups had little to lose from embracing female voices, unlike the Congregationalists and Presbyterians with their greater investments in denominational institutionalism. Capitalizing on new notions of feminine virtue as well as the growth of print culture, these women found venues to spread their messages largely without challenging the formal structures of the clerical establishment. While many worked in family or informal meetings, exhorting and praying rather than preaching, others took to the pulpit, and some were undeniably popular. Published narratives of their careers and spiritual journeys sold well and spread their stories.[64] If historians have disagreed as to whether this period was one which ultimately saw greater or lesser equality for women in religious realms, they concur that members and clergy of Dissenting denominations renegotiated the roles available for women as part of the process by which all Dissenters came to terms with their positions as moral leaders in a democratized political world with no church establishment.[65]

---

[62] Susan Juster, *Disorderly Women: Sexual Politics and Evangelicalism in Revolutionary New England* (Ithaca, NY, 1994), pp. 122-35.

[63] Heyrman, *Southern Cross*.

[64] Catherine Brekus, *Strangers and Pilgrims: Female Preaching in America, 1740-1845* (Chapel Hill, NC, 1998), pp. 118-61.

[65] A review of recent scholarship on Baptist women in the era reveals the strength of local trends, as some places saw increased opportunities for women and others saw them circumscribed. See Curtis D. Johnson, '"Disordered" Democracies: Gender Conflict and New York Baptist Women, 1791-1830', *Journal of Social History*, 47, 2 (2013), pp. 482-5.

CONCLUSION

In one of history's ironies, the principal challenge for Dissenting groups in the Western Atlantic world between 1787 and 1830 was not their status as Dissenters but its opposite, their position as culturally dominant players in a political environment where (for the United States) there was no church establishment from which to dissent. In the absence of legal struggles for legitimacy, American Dissenting leaders and communities worked to determine what kinds of roles they could play in the expanding nation. The dynamic growth of evangelical sects in the United States, particularly the Methodists and Baptists, also exerted force beyond the nation, as Canadian and Caribbean religious communities entered the orbit of the missionary establishments reaching outwards from the United States. That position of cultural dominance came with a price, however, as the opportunities to challenge traditional hierarchies of politics, race, and gender retreated. The denominations' inability to come to terms with slavery forms the most obvious example, leading to separate denominations for African Americans and eventually the fracturing of the white-dominated denominations. Religious liberty, in the form of legal disestablishment, was a complicated basis for religious community.

SELECT BIBLIOGRAPHY

Andrews, Dee E., *The Methodists and Revolutionary America, 1760–1800: The Shaping of an Evangelical Culture* (Princeton, NJ, 2000).

Balik, Shelby M., *Rally the Scattered Believers: Northern New England's Spiritual Geography* (Bloomington and Indianapolis, IN, 2014).

Bowers, J. D., *Joseph Priestley and English Unitarianism in America* (University Park, PA, 2007).

Brooke, John L., 'Cultures of Nationalism, Movements of Reform, and the Composite-Federal Polity: From Revolutionary Settlement to Antebellum Crisis', *Journal of the Early Republic*, 29, 1 (2009), pp. 1–33.

Conroy-Krutz, Emily L., *Christian Imperialism: Converting the World in the Early American Republic* (Ithaca, NY, 2015).

Curry, Thomas J., *The First Freedoms: Church and State in America to the Passage of the First Amendment* (New York, 1986).

Hatch, Nathan O., *The Democratization of American Christianity* (New Haven, CT, 1989).

Hempton, David, *Methodism: Empire of the Spirit* (New Haven, CT, 2005).

Hyerman, Christine Leigh, *Southern Cross: The Beginnings of the Bible Belt* (Chapel Hill, NC, 1997).

Irons, Charles F., *The Origins of Proslavery Christianity: White and Black Evangelicals in Colonial and Antebellum Virginia* (Chapel Hill, NC, 2008).
Juster, Susan, *Disorderly Women: Sexual Politics & Evangelicalism in Revolutionary New England* (Ithaca, NY, 1994).
Longfield, Bradley J., *Presbyterians and American Culture: A History* (Louisville, KY, 2013).
Mulder, Philip N., *A Controversial Spirit: Evangelical Awakenings in the South* (New York, 2002).
Najar, Monica, *Evangelizing the South: A Social History of Church and State in Early America* (New York, 2008).
Noll, Mark A., *America's God: From Jonathan Edwards to Abraham Lincoln* (New York, 2002).
Rawlyk, G. A., *The Canada Fire: Radical Evangelicalism in British North America, 1775–1812* (Kingston and Montreal, 1994).
Sassi, Jonathan, *A Republic of Righteousness: The Public Christianity of the Post-Revolutionary New England Clergy* (New York, 2001).
Semple, Neil, *The Lord's Dominion: The History of Canadian Methodism* (Kingston and Montreal, 1996).
Wigger, John H., *Taking Heaven by Storm: Methodism and the Rise of Popular Christianity in America* (Chicago and Urbana, IL, 1998).
Wright, Conrad, *The Beginnings of Unitarianism in America* (Hamden, CT, 1976).

Part III

Awakening

11

Revival

Michael J. McClymond

The British Evangelical Revival of the eighteenth and early nineteenth centuries has been called 'an attempt to return, after the spiritual lethargy of the late seventeenth century, to the religious fervour of an earlier age'.[1] What is meant generally by 'revival' should be clear enough. Yet the topic involves ambiguities. One question concerns the geographical scope of analysis. While it is possible to focus primarily on revivals and revivalists in the British Isles, such a focus ought not ignore the interchanges of ideas, practices, persons, and texts that linked British Protestants to Continental Europe and to the American colonies. Narratives of spiritual awakening in the eighteenth and early nineteenth centuries would be truncated—and perhaps distorted—if one were to exclude non-British elements. Recent authors have endeavoured to construct a pan-European and a transatlantic protestant revival narrative and have criticized earlier authors for their purportedly insular approach to revival in the British Isles.[2]

Another issue concerns the 'established' versus 'dissenting' distinction. Revival movements criss-crossed this ecclesiastical divide and often adopted a 'one-foot-in, one-foot-out' posture toward Anglicanism. John Wesley's Methodist societies began under the aegis of the Church of England and later

---

[1] Michael R. Watts, *The Dissenters: From the Reformation to the French Revolution* (Oxford, 1978), p. 374.

[2] On British–Continental connections, see W. Reginald Ward, 'Power and Piety: The Origins of Religious Revival in the Early Eighteenth Century', *Bulletin of the John Rylands University Library*, 63, 1 (1980), pp. 231–52; W. Reginald Ward, *The Protestant Evangelical Awakening* (Cambridge, 1992); and Colin J. Podmore, 'The Moravians and the Evangelical Revival in England, 1738–1748', *Transactions of the Moravian Historical Society*, 31 (2000), pp. 29–45. On British–American connections, see Michael J. Crawford, 'New England and the Scottish Religious Revivals of 1742', *American Presbyterians*, 69, 1 (1991), pp. 23–32 and Richard Carwardine, *Transatlantic Revivalism: Popular Evangelicalism in Britain and America, 1790–1865* (Westport, CT, 1978). On North American revivals, see Michael J. McClymond, ed., *Encyclopedia of Religious Revivals in America*, 2 vols. (Westport, CT, 2007). On early Australian evangelicalism, see Stuart Piggin, 'Going into All the World, 1788–1835', in his *Evangelical Christianity in Australia; Spirit, Word, and World* (Melbourne, 1991).

separated—though not all at the same time or in the same way. If one views Methodism as a single tradition, then it has to be categorized as *both* established *and* dissenting. A complete picture of revived Protestantism would include not only groups that finally left the Anglican fold but also the lay and clerical 'Methodists' who carried a revivalist ethos into nineteenth-century Anglicanism. Likewise, Welsh Calvinistic Methodists under Howel Harris and Daniel Rowland began in the Anglican fold and yet by the early nineteenth century had left. In Scotland, the evangelical awakening primarily took place within the Church of Scotland, rather than in the Scottish seceding churches, which largely stood aloof, just as did many of the older Dissenting groups in England.

The Moravians—who helped launch the evangelical awakening—were neither Dissenters as such nor members of the Established Church. On coming to England, they viewed themselves as members of a European sister church to the Church of England, and that—in its Fetter Lane Society—allowed Anglicans to be full members without relinquishing their Anglican identity. Perhaps the clearest case of a revival within the boundaries of British Dissent is that of the English Particular (i.e. Calvinistic) Baptists who were evangelicalized from 1770 to around 1800. This group began in Dissent and ended in Dissent. Yet their case was atypical. More often than not, revival movements began in the Established Church and remained officially within the Established Church from thirty to as long as seventy years before any formal separation took place. In other cases—as in the Moravian–Anglican relationship—the boundaries were always blurry. Wherever in eighteenth-century Britain one found *spiritual fervour*, there was often some crossing of boundaries—between Established and Dissenting Churches, between geographical regions (England, Scotland, Wales, Germany, America), between clergy and laypersons, and between male and female leadership. 'Revival' overflowed institutional, geographical, chronological, and social class or gender boundaries.[3]

ON 'REVIVALS' AND THEIR RELATIONSHIP TO ONE ANOTHER

How ought one to define 'revival'? While there is no unanimity in usage, the term is generally used for a time of *intensified spiritual experience* within some Christian group that has gathered to pray, worship, and/or hear preaching.

---

[3] Mark Noll speaks variously of evangelicalism 'As the Establishment', 'Alongside the Establishment', 'After the End of Establishment', 'Against Establishment', and 'Completely beyond Establishment' (*The Rise of Evangelicalism: The Age of Edwards, Whitefield and the Wesleys* (Leicester, 2004), pp. 195–232).

One person alone with God is not a 'revival'. A 'revival' is inherently corporate rather than individualistic. A group dynamic or spiritual impulse transmitted from person to person is part of what is meant. A 'revival' typically has a definite place and time attached to it. Since 'revivals' are times of intensified, corporate, spiritual experience, they are chiefly known through the reports of people who participated in or witnessed them.

Joseph Entwisle, a Wesleyan preacher in Yorkshire, during February 1794, offered what might be regarded as a typical eighteenth-century revival report:

> Preached at Woodhouse at noon... The Lord is pouring out his Spirit in a very extraordinary manner. Almost all the inhabitants of the village appear to be under religious concern. They have been praying night and day most of the week, generally continuing together from evening till morning.... [At another meeting after they had sat in silence for a considerable time, a poor woman fell upon her knees, and with an extraordinary loud and bitter cry, pleaded for mercy. While she continued crying, 'God be merciful to me a sinner', some of the company went out, and called upon one or two of the leaders, who came and held a meeting; in which several were brought into the liberty of the children of God.

In Entwisle's estimation, some of the religious services got out of hand:

> Our warm friends from Woodhouse... had gone beyond all bounds of decency, such screaming and bawling I never heard. Divided into small companies in different parts of the chapel, some singing, others praying, others praising, clapping of hands, etc. all was confusion and uproar. I was struck with amazement and consternation. What to do I could not tell. However, as there appeared to be no possibility of breaking up the meeting, I quietly withdrew. They continued thus until five o'clock in the morning. What shall I say to these things? I believe God is working very powerfully on the minds of many; but I think Satan, or, at least *the animal nature*, has a great hand in all this.

Soon after writing this journal entry, Entwisle took a more magnanimous view, commenting that the 'good work [is] going on with amazing rapidity in Birstal, Dewsbury, Bradford and Keighley circuits'.[4]

Several things are noticeable here. The defining mark of revival is present, i.e. a pervasive 'religious concern' among this group. Other common phenomena of revival appear—spontaneity, intense prayer, awareness of sinfulness, and emotional distress. The lay-orientation is also clear. A verbal outcry by a 'poor woman' caused those gathered to lay hold of leaders to take charge of the meeting. Finally, the sheer exuberance of the services caused Entwisle to

---

[4] T. Entwisle, *Memoir of the Reverend Joseph Entwisle* (London, 1867), pp. 110–13 (quoted in John Baxter, 'The Great Yorkshire revival 1792–6: A Study of Mass Revival Among the Methodists', *Sociological Yearbook of Religion in Britain*, 7 (1974), pp. 54–5).

wonder whether God's work was also accompanied by the involvement of 'Satan, or, at least *the animal nature*'. The issue of spiritual discernment was inescapable.

Eighteenth-century revivals were interwoven. This becomes clear if one considers the chronology of events and personal connections. The period from 1734 to 1738 was foundational. A powerful spiritual awakening, ensuing in hundreds of reported conversions, occurred in Jonathan Edwards's congregation in Northampton, Massachusetts, in 1734–5. George Whitefield was converted around Easter 1735. The two foremost eighteenth-century Welsh preachers of revival, Howel Harris and Daniel Rowland, also experienced conversion in this same year of 1735. In 1737, Whitefield began his celebrated preaching ministry in England, and Edwards's report of the revival in America—the *Faithful Narrative* (1737)—appeared that same year in London. Edwards's book was read by Wesley, Whitefield, and Harris, and raised expectations regarding a possible spiritual outpouring in Britain. Soon thereafter, John and Charles Wesley both experienced conversion in 1738.

Whitefield's links to the Wesley brothers were manifold. At Oxford in the early 1730s they all participated in the 'Holy Club'. In 1738, their paths crossed when Whitefield travelled to the American colony of Georgia as John Wesley was returning from it. In 1739, Whitefield left Wesley in charge of his work in and around Bristol, as Whitefield went to preach in the colonies—the time of America's 'Great Awakening'. Among the major revivalists, Howel Harris was first to preach outdoors. He convinced George Whitefield to do the same, and Whitefield later convinced John Wesley to follow suit. On arriving in the American colonies, George Whitefield preached from Jonathan Edwards's pulpit in Northampton, Massachusetts. While in America, Whitefield revisited the colony of Georgia, where John and Charles Wesley had served, and where Whitefield had set up his orphanage. John Wesley, in the last letter he wrote before his death in 1791, urged William Wilberforce to pursue the cause of abolitionism. Wilberforce had also come under the influence of the Anglican pastor and hymnodist, John Newton. Anglican evangelical author, Thomas Scott, was another of Newton's protégés. The deeper one looks into British revival history, the more connections one is apt to find.

If the primary direction of influence in mid-eighteenth-century revivalism was from Britain to America, then the direction of flow seems to have reversed by the early nineteenth century. The American revival preacher, Lorenzo Dow (sometimes called 'Crazy Dow' because of his unpredictable behaviour), influenced Hugh Bourne and William Clowes in 1809 to undertake the first Methodist-style camp meeting in England at Mow Cop. Opposition to this innovation led Bourne and Clowes to break away and found the Primitive Methodist denomination. Another flamboyant American preacher, Charles Finney, influenced the development of revivals in Britain indirectly through his writings and example during the 1820s and 1830s and then directly during his travel and preaching in Britain in 1849–51.[5]

THE EMERGENCE OF REVIVAL IN ENGLAND

Michael Watts traced the earliest manifestations of revival in the British Isles to American and/or Continental roots. He noted the fervent preaching of Theodore Frelinghuysen during the 1720s—a Dutch Reformed minister in the American colony of New Jersey. The American Presbyterian Gilbert Tennent was inspired by Frelinghuysen in 1726 to preach in a comparable way, attacking the 'presumptuous security' of those who formally adhered to the Christian faith but without genuine conviction. Watts also pointed to the impact of the Moravian community under Count Zinzendorf at Bertelsdorf in Saxony, which experienced a 1727 'Pentecost' of renewed religious fervour, and soon sent out missionaries to the West Indies (1732), to Greenland (1733), to the Indians of Surinam (1734), to the Hottentots of South Africa (1737), and to Ceylon (1737).[6] W. R. Ward traced Protestant awakenings in Britain back to persecuted German-speaking Protestants, in Silesia just after 1700, and in Salzburg during the 1730s. In both cases Protestants were persecuted by Catholic authorities and driven from their homes and places of worship. A 'Children's Revival' in Silesia took shape as younger people gathered outdoors for impromptu prayer, persuading their elders to join them, and not let the loss of church buildings put an end to their corporate worship.[7]

Three independent movements—American, Moravian, and Welsh—came into contact with Anglicanism and with one another through the 'Holy Club' at Oxford University. From 1729, this group met for study, prayer, and good works. George Whitefield noted that they were called 'Methodists... from their custom of regulating their time and planning the business of the day every morning'. The first 'Methodist' to come out as a revival preacher was George Whitefield—who, in time, proved to be the most popular of them all. Whitefield was also the chief connective link between the English, American, Welsh, and Scottish revivals. Ordained deacon in 1736, he answered a call to the infant colony of Georgia. Yet while waiting for his departure, Whitefield began preaching in 1737 to large and animated audiences in Bristol, Gloucester, and London. 'The doctrine of the new birth and justification by faith in Jesus Christ,' he wrote, 'made its way like lightning into the hearers' consciences. The arrows of conviction stuck fast.'[8]

---

[5] Carwardine, *Transatlantic Revivalism*, ch. 4.   [6] Watts, *The Dissenters*, pp. 394–6.
[7] Ward, *The Protestant Evangelical Awakening*.
[8] Watts, *The Dissenters*, p. 398 (citing George Whitefield, *Journals* (Edinburgh, 1960), pp. 48, 81).

From 1738 to 1741, Whitefield was nominally the parish minister in Savannah, Georgia. Yet throughout his career he devoted himself to itinerant evangelism rather than traditional pastoral work. Whitefield's travels did not allow for regular pastoral ministry; he crossed the Atlantic no fewer than thirteen times. His preaching impressed even the unbelievers. Lord Bolingbroke attributed to Whitefield 'the most commanding eloquence I ever heard in any person', while David Hume thought it 'worth going twenty miles to hear him'.[9] When the crowds grew too large for the churches, Whitefield went outdoors, noting that he could address 'ten times more people than I should if I had been confined to churches'.[10]

Together with Frelinghuysen, Tennent, and Edwards in America, and Harris in Wales, Whitefield embraced a Calvinist theology. The Wesley brothers, as Arminians, were in the minority among early 'Methodist' preachers, even though the label 'Methodist' eventually affixed itself to the denomination the Wesleys began. The eclipse of Whitefield's adherents by Wesley's had much to do with Whitefield's lack of success in organizing his followers, whom he once called a 'rope of sand' in contrast to the better-disciplined Wesleyan associations. Though a wooden meeting house had been built for Whitefield in London in 1741, Moorfields Tabernacle, it was Howel Harris who preached during Whitefield's absences. Harris bore responsibility for organizing the Welsh societies and did so skilfully. By 1750, there were 433 Welsh Calvinistic Methodist societies, but only twenty-nine English Calvinist Methodist societies.[11] In consequence, Welsh Methodism became decidedly Calvinistic.

Whitefield's followers, to be sure, were not wholly unorganized. Selina, countess of Huntingdon, was converted in the 1730s, and sought to give stability to the English Calvinistic Methodist societies. She appointed evangelical clergymen, including Whitefield, as her private chaplains, built chapels for them in fashionable resorts such as Brighton, Bath, and Tunbridge Wells, and invited them to speak to aristocratic gatherings at her London and Leicestershire homes. In 1768, Selina opened an evangelical training college at Trevecca. Yet her authority over the 'Connexion' was moral rather than legal, and she may have waited too long to provide formal structure. In 1790, the year before her death, she composed a 'plan of association' to give organization to her sixty-four chapels, yet the plan was never implemented.[12]

While Charles Wesley had founded the 'Methodist' or 'Holy Club' at Oxford in 1729, John—his older brother, and a Fellow of Lincoln College—soon emerged as the dominant figure. In the winter of 1735–6, the two brothers sailed to Georgia to minister in the colony and to convert the Native

---

[9] Luke Tyerman, *The Life of the Rev. George Whitefield*, 2 vols. (London, 1876–7), II, p. 194ff.
[10] Watts, *The Dissenters*, p. 399 (citing Whitefield, *Journals*, p. 84).
[11] Watts, *The Dissenters*, pp. 399–400.   [12] Watts, *The Dissenters*, pp. 400–1.

Americans. Yet the rigid spiritual discipline that they sought to impose provoked resentment. Instead of converting others, John Wesley came to doubt his own conversion. In Oxford he had devoted himself to 'visiting the prisons, assisting the poor and sick in town, and what other good I could'. He fasted two days each week. Yet all this abstinence and activity brought him no comfort, nor 'any assurance of acceptance with God'. It was the Moravians whom John met in America and in London who showed him a more excellent way'. Soon John Wesley came to rely on Christ alone for forgiveness. Charles Wesley returned to England in 1736, and John in 1738—both depressed at the failure of their mission. Back in England, Charles experienced conversion on Pentecost Sunday (21 May 1738), and wrote in a hymn: 'My chains fell off, my heart was free / I rose, went forth, and followed thee'. Three days later (24 May 1738), John went to a religious meeting at Aldersgate in London, at which, as he wrote, 'I felt my heart strangely warmed. I felt that I did trust in Christ, Christ alone, for my salvation; and an assurance was given me, that he had taken away my sins.' In March 1739, Whitefield asked John Wesley to take over his evangelistic work in Bristol, while Whitefield went to preach in America. Wesley accepted, though he could 'scarce reconcile' himself to Whitefield's 'strange way of preaching in the fields'. By April, Wesley 'submitted to be more vile, and proclaimed in the highways the glad tidings of salvation'.[13]

In the thirty years from 1740 to 1770, John Wesley by his own estimate had ridden more than 100,000 miles on horseback, and still had almost twenty more years of travel ahead of him. Wesley travelled twenty times to Scotland and twenty more times to Ireland. He was more inclined to the humdrum tasks of pastoral care than Whitefield was. As an ordained clergyman, Wesley had an authority over the Methodist societies under his charge that Howel Harris as a layman did not have.[14]

INTERNAL DIVISION AND EXTERNAL OPPOSITION

The earliest theological debate among the leaders of British revival began in October 1739, when the Moravian, Philip Molther, arrived in England and brought with him the doctrine of 'stillness'. According to this teaching, the way to attain faith was not by attending church, hearing sermons, or receiving the sacrament, but by being still and waiting for Christ. By contrast, John Wesley insisted that public worship, private devotion, fasting, and the Lord's

---

[13] Watts, *The Dissenters*, p. 402 (citing John Wesley, *The Journal of the Rev. John Wesley*, ed. N. Curnock, 8 vols. (London, 1909-16), I, pp. 467-9, 475-6, 167, 172-3).

[14] Watts, *The Dissenters*, p. 403 (citing Wesley, *Journal*, V, p. 361).

Supper were 'means of grace' that 'do ordinarily convey God's grace to unbelievers'. Molther denied that an unbeliever should perform good works, while Wesley thought he should 'do all the temporal good he can'. Wesley concluded that the Moravians were antinomians—i.e. denying that those saved by grace needed to obey God.

A more enduringly divisive conflict arose less than a year later. Though Whitefield left Wesley in charge of his ministry in Bristol, Wesley went against Whitefield's wishes by publishing his anti-Calvinist sermon, *Free Grace* (1740). The resulting theological rift between Calvinist and Arminian evangelicals ran deep and it remained unreconciled. Arminians rejected Calvinist predestination, were offended by what they took as the heartlessness of the Calvinist God, and regarded Calvinism as leading to antinomianism. Calvinists considered Arminianism a mistaken denial of God's sovereignty and suspected Arminians of teaching works-righteousness. In 1738 Wesley had experienced his conversion while listening to Luther's writings being read aloud. Yet just three years later, Wesley found Luther's commentary on Galatians to be 'muddy and confused', and viewed Luther's denigration of good works as the root cause of the Moravians' errors on grace and law.[15]

There was a lull in the Calvinist–Arminian controversy for more than twenty years. In 1768, six Calvinistic Methodists were expelled from St Edmund Hall, Oxford, and this led to a pamphlet war in which Calvinists and Arminians both claimed that theirs was the true Anglican teaching. At the Methodist Conference in 1770, Wesley defined faith and works in a way that struck Calvinists as essentially catholic, stating that 'whoever repents, should do "works meet for repentance"'. Good works were a condition for salvation. Wesley went so far as to defend the condemned heretic of ancient Britain, Pelagius, as 'a wise and an holy man'.[16] The Anglican Calvinist, Augustus Toplady, debated Wesley and then Wesley's associate, John Fletcher. At issue were the Calvinistic doctrine of predestination, the Wesleyan charge of antinomianism against the Calvinists, and what Calvinists regarded as the most dangerous delusion of all—the Wesleyan teaching on 'Christian perfection'.[17]

For Wesley, the goal of salvation was not forgiveness and assurance of salvation, but 'entire sanctification', 'perfect love', or 'Christian perfection'. This he defined as 'another name for universal holiness'. Christians, he said, could not in the present life be free from ignorance, yet could be 'free from outward sin'. This Christian ideal was drawn at least in part from William Law and Jeremy Taylor—part of Wesley's pre-conversion Anglican reading. Many

---

[15] Watts, *The Dissenters*, p. 429 (citing Wesley, *Journal*, II, pp. 329–30, 491, 476).

[16] Watts, *The Dissenters*, p. 431 (citing *Minutes of the Methodist Conferences* (London, 1812), p. 96 and John Wesley, *The Letters of the Rev. John Wesley*, ed. J. Telford, 8 vols. (London, 1931), IV, p. 158 and VI, p. 175).

[17] Patrick Philipp Streiff, *Reluctant Saint?: A Theological Biography of Fletcher of Madelay* (Peterborough, 2001).

of Wesley's followers, though, preferred to preach grace rather than insist on 'Christian perfection'. By 1772, Wesley admitted that he was losing the battle: 'I found almost all our preachers in every circuit have done with Christian perfection. They say they believe it; but they never preach it.'[18]

Throughout the mid to late eighteenth century, revival preachers faced fierce opposition. Anglican clergymen resented what they took as an intrusion into their sphere. Welsh clergymen complained to Griffith Jones in 1743 that the Methodist preachers 'damn all others in order to terrify the illiterate into their faction'. At Machynlleth in 1739, Howel Harris was prevented from preaching by a crowd 'threatening, swearing, and flinging stones', while someone fired a pistol at the evangelist. At Bala in 1741, both Harris and John Cennick were squirted with water from a fire engine. John Wesley, when preaching at St Ives in Cornwall, had a mob break into the room in which he was preaching and strike him on the head. When Charles Wesley addressed a congregation in Sheffield in 1743, the mob demolished the Methodists' meeting house. In Yorkshire in 1752, Thomas Lee was dragged through the sewer. At Stepney in 1772 a group of sailors 'swore they would hear no such doctrine as damnation', threw a Methodist preacher in a wheelbarrow, and dumped him into a pond. Not only preachers, but rank-and-file Methodists suffered too. Homes were ransacked, possessions looted, and women assaulted. Methodist artisans were deprived of work and Methodist farmers evicted.[19]

REVIVALS IN SCOTLAND

Scotland has a protestant revival tradition stretching back to the early seventeenth century and perhaps even earlier. Successive waves of Catholic and Anglican opposition to Presbyterianism kindled Scottish fervour. When Charles I ascended to the throne in 1625, some Scots feared that the king would restore Roman Catholicism there. An effort to introduce King Charles's new Prayer Book in St Giles Cathedral caused a riot.[20] Protestant–Catholic conflicts are one reason for the emergence of outdoor services. Most memorable was that held at the Kirk of Shotts in 1630, when 500 persons were reportedly converted at one time. Revivals occurred during Scottish 'Holy Fairs'—religious festivals that brought together multiple congregations for multi-day services of preaching and culminating in reception of the

---

[18] Watts, *The Dissenters*, pp. 432, 434 (citing John Wesley, *The Works of the Rev. John Wesley*, 14 vols., 3rd edn (London, 1831), VI, pp. 413–14, and Wesley, *Letters*, V, p. 314).

[19] Watts, *The Dissenters*, pp. 404–6; R. F. Wearmouth, *Methodism and the Common People of the Eighteenth Century* (London, 1945), p. 158; and Thomas Jackson, ed., *The Lives of Early Methodist Preachers*, 6 vols., 3rd edn (London, 1865–6) IV, pp. 158, i, 160.

[20] J. H. S. Burleigh, *A Church History of Scotland* (London, 1960), pp. 210, 216.

Lord's Supper.[21] Lay-led, private religious societies further stoked Scottish devotion. John Knox, in his *Letter of Wholesome Counsell* (1556), instructed that laymen's groups should pray and read Scripture together, expound the Scriptures, practise mutual confession of sins, and give thanks to God. Only the celebration of the Lord's Supper was to be omitted.[22]

In discussing Scottish revivals, one must distinguish the Highlands from the Lowlands. In remote parts of the Highlands and the Isles during the eighteenth century and early nineteenth century, church congregations were few and far between and pastoral ministry was scarce. Christian ministry in the Highlands was often combined with basic education. The Haldane brothers, who toured the Scottish Highlands in the 1790s, used such a strategy. Literacy increased among those learning to read the Bible. The religious and cultural impact was far-reaching.

By the early eighteenth century, a new challenge to evangelical faith appeared.[23] Scottish Presbyterian ministers influenced by the Enlightenment were preaching natural morality and the cultivation of moral goodness to the neglect of sin and redemption through Christ. Some university professors veered into Arminian or Arian teachings. The drift into liberalism helped galvanize evangelicals. In 1712, Parliament restored to protestant heritors the right to nominate ministers to vacant pulpits. Scottish evangelicals objected to church patronage as inimical to Presbyterian polity, as an infringement on the rights of lay church members, and as a tool for the elites to impose non-evangelical ministers on unwilling congregants. Yet the evangelical party was itself divided. Edward Fisher's *The Marrow of Modern Divinity* (1644), partially republished in 1718, fostered a more strident evangelicalism that insisted on the fullness and freeness of grace, the universal call to faith, and the sufficiency of Christ as the Saviour for all. Angered by doctrinal laxity in the Church, a number of 'Marrowmen', led by Ebenezer Erskine, seceded in 1733 to form the Associate Presbytery.

When Whitefield came to preach in Scotland in July 1741, he first met with leaders from the Associate Presbytery. These Seceders insisted that Whitefield preach only from their own pulpits, have nothing to do with the Church of Scotland, and that he officially renounce his own Anglicanism. Only days after arriving, Whitefield had fallen out with them, but was welcomed by evangelical ministers in the Church of Scotland. Over the next four months, Whitefield preached in some thirty towns, including Edinburgh, Glasgow, Aberdeen,

---

[21] Leigh Eric Schmidt, *Holy Fairs: Scottish Communions and American Revivals in the Early Modern Period* (Princeton, NJ, 1989).

[22] Burleigh, *A Church History of Scotland*, pp. 160, 268. See also Kenneth B. E. Roxburgh, 'The Scottish Evangelical Awakening of 1742 and the Religious Societies', *Journal of the United Reformed Church History Society*, 5, 5 (1994), pp. 266–73.

[23] The following paragraphs draw from Crawford, 'New England and the Scottish Religious Revivals', pp. 24–30.

and Dundee. While Whitefield's preaching stirred interest, widespread revival did not take shape until Whitefield came again to Scotland in 1742, to Cambuslang, at what was perhaps the most celebrated and most controversial revival episode in eighteenth-century Britain.[24]

The 'Cam'slang Wark' began in a rural parish five miles south-east of Glasgow, through minister William McCulloch's calculated effort to bring revival. Not known for his preaching skill, McCulloch was appointed to this congregation after it had lacked a minister for several years. After McCulloch organized his people into several groups to pray for spiritual awakening, the first stirrings appeared in February 1742, when one member of the church showed deep distress over her spiritual state, and then the spiritual concern spread to fifty parishioners. Numbers of the hopeful, the sceptical, and the curious began to appear, and McCulloch's fellow ministers, John Willison of Dundee, James Robe of Kilsyth, and John Maclaurin of Glasgow came to assist him. During spring and summer the movement grew until much of western Scotland was affected. The revival culminated in a vast outdoor communion service in July 1742, with Whitefield preaching, some 20,000 in attendance, and 1,700 receiving communion, and then—in unprecedented succession—a second summer service with 30,000 in attendance, and thirteen pastors administering communion to 3,000 persons.

What distinguished the Cambuslang Revival was not only its magnitude, but the intensity of the reported spiritual experiences. McCulloch's 1,300 page manuscript—*Examinations of Persons Under Spiritual Concern at Cambuslang*—included accounts of 108 persons affected by the revival. The manuscript included not only first-person narratives, but marginal comments from five ministers, indicating how clerics interpreted lay spiritual experiences. While neither McCulloch nor the other ministers wanted to publish unedited accounts (and the full versions did not appear until 2011), the manuscript bears eloquent witness to the range and intensity of Scottish lay spirituality during the time of evangelical awakening.[25]

Against Whitefield's advice, John Wesley made Scotland a part of his mission field, travelling there no fewer than twenty-two times between 1751 and 1790. Yet Wesley was less successful in Scotland than elsewhere. His preaching may have been less necessary there, for Wesley himself acknowledged that the Scots were spiritually better off than were the English. Whitefield saw no need for a Calvinistic Methodist Connexion in Scotland.

---

[24] T. C. Smout, 'Born Again at Cambuslang: New Evidence on Popular Religion and Literacy in Eighteenth-Century Scotland', *Past & Present*, 97, 1 (1982), pp. 114–27; D. Bruce Hindmarsh, '"The Word Came In With Power": Conversions at Cambuslang', in Hindmarsh, *The Evangelical Conversion Narrative: Spiritual Autobiography in Early Modern England* (Oxford. 2005), pp. 193–225.

[25] The first full transcription and publication was Keith Edward Beebe, *The McCulloch Examinations of the Cambuslang Revival (1742): A Critical Edition*, 2 vols. (Woodbridge, 2011).

akin to that in Wales. More ardent an Anglican than Whitefield, Wesley was also less sympathetic to Scottish ways. He established Wesleyan associations in Scotland, but they remained small. Another difficulty for Wesley in Scotland was his Arminianism, which ran against the theological sensibilities of Scottish evangelical leaders, such as Thomas Erskine, who steadfastly opposed him.[26]

If we include the earlier awakenings, then a list of noteworthy Scottish (and Ulster) awakenings would include: Edinburgh, 1596; Ulster, 1623–41; Stewarton, 1625; Kirk of Shotts, 1630; Cambuslang, 1742; Kilsyth, 1742–3; Balderknock, Kirkintilloch, 1742–3; Moulin, 1798–1800; the Isle of Arran, 1804 and 1812–13; Skye, 1812–14; and the Isle of Lewis, 1824–35.[27] Scottish revivals of the late 1700s and early 1800s not only brought a renewal of religious fervour, but a renewal of controversies over lay patronage and theological orthodoxy, pitting Evangelicals against Moderates during the Ten Years' Conflict (1834–43), and culminating in the Great Disruption of 1843, which resulted in the emergence of the Free Church of Scotland.[28]

REVIVALS IN WALES

In the early eighteenth century, Wales was still a predominantly agricultural society. Though Wales had been politically united to England since the time of Henry VIII, travel between England and Wales remained difficult. The Welsh sense of isolation was further heightened by their linguistic difference from England and Scotland. Early revival preachers in Wales noted that many hearers and converts knew no English at all. The ministry of the Anglican Church in Wales was largely unsuccessful. Few ministers could preach in Welsh. The Diocese of St David's covered half of Wales, included 300 parishes, and yet was an impoverished post that Anglican bishops viewed as a stepping-stone to a better position. Diocesan records reveal that clergy in this period were charged with sexual immorality, drunkenness, and neglect of duty. Many parishes were too poor to support a minister, so ministers had to divide their time among multiple parishes. Most families could not afford to buy books.

Against this backdrop, the Anglican minister, Griffith Jones, established free 'circulating' (i.e. movable) schools to provide basic education in the remote villages and countryside of Wales. These schools were strikingly successful. Between 1737 and 1761, Jones conducted 3,225 schools in 1,600 locations, and taught 200,000 students—a figure amounting to about half of the population

---

[26] Burleigh, *A Church History of Scotland*, pp. 293–5.
[27] See the Scottish revival narratives in Richard Owen Roberts, ed., *Scotland Saw His Glory: A History of Revivals in Scotland* (Wheaton, IL, 1995).
[28] Burleigh, *A Church History of Scotland*, pp. 337–62.

of Wales. A popular preacher, Jones was reported to the authorities—for the offence of attracting crowds. Just as important as Jones's educational work was the inspiration his example gave to others, including Howel Harris and Daniel Rowland, who emerged as two leading revival preachers of the eighteenth century in Wales.[29]

On Palm Sunday of 1735, Howel Harris was alarmed by the vicar's warning to those unfit to come to the Lord's Table. His breakthrough came on Pentecost Sunday. When Harris experienced conversion he was convinced 'that Christ died for me, and that all my sins were laid on him'. Harris said that he 'felt some insatiable desires after the salvation of poor sinners', and so started holding services in his mother's home, where her neighbours had been invited. Soon he was going house to house, and village to village, 'exhorting all those with whom I had formerly sinned'. Harris wrote: 'The word was attended with such power that many on the spot cried out to God for pardon of their sins.' Later in 1735, Daniel Rowland attended a service conducted by Griffith Jones and experienced his conversion.[30]

Rowland and Harris first met in 1737. Harris came to hear Rowland preach, and said that 'the first time I saw him he was surrounded with glory in the pulpit in Defynnog'.[31] By temperament, Rowland was steady while Harris was impetuous. Rowland was an ordained minister and remained within the Established Church (until finally forced out), while Harris was an irregular or lay preacher. Rowland travelled occasionally while Harris itinerated constantly. Harris was austere, humourless, imperious, and passionately devoted to evangelism, while Rowland could be light-hearted as well as serious. At first Harris tried to combine school teaching in daytime with 'exhorting' in the evening, making do with only two hours' or less sleep at night. He pushed himself relentlessly, often travelling twenty or thirty miles a day and preaching in multiple locations. The travel took a toll on Harris and may have helped to precipitate the emotional instability that preceded his break with Rowland in 1750. Yet by this point there were 433 religious societies in Wales and bordering regions. Michael Watts wrote that 'Harris, more than any other man, had begun a revolution in the religious life of Wales which was to determine the character of its people for 200 years.'[32]

By the end of 1738, Rowland was preaching in extra-parochial contexts, and facing the same sort of opposition that Wesley and Whitefield had experienced in England. When church doors were locked, Rowland preached outdoors. As events unfolded, Rowland took over much of the pastoral responsibility for those affected by the Welsh revival, while Harris was away travelling and

---

[29] Eifion Evans, *Daniel Rowland and the Great Awakening in Wales* (Edinburgh, 1985), pp. 9–20.
[30] Watts, *The Dissenters*, p. 396.
[31] Evans, *Daniel Rowland and the Great Awakening*, p. 52.
[32] Watts, *The Dissenters*, pp. 396–7.

preaching in London, Bristol, and Gloucester.[33] As noted already, Harris was himself often doing pastoral ministry in England, while Whitefield was absent in America and Scotland. Another leader in Welsh revival was William Williams Pantycelyn, converted in 1738, ordained in 1740, and best known as a hymnodist in the Welsh language. Among his songs is 'Guide Me, O Thou Great Jehovah'. A second-generation Welsh revival preacher was Thomas Charles (1755–1814), who led an awakening in Bala, North Wales, at the end of the eighteenth century.

LATE EIGHTEENTH-CENTURY AND EARLY NINETEENTH-CENTURY DEVELOPMENTS

One general trait in the second wave of evangelical revivals (c.1780–c.1830) was a self-conscious focus on human effort in advancing revivals and evangelism. Perspectives on American and British revivals began to shift. Observers often compared revivals of the 1740s to unanticipated 'showers of blessing'. Revivals of the early 1800s were 'harvests' resulting from diligent and wise application of human 'means'. From the 1770s onward, Jonathan Edwards's writings helped British Calvinistic Baptists adopt a more activist approach to ministry. John Sutcliff, John Ryland, Junior, and Andrew Fuller came to accept the legitimacy of calling hearers to faith (the 'duty faith' doctrine)—a theological shift that sanctioned the use of new evangelistic strategies. The protestant missionary pioneer William Carey referred to Edwards's writings as a 'second Bible'.[34] Scotland's leading evangelical in the early to mid nineteenth century, Thomas Chalmers, was another avid reader of Jonathan Edwards. Like the British Calvinistic Baptists, Chalmers found Edwards an inspiration for his labours in evangelism, church renewal, and social reform.

The evangelical revivals of the 1780s and 1790s occurred against the backdrop of Enlightenment attacks on Christian belief and the political insurgency of the French Revolution and Napoleonic era. Christianity itself was now on the defensive, and this meant that a presentation of gospel claims also had to address intellectual objections, especially in elite circles. In the newly formed United States of America, the president of Yale College (and grandson of Jonathan Edwards), Timothy Dwight, responded to a challenge from students to defend the veracity of the Bible, and Dwight's impassioned campus lectures in 1802–3 resulted in a student revival in which one-third of

---

[33] Evans, *Daniel Rowland and the Great Awakening*, pp. 81–5.
[34] Michael A. G. Haykin, *One Heart and One Soul: John Sutcliff of Olney, His Friends, and His Times* (Durham, 1994), pp. 139–71.

the Yale students made professions of faith. On both sides of the Atlantic, revival preaching became conjoined with Christian apologetics.[35]

Fear of political insurgency was another new factor after the outbreak of revolution in France. When the Scottish evangelicals, James and Robert Haldane, did revival preaching and teaching in the Scottish Highlands in the late 1790s, the Church of Scotland's General Assembly in 1799 not only lambasted 'vagrant teachers and Sunday Schools' but intimated that the Haldanes might be linked to atheistic and seditious opinions emanating from France.[36] To the authorities, all popular movements were suspect. Members of the Haldane family later helped to trigger religious revivals in Switzerland from the 1810s to the 1830s (there known as the *Reveil*).[37]

At the time of Wesley's death in 1791, there were 72,000 Wesleyan or Arminian Methodists in the British Isles and another 60,000 in North America.[38] The strong growth of Wesleyan Methodism through the latter part of the eighteenth century was due in no small part to itinerancy by Wesley and the preachers whom he appointed. Itinerancy was strongly associated with Wesleyan Methodists, occasionally with Anglicans, and rarely with Dissenters.[39]

During the final decades of the eighteenth century, the Anglican evangelical, John Newton, seemed to be everywhere and to be connected with everyone—a 'middleman' as he termed himself. Though ordained and serving in the Church of England, Newton maintained close ties with Dissenting evangelicals, and his bridge-building ministry foreshadowed the interdenominational British evangelicalism of the nineteenth century. A former slave-ship captain, Newton underwent a long pilgrimage toward abolitionism, and in later life counselled William Wilberforce and other members of the reformist 'Clapham Sect' in their campaign against the slave trade and for moral reform.[40] Wilberforce's Society for the Suppression of Vice (1802) was only one of many such organizations directed by upper-class Anglican evangelicals and devoted to the eradication of prostitution, illegal gambling, blasphemy, Sabbath-breaking, and other offences. From 1790 to 1830, evangelicalism in Britain to some extent entered a 'triumphant phase' and became a victim of its own

---

[35] David Bebbington has argued that evangelical revival was not an antithesis to eighteenth-century Enlightenment, but embodied many of the same traits. See David Bebbington, Revival and Enlightenment in Eighteenth-Century England', in Edith L. Blumhofer and Randall Balmer, eds, *Modern Christian Revivals* (Urbana, IL, 1993), pp. 17–41.

[36] Burleigh, *A Church History of Scotland*, 311–12.

[37] Timothy C. F. Stunt, *From Awakening to Secession: Radical Evangelicals in Switzerland and Britain, 1815–35* (Edinburgh, 2000).

[38] Watts, *The Dissenters*, p. 403 (citing Wesley, *Journal*, V, p. 361).

[39] Roger H. Martin, 'Evangelical Dissenters and Wesleyan-style Itinerant Ministries at the End of the Eighteenth Century', *Methodist History*, 16, 2 (1978), pp. 169–84.

[40] D. Bruce Hindmarsh, *John Newton and the English Evangelical Tradition* (Grand Rapids, MI, 2001 [1996]).

successes.[41] Evangelical moralism provoked counterreaction. Novelist Charlotte Brontë—though daughter of a moderately evangelical, clerical father—depicted evangelicalism in her novel *Jane Eyre* as harsh, joyless, and intolerant in the figure of the Reverend Brocklehurst.[42]

EXPLANATIONS FOR REVIVALS

How might one explain the emergence and prevalence of religious revival?[43] Participants often attributed revival to the power of God or agency of the Holy Spirit. Their impression of revival as something God-given was strengthened by the nearly simultaneous emergence of religious awakenings in different locations during the decade from 1734 to 1744. Such faith-based explanations are of course empirically untestable, and do not account for why revivals arrive at particular times and places. F. M. Davenport's *Primitive Traits in Religious Revivals* (1905) was among the first works to break away completely from theological explanations. Davenport appealed to crowd psychology. The skilful preacher played on the chords of imagination, weakening an audience's inhibitions, and leading hearers to suspend rational thought and to enter into emotional frenzy.[44]

In writings published between 1905 and 1913, the French scholar, Élie Halévy, examined Britain in 1815 and asked why it had not undergone the sort of revolution that occurred in France. On his view, Britain was favourable soil for revolution, and neither the British Constitution nor the Established Church could explain the nation's political stability. Halévy found his answer in England's Dissenters, stating that 'the despair of the working class was the raw material to which Methodist doctrine and discipline gave shape'. Methodism was an antidote to Jacobinism.[45] Religious revival substituted for political revolution—a way of releasing pent-up social energies.

Scholars have long debated Halévy's thesis. In *The Making of the English Working Class* (1963), E. P. Thompson drew out one of Halévy's

---

[41] Arthur Pollard, 'The Evangelical Revival: The Triumphant Phase (1790–1830)', *Churchman*, 107, 3 (1993), pp. 254–66.

[42] Michael Baumber, 'William Grimshaw, Patrick Brontë and the Evangelical Revival', *History Today* (November 1992), pp. 25–31. The American analogue might be Harriett Beecher Stowe's novel, *The Minister's Wooing* (1859), portraying a righteous though rigid preacher, modelled on Jonathan Edwards's disciple, Samuel Hopkins.

[43] Discussions of the 'why' of revivals include Watts, *The Dissenters*, pp. 406–28 and Michael J. Crawford, 'Origins of the Eighteenth-Century Evangelical Revival: England and New England Compared', *Journal of British Studies*, 26, 4 (1987), pp. 361–97.

[44] Watts, *The Dissenters*, pp. 409–10.

[45] Elissa S. Itzkin, 'The Halévy Thesis—A Working Hypothesis? English Revivalism: Antidote for Revolution and Radicalism, 1789–1815', *Church History*, 44, 1 (1974), p. 48.

implications—viz. that one should observe an inverse relationship between religious and political radicalism. When lower-class movements of political protest became stalled, according to Thompson, the energy of protest was rechannelled into religious revival.[46] Yet while the revivals of the 1790s–1810s might perhaps be explained in terms of a revolutionary situation, those of the 1730s and 1740s are harder to explain in this way. Another suggestion from Thompson is that the 'sin' involved in Methodist conversion was usually sexual in character, and often a covert struggle to overcome masturbation. There is some evidence for this—though the eighteenth-century texts are oblique.[47] A high proportion of early Welsh Calvinistic Methodists were unmarried women and men, and so attraction to revivalist religion might be correlated with sexual frustration and/or romantic disappointment.

Alan Gilbert traced Methodism's appeal in the early Industrial Revolution to its 'capacity for satisfying the profound associational and communal demands of people experiencing anomie... and social insecurity in a period of rapid social change'.[48] Yet Michael Watts has argued that early Methodist preachers, as a group, were not victims of social disorganization: 'A high proportion seem to have enjoyed secure family life, steady work, and modest prosperity.'[49] While the fact and the importance of eighteenth- and early nineteenth-century British revivals is not in doubt, the causes of these revivals remain a matter of debate.

SELECT BIBLIOGRAPHY

Bebbington, David, 'Revival and Enlightenment in Eighteenth-Century England', in Edith L. Blumhofer and Randall Balmer, eds, *Modern Christian Revivals* (Urbana, IL, 1993), pp. 17–41.
Beebe, Keith Edward, *The McCulloch Examinations of the Cambuslang Revival (1742): A Critical Edition—Conversion Narratives from the Scottish Evangelical Awakening*, 2 vols. (Woodbridge, 2011).
Carwardine, Richard, *Transatlantic Revivalism: Popular Evangelicalism in Britain and America, 1790–1865* (Westport, CT, 1978).
Crawford, Michael J., 'New England and the Scottish Religious Revivals of 1742', *American Presbyterians*, 69, 1 (1991), pp. 23–32.
Evans, Eifiion, *Daniel Rowland and the Great Awakening in Wales* (Edinburgh, 1985).

---

[46] E. P. Thompson, *The Making of the English Working Class* (London, 1963).
[47] Watts, *The Dissenters*, pp. 418–19. Whitefield said that he 'fell into abominable secret sin' aged sixteen and he asked why God gave him such passions when he was not permitted to gratify them (quoted p. 419).
[48] Alan D. Gilbert, *Religion and Society in Industrial England: Church, Chapel, and Social Change, 1740–1914* (London, 1976), p. 89.
[49] Watts, *The Dissenters*, p. 409.

Haykin, Michael A. G., *One Heart and One Soul: John Sutcliff of Olney, His Friends, and His Times* (Durham, 1994).

Hindmarsh, D. Bruce, *John Newton and the English Evangelical Tradition* (Grand Rapids, MI, 2001 [1996]).

Hindmarsh, D. Bruce, *The Evangelical Conversion Narrative: Spiritual Autobiography in Early Modern England* (Oxford, 2005).

Piggin, Stuart, *Evangelical Christianity in Australia: Spirit, Word, and World* (Melbourne, 1991).

Podmore, Colin, 'The Moravians and the Evangelical Revival in England, 1738–1748', *Transactions of the Moravian Historical Society*, 31 (2000), pp. 28–45.

Rawlyk, George A., ed., *Henry Alline: Selected Writings* (New York, 1987).

Roberts, Richard Owen, ed., *Scotland Saw His Glory: A History of Revivals in Scotland* (Wheaton, IL, 1995).

Schmidt, Leigh Eric, *Holy Fairs: Scottish Communions and American Revivals in the Early Modern Period* (Princeton, NJ, 1989).

Smout, T. C., 'Born Again at Cambuslang: New Evidence on Popular Religion and Literacy in Eighteenth-Century Scotland', *Past & Present*, 97, 1 (1982), pp. 114–27.

Stunt, Timothy C. F., *From Awakening to Secession: Radical Evangelicals in Switzerland and Britain, 1815–35* (Edinburgh, 2000).

Ward, W. R., 'Power and Piety: The Origins of Religious Revival in the Early Eighteenth Century', *Bulletin of the John Rylands University Library*, 63, 1 (1980), pp. 231–52.

Ward, W. R., *The Protestant Evangelical Awakening* (Cambridge, 1992).

Watts, Michael R., *The Dissenters: From the Reformation to the French Revolution* (Oxford, 1978).

12

Missionary Societies

Brian Stanley

NEW DISSENTING PATTERNS OF OVERSEAS MISSION

The Dissenting religious traditions that trace their origins to a variety of movements in English church history in the period from the late sixteenth to the eighteenth century now form prominent features of the global patchwork that is world Christianity. The diffusion of those traditions beyond the British Isles is partly the result of migration, some of it, as in the seventeenth century, impelled by a quest for religious freedom. But it is also the product of a quite deliberate process of religious propagation initiated by missionary societies formed in the years between the French Revolution and the repeal of the Test and Corporation Acts and shaped by the theological perspectives of the eighteenth-century evangelical awakenings. This turbulent period in British political history is thus of seminal significance in the globalization of Christian Dissenting traditions.

An older tradition of anglophone protestant scholarship tended to identify English evangelical Dissent as the cradle of the modern protestant missionary movement itself. According to this tradition, the Particular (Calvinistic) Baptist pioneer William Carey (1761–1834) deserves to be remembered as 'the father of modern missions'. More recent scholarship has eroded this narrative from two directions. First, Anglican historians have sought to rehabilitate the genuinely missionary credentials of the Society for the Propagation of the Gospel in Foreign Parts (SPG), awarded its royal charter by William III in 1701, and, to a lesser extent, of the Society for Promoting Christian Knowledge (SPCK), founded in 1698/9. Rowan Strong and Dan O'Connor have argued that the SPG was always more than a society designed to provide Anglican ministry to British settlers in the American colonies, and have thus claimed that the source of the foreign missionary imperative in protestant history should be traced to the orthodox High Church tradition of the eighteenth-century Church of England rather than to the Evangelical Revival and its impact on English

Dissent.¹ Second, much recent writing has pointed out that the deepest roots of evangelical protestant missions lie, not in English Dissent, but in the central European Pietist traditions that inspired the first protestant mission from Halle to the Danish colony of Tranquebar in 1706 and the diverse overseas missions mounted by the Moravian Brethren, beginning with their mission to the slave population of St Thomas in the Caribbean in 1732.

Both strands of historical revision have valid points to make. William Carey himself, in his celebrated pamphlet, *An Enquiry into the Obligations of Christians to Use Means for the Conversion of the Heathens* (1792), gladly conceded the second point by referring with admiration to both the Tranquebar mission and the Moravian missions, which subsequently influenced his own mission practice in Bengal. Carey's pamphlet in fact assembled as many examples as he could find to refute the allegation that the idea of mounting missions to the 'heathen' overseas was an unwarranted novelty. Nevertheless, it is therefore significant that he makes no mention of the SPG; he dismisses the 'bulk of the church of England' as little better than the 'Papists', 'either in knowledge or in holiness'.² The mission initiatives pioneered by English Dissenters at the close of the eighteenth century were not without precedent, but their novelty lay in their combination of two key features.

First, unlike the missions of the SPG, whose evangelistic work was limited to the British colonies or their adjacent territory, or the original Halle mission, which was under the auspices of the Danish crown, the geographical horizons of the new Dissenting missions were in principle unlimited. For obvious reasons Dissenters looked to no European monarch or state authority for sponsorship, and their chosen fields of labour bore no necessary relationship to the boundaries of any European empire. The original focus of Carey's evangelistic vision, stimulated by reading the recent accounts of Captain James Cook's voyages, was the South Pacific, not at that time a sphere of formal British control, although in the event the Baptist Missionary Society (BMS), formed largely on his initiative in October 1792, chose Bengal as its first field. Tahiti was, however, the first field of the London Missionary Society (LMS), originally known simply as 'The Missionary Society', whose formal foundation took place in London in September 1795.

The second and related innovatory characteristic of the English Dissenting missions, consequent upon their entire independence of state patronage, was their total reliance on voluntary mechanisms of philanthropic support. The idea of a voluntary society dedicated to the propagation of the Christian faith

---

[1] Rowan Strong, *Anglicanism and the British Empire, c.1700–1850* (Oxford, 2007), pp. 12–17; Daniel O'Connor and others, *Three Centuries of Mission: The United Society for the Propagation of the Gospel 1701–2000* (London and New York, 2000), pp. 7–44.

[2] William Carey, *An Enquiry into the Obligations of Christians to Use Means for the Conversion of the Heathens* (Leicester, 1792; facsimile edition edited by Ernest A. Payne, London, 1961), pp. 36–7, 65.

was not in itself new—the SPCK was one such. Since 1709 there had also been a Society in Scotland for Promoting Christian Knowledge (SSPCK), whose Royal Letters Patent defined its objects as 'the further promoting Christian Knowledge and increase of piety and virtue within Scotland especially in the Highlands, Islands and remote corners thereof... and for propagating the same in Popish and Infidel parts of the world'.[3] In dependence on that second object, the SSPCK began in 1730 to operate in North America; its most famous missionary, David Brainerd, ministered among the Mohican and Delaware Indians from 1742 to 1746. However, the English Dissenting missionary societies founded in the 1790s differed in their functional ecclesiology from both the SPCK, which remained consistently deferential to episcopal authority, and the SSPCK, which had close links to the Church of Scotland. Neither Particular Baptists nor Congregationalists possessed any national denominational structures (as opposed to regional associations) in the 1790s—the first Congregational Union (which proved short-lived) was not formed until 1806 and the first Baptist Union until 1812. Both the BMS and LMS were entirely independent voluntary agencies whose sole dependence on the giving of lay donors and subscribers was reflected in an elected governing committee (in the BMS case) or board of directors (in the LMS case).

Although ministers predominated in these early governing bodies, these were forms of governance patterned on the business model of the joint-stock company and were potentially wide open to lay influence. Fourteen of the first board of directors of the LMS were laymen, while twenty were ministers although the founding Plan of the Society made provision to ensure that at least 40 per cent of the directors came from outside London, there was no such limit on the percentage of laymen who could be elected.[4] The BMS, on the other hand, needed no such restriction on the percentage of London members: its roots were in the provinces, especially in the Northamptonshire Baptist Association, which extended well beyond the county of Northamptonshire. The founders of the Society were in fact wary of metropolitan culture and criticized the LMS for the ostentation and display of its annual public meetings in London. Only after the death in 1815 of its first secretary, Andrew Fuller, was the BMS gradually, and, not without difficulty, brought under the control of London money and business methods. The Society did not even have a London office till 1819. The transition implied an extension of the powers of the metropolitan committee over the missionaries in the field, and the

---

[3] Henry R. Sefton, 'The Scotch Society in the American Colonies in the Eighteenth Century', *Records of the Scottish Church History Society*, 17, 3 (1972), p. 170; D. E. Meek, 'Scottish Highlanders, North American Indians and the SSPCK', *Records of the Scottish Church History Society*, 23, 3 (1989), p. 383.

[4] Richard Lovett, *The History of the London Missionary Society 1795-1895*, 2 vols. (London, 1899), I, pp. 31, 39-40.

resulting tensions led to the painful separation of Carey's Serampore Mission in Bengal from the BMS in 1827, a breach that was not healed till 1837.[5]

This radically Nonconformist way of disseminating Christianity by means of autonomous voluntary societies that were structurally unrelated to any ecclesiastical or governmental authorities spread beyond the boundaries of English Dissent. It was adopted in the United States, where Congregationalists and Presbyterians established the first American foreign missionary society, the American Board of Commissioners for Foreign Missions, in Bradford, Massachusetts, in June 1810. The American Board soon became an exclusively Congregational body after the Presbyterians, and also the Dutch Reformed, withdrew to form their own missionary agencies. Similar societies were founded in continental Europe. In 1815 Würtemberg and Swiss Pietists associated with the Deutsche Christentumsgesellschaft (German Society for Christianity) established a seminary in Basle to train evangelists for work overseas. Initially the students trained in Basle were seconded to other societies, such as the Netherlands Missionary Society, founded in 1797 in direct imitation of the LMS, and the Church Missionary Society (CMS), founded by evangelical Anglicans on voluntary principles in 1799. After 1821, the Basle seminary evolved into the Basle Mission, and the links with other societies gradually weakened.

Despite the rapidity of its adoption on both sides of the Atlantic, the voluntary society model of mission never gained universal acceptance, even among British Nonconformists. The Moravian Church had by 1764 adopted a formal constitution, in which there was no separation between church and mission: one of their early bishops, E. R. Hassé, wrote that it was 'a cardinal principle that to be a Moravian and to further foreign missions are identical'.[6] Methodism reflected both its Anglican origins and John Wesley's theological indebtedness to Moravians in similarly resisting any separation between church and mission structures. Methodism began as a connection of local mission societies within the Church of England; whilst there was by 1818 a national Wesleyan Methodist Missionary Society, its missionaries were stationed by, and subject to, the Wesleyan Conference, and the Wesleyan Mission House in London was, in effect, the headquarters of the Wesleyan Methodist Connexion in Britain.[7] Whereas Baptists and Congregationalists had no church structures that were fit for missionary purpose, and hence turned in a spirit of gospel pragmatism to independent voluntary effort, Moravians and Methodists made the voluntary missionary society *into* the Church.

---

[5] Brian Stanley, *The History of the Baptist Missionary Society 1792-1992* (Edinburgh, 1992), pp. 29-35, 57-67.

[6] J. C. S. Mason, *The Moravian Church and the Missionary Awakening in England 1760-1800* (Woodbridge, 2001), p. 24.

[7] John Pritchard, *Methodists and their Missionary Societies 1760-1900* (Farnham, 2013), pp. 25, 85-6.

EXPLANATIONS

Why did the Dissenting missionary societies appear when they did? Although much of the history of eighteenth-century Dissent appears to be a story of hardening rationalism and a theological slide into Unitarianism, there were evangelical counter-currents flowing with increasing strength as the century proceeded. Among the Independents, both Isaac Watts and Philip Doddridge took a keen interest in reports of the missionary ventures of the Halle Pietists and the Moravians. Watts's famous missionary hymn, 'Jesus shall reign where'er the sun' was written as early as 1719. In September 1741 Doddridge met Count Nicholas von Zinzendorf, leading to regular mutual correspondence, and in 1742 he published proposals (that proved abortive) for the formation of a missionary society.[8] Among Particular Baptists, the dominance of hyper-Calvinism came under mounting challenge, especially from the 1770s, from a warmer and more evangelical strand of Calvinism associated with Bristol Baptist Academy and the theology of Andrew Fuller, pastor first at Soham in Cambridgeshire and from 1782 at Kettering, Northamptonshire. Fuller's *The Gospel Worthy of All Acceptation* (1785) channelled into English Dissent the evangelical moral philosophy of Jonathan Edwards and hence subverted the hyper-Calvinist position that human depravity made it pointless to appeal to the unconverted to repent and believe. Edwards's influence was also disseminated through his tract, *An Humble Attempt to Promote Explicit Agreement and Visible Union of God's People in Extraordinary Prayer* (1747). This began to circulate among the pastors of the Northamptonshire Baptist Association from 1784, and in 1789, one of them, the Bristol-trained John Sutcliff, minister at Olney in Buckinghamshire, republished Edwards's tract in a British edition. By the early 1790s regular monthly united prayer meetings for the universal spread of the Gospel were being held, according to Edwards's recipe, among Particular Baptists in many parts of England and Wales, notably in the Midlands, Yorkshire, and the Bristol area. Carey's *Enquiry* published on 12 May 1792, made extended reference to the united prayer movement, but urged that now was the time for '*exerting ourselves in the use of means* for the obtaining of those things we pray for' by the formation of a society for the propagation of the Gospel overseas.[9] Carey's plea was eventually heard on 2 October 1792, when thirteen Baptist ministers and laymen gathered in Kettering to pledge their subscriptions to enable the formation of the 'Particular Baptist Society for Propagating the Gospel among the heathen', later known as the Baptist Missionary Society. The prayer movement was also crucial in the genesis of the LMS, being adopted by Independents

---

[8] E. A. Payne, 'Doddridge and the Missionary Enterprise', in G. F. Nuttall, ed., *Philip Doddridge 1701–51* (London, 1951), pp. 79–101.

[9] Carey, *Enquiry*, pp. 81–5.

(Congregationalists) in Warwickshire in June 1793; one of the first acts of the LMS directors was to commend the prayer movement, which soon gave rise to four united monthly prayer meetings in different parts of London.[10]

Historians of imperialism are inclined to regard the missionary movement as an epiphenomenon of imperialism, and hence to explain the timing of the British missionary awakening by reference to developments in imperial history. To an extent such reasoning is incontrovertible. As already noted, Carey attributed his fascination with the spiritual condition of the non-European world to Captain Cook's *Voyages*, which form part of the story of European commercial penetration of the Pacific. The Pacific was the exotic 'New World' opening up to eighteenth-century European eyes, arousing something of the same degree of religious excitement as the discovery of the Americas had done in early sixteenth-century Spain, even though British annexation of any of the Pacific islands was still some way off. The BMS's eventual selection of Bengal rather than the Pacific as its first theatre of operations was fortuitous in the sense that an offer was received from a personal friend of John Sutcliff's, John Thomas, who had served there as a surgeon with the East India Company, to return to India as a missionary in the employ of the Society, with a companion (Carey then volunteered to be that companion). Without the growing involvement of the Company in Bengal, Thomas's offer would not have been forthcoming. Yet there is no evidence that the extent of British connection with Bengal provided the BMS committee in 1792 with anything more than a merely pragmatic argument in favour of accepting Thomas's offer. In fact one leading member of the committee, Samuel Pearce, minister of the Cannon Street church in Birmingham, had urged the adoption as the Society's first field of the Pelew Islands, a tiny archipelago to the East of the Philippines—hardly a location of strategic interest to Britain.[11] Occurring as it did within living memory of the traumatic loss of the American colonies, the evangelical missionary awakening in Britain in the 1790s had less to do with any renewed British enthusiasm for colonial expansion than with the consciousness of evangelical Christians across Europe and in North America that they were living on the cusp of the closing era of human history.

Jonathan Edwards's *Humble Attempt* was written against the backcloth of the 'Great Awakening' in New England. It expressed Edwards's conviction that the Awakening indicated the imminence of the final age in which the Holy Spirit would be poured out in unprecedented measure to bless Christian missionary efforts across the globe. That eschatological expectation was shared by the founders of the BMS and LMS, living as they did in the immediate

---

[10] Lovett, *History of the London Missionary Society*, I, p. 12; Ernest A. Payne, *The Prayer Call of 1784* (London, 1941), p. 11.

[11] S. P. Carey, *Samuel Pearce, MA: the Baptist Brainerd* (London, n.d.), pp. 139–40.

aftermath of the French Revolution. Melvill[e] Horne, second chaplain to the evangelical colony for freed slaves at Sierra Leone, wrote in his influential *Letters on Missions* (1790) that 'the latter ends of the world are fallen upon us'. With events in France in mind, Horne commented that 'the Roman Antichrist... is sinking under the reiterated strokes of divine vengeance'. Such portents constituted a sombre challenge to Christians to engage in 'more than apostolick labours' to bring the Gospel to the world.[12] 'The present age', reflected John Ryland, close friend of Carey and Fuller, in his Moderator's letter to the Northamptonshire Baptist Association in May 1792, 'seems pregnant with great events', with 'the nations of Europe in commotion'.[13] By 1798 French armies had set up a republic in Rome itself, dragged Pope Pius VI into exile, and Napoleon was in Egypt threatening the Ottoman hold on Palestine; evangelicals speculated that the restoration of the Jews to their homeland might be imminent. Buoyed by such expectations, English Dissenters organized themselves to convert the world to evangelical Christianity, confidently expecting divinely bestowed success. In the words of Carey's famous sermon, preached before the Northamptonshire Baptist Association on 30 May 1792, they expected 'great things' [from God], and therefore were obliged to 'attempt great things' [for God].[14] Moderate Calvinism proved extraordinarily effective in mobilizing evangelistic action.

Empire does not explain the missionary awakening itself, but it certainly helps to explain the choice of mission fields. The decision of the BMS to make India its first sphere of operations encouraged other societies to follow suit. In 1798 the LMS sent its first India missionary, Nathanael Forsyth, to Calcutta. The increasing prominence of India in parliamentary and public debate did much to raise the profile of India in the Christian conscience. The flood of 908 public petitions submitted to Parliament in 1813, the majority emanating from Dissenters, for the insertion of a 'pious' (pro-missionary) clause in the renewed East India Company Charter succeeded only in securing a very limited statement in the Charter conceding the responsibility of Britain to promote the 'religious and moral improvement' of the native inhabitants of India; all intending missionaries still had to apply to the Company for a licence, as had been the case previously. Nevertheless, the 1813 campaign was a watershed in bringing the missionary agenda of evangelical Dissent into the public sphere; from now on it would be very difficult for the East India

---

[12] Melvill Horne, *Letters on Missions; addressed to the Protestant ministers of the British churches* (Bristol, 1794), p. 20.

[13] John Rippon, *The Baptist Annual Register for 1790, 1791, 1792, and part of 1793. Including Sketches of the State of Religion among Different Denominations of Good Men at Home and Abroad* (London, 1793), pp. 438-9.

[14] For a discussion of the original form of Carey's slogan, see Stanley, *History of the Baptist Missionary Society*, pp. 13-14.

Company to refuse licences to evangelical missionaries.[15] The first Methodist missionary to India, James Lynch, moved from Ceylon to Madras in 1818, to work initially among the British military garrison there. Under the influence of Carey's fellow Serampore missionary William Ward, the Missionary Society of the General Baptist New Connexion, formed in Boston, Lincolnshire, on 26 June 1816, sent its first two missionaries, William Bampton and James Peggs, to India in 1821, to work in Orissa, to the south of Bengal. After his return to England in 1826 Peggs became a thorn in the side of the East India Company on account of his sustained pamphlet campaign against the Company's involvement in the management and support of Hindu temples. Peggs directed his invective particularly against the tax levied by the Company on pilgrims to the Jagannath temple at Puri, where the periodic deaths of Hindu devotees, crushed beneath the wheels of the large carriage (hence the English word 'juggernaut') carrying the deity as it passed through the crowded streets at the annual festival, became a symbol in the evangelical mind of the horrors of Hindu 'idolatry'.[16]

The evangelical relationship to empire was always ambiguous and many-sided. In the Cape Colony, LMS missionaries, notably the Scotsman John Philip, rapidly gained a reputation for outspoken defence of the interests of the 'Hottentot' (Khoikhoi) and Xhosa populations. Philip came to favour an extension of British colonial rule eastwards precisely because he wished to curtail the freedom of Boer (Afrikaner) settlers to exploit black labour. Similarly, in the Caribbean, BMS and LMS missionaries found themselves gradually propelled by planter opposition to their work among the slaves towards an explicitly emancipationist but also pro-imperial stance; their indignation with the planters' attacks on the chapels played a major role in the public campaign in Britain to bring plantation slavery to an end. Not every field in which the Dissenting missionary societies commenced work during this period lay within the domains of the East India Company or the British Empire. Although most scholarly attention has been directed to those BMS or LMS missions located within British India, the West Indies, or African colonies such as the Cape of Good Hope or Sierra Leone, fields that lay outside of the sphere of primary British influence included the BMS missions in Java (1813), and Sumatra (1818), and the LMS missions in Tahiti (1797), Canton (1807), Java (1814), Madagascar (1818), and Mongolia (1818).

---

[15] Penelope Carson, *The East India Company and Religion, 1698–1858* (Woodbridge, 2012), pp. 130–48.

[16] Kenneth Ingham, *Reformers in India, 1793–1833: An Account of the Work of Christian Missionaries on Behalf of Social Reform* (Cambridge, 1956), pp. 39–40. Peggs was not the first to publicize the Jagannath festival; this was the work of the East India Company chaplain Claudius Buchanan, in his *Christian Researches in Asia* (1811).

EVANGELICAL ECUMENISM

In his *Enquiry*, Carey appealed to 'every one who loves our Lord Jesus Christ in sincerity' to respond to the missionary challenge, yet conceded that 'in the present divided state of Christendom, it would be more likely for good to be done by each denomination engaging separately in the work, than if they were to embark in it conjointly'.[17] Experience would eventually confirm Carey's sober realism, but in the short term many of those who were prominent in the missionary awakening were confident that the historic divisions between Calvinists and Arminians, Baptists and paedobaptists, and perhaps even those between Church and Dissent, could be overcome by the force of the shared missionary dynamic. Melvill[e] Horne embodied in his own person the new spirit of evangelical ecumenism. Ordained to the Anglican ministry in 1786, he was appointed the following year by Wesley as superintendent of the Wolverhampton Methodist circuit. In 1797 he became (for one year) a director of The Missionary Society and preached for it during its May annual meetings, before in 1799 joining the committee of the newly founded Church Missionary Society. His *Letters on Missions* in 1794 had called for 'liberal Churchmen and conscientious Dissenters, pious Calvinists and pious Arminians' to 'embrace with fraternal arms', and insisted that missionaries should in a truly 'catholick spirit' confine themselves to teaching a simple Christianity that transcended such divisions, a vision that was fulfilled a year later in the formation of the LMS.[18] Thus the Scottish Independent David Bogue, minister at Gosport in Hampshire, entitled his sermon preached before the newly founded 'Missionary Society' in September 1795 'The Funeral of Bigotry':

> This is a new thing in the Christian church.... Here are Episcopalians, Methodists, Presbyterians, and Independents, all united in one society.... Behold us here assembled with one accord to attend the funeral of *bigotry*; And may she be buried so deep that not a particle of her dust may ever be thrown up on the face of the earth.[19]

The *Evangelical Magazine* reported that in response to these fine words the vast congregation 'could scarcely refrain from one general shout of joy' and pronounced that the scene 'was perhaps, never before beheld in our world'.[20] Evangelical unity was seen as a peculiar fruit of the last days: the 'funeral of bigotry' was a prelude to the marriage-supper of the Lamb. Bogue's ideas exercised an enduring influence on the LMS for years to come, not least

---

[17] Carey, *Enquiry*, p. 84.   [18] Horne, *Letters on Missions*, pp. 21, 60.
[19] *Sermons Preached in London at the Formation of the London Missionary Society* (London, 1795), p. 425.
[20] *Evangelical Magazine* 3 (1795), p. 425, cited in Roger H. Martin, *Evangelicals United: Ecumenical Stirrings in Pre-Victorian Britain, 1795–1830* (Metuchen, NJ, and London, 1983), p. 43.

through the many missionaries whom he trained in his Gosport Academy and Missionary Seminary, established in 1800. By the time of his death in 1825, the Gosport Seminary had educated nearly 40 per cent of the Society's missionaries, and 70 per cent of those sent to India.[21] Bogue's seminary also provided the template for the Anglo-Chinese College in Malacca, opened by Robert Morrison in 1818, and in this way its vision of non-denominational Christianity influenced the formative years of what the LMS called its 'Ultra-Ganges' mission and hence passed into the bloodstream of early Chinese Protestantism.[22]

The pan-evangelical sentiment extravagantly applauded in Bogue's sermon was in 1796 written into the constitution of the Society in what became known as the 'Fundamental Principle':

> As the union of Christians of various denominations in carrying on this great work is a most desirable object, so to prevent if possible, any cause of future dissension, it is declared to be a Fundamental Principle of the Missionary Society, that our design is not to send Presbyterianism, Independency, Episcopacy, or any other form of Church Order and Government, (about which there may be difference of opinion among serious persons) but the Glorious Gospel of the blessed God, and that it shall be left (as it ought to be left) to the minds of the persons whom God may call into the fellowship of His Son to assume for themselves such form of Church Government as to them shall appear most agreeable to the Word of God.[23]

The author of the Fundamental Principle was in fact a Scottish Presbyterian, Alexander Waugh, minister of the Scots Secession Church in London. As a minister of the Secession Church, Waugh was a rather Congregational sort of Presbyterian, and Andrew Walls has pointed out that the clause lurking in parenthesis in his Principle—'as it ought to be left'—introduced Congregationalism by the back door, since it asserted that the determination of church order was properly a matter for each identifiable unity of converts to decide, and if no particular system of church order were to be imposed upon them, what other unit could there be than the gathered congregation?[24] Waugh claimed that the Principle was not intended to downgrade denominational convictions, but simply to draw a distinction between the word of life in Scripture, in which there was no darkness at all, and the decrees on church

---

[21] F. Stuart Piggin, *Making Evangelical Missionaries 1789–1858: The Social Background, Motives and Training of British Protestant Missionaries to India* (Abingdon, 1984), p. 157.

[22] Christopher Daily, *Robert Morrison and the Protestant Plan for China* (Hong Kong, 2013).

[23] LMS Board Minutes, 9 May 1796, cited in I. M. Fletcher, 'The Fundamental Principle of the London Missionary Society', *Transactions of the Congregational Historical Society*, 19, 3 (1963), p. 138.

[24] Andrew F. Walls, 'Missionary Societies and the Fortunate Subversion of the Church', *Evangelical Quarterly*, 60, 2 (1988), p. 149.

order passed by human assemblies, which mixed truth and error and hence formed no part of the sacred deposit to be transmitted to the 'heathen'.[25] Such an easy distinction between the unchanging Gospel and the relativities of church order was characteristic of evangelical Dissent in the age before the Oxford Movement and the subsequent development of High Church or 'Catholic' forms of Nonconformity.[26]

In its early years The Missionary Society had some success in realizing the non-denominational ideal adumbrated by Horne and Bogue. It drew significant support from Scottish Presbyterians. Its early directors included Presbyterians, Anglicans, and the occasional Wesleyan Methodist. Its early missionaries included Anglicans (Orlando Dobbin from Northern Ireland and Henry Beidenback from London), Lutherans (among them W. T. Ringeltaube, missionary in South India), numerous Dutch Reformed (such as Johannes van der Kemp, the Society's controversial pioneer in the Cape Colony), and even an English Baptist (George Vason, one of the ill-fated *Duff* party to Tahiti in 1797, who ended up marrying a Tongan woman and abandoning the mission).[27] But the reality of support for the Society consistently failed to match the heights of Bogue's rhetoric. Baptists had their own society. From 1805 Wesleyans were encouraged annually to send their own contributions for overseas work to Wesley's lieutenant, Thomas Coke. The few Anglican clergy who supported the Society were generally of the 'irregular' variety, such as Rowland Hill, incumbent of the proprietary Surrey Chapel in London, or Thomas Haweis, instigator of the LMS Tahiti mission, who combined his position as rector of Aldwincle, Northamptonshire, with being chief trustee of the Countess of Huntingdon's Connexion. After the formation of the CMS in 1799, complaints multiplied from Anglican clergy about fund-raising by agents of The Missionary Society among Anglican donors who wrongly believed they were giving to the CMS. The decision in 1818 to rename the Society as the London Missionary Society was a belated recognition of what had been a reality almost from the outset: the Society had never succeeded in implementing its vision of becoming a mission supported equally by all evangelicals. The lines of division within Dissent were also hardening, as Calvinistic Methodists, English Presbyterians, and members of the Countess of

---

[25] James Hay and Henry Belfrage, *A Memoir of the Reverend Alexander Waugh, D.D.* (London, 1830), p. 216.

[26] See David M. Thompson, *Denominationalism and Dissent, 1795–1835: A Question of Identity*, Friends of Dr Williams's Library, 39th Lecture (London, 1985), pp. 11–12.

[27] Martin, *Evangelicals United*, p. 48, lists Vason, Dobbin, and Beidenback. James Sibree, ed., *London Missionary Society: A Register of Missionaries, Deputations, etc. from 1796 to 1923*, 4th edn. (London, 1923), lists Vason as 'Veeson' (No. 29, p. 2) and appears not to include Dobbin or Beidenback. On Vason, see C. W. Newbury, ed., *The History of the Tahitian Mission 1799–1830 Written by John Davies Missionary to the South Sea Islands With Supplementary Papers from the Correspondence of the Missionaries* (Hakluyt Society, second series, No. CXVI, Cambridge, 1961), p. xli.

Huntingdon's Connexion increasingly gravitated towards Congregationalism.[28] By 1818 the LMS was a predominantly Congregational body, even though it never repudiated its Fundamental Principle. The ideal of evangelical interdenominationalism lived on, most notably in the Religious Tract Society, established in 1799, and the British and Foreign Bible Society, founded in 1804. Another experiment in missionary ecumenism, the London Society for Promoting Christianity Amongst the Jews, proved less enduring; within six years of its foundation in 1809, its Dissenting members had withdrawn, leaving the Society to continue under specifically Anglican auspices.

In practice the form of church order planted by both the LMS and the BMS overseas would be a working compromise between congregational independency, Presbyterianism, and de facto Episcopalianism. The compromise was not so much the result of conscious theological reflection as of apparent missionary necessity. Where, as was generally the case in the nineteenth century, converts were scattered and few in number, and missionaries fewer still, it made sense to gather their small congregations into networks within a large district (much like a presbytery). Supervision of those district networks would for long—too long—remain the prerogative of the foreign missionary, whose role thus became quasi-episcopal. When over a century later, at the Tranquebar conference in 1919, the first outlines of a scheme of church union in South India were drafted, it was not accidental that the form of church order envisaged was a hybrid ingeniously dubbed 'episocopresbygationalism'.[29] More generally, it may be observed that a rigid adherence to congregational independency proved less amenable to export to the rest of the globe than other aspects of the English Dissenting heritage. Even the very idea of 'Dissent' tended to dissolve in contexts where Congregationalists, Baptists, or Methodists faced little or no religious competition from Anglican missions and achieved virtual monopoly status. This was most markedly the case in the island societies of the Pacific. In 1824 Henry Nott of the LMS crowned Pomare III as Christian monarch of Tahiti, the culmination of a process in which this paramount chief had subjugated his rivals and asserted his authority over the whole island. LMS missionaries had acted as his counsellors in the promulgation in 1819 of a code of nineteen laws of clearly Christian character. Although there was considerable variation between individual missionaries in their attitudes to the law code, it is hard to resist the conclusion that, in a real sense, Congregationalism had become the Established Church of a

---

[28] Martin, *Evangelicals United*, pp. 70–4.

[29] Bengt Sundkler, *Church of South India: The Movement towards Union 1900–1947*, rev. edn (London, 1965), pp. 99–102; Brian Stanley, 'The Reshaping of Christian Tradition: Western Denominational Identity in a Non-Western Context', in R. N. Swanson, ed., *Unity and Diversity in the Church* (Oxford, 1996), pp. 411–12.

Christian kingdom.³⁰ Similar patterns would be discernible later in the nineteenth century in the Methodist islands of Tonga and Fiji.

SCOTTISH MISSIONARY SOCIETIES

The London Missionary Society, as its eventual name suggests, had a strong base within the capital, in contrast to the early BMS. However, both the BMS and the LMS had close links to Scotland. Andrew Fuller made five fund-raising trips to Scotland between 1799 and 1813, and found strong support for the Society among the evangelical churches planted by the brothers Robert and James Alexander Haldane.³¹ In the LMS, Scottish influence extended to the heart of the Society's management. One of the two secretaries appointed by the Society in September 1795, the Church of Scotland minister John Love, was pastor of the Scots Church in Bishopsgate. Its first board of directors included such prominent Scots as David Bogue, Alexander Waugh, and the London leather merchant Robert Steven, a close friend of leading Anglican evangelicals such as Thomas Scott and John Newton. The formation of the LMS was followed by the establishment in February 1796 of the Glasgow and Edinburgh Missionary Societies, each closely modelled on the pattern of The Missionary Society. By 1797 they had sent out their first missionaries to Sierra Leone, working in close association with the LMS. In addition, no fewer than sixty-one local mission societies were set up in different parts of Scotland, though none of these sent out their own missionaries; they supported the LMS, and some also the BMS or the Moravians. They included societies in each of the Scottish universities which nurtured the missionary enthusiasm of those who became some of the first Scottish missionaries, Alexander Duff among them. The enduring influence of these Scottish societies in support of the LMS is revealed by the fact that eighty-one of the 475 missionaries appointed by the LMS between 1795 and 1845 came from Scotland.³²

After John Love left his London pastorate in 1800 to become minister of Clyde Street Chapel in Anderston, Glasgow, he was replaced as secretary of the LMS by George Burder, a Congregational minister from Coventry who had been a prime mover in the formation of the Society. Love then maintained his

---

³⁰ Kirsteen J. Murray, 'Missionary Kingdoms of the South Pacific? The Involvement of Missionaries from the London Missionary Society in Law Making at Tahiti, 1795–1847' (PhD thesis, University of Edinburgh, 2002), chapter 7.
³¹ Stanley, *History of the Baptist Missionary Society*, p. 20.
³² James M. Calder, *Scotland's March Past: The Share of Scottish Churches in the London Missionary Society* (London, 1945), p. 5; Andrew F. Walls, 'Missions: The Early Societies', in Nigel M. de S. Cameron and others, eds, *Dictionary of Scottish Church History & Theology* (Edinburgh, 1993), pp. 567–70.

missionary interests by assuming the secretaryship of the Glasgow Missionary Society. He would give his name in due course to the most famous Scottish mission station in Africa, Lovedale in the Cape Colony, which the Glasgow Missionary Society opened in 1824.

The early history of the Glasgow and Edinburgh Societies is a chequered one. They never attracted more than the well-wishes of any of the Presbyterian churches (in the case of the Church of Scotland, it was more a question of attracting suspicion) and remained largely dependent for their funding on contributions from Scottish Congregationalists. One of the missionaries dispatched by the Glasgow Society to Sierra Leone became involved in slave trading; another lost his faith and became an atheist lecturer. Of the two missionaries sent by the Edinburgh Society to Sierra Leone, one, Peter Greig, was murdered, and the other, Henry Brunton, was compelled by ill-health to withdraw after two years from his work among the Susu people, an area under Islamic influence 200 miles to the north of the Sierra Leone colony. Brunton, a member of the Associate Synod, nevertheless succeeded in publishing a Susu grammar and vocabulary; his grammar was the most detailed study to date of any African language. In 1802 the Society, having closed its Sierra Leone mission, sent him to pioneer a new mission among the Tatars of the Caucasus—Europe was not excluded from the mission horizons of this generation of Dissenters.[33] In 1819 the Edinburgh Missionary Society changed its name to the Scottish Missionary Society. It opened a new field in the Bombay Presidency in 1823 which passed into the control of the Church of Scotland mission in 1835, and thence, after the 1843 Disruption, into the Free Church mission. The Society also had a mission in Jamaica, originally planted by the Glasgow Missionary Society in 1800, that eventually, after the formation of the United Presbyterian Church in 1847, became the responsibility of the Board of Foreign Missions of that Church. The two Scottish societies petered out, squeezed between the continued attraction of the LMS to Scottish Dissenters and the instigation by the Church of Scotland of its own foreign mission efforts after the General Assembly of 1824.

WESLEYAN METHODISTS

It might have been expected that Methodists would have taken the lead in the organization of foreign missions from late eighteenth-century Britain. The first Methodist class meeting to be formed outside the British Isles began

---

[33] On Brunton, see P. E. H. Hair in Donald M. Lewis, ed., *The Blackwell Dictionary of Evangelical Biography*, 2 vols. (Oxford, 1995), I, p. 157.

meeting in Antigua as early as 1760 in the home of Nathaniel Gilbert, a planter who had come under the influence of John Wesley through his brother Francis; the meeting included some of Gilbert's own slaves. Gilbert, it should be noted, was Melville Horne's uncle. As Arminians, the theology of the Methodists seemed tailor-made for an enterprise aimed at the salvation of all. John Wesley's most famous statement, made in a letter to James Hervey in 1739, declared that 'I look upon all the world as my parish'.[34] In fact the Wesleyan Methodists were the last of the Nonconformist denominations to organize themselves on a national scale for overseas missions: the Wesleyan Methodist Missionary Society was not formed till 1818. Arminianism proved no more powerful a theological dynamic towards world mission than evangelical Calvinism, which derived its confidence in mission from the assurance that the salvation of the heathen formed part of the eternal purpose of God. Wesley's 1739 statement was in fact a defence of his supposed divine right, in contravention of Anglican episcopal order, to ignore parish boundaries in England in his preaching. He was unenthusiastic about the idea of diverting Methodist preachers and funds to the West or, still more, the East Indies, and lent only qualified support to the attempts of Thomas Coke from 1783 to establish a Methodist Society for Missions to the Heathen.[35]

Yet Wesley preached sermons, such as that on 'The General Spread of the Gospel' (1783), which rejoiced in the prospect of the fulfilment of the biblical promises of the whole earth being filled with the knowledge of the Lord. The apparent contradiction finds resolution in the fact that, for Wesley, the spread of the kingdom of God was a strictly sequential process, beginning with the restoration of primitive Christianity in the heart of Western Christendom, namely Oxford. 'From Oxford, where it first appeared, the little leaven' of 'pure and undefiled religion' could be observed spreading outwards, to northern England, Ireland, Holland, and North America. The next step, supposed Wesley, would be for it to spread to Roman Catholics in countries of protestant or mixed faith; from there it would pass to countries 'merely popish'. 'And may it not', he asked, 'be gradually diffused from thence to all that name the name of Christ in the various provinces of Turkey, in Abyssinia, yea, and in the remotest parts, not only of Europe, but of Asia, Africa, and America?' Then, and only then, would the 'Mahometans' and 'heathen' be convicted by the power of a revived primitive Christianity and be drawn to Christ.[36] Hence the first of Coke's mission appeals to secure Wesley's support was one in 1786 that limited the mission fields in view to the British Isles and British

---

[34] John Wesley to James Hervey, 20 March 1739, in John Telford, ed., *The Letters of the Rev. John Wesley*, 8 vols. (London, 1931), I, pp. 284–7.
[35] John A. Vickers, *Thomas Coke: Apostle of Methodism* (London, 1969), pp. 131–3.
[36] John Wesley, 'The General Spread of the Gospel', in Albert C. Outler, ed., *The Works of John Wesley, Volume 2: Sermons II, 34–70* (Nashville, TN, 1985), pp. 490–6.

North America: 'I greatly approve of your proposal', wrote Wesley to Coke on 12 March 1786, 'for raising a subscription in order to send missionaries to the Highlands of Scotland, the Islands of Jersey and Guernsey and the Leeward Islands, Quebec, Nova Scotia and Newfoundland.'[37] Coke's published *Address to the Pious and Benevolent* confessed that his hope of sending missionaries to British India had been postponed, since

> Mr Wesley thinks it imprudent to hazard at present the lives of any of our preachers, by sending them to so great a distance, and amidst so many uncertainties and difficulties; when so large a field of action is afforded us in countries to which we have so much easier admittance, and where the success, through the blessing of God, is more or less certain.[38]

In response to Coke's appeal, the 1786 Methodist Conference appointed one missionary, William Warrener, to Antigua, and two, William Hammett and John Clarke, to Newfoundland. Their appointment is sometimes hailed as the beginning of Methodist overseas missions, though the selection is somewhat arbitrary, since the first Conference of Methodist preachers in North America, convened in Baltimore in 1784, had appointed one preacher, Jeremiah Lambert, to Antigua, whilst another, John Baxter, was ordained by Coke in Baltimore in the summer of 1785 for ministry in Antigua. By 1793—the year in which Carey and John Thomas landed in Bengal—there were twelve Methodist missionaries working in ten Caribbean islands among a Methodist membership of 6,570.[39]

To this extent, the claim often made by Methodists that they were the first of the British Nonconformist bodies to initiate foreign missions is warranted. However, it would be equally plausible to present these early Wesleyan ventures as a Methodist variant of the long-established pattern laid down in the charter of the SPG of providing Anglican ministry to British subjects in the American colonies, a commission which many SPG spokesmen had from the beginning construed as including the evangelization of both North American Indians and slaves.[40] As late as 1813 the only Methodist mission field which did not fall within the limited geographical scope of the 1786 plan was Sierra Leone, and the initiative for the inception of the Methodist mission to the colony in 1811 came, not from Britain, but from Methodists among the Nova Scotian settlers who had arrived in 1792 and subsequently made several appeals to the

---

[37] Thomas Coke, *An Address to the Pious and Benevolent, Proposing an Annual Subscription for the Support of the Missionaries in the Highlands and Islands and Adjacent Islands of Scotland, the Isles of Jersey, Guernsey and Newfoundland, the West Indies, and the Provinces of Nova Scotia and Quebec* (London, 1786), cited in Vickers, *Thomas Coke*, p. 136.

[38] Coke, *An Address to the Pious and Benevolent*, p. [5], cited in Vickers, *Thomas Coke*, p. 137.

[39] Vickers, *Thomas Coke*, p. 172.

[40] Andrew Porter, *Religion versus Empire? British Protestant Missionaries and Overseas Expansion, 1700–1914* (Manchester, 2004), p. 18.

Methodist Conference to send preachers.[41] Thomas Coke's *Account of the Rise, Progress, and Present State of the Methodist Missions* (1804) ranked the manifest spiritual destitution of the Scots, Welsh, and Irish alongside that of the West Indian slaves.[42] Such assimilation of the causes of home and overseas mission was not restricted to Methodists. The BMS supported itinerant preaching tours in remote parts of England until as late as 1815–16, and many of the first Nonconformist foreign missionaries cut their evangelistic teeth through itinerant preaching in Britain.[43] Nevertheless, the traces of Wesley's preference for missionary labour in those parts of Christendom needing the renewing grace of vital religion for long remained evident within the history of Methodist missions, which continued throughout the nineteenth century to give a priority to work in Europe, as also among British settlers and soldiers in the non-European world, that was matched by no other section of Nonconformity.

Whether or not it is accepted that Methodists were late to adopt a genuinely global missionary vision, it is undeniable that the organization of Methodist overseas missionary activity remained haphazard and heavily dependent on Thomas Coke's personal fund-raising efforts for the remainder of his life. The multiple connexional responsibilities on both sides of the Atlantic that fell on his shoulders following Wesley's death in 1791 did not help. Only in 1813 did the Leeds District of Methodist societies, at the instigation of the great Wesleyan denominational architect Jabez Bunting, grasp the administrative nettle by forming its own District Missionary Society for the support of the overseas missions. Other Districts followed the Leeds example. In 1816 a connexional committee for the management of the missions was formed and Richard Watson, the ablest theological mind in Methodism, was appointed General Missionary Secretary. In 1818 these various regional and connexional efforts were united through the formation of the national Wesleyan Methodist Missionary Society. In 1821 Bunting joined Watson as joint secretary of the Missionary Society; they became the most powerful men in Methodism.[44] Thomas Coke did not live to see this realization of his dream: he died in 1814 en voyage for India, the field on which his heart was always set. With the blessing of the Methodist Conference he had planned to make the British Crown colony of Ceylon the headquarters of the Methodist mission to the Indian subcontinent, and Coke's companions on the voyage went on to make Ceylon the site of the first Methodist mission in Asia.

---

[41] A. F. Walls, 'A Christian Experiment: The Early Sierra Leone Colony', in G. J. Cuming, ed., *The Mission of the Church and the Propagation of the Faith* (Cambridge, 1970), pp. 107–29.

[42] Thomas Coke, *Account of the Rise, Progress, and Present State of the Methodist Missions* (London, 1804), pp. 6–7, 31, 35; cited in Alison Twells, *The Civilising Mission and the English Middle Class, 1792–1850: The 'Heathen' at Home and Overseas* (Basingstoke, 2009), p. 30.

[43] Stanley, *History of the Baptist Missionary Society*, pp. 18–19; Elizabeth Elbourne, *Blood Ground: Colonialism, Missions, and the Contest for Christianity in the Cape Colony and Britain, 1799–1853* (Montreal and London, 2002), p. 33.

[44] Pritchard, *Methodists and their Missionary Societies*, pp. 80–1.

CONCLUSION

Evangelical Dissent provided much of the dynamic fuelling the Protestant missionary expansion of the nineteenth century. Its voluntaryist assumptions proved ideally suited for funding and organizing the enterprise, though the churches that were planted in the non-European world would depart in many respects from English Dissenting models. Over time the differences between Anglicans and Nonconformists would diminish in the missionary context, which is one of the reasons why the ecumenical movement has found its strongest support among the so-called 'younger' churches of Asia, and, to a lesser extent, of Africa.

SELECT BIBLIOGRAPHY

Carson, Penelope, *The East India Company and Religion, 1698–1858* (Woodbridge, 2012).

Cox, Jeffrey, *The British Missionary Enterprise since 1700* (New York and London, 2008).

Elbourne, Elizabeth, *Blood Ground: Colonialism, Missions, and the Contest for Christianity in the Cape Colony and Britain, 1799–1853* (Montreal and London, 2002).

Lovett, Richard, *The History of the London Missionary Society 1795–1895*, 2 vols. (London, 1899).

Martin, Roger H., *Evangelicals United: Ecumenical Stirrings in Pre-Victorian Britain, 1795–1830* (Metuchen, NJ, and London, 1983).

Mason, J. C. S., *The Moravian Church and the Missionary Awakening in England 1760–1800* (Woodbridge, 2001).

Payne, Ernest A., *The Prayer Call of 1784* (London, 1941).

Piggin, F. Stuart, *Making Evangelical Missionaries 1789–1858: The Social Background, Motives and Training of British Protestant Missionaries to India* (Abingdon, 1984).

Porter, Andrew, *Religion versus Empire? British Protestant Missionaries and Overseas Expansion, 1700–1914* (Manchester, 2004).

Pritchard, John, *Methodists and their Missionary Societies 1760–1900* (Farnham, 2013).

Stanley, Brian, *The History of the Baptist Missionary Society 1792–1992* (Edinburgh, 1992).

Twells, Alison, *The Civilising Mission and the English Middle Class, 1792–1850: The 'Heathen' at Home and Overseas* (Basingstoke, 2009).

Vickers, John A., *Thomas Coke: Apostle of Methodism* (London, 1969).

Walls, Andrew F., 'Missions: The Early Societies', in Cameron, Nigel M. de S. and others, eds, *Dictionary of Scottish Church History & Theology* (Edinburgh, 1993), pp. 567–70.

Part IV

Context

13

Toleration, Dissent, and the State in Britain

Andrew C. Thompson

It is tempting to tell a story of how the political position of protestant Dissenters within Britain was transformed between the late 1680s and the early 1830s. During that century and a half, Dissenters moved from being an oppressed and persecuted minority, denied both freedom of worship and basic political rights, to a self-confident and growing group, whose voice increasingly commanded attention on the national stage. While superficially attractive, the question of how Dissenters were best able to secure their religious and political rights is more complicated than a triumphalist tale of persecution to toleration to power. Borrowing from David Hempton's recent work suggests two important warnings for anyone tempted to follow the simple path. First, there is the need to remember the transnational aspects of Dissenting experience and, second, in a resort to metaphor, it is vital not to 'flatten out' lived experience.[1] Within Britain and Ireland and the wider Atlantic world, the legal position of, and context for, Dissent varied considerably. Much of the attention here is given to campaigns focused on the imperial centre but this does not mean that concerns about position and exclusion were simply the business of a metropolitan elite.

This chapter explores a variety of contexts that arise from Dissenters' encounters with the state. Central to these are the conflicts between the principle of establishment and what freedom of worship meant in practice. In this respect, thinking about the impact of the legislative changes of the Glorious Revolution of 1688–9 is both necessary and appropriate. Yet the right to worship was the beginning, rather than the end, of a wider debate about the limits of toleration, the extent to which political rights could be tied to particular forms of religious adherence, and larger questions about textual interpretation and the legitimacy of requiring subscription to particular forms of words as a precondition for the granting of full rights. Attempts to alter

---

[1] David Hempton, *The Church in the Long Eighteenth Century* (London, 2011), pp. 3, 104.

particular pieces of legislation required not just intellectual justification but also practical advocacy. It is important, therefore, to consider some of the mechanisms by which Dissenters were able to exert influence. Traditionally, there has been more of a focus on questions of organizational effectiveness than on the message itself. However, as historians have become increasingly interested in language and argument, it is also worth placing Dissenting campaigns within a broader framework of participation in politics and the public sphere.[2] Unlike in some other areas of this volume, it is possible to think about 'Dissent' as a relatively undifferentiated category when it comes to relations with the state. Although there were some differences of approach between Quakers and Presbyterians, it was also possible to think about a 'Dissenting interest', seeking to exert political influence at both a local and national level. Toleration, then, provides a lens through which to explore a range of interconnected issues.

Beyond seeking to understand what changed for Dissenters in this period, it is also worth exploring the reasons why these changes took place and what their significance was. The publication in 1985 of J. C. D. Clark's *English Society* has reignited a debate about the connections between theological beliefs and political affiliation.[3] Earlier generations of Unitarian historians were keen to show the leading role that theological heterodoxy, especially in relation to the Trinity, had played in the growth of liberty. Reversing the moral polarities, Clark posits a strong causal connection between theological scepticism, the growth of political radicalism, and the eventual collapse of the 'protestant constitution' in Britain. Moving attention beyond simply England, as James E. Bradley has done, suggests that issues of ecclesiology were just as important as theology in promoting the politics of change.[4] Indeed, it was the position of marginalization and exclusion, just as much as the development of ideas, that mattered.[5]

THE QUESTION OF ESTABLISHMENT

Bradley argues that in England, Scotland, and Ireland, protestant Dissenters were able to view the structures of the Established Churches as 'contributing to a species of slavery, and each served as a stimulus for the Dissenters to

---

[2] James Van Horn Melton, *The Rise of the Public in Enlightenment Europe* (Cambridge, 2001).
[3] J. C. D. Clark, *English Society* (Cambridge, 1985).
[4] James E. Bradley, 'The Religious Origins of Radical Politics in England, Scotland, and Ireland, 1662–1800', in James E. Bradley and Dale K. Van Kley, eds, *Religion and Politics in Enlightenment Europe* (Notre Dame, IN, 2001), pp. 187–253.
[5] Ibid., pp. 191–2.

sympathize with the claims of oppressed peoples and radical causes'.⁶ This is a useful reminder of the importance of perception when it comes to questions of personal position and identity. The language used during these struggles was frequently emotive and suggestive of the worldly trials that the path of discipleship entailed. It is also clear that debates about religious and political freedoms took place against a backdrop of state sponsorship or even direct control of ecclesiastical structures. Since the Reformation, European states had struggled with the question of how to deal with religious minorities. The pragmatic solution that many monarchs and governments had adopted was that associated with the Religious Peace of Augsburg (1555)—'cuis region, eius religio' ('of the prince, his religion'). Indeed, the treaties of Westphalia (1648), which brought the Thirty Years War to an end, had sought to set this practice in stone by fixing the confessional identities of states within the Holy Roman Empire—the position of a state in 1624 was seen as normative. The logic behind this approach was readily apparent. Secular and spiritual hierarchies were seen as mutually reinforcing, thus a challenge in one sphere was likely to lead to negative consequences in the other. Mono-confessional states were seen as desirable because they were more likely to engender political stability Religious diversity, by contrast, was a recipe for anarchy.

It was this form of argument that was increasingly challenged in the late seventeenth century. The consequences of this transformation were several. As W. R. Ward argued, the inability of state churches to cope with or assimilate minority groups effectively was a significant contributory factor to the Europe-wide process of awakening that took place in the early eighteenth century.⁷ There were other practical considerations too. Both population growth and migration frequently outpaced the ability of parish-based church structures to change to meet demand.⁸ This was true within Britain itself but the effect was magnified across the Atlantic. Demand for people was such that it was difficult to impose strict religious criteria about who might be allowed or encouraged to become part of new settler populations. Protestantism was often to become a more important marker of true religion in such contexts than whether or not church structures enjoyed official approval.⁹

Intellectually, writers such as Edmund Calamy (1671–1732) and John Shute Barrington (1678–1734) were keen to produce works defending the Dissenting position in the early eighteenth century. Calamy's *Defence of Moderate Non-conformity* (1703–5) and Barrington's *The Rights of Protestant Dissenters* (1704–5) were both published in the context of attempts to curtail Dissenting political rights. Both made the case that there was no necessary connection between Dissenting religious belief and attacks on established secular power,

---

⁶ Ibid., p. 234.
⁷ W. R. Ward, *Christianity under the Ancien Régime* (Cambridge, 1999), pp. 71–2.
⁸ Hempton, *Church in the Long Eighteenth Century*, p. 170.   ⁹ Ibid., p. 28.

thus seeking to deflect the impression of Dissenters as puritan sectaries, hell-bent on bringing down the monarchy and introducing republicanism, as it was claimed their seventeenth-century forebears had been. These two authors are typical, in many ways, of Dissenting polemicists and leaders in the early eighteenth century. One was a minister, the other a merchant who ended his political career in the House of Lords. They were keen to harness the power of the press to make their case and were also interested in using history as a means to further their arguments and construct a sense of Dissenting identity. Moreover, they had also grown to adulthood in a period in which Dissenting rights had been distinctly more precarious than they now were—hence the memory of past wrongs loomed large in their thinking.

It is worth reiterating that it was the sense of political exclusion, rather than particular theological positions, that mattered when it came to thinking about the validity of establishment. For all the previous emphasis on a supposedly radical 'Calvinist international', there were also places where Calvinism represented the status quo. Dale Van Kley has pointed to the 'establishment' position of a Calvinist church in the United Provinces and Geneva.[10] He could easily have added Massachusetts and Scotland (after 1688–9) to his list as well. In Scotland, in particular, as Stewart J. Brown points out elsewhere in this volume,[11] arguments about patronage and presentation to livings rapidly came to the fore with sociological and ecclesiological factors serving to exacerbate tensions. Moreover, while later generations of Calvinists were keen to distance themselves from some of their Genevan forebears' positions, the burning of Michael Servetus in 1553 left a lasting impression.[12] Connections between religious and political power, then, mattered for Dissenters.

THE CONTEXT OF STATE POWER

Much of the rest of this chapter is concerned with attempts by Dissenters to regularize and improve their position in relation to the state by removing perceived legislative anomalies and extending political rights. Such discussions should not, however, neglect the role and agency of the state. Many governments in the early modern period were keen to enhance their power and diminish the position of rival centres of authority, such as churches. Indeed, one of the major impulses behind the confessional-state model that has

---

[10] Dale K. Van Kley, 'Piety and Politics in the Century of Lights', in Mark Goldie and Robert Wokler, eds, *The Cambridge History of Eighteenth-Century Political Thought* (Cambridge, 2006), p. 139.
[11] See ch. 7, 'Protestant Dissent in Scotland'.
[12] Richard H. Popkin and Mark Goldie, 'Scepticism, Priestcraft and Toleration', in Goldie and Wokler, eds, *Cambridge History of Eighteenth-Century Political Thought*, p. 96.

become popular in describing developments across much of Europe in the period is the notion that it was essentially Erastian. Likewise, in a period which is still frequently associated with 'enlightenment', it is also worth recalling that the improvement of the functioning of state apparatus could easily go hand in hand with attempts to centralize power.

Authorities might be interested in reducing the power of the Established Church but it did not necessarily follow from this that they were keen to extend greater religious rights to individuals or groups. As Jeffrey Collins has pointed out, 'states usually viewed corporate religion more as a rival than as helpmeet and could prudentially promote the atomization and privatization of religion in the interest of their own autonomy'.[13] Within Britain, such moves could rely on reasonably well-established structures of coercion. Across the Atlantic, however, as the eighteenth century went on, it became clear that state structures were less capable of dealing with a coalition of religious liberty, combining deists and evangelicals, that had a strong dislike of Established Churches, recognized natural rights, was wary of the consolidation of political power, and emphasized the importance of providence and virtue.[14] The lack of deeply embedded state structures and the inability to invoke traditional models of authority was clearly important too. Any consideration of how 'successful' or otherwise Dissenting attempts were in promoting change has to remain alive to the realities of power.

TOLERATION IN CONTEXT

Toleration, in its various forms, has been central to understanding the political role and importance of Dissent. In eras in which progressive narratives of historical development commanded wider acceptance than they do now, it was easy to connect the growth of more tolerant societies to the inevitable triumph of liberal modernity; examples could be found in the historical writings of the great Whig historians Lecky, Macaulay, and Gardiner and, more recently, William Haller's work on Puritanism and W. K. Jordan's writings specifically on toleration also fit into this mould.[15] More recent work has tended to question a triumphalist reading of the contribution of early Dissenters to the growth of religious liberty.

---

[13] Jeffrey R. Collins, 'Redeeming the Enlightenment: New Histories of Religious Toleration', *Journal of Modern History*, 81, 3 (2009), p. 619.
[14] Hempton, *Church in the Long Eighteenth Century*, p. 190.
[15] William Haller, *The Rise of Puritanism* (New York, 1938); W. K. Jordan, *The Development of Religious Toleration in England*, 2 vols. (London, 1932–8); Alexandra Walsham, *Charitable Hatred: Tolerance and Intolerance in England, 1500–1700* (Manchester, 2006), p. 6.

This critique has taken several forms. More emphasis is placed now on the importance of Quakers and, particularly, Socinians as early advocates of toleration.[16] The contribution of the puritan mainstream has been concomitantly downgraded. Puritanism itself has been subject to serious historiographical scrutiny so a simple account of a straightforward transition from Puritan to Dissenter (thus enabling the spirit of liberal modernity to be kept alive) is no longer as tenable. Part of the reason for this is that the evidence of early generations of Dissenters actually putting ideas of toleration into practice, when given the opportunity, is mixed. A useful distinction could be drawn between those who favoured a model of gathered congregations and were willing to work outside existing ecclesiastical structures and those who wished to reform the governance and ceremonies of the Established Church, which they regarded as 'but partly reformed'.

Toleration in the sixteenth and seventeenth centuries was frequently regarded as a vice, rather than a virtue. As Alex Walsham points out, knowingly allowing someone to profess a form of false belief might be regarded as a form of spiritual murder because it put an individual's eternal fate into jeopardy.[17] Indeed, Ethan Shagan's recent work has shown how for many mid-seventeenth-century authors, moderation was seen as occupying a middle ground between tyrannical persecution and sinful toleration. Those that did argue for a wider religious toleration tended to accompany their arguments with claims about the need to restrain other forms of moral and religious excess, such as drunkenness, blasphemy, or atheism. The language of moderation in this period is best seen as reflecting the role of a moderator, rather than being a description of moderate behaviour.[18] As he puts it, 'religious moderation was the reasonable restraint of error'.[19]

Nevertheless, by the end of the seventeenth century, change was clearly discernible. Walsham attributes the altered situation not to shifts in ideas but rather to the practical realities of having to live side by side with neighbours of different faiths and none. She is reluctant to privilege either new ideas or new legislation over the practical parochial situation.[20] From a rather different perspective, John Marshall emphasizes the 1680s as being a crucial decade for arguments for and against toleration.[21] He links toleration to the development of the republic of letters and regards toleration as being the essential value of the early Enlightenment. Yet even he is quick to note that toleration in the United Provinces, widely regarded as one of the most tolerant of European societies in the period, was not the result of positive legislative change but,

---

[16] Sarah Mortimer, *Reason and Religion in the English Revolution* (Cambridge, 2010).
[17] Walsham, *Charitable Hatred*, p. 228.
[18] Ethan H. Shagan, *The Rule of Moderation* (Cambridge, 2011). [19] Ibid., p. 298.
[20] Walsham, *Charitable Hatred*, ch. 5.
[21] John Marshall, *John Locke, Toleration and Early Enlightenment Culture* (Cambridge, 2006).

rather, of the non-enforcement of existing laws. Here, as elsewhere, princely and magisterial intervention, or lack thereof, was crucial for determining the levels of permissible tolerance.[22]

Bearing these suggestions in mind, it is nevertheless still possible to point to some important intellectual transformations. One was a move away from an Old Testament emphasis on the importance of physical force to an appreciation of spiritual force more associated with New Testament writers. In particular, it was argued that Christ had not shown himself to be intolerant of others but, rather, that he had welcomed all who wished to come and follow him. Another was the belief that forcing conscience was a greater sin than false belief itself (this view was famously expounded in John Locke's *Letter on Toleration*, published anonymously in 1689). There was also the practical argument that toleration seemed to favour civil peace and economic prosperity.[23] Ends and means were sometimes confused. Nevertheless, practical examples of other European states were used to suggest that there was wisdom and wealth to be found in pursuing a policy of toleration. Spain, in particular, was singled out as a monarchy whose persecuting religious policies had, ultimately, contributed to its economic decline. More generally, a historical sense developed whereby magisterial intolerance was viewed as characteristic of ignorant and barbaric regimes. Histories of the inquisition helped to reinforce this idea, as did a sense of the 'middle ages' as a distinctive historical period from which 'modern' history emerged at the Reformation.[24]

BEYOND 1689

It is within this nexus of ideas and explanations that the changes in the legal position of Dissent occasioned by the political revolution of 1688-9 should be seen. For some Dissenters, James II's 'Declaration of Indulgence' (1687) had provided an important taste of freedom and a welcome relief. Nevertheless, one of the impulses behind the removal of James II had been a sense that the Church of England and, more generally, the protestant state would be difficult to defend in the longer term under a popish prince. The birth of a son to James and his wife in June 1688, thus offering the prospect of a permanent reversion to monarchical Catholicism, had a salutary effect in terms of focusing minds. Following James's military defeat and departure into exile, the Convention Parliament offered the (apparently vacant) thrones to William and Mary.

William III had been Stadtholder of the United Provinces since 1672 and had ruled over a state with a significant degree of de facto toleration, even

---

[22] Ibid., pp. 3-4. [23] Shagan, *Rule of Moderation*, p. 298.
[24] Marshall, *John Locke, Toleration*, p. 618.

though the Stadtholder himself was committed to the Calvinist theology and Presbyterian government of the Dutch Reformed Church. He was probably personally inclined towards tolerance and royal instincts were important in this regard.[25] That said, he was also aware that sometimes his personal views had to be sacrificed in favour of his larger aim of building a successful coalition to combat the power of Louis XIV. Thus, although the king sought to influence Parliament in March 1689 to remove some of the civil disabilities faced by Dissenters, he quickly retreated in the face of a strong backlash.

Royal intervention came at a point when the future of the ecclesiastical settlement brought about by the Orangist coup still hung in the balance. Godly Protestants had been quick to ascribe William's landing at Torbay on 5 November 1688 to the workings of providence. The practical details of deliverance proved more problematic. Among the possible solutions to the problems of protestant division, two in particular commanded significant attention. The first was a proposal for comprehension to bring those who had been excluded by the Act of Uniformity (1662) back within the Church of England.[26] Such a move was not without its difficulties. It entailed a significant revision of the terms of the 1662 Act such as on the questions of the necessity of episcopal ordination, subscription to the Thirty-Nine Articles including those on church government, and giving both assent and consent to the liturgical order set out in the Book of Common Prayer.

Daniel Finch, earl of Nottingham, introduced a Comprehension Bill into Parliament in March 1689. The fuss over attempts to remove the religious test persuaded the king that it was worth paying attention to his advice on ecclesiastical matters. In the course of its parliamentary progress, various suggestions were made about referring disputed ceremonies to a commission for further negotiation but there was a core of Church of England opinion that would allow neither alteration of the Thirty-Nine Articles nor optional use of the prayer book. Thus, the broader attempt at comprehension faltered. Instead an 'Act for Exempting their Majestyes Protestant Subjects Dissenting from the Church of England from the Penalties of certaine Lawes' eventually received royal assent in May 1689. Although it became widely known as the Toleration Act, the full title gives a proper sense of its more limited scope. It allowed freedom of worship to those prepared to take the oaths of allegiance and supremacy and who were also prepared to make a declaration against transubstantiation (this meant that Catholics could not claim its benefits). Additionally, it was necessary for Dissenters to register their meeting houses and

---

[25] Tony Claydon, *William III* (Harlow, 2002), p. 38.
[26] John Spurr, 'The Church of England, Comprehension and the Toleration Act of 1689', *English Historical Review*, 104, 413 (1989) and Roger Thomas, 'Comprehension and Indulgence', in Geoffrey F. Nuttall and Owen Chadwick, eds, *From Uniformity to Unity* (London, 1962), pp. 189–253.

no worship could take place behind locked doors. Dissenting ministers prepared to subscribe to those of the Thirty-Nine Articles that did not deal with church government were exempted from the penalties of the Act of Uniformity; Baptists did not have to subscribe to the article on infant baptism and Quakers could make an affirmation, rather than swear oaths. Those who denied the Trinity were excluded, as were Catholics and atheists.

In Scotland William had also had to moderate his tolerationist instincts. His desire to conciliate the Episcopalian clergy and create a broad religious settlement ran up against the strength of support for the exiled Stuarts in their ranks. In June 1689 he approved an act abolishing episcopacy and had to accept the victory of Presbyterians. In Ireland, William had triumphed militarily but was prepared to grant toleration to Catholics under the Treaty of Limerick. Pressure from the Irish Parliament throughout the 1690s led to increasing restrictions on Catholic worship and political action.

The changed legislative situation represented a compromise. It was also unclear whether it would be a permanent solution. Given the rapidity of religious change within Britain and Ireland over the previous century and a half, it was far from obvious that the freedom of worship now enjoyed was irreversible. Indeed, the sense of contingency felt by Dissenters at the time can be witnessed through the provisions within the trust deeds of many meeting houses established between 1689 and 1714 about what should happen if Dissenting worship were proscribed again. In such circumstances, the trustees were frequently obliged to sell up and distribute the proceeds to the poor.[27]

This gives an appropriate sense of how contested toleration still was under the last two Stuarts. As has become readily apparent, royal attitudes were important. It is also interesting how much both contemporary sermons and later histories of Dissent in this period tended to adopt a strongly providential point of view.[28] William was praised as a deliverer, brought down the channel on a protestant wind. Following his successful invasion and his consolidation of power, the court sponsorship for campaigns of moral reform was seen as contrasting strongly with the perceived moral laxity of the Restoration court.[29] Later Dissenting historians were keen to make the link between William as the initiator of Dissenting liberties and the Hanoverians as the fulfillers and consolidators of these aims. Writing in their *History of Dissenters*, David Bogue and James Bennett noted that 'the same kind of providence which had already saved us by one foreign prince, again rescued us by another, and employed the house of Hanover to perfect what had been begun by that

---

[27] Michael R. Watts, *The Dissenters: From the Reformation to the French Revolution* (Oxford, 1978), p. 263.

[28] For a similar point in the context of abolitionism, see John Coffey, '"Tremble, Britannia!": Fear, Providence and the Abolition of the Slave Trade, 1758–1807', *English Historical Review*, 127, 527 (2012), pp. 844–81.

[29] Tony Claydon, *William III and the Godly Revolution* (Cambridge, 1996), chs 1 and 4.

of Orange'.[30] Bogue and Bennett's chronology is interesting in a number of ways. It emphasizes a sense that Dissenters were part of a global protestant family that stretched beyond Britain but it is also interesting for its omissions: why was Queen Anne passed over in silence?

THE EARLY CHALLENGE OF TOLERATION

Moving away from teleological accounts where the ultimate triumph of toleration is asserted, rather than explained, is crucial. It took time to establish toleration as an accepted part of the political framework and even longer to make it non-negotiable. Indeed, there were several attempts to reshape the scope and extent of toleration during Anne's reign (1702–14).

Anne herself was in an awkward position. Her serious and serial gynaecological misfortune meant that she had no children to succeed her. Consequently, William, her brother-in-law, had taken steps to regulate the succession through the Act of Settlement (1701). The Act reinforced the principle already established in the Bill of Rights (1689) that all future monarchs must be a Protestant and married to Protestants. The immediate consequence of the Act was that after Anne, her nearest protestant relative the dowager Electress Sophia of Hanover, a granddaughter of James I and VI, was placed next in line to the throne. The number of closer blood relations who had been excluded from the succession was significant. Moreover, Anne's reign provided plenty of opportunities for those unhappy about the prospect of the hereditary principle being stretched to such an extent to make trouble.

Politically speaking, most of those who held such views were best described as Tories. They had been strong opponents of attempts to exclude the future James II from the line of succession during the Exclusion Crisis (1679–81) and, in addition to their support for hereditary rights, were also reluctant to permit resistance to authority, which they viewed as divinely ordained. The changes of 1688–9 had, therefore, been difficult to accept, although the fact that Mary and Anne were both daughters of James II had helped. Further dilution of the hereditary principle was, however, deeply suspect. They were also strong supporters of the Church of England and the mutual interdependence of hierarchical structures in Church and state.

Their opponents were known as Whigs. They remained concerned that a non-protestant ruler was dangerous for the continued existence of Protestantism within Britain. Therefore, they were willing to support Dissenters and enhanced rights for them as part of a broader anti-Catholic coalition. Within

---

[30] David Bogue and James Bennett, *History of Dissenters from the Revolution in 1688, to the Year 1808*, 4 vols. (London, 1808–12), III, p. 115.

public debates, Whigs were often associated with the new financial interests of the City of London, whereas the Tories were seen as the party of the older land-owning elite.

This background is important for understanding the form that the Tory parliamentary assault on Dissenters' rights took under Anne. Anne, like William before her, was keen to stand above party and initially favoured a mixed administration of Whigs and Tories. Hard-line Tories, anxious about the fate of the Church of England, hoped to derail government tax legislation by adding clauses ('tacking') on to the relevant bills. Between 1702 and 1704, Tory MPs included clauses attempting to outlaw the practice of Occasional Conformity in the Land Tax bill.

To understand the significance of this move, it is necessary to return to the political restrictions that had been placed on Dissenters during the restoration period. In addition to the Act of Uniformity, Dissenters were also subject to the provisions of the Corporation Act (1661) and the Test Act (1673). The Corporation Act had made holding an office in a town or city corporation subject to having taken communion within the Church of England on at least one occasion in the previous twelve months. The Test Act expanded these provisions to include all civil and military offices, added a declaration against transubstantiation (Catholics, rather than Presbyterians, were the original intended targets), and required taking communion within three months of election.[31] There were similar provisions in the Irish Popery Act (1704), which included a 'test clause', requiring the annual taking of communion within the Church of Ireland for all civil and military officeholders.[32]

The fact that taking communion was only annual provided a potential loophole for Dissenters. For those prepared to do it, they could attend the parish church once a year but continue to worship in a meeting house for the rest of the time. As John Ramsbottom has noted, the practice of 'partial conformity' was not uncommon amongst Presbyterians in the Restoration period; many still considered themselves as members of the parish, even if they were semi-separated.[33] The granting of freedom of worship to Dissenters made the practice of Occasional Conformity—simply attending the parish church to qualify for office—more visible. One of the most flagrant instances was that of Sir Humphrey Edwin (1642–1707) who became Lord Mayor of London in 1697. He had no qualms about taking the sacrament to qualify for office and then attended Dissenting meetings, accompanied by the civic regalia and trappings of his office. Daniel Defoe published a tract

---

[31] Watts, *The Dissenters*, ch. 3.
[32] D. W. Hayton, *Ruling Ireland, 1685–1742* (Woodbridge, 2004), ch. 6.
[33] John D. Ramsbottom, 'Presbyterians and "Partial Conformity" in the Restoration Church of England', *Journal of Ecclesiastical History*, 43, 2 (1992), pp. 249–70.

criticizing Occasional Conformity, igniting a debate that would continue for two decades.[34]

Attempts to outlaw Occasional Conformity between 1702 and 1704 foundered in the House of Lords. Yet following the election of a Tory-dominated administration in the General Election of 1710, the political situation seemed more propitious. Ironically, it was a combination of the ministry's opponents that ensured the passage of the Occasional Conformity bill (1711). The Whigs were anxious to derail the new administration's attempts to end the war of the Spanish Succession without reference to Britain's allies. Consequently, they agreed to support Nottingham's desire to limit Occasional Conformity in exchange for his help in attacking the government's peace plans. Attempts to stop the peace were unsuccessful, as Anne created more peers to ensure that the settlement would pass. Yet Occasional Conformity still became illegal in March 1712. Dissenting rights were further restricted by the passing of the Schism Act (1714). Those wanting to keep a school were required to have an episcopal licence and also needed to demonstrate that they were Anglican communicants. Undermining the Dissenting academies where Dissenters could receive a higher education outside Oxford and Cambridge was a clear aim.

PROVIDENTIAL REDEMPTION?

Yet on the very day that the Schism Act was due to come into effect (1 August 1714), following a prolonged period of ill-health, Anne died. Despite the doubts that had been expressed about the fate of the succession on her demise, Georg Ludwig, the Electress Sophia's eldest son, was proclaimed as George I with little immediate resistance. Thomas Bradbury claimed the honour of being the first minister to pray publicly for the new king, having been alerted to the change of dynasty via a handkerchief dropped from the gallery of his meeting house while he was preaching.[35]

The London Dissenting ministers went to court to present a loyal address shortly afterwards. Someone suggested that Bradbury's sober garb was more appropriate for a funeral than an audience at court. He quickly retorted that they had come to a resurrection.[36] Dissenters were over-represented in

[34] Yannick Deschamps, 'Daniel Defoe's Contribution to the Dispute over Occasional Conformity: An Insight into Dissent and "Moderation" in the Early Eighteenth Century', *Eighteenth-Century Studies*, 46, 3 (2013), pp. 349–61.

[35] John Handby Thompson, 'Bradbury, Thomas (1676/7–1759)', *Oxford Dictionary of National Biography* (Oxford, 2004) [http://www.oxforddnb.com/view/article/3169, accessed 8 July 2015].

[36] Edmund Calamy, *An historical account of my own life, with some reflections of the times I have lived in (1671–1731)*, ed. J. T. Rutt, 2 vols. (London, 1829), II, p. 301.

sermons preached to mark the Hanoverian accession, suggesting the high hopes that were invested in the new dynasty as friends of religious liberty.[37]

Contemporaries tended to refer to the events of 1714 as the protestant, as opposed to Hanoverian, succession. Although aspects of the Revolution Settlement of 1688–9 still provoked controversy, there was now less of a willingness to alter it fundamentally, such as through the repeal of the Toleration Act. Consequently, the attention of Dissenters moved away from basic security towards the raft of other civil disabilities under which they suffered. There was a strong desire to see the repeal of the legislation passed in the last years of Anne's reign.[38] The Sunderland–Stanhope ministry wanted to go further and repeal the Test and Corporation Acts completely. In this, they were to be disappointed, partly because of opposition from bishops in the House of Lords and partly because of opposition from Robert Walpole and Viscount Townshend, who had broken with the administration. Indeed, it would take more than a century before Dissenters were ultimately able to secure the repeal of the Test and Corporation Acts in 1828. The Occasional Conformity and Schism bills were, however, removed from the statute book.

Other than the problems of political division amongst the elite, one of the other difficulties that Dissenters backing repeal in the late 1710s faced was a continuing campaign to question the sincerity of their motives. Again, the earl of Nottingham was involved. As the ministry's appeal legislation was in the Lords in December 1718, Nottingham introduced the house to the disputes that were taking place between Dissenters in Exeter and suggested that any new legislation should include a specific requirement for officeholders to profess their Trinitarian orthodoxy.[39]

Nottingham clearly wanted to cause trouble. The Exeter Assembly, the ministerial association for Devon and Cornwall, had become concerned about the Trinitarian orthodoxy of the students at the Exeter Academy and one of Exeter's ministers, James Peirce, a leading Dissenting controversialist.[40] They had asked Peirce to make a specific declaration of his belief in the Trinity, even though the Toleration Act required this anyway. Peirce's preaching and professions were sufficiently ambiguous to mean that the Exeter Assembly and the lay financial committee referred the matter to the London Dissenting ministers for further advice on what to do. Nottingham's suggestion that those who were now appealing for an easing of their political marginalization were theologically suspect was tactically astute. The London

---

[37] James Caudle, 'Measures of Allegiance: Sermon Culture and the Creation of a Public Discourse of Obedience and Resistance in Georgian Britain, 1714–1760' (unpublished PhD dissertation, Yale, 1996).
[38] David L. Wykes, 'Religious Dissent, the Church, and the Repeal of the Occasional Conformity and Schism Acts, 1714–19', in Robert Cornwall and William Gibson, eds, *Religion, Politics and Dissent, 1660–1832* (Farnham, 2010), pp. 165–83.
[39] Ibid., pp. 177–9.   [40] Watts, *The Dissenters*, pp. 374–5.

ministers met in February 1719 at Salters' Hall to debate the matter. After a lengthy discussion, the assembly resolved by fifty-seven to fifty-three not to require specific adherence to human formularies on particular doctrines, beyond those contained within divine Scripture.[41] The minority reconvened in March 1719 to subscribe to a specific Trinitarian declaration. This led to the terminology of subscribers and non-subscribers becoming the standard way to differentiate between the two sides.

Debate about subscription continued to be important throughout the eighteenth century. Irish Presbyterians had similar debates about the value and necessity of subscribing to the Westminster Confession, partly prompted by the influence of 'New Light' thinking from the 1720s onwards.[42] Likewise, although issues about the control of patronage and presentation to livings were initially important in Scotland, subscription also played a role in the various divisions within Scottish Presbyterianism. It is also important to remember that the issue of the proper place of the civil magistrate in religious affairs had become prominent in the aftermath of the Bangorian controversy, sparked when Benjamin Hoadly, a leading Whig Erastian, had preached (and crucially published) a sermon to George I on the text 'My kingdom is not of this world' [John 18:36].[43]

There were two separate, but connected, issues that related to Dissenting political participation. At a practical level, objections were advanced to the notion that religious and political identity were inextricably linked, such that qualification for civic office required particular religious observance. This was another way of arguing against the structures of authority that followed from church establishment. It also provided an opportunity to suggest that the existence of a sacramental test demeaned religious practice by making it the gateway to worldly advancement. These sorts of arguments, along with claims about the need to question established authority, associated with enlightened rationalism, helped, in the longer term, to make religious faith more a matter of private faith than public commitment.

Related to these views was the claim that in religious matters, private judgement was sovereign.[44] A consequence of this was that discrimination on grounds of religion was illegitimate which was also, of course, an assertion of how its advocates wanted the world to be, as opposed to how it was. Its supporters claimed that the right of private judgement was intrinsic to religion

---

[41] Roger Thomas, 'The Non-Subscription Controversy amongst Dissenters in 1719: The Salters' Hall Debate', *Journal of Ecclesiastical History*, 4, 2 (1953).

[42] Ian McBride, *Eighteenth-Century Ireland* (Dublin, 2009), pp. 77–81. See also ch. 6 in this volume: Andrew Holmes, 'Protestant Dissent in Ireland'.

[43] Andrew Starkie, *The Church of England and the Bangorian Controversy, 1716–1721* (Woodbridge, 2007).

[44] Andrew C. Thompson, 'Popery, Politics and Private Judgement in Early Hanoverian Britain', *Historical Journal*, 45, 2 (2002), pp. 333–56.

itself and evidence of this could be found both in Scripture and in the workings of providence. Interestingly, debates about subscription raised the question of whether the rights of private judgement were being upheld in practice.

LEGISLATIVE CHANGE AND POLITICAL ORGANIZATION

The next concerted attempt to improve the legal position of Dissenters did not come until the 1730s. Simultaneously, Quakers were also seeking legislative change. Quaker campaigning had focused on two particular issues since 1689. The first was a desire to secure permission to make an affirmation, rather than swear an oath, in a variety of public contexts. The Toleration Act had allowed this as a means to gain its benefits and the Affirmation Act (1696) extended the right to substitute affirmation for oath. However, Quakers first had to ensure that the Affirmation Act was made perpetual. If this were achieved, it would then be necessary to monitor that new legislation did not override it. The second major issue of concern was over the payment of tithes. Given the Quaker emphasis on passive resistance, the principle at stake here was not that Quakers would be entirely exempted from tithe payment but that the legal process to force them to do so should work as expeditiously as possible.[45]

Quaker attempts to influence policy in these directions were helped by the existence of an effective lobbying group in London. Since 1675, the 'Meeting for Sufferings' had acted as a focal point for local complaints and it was this body that suggested in 1732 to Robert Walpole, now one of the leading ministers, that they desired further redress. Walpole's political strategy since replacing Stanhope and Sunderland in 1721 was driven by a desire for 'low temperature' politics. He had noted how controversial religious issues could be in Parliament and so set out to avoid them, if at all possible. The timing of the Quaker move was less than ideal. An election was due in 1734 and Walpole was keen to ensure that his opponents, including some inveterate Tories, could not revive the cry of the 'Church in Danger' that had been used extensively between 1688 and 1714. Nevertheless a bill to address tithe complaints was presented to Parliament in 1736, although it was eventually defeated in the Lords with the help of the episcopal bench.

Renewed attempts were also made in 1736 by other Dissenters to press the case for repeal of the Test and Corporation Acts.[46] Dissenters of all stripes

---

[45] N. C. Hunt, *Two Early Political Associations* (Oxford, 1961), chs 4–6.
[46] Andrew C. Thompson, 'Contesting the Test Act: Dissent, Parliament and the Public in the 1730s', in Stephen Taylor and David L. Wykes, eds, *Parliament and Dissent* (Edinburgh, 2005), pp. 58–70.

made extensive use of the press and pamphlets to influence political opinion. Articles were written in newspapers and letters sent to MPs to make them aware of Dissenters' claims. This was also the period which witnessed the foundation of a separate lay pressure group to advance the claims of Presbyterians, Independents, and Baptists. The London Dissenting Deputies developed to complement existing bodies such as the fund boards and London Dissenting ministers. Their first chairman was Samuel Holden, a respected and well-connected London merchant.[47] Holden's view, despite pressure from within London and further afield to press Dissenting concerns in Parliament, was that the time was not yet ripe to pursue vigorous action.

Why these concerns resurfaced in the 1730s is an interesting question. One explanation might be that the Test and Corporation Acts were irritating but typically affected a relatively small proportion of Dissenters. Some historians have argued that the passing of Indemnity Acts effectively removed most Dissenting complaints.[48] The problem with this view is that although Indemnity Acts provided a means to avoid the penalties for non-compliance with the Acts, taking the sacramental test by a specified date was still required. Indemnity Acts were also far from annual initially.[49] Moreover, in the early 1730s the practice of electing known Dissenters to the office of Sheriff in the City of London and then using the resultant fines to fund building projects accelerated—such was its eventual extent that the Mansion House was largely erected from the proceeds.[50]

A parliamentary attempt to gain repeal was eventually made in 1736. Following its failure, Holden resigned to be replaced by the more activist former minister, turned physician, Benjamin Avery. There was a further attempt to secure repeal in 1739 which, again, failed, despite attempts to emphasize Dissenters' continuing affection towards, and support for, Walpole's regime and the illegitimacy of sacramental tests in general.[51]

The efforts by Quakers and the Dissenting Deputies in the 1730s have been accorded differing significance. For N. C. Hunt, both were examples of 'early political associations'. They were, therefore, the precursors of more modern forms of political organization that were, later, to prove instrumental to modern forms of politics. Hunt was keen to emphasize the extent to which the Deputies were able to model themselves on Quakers' earlier efforts but the

---

[47] N. C. Hunt, 'Sir Robert Walpole, Samuel Holden, and the Dissenting Deputies', *Friends of Dr Williams's Library Eleventh Lecture* (London, 1957).

[48] Clark, *English Society*, p. 376.

[49] K. R. M. Short, 'The English Indemnity Acts, 1726–1867', *Church History*, 42, 3 (1973), pp. 366–76.

[50] Hunt, *Two Early Political Associations*, p. 128.

[51] Bernard Lord Manning, *The Protestant Dissenting Deputies*, ed. Ormerod Greenwood (Cambridge, 1952), p. 30.

importance of both was because 'they held the key to the future'.[52] More recent analysis of the Deputies' contribution has stressed the role that they, and religious ideas more generally, played in opening up public debate.[53] Legislative success was not, therefore, the only way of judging their achievement.

FURTHER DISSENTING PRESSURE FOR LEGISLATIVE CHANGE

After 1739, much of the Deputies' activity was focused on more 'local' issues, such as the refusal to bury Dissenters in Anglican churchyards, because of doubts over the legitimacy of their baptism. The campaign to prevent the City from electing Dissenters to office simply to secure the fine income was ultimately successful. In 1767, Lord Mansfield ruled that one could not criminalize the refusal to take the sacramental test and that by doing so, Dissenters rendered themselves ineligible for election to office.[54]

Direct parliamentary action resumed in the 1770s with a campaign against the need to subscribe to those of the Thirty-Nine Articles required by the original act in order to secure the benefits of toleration.[55] Part of the motivation was related to a more general concern about the legitimacy of requiring subscription to Trinitarian formulae that encompassed the Church of England too. Yet questions about the proper demarcation of religious and civic authority were also part of the debate. Petitions to Parliament from around the country played a greater role than in previous campaigns—again, the rise of this form of political action was part of a more general trend.[56] Likewise, there was also awareness of the British context for these debates: Irish Dissenters, for example, were not required to subscribe to benefit from toleration. Opponents of the change argued that it would contravene the Act of Union (1707) with Scotland because this had declared the Act of Uniformity to be perpetual and the proposed changes sought to undermine the latter.

The attempts by the Deputies to hasten the repeal cause in the late 1780s adopted the practice of a United Committee, formed specifically for the purpose, and this was to become the standard operational model in all subsequent attempts to achieve legislative change. Building on previous

[52] Hunt, *Two Early Political Associations*, p. 180.
[53] James E. Bradley, 'The Public, Parliament and the Protestant Dissenting Deputies', in Taylor and Wykes, eds, *Parliament and Dissent*, pp. 71–90.
[54] Manning, *Protestant Dissenting Deputies*, p. 125.
[55] G. M. Ditchfield, '"How Narrow will the Limits of this Toleration Appear?" Dissenting Petitions to Parliament, 1772–73', in Taylor and Wykes, eds, *Parliament and Dissent*, pp. 91–106.
[56] A theme emphasized in James E. Bradley, *Religion, Revolution and English Radicalism* (Cambridge, 1990).

campaign experience, local committees encouraged petitions and propaganda. Charles James Fox, leader of the opposition Whigs, also took up the cause, seeing it as part of his general assault on Pitt the Younger and George III's government—Fox believed the monarch had become too powerful and that Pitt was simply the king's puppet. Despite, or perhaps because of, Fox's support, little progress was made. Motions to repeal the Test and Corporation Acts were defeated in 1787 and again in 1789, although the margin of defeat was narrower on the second occasion. In 1790, with revolution spreading across the channel, Fox was again defeated, this time by a significant majority.[57]

The period of the French revolutionary and Napoleonic Wars was not necessarily the most auspicious time for promoting further claims for religious liberty. Richard Price's meeting house had been burnt down by a loyalist mob in 1790. While some welcomed the changes taking place in France as the dawning of a new era, loyalist sentiment also grew significantly. Prolonged conflict enhanced suspicions of political and religious difference and also meant that domestic issues were subjugated to wider strategic imperatives. The question of repeal resurfaced after Napoleon's defeat. There were a series of stillborn campaigns in the decade after 1817. A new United Committee was formed in 1827, bringing together various Dissenting interest groups and it was this body that was to be central to the ultimate success of repeal in May 1828. The Deputies now had an MP, William Smith, as their chairman and considerable care was taken to manage the whole process, through direct contacts with MPs and peers, petitioning, and other publications. Many of the arguments advanced were familiar from earlier campaigns. There was an absolute right of private judgement when it came to religious matters and the Dissenters had repeatedly proved their loyalty to the House of Hanover and were, therefore, deserving of some form of further relief.[58] Unlike in previous campaigns, the United Committee also expressed its support for the idea of Catholic Emancipation, which was also in agitation at this juncture.

The parliamentary campaign did not proceed entirely as planned. Although there was a clear majority in the Commons willing to remove the sacramental test, it was unclear as to whether attempts would be made in the Lords to introduce a new form of declaration or oath. Lord John Russell, who was one of the leading parliamentary figures backing repeal, was anxious that Dissenters showed themselves to be accommodating to a new moderate declaration, even though none was required of Irish Dissenters.[59] Ultimately, fears that the former Lord Chancellor, Eldon, might cause trouble about repeal in the Lords were unfounded. The Sacramental Test Act (1828) did require some office-holders to swear an oath not to undermine those churches established by law

---

[57] Manning, *Protestant Dissenting Deputies*, pp. 217–18.
[58] Ibid., p. 221.   [59] Ibid., pp. 236–8.

but those involved with revenue collection and most lower-ranking army and naval officers were exempted, even from this provision.[60]

The United Committee and the Deputies were naturally pleased with the outcome. A subcommittee was convened to organize a celebratory dinner in the Freemasons' Tavern for several hundred guests. The menu was lavish and the speeches, at more than six hours, lengthy. The Duke of Sussex, George III's sixth son, and nine other peers were present, along with a number of other MPs and notables. Sussex proposed the health of Charles James Fox and other previous campaigners for liberty. The health of the Established Church and of the ejectees of 1662 and of many more was also proposed.[61]

The intellectual climate in the 1820s was rather different from the 1680s. Yet, given the persistent hold that the idea of the necessity of membership of the Established Church being the only sure guarantee of proper political behaviour enjoyed, more than ideas had to change for Dissenting repeal attempts to succeed. Although Lord John Russell was important to the parliamentary campaign, the willingness of Sir Robert Peel, as Home Secretary, to seek a compromise settlement was also vital.[62] By contrast with the 1780s and 1730s, when neither Walpole nor Pitt the Younger was willing to give government backing to repeal, Peel was prepared to strike a deal. This is a useful reminder of the extent to which Dissenting campaigns for legislative change however effective they were at mobilizing opinion, also had to overcome the hurdle of persuading Parliament as well. For much of the eighteenth century, administrations were formed largely by various different sorts of Whigs. Walpole knew that a failure to support Dissenting demands for reform would probably not have serious political consequences. Although Dissenters were an important electoral interest in some boroughs, they were unlikely to switch their allegiance to the opposition. Likewise, in the 1780s, support from Charles James Fox may not have been an unmitigated blessing, given the strong reactions, both positive and negative, that his repeated attacks on the supposedly overbearing power of George III had provoked.

Dissenters were very often, although not invariably,[63] friends and supporters of the Whig interest, as well as the principles of the protestant succession, as embodied in William III and then the House of Hanover. Their loyalty was often taken as read. Yet, if Dissenters' political demands were not always met as quickly as they might have been, there were ways in

---

[60] Richard A. Gaunt, 'Peel's Other Repeal: The Test and Corporation Acts, 1828', in Clyve Jones and James Kelly, eds, *Parliament, Politics and Policy in Britain and Ireland, c.1680–1832: Essays in Honour of D. W. Hayton* (Oxford, 2014), p. 259.

[61] Manning, *Protestant Dissenting Deputies*, pp. 245–50.

[62] Gaunt, 'Peel's Other Repeal', pp. 260–2.

[63] See William Gibson, 'Dissenters, Anglicans and Elections after the Toleration Act, 1689–1710', in Cornwall and Gibson, eds, *Religion, Politics and Dissent*, p. 139 for Dissenting support for the Tories in 1710.

which they were able to shape, in a variety of ways, the debate about their demands. Pamphlets and petitions could have an immediate impact but the ways in which Dissenting writers contributed towards a broadly 'whiggish' account of the rise of liberty are also revealing. Writers like Daniel Neal, John Oldmixon, and Paul de Rapin de Thoyras all had Dissenting connections and moved in worlds in which the history of Protestantism was more than that of the Church of England. Through their historical writing, they helped shape a view of British history as being about a struggle for toleration and liberty in which the nasty Stuarts and high-flying Anglican clerics were the enemies of the ultimate triumph of providence. For all the slowness of legislative reform, the history of toleration was, for a very long while, written by the losers and forgotten by the winners.

SELECT BIBLIOGRAPHY

Bradley, James E., 'The Religious Origins of Radical Politics in England, Scotland, and Ireland, 1662–1800', in Bradley, James E. and Van Kley, Dale K., eds, *Religion and Politics in Enlightenment Europe* (Notre Dame, IN, 2001), pp. 187–253.

Bradley, James E., 'The Public, Parliament and the Protestant Dissenting Deputies', in Taylor, Stephen and Wykes, David L., eds, *Parliament and Dissent* (Edinburgh, 2005), pp. 71–90.

Calamy, Edmund, *An historical account of my own life, with some reflections of the times I have lived in (1671–1731)*, ed. J. T. Rutt, 2 vols. (London, 1829).

Collins, Jeffrey R., 'Redeeming the Enlightenment: New Histories of Religious Toleration', *Journal of Modern History*, 81, 3 (2009), pp. 607–36.

Ditchfield, G. M., '"How Narrow will the Limits of this Toleration Appear?" Dissenting Petitions to Parliament, 1772–73', in Taylor, Stephen and Wykes, David L., eds, *Parliament and Dissent* (Edinburgh, 2005), pp. 91–106.

Gaunt, Richard A., 'Peel's Other Repeal: The Test and Corporation Acts, 1828', in Jones, Clyve and Kelly, James, eds, *Parliament, Politics and Policy in Britain and Ireland, c.1680–1832: Essays in Honour of D. W. Hayton* (Oxford, 2014), pp. 243–62.

Hunt, N. C., *Two Early Political Associations* (Oxford, 1961).

Manning, Bernard Lord, *The Protestant Dissenting Deputies*, ed. Ormerod Greenwood (Cambridge, 1952).

Shagan, Ethan, *The Rule of Moderation* (Cambridge, 2011).

Short, K. R. M., 'The English Indemnity Acts, 1726–1867', *Church History*, 42, 3 (1973), pp. 366–76.

Spurr, John, 'The Church of England, Comprehension and the Toleration Act of 1689', *English Historical Review*, 104, 413 (1989), pp. 927–46.

Thompson, Andrew C., 'Popery, Politics and Private Judgement in Early Hanoverian Britain', *Historical Journal*, 45, 2 (2002), pp. 333–56.

Thompson, Andrew C., 'Contesting the Test Act: Dissent, Parliament and the Public in the 1730s', in Taylor, Stephen and Wykes, David L., eds, *Parliament and Dissent* (Edinburgh, 2005), pp. 58–70.

Walsham, Alexandra, *Charitable Hatred: Tolerance and Intolerance in England, 1500–1700* (Manchester, 2006).

Watts, Michael, *The Dissenters: From the Reformation to the French Revolution* (Oxford, 1978).

Wykes, David L., 'Religious Dissent, the Church, and the Repeal of the Occasional Conformity and Schism Acts, 1714–19', in Cornwall, Robert D. and Gibson, William, eds, *Religion, Politics and Dissent, 1660–1832* (Farnham, 2010), pp. 165–83.

14

Abolitionism and the Social Conscience

G. M. Ditchfield

INTRODUCTION

The abolition of the British slave trade in 1806–7 and the emancipation of slaves in the British Empire in 1833–4 have been and remain subjects of intense historical interest and polemical controversy. Explanations for abolition in 1806–7 in particular have provoked debate and sharp differences of interpretation. For many years in the nineteenth and early twentieth centuries, the priority, especially in Britain, was accorded to the altruistic efforts of leading individual abolitionists, notably Granville Sharp, Thomas Clarkson, and William Wilberforce, who, inspired by their Anglican evangelical values, helped to create a movement which ultimately won a historic victory. This view was not without an element of self-congratulation and amounted to a source of national pride.[1] The publication in 1944 of Eric Williams's *Capitalism and Slavery*, however, changed the entire pattern of the debate. Williams postulated a decline in the profitability both of the slave trade and of the British sugar-producing islands in the Caribbean which led an increasingly industrializing nation to perceive the slave trade as an obstruction to economic progress. Williams's 'decline' theory seriously diminished the role of abolitionists and their campaigns and substituted longer-term commercial and social factors. By thus downgrading almost to the point of dismissal the notion of humanitarian motivation, his work changed the entire character of the historiography of abolitionism.[2]

From the late 1960s and 1970s, Williams's view was itself seriously questioned. Roger Anstey not only rejected the 'decline' theory but reasserted the

---

[1] Classic examples are Reginald Coupland, *The British Anti-Slavery Movement* (London, 1933) and Frank J. Klingberg, *The Anti-Slavery Movement in England* (New Haven, CT and London, 1926). For a succinct analysis of the relevant historiography, see David Turley, 'British Antislavery Reassessed', in Arthur Burns and Joanna Innes, eds, *Rethinking the Age of Reform: Britain 1780–1850* (Cambridge, 2003), pp. 182–99.

[2] Eric Williams, *Capitalism and Slavery* (1944: New York edn 1966).

contribution of the abolitionists, although without attributing their efforts solely to unqualified altruism, and explained their success in 1806-7 by a combination of guile, skilful parliamentary tactics, and a shrewd appeal to the national interest. Anstey believed that the abolitionist dynamic was largely the result of the ways in which evangelical religion—within the Church of England, the recently formed Methodist movements, and among the Dissenting denominations—brought about the fundamental changes in the intellectual and moral climate which made the trade and slavery itself indefensible.[3] At the same time, Seymour Drescher also rejected the 'decline' theory and demonstrated that the profitability of the slave trade and of the sugar which the Caribbean plantations exported had reached new heights by the time of abolition. To Drescher, however, abolition was to be explained less by an evangelical world-view than by the growth of expertly mobilized popular pressure, especially through the mass organization of petitions, made possible by the rapid demographic expansion of the middle and working classes which was central to the emergence of industrial capitalism and urbanization.[4] To these conflicting interpretations has been added more recently the claim that in many cases slaves themselves contributed to the ending of the trade and, more particularly, to their own emancipation in 1833-4.[5] Successive slave uprisings not only drew public attention to the horrors of slavery and the cruelty with which the rebellions were suppressed, but showed that liberated slaves were capable of self-government. This latter view, although with potentially unfavourable implications for the importance of abolitionist campaigning, was one which some contemporary Nonconformists encouraged. In 1823 the Unitarian attorney James Losh praised the republic of Santo Domingo, both for its successful struggle for liberty in 1791 and for the peaceful and responsible quality of its government thereafter, and asked 'If the people of St. Domingo, without any assistance, had done so much, what might not be done in Jamaica, with the aid and co-operation of the British Government?'[6] The Baptist missionary William Knibb's reports of the Jamaica rebellion in December 1831 and its consequences helped to persuade the British government of the need for immediate emancipation.[7]

---

[3] Roger Anstey, 'Capitalism and Slavery: A Critique', *Economic History Review*, 2nd Ser. 21, 2 (1968), pp. 307-20; Roger Anstey, *The Atlantic Slave Trade and British Abolition 1760-1810* (London, 1975), Part One.
[4] Seymour Drescher, *Econocide: British Slavery in the Era of Abolition* (Pittsburg, PA, 1977).
[5] See the essays in Seymour Drescher and Pieter C. Emmer, eds, *Who Abolished Slavery? Slave Revolts and Abolitionism: A Debate with João Pedro Marques* (New York and Oxford, 2010), especially Robin Blackburne, 'The Role of Slave Resistance in Slave Emancipation', pp. 169-77.
[6] For example, *A Sketch of the Speech of James Losh, Esq, delivered in the Guildhall, Newcastle upon Tyne, on Tuesday April 29th, 1823* (Newcastle upon Tyne, 1823), pp. 6-7.
[7] J. N. Hinton, *Memoir of William Knibb* (London, 1849), pp. 147-53.

These debates are vital to an understanding of the contributions of campaigners to the abolition of the trade and to emancipation. Historians of religious traditions and institutions, non-Dissenting as well as Dissenting, have on the whole been reluctant to interpret abolition in 1806–7 as the result of long-term (and at the time perhaps not fully comprehended) 'vast, impersonal forces'. They continue to emphasize the positive role of the abolitionists, inspired by theories of Christian liberty and benevolence, under the guidance of divine providence. Those sympathetic to the nonconformist tradition and its progressive ethos do so with particular zeal and commitment, and it is not difficult to understand why. For Nonconformity, these efforts were central to its self-understanding and identity. Anti-slavery was inextricably associated with religious liberalism and civil equality, and subsequently with nineteenth-century parliamentary and municipal reform. Denominational historians understandably play up the abolitionist efforts of their precursors. Central to the ethos of Dissent were the voluntary principle, the private conscience, the preaching ministry, and the conviction that the endeavours of individual people, leading to public action, were capable of bringing about moral reformation and significant changes in public policy. With reference to anti-slavery, the distinguished scholar and senior Methodist minister Gordon Rupp wrote that 'William Wilberforce, making due and lawful use of the machinery of politics and law, proved that Christian politics are the art of the impossible.'[8]

This type of historical writing often led to a biographical approach, as well as detailed local studies of the efforts of specific congregations, with whiggish emphases upon 'progress', 'improvement', and the march of humanity towards the sunlit uplands. Of course, the individuals concerned did not think, write, and campaign in a vacuum. Without the expansion of print culture and developments in transport, the growth of a professional, commercial reading public, and the large concentrations of population in important manufacturing centres—all central to abolitionism—these campaigns and their popular mobilization would have made a far smaller impact. On the other hand, the involvement and initiatives of individuals cannot be too far downgraded without losing a sense of proportion; many thousands of individuals took the decision—no doubt for different reasons—to sign a petition, or—an even firmer sign of commitment—to pay a subscription to an abolitionist society. Moreover, irrespective of the reasons for abolition and emancipation, abolitionist movements internationally tell us a great deal about the character of the societies in which they functioned. And with regard to British abolitionism and moves for emancipation, protestant Nonconformity was central. One of the attractions of abolitionism and anti-slavery to Dissenters was their acute

---

[8] G. Rupp, *Religion in England 1688–1791* (Oxford, 1986), p. 526.

awareness of their own civil disabilities, leading perhaps to a sense of affinity with the victims of slavery (although not always with their catholic compatriots) as fellow-sufferers. Nonconformists were excluded from most officeholding at national level (although not from the franchise or membership of Parliament) by the sacramental provisions of the Test Act of 1673 and from much of local government (although with significant exceptions, such as Bristol and Nottingham) through the Corporation Act and the very limited nature of the local government franchise. Similarly, the parochial system discriminated heavily against Nonconformists by obliging them to pay tithes and church rates, and denying them equal status for the registration of their baptisms, marriages, and burials. It was not surprising that Dissenters supported anti-slavery campaigns in far higher proportions than did the population as a whole. Some of them sensed a common cause between Dissenters and slaves. Immediately after the House of Commons rejected the motion for repeal of the Test and Corporation Acts in March 1790, the Liverpool Unitarian Elizabeth Nicholson wrote, 'So the Dissenters expectations if they had any are over and I suppose the African will share the same fate.'[9]

NONCONFORMITY AND ABOLITIONISM

Hostility to the principle of enslavement may be found within the older puritan tradition which formed an essential component of eighteenth-century Dissent. During the 1660s Richard Baxter denounced the slave trade and slave traders in his *Chapters from a Christian Directory*, a work published in 1673 and influential for decades thereafter. The influence of the older Nonconformity can be seen in the way in which William Wilberforce attributed his evangelical conversion in the mid-1780s in large part to Philip Doddridge's *The Rise and Progress of Religion in the Soul*, first published in 1745. Doddridge, as a much-admired Independent minister and tutor at the Northampton academy during the 1730s and 1740s, advocated meticulous observance of worship and private study combined with the need to awaken to a deeply personal sense of sin—a sense which could easily be transferred to a broader national arena and applied to one's nation as a whole. Inasmuch as Wilberforce's conversion was an essential prerequisite for his decision to take up the cause of abolitionism, the older Nonconformity can be credited with much of the responsibility.[10] Of

---

[9] Quoted in William McCarthy, *Anna Letitia Barbauld: Voice of the Enlightenment* (Baltimore, MD and London, 2008), p. 291.

[10] Seymour Drescher, 'Capitalism and Abolition: Values and Forces in Britain, 1783–1814', in Roger Anstey and P. E. H. Hair, eds, *Liverpool, the African Slave Trade, and Abolition: Essays to Illustrate Current Knowledge and Research* ([Liverpool], 1976), pp. 177, 193; John Pollock, *Wilberforce* (London, 1977), pp. 34–5.

the famous Dissenting academy at Warrington, which between 1757 and 1783 educated some four hundred students, its historian asserted that its tutors were 'Anti-Slavery to a man'.[11] The family of John Aikin, divinity tutor from 1761 to 1780, bears out this claim, notably through his daughter Anna Letitia, the future Mrs Barbauld, and his son John Aikin, physician and pamphleteer, while of its former students, Henry Beaufoy became a prominent abolitionist member of Parliament, and John Prior Estlin, Unitarian minister in Bristol, played a leading role in abolitionist activity in that city with its heavy involvement in the slave trade.

Over the same period, objections to the slave trade were voiced increasingly within the Church of England by representatives of the latitudinarian tradition as well as by its evangelical 'wing'. Latitudinarianism, with its consistent sympathy with the principle of (protestant) religious pluralism, favoured a cautious removal of Dissenters' grievances and in many cases moved towards cooperation with Dissent, notably in criticism of the use of force against the American colonists in the 1770s.[12] Francis Blackburne, archdeacon of Cleveland and a powerful critic of the 'Confessional State', seemed to anticipate a public campaign when he wrote in 1756, 'Blessings on the Heart of any Man who will Ease our public of the horrid guilt of our Slave Trade, and bring us to a proper humiliation [fo]r that more than Pagan, that most inhuman Merchandise, which has indeed the Apocalyptical Mark upon it with a Vengeance.'[13] John Jebb, who resigned his Anglican livings and took up such radical causes as universal male suffrage, and Laurence Sterne, something of a maverick as a clerical incumbent of two Yorkshire parishes but with lifetime and posthumous fame as a 'sentimental' novelist, both expressed hostility to the trade.[14] Jebb and Sterne died before the public campaign for abolition began. Significantly, they, and Blackburne, were all graduates of Cambridge University, where latitudinarian and whig religious and political values tended to predominate. In the earliest moves for abolition, Cambridge was far more energetic than Oxford.[15]

With the beginning of popular campaigning in the later 1780s, however, Latitudinarianism could not provide abolitionism with the two major assets

---

[11] H. McLachlan, *Warrington Academy: Its History and Influence* (Manchester, 1943), p. 19.

[12] See John Gascoigne, 'Anglican Latitudinarianism, Rational Dissent and Political Radicalism in the Late Eighteenth Century', in Knud Haakonssen, ed., *Enlightenment and Religion: Rational Dissent in Eighteenth-Century Britain* (Cambridge, 1996), pp. 219–40.

[13] Dr Williams's Library (hereafter DWL), Blackburne Letters, MS 12.52 (22), Blackburne to Theophilus Lindsey, 21 Dec. 1756.

[14] Anthony Page, *John Jebb and the Enlightenment Origins of British Radicalism* (Westport, CT and London, 2003), pp. 225–6; Ian Campbell Ross, *Laurence Sterne: A Life* (Oxford, 2001), pp. 349–52.

[15] As was commented in a caustic note by the whiggish Lord Chedworth, a Suffolk magistrate; see *Letters from the late Lord Chedworth to the Rev. Thomas Crompton; written in the period from Jan. 1780 to May 1795* (London, 1828), p. 99.

which Dissent could offer. In the first place, the three older Dissenting denominations—Presbyterians, Congregationalists (or Independents), and Baptists—could bring to bear much experience of regional organization, such as the Cheshire Classis and the associated ministers of the West Riding of Yorkshire. At the national level, the Protestant Dissenting Deputies, founded in 1732, a body of lay Dissenters based in London but with correspondents from all over the country, had gradually accumulated respectability through successful litigation and access to a range of political contacts in pursuing redress of their grievances. The 'General Body of Protestant Dissenting Ministers of the Three Denominations', also London-based, originating in the reign of Queen Anne and reconstituted in 1727, was the clerical equivalent, and had recent experience of organizing petitions in 1772–3 for relaxation of subscription to the doctrinal articles for Dissenting ministers, which were approved in the House of Commons but rejected by the House of Lords.[16] Success in the lower, followed by frustration in the upper, chamber was an experience which abolitionists would soon share. Between 1786 and 1790, the Dissenting Deputies set up a committee to petition for the repeal of the Test and Corporation Acts, with representatives in each English county; they repeated the process, with more success, in 1827–8.[17] The Society of Friends had for decades possessed a well-organized and well-documented structure of particular meetings at a town and village level, quarterly meetings at county level, and a national Yearly Meeting in London, the purposes of which, in addition to worship, were to administer discipline and take up the grievances which bore heavily upon Quakers, notably the compulsory payment of tithes

Second, Dissenters could also contribute large and rapid increases in their numbers during the period of abolitionism. Although in the middle years of the eighteenth century many Dissenters had expressed anxiety that their congregations were dwindling, from the 1790s the numbers of Dissenting congregations and adherents grew at a faster rate than that of the population as a whole. Michael Watts estimated that the proportion of Dissenters in the population of England rose from 6.21 per cent in 1715–18 to 17.02 per cent at the religious census of 1851; the comparable increase in Wales was from 5.74 per cent to 45.50 per cent.[18] The English Presbyterians (increasingly

[16] John Stephens, 'The London Ministers and Subscription, 1772–1779', *Enlightenment and Dissent*, 1 (1982); G. M. Ditchfield, '"How Narrow will the Limits of this Toleration Appear?" Dissenting Petitions to Parliament, 1772–1773', in Stephen Taylor and David L. Wykes, eds, *Parliament and Dissent* (Edinburgh, 2005), pp. 91–106.

[17] Thomas W. Davis, ed., *Committees for Repeal of the Test and Corporation Acts: Minutes 1786–90 and 1827–8* (London, 1978).

[18] Michael Watts, *The Dissenters. Volume II: The Expansion of Evangelical Nonconformity* (Oxford, 1995), p. 29. Clive Field has estimated that the numbers of Congregationalists in England and Wales increased from approximately 60,000 in 1760 to 225,000 in 1800 and to 725,000 in 1840; the comparable figures for Baptists were 26,000 in 1760, 150,000 in 1800, and 500,000 in 1840. Dr Field further estimated that the numbers of Wesleyan Methodists, now

Unitarian in doctrine) and the Quakers, relatively uninfluenced by the Evangelical revival, lost support, although still retaining influence beyond their numbers. By contrast, the Congregationalists and Particular Baptists responded so much more favourably to evangelical teaching, preaching, and conversion that their numbers rose substantially, with the former quite clearly the largest of the older Dissenting denominations by the mid-nineteenth century. In addition, the Wesleyan Methodists and other Methodist groupings, which also experienced phases of revivalism and substantial (if irregular) gains in their numbers, came to see themselves as Dissenting denominations, as even the Wesleyans moved (or were pushed) away from the Church of England. Here were the boots on the ground which formed much of the abolitionist rank and file.

Perhaps because of their commitment to pacifism, perhaps because of their extensive transatlantic connections, and perhaps because their organization was the most efficient of all the Dissenting groupings, Quakers were the first to take action against the slave trade. From the late 1750s the publications of the former schoolteacher Anthony Benezet of Philadelphia, drawing on traditional Quaker teachings of the law of love, the golden rule, and importance of the good neighbour, beginning with his *Observations on the inslaving, importing and purchasing of Negroes* (1759), made a large and growing impression. An indication of the ways in which Quaker attitudes in the northern colonies were changing was evident in the decision in 1758 by the Philadelphia Yearly Meeting to condemn the practice of slave trading and at the same time to render more difficult the continued slave-holding by members of its Quaker communities.[19] In 1761 the London Yearly Meeting also denounced the trade and declared involvement in it to be worthy of disownment, the ultimate Quaker penalty for those of its adherents who breached its rules. That the point needed to be made is a reminder that some Dissenters (including Quakers) were still involved in the slave trade and slave-ownership and found it possible to reconcile such involvement with Christian belief.[20] Six years later the London Meeting for Sufferings circulated Benezet's tract of 1759, and from 1772, stimulated by visits from John Woolman and other American Quakers, began to debate the matter more frequently, although also with caution. In 1783 the London Yearly Meeting organized a petition to the House of Commons, circulated Benezet's pamphlet *The Case of our Fellow-Creatures the Oppressed Africans*, linked up with more than one hundred provincial correspondents, and set up what amounted to

---

moving from the Church of England towards Nonconformity after the death of their founder in 1791, rose from 265,000 in 1800 to 1,150,000 in 1840. See Clive D. Field, 'Counting Religion in England and Wales: The Long Eighteenth Century, c.1680–c.1840', *Journal of Ecclesiastical History*, 63, 4 (2012), p. 710.

[19] Brycchan Carey, *Quaker Rhetoric and the Birth of American Antislavery, 1657–1761* (New Haven, CT and London, 2012), pp. 206–13.

[20] Some examples may be found in Watts, *The Dissenters*, II, pp. 438–9.

'a permanent slave trade Committee of the Meeting for Sufferings'.[21] Thomas Clarkson's *Essay on the Slavery and Commerce of the Human Species, particularly the African* (1786), a work rightly credited with alerting the British public to the shocking nature of the middle passage, was published by the Quaker bookseller James Phillips. From 1787, when the Meeting for Sufferings decided on a further petition, its efforts became subsumed in the broader, multi-denominational abolitionist campaigns. But the Quaker initiative was undeniable. When the Society for Effecting the Abolition of the Slave Trade (the Abolition Society) was constituted in May 1787, nine of the original twelve members of its committee were Quakers.[22] Their efforts were praised from many directions. Preaching before the university of Cambridge in 1788 the latitudinarian Peter Peckard, Master of Magdalene College, declared that 'A very respectable Sect of our dissenting brethren ... have in respect of the Slave Trade set us a very amiable example. May we have the virtue to follow it!'[23] The radical Dissenting minister Richard Price of Hackney commented that 'their zeal in this instance does them peculiar honour'.[24]

Dissenters more generally contributed to abolitionism an awareness of international developments from which encouragement could be drawn. The qualified abolition of slavery in Pennsylvania (1780) and similar moves in other New England colonies, improvements in the legal position of the Huguenots in France in the mid-1780s, and the Virginia Statute of 1786 all seemed to point towards a providentially ordained enlightened future in which slavery and religious intolerance would alike be swept aside. So did the restrictions placed by Denmark upon its slave trade in 1792.[25] In some quarters, especially among those Rational Dissenters who rejected the Calvinism of the older Dissent, abolition became associated with millenarianism. Joseph Priestley told his Birmingham congregation in 1788 that 'It seems to be the intention of Divine Providence that every thing should be brought to perfection by degrees ... and certainly the present state of things is gradually bringing on a state of universal peace and happiness, which must ... imply the abolition of slavery, as well as of every other evil.'[26] Josiah Wedgwood, with his connections to radically minded members of the Lunar Society of Birmingham produced in 1787 his famous cameo of the kneeling slave with the slogan 'Am

---

[21] Anstey, *Atlantic Slave Trade*, p. 229.
[22] *A List of the Society instituted in 1787, for the Purpose of Effecting the abolition of the Slave Trade* (London, 1788), unpaginated list of the Committee.
[23] Peter Peckard, *Justice and mercy recommended, particularly with reference to the slave trade* (Cambridge, 1788), p. vi.
[24] W. Bernard Peach and D. O. Thomas, eds, *The Correspondence of Richard Price*. 3 vols. (Cardiff and Durham, NC, 1983-94), III, 146.
[25] Hugh Thomas, *The Slave Trade: The History of the Atlantic Slave Trade 1440-1870* (New York, 1997), p. 525.
[26] Joseph Priestley, *A Sermon on the Subject of the Slave Trade* (Birmingham, 1788), p. 36.

I not a man and a brother?' Although in some quarters subsequently perceived as condescending,[27] its adoption as the seal of the London Committee of the Abolition Society helped to make it a powerfully emotive image. Dissenters, too, were quick to emphasize the second of the two meanings assigned by Samuel Johnson's *Dictionary of the English Language* (1755) to the word 'traffick', namely 'to trade meanly or mercenarily'. The London Quaker William Allen, in urging a boycott of West India sugar in 1792, was characteristic in describing the slave trade as 'this inhuman traffic', and 'a traffic which is equally at variance with the true principles of Commerce and every sentiment of Justice and Humanity'.[28]

NONCONFORMIST INVOLVEMENT IN ABOLITIONIST CAMPAIGNING

Petitioning was far from new in the 1780s. Effective petitioning and instructions to MPs had helped to defeat Walpole's excise scheme in 1733 and Pitt's Irish trade proposals in 1785. The first large-scale petition for abolition of the slave trade in 1788, however, broke new ground by its unprecedented involvement of non-elite, as well as elite, opinion. The lead was provided by the London Committee of the Abolition Society, and, nationally, more than one hundred petitions were delivered to Parliament. The petition from Manchester attracted the highest response, with a total of 11,000 signatures, compared with 2,000 from Sheffield and 1,800 from York.[29] Much of the impetus was provided by the town's Literary and Philosophical Society and the Unitarian Cross Street Chapel, together with much mercantile and artisan opinion, while the strong Dissenting involvement is evident from the published lists of subscribers.[30] Probably Manchester's creaking manorial system of local government encouraged this widened political participation, which included pressure for incorporation and parliamentary representation. One measure of the impact of these petitions was the passage in Parliament in 1788 of the Slave Limitation Act, known from the name of its proposer Sir William Dolben as 'Dolben's Act', which regulated the numbers of slaves and the physical conditions in ships engaged in the middle passage. Although a source

---

[27] David Brion Davis, 'Slave Revolts and Abolitionism', in Drescher and Emmer, eds, *Who Abolished Slavery?*, p. 163.

[28] William Allen, *The Duty of abstaining from the use of West India Produce* (London, 1792), pp. 23, iv; see also p. 14.

[29] Seymour Drescher, *Capitalism and Antislavery: British Mobilization in Comparative Perspective* (Oxford and New York, 1986), pp. 70–8.

[30] *Manchester Mercury*, 1 and 15 Jan. 1788.

of anxiety to some abolitionists because of its seeming legitimization of the trade, the act was also an opportunity for statements of further intention. Endorsing the bill in the House of Commons on 18 June 1788, Henry Beaufoy, with his Quaker background and Dissenting education, distinguished between what was '*attainable*' and 'what is *desirable*', concluding that 'To the memory of former parliaments the horrors of this traffick will be an eternal reproach.'[31] The petition from the General Body of Dissenting Ministers focused upon the 'desirable' by demanding the complete abolition of slavery.[32]

Dolben's Act also illuminated several of the arguments which many Dissenters were particularly concerned to deploy during the abolition campaigns, and which had the additional advantage of promoting their own interests. It was essential to the Bible-centrism of the nonconformist tradition that it should respond effectively to the claim that slavery was sanctioned, or at least, not specifically condemned, by Scripture. Representative among vehement examples of such responses are sermons by the Baptist minister Robert Robinson of Cambridge in 1788 and by the Methodist Joseph Benson of Hull ten years later.[33] And Dissenters took even more pains than many abolitionists to stress the fundamental equality of humanity, irrespective of ethnicity, in terms of intellectual ability and moral potential. In 1788 Priestley declared that 'Christianity teaches us to consider all mankind as *brethren*, equally the subjects of God's moral government here, and alike heirs of immortality hereafter', and insisted that Africans 'were no means inferior to Europeans in point of understanding'.[34]

Such a view was of course consistent with religious equality, with equal treatment for all (protestant) religions and without any imposition of a state church. And it was no coincidence that a firm reassertion of that principle was made by Andrew Thomson, minister of St George's Church, Edinburgh and an adherent of the anti-patronage party of the Church of Scotland on the eve of emancipation, who maintained that 'A difference may subsist in the degree of personal endowments, in external circumstances, in what may be called the mere accidents of created existence' but that there was no distinction between slaves and the rest of humanity 'as rational, accountable, immortal creatures'.[35] Furthermore, as a means of emphasizing their own patriotism in a period when Dissent was suspected of sympathy with the French Revolution, Dissenters were keen to argue that abolition, far from threatening radical change, would

---

[31] *The Speech of Mr Beaufoy... on a Bill for regulating the Conveyance of Negroes from Africa to the West Indies* (London, 1789), pp. 11, 20.

[32] DWL MS 38.106, pp. 279–82 (Minute Books of the General Body of Dissenting Ministers, 5 Feb. 1788).

[33] Robert Robinson, *Slavery inconsistent with the Spirit of Christianity* (Cambridge, 1788); Joseph Benson, *A Sermon preached at the Methodist Chapel, at Hull, on Wednesday, the 7th of March, 1798, being the day appointed for a national fast* (London, 1798).

[34] Priestley, *Sermon... on the Slave Trade*, pp. 15, 20.

[35] Andrew Thomson, *Slavery condemned by Christianity* (Edinburgh, 1847), p. 13.

benefit the national interest, for example by saving the lives of sailors. Henry Beaufoy in June 1788 pointed out that 'the trade to Africa has invariably proved, not the nursery, but the grave of the British seamen', and contrasted the middle passage with the Newfoundland fisheries, which were essential for the training of merchant seamen, who could be drafted into the royal navy in wartime.[36] The continuity over many years of this line of argument may be seen in the prediction by the Liverpool Society for the Abolition of Slavery that emancipation would actually be advantageous to West India planters as well as to the British Empire as a whole.[37] And in 1788 Helen Maria Williams, a member of the Princes Street Presbyterian congregation, Westminster, expressed in verse the boost to British pride and self-esteem which would follow a clear lead if the nation were to set an example of abolitionism; Britain could be 'first of EUROPE's polish'd lands, / To ease the Captive's iron bands!'. It is reasonable to conclude that her congregation agreed; its minister, Andrew Kippis, was one of the first subscribers to the Anti-Slavery Society in 1787.[38]

As the evidence for the popularity of abolitionism grew, and as the defence of the slave trade was increasing the preserve of those with a financial stake in its continuance, some Dissenters hoped that their highly visible involvement in this cause would ease public antipathy towards them. Whereas Priestley and the High Church bishop of St David's, Samuel Horsley, had engaged in bitter theological controversy during the 1780s, abolitionism was probably the only public issue on which they were in agreement. Claiming that abolitionism was the cause of '*humanity*, and our common *Christianity*', Priestley declared himself to be 'peculiarly happy that, in recommending the relief of the distressed African slaves, I can join heartily with every denomination of Christians in the country, the catholics, the members of the establishment, and dissenters of all denominations'.[39] Other sympathizers with Unitarianism were equally hopeful.[40] In the short-term they were too optimistic as regards cooperation with High Churchmen in the aftermath of the Birmingham riots of 1791, since in some areas, High Church Anglicans were unwilling to support a society 'dominated by nonconformists'.[41] But Priestley was right to detect a unifying process between evangelical and 'rational' (i.e. non- or anti-Trinitarian) Dissenters. The Dissenting banker Samuel Kenrick wrote from Worcestershire in 1792 that 'the Methodists are the most violent

---

[36] *Speech of Mr Beaufoy*, pp. 15, 20.
[37] *An Address from the Liverpool Society for the Abolition of Slavery* (Liverpool, 1824), p. 6.
[38] Helen Maria Williams, *A Poem on the Bill lately passed for regulating the slave trade* (London, 1788), pp. 3, 26.
[39] Priestley, *Sermon on... the Slave Trade*, p. 33.
[40] John Rylands University Library of Manchester, UCC/2/34/1/44, William Tayleur to Theophilus Lindsey, Feb. 1788.
[41] Clare Midgley, *Women against Slavery: The British Campaigns, 1780–1870* (London and New York, 1992), p. 18.

anti-revolutionists we have, & yet we all join for the abolition of the Slave Trade'.[42] Admittedly, Dissenters and indeed evangelicals more generally, while proclaiming a common humanitarianism, did not share identical priorities in advocating abolition. Many evangelicals among the older nonconformist denominations and within the New Dissent represented mainly by Methodism, were much motivated by an urge to appease God by removing a hideous national sin; 'rational' Dissenters placed much more emphasis upon the rights of man, although so also did some Methodists, notably Samuel Bradburn of Manchester. It has been suggested that Calvinists were perhaps less likely than Arminians to give active support to abolition.[43] George Whitefield had not only defended slavery but purchased slaves, as had the Countess of Huntingdon's Connexion, in effect a Dissenting sect by the later 1780s, and the countess herself had been admonished by Anthony Benezet for her Connexion's practice of slavery.[44] However, most Congregationalists and Particular Baptists, influenced by more moderate forms of Calvinism, were strongly supportive of abolitionism and emancipation.

This sometimes uneasy coalition was greatly stimulated by Wilberforce's introduction into the House of Commons in April 1791 of a motion for abolition. Its defeat gave rise the following year to an even greater display of mass petitioning than in 1788. As before, Manchester's participation was prominent; the Methodist minister Samuel Bradburn in 1792 reported that 'some hundreds signed it in the Chapel at the Communion Table, on the Lord's Day'.[45] The combined number of signatures in Manchester, Sheffield, Edinburgh, and Glasgow has been estimated at 43,000 and the national total at approximately 400,000.[46] The inclusiveness of the petitioning was striking. Dissenters in the principal slave-trading ports, notably Liverpool (with the Quaker Rathbone family and the Unitarian William Roscoe as leaders), Bristol, and London were well represented, although not without obstruction from slaving interests. And while convention frowned upon the signing of petitions by women, there were exceptions in 1792. The *Newcastle Courant* reported that signatories included 'Ladies anxiously desiring to show their abhorrence of this abominable trade'.[47] Moreover, women could and did pay

---

[42] DWL, Kenrick Papers, MS 24.157 (173), Samuel Kenrick to James Wodrow, 10 Apr. 1792
[43] Boyd Hilton, *A Mad, Bad, and Dangerous People? England 1783–1846* (Oxford, 2006) p. 187, n. 229.
[44] Boyd Stanley Schlenther, *Queen of the Methodists: The Countess of Huntingdon and the Eighteenth-Century Crisis of Faith* (Durham, 1997), pp. 90–1. The contrast with John Wesley's *Thoughts on Slavery* (London, 1774) is obvious.
[45] Samuel Bradburn, *An Address to the People called Methodists; concerning the evil of encouraging the Slave Trade* (Manchester, 1792), p. 13.
[46] Drescher, *Capitalism and Antislavery*, pp. 82, 219, n. 59; J. R. Oldfield, *Popular Politics and British Anti-Slavery: The Mobilization of Public Opinion against the Slave Trade, 1787–1807* (Manchester, 1995), p. 114.
[47] Quoted in Drescher, *Capitalism and Antislavery*, p. 221, n. 69.

subscriptions to abolitionist societies, as in Manchester.[48] Such female involvement gave a particular prominence to Dissenters—from Unitarians, with their advanced views on women's rights, to Methodists with their relatively unlettered female preachers in the later eighteenth century.[49] On 6 January 1790 Stephen Fuller, the agent for Jamaica and a leading coordinator of the opposition to abolition, grudgingly acknowledged the effectiveness of Dissenters' endeavours by commenting that Wilberforce would 'meet with sufficient encouragement from the Dissenters, who never give up any thing'; on 7 December 1791 he noted that 'the Children of the Dissenters schools are not to be suffer'd to use sugar, and being educated & trained up to do without it, it is concluded they will never know the want of it'.[50]

Fuller's verdict was justified by the vote in the House of Commons in April 1792 for the gradual abolition of the trade—evidently the 'sense of the nation' against the 'traffick' had some effect. The decision was not as dramatic as first appeared, and the Commons' initiative was frustrated by repeated postponements in the House of Lords. Wilberforce's abolition motions in 1793 and 1794 were unsuccessful.[51] And the defeat of his motion in 1796 by only four votes is partly explained by the thin attendance in the Commons. But as the wider consequences of the French Revolution frightened many abolitionists from public identification with any type of reform, Dissenters probably contributed an even higher proportion of public support, as distinct from private sympathy, for anti-slavery than before. In Norwich, *The Cabinet*, a short-lived journal run by some of the city's Dissenters in 1794–5, continued to urge abolition, as did Dissenting periodicals such as the *Analytical Review* and the *Monthly Magazine*.[52] When in 1799 the evangelical Henry Thornton's Slave Trade Limitation Bill passed in the Commons but was narrowly lost in the Lords, the Particular Baptist Andrew Fuller took the lead in castigating the defenders of 'that iniquitous traffic' as among the worst of sinners.[53] When abolition of the trade to foreign territories in 1806 and of the entire British slave trade in 1807 were both carried, their enactment owed more, as Roger Anstey has demonstrated, to dextrous parliamentary manoeuvring than to mass petitioning.[54] Hence when the Protestant Dissenting Deputies expressed support for the act of 1807, they did not cite public opinion but cautiously

---

[48] *Manchester Mercury*, 3 Apr. 1792.

[49] Midgley, *Women against Slavery*, pp. 16–25.

[50] M. W. McCahill, ed., *The Correspondence of Stephen Fuller, 1788–1795: Jamaica, the West India Interest at Westminster and the Campaign to Preserve the Slave Trade* (Parliamentary History Yearbook Trust, Chichester, 2014), pp. 130, 176.

[51] Anstey, *Atlantic Slave Trade*, pp. 276–80.

[52] See Gina Luria Walker, *Mary Hays (1759–1843): The Growth of a Woman's Mind* (Aldershot and Burlington, VT, 2006), pp. 164–5, 180, n. 33.

[53] Andrew Fuller, *The Gospel its own Witness: or the holy nature, and divine harmony, of the Christian Religion* (Clipstone, 1799), p. 14.

[54] Anstey, *Atlantic Slave Trade*, chs 15 and 16.

THE SOCIAL CONSCIENCE

The enactment of abolition gave its supporters new targets. One of the first was a further petitioning campaign against the renewal of the French trade, as permitted by the peace treaty with post-Napoleonic France, in 1814. Again, the Dissenting involvement was intense. The Dissenting Deputies, while usually cautious, organized one of the petitions and it was presented to the House of Commons by their chairman, the long-serving Dissenting MP William Smith.[56] So did the General Body of Dissenting Ministers.[57] The campaign as a whole claimed some 750,000 signatures, although the precise figure cannot be verified.[58] At the same time, the expansion of overseas missions, Dissenting and non-denominational, greatly increased the amount of evidence whereby this hope could be assessed. It has been suggested that nonconformist missionaries were often more outspoken in criticizing the authorities in the British slave-holding colonies than were their Anglican counterparts,[59] and there is evidence that they were more frequent targets of hostility from planter interests. In October 1823 the Wesleyan Methodist chapel in Barbados was destroyed by fire and the life of its minister, William James Shrewsbury, threatened following his complaints about the ill-treatment of slaves on the island. Two years later, Shrewsbury's ill-treatment was raised in the House of Commons by Thomas Fowell Buxton and the veteran Unitarian MP William Smith.[60] The Congregationalist missionary in British Guiana, John Smith, refused to take up arms against the slave rebellion in Demerara in 1824, was sentenced to death, and died in prison. He became known as the 'Demerara Martyr' and when Henry Brougham took up his case in the House of Commons on 1 June 1824 he gave considerable publicity to the Anti-Slavery Society founded the previous year.[61] The Baptist missionary William Knibb became a popular hero after his exposure of the cruelties which accompanied the slave rebellion in Jamaica in 1831–2.[62]

---

[55] B. L. Manning, *The Protestant Dissenting Deputies* (Cambridge, 1952), p. 471.
[56] Manning, *Dissenting Deputies*, p. 472.   [57] DWL, MS 38.107, pp. 107–12.
[58] Drescher, *Capitalism and Antislavery*, p. 82.
[59] Ian M. Randall, 'Nonconformists and Overseas Mission', in Robert Pope, ed., *T & T Clark Companion to Nonconformity* (London and New York, 2013), p. 291.
[60] *Parliamentary Debates*, NS, XIII, 1285–347.
[61] *Parliamentary Debates*, NS, XI, 961–1075.
[62] John Howard Hinton, *Memoir of William Knibb, Missionary in Jamaica* (London, 1847), pp. 143–53.

In the years immediately before emancipation, Nonconformists were particularly emphatic in their assertion of the advantages of free over slave labour, with the Liverpool Quaker James Cropper and the Newcastle attorney James Losh among the vanguard.[63] It was a perception entirely consistent not only with economic free-market principles but also with religious liberty in an open market, a step towards which followed with the repeal of the sacramental provisions of the Test and Corporation Acts in 1828. The 'free labour' policy informed both the gradualist policy of the Anti-Slavery Society and the more urgent demands for immediate emancipation propounded by the Society's 'Agency Committee' which emerged in 1831–2 under the leadership of the Birmingham Quaker Joseph Sturge. Significantly, the Protestant Dissenting Deputies, despite their initial concern about a display of excessive militancy, lent their support to the Anti-Slavery Society and petitioned for emancipation in 1830 and 1832. At the moment of emancipation in 1833, however, the sense of triumph was severely tempered in Dissenting eyes by the defects of the measure. The *Congregational Magazine* spoke for many Dissenters in deploring the 'obnoxious' imposition of 'apprenticeship' upon the freed slaves, and expressed incredulity and outrage at what it called the 'gift' of £20 million paid by the British government as compensation to the owners of slave plantations.[64] There was certainly no complacency; the Dissenting element in the post-1833 anti-slavery movement now moved on to contribute substantially to attacks upon 'apprenticeship' and upon slavery in non-British colonies.[65]

Nonetheless, their commitment to abolitionism helped to expose Nonconformists to the complaint which had become familiar over the previous forty years, namely that while expostulating indignantly about the plight of colonial slaves, they were relatively indifferent to the condition of the poor in Britain—'Shewing their humanity at the expense of others'.[66] The allegation, famously caricatured by Charles Dickens in *Bleak House*, implied that abolitionists could afford the luxury of gratifying their consciences at the expense of distant planters, whose demise would hardly undermine their economic interests and social status. State intervention to regulate factory conditions and alleviate poverty, by contrast, risked threatening their profits and privileges as employers, shareholders, and taxpayers.[67] The abolitionist moral

---

[63] James Cropper, *A Vindication of a Loan of £15,000,000 to the West India Planters* (London, 1833), pp. 7, 11–14; *Sketch of the Speech of James Losh*, pp. 5–8. The best guide to this debate is Seymour Drescher, *The Mighty Experiment: Free Labor versus Slavery in British Emancipation* (Oxford, 2002).

[64] *Congregational Magazine*, n.s., IX (1833), pp. 501–2; see also Manning, *Protestant Dissenting Deputies*, pp. 472–3 and Cropper, *Vindication of a Loan*, pp. 4–7.

[65] See Howard Temperley, *British Antislavery 1833–1870* (London, 1972).

[66] *The Speech of James Losh ... Newcastle upon Tyne ... 31 March 1824* (Newcastle, 1824), p. 4.

[67] There is a neat sketch of this allegation in Hilton, *Mad, Bad and Dangerous People*, pp. 186–7.

indignation, it seemed, was highly selective; hence, probably, the hostility to anti-slavery on the part of many Chartists in the 1840s, to whom abolitionists, especially Nonconformists, were capitalists whose sole motive for seeking lower prices by removing bounties on Caribbean sugar or tariffs on imported corn was to create an opportunity for reducing wages.[68] What became known as the 'Nonconformist Conscience' in the nineteenth century had as its essence standards of public and private morality, non-denominational education, the removal of all remaining legal discrimination against non-Anglicans, and the disestablishment of the Church of England.[69] Such a libertarian ethos demanded a contraction, rather than an augmentation, of the role of the state, and rejected any suggestion that redistribution of wealth should be undertaken by governments. Hence the expressions 'Nonconformist Conscience' and 'Social Conscience' are not coterminous. The latter concept, when applied to Nonconformity, expressed itself in the stirrings in the minds of individual Nonconformists to follow the Christian duty of charity—or philanthropy—on their own initiatives.

The nonconformist preference was for private philanthropy, individual and collective, over state intervention. To some extent this resulted from suspicion of a state in which power, nationally and locally, remained for the most part in the hands of those hostile to them. Until 1828–9 the state defined itself in terms of Trinitarian Anglicanism and the after-effects of that definition lingered thereafter. Nonconformist suspicion of the state had increased by its involvement in warfare between 1775 and 1815, itself a cause of poverty as well as unnecessary expenditure. Predictably, Nonconformists were prominent in campaigns for peace between 1804 and 1814.[70] For many of them 'Conscience' meant above all the individual liberty to worship and serve God unhindered by control from any secular institution. Slavery and war were both serious obstacles to these ideals. But the same impulses which impelled such energetic involvement in abolition and emancipation were equally powerfully directed at poverty in Britain. Colonial slaves and the British poor were interlocking, not alternative, causes. When in 1814 the Quaker William Marten of Lewes collected 693 signatures for a petition against the slave trade, he also raised £123 for the York retreat, a charitable organization for the mentally ill. On Marten's death in 1823 a newspaper obituary described him as 'a man of eminent piety and the most diffuse benevolences'.[71]

---

[68] Patricia Hollis, 'Anti-Slavery and British Working-Class Radicalism in the Years of Reform', in Christine Bolt and Seymour Drescher, eds, *Anti-Slavery, Religion and Reform: Essays in Memory of Roger Anstey* (Folkestone and Hamden, CT, 1980), pp. 294–315.

[69] These are the issues delineated in Robert Pope, 'The Nonconformist Conscience', in Pope, ed., *T & T Clark Companion to Nonconformity*, pp. 437–58.

[70] See J. E. Cookson, *The Friends of Peace: Anti-War Liberalism in England, 1793–1815* (Cambridge, 1982).

[71] David Hitchin, *Quakers in Lewes: An Informal History* (n.p., 2010), p. 59.

Very many examples of nonconformist concern for and efforts to relieve poverty—among members of their own denominations and nationally—may be adduced, and a large proportion of them was undertaken by high-profile abolitionists. When James Losh complained in 1823 that the high duties upon slave-produced sugar amounted to a 'bounty' of some two million pounds per annum to unworthy Caribbean planters, he added that such a sum 'would support a large proportion of our poor'.[72] It was no accident that this was the period in which nonconformist denominations opened domestic, as well as overseas, missions; and whereas 'home' missions focused upon preaching and revivalism, the purpose of domestic missions was the alleviation of poverty, especially in large cities.[73] The Quakers James Cropper and Joseph Sturge were almost all-embracing in their philanthropic works. John Howard was far from alone in his involvement in prison reform; for example, the Dissenter, Manchester abolitionist, and Salford magistrate Thomas Butterworth Bayley was a leader in prison reform, combining rigorous enforcement of regulations with 'an emphasis on individual moral regeneration'.[74] Mary Carpenter, the daughter of a Unitarian minister in Bristol, made a major contribution to the education of the poor through her opening of 'ragged schools'; her biographer observes that 'she felt strongly that anti-slavery enthusiasm should not be used, as sometimes in the past, to muffle social injustice at home'.[75] As Seymour Drescher showed, anti-slavery stimulated working-class support on an unprecedented scale; and in so doing it was always likely to broaden awareness of wider social issues and to stimulate private philanthropic and conscience-related initiatives including penal reform, public health, household impoverishment, and education. Not until the later nineteenth century did significant leaders of Nonconformity begin to look towards more state intervention and expenditure for the relief of poverty—achieving 'social righteousness' by legislation.[76]

The ultimate responsibility (or credit) for abolitionism and the emancipation of slaves does not admit easy explanations. What may be asserted with confidence, however, is that anti-slavery in all its dimensions revealed much about the character of the nonconformist tradition and was fundamental to its

---

[72] *Sketch of the Speech of James Losh*, p. 6.

[73] See David Ceri Jones, 'Nonconformists and Home Mission', in Pope, ed, *T & T Clark Companion to Nonconformity*, pp. 353–80. For a case study of domestic missions, see David Turley, 'The Anglo-American Unitarian Connexion and Urban Poverty', in Hugh Cunningham and Joanna Innes, eds, *Charity, Philanthropy and Reform: From the 1690s to 1850* (Basingstoke and New York, 1998), pp. 228–42.

[74] Margaret DeLacy, *Prison Reform in Lancashire, 1700–1850: A Study in Local Administration* (Manchester, 1986), pp. 70–4, quotation at p. 73.

[75] Jo Manton, *Mary Carpenter and the Children of the Streets* (London, 1976), p. 78.

[76] See David M. Thompson, 'The Emergence of the Nonconformist Social Gospel in England', in Keith Robbins, ed., *Protestant Evangelicalism: Britain, Ireland, Germany and America, c.1750–c.1950. Essays in Honour of W. R. Ward* (Oxford, 1990), pp. 255–80.

social conscience. Anti-slavery greatly enhanced the role, respectability, and influence of Nonconformity in British society; probably it helped to rescue it from the disrepute which some of its adherents incurred after the French Revolution—'the solvent of heresy's stain'.[77] Of all the causes associated with Nonconformity, anti-slavery was by far the least divisive and most unifying in relations between Nonconformists and the communities in which they lived.

SELECT BIBLIOGRAPHY

Anstey, Roger, *The Atlantic Slave Trade and British Abolition* (London, 1975).
Davis, David Brion, *The Problem of Slavery in an Age of Revolution 1770–1823* (Ithaca, NY and London, 1975).
Drescher, Seymour, *Capitalism and Antislavery: British Mobilization in Comparative Perspective* (Oxford and New York, 1986).
Drescher, Seymour, *The Mighty Experiment: Free Labor versus Slavery in British Emancipation* (Oxford, 2002).
Drescher, Seymour and Emmer, Pieter C., eds, *Who Abolished Slavery? Slave Revolts and Abolitionism: A Debate with João Pedro Marques* (New York and Oxford, 2010).
Essig, James D., *The Bonds of Wickedness: American Evangelicals against Slavery 1770–1808* (Philadelphia, PA, 1982).
Field, Clive D., 'Counting Religion in England and Wales: The Long Eighteenth Century, c.1680–c.1840', *Journal of Ecclesiastical History*, 63, 4 (2012), pp. 693–720.
Midgley, Clare, *Women against Slavery: The British Campaigns, 1780–1870* (London and New York, 1992).
Oldfield, J. R., *Popular Politics and British Anti-Slavery: The Mobilization of Public Opinion against the Slave Trade, 1787–1807* (Manchester, 1995).
Pollock, John, *Wilberforce* (London, 1977).
Thompson, David M., 'The Emergence of the Nonconformist Social Gospel in England', in Robbins, Keith, ed., *Protestant Evangelicalism: Britain, Ireland, Germany and America, c.1750–c.1950. Essays in Honour of W. R. Ward* (Oxford, 1990), pp. 255–80.
Turley, David, *The Culture of English Antislavery, 1780–1860* (London, 1991).
Walker, Gina Luria, *Mary Hays (1759–1843): The Growth of a Woman's Mind* (Aldershot and Burlington, VT, 2006).
Watts, Michael, *The Dissenters. Volume II: The Expansion of Evangelical Nonconformity* (Oxford, 1995).

---

[77] As suggested by D. C. Strange, *British Unitarians against American Slavery* (Rutherford, NJ, 1984); the author's conclusions could be extended to Nonconformity as a whole.

Part V

Congregations and Living

15

Theology and the Bible

David M. Thompson

Any historian of Dissenting religious thought faces a twofold challenge: first, to overcome the 'victim mentality' that has dogged much earlier writing (with some honourable exceptions), and second, to overcome the imposition of later denominational labels on a more fluid situation. We know relatively little about the beliefs and attitudes of ordinary Dissenters in the eighteenth century: it is, for example, unlikely that most members of congregations could give a coherent account of the Chalcedonian definition of the two natures of Christ (any more than they could today), even though the Trinity became one of the most keenly contested doctrines among some Dissenters.

Ideas are articulated by people, and much therefore depends on the people selected. In an age when modern footnotes were rare and direct quotations even more so, influence is essentially inferential. A 'tradition' is more than a string of books and authors over a chronological period. There were confessions of faith, but no equivalent to subscription to the Thirty-Nine Articles at the ordination of Anglican ministers; though there could be, and often was, extensive questioning by fellow-ministers beforehand. The lack of access to the Universities of Oxford and Cambridge, with their opportunities for future patrons and beneficiaries to meet, meant that Dissent lacked even a simple structure for the education and placement of its ministers. This need was acutely felt by the second generation, who had not completed or begun their university education before 1662. The solutions were the development of associations (for the ministers in an area) and academies (for education), which filled the gaps. They were responses by individual ministers, who found the meetings helpful, and educated the sons of sympathetic families, particularly those who already offered such ministers chaplaincies. Only with the formation of the Presbyterian Fund (1690), the Congregational Fund (1695), and the Particular Baptist Fund (1717—always much smaller) was anything like a confessional test of faith used to support intending ministers.

Academies were not essential for all. A rural church with a good number of members might choose ministers from those within its own membership with a gift for preaching for the whole of the eighteenth century. Such churches were self-supporting, self-sufficient—and probably relatively isolated or inward-looking. But in any small market town after 1688, and certainly in larger towns, members had wider aspirations in looking for their ministers. Members involved in trade could experience worship and preaching in other congregations on their travels.

Sometimes a minister whom a church had called in good faith began to preach in ways that struck some of the leaders of the congregation as dubious, and there was a conflict. Occasionally the minister would leave; less often the congregation would leave the minister, either a majority or a minority. For example, the Great Meeting in Cambridge (1687)[1] called its first minister in 1691: Joseph Hussey, a Presbyterian. In 1694 he proposed the adoption of a church covenant, which was accepted, and the church became Independent. When Hussey moved to London in 1721, the congregation divided over the appointment of a successor; a group of members moved to a building in the Stone Yard (round the corner) and formed what eventually became St Andrew's Street Baptist Church. This was a relatively peaceful (and an early) division, but such events continued through the century. Since many buildings were still rented rather than held on trust, that was easier than it became when trust deeds contained doctrinal clauses.

A brief account can only sketch some leading themes, and these are fairly clear. The turning point for eighteenth-century theology was the Toleration Act of 1689. Censorship of the theological press was effectively ended by Parliament in 1640; and, the attempt to suppress religious opposition to the Restoration regime from 1660 was at best partially successful. Many regarded the Civil War and Commonwealth as having opened the floodgates to all manner of dangerous theological and political speculations; but the link between political and theological orthodoxy remained a commonplace of medieval and early modern thought that was difficult to dislodge.

Opposition to religious toleration therefore was based on memories of the past. In the rather frenzied political atmosphere of the late seventeenth century, freedom of speech for the wilder Quaker speculations was bad enough; but even the moderate Richard Baxter (1615–1691) was a threat. His *True History of Councils enlarged and defended* (1682) cast doubts on the binding nature of the Nicene Creed, because of the politicking of the pro-Trinitarian bishops at the Councils of Nicaea and Constantinople. This strengthened his anxiety over the imposition of any human definition of faith.[2] For Baxter this was another

---

[1] Registration date under James II's Declaration of Indulgence.
[2] Paul C. H. Lim, *Mystery Unveiled: The Crisis of the Trinity in Early Modern England* (New York, 2012), pp. 255–60.

nail in the coffin of episcopacy, accentuated by his own treatment by the High Church bishops at the Savoy Conference in 1661. He was imprisoned by Judge Jeffreys as late as 1685, on a charge that certain passages in his *Paraphrases of the New Testament* (1683) were seditious.[3]

Theologically the link between the arguments for the Trinity and those for transubstantiation (based on the same metaphysical assumptions) strengthened the belief of Reformed Protestants in *sola scriptura* as the guide for safe doctrine. The problem was that a multitude of conflicting arguments, all based on Scripture, had been produced since 1640, without any consensus on the disputed points. For the Church of England that was less important, since its self-understanding left room for reason; and it was more concerned to demonstrate the improbable hypothesis that its continuity in no sense depended on the Church of Rome and its corruptions. Dissenters, however, hoped that *sola scriptura* would lead them to the promised land of theological certainty.

Those who thought new thoughts were able in a new way to survive. The development of great libraries no longer under the direct control of the Church, in universities and colleges, and in the homes of the gentry, created new access to learning.[4] Religious dissent did not disappear after the Restoration. Instead England and Wales, and later Scotland, had to come to terms with a new reality—a permanently plural religious society, even including tendencies to atheism. Moreover, earlier historians of Dissent have not always acknowledged the extent to which many of its controversies followed those in the Established Church.

THE MAIN ISSUES

Four questions preoccupied Dissenting theologians during the century: biblical interpretation, sacraments, the incarnation and the Trinity, and finally Calvinism and its moderation. Theologically the Quakers did not move significantly beyond the work of the Scottish Quaker, Robert Barclay, in his *Apology for the true Christian divinity* (1675). He had set out Friends' position in fifteen propositions (including universal salvation, their attitude to the sacraments, and a limited view of the power of the civil magistrate in matters of personal religious conviction).

For those who in some way stood in the tradition of John Calvin, the issues were different. Predestination and reprobation still loomed large (even though

---

[3] N. H. Keeble and Geoffrey Nuttall, *Calendar of the Correspondence of Richard Baxter*, 2 vols. (Oxford, 1991), II, pp. 267, 271–2, 281, 283–4.

[4] For an analysis of Socinian books in some seventeenth-century libraries, see H. John McLachlan, *Socinianism in Seventeenth-Century England* (Oxford, 1951), pp. 103–48.

these were not prominent matters in Calvin's *Institutes*.[5] Broadly speaking, Presbyterians, Independents, and Particular Baptists followed Calvin's teaching on limited atonement: their differences arose over church order and discipline, exemplified in what was omitted from the Westminster Confession of 1646/7 by the Savoy Declaration of 1658.[6] The substantial identity of the two documents led (perhaps confusingly) to the 'Westminster standards' remaining the starting point for much Dissenting theology in the eighteenth century. Particular Baptists had their own Confessions, which rejected infant baptism. In contrast the General Baptists believed in a general offer of the Gospel, and rejected Calvin's teaching on election.

The only links within these groups were bonds of fellowship, not organization. English Dissenters were also more eclectic in the extent to which they followed the continental Reformers. Intellectually speaking both the English Channel and the North Sea were wider than mileage alone would suggest, though the Netherlands remained an important theological resource, especially for the Socinian ideas driven out of Poland.

Dissenters welcomed the Toleration Act, and the language of rights and toleration borrowed from John Locke had a theological impact of sorts. Yet it was still rare to find a theologian writing with any acknowledgement of the *legitimacy* of alternative points of view. The slowness of this point to penetrate Dissenting minds is well illustrated by the different uses to which Richard Baxter's phrases, 'catholic Christianity' or 'mere Christianity', were put. For Baxter they represented both a common inheritance on which all Christians might be expected to agree, as well as a reason never to persecute those with whom one might disagree.

Philip Doddridge (1702–1751) was tutor of Northampton Academy during his ministry at Northampton from 1729 to his death. He was also against

---

[5] For this discussion, see John Calvin, *Institutes of the Christian Religion* (1559 text), ed. John T McNeill, trans. Ford Lewis Battles, Library of Christian Classics, vols xx–xxi (London, 1960), Book III, pp. 920–87. Calvin discusses the Scripture testimonies, and refutes contrary arguments in the following two chapters; but at the outset of his discussion in ch. 21 he warns against imprudent human curiosity into divine wisdom (p. 922). Reprobation is discussed explicitly in ch. 24, pp. 978–87. The *Articles concerning Predestination*, the precise date of which is uncertain, set out a shorter and less nuanced statement in propositional form: Introduction and trans. J. K. S. Reid, Library of Christian Classics, vol. xxii (London, 1954), pp. 178–80.

[6] In brief, the Presbyterians only accepted episcopal authority when bishops acted in consultation with their ministers (or presbytery). After episcopacy disappeared in Scotland in 1689, the issue died; nor was there a church-wide presbytery structure in England until the early nineteenth century. Locally, Presbyterian ministers could decide matters of discipline in consultation with the elders of their local congregation. Independents believed that each local church contained all the elements of the Church universal within its own fellowship: thus, the local church meeting of covenanted believers had sole power to call ministers and act in matters of discipline; bishops were redundant. Elders existed to advise the minister, but not to decide alone. Both groups were strongly influenced by Calvin, but neither to the same extent as comparable groups in Switzerland, France, the Netherlands, or Germany. Among Particular Baptists there was greater equality between minister and elders; the minister was sometimes referred to as the 'preaching elder'.

subscription to human creeds and confessions, fearing that they harmed Christian unity. In his *Course of Lectures on the Principal Subjects in Pneumatology, Ethics and Divinity* (posthumously published in 1763),[7] Doddridge discarded the work of Franco Burgersdijk (1590–1635) on Logic, on which he had been brought up (along with John Locke) at John Jennings's Academy, and relied entirely on Locke and Isaac Watts's *Philosophical Essays*. Doddridge did not agree with everything that Locke wrote, but set out his lectures so as to consider opposing views to his own,[8] following a pattern comparable to that in Isaac Newton's *Principia Mathematica*. Jonathan Edwards in America did the same in his work, but Doddridge's Lectures were published after Edwards's death, so although Edwards does refer to Doddridge, the works cited are those published in his own lifetime. The pattern of arguing a case, as it were by disputation, was traditional in both Oxford and Cambridge, although in Cambridge the emphasis was more mathematical and Locke was adopted earlier.

For those like the entirely orthodox Edmund Calamy (1671–1732), who used toleration as a reason to support non-subscription to the agreement proposed at Salters' Hall in 1719, its rationale had imperceptibly begun to shift towards tolerating differences of opinion rather than expecting agreement on fundamental articles of faith. By 1788 Richard Price (1723–1791) also from orthodox Presbyterian parentage but moving towards Unitarianism misleadingly invoked the inheritance of 1662 as a simple defence of religious liberty. But without having either the desire, or the opportunity, to persecute those of different opinions, Unitarians nevertheless argued that their understanding of Christianity made most obvious sense biblically and rationally.

The day-to-day life of people in the parishes of England and Wales did not, by the eighteenth century, reflect the tense, even febrile atmosphere of the century before. The sporadic attacks on meeting houses in 1714 and the infamous burning down of Joseph Priestley's chapel in Birmingham in 1791 were exceptional. Dissenting ministers, such as Isaac Watts, were still invited to serve as chaplains to the gentry; and Dissenting meetings were held in the halls of London livery companies. The end of that practice was a sign of the prosperity that financed new chapels, not intolerance by the companies. Dissenting ministers like Philip Doddridge and Robert Hall were entertained

---

[7] The first edition was published in London in 1763, and four further editions followed in 1776, 1794, and 1799 culminating in the version published in E. Williams and E. Parsons, eds, *Works of the Revd P. Doddridge DD* (Leeds, 1802–5). In each edition, the various editors updated references.

[8] See Isabel Rivers, *The Defence of Truth through the Knowledge of Error: Philip Doddridge's Academy Lectures* (London, 2003). Doddridge was certainly unusual in recommending his students to read Deist writers such as Tindal as well as more orthodox works; but he himself remained firmly orthodox theologically, even later attracting criticism from more heterodox writers for begging some of the propositions he sought to prove.

in Cambridge colleges later in the century (though some colleges changed their dining hours to prevent undergraduates hearing Hall's sermons). In country villages 'peaceful co-existence' meant some loss of the former social stigma of Dissent. The building of chapels focused Dissenting life in certain places and reduced its earlier geographical spread. Nevertheless, Dissenters still wrote in terms of struggle, persecution, and martyrdom as a ground-bass to other theological issues, discussed often with lively vigour, and sometimes with exhausting tedium.

SOLA SCRIPTURA AND THE UNDERSTANDING OF SCRIPTURE

The underlying issue for all Protestant Dissenters was the principle of *sola scriptura*, coupled with the right of private judgement. At first this protestant principle simply meant testing the practices of the medieval Catholic Church against Scripture. Writing a constructive theology, however, was more complicated. What was the biblical understanding of the nature of God or Jesus Christ? Was original sin hereditary, as taught by St Augustine, and followed by Luther and Calvin? What patterns of church government were self-evident in Scripture? How were baptism and the Lord's Supper to be understood? How should theologians handle the many textual variants in the Bible, complicated by the New Testament's use of the Septuagint (the Greek version of the Old Testament), rather than the Hebrew text that Renaissance Humanists regarded as the original? The different answers, when linked to the 'right of private judgement', seemed to make theological decisions by the Church impossible.

Many, if not all, of the Greek concepts used to formulate the theology of the post-Nicene Church were dismissed. Whenever a theologian expressed distrust of 'metaphysics', that usually referred to the metaphysical assumptions of the Greek classical authors (often misunderstood, from a twenty-first century perspective). Similarly, 'Platonism' often meant little more than typology and allegory.[9]

This strategy for scriptural interpretation significantly reduced the range of understandings available. Medieval theology had used the Old Testament for Christian theology in several ways—analogical, typological, literal, or allegorical. There was a strong impulse to disregard all but the literal after the Reformation: multiple meanings were excluded. Even numbers could be treated 'literally', enabling the calculation of the age of the earth (as by Archbishop Ussher who dated the creation in 4004 BC), or the date of the Second Coming

---

[9] Lim, *Mystery Unveiled*, pp. 309–28.

(based on numbers given in Revelation, Daniel, and Ezekiel). A literal reading of Revelation seemed to offer conclusive proof that the Pope was Anti-Christ, such that this view was confidently inserted in the Westminster Confession; but curiously it depended on an analogical or allegorical reading of Rome for 'Babylon' in the text. This was the origin of the biblical literalism that characterized twentieth-century fundamentalism.[10]

Sola scriptura therefore put biblical interpretation, especially of the New Testament, at the centre of doctrinal controversy. The Old Testament attracted less controversy. The great English Hebraist, John Lightfoot (1602–1675), for example, was a member of the Westminster Assembly, who often sided with the Presbyterians against the Independent minority, and was occasionally outspoken, as when he criticized erroneous opinions about the millennium, which happened 'when mechanicks, unlettered and ignorant men will take upon them to bee preachers'.[11] He was disgusted by the acrimony at the Savoy Conference, but was selective in his observance of the Prayer Book, both in the prayers and the rubrics (he never wore a surplice). Lightfoot could have served in either an episcopal or a Presbyterian establishment, so long as there was no attempt to assert clerical control of civil government.[12]

By the eighteenth century the only translation of Scripture permitted was the King James Version (KJV) of 1611. (The 1560 Geneva Bible was banned in 1640.) The KJV's slightly antiquated style led to the flourishing of biblical paraphrases, which had begun with the Paraphrases of Desiderius Erasmus in the early sixteenth century. A Paraphrase typically gave the original text, with a paraphrase for difficult verses alongside notes on points of more general interest with longer comments at the end of chapters or groups of chapters.[13] Richard Baxter's *Paraphrase of the New Testament* began as a Paraphrase on Romans, since it was 'hard to understand'.[14] Detailed commentary on difficult doctrinal points was placed in a series of Notes of essay length: for example, he

---

[10] McLachlan was unnecessarily puzzled by the fact that Socinianism seemed to be a 'halfway house between medievalism and modernism': *Socinianism in Seventeenth-Century England*, p. 12. Only when *sola scriptura* had been abandoned was modern Unitarianism possible.

[11] J. Lightfoot, *A Sermon preached before the Honourable House of Commons at Margarets Westminster, upon the 26 day of August 1645* (London, 1645), p. 31. Having already written on Exodus and Acts in the 1640s, he published a four-part *Harmony of the Four Evangelists* (1644–58). His major work on the Hebrew Bible reached its climax in the later 1650s.

[12] Newton E. Key, 'Lightfoot, John (1602–1675)', *Oxford Dictionary of National Biography* (hereafter *ODNB*), Oxford University Press, 2004 [http://www.oxforddnb.com/view/article/16648, accessed 21 July 2015].

[13] An online check in the Cambridge University Library catalogue (including the Bible Society catalogue) for 'Paraphrase New Testament' yielded 330 entries. Most of these were duplicates of a small group of around half a dozen main Paraphrases held in different college libraries, but they also indicate the number of editions and the fact that new paraphrases continued to be published in the nineteenth and twentieth centuries.

[14] Richard Baxter, *A Paraphrase on the New Testament with Notes Doctrinal and Practical* (London, 1685), p. i.

explained Paul's understanding of election in Romans and always linked baptism to covenant as well as profession of faith.

Baxter pointed out the danger of giving too little or too much emphasis to the sacred Scriptures: on the one hand, those who denied it to be God's infallible word unless supplemented by other written or oral testimonies, made 'Church-concord utterly impossible'; on the other hand, those who denied the existence of the Church or an infallible rule of life before the Scriptures were written down, and even denied the possibility of human imperfections in transcription, were simply wrong. Similarly, it was an error either to disregard the Old Testament completely or to give it the same authority as the New.[15] He warned against 'Fanaticks' (i.e. the Quakers) who would test the Scriptures by the Spirit, rather than vice versa; and affirmed that the Spirit was given to the faithful 'not to reveal to them a new Law, and Gospel, but to enable them to understand, believe, love and obey that already revealed'.[16]

Baxter was explicitly writing for a domestic context, in which masters might instruct their servants or parents their children on the meaning of Scripture. The apogee of such books was probably Philip Doddridge's *Family Expositor* (1739–56).[17] It only covered the New Testament—in six volumes (only three were edited by Doddridge, with the remainder left to Job Orton). It combined the text of the KJV, a paraphrase, and a series of notes, and was still being reprinted in the nineteenth century, along with later imitations. Such Paraphrases illustrate the extent of the knowledge of texts and versions of Scripture then current—thus Baxter commented on whether John 8:1–11 was apocryphal, the authorship of the Letter to the Hebrews, and the authenticity of 1 John 5:7–8: in each case he saw no reason to alter the traditional view. He also described how doctrinal or ecclesiological positions may be inferred from particular texts: here his particular target was Hammond's Paraphrase of 1653 defending the Church of England's use of Scripture.[18]

The pre-eminent biblical commentator of his day was Matthew Henry (1662–1714).[19] Ordained 'in great privacy' in 1687, he became minister at

---

[15] Ibid., pp. 1–2. [16] Ibid., p. 3.

[17] Philip Doddridge, *Family Expositor: or A paraphrase and version of the New Testament; with critical notes, and a practical improvement of each section* (London, 1739–56).

[18] Henry Hammond, *A paraphrase and annotations upon all the books of the New Testament: Briefly explaining the difficult phrases thereof* (London, 1653). Hammond (1605–1660) was Chaplain to Charles I and President of Magdalen College, Oxford. Since it was a folio volume of 1,000 pages, it was hardly bedtime reading.

[19] His father, Philip Henry, had been ejected and vacated his parsonage a month before Matthew was born. Matthew was educated at home by his father and his father's students, and in 1680 went to Thomas Doolittle's Academy in London, just in time to encounter intensified persecution of Dissenters. He returned home and went back to London only in 1685 to study Law at Gray's Inn (whilst at the same time continuing his divinity studies). Henry's *Commentary on the whole Bible* is still in print.

Chester, supported the Cheshire classis, founded in March 1691, and was much called upon to take part in ordinations. Matthew Henry's *Exposition of the Old and New Testaments* was begun in 1704; the four volumes on the Old Testament were published in folio between 1707 and 1712, the fifth volume on the New Testament (as far as Acts) was in press when he died; and the final volume was completed by thirteen other nonconformist ministers.[20]

Henry's assumptions and methods are typical of the moderate expositor of Scripture in his time. His underlying propositions were: religion was the one thing needful; divine revelation was necessary to true religion; this could be found only in the Scriptures of the Old and New Testaments; these were designed for our learning; and also to be the settled standing rule of our faith and practice; and thus it was the duty of all Christians to search the Scriptures and the office of ministers to assist them in this task.[21] The underlying authority of Scripture was self-evident, though it was proved to believer and non-believer alike by 'the many incontestable miracles wrought by Moses and the prophets, Christ and his apostles'. Scripture was intended first to revive the universal and perpetual law of nature, the very remains (or ruins) of which in natural conscience suggest that there must be 'a fairer copy elsewhere; and second 'to reveal the universal and perpetual law of grace which God's common beneficence to the children of men...gives us some ground to expect'.[22]

Henry claimed no special gifts for his task, save the time left over from preparing sermons he had used in 'drawing up expositions upon some parts of the New Testament'.[23] He paid tribute to the work of those learned in the languages and in ancient usages, the philology of the critics (which he thought of more advantage to religion than the philosophy of the school-divines), and even those learned in the arts of war, who had done great work in defending the garden of the Lord against the powers of darkness. Henry asked 'not only *what is this?* but *What is this to us?*'[24] That personal application explains his appeal.

He focused on what is '*profitable for doctrine, for reproof, for correction, for instruction in righteousness*' (2 Tim. 3:16). He did not trouble the reader with

---

[20] *Exposition* rather than *Commentary* was the original title, though the latter is used universally today. See also David L. Wykes, 'Henry, Matthew (1662–1714)', *ODNB*, Oxford University Press, 2004 [http://www.oxforddnb.com/view/article/12975, accessed 15 July 2015].

[21] *Matthew Henry's Commentary on the whole Bible*, 6 vols. (McLean, VA, n.d. [c.1980]), I, pp. iii–vi. This version, based on a possibly late nineteenth-century text printed by M. Thoms, Warwick Square, London, is the commonest available today, issued by various publishers. I have cited it rather than the original eighteenth-century editions, because of its ready availability. The first volume, at least for the first two editions, was entitled *An Exposition of the Five Books of Moses* (folio, 2 edn, London, 1710) and the Preface occupied eight pages; the 1790 edition, published in Edinburgh, was entitled *An Exposition of the Old and New Testament in six volumes*, and the Preface occupied nine pages.

[22] Ibid., I, p. v. [23] Ibid., I, p. vi. [24] Ibid., I, p. v (italics original).

problems of chronology, genealogy, or chorography (i.e. maps).²⁵ He regarded the history of the Jewish people as a type for the history of the Church, so there were important lessons about the consequences of failing to follow God's way. The constant tranquility and prosperity of the Church should not be expected; yet we need not fear 'its utter extirpation'. Henry therefore still accepted some degree of typology, just as he did when seeking for prophecies of Christ in the Old Testament.

The historical books were easy compared with the Writings and the Prophets, which contained 'many things dark and hard to understand'. In a charming metaphor Henry commented that if the waters of the sanctuary thus far have been up to the ankles or knees, now we were up to our loins—with a warning that with the Prophets we would be in 'water to swim in' (Ezek. 47:3–5) or 'depths in which an elephant will not find footing'.²⁶ Henry believed both that prophecy is essentially the prediction of events yet to come, and also that the subject of most of the prophetic books is the Messiah, i.e. Jesus Christ. Thus the prophetic books were most dependent on divine inspiration.²⁷ Henry also noted sadly that the prophets 'were generally hated and abused in their several generations by those that lived with them'.²⁸ Henry's *Exposition* summed up the traditional Dissenting view of Scripture and its interpretation. Its massive scale (particularly by one person) left it unrivalled for more than a century, and its method and conclusions became normative for ordinary Dissenters—the men and women in the pew.

Nathaniel Lardner (1684–1768) was very different.²⁹ After study in London and Leiden he began a series of public lectures at the Old Jewry in 1723, which became in due course his magnum opus—*The Credibility of the Gospel History* (12 vols, 1727–55).³⁰ This work remained a standard authority until the generation of J. B. Lightfoot and B. F. Westcott. His long period of study showed itself, first in the depth of his patristic studies, and second in his knowledge of contemporary sources from Jews (such as Josephus), Romans (such as Pliny), and places in the Orthodox world. He systematically considered almost every text that was currently known, which might shed light on the historicity of the Gospel narratives. In effect, he was a one-man Jesus seminar for the eighteenth century. His work was soon translated into Dutch,

---

²⁵ Ibid., II, p. iii (italics original).   ²⁶ Ibid., III, p. iii.
²⁷ Ibid., IV, pp. v–ix.   ²⁸ Ibid., IV, p. xi.
²⁹ His father was an Independent minister but Nathaniel attended the Academy run by the Presbyterian, Joshua Oldfield, in Hoxton Square, London, followed by a period of study at Leiden. On his return to London (1703) he joined the Independent congregation in Miles Lane, and continued his studies for a further six years before preaching his first sermon. He was domestic chaplain to Lady Treby (1713–21).
³⁰ Alexander Gordon, 'Lardner, Nathaniel (1684–1768)', rev. Alan P. F. Sell, *ODNB*, Oxford University Press, Oct. 2009 [http://www.oxforddnb.com/view/article/16069, accessed 22 Aug 2015].

and into German by the biblical scholar, J. D. Michaelis (1717–1791). Lardner's historical conclusions were generally traditional: there was no suggestion of textual criticism, which was already beginning in the Church of England.[31] Nor did he share David Hume's difficulties over miracles in the Gospel story.

The nature of Bible study revealed that, despite its development under Dissenting divines, its controversial use had changed very little. People on different sides threw contrasting bundles of texts at one another like snowballs, with little reference to context. Since only the number of relevant texts was counted, the modern approach through 'families' of manuscripts was not yet appreciated. The Anglican, Richard Bentley's distinction between manuscripts from different countries was closer to today.[32]

THE DOCTRINE OF THE SACRAMENTS

Although Dissenters rejected transubstantiation, classical Dissent did attempt to acknowledge a real presence of Christ in the Last Supper. Both Baxter and Henry in commenting on Matthew's text used the term 'sacrament'. Baxter identified three actions: blessing, by prayer to God; breaking, the breaking of Christ's body as the sacrifice for sin; and giving, as Christ gives himself to believing receivers, with and for spiritual and everlasting life. He argued that the bread, once offered with the words 'This is my body', was no longer mere bread, because it had the form of Christ's sacramental body. Similarly the cup was representatively or sacramentally Christ's blood.[33]

Matthew Henry went further: 'The body of Christ is signified and represented by bread; he had said formerly (John vi, 35) *I am the Bread of life*, upon which metaphor this sacrament is built; as the life of the body is supported by bread, which is put for all bodily nourishment (iv, 4; vi, 11) so the life of the soul is supported and maintained by Christ's mediation.'[34] Nevertheless in describing the regular breaking of bread in Acts 2, he wrote: 'They frequently

---

[31] Dr John Mill's edition of the Greek New Testament of 1707 established inter alia the inauthenticity of 1 John 5:7 in the Vulgate, amid a long list of variant textual readings. The list alarmed many, but as Richard Bentley pointed out, 'Dr Mill did not make and coin them, he only exhibited them to our view. If Religion therefore was true before, though such Various Readings were in being; it will still be as true and consequently as safe still, though every body sees them'. Phileleutherus Lipsiensis [Bentley], *Remarks upon a late Discourse of Free-Thinking* (London, 1737), pp. 93–4. Bentley developed his point about 1 John 5 in his exercise for the Regius Chair of Divinity at Cambridge: Hugh de Quehen, 'Bentley, Richard (1662–1742)', *ODNB*, Oxford University Press, Jan. 2008 [http://www.oxforddnb.com/view/article/2169, accessed 14 Feb. 2016]; Adam Fox, *John Mill and Richard Bentley: A Study of the Textual Criticism of the New Testament, 1675–1729* (Oxford, 1954), pp. 105–26.

[32] Fox, *Mill and Bentley*, pp. 45–6.   [33] Baxter, *Paraphrase*, Matthew 26:26–7.

[34] Henry, *Commentary*, V, pp. 224–5.

joined in the *ordinance* of the Lord's supper; they continued in *breaking of bread*, in celebrating that memorial of their Master's death, as those that were not ashamed to own their relation to, and their dependence upon, Christ and him crucified.'[35] The use of 'ordinance' (rather than 'sacrament') and 'memorial' (though 'memorial' is used in that context in the Roman canon of the Mass and the *Book of Common Prayer*) became more customary.

Despite their usual literal interpretation, many Dissenters were uneasy with such an understanding of the words attributed to Jesus at the Last Supper—'This is my body', 'This is my blood'. Isaac Watts did not shrink from such literalism in his *Hymns for the Lord's Supper*. Hymn 2 is still sung ('Jesus invites his saints') including, 'For food he gives his flesh / He bids us drink his blood', though nineteenth-century editors omitted the relevant verses, or sometimes the whole hymn. But it is not unique. Hymn 19 is in no modern hymnbook; its first verse reads: 'At thy command, our dearest Lord / Here we attend thy dying feast; / Thy blood like wine adorns thy board, / And thine own flesh feeds every guest.' Note 'Thy blood like wine' not 'wine like thy blood'; and there are others too. The transfer of 'When I survey the wondrous cross' from its original context in *Hymns for the Lord's Supper* to passion-tide more generally context misses the significance of Christ's death on the cross in all its detail as the pattern for an understanding of the Supper.[36]

On baptism differences among Dissenters were sharper—at least in practice. Particular Baptists declined to practise infant baptism; but initially they were rarely enthusiastic to re-baptize and did not exclude those baptized in infancy from communion, because they did not believe in any sacramental action in baptism. Faith was what led to incorporation in the covenant. Independents were similar, and Baxter was scrupulous in the draft alternative he produced for the *Prayer Book*, always to refer to 'covenant-baptism'. Mixed congregations, in which some wanted infant baptism for their children and others did not, seem to have been more common than often supposed. John Bunyan's congregation in Bedford was one such; and division would not have happened in Cambridge in 1721 if there had not been members of both convictions. Obviously some congregations began on a Baptist basis and continued as such; but a more denominationally divided Dissent may have come later and more gradually than often realized. Philip Doddridge, when lecturing about baptism, reminded his students that they might find persons of both persuasions in their congregations, and that therefore they should speak tenderly on the subject.[37]

---

[35] Ibid., VI, p. 28.

[36] I. Watts, DD, *Hymns and Spiritual Songs. Book 3: Prepared for the Lord's Supper* (London, 1811), Hymns 2 and 19, pp. 237, 252. 'Nature with open volume stands' (Hymn 10) is also part of this book.

[37] 'A Course of Lectures on Pneumatology, Ethics and Divinity', *The Works of the Rev P. Doddridge, DD* (Leeds, 1804), V, Lecture CCV, §13, p. 334; 'Lectures on Preaching and the several branches of the Ministerial Office', ibid., V, Lecture XIX, pp. 482–5, especially §2.

Later in the century some more conservative ministers pressed for restrictions on the admission of those baptized in infancy to communion, since it was inconsistent both to deny the validity of infant baptism, and to accept those without a valid baptism at the Supper. Two prominent advocates of this position were John Gill (1697–1771) of Southwark, and Abraham Booth (1734–1806) of Goodman's Fields, London. Gill wrote a *Treatise on the Doctrine of the Trinity* (1731), designed to check the spread of Sabellian ideas among Particular Baptists. In *The Cause of God and Truth* (4 vols, 1735–8) he defended the five points of Calvinism. His *Body of Doctrinal and Practical Divinity* (1769–70) was claimed to be in the library of most Baptist ministers. Booth was initially converted by General Baptists of the New Connexion, but over time he was drawn to a more conservative position, expressed in *Paedobaptism Examined* (1784), a criticism of Matthew Henry.

The development of what were to become Strict and Particular Baptist churches belongs to the nineteenth century; but its origins lie in the, often itinerant, influence of preachers like William Gadsby from the 1790s and 1800s. They were influenced by the development of a moderate Calvinism among Particular Baptists (see later in this chapter).

THE DOCTRINE OF GOD

Controversy over the incarnation and the Trinity was not the exclusive preserve of Dissenters, as some historians have implied. Nor is the widespread use of the term 'Arian' or even 'Socinian' particularly helpful in clarifying what various writers meant theologically, despite being used at the time.[38] The Trinitarian controversy vexed the Church of England throughout the eighteenth century, without any change in the official position. But whenever changes in the terms for the toleration of Dissenters were proposed, the discussion intensified in heat, if not light.

The Italian reformer, Fausto Paulo Sozini (1539–1604), more generally known as Faustus Socinus, left Florence and ended up in Poland. He argued against Anselm's understanding of atonement, preferring an exemplarism more akin to Peter Abelard, and also the pre-existence and divinity of Christ, though that was not the most important issue for him. He preferred a Zwinglian understanding of the sacraments, and argued for religious toleration and the separation of Church and state. The use of coded language (such as 'mere Christianity') to refer to some of these points makes it difficult to decide whether an author's use of such a phrase is in code or not.

---

[38] Arian generally entailed a denial of Christ's pre-existence, whereas Socinians regarded Jesus as a man, whose death was exemplary.

Some have seen John Locke's argument that the fundamental article of Christian belief was that Jesus was the Messiah as Socinian rather than minimalist.[39] Many English Dissenters were not interested in the patristic explanations of Christ's person, since they depended on unbiblical and (in their view) unnecessary 'metaphysics'.[40] The abandonment of the *Book of Common Prayer*, and the regular use of the Nicene and 'Athanasian' Creeds,[41] left only the relatively simpler language of the Apostles' Creed within the collective memory.

Within Dissent the turning point was the meetings of the London ministers at Salters' Hall in February–March 1719. Several issues were at stake: subscription to the doctrine of the Trinity, toleration of private judgement, powers of ministerial jurisdiction outside the local congregation, the right of trustees (not usually ministers) to determine doctrine for local congregations, and the freedom of ministers to affirm their faith in scriptural terms alone. The final decisions at Salters' Hall demonstrated an inability to separate these issues clearly. On 24 February 1719 all agreed that error justified congregations in withdrawing from their ministers, that congregations had a right to judge what was error, that there should be charity in cases of doubt, and certainty that what was alleged was true before any action was taken. Here the agreement ended. A resolution in favour of subscription was put to the meeting; a division was called for; ministers against subscription voted against; those that were 'for the Trinity' voted in favour. The result was fifty-seven against subscription and fifty-four in favour: 'one party believed they were fighting against intolerance and the other against heresy'.[42] At an adjourned

---

[39] John Locke, *The Reasonableness of Christianity as delivered in the Scriptures* [1695], ed. John C. Higgins-Biddle (Oxford, 1999), p. 23. He was almost immediately attacked by John Edwards, a Calvinist Fellow of St John's College, Cambridge, in *Some Thoughts concerning the several causes and occasions of Atheism* (London, 1695), and *Socinian Unmask'd* (London, 1696). The controversy led Locke to publish two responses: John Locke, *Vindications of the Reasonableness of Christianity*, ed. Victor Nuovo (Oxford, 2012).

[40] William Ames, *The Marrow of Theology (Medulla Theologicae)* [1st Latin edition, 1623], trans. and ed. John Dystryka Eusden (Durham, NC, 1968). Ames (1576–1633) fled to Holland in 1610 and spent the rest of his life there. Although he accepted some of Aristotle, he had little time for Plato, and was really influenced by the French logician Peter Ramus. The *Marrow* is an application of Ramist logic to Scripture, and was used in several Dissenting academies. 'Platonism' was often used to describe any figurative rather than literal interpretation of Scripture: Lim, *Mystery Unveiled*, pp. 309–18.

[41] Cranmer included the 'Athanasian' Creed in the *Prayer Book*, because it was a regular part of Prime in the monastic offices. The rubric indicating when it was to be said or sung varied in the sixteenth century and subsequently. Its origin seems to have been in the fifth century and it became common in the Western Church from the eighth century. The Nicene Creed was originally less used, beginning in Spain and Gaul as an anti-Arian creed, followed by Antioch, Alexandria, Constantinople, and finally Rome from the tenth century: Francis Proctor and Walter Howard Frere, *A New History of the Book of Common Prayer* (London, 1955), pp. 388–9. John Biddle (1614–1662) was one of the earliest English writers to adopt a Socinian Christology.

[42] J. Hay Colligan, *The Arian Movement in England* (Manchester, 1913), p. 56.

meeting in March those in favour declared that they would subscribe individually. Although they numbered sixty, as against the fifty non-subscribers, the subscribers withdrew. The non-subscribers declared that they aimed for peace with truth; they believed they had the backing of a majority of the London laity; they disowned Arian doctrine and believed in the 'proper divinity of Jesus Christ'; but they would not condemn anyone who declared his faith only in Scripture-terms.

What led to Salters' Hall? A bright young minister in Exeter, James Peirce, who was also an assistant at Joseph Hallett's Academy, had encountered the heterodox views of some Remonstrant thinkers during studies in Holland, and also met both Sir Isaac Newton and William Whiston during a brief ministry at Green Street, Cambridge.[43] Peirce accepted Whiston's view of early Christianity, and was also convinced by Samuel Clarke's *Scripture Doctrine of the Trinity* (1712), which he may have used in his teaching.[44] In 1718 Peirce and others gave a private certificate to Hubert Stogden, a student who also accepted Clarke's views, to secure his ordination at Shepton Mallet. The Devon and Cornwall Association of Ministers asked Peirce to preach two sermons to prove his orthodoxy, one on the Satisfaction of Christ (1 John 2:2), and the other on the Trinity (1 John 5:7). Both doctrines were tests for Socinianism. On 9–11 September Peirce's case was discussed, but the Association failed to persuade him to accept the majority view in favour of the Trinity.[45]

Thirteen gentlemen, who administered the finances of all three Exeter congregations, tried to mediate, and both they and Peirce appealed privately to the London ministers to make a declaration on subscription to the Trinity. The reluctance of the London ministers to intervene led to decisions being taken in parallel in London and Exeter. In the resulting deadlock a group of London gentlemen, anxious for the reputation of Dissent, called the meeting at Salters' Hall. This intervention was an effort to calm things down when there was a political campaign to repeal the Schism Acts. The Bangorian controversy in the Church of England was fresh in people's minds.[46] Although there were Presbyterians and Independents on both sides, Salters' Hall proved to be the

---

[43] Both held heterodox views; Whiston succeeded Newton in his chair, and later lost it because of his views.

[44] Clarke's book was a characteristic post-Reformation attempt to prove classical Trinitarian doctrine on the basis of Scripture alone. A series of critical books and pamphlets appeared from other Anglicans, and Clarke was forced to defend his views before Convocation in 1714. However, supported by his patron, he lived peacefully until his death in 1729.

[45] Allan Brockett, *Nonconformity in Exeter 1650–1875* (Manchester, 1962), pp. 74–106; Colligan, *Arian Movement in England*, pp. 44–59; J. Hay Colligan, *Eighteenth-Century Nonconformity* (London, 1915), pp. 23–33.

[46] Benjamin Hoadly, Bishop of Bangor, claimed in a sermon before the King that there was no scriptural authority for any particular form of church order; and Dissenters thought it wise to avoid being caught up in the ensuing internal controversy in the Church of England.

turning point in Presbyterian–Independent relations. Presbyterian reluctance to insist on subscription contrasted with Independent insistence on the 'Westminster standards'! Many of the later disputes between the two groups, over the interpretation or drafting of trust deeds of chapel property, were affected by the Exeter controversy. Some Independent congregations became Presbyterian and many more went the opposite way. Interestingly, subscription was usually discussed in relation to the Catechism rather than the Confession, suggesting a concern over what members were taught.

Two points stand out: first, the whole controversy and its subsequent development turned on what *ministers* were prepared to affirm theologically—consequently a change of minister became a crucial point in a congregation's life; second, notwithstanding the acknowledgement of the congregation's right to judge what constituted error, the Exeter controversy had exposed the importance of trustees (and trust deeds) in determining doctrine.[47]

Many ordinary Dissenters were persuaded by arguments based on the plain meaning of Scripture; and the post-biblical development of Trinitarian theology in the Christian creeds was one of the strongest arguments that various heterodox preachers used against it. Furthermore, whereas ministers like Matthew Henry, Nathaniel Lardner, and Isaac Watts were theologically and historically sophisticated, many of their congregations were not. As the philosophical assumptions of John Locke were absorbed, the ancient world, which shaped Christian theology, came to seem a very different place from that of eighteenth-century Dissenters.

It is easy to misunderstand what was going on. Colligan categorized subscribers as the 'conservative' and non-subscribers as the 'progressive' party.[48] Such terms are misleading. The positions of Peirce, and even Whiston, betray a literalism in the understanding of Scripture, which is more like modern fundamentalism than anything regarded as 'progressive' today. But the emphasis placed on *sola scriptura*, and even the concern to discover the exact original text, did not as yet bring awareness of the historical context of either the Scriptures, or those who followed them in formulating the doctrine of the Church. There was no sense that the translation of the Christian message is not just a word-by-word exercise, but entails understanding the conceptual world of both past and present.

The interest of Whiston—and indeed Newton—in discovering instances of the literal fulfilment of prophecies is unsurprising, even though they are not usually compatible with religion based on reason. The explanation is simple: the religion of these early 'Socinians' was not based on reason alone. It may seem strange that such a fascination co-existed with advances in mathematics

---

[47] This made the advice given by Richard Baxter and Matthew Henry, commenting on Matthew 18:17 concerning disagreement in the church, redundant.

[48] Colligan, *Arian Movement*, p. 55.

and physics, which changed the understanding of the modern world; but that is to underestimate the appeal of *sola scriptura*. Nathaniel Lardner concluded his *Essay on the Logos*, after an exhaustive examination of biblical texts, by saying 'I think I have above shown *from scripture*, that Jesus Christ was a man like unto us, or having a human soul, as well as a human body...I think myself therein both a catholic, and a scriptural Christian. It has been the general belief of the church of Christ in all ages.'[49] But he only published that letter eight years after he had left pastoral charge.

The Exeter controversy also affected Baptists in the south-west. The General Baptists in the eighteenth century were drawn further along the lines of heterodoxy than the Particulars, who retained a firm allegiance to 'Calvinism'. By the end of the century many General Baptist congregations had adopted heterodox views of Christology. It was a different story for Particular Baptists. Edward Foskett, minister of Broadmead Baptist Church, had established the academy that later became Bristol Baptist College. He and others were alarmed by the outcome of the Exeter disputes. Bristol was a key place as the meeting point of Baptists in South Wales and those in Wiltshire. Foskett was a leader in establishing in 1732 a separate Baptist association based on the acceptance of the Particular Baptists' Second London Confession (1689).[50]

By mid-century such differences were becoming sharper, not least in the academies. The ambiguities persisted: Trinitarian Independents insisted that the 1779 Act of Parliament, granting greater liberty for nonconformist ministers and schoolmasters, extended only to 'the Exercise of Religion permitted and allowed by Law'.[51] Dissenters' sympathy for American independence did not assist them. The foundation of the Essex Street meeting in 1774 on an explicitly Unitarian basis accentuated problems. It followed the failure of the Feathers Tavern Petition of 1772, seeking to relax the law on subscription. The leaders were primarily ex-Anglicans, led by Theophilus Lindsey (1723–1808), whose Unitarian views owed much to Archdeacon Francis Blackburne. Lindsey had originally hoped to reform the Church of England from within. The French Revolution overshadowed the centenary of 1688. Richard Price's *Discourse on the Love of One's Country* provoked keen Tory antagonism and even brought down the wrath of Edmund Burke. The New Meeting in Birmingham was attacked and destroyed.

---

[49] The Letter was written in 1730, but not published until 1759: *A Letter concerning the question whether the Logos supplied the place of a human soul in the person of Jesus Christ*, in *The Works of Nathaniel Lardner, DD*, 5 vols. (London, 1815), V, pp. 371–431, quotation from p. 394; emphasis mine.

[50] Michael A. G. Haykin, 'Foskett, Bernard (1685–1758)', *ODNB*, Oxford University Press, Jan. 2008 [http://www.oxforddnb.com/view/article/71073, accessed 29 Feb. 2016].

[51] 'An Act for the further Relief of Protestant Dissenting Ministers and Schoolmasters', 19 Geo III, c. 44, E. Neville Williams, *The Eighteenth-Century Constitution* (Cambridge, 1960), pp. 345–6. Unitarianism was still illegal.

Its minister was Joseph Priestley (1733–1804), one of the great Dissenting polymaths of the century. Joseph was brought up principally by his father's older sister, Sarah Keighly and her husband at Old Hall, Heckmondwike, Yorkshire. A serious illness when he was sixteen led him to doubt whether he had experienced the 'new birth'. He discovered that several ministers did not believe a new birth was necessary, nor that the sin of Adam had condemned humankind for ever to the wrath of God. When Priestley applied for membership at the Heckmondwike Independent church, the elders rejected him because of his unsound opinions about the sin of Adam.[52] Nevertheless he registered at Doddridge's Academy, now at Daventry under Caleb Ashworth. His treatise on *The Scripture Doctrine of Remission* (1761) analysed the relevant Old and New Testament texts in their context, rather than as proofs for a doctrine of atonement. He argued that all the Scripture references suggested that, if sinners repented of their sins before God, they would receive remission. Only on page 90 of his 95-page work, did he refer to *Hebrews*, describing verses 14 or 28 (it is not clear which) of Hebrews 9 without quoting them in full, as 'a bold figure', indicating that Christ's death relieved us of the burden of dead works. This, in his view, rescued Christianity from the disguise that both Jews and Christians had placed upon it. In 1761 he was appointed by Warrington Academy to teach English Literature, Rhetoric, and Natural Science. Six years later he became minister of Mill Hill chapel, Leeds, where he moved to complete anti-Trinitarianism, as a result of reading 'with care' Lardner's *Essay on the Logos*.[53] Priestley's *Institutes of Natural and Revealed Religion* (3 vols., 1772–4) argued that natural religion took primacy over revealed religion, and the latter had to be read in the light of the former; thus the original religion of human beings had been Unitarian.[54]

After serving Lord Shelburne as Librarian–Companion (1773–80), he received a pension and retired to Birmingham; within a few months he became minister of the New Meeting, one of the largest and wealthiest Dissenting congregations in England. Priestley preached regularly and conducted a Sunday class for children and young adults of nearly 150; and led the establishment of Sunday Schools by the Old and New Meetings. He also resumed his controversial theological writing—two volumes on *Corruptions in Christianity* (1782), four on *Early Opinions concerning Jesus Christ* (1786), and two on *A General History*

---

[52] Robert E. Schofield, *The Enlightenment of Joseph Priestley* (University Park, PA, 1997), p. 1.
[53] Ibid., p. 172.
[54] Ibid., pp. 172–8, 187–201. Although Schofield is puzzled by the 'curious mixture of uncritical conservatism, of forced anti-Trinitarianism, and of noteworthy insights' in Priestley's *Theological Repository* (1773–8), I suggest that this is only because he is committed to seeing Priestley as 'in the tradition of "modern" rationalist biblical criticism' leading to (some of) the German nineteenth-century critics: *Enlightenment*, pp. 188, 201. Priestley postulates an original perfection, a secularized Christianity corrupted by 'oriental and Indian philosophy', followed by slow rational progress; in other words, he reflects the prejudices of his age.

of the *Christian Church* (1790). When he welcomed the French Revolution in his *Letters to Edmund Burke* (1791), the local political establishment acquiesced in the 'church and king' mob destroying his chapel, house, laboratory, library, and most of his possessions. Priestley left England for Pennsylvania in 1794, and never again assumed pastoral charge of a congregation. Unitarianism was legalized in 1813, following the amendments to the Toleration Act in 1812, but failed to grow.

THE 'MODERATION' OF CALVINISM

The final issue was on the 'Calvinist' side of Dissent, increasingly represented by Independents and Baptists rather than Presbyterians, where disputes about election, predestination, and reprobation assumed an increasingly inward-looking character more concerned with theological precision than evangelism. They failed to see that predestination should be understood retrospectively (e.g. Rom. 8:28–30), rather than prospectively. The rise of Methodism, whether that of John and Charles Wesley in England, George Whitefield in England and America, or Howel Harris in Wales, crystallized the issue. By the mid-century Old Dissent lost the theological initiative on both sides of the Atlantic. Only the Baptists, with difficulty, emphasized evangelism.

John Wesley understood and advertised himself as an 'Arminian', meaning that the Gospel was for everyone and should be preached to everyone. From the first Conference of his Preachers in England in 1744, rapid growth followed almost wherever they went. This new appearance on the nonconformist scene (for Wesley always denied being a Dissenter) was bound to affect the Old Dissent, which had fallen on hard times in the 1730s and 1740s. Yet traditional Dissenters had begun with itinerant (and outdoor) preaching before devising theological justifications for doing so. Within the Independent and Particular Baptist traditions two men were particularly associated with 'evangelical Calvinism': the Independent, Edward Williams (1750–1813); and the Particular Baptist, Andrew Fuller (1754–1815). Of the two, Fuller is the better known, although neither has received the attention he deserves. Behind both men, however, lay the figure of Jonathan Edwards (1703–1758), probably the main English-speaking theologian in the traditions represented by English and Welsh Dissent.

Edwards studied at Yale, and served both Presbyterian and Congregational congregations. He was minister at Northampton, Massachusetts (1726–50), and from George Whitefield's first visit to America he supported revivals of religion. In 1746 he wrote a public defence of the revival in Northampton; and indirectly this was the cause of the breakdown in his relationship with the leaders of the congregation. He proposed to require evidence of a feeling of grace from all who presented themselves for communion; and in 1750 he was dismissed. After ministering in Stockbridge, a small community on the colony's border, subject to attacks from Native Americans, he was invited in 1757 to become president of Princeton College, New Jersey, taking up office in 1758. Within a few months he died after a smallpox inoculation.

Edwards defended Calvin's teaching on justification and predestination in terms that took account of the new philosophy of Locke and his successors. At one crucial point he modified Calvin's teaching. Calvin had insisted that both predestination and reprobation were the actions of God, unaffected by human action, in order to safeguard the belief that salvation was only of God's grace. Edwards retained the belief that predestination was before the Fall, not least because God was outside time; but suggested God's judgement depended on what people had done in their lives. This is explained in his *Seven Sermons on Important Subjects*. Although perhaps his best-known sermon is 'Sinners in the Hands of an Angry God', preached at Enfield, Massachusetts, on 8 July 1741, at a time of great awakenings, probably fewer people have actually read it; and the *Seven Sermons* are less well known. The first, 'God the best Portion of the Christian', preached in April 1736, invites the congregation to consider whether it loves God above all things, or only as a way of avoiding hell; the second on 'Divine Sovereignty' (June 1736) emphasizes that true acknowledgement of the divinity of God entails acceptance that rewards depend on God's mercy, not our righteousness and that God has the right to show mercy to his enemies; the third on 'Pardon for the greatest Sinners' (undated, but probably before 1733) was to encourage even the greatest sinner to turn to God for mercy; and the fourth on 'The Prayer-hearing God' (January 1735) emphasized that God hears our prayers.[55] Thus although no one could earn salvation, one could lose it.[56]

The thrust of what is set out here in occasional sermons is amplified in his *Remarks on Important Theological Controversies*, which touches on the vexed question of predestination. Edwards argues that the Arminian scheme is inconsistent, because there can be no such thing as 'conditional election'. As a Reformed theologian he always opposes the idea that anyone can achieve salvation by their own merit. Edwards was more aware than many of the problems in translating God's eternal decrees into a chronological sequence. Hence he resorts to the underlying logic of prior and posterior action to explain how the decrees fit together. The glory of God and God's goodness are prior; creation and the eternal glory of the elect follow from God's

---

[55] Jonathan Edwards, *Seven Sermons on Important Subjects*, in Edward Hickman, ed., *The Works of Jonathan Edwards*, 2 vols. (Edinburgh, 1834, reprinted 1976), II, pp. 104–18.

[56] Jonathan Edwards, *Miscellaneous Remarks on Important Subjects*, ch. iv and ch. vii §9 in *Works*, II, pp. 470–2, 481; cf. Conrad Cherry, *The Theology of Jonathan Edwards: A Reappraisal*, new edn, with forward by Stephen J. Stein (Bloomington, IN, 1990), pp. 93–6.

goodness. Only after the Fall can it be affirmed that the reprobation of the unrighteous is decreed, as a manifestation of God's justice, just as God's mercy to the repentant is also a manifestation of God's justice.[57]

The placing of the decree of election to glory in a prior position to the decree of reprobation justified the possibility of preaching salvation in Christ to all who repent, and therefore overcame the arguments of double-predestinarians who saw no point in doing so. Whereas Wesley and other 'Arminians' emphasized human free will in choosing salvation, Edwards argued that human free will in this sense was logically inconsistent;[58] his movement was made in relation to God's action rather than human action. It was a small shift with great theological significance, which opened the way for English Calvinists among both Baptists and Independents to become evangelical.

The link between Edwards and English Baptists was almost immediate from his publication of *The Life of David Brainerd* in 1748, and the key people in spreading this were John Ryland, Jnr (1723-1792) and John Sutcliff (1752-1814). This was reflected in various references to Edwards in the Northamptonshire Association Annual Letters written by Sutcliff, calling on the churches to pray for revival. But Sutcliff's influence on two self-taught ministers in the Association, Andrew Fuller and William Carey, was perhaps the most important.[59]

Sutcliff did not write any significant books, whereas Andrew Fuller became the one most often remembered (or vilified) for preaching 'moderate Calvinism', or 'modern Calvinism' (hence the phrase 'the Modern Controversy', often used to describe the mid-century arguments). Born in Wicken, Cambridgeshire, in 1754, his family moved to nearby Soham, where Andrew was converted, baptized, and in 1775 ordained as minister of Soham Baptist church. He first read Edwards on the *Freedom of the Will* in 1777 and *Religious Affections* in 1780. In 1783 he moved to be minister of Kettering Baptist church, and in 1785 published his best-known book, *The Gospel Worthy of All Acceptation*.[60] Picking up Edwards's distinction between natural and moral ability, and inability, Fuller concluded that the hyper-Calvinist insistence that a 'subjective warrant' was necessary for

---

[57] Edwards, *Miscellaneous Remarks*, in *Works*, II, pp. 540-1.

[58] Edwards argued that there was always a prior cause for any human action; crucially, however, repentance (which he believed to be the condition of salvation, rather than righteousness) did depend on human action: Jonathan Edwards, *Freedom of the Will*, ed. Paul Ramsey (New Haven, CT, 1957), pp. 70-4, 172-4, 188-9, 193-4, 204-12, 215-16, 237-8, 248-56, 320-7, 465-70.

[59] Roger Hayden, *Continuity and Change: Evangelical Calvinism among Eighteenth-Century Baptist Ministers Trained at Bristol Academy, 1690-1791* (Milton under Wychwood, 2006), pp. 194-202.

[60] Andrew Fuller, *The Gospel of Christ Worthy of All Acceptation: or the Obligations of Men Fully to Credit and Cordially to Approve, Whatever God Makes Known, Where in is Considered the Nature of Faith in Christ, and the Duty of Those Where the Gospel Comes in that Matter* (Northampton, 1785).

anyone to approach God for salvation was mistaken.⁶¹ This led to conflict both with Particular Baptists like William Button and John Martin, who took the traditional view of Gill and John Brine on the one hand, and also with Dan Taylor, the leading spokesman of the General Baptists of the New Connexion, who maintained an 'Arminian' position. By moving to Kettering, Fuller found more congenial theological company among the ministers of the Northamptonshire Association: John Sutcliff, John Ryland, Jnr, and later William Carey. Sutcliff provided the material (from an impeccable Calvinist source) that Fuller needed. Fuller's book therefore met a need, which rapidly aroused a response among Baptists throughout the country. It is often associated with the formation of the Baptist Missionary Society in 1792, and a willingness to engage in overseas missions, principally because of the urging of Carey. But its effect in revitalizing Baptist life within England and Wales was just as significant, if rather less glamorous.

Edward Williams (1750–1813) was born in Glanclwyd, Bodfari, a few miles from Denbigh in North Wales to a farming couple, Thomas and Ann Williams. After the failure of his parents' wish that he should enter the Anglican ministry, a neighbour, who was a (Calvinistic) Methodist preacher, took Edward to hear Daniel Rowland, the great Welsh preacher. Edward was converted by a Methodist lay preacher and joined the Independent church in Denbigh, whose minister was Daniel Lloyd. In 1771 he entered the Abergavenny Academy under Benjamin Davies, which taught Lloyd's high Calvinism. He was also strongly influenced by the importance of reason in religion. After a pastorate in Ross-on-Wye, he moved to Oswestry in 1777; and in 1781 he persuaded the Congregational Fund Board to move their academy from Abergavenny to Oswestry, where he became principal.⁶²

While at Oswestry Williams wrote his first book, *Antipaedobaptism Examined* (1789), in response to Abraham Booth's book on *Paedobaptism* (1784). He reasoned that baptism was a positive institution as the covenant seal adapted to Christianity, but its qualifications and mode related to baptism as a moral institution. In the latter respect, qualifications were irrelevant since baptism was an act of sovereign efficacious grace, 'the Holy Spirit therein executing the decree of election'.⁶³ He used the same distinction later, when tackling the apparent arbitrariness of Calvinism's emphasis on the primacy of God's action in election, independent of human agency.

After a brief ministry at Carrs Lane, Birmingham, in 1795 the Rotherham Independent Academy called him to be principal, where he remained until his death. His *Syllabus of Lectures on the most important subjects in Theology*

---

[61] Chris Chun, *The Legacy of Jonathan Edwards in the Theology of Andrew Fuller* (Leiden, 2012), pp. 32–3.
[62] W. T. Owen, *Edward Williams, DD* (Cardiff, 1963), pp. 1–34.
[63] Quoted in Owen, *Williams*, p. 39.

(1812) significantly influenced John Pye Smith, one of his most brilliant pupils.[64] This was the period of his decisive writing on election and predestination. In 1809 Williams published his *Essay on the Equity of Divine Government and the Sovereignty of Divine Grace*, a second edition of which was published (with significant alterations) in 1813.[65] In order for Christian teaching to avoid the pernicious effects of human traditions, it was necessary to regard the church 'as a *voluntary society* taking the SACRED SCRIPTURES as its *only* director, relative to faith, worship and practice'.[66] This did not mean rejecting the Newtonian system, because the laws of matter and motion were not essential to salvation; nor was it reasonable to decide every legislative or legal matter by reference to the sacred Scriptures.[67] Williams declared that Calvin was clear, scriptural, and argumentatively strong on the doctrines of grace, but less so on reprobation and free will; on the event of sin his positions were 'bold and rash, and the consequences alarming'.[68] Instead, Williams proposed 'Modern Calvinism', defined as 'that system of religion which represents the Sovereignty of divine Grace, without encroaching on the Equity of divine Government. Modern Arminianism by contrast represented the Equity of divine Government in such a way as to encroach on the Sovereignty of divine Grace.[69] Thus Calvin's position that both election and reprobation must be decreed in advance was countered, and punishment for sin became solely dependent on human failure to follow God's will.[70] In the *Essay* and the *Defence* Williams drew on the arguments deployed by Jonathan Edwards in *The Freedom of Will* (1754).

Coleridge misunderstood both Edwards and Williams in an oft-quoted passage in *Aids to Reflection*, by suggesting that each represented the high Calvinist position, in which human free will was reduced to a cipher, and the universe was represented as a machine—whereas the opposite was the case. On the other hand, Coleridge rightly observed that none of the writers, including Calvin himself, noted that the context for the text used from St Paul (and the supporting texts that Paul cited from the Old Testament) referred to nations rather than individuals (particularly, Christians rather than Jews).[71] Coleridge

---

[64] *A Syllabus of Lectures on the most important subjects in Theology* ([Rotherham], 1812). This rare book is anonymous, but has been identified as being by Williams. The copy in Dr Williams's Library is signed by William Harris of Cambridge, and Harris has written Williams's name on the title page.
[65] Edward Williams, *Essay on the Equity of Divine Government and the Sovereignty of Divine Grace*, 2nd edn (London 1813).
[66] Ibid., p. 77 (emphases original). [67] Ibid., pp. 97–8.
[68] Ibid., p. 142. [69] Ibid., pp. 144–5.
[70] Williams defended the same position in his book, *A Defence of Modern Calvinism* (1812), which was based on an examination of the Bishop of Lincoln's work, *A Refutation of Modern Calvinism* (1809).
[71] 'The doctrine of modern Calvinism as laid down by Jonathan Edwards and the late Dr Williams, which represents a will absolutely passive, clay in the hands of a Potter, destroys

disregarded the 'replacement theology' that had been read into Romans 9–11, where Paul was addressing precisely the opposite problem: could or would God break his pledge to his people (and Paul's)—the Jews?

The revitalized Calvinism among both Baptists and Independents gave Old Dissent an evangelical initiative to rival the Wesleyan movement. The full fruits of this were seen in the early nineteenth century, when the fears surrounding the French Revolution and the domestic tensions of the 1790s were replaced by a calmer atmosphere in the 1800s and 1810s. Then chapel expansion began in earnest.

There were some unexpected consequences. Some Independent congregations became Particular Baptist (of a strict kind) in order to preserve the older Calvinism. The church at Isleham in Cambridgeshire (a mile or two from Fuller's former church in Soham) was one, when it called a new minister in 1806.[72] Among Independents there developed a greater, almost defiant, emphasis on infant baptism.[73] Alongside this relaxation of traditional 'Calvinist' emphases on election and reprobation, there was also a weakening of the understanding of the sacramental emphasis, both in baptism and Holy Communion. This led directly to the rather 'weak' doctrine set out in the Congregational Union's *Declaration of the Faith, Church Order, and Discipline of the Congregational or Independent Dissenters* of 1833, which R. W. Dale called Calvinism in decay.[74]

---

all Will, takes away its essence and definition... It was in strict consistency therefore, that these Writers supported the Necessitarian Scheme, and made the relation of Cause and Effect the Law of the Universe, subjecting to its mechanism the moral World no less than the material or physical': S. T. Coleridge, *Aids to Reflection*, ed. John Beer, 'Aphorism on Spiritual Religion B I', in *The Collected Works of Samuel Taylor Coleridge*, vol. IX (Princeton, NJ, 1993), pp. 158–60. Compare Coleridge's comments on reading Williams in a short essay accompanying a letter to Captain Brabant, March 1815: *Collected Works, Shorter Works and Fragments*, vol. XI, ed. H. J. Jackson and J. R. de J. Jackson (Princeton, NJ, 1995), I, pp. 396–401. See further, Timothy Whelan, 'Coleridge, Jonathan Edwards, and the "edifice of Fatalism"', *Romanticism*, 21, 3 (2015), pp. 280–300.

[72] Samuel Lambert was pastor for fifty-two years (1753–1805); his son-in-law was Robert Fuller, brother of Andrew Fuller (who baptized several members in the late 1790s), and by the time of his death the majority of members had adopted Baptist principles. His successor, Hugh McKenzie, from 1806 was a Baptist, and the church became a Baptist congregation: Kenneth A. C. Parsons, ed., *The Church Book of the Independent Church (now Pound Lane Baptist) Isleham 1693–1805*, (Cambridge, 1984).

[73] See John Pye Smith, *First lines of theology: in the form of a syllabus prepared for the use of students in the Old College, Homerton*, ed. William Farrar (London, 1854). Pye Smith dominated one section of Independent theological thought for half a century until 1850.

[74] R. W. Dale, *History of English Congregationalism*, ed. A. W. W. Dale (London, 1907), pp. 699–709. Dale was critical of the way in which even a moderate statement had been weakened in discussion, especially on key doctrines such as the Trinity, the atonement, justification by faith, and the sacraments. Scathingly he explained this by the lack of education and theological isolation of most of those who approved the Statement: cf. John Stoughton, *Reminiscences of Congregationalism fifty years ago* (London, 1881), pp. 41–58.

CONCLUSION

Protestant Dissent had never been a unified movement, but rather a collection of different groups with differing agendas. The sharp decline of the Presbyterians—originally the largest group and the one most open to reconciliation with the Church of England—meant that separation would be a permanent feature of English Christianity, despite the cordial personal relationships of the mid-eighteenth century. Instead, the various groups gradually developed more sharply differentiated identities. Quakers also became more introverted as the eighteenth century progressed, though collectively they prospered perhaps more than their orthodox rivals. Their attention was drawn into good works outside the Church, particularly anti-slavery. The distinction between evangelicals in Dissent and those in the Church of England and Methodism became less clear.

Among the Old Dissent the chief continental influence remained that of the Netherlands, particularly among the Remonstrants, notably Hugo Grotius. This was especially true as long as most theology was written in Latin; that declined in the later eighteenth century. The withdrawal of the subscribers from Salters' Hall in 1719 effectively represented the triumph of private judgement over the seventeenth-century confessions of faith—objectively, theological anarchy. The Westminster Assembly had been summoned to prepare a new national basis of faith. Although accepted in Scotland, the English Parliament declined to accept it; and by the eighteenth century it had become the badge of a party. Apart from the New Connexion of General Baptists no new confessions of faith were prepared in eighteenth-century England. (Seceder Presbyterians in Scotland did prepare an additional statement to the Westminster Confession.) The Unitarians did not prepare a Confession of Faith before Unitarianism was legalized in 1813, nor in the nineteenth century. The only examples of anything comparable to a Confession were the doctrinal articles incorporated in the trust deeds of individual congregations after it became clear that 'the principles of Protestant Dissenters' was not a sufficiently clear phrase for the lawyers. From a twenty-first century perspective, there were two different failures in Dissenting theology: first, they did not know enough about the philosophical background to patristic theology; second, they did not appreciate that Christian doctrine is not a completed task, but an ongoing one. Hence, like most Protestants, they sought to reason syllogistically either from Nicene or Chalcedonian conclusions, or from Scripture, to justify their conclusions by reference to some supposedly complete standard of another age.

By the end of the century the future seemed to lie with an activist and superficially orthodox Nonconformity—some distance from seventeenth-century Puritanism. Nonconformist growth led to a revival of concern for greater civil liberties, and the political involvement of Dissenters also reflected a growing difference between the more comfortable atmosphere of London Dissent (of all shades) and the more exposed nature of Dissenters in the provincial corporate towns, and the new industrialized towns of a changing economic environment. Neither Unitarians nor Quakers, for rather different reasons, gained from the theological impetus of the evangelical revival. By the 1820s Dissent was already facing more substantial theological challenges from both biblical criticism and scientific discoveries that posed new challenges to the credibility of Christianity. The divisions these created bore no relation to those of the seventeenth century from which Dissent had sprung.

SELECT BIBLIOGRAPHY

This Bibliography largely excludes books cited in the text; nor does it refer to the ongoing Yale edition of the *Works of Jonathan Edwards*, which has the disadvantage of seeking to arrange the Sermons chronologically, making it difficult to find those published in separate sets in the eighteenth and nineteenth centuries. For those, the simpler method is to consult the older Banner of Truth Trust edition in two volumes.

Cherry, Conrad, *The Theology of Jonathan Edwards: A Reappraisal* (new edn, with forward by Stephen J. Stein, Bloomington, IN, 1990).
Chun, Chris, *The Legacy of Jonathan Edwards in the Theology of Andrew Fuller* (Leiden, 2012).
Copson, Stephen and Morden, Peter J., eds, *Challenge and Change: English Baptist Life in the Eighteenth Century* (Didcot, 2017).
Cornwall, Robert D. and Gibson, William, eds, *Religion, Politics and Dissent, 1660–1832* (Farnham, 2010).
Hayden, Roger, *Continuity and Change: Evangelical Calvinism among Eighteenth-Century Baptist Ministers Trained at Bristol Academy, 1690–1791* (Milton under Wychwood, 2006).
Lim, Paul C. H., *Mystery Unveiled: The Crisis of the Trinity in Early Modern England* (New York, 2012).
Mandelbrote, Scott and Ledger-Lomas, Michael, eds, *Dissent and the Bible in Britain, c.1650–1950* (Oxford, 2013).
Morden, Peter J., *The Life and Thought of Andrew Fuller (1754–1815)* (Milton Keynes, 2015).
Pfizenmaier, Thomas C., *The Trinitarian Theology of Dr Samuel Clarke (1675–1729): Context, Sources, and Controversy* (Leiden, 1997).
Pope, Robert, ed., *T & T Clark Companion to Nonconformity* (London, 2013).
Rivers, Isabel, *Reason, Grace and Sentiment: A Study of the Language of Religion and Ethics in England, 1660–1780. Volume I, Whichcote to Wesley* (Cambridge, 1991).
Rivers, Isabel, *The Defence of Truth through the Knowledge of Error: Philip Doddridge's Academy Lectures* (London, 2003).

Rivers, Isabel and Wykes, David, eds, *Joseph Priestley: Scientist, Philosopher, and Theologian* (Oxford, 2008).
Schofield, Robert E., *The Enlightenment of Joseph Priestley: A Study of His Life and Work from 1733 to 1773* (University Park, PA, 1997).
Schofield, Robert E., *The Enlightened Joseph Priestley: A Study of His Life and Work from 1773 to 1804* (University Park, PA, 2004).
Sell, Alan P. F., *Philosophy, Dissent and Nonconformity, 1689–1920* (Cambridge, 2004).
Sell, Alan P. F., with Hall, David J., and Sellers, Ian, eds, *English Protestant Nonconformist Texts, Volume 2: The Eighteenth Century* (Aldershot, 2006).

16

Sermons

Françoise Deconinck-Brossard

Despite the recent surge of scholarship on 'sermon studies' that has led to the publication of several major works highlighting the key significance of the eighteenth-century pulpit in British society,[1] the question of the specificity of the Dissenting sermon culture remains underexplored.[2] The pulpit played such a significant part in nonconformist worship, even architecturally, that it contributed to the construction of a Dissenting identity.

This chapter discusses printed sermons and manuscript records, without forgetting to mention their physical characteristics. It will seek to address not only 'the most basic questions of early modern preaching—where, when, and to whom sermons were delivered',[3] but also what they dealt with, and how they were received. Both typical and rare features will be examined.

PRINTED SERMONS

Until the advent of electronic databases that have radically transformed the approach to sermon studies, not least by making the full text of much

---

[1] For the period prior to 1720, see Peter McCullough and others, eds, *The Oxford Handbook of the Early Modern Sermon* (Oxford, 2011); cf. Keith A. Francis and William Gibson, eds, *The Oxford Handbook of the British Sermon 1689–1901* (Oxford, 2012). Jennifer Farooq, *Preaching in Eighteenth-Century London* (Woodbridge, 2013) never neglects the Dissenting pulpit, but focuses on the first six decades of the century. See also Lori Anne Ferrell and Peter McCullough, eds, *The English Sermon Revised* (Manchester, 2000), and Robert Hole, *Pulpits, Politics and Public Order in England 1760–1832* (Cambridge, 1989).
A new, peer-reviewed online journal, *Sermon Studies*, was launched in 2015: see http://mds.marshall.edu/sermonstudies/ [accessed 9 March 2016].

[2] See esp. the subchapter on 'Nonconformist Sermons in Print', in Rosemary Dixon, 'Sermons in Print, 1660–1700', *Handbook of the Early Modern Sermon*, pp. 470–4; Farooq, *Preaching*, esp. 'Nonconformist Preaching', pp. 28–34.

[3] Emma Rhatigan, 'Preaching Venues: Architecture and Auditories', in *Handbook of the Early Modern Sermon*, p. 87.

printed material available online,⁴ one of the major bibliographic sources for seventeenth- and eighteenth-century preaching was the last edition of a catalogue published in 1753 by an almost obscure compiler,⁵ Sampson Letsome.⁶ The work was originally designed to provide theology students with useful references for biblical commentary, but the title of the last edition indicates that it also aimed at a wider market of ministers who might want to find inspiration when preparing their sermons. There is evidence, among the several copies that have survived, that the book remained in use, among Anglicans and Dissenters, well into the nineteenth century,⁷ so that it remains a significant primary source, all the more so as it can easily be supplemented with the online databases that have revolutionized seventeenth- and eighteenth-century studies.⁸ In spite of Letsome's attempts to give a comprehensive account of English sermon literature since the Restoration, his book is far from complete. His work was expanded thirty years later by another Anglican compiler, John Cooke.⁹ Cooke reckoned that his predecessor had omitted 'several thousand Discourses',¹⁰ and marked his own additions with an asterisk. His catalogue is

---

⁴ For works printed before 1701, see *Early English Books Online* (hereafter *EEBO*), and *Eighteenth-Century Collections Online* (hereafter *ECCO*) for the eighteenth century.

⁵ *The Preacher's Assistant, In Two Parts. Part I. A Series Of the Texts of all the Sermons and Discourses Preached upon, and Published Since the Restoration to the Present Time. Part II. An Historical Register Of all the Authors in the Series, Containing, A Succinct View of their Several Works* (London, 1753).

Nineteen years earlier, Letsome had already published a smaller, less elaborate *Index*, similarly arranged in order of biblical text: *An Index to the Sermons, Published since the Restoration. Pointing out the Texts in the Order they Lie in the Bible, Shewing the Occasion on Which they were Preached and Directing to the Volume and Page where they Occur* (London, 1734).

⁶ Information about Letsome's biography is incomplete. At the age of 18 he matriculated at Magdalen Hall, Oxford in February 1722, graduated BA in 1728, and proceeded MA in 1729, the year when he was ordained priest. In 1739 he co-edited a collection of the Boyle lectures. In 1748 he became the domestic chaplain to the politician John Carteret, Earl of Granville, and in 1751 'Vicar of Thame in Oxfordshire'. He was later appointed rector of Hatford (Berkshire), and died in 1760 or 1761: see *Clergy of the Church of England database* (hereafter *CCEd*), Person ID 51482 [accessed 29 February 2016].

⁷ For instance, a two-volume interleaved copy in Dr Williams's Library (DWL) has copious annotations in several hands, including many references to nineteenth-century publications (shelfmark: 3008.C.1). Another interleaved copy, in Durham University library (DUL shelfmark Bamburgh M.5.17–18), inscribed by Thomas Sharp (1725–1772) in his student days at Trinity College, Cambridge, remained in his library at Bamburgh in Northumberland where he was the perpetual curate from 1757 until his death (*CCEd* Person ID: 20292).

⁸ Especially the *English Short Title Catalogue*: see http://estc.bl.uk/F/?func=file&file_name=login-bl-estc (hereafter *ESTC*) for items published before 1801.

⁹ *The Preacher's Assistant, (After the Manner of Mr. Letsome) Containing a Series of the Texts of Sermons and Discourses Published either Singly, or in Volumes, by Divines of the Church of England and by the Dissenting Clergy, since the Restoration to the present Time, Specifying also the Several Authors alphabetically Arranged under each Text—with the Size, Date, Occasion, and Subject-matter of each Sermon or Discourse*, 2 vols. (London, 1783). The copy in DWL has two inscriptions dated 1827 and 1831 by one 'Wᵐ Brown'.

Not all asterisks in Cooke's edition are justified.

¹⁰ Cooke, *Preacher's Assistant*, I, p. iii.

almost twice as long as Letsome's.[11] In both works, Dissenters are singled out by italics, as if they were a homogeneous group. As clergymen of the established church, Cooke[12] and Letsome might have been more sensitive to the Nonconformity of the three major Dissenting denominations than to their disagreements in matters of doctrine or church polity.[13] In spite of their divisions, a sense of the 'underlying unity'[14] of Nonconformists could be inferred, for instance, from the annual meeting of the body of their London ministers, where an eminent preacher was invited to deliver the sermon.[15] Besides, many eighteenth- and early nineteenth-century sources referred to 'the Dissenting Interest'.[16] Some even lamented what they considered as its decline: 'If Grey hairs were ever upon Protestant Dissenters, they are now upon y^m of all three Denominations of wch general decays I would assign ye following Reasons'.[17] Neither Quakers nor Methodists were usually included in this group, although there is evidence, especially from episcopal visitation returns, that many Church of England clergymen considered the latter as Dissenters too. However, Wesleyan Methodists or other revival groups had not yet formally separated from the established

---

[11] There are 13,734 records in Letsome, in contrast with over 24,000 in Cooke.

I shall ever be grateful to the University of Sheffield for their assistance in 1985 with the design of a database based on Letsome's catalogue, while I was a visiting lecturer there.

I am equally indebted both to the late John Gordon Spaulding, and to the IBM Almaden Research Center in California. The former kindly sent me his data on loan in 1992, so that I might compare his computerization of Cooke's catalogue with my own digital version of Letsome. Without the help of the Almaden Center, where I was on sabbatical leave, I would have been unable to read Spaulding's data. His work has since been published as *Pulpit Publications 1660-1782 being a New Edition of 'The Preacher's Assistant': A Bibliography, with Introductory Matter, Indexes, Statistical Tables, and other Interpretive Apparatus*, 6 vols. (New York, 1996).

[12] Even less is known about John Cooke (*CCEd* Person ID: 12322) than Letsome; see 'The Reverend John Cooke: 1742-1794: A Brief Sketch of His Life and Work', in Spaulding, *Pulpit Publications*, II, xiii-xv.

[13] Isabel Rivers and David Wykes give a very clear summary of 'developments in eighteenth-century Dissent' in the Introduction to *Dissenting Praise: Religious Dissent and the Hymn in England and Wales* (Oxford, 2011), pp. 4-6. On the nonconformist 'spectrum', see Isabel Rivers, *Reason, Grace, and Sentiment: A Study of the Language of Religion and Ethics in England 1660-1780. Volume I, Whichcote to Wesley* (Cambridge, 1991), pp. 95-9.

[14] James E. Bradley, *Religion, Revolution and English Radicalism: Non-Conformity in Eighteenth-Century Politics and Society* (Cambridge, 1990), p. 53.

[15] At least six parchment-bound quarto manuscript sermons have survived for 1731-36 (DWL MS 24.38-43): 'Gospel Ministers The *Salt* of the Earth', preached by Edmund Calamy on 28 Oct. 1731; 'Of Ministers Commending themselves to the Consciences of men', by W[illiam] Harris (21 Nov. 1733); 'The Pastoral Care, True Love to Christ', by B[enjamin] Grosvenor (13 Nov. 1734); 'The Wisdom of Winning Souls', by Daniel Neal; as well as two untitled sermons by Joshua Bayes on 1 Tim. 4:16 (23 Nov. 1732) and John Newman on 1 Thess. 2:4.

[16] Bradley, *Religion, Revolution*, p. 53. One century separates [Strickland Gough], *An Enquiry into the Causes of the Decay of the Dissenting Interest. In a Letter to a Dissenting Minister* (London, 1730) from [Walter Wilson], *Remarks upon the Present State of the Dissenting Interest, with Hints for its Improvement by Means of a Consolidated Union* (London, 1831).

[17] 'The Substance of Several Sermons Preached by y^e Rev^d. M^r. Robt. Bragg$^{<e>}$, Minister of y^e Gospel in Lime-Street. Lon<d>on 1732', DWL MS 24.33, p. 124.

church, so most of their preachers were not, strictly speaking, Dissenters. Therefore their names are rightly printed in Roman type, like those of their Church of England counterparts, in both editions of the *Preacher's Assistant*.[18]

Interestingly enough, the proportion of Dissenting sermons was almost three times as high in Cooke (19 per cent) as in Letsome (6.7 per cent).[19] Even the former's figure is much lower than has been found in Jennifer Farooq's survey of London printed sermons in the first six decades of the eighteenth century (35 per cent).[20] This could suggest that the capital city was over-represented in the publication of Dissenting sermons. Indeed, almost half of the preachers for whom Letsome provides geographical information were based in London and the surrounding area. His 'Historical Register' also mentioned English towns and cities like Oxford, Leeds, Derby, Exeter, Portsmouth, and 'Sarum', as well as counties such as Hertfordshire, Dorset, and Somerset. These provincial centres may have played an important part in the publication of Dissenting sermons, but the list hardly represents the geography of eighteenth-century Dissent as a whole. It is worth noting that Letsome did not omit Scotland, Ireland, or even New England. South of the Scottish border, members of the Kirk were regarded as Nonconformists. Logically enough, the name of a preacher from the Scots Church in London, John Cumming,[21] was printed in italics like those of English Dissenters. More surprisingly, Henry Scougal, a minister in the Church of Scotland before the reintroduction of Presbyterianism by the 1688 revolution,[22] was treated as if he were a Dissenter,[23] probably because his sermons were reprinted in the eighteenth century. Letsome and Cooke did not necessarily refer to the first edition of the works that they listed, for they relied heavily on the holdings and catalogues of public libraries, private collections,[24] booksellers, and auctioneers. In the thriving market of sermon literature

---

[18] For obvious examples, see references to Charles and John Wesley, as well as George Whitefield: Cooke, *Preacher's Assistant*, II, pp. 364, 370.

[19] See my quantitative analysis of Cooke and Letsome, 'Eighteenth-Century Sermons and the Age', in W. M. Jacob and Nigel Yates, eds, *Crown and Mitre: Religion and Society in Northern Europe since the Reformation* (Woodbridge, 1993), figure 1, p. 107—where, incidentally, the figures for 'C.o.E.' should be 12,742 for the period 1660–1753, and 18,591 for 1660–1782.

[20] Her analysis is based on items identified from the *ESTC*: Farooq, *Preaching*, esp. figure 1, p. 66 and n. 3, p. 40.

[21] *Surman Index Online* (http://surman.english.qmul.ac.uk/ [accessed 2 July 2016]), id: 6226; see Letsome, *Preacher's Assistant*, II, p. 56.

[22] Clare Jackson, 'Scougal, Henry (1650–1678)', *Oxford Dictionary of National Biography* (hereafter *ODNB*), Oxford University Press, 2004 [http://www.oxforddnb.com/view/article/24941, accessed 10 Aug. 2016].

[23] Letsome, *Preacher's Assistant*, I, pp. 33, 91, 147, and II, p. 171.

[24] Letsome's own collection of over 200 volumes is now part of the 'King's Library' at the British Library (hereafter BL): see Frederick Augusta Barnard, *Bibliothecæ Regiæ Catalogus* (London, 1820–9), V, p. 166.

many discourses went through several editions, and thus had a lasting impact on the reading public.

OCCASION AND SUBJECT-MATTER

Many of the topics that were dealt with in the printed sermons listed by Letsome or Cooke did not differ significantly from the subjects that were addressed in discourses published by Anglican clerics. The prevailing trend was the emphasis on 'practical' issues.[25] Dissenting preachers inveighed against anger, slander, covetousness, cowardice, censoriousness, lukewarmness,[26] or drunkenness,[27] warned their flocks against the danger of riches or evil habits,[28] and advocated 'Constancy & Perseverance', patience, peaceableness, sincerity, and temperance.[29] Some were keen to underline the Christian foundation of their concern for morality, therefore preached on Christian fortitude, Christian humility, or Christian meekness.[30] Most importantly, they favoured the societies for the reformation of manners, especially in the first decades of the century.[31] They also supported charities, particularly schools[32] and sometimes hospitals or 'infirmaries'. Indeed, some of these charities were interdenominational.[33] However, there could be variations in sermon styles. For instance, when in 1777 the Presbyterian minister Joseph Towers (who became an Arian at an early stage in his life)[34] preached for the benefit of the oldest nonconformist charity school, he not only addressed the audience of potential benefactors, as was common practice, but he also spoke to the pupils as his 'young friends',[35] an unusual approach in charity sermons, and perhaps

[25] Deconinck-Brossard, 'Eighteenth-Century Sermons', pp. 109–11.
[26] Letsome, *Preacher's Assistant*, I, pp. 219, 8, 142, 74, 114, and 249.
[27] Cooke, *Preacher's Assistant*, I, pp. 115 and 118.
[28] Letsome, *Preacher's Assistant*, I, pp. 238 and 89.
[29] Letsome, *Preacher's Assistant*, I, pp. 205, 263, 188, 196, 153, 150, and 263.
[30] Letsome, *Preacher's Assistant*, I, pp. 263 and 229.
[31] All but three of the sermons listed by Cooke on the subject were published before 1740: see, for instance, Cooke, *Preacher's Assistant*, I, pp. 3, 11, 15, 24, 29, 46, 47, 52, 82, 108, 111, 120, 128, 135, 143, 147, 168, and 169; II, pp. 86, 217, 309, and 312.
[32] Cooke, *Preacher's Assistant*, I, pp. 5, 10, 21, 53, 74, 110, and 117; II, pp. 26, 68, 202, 245, 341, and 378.
[33] See, for instance, Philip Doddridge, *Compassion to the Sick Recommended and Urged, in a Sermon Preached at Northampton, September 4, 1743. In Favour of a Design then Opening to Erect a County Infirmary there for the Relief of the Poor Sick and Lame. Published at the Request of Several who Heard it* (London, 1743), p. xii.
[34] Alexander Gordon, 'Towers, Joseph (1737–1799)', rev. M. J. Mercer, *ODNB*, Oxford University Press, 2004 [http://www.oxforddnb.com/view/article/27588, accessed 25 Aug. 2016].
[35] Joseph Towers, *The Professors of the Gospel under the Strongest Obligations to Labour to Distinguish Themselves by an Eminent Degree of Piety and Virtue. A Sermon Preached at*

a feature of the 'affectionate' tradition of Old Dissent.³⁶ The recurrence of the word 'affectionate' in Dissenting sermons is noteworthy.

As far as political issues were concerned, Dissenting preachers were keen to publish sermons showing their loyalty to the Crown. Until the age of the American and French revolutions, most were devoted Hanoverians. They observed national commemorations such as the sovereign's accession, coronation, or official birthday.³⁷ Ferdinando Shaw, who ministered at Derby, even marked the birthday of Frederick, prince of Wales,³⁸ although the day had not been officially set aside as a particular occasion for special worship.³⁹ One of the few funeral sermons published after the death of William III was preached by a Dissenter.⁴⁰

However, Nonconformists rarely published 30 January sermons, largely because they disagreed with the official interpretation of the regicide as the 'martyrdom' of Charles I. The only exception in Letsome's catalogue seems to be the Presbyterian controversialist James Peirce.⁴¹ On two occasions, he claimed that, as the date of his lecture happened to fall on that day, he had taken the opportunity 'to say something in our own vindication',⁴² and offered a Dissenting interpretation of history. Similarly, the Church of Scotland minister James Anderson's publication of a polemical sermon preached on 30 January 1715 sought to prove that Presbyterians were *No King-Killers*.⁴³ By contrast, the 5 November anniversary, commemorating the 'glorious' revolution⁴⁴ as well as

---

St. Thomas's, January 1, 1777, for the Benefit of the Charity-School in Gravel-Lane, Southwark (London, 1777), p. 22.

³⁶ Rivers, *Reason, Grace, and Sentiment*, I, chapter 4.

³⁷ On the significance of these special occasions, see the introduction to Nathalie Mears et al., eds, *National Prayers: Special Worship since the Reformation*, I (Woodbridge, 2013), esp. pp. l–liv.

³⁸ *A Sermon Preached on the Birth-day of His Royal Highness Frederick Lewis, Prince of Wales and Electoral Prince of Brunswick-Lunenburgh; At Derby, Jan. 19, 1728/9. By Ferdinando Shaw M. A.* (London, 1729).

³⁹ 'Analytical List of Particular Occasions of Special Worship, 1533–2012', in Mears et al. *National Prayers*, n.p. [post p. cxii].

⁴⁰ *A Sermon, Occasionally Preached on the Funeral Of our late Soveraign William the III. King of England, Scotland, France and Ireland; who was Solemnly Interr'd in Henry the 7th. Chappel in the Abby of Westminster. On Sunday April the 12. 1702 By William Bentley. D.D.* (London, 1702)

⁴¹ Surman Index id: 22109; David L. Wykes, 'Peirce, James (1674–1726)', *ODNB*, Oxford University Press, 2004; online edn, Jan. 2008 [http://www.oxforddnb.com/view/article/21782, accessed 10 Aug. 2016].

⁴² 'The Curse Causeless. A Sermon Preach'd at Exon, Jan. 30, 1716–17', sermon III in the posthumous collection of *Fifteen Sermons on Several Occasions, Eight of which were Never Before Printed* (London, 1728), p. 90. See also sermon VII, ibid., 'Christ's Kingdom Advanc'd by Peace. A Sermon Preach'd at Exon, January 30, 1722'.

⁴³ James Anderson, *No King-Killers. A Sermon Preach'd in Swallow-Street, St. James's, on January 30. 1714/15* (London, 1715); Francis Espinasse, 'Anderson, James (bap. 1679, d. 1739)', rev. S. J. Skedd, *ODNB*, Oxford University Press, 2004; online edn, Jan. 2006 [http://www.oxforddnb.com/view/article/474, accessed 10 Aug. 2016].

⁴⁴ The earliest occurrence of this phrase documented in the *Oxford English Dictionary* (http://www.oed.com/) [accessed 9 May 2016] quotes a sermon preached by the Independent minister

the discovery of the gunpowder plot, naturally appealed to protestant audiences. In the late eighteenth century, this commemoration became the ideal platform for Dissenting preachers to disseminate their political opinions. The 'great majority' held pro-American views.[45] In the peroration of a sermon reminding his audience of the 'repeated interpositions of divine providence' commemorated on that 'auspicious day',[46] the Particular Baptist minister Caleb Evans[47] typically alluded to the 'most unhappy war'[48] in which the country was now engaged against the American colonists. In the following decade, the London Revolution Society preferred to hold its anniversary celebrations on the fourth of November (William III's birthday) in order to dissociate the commemoration of the 1688 revolution from Guy Fawkes' day.[49] The sermon preached by the Arian philosopher and political radical Richard Price[50] for the Society's second memorial famously triggered much controversy. The author praised not only the principles of 1688 but also the American and French equally 'glorious'[51] revolutions 'in which every friend to mankind [was] now exulting'.[52] That this sermon should have set the terms of the British debate on the French revolution only shows how influential the Dissenting pulpit could be in spite of its minority status, as G. M. Ditchfield has convincingly argued.[53]

The providentialism underlying the discourse on divine intervention in history could also be illustrated in discourses interpreting or commemorating 'acts of God' like storms, earthquakes, plague epidemics, and the fire of

---

Thomas Bradbury on 5 Nov. 1716, *The Establishment of the Kingdom in the Hand of Solomon, Applied to the Revolution and the Reign of King George* (London, 1716, 3rd edn), p. 4. For another instance of this term in eighteenth-century Dissenting pulpit literature, see Caleb Evans, *The Remembrance of Former Days. A Sermon Preached at Broad-mead, Bristol, November 5, 1778* (Bristol, n.d. [1778]), p. 27.

However, Ulrich Niggemann has argued that the phrase was used as early as the 1690s by 'the Revolution propaganda' that borrowed it from even earlier sources: 'Some Remarks on the Origins of the Term "Glorious Revolution"', *The Seventeenth Century*, 27, 4 (2012), pp. 477–87. I owe this reference to Clotilde Prunier.

[45] Bradley, *Religion, Revolution*, p. 189.
[46] Evans, *Remembrance of Former Days*, p. 6.
[47] Roger Hayden, 'Evans, Caleb (1737–1791)', *ODNB*, Oxford University Press, 2004 [http://www.oxforddnb.com/view/article/40192, accessed 10 Aug. 2016].
[48] Evans, *Remembrance of Former Days*, p. 31. For other instances of Dissenting preachers' condemnation of what they considered as an unjust war, see Bradley, *Religion, Revolution*, p. 149.
[49] Rémy Duthille, 'London Revolution Society (*act.* 1788–1793)', *ODNB*, Oxford University Press, 2004 [http://oxfordindex.oup.com/view/10.1093/ref:odnb/96833, accessed 10 Aug. 2016].
[50] D. O. Thomas, 'Price, Richard (1723–1791)', *ODNB*, Oxford University Press, 2004; online edn, May 2005 [http://www.oxforddnb.com/view/article/22761, accessed 10 Aug. 2016].
[51] Richard Price, *A Discourse on the Love of our Country, Delivered on Nov. 4, 1789, at the Meeting-house in the Old Jewry, to the Society for Commemorating the Revolution in Great Britain* (London, 1789), p. 49.
[52] Ibid., p. 14.
[53] G. M. Ditchfield, 'Sermons in the Age of the American and French Revolutions', in *Oxford Handbook of the British Sermon*, pp. 285–6.

London. In Ireland the anniversary of the 'deliverance' from the 1641 rebellion was regularly commemorated on 23 October. The eminent Presbyterian minister Joseph Boyse[54] published several thanksgiving sermons on the subject.[55] Besides, Dissenting preachers joined their Anglican counterparts in keeping the appointed fasts during periods of national crisis, and giving thanks for happy outcomes such as naval and military victories. Like Daniel Defoe and his English co-religionists, the Baptist minister Joseph Stennett praised the union of England and Scotland in 1707.[56] In 1746 many Dissenting preachers rejoiced after the defeat of the Jacobite rebellion that had exercised their fears of religious and political oppression, in much the same terms as their colleagues from the established church.[57]

The related theme of 'God with us, while we are with Him' was treated by the popular preacher John Evans[58] after the election of the Presbyterian Sir John Fryer as Mayor of London,[59] a rare instance in Letsome's catalogue of a Dissenter being invited to publish a sermon on this important civic occasion. Evans preached in the Hand-Alley Meeting House. Nonconformist preachers were officially deprived of the opportunity to address the influential audiences of the Houses of Parliament, the sovereign, the court, the Lord Mayor of London, county assizes, or the two English universities, at whose request prominent Anglican divines printed many sermons.

A QUESTION OF IDENTITY

The congregations whom Dissenting preachers did address could generally be identified by the place of delivery that was referred to in the lengthy titles or the paratext of eighteenth-century publications. Sometimes, however, there

---

[54] A. W. Godfrey Brown, 'Boyse, Joseph (1660–1728)', *ODNB*, Oxford University Press, 2004 [http://www.oxforddnb.com/view/article/3151, accessed 10 Aug. 2016].

[55] Sermons I, II, XXXIV, and XXXV in volume I of *The Works of the Reverend and Learned Mr. Joseph Boyse, of Dublin. Being a Complete Collection of all the Discourses, Sermons, and Other Tracts, which have been already Published. To which are Added, Several Other Sermons [...], Never before Published* (London, 1728).

[56] *A Sermon Preach'd on the First of May, 1707. Being the Day Appointed for a Publick Thanksgiving for the Happy Union of England and Scotland. By Joseph Stennett* (London, 1707).

[57] See my article on 'The Churches and the '45', in W. J. Sheils, ed., *The Church and War* (Oxford, 1983), pp. 253–62. In the same volume, see also D. Napthine and W. A. Speck, 'Clergymen and Conflict 1660–1763', pp. 231–51.

[58] *Dissenting Academies Online: Database and Encyclopedia*, http://dissacad.english.qmul.ac.uk/ (hereafter *D & E*) [accessed 13 July 2016], person id: 1406; Alsager Vian, 'Evans, John (1679/80–1730)', rev. S. J. Skedd, *ODNB*, Oxford University Press, 2004 [http://www.oxforddnb.com/view/article/8962, accessed 10 Aug. 2016].

[59] John Evans, *God with us, while we are with Him. A Sermon Preached at Hand-Alley, In London, October the 9th, M.DCC.XX. Humbly Dedicated to my Lord Mayor* (London, 1720).

was a particular mention of specific audiences 'before' whom sermons were delivered. Unsurprisingly, nonconformist preachers addressed distinctly Dissenting bodies like synods and associations of ministers. Likewise, ordination sermons were probably intended primarily for the use of nonconformist hearers and readers. An especially interesting category of listeners were young people.[60] Not only did they need 'advice'[61] and instruction, but they were an essential link in the chain of nonconformist heritage. Philip Doddridge thus asked his young hearers to contemplate the long line of unborn children who would be brought up in the legacy of the Dissenting tradition: 'there may be Thousands of your *remote Descendents*, who... may owe their Religion and their Happiness to *you*'.[62]

That sense of identity was reinforced by funeral orations, by far the largest single category of printed nonconformist sermons listed in Cooke and Letsome.[63] It is not surprising to find that the genre was more widespread among Dissenters than Anglicans, since there was no provision for sermons in the burial rites of the *Book of Common Prayer*.[64] A biographical encomium of the deceased generally served as the 'application' or 'improvement' that concluded a discourse starting, as usual, with a biblical epigraph and an exegesis of its context, followed by theological 'doctrine' or argument. The introductory Scripture quotation had sometimes been selected by the departed[65]—probably the only circumstance when the preacher was ostensibly deprived of his choice of 'text'.[66] Apart from the standard religious comforts to the bereaved, observations on the vanity of worldly pursuits that should discourage the faithful from procrastination, and the reiteration of the belief in the last four things, memoirs of the lives of leading nonconformist ministers or pious lay men, women and children[67] provided Dissenting communities with role models, however idealized they may sometimes have been.

---

[60] The next few lines borrow heavily from my article on 'Philip Doddridge and Children', *Journal of the United Reformed Church History Society*, 7, 2 (2003), pp. 74–89 (here 88–9).

[61] e.g. Joseph Stennett, *Advice to the Young, or, The Reasonableness and Advantages of an Early Conversion to God Demonstrated, in Three Discourses on Ecclesiastes xii, 1* (London, 1695).

[62] Philip Doddridge, 'The Importance of the Rising Generation', no. I in *Sermons to Young Persons* (London, 2nd edn, 1737), p. 43.

[63] F. Deconinck-Brossard, 'Eighteenth-Century Sermons', pp. 110–11, esp. figure 3A. Cf. Farooq, *Preaching*, quoting p. 42 a proportion of 21 per cent of all printed Dissenting sermons in her corpus.

[64] See Brian Cummings, ed., *The Book of Common Prayer: The Texts of 1549, 1559, and 1662* (Oxford, 2011), p. 782, n. 451; Penny Pritchard, 'The Protestant Funeral Sermon in England, 1688–1800', in *Handbook of the British Sermon*, pp. 322–37. For a small case study of manuscript nonconformist funeral sermons, see Don Gilbert, 'A Worcestershire Sermon-Book of 1751–1802', *Journal of the United Reformed History Society*, 7, 2 (2003), pp. 108–13.

[65] e.g. Joseph Stennett, *The Rest of the People of God. A Funeral Sermon Occasion'd by the Death of the Reverend Mr. John Piggott, Late Minister of the Gospel* (London, 1713), pp. 3–4.

[66] Cf. Pritchard, 'The Protestant Funeral Sermon', esp. p. 326.

[67] Alan Ruston discusses funeral sermons of lay people as well as ministers in *Those Eighteenth-Century Divines: Writing for the New Dictionary of National Biography* (London, 2001), pp. 5–7.

DOCTRINE

Speaking thus from the grave, as it were, through a pre-selected text of his choice, the deceased minister could continue to preach 'the sacred Doctrine he so often inculcated on [the] Minds'[68] of his congregation. Indeed, doctrinal matters were common sermon topics among Dissenters, and more widespread than in the established church.[69] Unsurprisingly, some Nonconformists discoursed on the core tenets of Protestant theology. They discussed justification by faith and the small number of the elect. Several eminent nonconformist ministers delivered lectures at Salters' Hall in order to refute Roman Catholic beliefs,[70] criticizing transubstantiation frequently.[71] Anti-Catholic polemic was widespread, not only in doctrinal sermons, but also in the political discourse of the nonconformist pulpit. However, a sense that the 'danger of Popery' had 'much diminished' in Britain since the seventeenth century evolved slowly, even though it was necessary for Dissenters to remain on their guard 'against its propagation and increase'.[72]

Eighteenth-century Dissenting sermons also reflected contemporary issues. In two Salters' Hall lectures, the Presbyterian William Harris[73] argued against the religious controversialist Thomas Woolston's best-selling *Discourse of Miracles* in the very Lockean terms of the *Reasonableness of Believing in Christ*.[74] Likewise, the General Baptist James Foster's approach to the issue of the relationship between 'natural' and 'revealed' religion was more typical of the age of the Enlightenment than of Calvinist theology. Like many of his Anglican colleagues, this very popular preacher[75] argued that reason and revelation 'are so far from representing things in *opposite* views, and *disagreeing* colours, that they add *a lustre* to each other'.[76]

---

[68] Stennett, *The Rest of the People of God*, pp. 4–5.

[69] Deconinck-Brossard, 'Eighteenth-Century Sermons', pp. 110–11, esp. figure 3A.

[70] Jabez Earle, *The Popish Doctrine of Purgatory Repugnant to the Scripture Account of Remission through the Blood of Christ* (London, 1735).

[71] George Benson, 'The absurd nature of transubtantiation', and 'The terrible consequences of transubstantiation', respectively nos. VII and VIII in *Sermons on the Following Subjects* (London, 1748), pp. 171–98 and 199–219.

[72] Towers, *The Professors of the Gospel*, p. 21; cf. J. Bennett, *Memoirs of the Life of the Rev. David Bogue, D. D.* (London, 1827), p. 156, quoted in David M. Thompson, *Denominationalism and Dissent, 1795–1835: A Question of Identity* (London, 1985), p. 10.

[73] Alan Ruston, 'Harris, William (1675–1740)', *ODNB*, Oxford University Press, 2004; online edn, May 2009 [http://www.oxforddnb.com/view/article/12425, accessed 10 Aug. 2016].

[74] William Harris, *The Reasonableness of Believing in Christ, and the Unreasonableness of Infidelity* (London, 1729).

[75] Leslie Stephen, 'Foster, James (1697–1753)', rev. Jim Benedict, *ODNB*, Oxford University Press, 2004; online edn, Jan. 2008 [http://www.oxforddnb.com/view/article/9958, accessed 10 Aug. 2016].

[76] James Foster, 'Of the Distinct Offices and Uses of Reason and Revelation', sermon IV in *Sermons on the Following Subjects*, vol. 4 (London, 1744), p. 76.

The Presbyterian minister Henry Grove, who had read Locke and Le Clerc in his formative years at Taunton Academy,[77] and later preached on the 'reasonableness of religion',[78] derived 'from a close and critical study of the *scriptures*' the idea that revelation complemented reason.[79] Given the Protestant principle of *sola scriptura*, it should come as no surprise that Dissenting preachers emphasized the authority of the Bible. It took the Presbyterian historian Edmund Calamy no fewer than fourteen lectures at Salters' Hall to discuss the inspiration of holy writ.[80] As for James Foster, he devoted a whole sermon to methods of reading Scripture 'profitably'.[81] All neoclassical sermons, of whatever denomination, were naturally based on intertextuality, since preachers usually built their discourses on an introductory Biblical verse. Particularly representative features of nonconformist preachers' choice of 'text' include the prevalence of New Testament quotations, the insistence on wisdom literature, and the fondness for Pauline epistles.[82] In order to contextualize the epigraph, develop the doctrinal points that derived from it, and enforce the duties that followed, preachers usually supported their argument with further Scripture quotations, usually printed in italics, and documented with precise references in the margins or in footnotes.

AUDIENCE, PUBLICATION, AND READERSHIP

Outside the captive audience of Dissenting congregations, a rare instance of corporate attendance was 'the Weavers company upon their anniversary day for chusing a Master',[83] whom the nonconformist minister Thomas Emlyn addressed at Dublin on 1 May 1700. The sermon was published posthumously in the preacher's collected *Works* forty-two years later—an interesting, and rather extreme, example of delayed pulpit publication. Going to press was never guaranteed. In this instance, the Weavers perhaps refrained from

---

[77] *Sermons and Tracts: Being the Posthumous Works of the Late Reverend Mr. Henry Grove, of Taunton*, ed. Thomas Amory (London, 1740), vol. 1, p. xiv; cf. Mark Burden, 'A Biographical Dictionary of Tutors at the Dissenters' Private Academies, 1660–1729', Dr Williams's Centre for Dissenting Studies (2013), http://www.qmulreligionandliterature.co.uk/online-publications/a-biographical-dictionary/ [accessed 29 Apr. 2016], p. 235.

[78] Grove, sermon I in *Sermons and Tracts*, I, pp. 1–39.

[79] Grove, *Sermons and Tracts*, I, p. xxiii.

[80] Edmund Calamy, *The Inspiration of the Holy Writings of the Old and New Testament Consider'd and Improv'd* (London, 1710).

[81] Foster, 'Rules for the profitable reading of the Holy Scriptures', no. X in *Sermons on the Following Subjects*, II (London, 1735), pp. 160–78.

[82] Françoise Deconinck-Brossard, 'Patterns of Preaching among Eighteenth-Century Dissenters', *Journal of the United Reformed Church History Society*, 6, 1 (1997), pp. 5–16 (here p. 10).

[83] 'Diligence the likeliest way to rise in the world', sermon IX in *The Works of Mr. Thomas Emlyn*, 3 vols. (London, 1742; 4th edn, 1746), III, p. 179n.

sponsoring print on account of the author's dismissal from the ministry for heresy. Though he held Unitarian views, Emlyn claimed that he never preached Unitarianism.[84] Indeed, his discourse on Proverbs 22:29 only illustrated the prevailing work ethic. He advised weavers to 'hate idleness', and use their hard-earned money to employ, or if necessary relieve, the industrious poor. The editor found it necessary to footnote the preacher's brief allusion to English laws prohibiting the exportation of Irish textiles.[85]

Another unusual audience consisted of those imprisoned for debt, whom James Anderson addressed in the wake of the passing of the 'insolvent debtors relief act' (10 Geo.2 c.26). The preacher dedicated his publication to Robert Walpole, and used the opportunity to ask his listeners to pray for the king, '*the kind and happy* FATHER *of a dutiful and affectionate People, the* DEFENDER *of the Protestant-Christian Faith, and the* DELIVERER *of the Oppress'd and Distress'd*'.[86] Like many other sermons, it was supposedly printed 'at the request' of the hearers, but one may wonder how insolvent debtors could afford to sponsor such a publication.

Private sponsoring was not the only possible source of funding for printing sermons. Preachers who could not, or would not, resort to the financial support of wealthy individuals could publish volumes by subscription. Thus, a collection of sermons by Joseph Morris, 'minister of the gospel in London',[87] began with a list of 655 subscribers.[88] Even though one example cannot be statistically significant, it can shed some light on the readership of printed Dissenting sermons. Not surprisingly, the purchasers of this volume were predominantly male. A small minority were described as 'gentlemen' (1.98 per cent) or 'esquires' (2.13 per cent). The occupations of approximately one in five subscribers were specified. They included seven merchants, two wholesale linen drapers, three ironmongers, as well as craftsmen (a tanner, an engraver, and a cabinet maker), and tradesmen (three mercers, a grocer, and a printseller). The medical world was represented by six surgeons, one physician, and

---

[84] Alexander Gordon, 'Emlyn, Thomas (1663-1741)', rev. H. J. McLachlan, *ODNB*, Oxford University Press, 2004 [http://www.oxforddnb.com/view/article/8793, accessed 10 Aug. 2016].

[85] Emlyn, *Works*, III, p. 196n.

[86] James Anderson, *The Lord Looseth the Prisoners: A Sermon Preach'd in Prujean Court Old Bailey, London; on Sunday the 3d of July 1737. To the Prisoners for Debt that Reside in the Rules of the Fleet-Prison, On Occasion Of the late Act of Parliament for Insolvents* (London, 1737), p. 31.

[87] Letsome, *Preacher's Assistant*, II, p. 138. No relevant information has been found in the *Surman Index*, the *D & E*, or the *ODNB*. According to the *ESTC*, he lived c.1685-1755.

[88] Joseph Morris, *Sermons on the Following Subjects: Elijah's Prayer, That it Might not Rain, Considered. Wherein Charity Excels Faith and Hope. The Condemnation of Unbelievers Just. Elijah's Calling down Fire from Heaven Vindicated. The Reasons why Christians should always Rejoice. A Defence of Elisha's Curse. Faith a Reasonable Condition of Salvation. The Unbelief of the Citizens of Nazareth Unreasonable. Of God's not Giving Men Hearts to Perceive. Holiness the Design of the Gospel. Real Holiness more Excellent and Necessary than Positive Rites. Of Sins of Omission with Respect to Moral Duties. Mutual Love the Distinguishing Mark of true Christians* (London, 1743).

eleven apothecaries, and the legal professions by four 'attorney[s] at law'. By far the largest single category (11.14 per cent) consisted of ministers of religion, including at least five clergymen from the established church. A few clerics were also involved in teaching activities, and were joined by a handful of other schoolmasters, as well as a 'professor of rhetoric in Gresham College'. This last subscriber was one of two who could add 'FRS' to their names. The list also showed an interesting proportion of women (5.03 per cent). Some of these female readers subscribed at the same time as their husbands or relations; others seemed to appear on the list in their own right. Furthermore, the wide geographical distribution of the subscribers is noteworthy, even though only three-quarters of their addresses, scattered in approximately 130 distinct locations, are specified. The London area, arguably the main English centre for preaching, was naturally the location with the largest number of readers, all the more so as the author ministered there. A significant proportion of subscribers came from Lincolnshire, where the preacher perhaps had personal connections. By contrast, only one reader appeared in almost half of the other places mentioned. While only one subscriber from 'North Britain' was identified, one striking feature is the number located in Boston (4.88 per cent).

MANUSCRIPTS

Whatever their source of funding, there is no comparison between the small number of sermons that went to press and the large quantities that were preached every week. Letsome listed over seven hundred items published by approximately one hundred and fifty Dissenters between 1689 and 1753. For the same period, Cooke recorded over eighteen hundred items, as well as over two thousand for the next three decades, which underlines the sharp increase in the publication of Dissenting sermons in the latter half of the century.[89] Even the 3,676 discourses identified by the *English Short Title Catalogue* as being published by London preachers of all denominations in the first six decades of the eighteenth century[90] do not compare with the large contemporary output. At the rate of two sermons every Sunday, not to mention weekly lectures—a Dissenting specificity—and special occasions, almost fifteen thousand would have been heard in any preaching venue during the period under review, and the figure would of course need to be multiplied by the number of pulpits. Scholars have therefore now begun to recognize that

---

[89] Deconinck-Brossard, 'Eighteenth-Century Sermons', pp. 108–9, esp. figure 2; Farooq, *Preaching*, p. 61.
[90] Farooq, *Preaching*, p. 40, n. 3.

manuscript records complement printed sermons.[91] The evidence comes from a variety of sources. Sermon outlines, drafts, and fair copies written by preachers document the view from the pulpit, whereas diaries, correspondence, or other notes taken by hearers enable historians to glimpse the response from the pew.

It was not unusual for preachers to number their sermons consecutively, and write fair copies into small booklets that would be easily carried into the pulpit. The format also made it easy to archive them for future use. Like their Anglican counterparts, many Dissenting preachers were wont to deliver the same sermon several times, either in different venues or at the same place over the years.[92] They often recorded the dates and places of preaching on the title page of each discourse.[93] The evidence to be drawn from the notes of Peter Emans on his collection of forty-six sermons preached in at least forty-two different venues between July 1757 (when he had just finished his course at Mile End Academy) and May 1775 shows that on average he repeated them approximately seven times each,[94] which seems to reflect standard practice.[95] Some sermons were recycled more often than others, perhaps as a result of a process of trial and error. Lack of documentary evidence often makes it difficult to know whether they were more popular with the preacher or with the congregation or both. Emans's favourite texts suggest that this preacher, who began his career as an Independent and later ministered to Unitarian congregations,[96] was particularly fond of drawing the 'practical' applications of Pauline epistles and wisdom literature.[97] Sixteen sermon manuscripts[98] by the Devon minister John Kiddel(l) or Kiddle (1720–1810), who, like many

---

[91] Ian M. Green, *Continuity and Change in Protestant Preaching in Early Modern England* (London, 2009); John Spurr, *The Laity and Preaching in Post-Reformation England* (London, 2013); Farooq, esp. 'The nature of preaching in London: Manuscript versus printed sermons', *Preaching*, pp. 144–9.
For the period up to 1715, see the *Gateway to Early Modern Manuscript Sermons* (hereafter *GEMMS*) project: http://www.gemmsproject.blogspot.fr/search/label/Database [accessed 9 Mar. 2016].

[92] One striking example in the Church of England is John Sharp (1723–1792), vicar of Hartburn, prebendary of Durham, and archdeacon of Northumberland, who repeated approximately forty-five manuscript sermons in the course of a forty-three-year ministry.

[93] One only needs to remember parson Yorick's comments on his sermons to realize how common it was for eighteenth-century preachers of all denominations to 'chronicle the time, the place, and the occasion of [their] being preached': Laurence Sterne, *The Life and Opinions of Tristram Shandy, Gentleman*, ed. Melvyn New and Joan New (Gainesville, 1978), pp. 513–14.

[94] DWL MS 28.53. The catalogue of DWL manuscripts is less precise: 'composed in the 1750's and 1760's [sic] and preached in a variety of places': http://dwlib.co.uk.gridhosted.co.uk/wp-content/uploads/2013/10/DWL-MSS-ALL.pdf [accessed 4 Apr. 2016], p. 80.

[95] In a sample of approximately four hundred manuscript sermons of all denominations, Farooq has found that over half were preached multiple times, 'most frequently five or more times': *Preaching*, p. 145.

[96] *Surman Index* id: 8805; *D & E* person id: 6245.

[97] For a more detailed analysis, see Deconinck-Brossard, 'Patterns of Preaching', pp. 14–15.

[98] DWL MS 28.52 (1–16).

Presbyterian ministers, ended his career as a Unitarian,[99] were reused less extensively; they display the same taste for wisdom literature; hence, probably, the emphasis on 'practical' subjects. Similarly, Joseph Towers read six manuscript sermons twenty-nine times,[100] a typical average of five preachments per discourse. However, two sermons composed in the last two years of Towers's career were only used once. Perhaps the opportunity to recycle them never arose before his death. His declining health might have made him choose to discourse on Ecclesiastes 9:10 on New Year's Day 1797, when he commented on the shortness of human life. In this context, he insisted on his favourite theme, the need to practise both 'piety and virtue'.[101] The unorthodox emphasis on good works shows that the preacher shared his contemporaries' outlook on poor relief. Many a charity sermon, of whatever denomination, conveyed the idea that the interdependence of rich and poor implied that the former had a moral duty to assist the deserving poor:

> As all men in society partake of its benefits, every individual in it should contribute somewhat to the common good. The man of opulence derives great advantage from the labours of others...and, as he necessarily enjoys much leisure, he ought to employ a part of that, as well as of his fortune, in promoting the interests of his country, in assisting the indigent & unhappy, in being the patron of the poor, & the friend of merit.[102]

Towers even went so far as to suggest that his congregation should 'distinguish [themselves] by a benevolence at once active & extensive'.[103] The recurrent idea is in keeping with the main theme of a charity sermon published earlier by the same preacher. With a self-righteous attitude of superiority, Towers recommended that those 'who make a serious profession of Religion'[104] endeavour to 'distinguish [themselves] from those around [them]',[105] in a country where the Gospel is only 'externally professed',[106] by better 'piety and virtue'.[107]

IMPROVISATION AND SHORTHAND

One feature that often distinguished Dissenting preachers from their Anglican contemporaries was the tradition of extemporization, which leaves fewer traces for the historian than complete scripts. For instance, the surviving record for two of Philip Doddridge's unpublished sermons are brief shorthand

---

[99] *Surman Index* id: 31054; *D & E* person id: 1488. [100] DWL MS 28.14 (1–6).
[101] DWL MS 28.14 (2).   [102] Ibid., pp. 42–4.   [103] DWL MS 28.14 (4), p. 67.
[104] Towers, *The Professors of the Gospel*, p. 10.   [105] Ibid., p. 3.
[106] Ibid., p. 10.   [107] Ibid., p. 3.

outlines.[108] The famous Independent preacher[109] would have only carried a small single sheet of paper folded into two (approximately 10 cm × 15.8 cm) into the pulpit. At the top of the page, the title, sermon number, and reference of the Biblical epigraph are written in longhand, as well as the references of other Scripture texts quoted in the body of the discourse, and the place and date of delivery at the end of the sermon. The rest is a simple outline, with only the introduction, the list of 'heads' or main points, and the conclusion written in neat shorthand characters (approximately 1 mm high). This kind of detailed plan would help structure improvised speech, and the beauty of the characters suggests a high degree of preparedness. For many of Doddridge's fellow ministers, preaching from notes, far from being 'extempore effusions',[110] often resulted from careful preliminary study. In this respect, Quakers differed from other Dissenting denominations, since they believed that preaching should be completely improvised without any form of preparation.[111] Only one preaching occurrence is recorded for each of the two above-mentioned shorthand outlines by Doddridge, respectively on 7 October 1739 and on 5 November 1750, so it is reasonable to imagine that they were less general than oft-recycled discourses. They are identified as numbers '775' and '1424', which suggests that in the eleven-year interval he delivered more than six hundred distinct sermons, whereas a repertoire of approximately fifty compositions was enough for those preachers who did not scruple to repeat their sermons multiple times every year.

Shorthand notes were not always synonymous with improvisation, however. In the same archive of Doddridge papers, another item seems to be a full script, of what may have been Doddridge's last sermon in England, preached at Northampton on 14 April 1751, and repeated a few weeks later in Isaac Watts's meeting house.[112] Admittedly, a posthumous longhand transcript states in an 'Advertisement' that it was 'more fully written than usual'.[113]

Neither was preaching from shorthand distinctive to nonconformist preaching. The eminent Anglican ecclesiastical family of the Sharps were 'a dynasty of shorthanders'.[114] Thomas Sharp senior advised his son John to

---

[108] 'N° 775 Christ Servants not left orphans on Jn XIV.18', and 'N° 1424 Of returning back into Egypt', DWL MS 24.179 (5–6).

[109] Isabel Rivers, 'Doddridge, Philip (1702–1751)', *ODNB*, Oxford University Press, 2004; online edn, Oct. 2009 [http://www.oxforddnb.com/view/article/7746, accessed 10 Aug. 2016].

[110] Nathaniel Lardner, *A Sermon Preached at Pinners-Hall, On Occasion of the Death of the Late Learned and Reverend Jeremiah Hunt, D.D. Who Departed this Life Sept. 5. 1744. in the 67. Year of his Age* (London, 1744), p. 35.

[111] Farooq, *Preaching*, p. 10, n. 34.   [112] DWL MS 24.179 (7).

[113] DWL MS 24.179 (9), n.p.

[114] Timothy Underhill, 'John Byrom and Shorthand in Early Eighteenth-Century Cambridge', *Transactions of the Cambridge Bibliographical Society*, 15, 2 (2013), p. 233. I am grateful to the author for sending me an excerpt from a draft of this article before its publication.

'make constant use of' shorthand and 'preach from it'.[115] The stenography may have been different: Doddridge and many Dissenting academies recommended Rich,[116] the Sharps used Shelton,[117] and the Wesleys used Byrom, but the approach was similar.

Some Dissenters shifted from one preaching style to another at different stages of their careers or when they addressed different congregations. Thus, when the Presbyterian minister John Abernethy (1680–1740), who had a great gift for improvisation,[118] moved to Dublin, he adopted the method of writing 'all his sermons at full length, all legible', according to his biographer, and 'composed one almost every week'.[119] Much of the prescriptive literature about the art of preaching, both Anglican and Dissenting, explained that it was easier to improvise in smaller locations than in large towns or cities.[120]

Shorthand was useful, not only for ministers to prepare their sermons, but also for members of the congregation to record what they heard. Ministerial students in the Dissenting academies were expected to give a faithful account of what they had heard on Sundays.[121] This exercise played a significant part in the training of future preachers. It helped them to assess quality, and thus develop their critical spirit, as well as find homiletic examples to imitate and devotional material to reflect on. Some of the manuscripts that have survived look like notes that were taken on the spur of the moment. The size and shape of his oblong duodecimo flip top[122] notepad, much like a modern-day reporter's notebook, probably helped Joshua Sager, an Independent student at Richard Frankland's Academy in the 1680s,[123] write down the outlines of

---

[115] Thomas Sharp to his son John, 22 Nov. 1748, Northumberland Archives NRO 00452/C/3/2/1/1. This, and several other manuscript letters of advice from Thomas Sharp to his son lately entered into orders, form the groundwork for the prescriptive *Discourses on Preaching, or Directions towards Attaining the Best Manner of Discharging the Duties of the Pulpit: Delivered in Three Visitation Charges*, published almost ten years later (London, 1757; 3rd edn, 1787).

[116] Françoise Deconinck-Brossard, 'La sténographie de Philip Doddridge (1702-1751)', *XVII-XVIII: Bulletin de la Société d'Études anglo-américaines des XVIIè et XVIIIè siècles*, 12 (June 1981), pp. 29–43, http://www.persee.fr/web/revues/home/prescript/article/xvii_0291-3798_1981_num_12_1_1874 [accessed 9 Mar. 2016].

[117] Underhill, 'John Byrom', p. 234.

[118] M. A. Stewart, 'Abernethy, John (1680–1740)', *ODNB*, Oxford University Press, 2004 [http://www.oxforddnb.com/view/article/48, accessed 10 Aug. 2016].

[119] John Abernethy, *Sermons on Various Subjects*, ed. James Duchal (3rd edn, London, 1762), p. lxxviii.

[120] For instance, 'Lectures on Preaching, and the Several Branches of the Ministerial Office', in *The Works of the Rev. P. Doddridge*, ed. Edward Williams and Edward Parsons (Leeds, 1802–5), V, pp. 464–5. See my chapter on 'The Art of Preaching', in *Preaching, Sermon and Cultural Change in the Long Eighteenth Century*, ed. Joris van Eijnatten (Leiden, 2009), pp. 95–130 (here 118–19).

[121] The following paragraph draws on the chapter on 'Preaching and Practical Divinity' by Tessa Whitehouse and Françoise Deconinck-Brossard, to be published in *A History of the Dissenting Academies in the British Isles, 1660–1860*, ed. Isabel Rivers (Cambridge, forthcoming).

[122] The phrase is borrowed from Spurr, *Laity and Preaching*, p. 17.

[123] D & E person id: 2208.

discourses delivered by visiting preachers.[124] However, many other sermon notes that have survived, even when they are in shorthand, seem to be too tidy to have been written in haste. They probably result from the second stage of the exercise, which consisted in transcribing the notes and 'Writing 'em Down orderly', as John Collett Ryland, a student at Bristol Baptist College in the 1740s, noted.[125] The process could be time-consuming. Thus, it may have taken two years for the sermons preached in 1732 by the Congregationalist minister Robert Bragge to be 'newly transcribed into longhand'.[126]

SERMON NOTES

Whether in shorthand or longhand, writing sermon notes was also common practice among the laity. One of the simplest records is the diary of sermon attendance that is to be found in the commonplace book of Richard Livett, perhaps a Bedfordshire farmer, who listed the sermons he heard between January 1736 and December 1745.[127] He noted the Biblical epigraphs, the dates of the sermons, the places where they were preached, the names of the preachers, and a few memoranda. Livett does not seem to have been a very regular churchgoer, especially in the earlier years of the diary, before what is likely to have been an experience of conversion. Agricultural work may have kept him too busy in summer. When he did go to church, he typically attended two sermons on the same day, morning and evening. He heard fifty preachers in twenty-three different places over a decade. Most were Independents, but the diarist was also acquainted with several Baptists, and on two occasions he went to listen to George Whitefield who was visiting the area—an interesting conjunction of Old Dissent with nascent Methodism. Each minister was identified by a remark about the place that he served. Similarly, meeting houses were often referred to by the minister's name, with an interesting possessive case, rather than their location. Thus, Emans recorded preaching at 'Dr Fordyce's', 'Mr Kippis's', or 'Revd Mr Thompson's', inter alia.[128] Livett almost always travelled some distance to hear sermons. His diary also provides evidence of some itinerancy among preachers.

---

[124] Joshua Sager (elsewhere 'Sagar'), 'Sermon notes', BL Add MS 54185.
[125] John Collett Ryland, Regent's Park College, Oxford, Angus Library, 6.e.27(1), n.p. *D & E* person id: 181.
[126] DWL MS 24.33, verso of title page.
[127] DWL MS 24.64. The end of this paragraph borrows heavily from my detailed analysis in 'Patterns of Preaching', esp. pp. 5–11.
[128] DWL MS 28.53(2), respectively fos. 46v (01/02/1761), 145v (06/05/1764), and 187v (20/11/1757).

Another, more detailed, example of a layman's record of sermon attendance was kept by a Mr Marriot, a writer of the repertories at Guildhall, between 13 April 1701 and 11 February 1704.[129] The duodecimo diary began when the congregation to whom the English Presbyterian John Shower ministered[130] moved to new premises in the Old Jewry. The first entry suggests that one of the purposes of writing down notes was to memorize sermons for devotional purposes: 'How many good Sermons have I heard in ye old place, how few did I mind and how much fewer do I remember.'[131] Unlike Livett, Marriot commented on the sermons he attended. For instance, he heard Shower preach 'a pleasing Sermon' on 11 January 1702.[132] Marriot probably shared with his contemporaries the taste for a plain preaching style that had been initiated by the Puritans, then advocated by Dissenters and Anglicans alike after the Restoration. He noted on 13 September 1701 that Shower gave 'a very good plane' sermon.[133] However, Marriot disliked extreme plainness. Another preacher, 'Mr Flow', had delivered a sermon that was 'very plain, I think too plain for such an Auditory'.[134] He thus agreed with many *artes prædicandi* on the commonplace, and common sense, idea that the preacher should adjust his style to the abilities of the congregation. Given the reluctance to celebrate Christmas that Nonconformists sometimes inherited from their puritan forebears, it is interesting to notice that on Christmas Day 1701, Marriot found Shower's sermon 'suiteable'.[135] By contrast, Livett did not record any Christmas sermon for 1736, 1737, 1739, or 1743.[136] Like Livett and many other 'sermon-tasters',[137] Marriot visited several places of worship in order to hear other ministers preach: 'In ye Afternoon I was led by curiosity to go hear Mr Robinson... who preacht from 4. Philip^s.6^v. ye first part of ye verse.'[138] Preachers catered for the same congregation for many years, and occasionally paid visits to neighbouring communities: 'In ye Morning I went to Mr Stretton's here I heard Mr Allaxander on 2 Peter. 3. 14.'[139] This suggests that there was great stability in nonconformist pulpits, as well as a kind of preaching network among Dissenting denominations. Quakers were perhaps the exception to the rule.[140] When Marriot attended a Quaker meeting, he was disappointed because the preacher whom he had expected to hear remained silent.[141]

---

[129] BL Add MS 22490.

[130] *D & E* person id: 1165; M. J. Mercer, 'Shower, John (*bap.* 1657, *d.* 1715)', *ODNB*, Oxford University Press, 2004 [http://www.oxforddnb.com/view/article/25472, accessed 10 Aug. 2016].

[131] BL Add MS 22490, 13 April 1701, fo. 3r.

[132] Ibid., fo. 3r.   [133] Ibid., fo. 20r.   [134] BL Add MS 22490, 8 June 1701, fo. 8r.

[135] Ibid., fo. 23r.   [136] Deconinck-Brossard, 'Patterns of Preaching', p. 6.

[137] The word is used *passim* by Farooq.   [138] BL Add MS 22490, 27 Apr. 1701, fo. 4r.

[139] Ibid., 29 June 1701, fo. 10r.

[140] On eighteenth-century Quaker sermons, see Michael Graves, 'The British Quaker Sermon, 1689–1901', in *Oxford Handbook of the British Sermon*, esp. pp. 106–8.

[141] BL Add MS 22490, fo. 23r.

Marriot's judgement on the quality of what he heard was not the aesthetic or literary performance, but rather the effect that the discourse had on his own emotions. One recurring phrase in his journal is whether, how, or how long he 'was affected' by what had been preached. Whether the Biblical epigraph, or indeed the sermon, was repeated, did not matter so much as the emotional response that it triggered: 'Mr Shower preacht another anual sermon to yong People on ye last year's Text [Prov. 3.15, 16, 17.] which I heard and liked as well as his... sermon last year on ye Text, but I was not so much nor so long affected with it.'[142] This is in keeping with the 'affectionate' strain of Old Dissent, that emphasized the rhetoric of the 'passions'.[143] However, even 'a very serious affecting sermon' by Shower, who had the reputation of being an emotional preacher,[144] was no guarantee that the diarist would be 'much affected'.[145] Sometimes circumstances like the 'uneavenness' of the preacher's voice[146] or extreme weather conditions[147] prevented Marriot from heeding the words of the minister. However, 'the best sermon' that he heard 'made [him] greatly in love w^{ith} the preacher, but especially with his Doctrine'.[148] The diarist then summarized the main doctrinal point and explained what its effect consisted in: 'The happiness of being related to God was so extraordinarily illustrated and set forth by him as made me in reality to wish it was [sic] my Condition.'[149] Unfortunately those remarkable illustrations are lost for ever, and the brief summary makes it difficult for the historian to understand the appeal of that particular sermon: 'None of ye sermons here recorded had so great an Effect on me as this.'[150]

Marriot's comments on the preachers' 'spirituality'[151] or 'divinity'[152] as much as on their 'ingenuity'[153] convey the same approach as what is exemplified in several calligraphed sermon books compiled by lay hearers. Sometimes the discourse was transcribed verbatim,[154] sometimes it was summarized so that only the 'substance' was copied. When the outline of the discourse is highlighted in black letter and in bold or larger characters, or the 'heads' numbered consecutively in the left-hand margin,[155] the layout visually emphasizes the standard tripartite sermon structure, very similar to the outline of printed sermons. The preacher began with a critical examination of the Biblical epigraph or 'text', then expounded the 'doctrine' that could be derived from it, and concluded with

---

[142] Ibid., 4 May 1701, fo. 4r. [143] Rivers, *Reason, Grace, and Sentiment*, I, pp. 188–96.
[144] Mercer, 'Shower'. [145] BL Add MS 22490, 28 Dec. 1701, fo. 23r.
[146] Ibid., 27 Apr. 1701, fo. 4r. [147] Ibid., 29 June 1701, fo. 10r.
[148] Ibid., 29 June 1701, fo. 12r. [149] Ibid., 29 June 1701, fo. 12r.
[150] Ibid., 29 June 1701, fo. 12r. [151] Ibid., 27 Apr. 1701, fo. 4r.
[152] Ibid., 27 Apr. 1701, fo. 4r. [153] Ibid., 27 Apr. 1701, fo. 4r.
[154] For instance, 'Sermons transcribed by Eliz. Cooke', in beautiful copperplate handwriting within a frame delineated by red ink margins, DWL shelfmark: NCL L. 6/6–7.
[155] See, for example, the book of sermon notes written by Benjamin Coles and his homonymous son, DWL MS 28.13.

the 'application' enforcing the moral duties that ensued. In the quarto leather-bound manuscript volume containing notes on sermons preached by Robert Bragge, one discourse on Philippians 1:21 ends thus:

> One word by way of **Application** & so I have done.
> You have heard under 12. Heads What it is 𝕿𝖔 𝕷𝖎𝖛𝖊 𝖙𝖔 𝖃. We therefore y^t believe, should not only Lament our Living so long in Sin, but our Living so long to our selves as we did all of us during ye days of our Unregeneracy Not only were you serving divers Lusts & pleasures then, but your serving Carnal Corrupt Self Should be matter of Humiliation to you. This Opens into a very large prospect of Shame & Sorrow.[156]

Twelve 'heads' would have been an unusually long number of points, even in a Dissenting pulpit. The minister was dubbed 'eternal Bragge' in a contemporary poem, alluding to his exhaustive preaching style. He was reported to have spent four months developing the mysteries of Joseph's coat (Genesis 37:3).[157] Delivering a series of sermons on the same text was, however, far from unusual. Between 4 June and 6 August 1732 he preached ten times on the beginning of Philippians 1:21, 'For me to live is Christ'.[158] The practice of preaching several sermons on a single Scripture quotation is much more widespread in manuscript sources than in print, and more common among Dissenters than Anglicans; the number of discourses in each series tends to be smaller in Anglican than nonconformist pulpits.[159] Each sermon was both a separate unit, and part of the larger composite entity. Therefore it made sense to bind them in the same volume, as in the case of Bragge's sermons 'on ye awefull Subject of Death'.[160] Furthermore, a series allowed the preacher to build up a lasting relationship with the congregation of regular attenders. Ministers or compilers of sermon notes frequently advertised future subjects or epigraphs, as in the calligraphed last page of Bragge's sermons (Fig. 16.1):

> 𝕴𝖋 **God** spare life, I design ye Next Oppor-
> tunity to take for my text, One half of
> as famous a Chapter as any in the
> New testament, 𝖆𝖓𝖉 therefore I
> wish you would all of you
> bring yor Bibles along wth
> you. its half such a
> chapter as deserves
> diligently to be
> Enquired
> into
> [.][161]

---

[156] DWL MS 24.33, p. 18.
[157] Walter Wilson, *The History and Antiquities of Dissenting Churches and Meeting Houses in London, Westminster, and Southwark*, 4 vols. (London, 1808), I, p. 247.
[158] DWL MS 24.33, p. 36.   [159] Farooq, *Preaching*, p. 147.
[160] DWL MS 24.33, p. 1.   [161] DWL MS 24.33, p. 350.

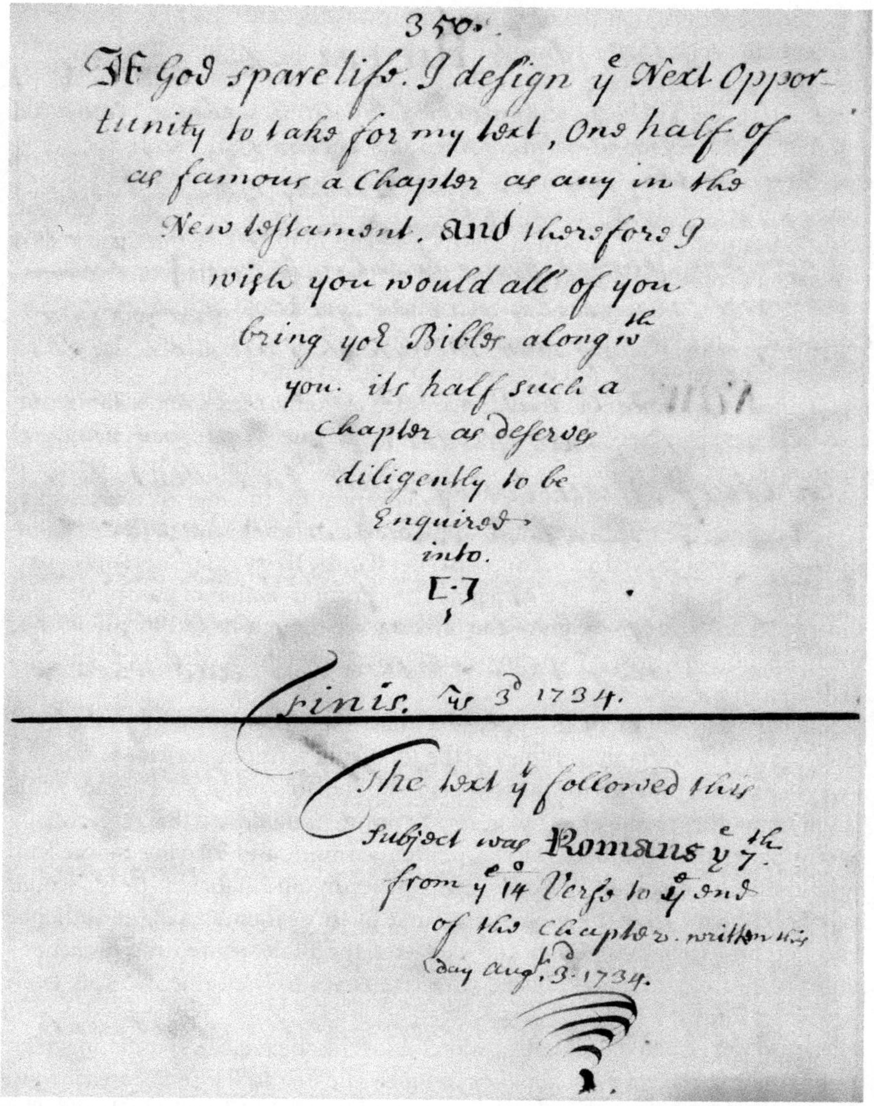

> 350.
>
> If God spare life. I design ye Next Opportunity to take for my text, One half of as famous a Chapter as any in the New Testament. and therefore I wish you would all of you bring yor Bibles along wth you. its half such a Chapter as deserves diligently to be Enquired into.
> [-]
>
> ――――――――――――――
>
> Finis. Ju 3d 1734.
>
> The text yt followed this Subject was Romans ye 7th from ye 14 Verse to ye end of this Chapter. written this day augt 3. 1734.

Fig. 16.1 'The Substance of Several Sermons Preached By ye Revd Robt Bragg<e> Minister of ye Gospel In Lime-Street London'.
© Trustees of Dr Williams's Library, London.

A footnote specifies that the text in question was the latter half of the seventh chapter of the epistle to the Romans. Choosing this unusually long epigraph from the book that has played the most significant part in the development of Protestant thought since the Reformation was a doctrinal statement. Whilst little difference may be found between Anglicans and Nonconformists for some categories of sermons (like charity sermons, as mentioned above), one major Dissenting specificity lay in some preachers' emphasis on the essentials of the Christian faith from a Reformed viewpoint. The ministers of the three major Dissenting denominations were reminded by Daniel Neal at their annual meeting in 1736 that 'the reigning Subjects of the Pulpit' should be 'the Doctrines of Christ' rather than the tenets of 'natural Religion'.[162] As a result, the word 'Christ' and its abbreviation 'X' often stand out of the manuscripts because they are highlighted by a number of visual devices such as gothic script, underlining, and bold or larger characters. Bragge and others were acutely aware that 'enlarg[ing] on the true and proper divinity of Christ' was a way of 'lifting up [the] standard against the Arians and Socinians'.[163] By contrast, by the end of the century, Towers defined the true professors of the Gospel as 'the followers of Jesus',[164] and diversely referred to God as 'the Supreme Being', 'the Deity', 'the Supreme Parent and Judge of the universe', 'the Almighty', 'the gracious Father of our spirits', and 'the great Lord and Sovereign of the universe',[165] though he did mention once 'the mediation of Christ',[166] whom he also called 'our Divine Master',[167] and 'the Divine Author of our religion'.[168]

The atypical length of his next text may explain why Bragge asked the congregation to bring their Bibles to the following sermon. Perhaps it was not always common practice for the hearers to be able to consult their Bibles while listening to the preacher. The many Scripture references that are usually intermingled with the body of the written sermon, and visually marked up by underlining or bold characters in manuscript, and italics in print, would have been identified in the spoken discourse by those members of the audience who had an extensive enough knowledge of the Bible, shared the preacher's biblical culture, and could engage with references to the same excerpts from the sacred writings.

Manuscript notebooks did not always follow the chronological order in which the sermons had been preached. For instance, the first in the series preached in 1747–8 by 'Mr Hall' on Revelation 1:5–6 is bound in the wrong order.[169] The

---

[162] Daniel Neal, 'The Wisdom of winning Souls', DWL MS 24.43, p. 15 (fo. 10r).
[163] Robert Bragge, *The Spirit's Standard Lifted up and Display'd against Error*, in *A Defence of Some Important Doctrines of the Gospel*, in *Twenty-six Sermons, Most of Which were Preached in Lime-Street. By Several Ministers* (London, 1732), p. 25.
[164] Towers, *The Professors of the Gospel*, p. 11.
[165] Ibid., respectively pp. 4, 8, 12, 17, 18, and 24.   [166] Ibid., p. 9.
[167] Ibid., p. 11.   [168] Ibid., pp. 12 and 16.   [169] DWL NCL L.6/6, p. 69.

prefaces to Bragge's sermons appear after the discourse.[170] The compilation and rearrangement of such books was a construct. Sometimes selected quotations, more akin to commonplacing than preaching, were interspersed in the collection. Thus, in the book kept by Benjamin Coles and his son,[171] 'some choice sentences' of the Independent minister Thomas Cole appear between notes on two of his sermons. In spite of the calligraphy, the flourish,[172] and decorated initials, some of the scribes do not appear to have been professional, but rather lay churchgoers who valued the sermons that they heard. The clumsy calligraphy on the title page of the notes to Bragge's sermons seems to be the work of an amateur copyist who miscalculated the amount of space necessary to write the preacher's name, and also omitted one letter, later added in superscript, in the place name on the last line.[173] The writing and binding of these volumes was truly a labour of love. However, when much time elapsed between the delivery of the sermon and its transcription, there was always a risk of inaccuracy. In his notes on a funeral sermon preached by Daniel Neal, the younger Benjamin Coles wrote out the text from Psalm 23:4 as 'though I walk throw the value of the Shadow of Death'.[174] The error may be due to the fact that most shorthand systems were consonantic.

Such elaborate books of sermon notes were obviously written in order to be kept for future reference. Re-reading them would help reiterate the effect of the discourse and memorize it. An interesting address to the implied reader of the notes on Bragge's sermons even specifies that 'wheresoever ye Reader shall find words y^t are written in a Crotchet which is marked thus [...] they were mentioned twice, & in Reading they may be twice gone over'.[175] That printed sermons do not provide evidence of such emphasis through repetition does not mean that it did not take place in the pulpit. The remark conveys an acute sense, shared by the preacher and the transcriber, of the ephemeral nature of the spoken word, and sheds light on reading practices. Neither delivering a sermon, nor reading a transcript at home, whether silently or 'in the family', were necessarily linear processes.

Of course, the transcriber was the book's first reader, but the volume may also have been intended to be circulated, thus possibly extending the preacher's audience beyond the pale of his meeting house. For instance, the 'Courteous Reader' to whom the scribe appealed in the notes on Bragge's sermons[176] might have been an outsider. Besides, the copyist only signed his/her work with his/her initials 'I:D:' in 1734, but by 1744 the book had become the property of 'Eliz. Picart'.[177] In this respect the manuscript volume may be an example of scribal publication. Like any other book, it could have a long shelf life. Emans's

---

[170] 'Some Prefaces which belong unto ye foregoing Sermons', DWL MS 24.33, p. 95.
[171] DWL MS 28.13, pp. 35–42. [172] DWL MS 28.13, fos. 1, 2, and 177v.
[173] DWL MS 24.33. [174] DWL MS 28.13, p. 70 (fo. 34r).
[175] DWL MS 24.33, p. 267. [176] Ibid., p. 212. [177] Ibid., verso of title page.

manuscript sermons, for which the last record of delivery by their author is in 1775, were preached posthumously at least five times between 1812 and 1815 at Oldbury, Shropshire, perhaps by Timothy Davis (1786–1849) who had just begun a Unitarian ministry there.[178] How Davis acquired the text is a mystery. There is no evidence that Emans ever ministered in Shropshire.[179]

Manuscripts and printed books complement and inform each other. The layout of some manuscripts imitates print. For instance, black frames copy the title pages of published funeral sermons.[180] Sometimes the volumes look as if they were designed for publication. If his collection was meant to remain for private use, why did Emans, for instance, bother to refute an accusation of plagiarism?[181] Besides, much thematic continuity is to be found between the manuscript records of numerous unpublished sermons by such preachers as Shower, Bragge, Doddridge, Emans, Towers, and their much smaller printed output. Ideally, one would dream of finding archival material that would match notes prepared by one or several preachers with notes taken by a member of the congregation, and the printed version of the same discourse. Unfortunately, so far this dream has not come true.[182]

General conclusions about the eighteenth-century Dissenting pulpit are elusive. In many cases there was no clear-cut distinction between Nonconformists and Anglicans,[183] as if genre mattered more than denomination. Many features that have been discussed in this chapter have also been documented for Anglican sermons, though sometimes with a clearly distinctive difference in emphasis. Funeral sermons reinforced among Dissenters a sense of identity supported by a culture of extemporization, shorthand notation, and scribal publication. However, the doctrinal divisions between orthodox Calvinists on the one hand, and Arians, Socinians, or Unitarians on the other hand ran through the three major nonconformist denominations, so that there was no single Dissenting voice, in spite of the denominational blurring that has already been noticed among eighteenth-century nonconformists.[184]

---

[178] *D & E* person id: 8718; George Eyre Evans, *The Registers of The Old Dissenting Chapel, Oldbury, 1715–1745, 1759–1813* (Shropshire Parish Register Society, 1903), p.v.
There is evidence of a similar feature in the Church of England. Although they were not bound in book form, some of the manuscript sermons composed by John Sharp (1723–1792) were re-used after his death, probably by Andrew Bowlt, the curate who married his niece.

[179] Once he had become a Unitarian, he was a pastor at Nottingham and Coventry. In his early career he had worked with Congregationalist congregations at Ipswich and Dorking. His surviving manuscript sermons record preachments in East Anglia, Surrey, Berkshire, Middlesex, and Kent.

[180] For example, DWL MS 28.13, fo. 168r.

[181] DWL MS 28.53 (2), fo. 173v. The accusation turns out to be well founded: see Deconinck-Brossard, 'Patterns of Preaching', pp. 14–15.

[182] Scholars researching the works of John Donne have been more fortunate. See http://www.cems-oxford.org/donne/sermons-in-manuscript-1 [accessed 30 June 2016].

[183] Farooq comes to a similar conclusion: *Preaching*, p. 177.

[184] Deconinck-Brossard, 'Patterns of Preaching', pp. 8–9.

SELECT BIBLIOGRAPHY

Deconinck-Brossard, Françoise, *Vie politique, sociale et religieuse en Grande-Bretagne d'après les sermons prêchés ou publiés dans le Nord de l'Angleterre, 1738–1760*, 2 vols. (Paris, 1984).
Farooq, Jennifer, *Preaching in Eighteenth-Century London* (Woodbridge, 2013).
Ferrell, Lori Anne and McCullough, Peter, eds, *The English Sermon Revised* (Manchester, 2000).
Francis, Keith A. and Gibson, William, eds, *The Oxford Handbook of the British Sermon 1689–1901* (Oxford, 2012).
Green, Ian M., *Continuity and Change in Protestant Preaching in Early Modern England* (London, 2009).
Hole, Robert, *Pulpits, Politics and Public Order in England 1760–1832* (Cambridge, 1989).
McCullough, Peter et al., eds, *The Oxford Handbook of the Early Modern Sermon* (Oxford, 2011).
Robinson, F. J. G. and Wallis, P. J., *Book Subscription Lists: A Revised Guide* (Newcastle, 1975).
Spurr, John, *The Laity and Preaching in Post-Reformation England* (London, 2013).
Stout, Harry S., *The New England Soul: Preaching and Religious Culture in Colonial New England* (Oxford, 1986).
Wallis, P. J., *Book Subscription Lists: Extended Supplement to the Revised Guide*, ed. Ruth Wallis (Newcastle, 1996).

Selected Online Resources

Dissenting Academies Online: Database and Encyclopedia (D & E): http://dissacad english.qmul.ac.uk/.
English Short Title Catalogue (ESTC): http://estc.bl.uk/F/?func=file&file_name=login-bl-estc.
Gateway to Early Modern Manuscript Sermons (GEMMS) project: http://www.gemmsproject.blogspot.fr/search/label/Database.
Surman Index Online: http://surman.english.qmul.ac.uk/.

17

Dissenting Hymnody

J. R. Watson

INTRODUCTION: KEACH AND STENNETT

In the turbulent religious times of the nineteenth century, Matthew Arnold deplored what he called 'the Dissidence of Dissent and the Protestantism of the Protestant religion'. In chapter one of *Culture and Anarchy* he noted it as the motto of a newspaper ('written with great sincerity and ability') entitled the *Nonconformist*, 'a life of jealousy of the Establishment, disputes, tea-meetings, openings of chapels, sermons'. He contrasted it with 'an ideal of a human life completing itself on all sides, and aspiring with all its organs after sweetness, light, and perfection.'

The urbane Arnold had forgotten, if he ever knew, the need for English Dissent to establish itself in the national life. In the years after 1662, that need was urgent and, in retrospect, much more attractive than Victorian Nonconformity. It was forged out of persecution and imprisonment, and its worship developed out of a stubborn determination. Not only did the Dissenters ask 'chiefly to be left alone to worship God in their own way',[1] but they also asserted their own identity against that of their persecutors in the years of the Clarendon Code. This gave to their hymnody an edge, a driving force that set it apart from the psalms and hymns of the Church of England, from Tate and Brady's *New Version of the Psalms of David* or Addison's hymns in *The Spectator*. Even the act of writing hymns was a deliberate assertion of independence, of difference; singing them was to risk discovery and imprisonment, even after the Declaration of Indulgence of 1672: 'as their Lord went from the supper to the garden, and from thence to the cross, so they had often left the Lord's table to appear at the magistrate's bar, and from thence be dragged to prison'.[2]

---

[1] Michael Watts, *The Dissenters: From the Reformation to the French Revolution* (Oxford, 1978), p. 2.
[2] Howard Malcolm, preface to Benjamin Keach, *Travels of True Godliness* (Boston, 1831), p. 9.

The Lord's Supper was the occasion for the earliest hymns of Benjamin Keach (1640–1704), an innovative Particular Baptist. He introduced hymn singing in his chapel at Southwark in the 1670s, at a point in the service when members of the congregation who disagreed with hymn singing could leave. Later he extended the practice to other parts of the service, and on most Sundays, and thereby caused controversy. His fellow Baptist Isaac Marlow attacked hymn singing in *A Discourse Concerning Singing* (1690), arguing that it was a distraction from the simplicity of worship. Keach responded in 1691 with *A Breach Repair'd in God's Worship*, citing David and his psalms as a precedent (as Isaac Watts and Simon Browne were to do after him). In the following year he published *The Banquetting-House, or, A Feast of Fat Things*, a major collection designed to help those who 'would gladly have a little help in order to the understanding of Metaphorical Scripture'.[3] Keach loved metaphors: he had written a huge book entitled *Tropologia, A Key to Open Scripture Metaphors* in 1681, and he saw the imaginative possibilities of figures of speech. His own application of his theory was dogged and uninspired, but their very doggedness was an example of the defiant hymnody of Dissent. From his last book, *A Feast of Fat Things full of Marrow* (1696) comes his exposition of 'Ye are the salt of the earth':

> If Saints, O Lord, do Season all
>   amongst whom they do Live,
> Salt all with Grace, both Great and Small
>   They may Sweet Relish give;
>
> And blessed be thy glorious Name,
>   in England Salt is found;
> Some Savoury Souls who do Proclaim
>   the Grace which doth abound.

There can have been no doubt in Keach's mind that the savoury souls were to be found in his chapel, and in others like it, and that the central act of worship was The Lord's Supper (as Dissenters termed it, not Holy Communion). His successor in Baptist hymn writing, Joseph Stennett (1663–1713), must have been of the same mind, for he published *Hymns in Commemoration of the Sufferings of our Blessed Saviour Jesus Christ, compos'd for the Celebration of his Holy Supper* in 1697. As the title indicates, Stennett was concerned to bring the events of the Passion before his congregation: they were to be constantly reminded of the Cross. The phrases 'The body of our Lord Jesus Christ, which was given for thee' and 'The Blood of our Lord Jesus Christ, which was shed

---

[3] Benjamin Keach, *The Banquetting-House* (London, 1692), p. 1.

for thee' were not simply part of the liturgy, but were brought before the participant in all their horror and glory:

> Remember all his Acts of Love,
>   His Torments every one:
> Whom Angels fear'd, him Mortals jeer'd,
>   Blasphem'd, and spat upon.
>
> See's Head all torn with Thorns, his Face
>   (Divinely bright before)
> Now marr'd more than the Sons of Men;
>   Reaking with Sweat and Gore.
>
> See cruel Nails in's Hands and Feet,
>   Piercing the tender Veins:
> See how each Wound the blushing Ground
>   With precious Tincture stains.
>
> See his pierc'd Side spouting out Blood
>   And Water through the Wound,...
>   (Hymn VII)

Stennett was trying, again and again, to awaken in the singers' minds the redeeming love of God in Jesus Christ, and its cost. Hymn after hymn depicted spitting in the face, bleeding wounds, and dying groans. They were designed to jolt people out of complacency, out of an unperturbed acceptance of a narrative they had heard many times before. Stennett wanted to remind them of what he called 'amazing love':

> Amazing Love! 'Tis Infinite!
>   No Thoughts its endless Depth can sound;...
>   (Hymn VI)

'Amazing love' and the adjective 'amazing' occur again and again in eighteenth-century Dissenting hymnody. Similarly, the word 'awake' was used, very often, to remind congregations not to fall asleep, either literally or (more important) metaphorically. Hogarth's engraving 'The Sleeping Congregation' of 1736 is a reminder of the former: it depicts a bewigged and cross-looking Church of England clergyman reading a sermon to a congregation that has long since become oblivious, fallen on one another's shoulders with their eyes firmly closed. The only person not asleep is the Parish Clerk, who casts lascivious eyes on the breasts of a sleeping young woman in the foreground (Fig. 17.1). Dissenting hymnody, and all aspects of a Dissenting service, were designed to keep people in a state of physical wakefulness (and, of course, of propriety); worship was a 'wake-up call', a summons to people to realize and celebrate the wonder of the saving love of Jesus Christ in his death on the Cross. Thus the Independent minister Simon Browne (1680–1732), who published *Hymns and Spiritual Songs* in 1720, had no doubts: 'Poetry enlivens praise' and 'Musick still heightens the power of Poetry, and gives it

Dissenting Hymnody 361

Fig. 17.1 'The Sleeping Congregation' (1736) William Hogarth.
Courtesy of the Lewis Walpole Library, Yale University. The polar opposite of the effect Dissenting hymns were supposed to achieve.

fresh force to engage and affect the mind.' The mind is 'most in tune for the work of praise, when its powers are in most vigorous exercise: When the thoughts are bright and intense, the passions warm, and the whole soul awake.'[4]

[4] Simon Browne, *Hymns and Spiritual Songs* (London, 1720), Preface, n.p.

ISAAC WATTS

The writings of Isaac Watts (1674–1748) were so dominant, particularly among Independents, and his influence so widespread, that he shaped the expression of Dissenting sensibility for more than a hundred years. He was educated at a Dissenting academy, having turned down the chance of going to Oxford or Cambridge: in Samuel Johnson's words, 'he declared his resolution of taking his lot with the Dissenters'.[5] Since his father had been imprisoned for his beliefs, it would surely have been unthinkable for the young Isaac to have turned Anglican. The problem was the worship. The dogged psalms and hymns of William Barton were uninspiring; as his brother Enoch wrote, 'honest Barton chimes us asleep'.[6] Wakefulness was all. There are three hymns beginning 'Awake' in *Hymns and Spiritual Songs* (1707, 1709):

'Awake my Heart, arise my Tongue' (Book I, hymn XX)
'Awake, my zeal, awake my love' (Book I, hymn XLVI)
'Awake our souls, away our fears' (Book I, hymn XLVIII).

Words such as 'awake' and 'arise' are frequently found. At one point Watts laments his own failure: 'My drowsie Powers, why sleep ye so? / Awake my Sluggish soul!' (Book II, hymn XXV). There is another opening 'Awake' in *The Psalms of David* (1719):

> Awake, ye Saints: To praise your King
> Your sweetest Passions raise;
> Your pious Pleasure, while you sing,
> Increasing with the Praise.
> (Psalm CXXXV)

Compressed into this verse are 'sweet Passions', and 'pious Pleasure', both an obvious rejection of worldly and profane activity, and also a renunciation of sinful passion and trivial pleasure that is as demanding as a discipline of a monastery. However, pleasure increases as divine worship proceeds:

> Religion never was design'd
> To make our pleasures less.
> ('Come, we that love the Lord',
> Book II, hymn XXX)

Those who are to enjoy such privileges are the saints ('Awake, ye Saints'), who are the congregation of the faithful. The Dissenting poet has here appropriated the word that was formerly used to denote those of exceptional holiness and

---

[5] Samuel Johnson, *The Lives of the Most Eminent English Poets; With Critical Observations on Their Works*, ed. Roger Lonsdale, 4 vols. (Oxford, 2006), IV, p. 105.

[6] Thomas Milner, *The Life, Times, and Correspondence of the Rev. Isaac Watts, D.D.* (London, 1845), p. 177.

sanctity, in whose name signs and wonders were performed. Now the 'Saints' are the members of the Gathered Church:

> We are a Garden wall'd around,
> Chosen, and made peculiar Ground;
> A little spot inclos'd by Grace
> Out of the World's wide Wilderness.
> (Book I, hymn LXXIV)

Donald Davie offered this as an example of Watts as 'a poet of the tribal lay': the Dissenters 'conceived themselves to be, very exactly, "a tribe", a chosen people just as ancient Israelites were chosen, in tension with their neighbours just as ancient Israel was'.[7]

The enduring appeal of his hymns for Dissenters was based precisely, for Watts was a precise man, on the threefold division of the books of *Hymns and Spiritual Songs*: 'I. Collected from the Holy Scriptures'; 'II. Composed on Divine Subjects, Conformable to the Word of God'; 'III. Prepared for the holy Ordinance of the Lord's Supper'. The first emphasizes the centrality of the Bible in worship and belief; the second allows an exploration of the soul on pilgrimage, creating what John Wesley was later, and for the same reason, to call 'a little body of experimental and practical divinity';[8] and the third draws attention, as Stennett had done, to the Lord's Supper as an act of suffering and redemption, in which the pardoned sinners were privileged to participate.

Watts's hymns were situated at the centre of Dissenting experience, and his version of *The Psalms of David*, which he regarded as his greatest work, was naturally influenced by it. I have argued elsewhere that his metrical psalms were not just Christianized, which is the avowed purpose as stated in the Preface, but shaped into a justification of Dissent.[9] Although many of the psalms are devoted to praise and prayer, there are others, especially those from 1 to 17, which are particularly concerned with the division between the godly and the ungodly. Psalm 7 was entitled 'God's Care of his People. and Punishment of Persecutors'; and Part 1 of Psalm 35 was entitled 'Prayer and Faith of Persecuted Saints; or, Imprecations mix'd with Charity'. The paraphrase of Psalm 35 allowed him to remember recent persecution, and

---

[7] Donald Davie, *A Gathered Church: The Literature of the English Dissenting Interest, 1700–1930* (London and Henley, 1978), p. 28.

[8] John Wesley, 'Preface' to Franz Hildebrandt and Oliver A. Beckerlegge, eds, *A Collection of Hymns for the Use of the People called Methodists (London, 1780): The Works of John Wesley*, Vol. 7 (Oxford, 1983), p. 74.

[9] J. R. Watson, 'The Hymns of Isaac Watts and the Tradition of Dissent', in Isabel Rivers and David L. Wykes, eds, *Dissenting Praise: Religious Dissent and the Hymn in England and Wales* (Oxford, 2011).

the men of blood, but to hope that there might be some who could be touched by grace:

> They love the Road that leads to Hell;
>   Then let the Rebels dye,
> Whose Malice is implacable
>   Against the Lord on high.
>
> But if Thou hast a chosen few
>   Amongst that impious Race,
> Divide them from the bloody Crew
> By thy surprizing Grace.

'Surprizing Grace' is a variant on the better known 'Amazing Grace'. It is a variant with a purpose: to a Dissenter the gift of grace is, or should be, a perpetual cause for astonishment. It is guaranteed to surprise, and through that surprise it continues to awake the soul.

WOMEN AND DISSENT

One of the ways in which Dissenters showed their independence and originality of thought was through their respect for women. One of the earliest women hymn writers was Elizabeth Rowe (1674–1737). She was an exact contemporary of Isaac Watts. Her father was a nonconformist minister who, like his, had been imprisoned for his beliefs; and she married Thomas Rowe, a Dissenter who died young. She wrote poems from an early age, contributing them to a periodical, *The Athenian Mercury*, edited by John Dunton (1659–1733). Dunton married Elizabeth Annesley, the daughter of the celebrated Puritan minister Samuel Annesley, ejected in 1662 from St Giles, Cripplegate; another of his daughters, Susanna, married Samuel Wesley, father of John and Charles, and became 'the mother of Methodism'. Into this circle came Elizabeth Rowe, publishing her poems under the names of 'Philomela' or 'The Pindarick Lady'. Evidently she had no wish to conceal her gender. She corresponded with Watts: in the second edition of his *Horae Lyricae* (1709), he addressed a poem to her entitled 'To Mrs. Singer. On the Sight of some of her Divine Poems Never Printed. July 19th, 1706'. Watts was extravagant in his praise, although he was clearly adopting a persona. He hears her 'Harmonious Notes':

> At once my Strings all silent lie,
> At once my fainting Muse was lost
> In the superior Sweetness drown'd.
> In vain I bid my tuneful Powers unite;
>   My Soul retir'd, and left my Tongue,
> I was all Ear, and PHILOMELA's Song
>   Was all divine Delight.

Presumably she had sent Watts some of her work in manuscript; and with others she had already published *Divine Hymns and Poems on Several Occasions... by Philomela and other ingenious persons* (1704), revised as *A Collection of Divine Hymns and Poems* (1709). Watts certainly thought highly of her work, for after her death he edited her *Devout Exercises of the Heart in Meditation and Soliloquy. Prayer and Praise* ('by the late Pious and Ingenious Mrs. Rowe') in 1738. It had a fulsome preface, extolling her virtues as woman and poet ('as her Virtues were sublime, so her Genius was bright and sparkling, and the Vivacity of her Imagination had a Tincture of the Muse almost from her Childhood', pp. xi–xii). Her work was read by Charles Wesley, who borrowed phrases from it (James Dale has demonstrated that 'Christ, whose glory fills the skies' owes much to one of her hymns, 'In vain the dusky Night retires').[10]

She may also have been an example and encouragement to Anne Steele (1716–1778), the first woman hymn writer to become widely known. While Rowe called herself 'Philomela', Steele used the name 'Theodosia'. Her *Poems on Subjects Chiefly Devotional* appeared in 1760, and featured largely in a major Baptist production, *A Collection of Hymns Adapted to Public Worship* (Bristol, 1769), edited by John Ash (1724–1779) and Caleb Evans (1737–1791). Steele was dramatic and forceful, drawing on the hymns of Watts, but injecting the language with the intensity of Joseph Stennett:

> Stretch'd on the cross the Saviour dies;
> Hark! his expiring groans arise!
> See, from his hands, his feet, his side,
> Rolls down the sacred crimson tide!

Her hymns often begin with her experience, rather than with a scriptural text, and in this she follows Watts and anticipates Wesley. Her heart is frequently invoked as the centre of her passionate love and wonder. As Watts brackets love and sorrow in 'When I survey the wondrous cross', Steele links grief and wonder, echoing Watts's 'flow mingled down':

> Can I survey this scene of woe,
> Where mingling grief and wonder flow;
> And yet my heart unmov'd remain,
> Insensible to love or pain?

This concentration on the heart, the direct engagement of the individual self with the mystery of the Passion, leads to the celebration of 'surprising grace', following Watts again. It is vividly applied to her own sinful condition:

> Dear Lord, and shall thy Spirit rest
> In such a wretched heart as mine?
> Unworthy dwelling! Glorious guest!
> Favour astonishing, divine!

---

[10] James Dale, 'Holy Larceny? Elizabeth Rowe's Poetry in Charles Wesley's Hymns', *Proceedings of the Charles Wesley Society*, 3 (1996), pp. 5–20.

To this should be added her reverence for the Bible. One of her hymns that has (just) survived into the present age is 'Father of mercies, in thy word / What endless glory shines'. This places her in the tradition of Watts's Book I, 'Collected from the Holy Scriptures', and of her younger contemporary Benjamin Beddome, whose hymns were first written to be sung after the sermon, so that the emphasis shifts from personal intimacy to public worship.

DISSENTING HYMNODY AND PUBLIC WORSHIP

Beddome (1717–1795) was a Baptist minister, who was conscious of his own status and that of his denomination. His 'Morning before Baptism; or, at the Water Side, Psalm cxix. 32' begins 'How great, how solemn is the Work, / Which we attend To-day!'. His 'Signification of Baptism' claimed the Sacrament of Believer's Baptism as being in the line of succession to the Baptism of Jesus, and as the counter to the pre-baptismal state of sin:

> Lo, this sacred institution
>   Shows the state that we are in,
> All the subjects of pollution,
>   All unholy and unclean.
>
> 'Twas the Lord the rite appointed,
>   We his precepts must fulfil,
> With our duty new acquainted,
>   Yield obedience to his will.
>
> Now we sink beneath the waters,
>   Emblem of our death to sin;
> Thence ascending, grace has taught us,
>   We our lives anew begin.

Beddome was friendly with Anne Steele (as Nancy Cho discovered, he proposed marriage to her in 1742).[11] Thirteen of his hymns appeared in Ash and Evans's 1769 book, and thirty-six in one of the most popular Dissenting worship books of the century, John Rippon's *A Selection of Hymns* of 1787, which will be discussed below (a full edition of Beddome's hymns did not appear until 1818).[12] Apart from his specifically Baptist hymns, they were clear and unpretentious, with a

---

[11] J. R. Watson and Nancy Cho, 'Anne Steele's Drowned Fiancé', *British Journal of Eighteenth-Century Studies*, 28, 1 (2005), pp. 117–21.

[12] *Hymns Adapted to Public Worship, or Family Devotion: now first published, from the manuscripts of the late B. Beddome. With a recommendatory preface by the Rev R. Hall, A.M.* (London, 1818).

Dissenter's straightforwardness, designed to follow the sermon and reinforce its text. As Horton Davies has observed, the Dissenters regarded the sermon as 'the chief regular means of grace'.[13] Thus in 'The humble Publican, Luke xviii. 13', number 236 in Rippon's *Selection*, the drama is brought out more forcefully, as the singer places himself or herself in the place of the sinner:

> Lord with a griev'd and aching Heart,
> To thee I look – to thee I cry;
> Supply my Wants, and ease my Smart,
> O help me soon, or else I die.

Beddome was the most irenic of Dissenters, perhaps because he was a generation younger than Watts, and further from the memory of persecution and imprisonment. His 'Christian Love, Gal. iii. 28' is a plea for an ecumenicity that might have been written in the late twentieth century:

> Let Party Names no more
>   The Christian World o'erspread;
> Gentile and Jew, and Bond and Free,
>   Are one in Christ their Head.
>
> Among the Saints on Earth,
>   Let mutual Love be found;
> Heirs of the same Inheritance,
>   With mutual Blessings crown'd.
>
> Let Envy, Child of Hell
>   Be banish'd far away;
> These should in strictest Friendship dwell
>   Who the same Lord obey.
>
> Thus will the Church below
>   Resemble that above,
> Where Streams of Pleasure ever flow,
>   And every Heart is Love.
>   (Rippon, *Selection of Hymns*, CCLV)

Beddome's hymns reflect a growing confidence, as Dissenters began to feel more secure. In 'Peace prayed for' (Rippon, DXXX), they suggest a link between Dissent and a prosperous economy:

> Let Peace descend with balmy Wing,
> And all its Blessings round her shed;
> Her Liberties be well secur'd,
> And Commerce lift its fainting Head.

---

[13] Horton Davies, *Worship and Theology in England from Watts and Wesley to Maurice, 1690–1850* (Princeton, NJ, 1961), p. 31.

PHILIP DODDRIDGE

By 1750 Dissenting hymns were no longer prickly with antagonism towards the established order of Church and state. This is nowhere more clearly demonstrated than in the hymns of the Independent minister Philip Doddridge (1702–1751), whose hymns, like Beddome's, were written for public worship. They were published after his death by his friend Job Orton as *Hymns Founded on Various Texts in the Holy Scriptures* (1755), containing 370 hymns. Each hymn was preceded by a scriptural text, all arranged in order of the books of the Bible, re-affirming the centrality and authority of Holy Scripture. Like his great Dissenting predecessor, John Bunyan, Doddridge saw himself and his congregation as pilgrims:

> O God of Jacob, by whose Hand
> Thine Israel still is fed,
> Who thro' this weary Pilgrimage
> Hast all our Fathers led.
> ('Jacob's Vow. Genesis xviii.
> 20–22'. Hymn IV)

This verse reminds the singer of the inheritance of the Saints, the providence of God, and the privileges of Israel. The 'Fathers' are the persecuted predecessors of Doddridge's congregation, and his people are an eighteenth-century Israel, 'in tension with their neighbours', as Davie observed. Doddridge's hymns are capable of being read on two levels: as general aspirations that are common to all Christians, and that have continued to make them useful and well known; and as expressions of the peculiar (special) grace vouchsafed to members of a Gathered Church:

> The Lord with Pleasure views his Saints,
> And calls them all his own;
> And low He bows to their Complaints,
> And pities ev'ry Groan.
>
> In all the Joys they here possess,
> He takes a tender Part;
> And, when they rise to heav'nly Bliss,
> Complacence fills his Heart.
> ('God's Complacency in the Prophecy of
> his Servants. Psalm xxxv. 27'. Hymn XXXVII)

The 'complacency', or contentment, here places God in an intimate relationship with a particular people, although they have to work hard to earn his interest. The pilgrimage may be watched over by an encouraging and benevolent figure, but it is a strenuous occupation, requiring commitment and attention:

> Awake, my Soul, stretch ev'ry Nerve
> And press with Vigour on:
> A heav'nly Race demands thy Zeal,
> And an immortal Crown.
> ('Pressing on in the Christian Race.
> Phil. iii. 12–14'. Hymn CCXCVI)

The phrase 'stretch ev'ry Nerve' is at the heart of the Dissenting experience, and so is the title of the hymn. It emphasizes not only the necessary wakefulness, but the requirement that an attentive congregation should be awake for a purpose—to stretch every nerve, to be fully alive, to be ready at all times for love and service, pressing on.

Four more hymns by Doddridge begin with the word 'Awake':

Awake, my drowsy Soul, awake ('Christian Watchfulness. Mark xiii. 37'. Hymn CXCIX)

Awake, my Soul, to meet the Day ('A Morning-HYMN, to be used at awaking and rising'. Hymn CCCLXII)

Awake, our Souls, and bless his Name ('Christ the Door. John x. 9'. Hymn CCXXVIII)

Awake, ye Saints, and raise your Eyes ('The near Approach of Salvation, an Encouragement to Diligence and Love. Rom. xiii. 11'. Hymn CCLXIV).

Although the second of these has much in common with Thomas Ken's 'Awake, my soul, and with the sun', it goes on to place a particular stress on the need for wakefulness in an age of sleep:

> The Work of each immortal Soul
> Attentive Care demands;
> Think then what painful Labours wait
> The faithful Pastor's Hands.

The mention of the pastor is rare in Doddridge's hymnody; but 'Attentive Care' recalls Bunyan's Mr Greatheart, that indefatigable conductor of souls to the Celestial City.

SELECTIONS OF HYMNS

One feature of Dissenting worship was the provision of hymnals. This was not unique to Dissent, for evangelical clergy such as Martin Madan, Richard Conyers, and Augustus Montague Toplady produced them in the 1760s and 1770s. But there were notable Dissenting collections: at first selections from Isaac Watts, and then supplements to those selections. Two Baptists, Caleb

Evans and John Ash, produced the book mentioned above, *Hymns Adapted to Public Worship* (Bristol, 1769). Beddome's hymns appeared in that selection, together with those of other Baptists such as Joseph Stennett, Daniel Turner (1710–1798), and Benjamin Wallin (1711–1782). Non-Baptists included were James Merrick, whose metrical translations of the psalms had appeared in 1765, and Philip Doddridge; but for the most part the selection was Baptist in origin and use. Anne Steele was a prominent contributor, with sixty-two hymns (the Steele family in Hampshire was friendly with the Ash and Evans families in Bristol). The 'Bristol Book', as it came to be known, went through a number of editions, including one (1801) edited by Isaac James, a Deacon at the Broadmead Church where Evans and his father had been pastors.

It was overtaken in popularity, however, by John Rippon's *A Selection of Hymns, from the best authors* (1787). Once again personal Dissenting connections can be observed: John Rippon (1751–1836) was a student at the Baptist College at Bristol, where Hugh Evans, father of Caleb, was Principal. This substantial collection contained 588 hymns, added to in successive editions, so that by 1828 there were 803 hymns. After Rippon's death there was a 'Comprehensive Rippon' of 1844 with no fewer than 1,174 hymns. Because the 1787 book was designed to supplement the hymns and psalms of Isaac Watts, there were only thirty-eight hymns by him, those that had not been used in previous collections; but there were eighty-nine by Doddridge, forty-five by Steele, and thirty-nine by Beddome. Samuel Stennett (1727–1795), grandson of Joseph, who had published *A Collection of Hymns for the use of Christians of all Denominations* in 1782, was represented by thirty-eight hymns, two of which became well known, 'Majestic sweetness sits enthroned' and 'On Jordan's stormy banks I stand'.

Rippon's *Selection* became so famous that it is sometimes forgotten that it was preceded by others. William Enfield (1741–1797), a Presbyterian, published a collection, *Hymns for Public Worship* (Warrington, 1772), which is notable for having included five hymns by Anna Letitia Barbauld (1743–1825), including 'Praise to God, immortal praise'. Enfield and Barbauld had Unitarian leanings: they were typical of a tendency towards Arianism, or 'Semi-Arianism', so-called by Horton Davies, who noted a class of 'Presbyterian-Arian ministers'.[14] They included many of the most distinguished thinkers of the century, who were Dissenters precisely because they had enquiring and independent minds. In worship, and in liturgy, they were descended from the Puritan clergy ejected in 1662; and they were true children of the Enlightenment. Dissent was their natural home.

More orthodox was an Independent collection, edited by George Burder (1752–1832), *A Collection of Hymns from Various Authors. Intended as a Supplement to Dr Watts's Hymns, and Imitations of the Psalms* (Coventry,

---

[14] Davies, *Worship and Theology in England, 1690–1850*, p. 83.

1784, with later enlarged editions up to the twenty-fifth in 1827). Burder, who went on to edit the *Works* of Watts in six volumes (1810–11), was careful to limit the collection to hymns that were not by Watts, respecting the integrity of the publications of his great predecessor. His book contained hymns by Newton and Cowper, from *Olney Hymns* (1779), and a considerable number by Charles Wesley. The Methodists were starting to influence Dissenting culture.

THE METHODISTS

Methodism began as a movement within the Church of England, but its subsequent development—field-preaching, opening its own chapels, printing its own hymn books and other material, and finally taking the decisive step, strongly opposed by Charles Wesley (1707–1788), of ordaining superintendents to minister to the newly independent Americans in 1784—led it eventually into a new identity as a Dissenting church. It was associated with hymn-singing from the very beginning, although the saying that 'Methodism was born in song' (the opening sentence of the preface to the 1933 *Methodist Hymn Book*) is an oversimplification. Methodism was born in response to the idle and worldly society of Oxford, which led to the foundation of the Holy Club, and the adoption of a discipline that led to the nickname 'Methodist'. John Wesley (1703–1791) became fully conscious of the value of hymn singing when he observed, and then joined, the Moravian missionaries on the voyage to Georgia in 1735–6. Five of his translations from the German appeared in his first hymn book, the *Collection of Psalms and Hymns* printed in Charles-Town (now Charleston), South Carolina in 1737, including twenty-one metrical psalms and forty-nine hymns, of which thirty-five were by Isaac Watts. Back in Britain, John and Charles Wesley produced books with remarkable frequency; there were also three tune books, *A Collection of Tunes, Set to Music, as they are commonly sung at the Foundery* (1742), *Select Hymns, with Tunes Annext* (1761), and *Sacred Harmony: or, a choice Collection of Psalms and Hymns set to Music* (1780).

There is evidence that the Methodists were able to sing their faith in a way that made their worship much more attractive than the 'lining out' of Church of England services, in which the parish clerk sang the line and the congregation repeated it (John Wesley had been influenced by the Moravians' 'Singstunde', the 'singing hour' in which they practised hymn singing). Throughout most of his lifetime, however, Wesley endeavoured to keep his people within the fold of the Established Church, and in his *Reasons against a Separation from the Church of England* (1760) he dissented from Dissent, in musical matters at any rate. He described Dissenters as singing 'in a slow, drawling manner', whereas 'we sing swift, both because it saves time, and because it tends to awake and enliven the soul'.[15] This throws some light on the actual singing that took place in other Dissenting chapels, as well as highlighting once again the virtue of wakefulness (and of not wasting time, an obsession with John Wesley). The hymns of the Methodists were certainly designed to enliven as well as instruct. They did so by the astonishing vigour of their language, the sheer bravado of the verse:

>Where shall my wond'ring Soul begin?
> How shall I All to Heaven aspire?
>A Slave redeem'd from Death and Sin,
> A Brand pluck'd from Eternal Fire,
>How shall I equal Triumphs raise,
>And sing my great Deliverer's Praise!
>
>O how shall I the Goodness tell,
> Father, which Thou to me hast show'd,
>That I, a Child of Wrath, and Hell,
> I should be call'd a Child of GOD!
>Should know, should feel my Sins forgiven,
>Blest with this Antepast of Heaven!

In this hymn on his 'conversion' in 1738 Charles Wesley compresses a multitude of impressions into this verse: wonder, the hope of heaven, the redeemed slave, the brand saved from the burning, the child of God; and then comes the complementary line in verse 2 to the opening: 'O how shall I?... Where shall I begin?' He is asking the question of all great poets: how do I find words to express the wonder of the originating thought?

Not only does he know this, he *feels* it: this is not an intellectual exercise but a complete response from the whole self. And finally the astonishing 'Antepast', the foretaste of heaven, comes to conclude the opening movement of the hymn. In later verses he turns outward from himself to the London of his own day, with its 'Harlots and Publicans, and Thieves' (verse 5) and its '*Magdalens in Lust*' (verse 6). Not only does this astonishing hymn produce the question: 'how can I find words for the wonder that has overcome me?' It also commits the receiver of this new birth to a life of evangelism and social justice.

Charles Wesley was a writer of such variety of subject-matter, of technique, and of acute psychological insight, that verses such as those just quoted give a partial insight only into his amazing work. He was a staunch member of the Church of England to the end of his life, refusing to be buried in the double grave at City Road chapel that John had ordered for himself and his brother, and insisting on interment at his parish church. In the context of Dissenting hymnody, however, he provided a vast corpus of hymns that followed Watts,

---

[15] Quoted in Carlton R. Young, *Music of the Heart: John & Charles Wesley on Music and Musicians* (Carol Stream, IL, 1995), p. 65.

Doddridge, and Steele in being 'experimental' (concerned with religious 'experience' of all kinds) and biblical (his *Short Hymns on Select Passages of the Holy Scriptures* of 1762 contained no fewer than 1,478 paraphrases of the Old Testament and 870 of the New). As recorded above, anthologists such as George Burder drew on his work; he brought to life, as if in a sermon, episodes such as Jacob and the angel. Isaac Watts said that 'that single poem, *Wrestling Jacob*, was worth all the verse he himself had written'.[16] We have seen Watts's tendency to praise others extravagantly in the case of Elizabeth Rowe; but there seems no reason to dispute his genuine admiration at this point, for 'Come, O Thou Traveller unknown' is one of the great religious poems of the century. Like so many of Charles Wesley's hymns, it sparks the reader or singer into wakeful attention, to hear the whisper:

> I need not tell Thee who I am,
>   My Misery, or Sin, declare,
> Thyself hast call'd me by my Name,
>   Look on Thy Hands, and read it there,
> But who, I ask Thee, who art Thou,
>   Tell me Thy Name, and tell me now?...
>
> 'Tis Love, 'tis Love! Thou diedst for Me,
>   I hear Thy Whisper in my Heart,
> The Morning breaks, the Shadows flee:
>   Pure UNIVERSAL LOVE Thou art,
> To me, to All Thy Bowels move,
>   The Nature, and Thy Name is LOVE.

These are two verses of the original fourteen; but they show something of the genius with which the encounter with the Other in the darkness is presented.

The proliferation of Wesleyan books led John Wesley to produce what became known as 'the Large Hymn Book', *A Collection of Hymns for the Use of the People called Methodists*. It has been much praised. It was even described by Bernard Manning as being comparable to Leonardo da Vinci's 'Last Supper' or King's College Chapel, Cambridge.[17] Such extravagance over-praises the book, and does not do justice to its precise but idiosyncratic arrangement. It should be remembered that many eighteenth-century collections included a multitude of hymns in no apparent order; Wesley was concerned to provide a structure in which the hymns represented, and expressed, the states of mind which a believer might be expected to go through.

It was in five parts. The first was introductory, exhorting people to 'return to God' and describing 'the pleasantness of Religion'. The second distinguished between 'formal Religion' and 'inward Religion'. The third recognized the

---

[16] John Wesley's obituary tribute to his brother, *Minutes of the Methodist Conference* (1788), p. 5, quoted in Frank Baker, *Representative Verse of Charles Wesley* (London, 1962), p. 37.
[17] Bernard Manning, *The Hymns of Wesley and Watts* (London, 1942), p. 14.

difficulties of the spiritual life, with sections on repentance, conviction of sin, backsliding, and recovery. The fourth showed believers in various states of religious activity, 'Rejoicing, Fighting, Praying, Watching, Working, Suffering, Groaning for full Redemption, Brought to the Birth, Saved, Interceding for the World'. The final section was for the Society, 'meeting, giving thanks, praying, and parting'. The first three stages of this arrangement charted a progress or spiritual pilgrimage, from a first approach to belief, through a guided perception of true and false religion, then through the difficult stages of repentance, backsliding, and recovery. The result is a hymnic version of *The Pilgrim's Progress*, Part 1, in which an individual Christian pursues his or her way from stage to stage of the religious life, learning, suffering, and being helped along the way. The two final parts are closer to Bunyan's Part 2, in which the 'Believers' (in the plural, like the group led by Mr Greatheart) are found rejoicing, fighting, praying, watching, working, and suffering. The fighting section, in particular, has echoes of Mr Valiant-for-Truth:

> Surrounded by a host of foes,
> Stormed by a host of foes within,
> Nor swift to fly, nor strong to' oppose,
> Single against hell, earth, and sin;
> Single, yet undismay'd I am,
> I dare believe in Jesu's name.
> 			(Hymn CCLXI)

This section also includes 'Soldiers of Christ, arise', and 'Jesus, the conqueror reigns'. Having been courageous, the believers can then watch and pray, and intercede for the world. The final section, 'For the Society', is a recognition of the fellowship of believers, and of Wesley's insistence that one could not be a solitary Christian.

The 1780 book was a remarkable statement. Wesley's preface pointed out that the hymns were 'not carelessly jumbled together, but carefully ranged under proper heads, according to the experience of real Christians' (p. iv). That experience had nothing to do with the church's year from Advent to Trinity, or the Great Festivals of Christmas, or Easter, or Pentecost (although all of these had featured in Charles Wesley's hymns). It was the progress of the soul that was the subject of the book, individually for the most part, and in fellowship at the end. The descent from Bunyan is clear: the book was, Wesley continued, 'a little body of experimental and practical divinity'.

Experimental emphasized Christian experience. Practical pointed to the practice of the Christian life. Both stood in the tradition of Dissent, however much John Wesley may have protested that he had 'reasons against separation' from the Church of England (though that was twenty years earlier). They deliberately set aside the liturgical structures of the Church, for there was more important business in hand. They also made no provision for Holy

Communion (Methodists were urged to attend their parish church). But even though they might have done so, the 'Large Hymn Book' of 1780 offered a rich spiritual life and a comforting Christian fellowship in the local Methodist Society. It offered, also, a supercharged expression of evangelical belief. It began with Charles Wesley's 'O for a thousand tongues to sing / My dear Redeemer's praise!', which may have been an imitation of the German of Johann Mentzner, 'O dass ich tausend Zungen hätte', but which also multiplied a thousand-fold the opening line of Isaac Watts's 'Begin, my tongue, some heavenly theme'. Throughout the 1780 hymn book there is a sense of increased urgency, of an even more strenuous religious effort than that envisaged by Doddridge.

Wesley had previously used hymns to inculcate doctrine. The most conspicuous example of this is the volume entitled *Hymns on God's Everlasting Love* (1742), which was an Arminian refutation of the Calvinistic Methodist movement led by George Whitefield (1714–1770). Whitefield had been a member of the Holy Club at Oxford, and it was he who first encouraged John Wesley to preach in the open air; but Whitefield's Calvinism drove them apart. He became closely associated with Selina Hastings, countess of Huntingdon, who used her wealth and position to promote her own kind of Methodism; on the title page of his *Hymns for Social Worship* (1753), Whitefield described himself as her chaplain. One of his followers was John Cennick (1718–1755), who wrote 'Children of the heavenly King' and the charming 'Ere I sleep, for every favour', and who later joined the Moravians. Cennick's daughter married John Swertner (1714–1813), who edited the British Moravian hymnal *A Collection of Hymns for the Use of the Protestant Church of the United Brethren* (1789, enlarged 1801).

Whitefield's authorship of hymns is uncertain, although he and the countess were responsible for many Dissenting hymnals, and he is remembered for his alteration of Charles Wesley's 'Hark! how all the welkin rings' to 'Hark, the herald angels sing'. His Dissenting credentials are impeccable: shortly after his ordination he was banned from London pulpits for criticizing the clergy, and he established a tabernacle at Moorfields in 1741 and a chapel in Tottenham Court Road in 1756. He was by all accounts a charismatic preacher, so effective that he was the subject of another of Hogarth's satirical engravings, 'Credulity, Superstition and Fanaticism' (1762). He visited America on no fewer than seven occasions, and was instrumental in the 'Great Awakening' of 1739–41. He was closely associated in the public mind with Wesley: William Blake (1757–1827), a Dissenter who was at one time associated with the Swedenborgians, praised 'Whitefield and Westley' as 'men who devote / Their life's whole comfort to intire scorn & injury & death' (*Milton*, Book I, plate 23). However threatening they seemed to the Established Church and to moralists such as Hogarth and Fielding (in *Tom Jones* the sneaking Blifil becomes a Methodist), they were gripped by the need to pursue their pilgrimage with the utmost zeal; in Doddridge's words, to 'stretch ev'ry Nerve'.

376 J. R. Watson

FREE GRACE

The Methodists preached 'Free Grace', the title of Charles Wesley's great hymn, 'And can it be, that I should gain', probably written shortly after his 'conversion' in 1738. Into that word 'grace' are imported ideas of forgiveness and mercy, and an undeserved acceptance of the sinner (Fig. 17.2). Watts and

Fig. 17.2 'Credulity, Superstition and Fanaticism' (1762) William Hogarth.
Courtesy of the Lewis Walpole Library, Yale University. George Whitfield in his pulpit. Note the musical notes in the top right that provide a scale to indicate the intensity of his preaching.

Steele, as we have seen, called it 'surprizing grace'. Philip Doddridge celebrated it in 'Grace, 'tis a charming sound', a hymn based on Ephesians 2:5: 'Even when we were dead in sins, [God] hath quickened us together with Christ, (by grace ye are saved;)'. By 'charming', Doddridge would have meant 'a sound that has a supernatural power to change things', like a witch's spell, only benign and holy. Every verse began with 'Grace':

'Grace, 'tis a charming sound'
'Grace first contriv'd a Way'
'Grace taught my wand'ring Feet'
'Grace all the work shall crown'.

Toplady altered the hymn, and John Newton imitated it, in the far better known 'Amazing grace! (how sweet the sound)'. An example from America, following Whitefield's preaching and the Great Awakening, was the Presbyterian Samuel Davies's 'Great God of wonders!' with its rhetorical refrain:

> Who is a pard'ning God like Thee
> And who has grace so rich and free?

The concept of grace, undeserved and freely given, was fundamental to the teaching and the hymnody of eighteenth-century Dissent. The first hymn in the Methodist *Collection of Hymns* of 1780 contained the verse:

> Look unto him, ye nations, own
>   Your God, ye fallen race;
> Look, and be sav'd through faith alone,
>   Be justified by grace!

The reference back to Reformation teaching is evident. A hymn by Charles Wesley, 'My gracious, loving Lord' (no. XC in 1780), sets it out plainly. The singer is 'a goodly formal saint' (formal religion was practised by 'professors', who were particularly abhorred by Dissenters). He becomes so ashamed that at the end he records:

> I fell on the atoning Lamb,
>   And I was saved by grace.

Perhaps the most dramatic example is the hymn by the Baptist minister Robert Robinson (1735–1790), who described himself as 'reborn...by the powerful preaching of George Whitefield' ('Renatus Sabbati die, Maii 24, 1752, per predicationem potentem Georgii Whitefield'). His 'Come, thou fount of every blessing' (no. DIX in Rippon, *Selection of Hymns*) is a moving account of the blessings on his pilgrimage, and his hopes for the future. It begins:

> Come, thou Fount of every Blessing,
>   Tune my Heart to sing thy Grace!
> Streams of Mercy never ceasing,
>   Call for Songs of loudest Praise:...

The second verse draws on the Dissenter's familiarity with the Bible, in this case 1 Samuel 7:12, in which Samuel set up a stone to record that 'Hitherto hath the Lord helped us'. Every Dissenter would be expected to pick up the reference:

> Here I raise my Ebenezer,
>   Hither by thy Help I'm come;
> And I hope by thy good Pleasure,
>   Safely to arrive at Home;
>
> Jesus sought me, when a Stranger
>   Wandering from the Fold of God;
> He to save my Soul from Danger
>   Interpos'd with precious Blood.

Verse 3 sees grace as a gift, and prays for it to become a chain:

> O! to Grace how great a Debtor,
> Daily I'm constrain'd to be!
> Let that Grace, Lord, like a Fetter,
> Bind my wandering Heart to thee! ...

In his *Memoirs of the Life and Writings of Robert Robinson*, George Dyer described this as 'written by him, when among the Methodists; one is well known, and much admired by the Methodists, and such as, in contradistinction to the *rational* dissenters, call themselves *evangelical*'.[18] Dyer was an eccentric character, as the letters of his friend Charles Lamb make abundantly and hilariously clear, but his distinction between rational Dissent and evangelical Dissent is one that will be discussed briefly in the final section of this chapter.

THE MISSION FIELD

Dissenters were committed to evangelism, in a wider sense than that envisaged by Dyer. One of the functions of the various churches in Britain was to preach the good news to 'the poor', by which was meant the unchurched multitudes who had no hope or purpose in life. George Eliot, whose much admired aunt, Mrs Samuel Evans, was a Methodist local preacher, described the early Wesleyans much as Blake had done, as enduring hardship for Christ, feeding 'on the hips and haws of the Cornwall hedges, after exhausting limbs and lungs in carrying a divine message to the poor' (*Adam Bede*, chapter 3). The other great imperative

---

[18] George Dyer, *Memoirs of the Life and Writings of Robert Robinson, late Minister of the Dissenting Congregation, in St Andrew's Parish, Cambridge* (London, 1796), p. 253.

was overseas missions, and this became a pressing commitment.[19] There are signs of missionary endeavour in the hymns of Dissenters from the beginning: Isaac Watts's 'Jesus shall reign where're the sun' hoped that 'People and realms of every tongue' would 'Dwell on his love with sweetest song' (Psalm LXXII) and his 'Great God, whose universal sway', from the same Psalm, has the verse:

> The heathen Lands, that lie beneath
> The Shades of overspreading Death,
> Revive at his first dawning Light,
> And Deserts blossom at the Sight.

John Ryland (1753–1825), who was instrumental in the founding of the Baptist Missionary Society (BMS), wrote 'Let us sing the King Messiah', a paraphrase of Psalm 45, for a missionary meeting in Bristol in 1798, urging the Messiah to 'Gird thy sword on, mighty Hero' to 'assert thy right' and 'Ride triumphant / All around the conquered globe'.

The most remarkable achievement of the BMS was the Serampore Mission in India, staffed by Joshua Marshman (1768–1837), William Carey (1761–1834), and William Ward (1769–1823). One of those converted was a carpenter, Krishna Pal (1764–1822), who wrote a hymn in Bengali, 'Je Jone Apon Pam', translated by Carey and versified by Marshman as 'O thou my soul, forget no more'. It was published by the BMS in 1830. The London Missionary Society (LMS) was similarly active: it was at one of its meetings in 1825 that 'Thou, whose almighty word' was first quoted (although it had probably been written earlier, in 1813). The author, John Marriott (1780–1825), was an Anglican, but his hymn evidently made its way into the LMS, a Society in which Dissent and established religion found common cause.

JAMES MONTGOMERY

The outstanding hymn writer of the Dissenting missionary tradition was James Montgomery. His parents had been Moravian missionaries in the West Indies. He was educated at the Moravian school at Fulneck, and he inherited their commitment, although he never became a missionary himself. He was an active member of the Yorkshire branch of the LMS, and his hymns were enthusiastic in their support of its work. His 'Hark! The song of Jubilee' was written in 1819 to celebrate 'the renunciation of Idolatry, and acknowledgment of the Gospel, in the Georgian Isles of the South Seas'. These were the islands around Tahiti, which were the centre of much missionary activity: Christianity was adopted as

---

[19] See ch. 12 in the current volume, Brian Stanley 'Missionary Societies'.

the official religion after 1815.[20] One of his best known hymns, 'Hail to the Lord's Anointed', is characteristic of his confidence:

> Arabia's desert ranger
>   To him shall bow the knee,
> The Ethiopian stranger
>   His glory come to see;
>
> With offerings of devotion,
>   Ships from the isles shall meet,
> To pour the wealth of ocean
>   In tribute at his feet.
>
> Kings shall fall down before him,
>   And gold and incense bring;
> All nations shall adore him,
>   His praise all people sing....

The reference to gold and incense is a reminder that this is an Epiphany hymn, but, typically for a Dissenter, Montgomery subordinates the liturgical 'Manifestation of Christ to the Gentiles' to a geography that brings out the importance of mission. He does so again in the hymn that is a paraphrase of the Lord's Prayer, where 'Hallowed be thy name' becomes:

> Our heavenly Father, hear
>   The prayer we offer now;
> Thy name be hallowed far and near,
>   To Thee all nations bow.

Montgomery was acutely aware of the demands that missionary work made upon people. His 'Home, kindred, friends, and country' was a moving tribute:

> Home, kindred, friends, and country – these
>   Are things with which we never part;
> From clime to clime, o'er land and seas,
>   We bear them with us in our heart;
> And yet 'tis hard to feel resigned
> When these, all these, are left behind.

Montgomery went on to say that for missionaries there is a compensating glory, and comfort that they thought had been lost:

> Take up your cross, and say 'Farewell!'
>   Go forth without the camp to Him
> Who left Heaven's throne with men to dwell,
>   Who died His murderers to redeem:
> O tell his name in every ear!
> Doubt not, the dead themselves will hear, –

---

[20] See C. W. Newbury, *The History of the Tahitian Mission, 1799–1830* (London, 1961).

> Hear, and come forth to life anew;
>   Then, while the Gentiles' courts they fill,
> Shall not your Saviour's words stand true?
>   Home, kindred, friends, and country, still
> In earth's far deserts you shall find,
>   Yet lose not those you left behind.

This is Montgomery's perception of the personal cost, the loss and the gain. His hymn on 'The Lord's Day' is suffused with a vision of the Christianized globe that anticipates John Ellerton's 'The day thou gavest, Lord, is ended':

> People of many a tribe and tongue,
>   Men of strange colours, climates, lands,
> Have heard Thy truth, Thy glory sung,
>   And offered prayer in distant lands.
>
> Soon as the light of morning broke
>   O'er island, continent, or deep,
> Thy far-spread family awoke,
>   Sabbath around the world to keep.
>
> From east to west, the sun surveyed,
>   From north to south, adoring throngs;
> And still, when evening stretched her shade,
>   The stars came out to hear their songs.

The last line is an example of the simple beauty of which Dissenting hymnody was capable. Montgomery, who was a newspaper editor as well as a poet friendly with Shelley and admired by Byron, had an economy with words, and a Dissenting plainness that Donald Davie called 'classical'. Writing of Charles Wesley, he singled out the line 'This man receiveth sinners still' as having an absolute precision and weight;[21] Montgomery could use the plain simplicity of Dissenting worship and thought to produce a similar effect.

He was also the great hymn writer of the Sunday School movement. This had begun in the 1780s, and its foundation is generally associated with Robert Raikes, a member of the Church of England. But the first Sunday School in London was the work of Rowland Hill (1744–1833) at the Surrey Chapel, an independent institution that had Congregational and Methodist origins. Montgomery was the greatest hymn writer of the movement: for many years he wrote hymns to be sung at the Whitsuntide Festivals of the Sheffield Sunday School Union. These were attended by children of all denominations, who paraded through the streets in their best new clothes, although there were individual church occasions also; for them Montgomery wrote 'Sing we the song of those who stand', and 'Stand up and bless the Lord', the latter specifically for the Wesleyans.

---

[21] Donald Davie, *Purity of Diction in English Verse* (revised edition, London, 1967), pp. 72–3.

CONCLUSION: RATIONAL DISSENT AND EVANGELICAL DISSENT

When George Dyer drew a distinction between 'Rational' and 'Evangelical' Dissent, he was probably thinking of Unitarians or 'Semi-Arians' as opposed to others. But there is another way in which the endless fluidity of different Dissenting traditions points forward to the nineteenth century. While there were Baptist, Congregational, and Wesleyan Churches that continued to act in a traditional manner, there were invariably many others that went their own way (Hill's Surrey Chapel was a good example). There were splinter groups of many kinds: there was a natural tendency for Dissenters, who felt passionately about their beliefs, to create particular spaces for those beliefs to flourish. Each church, or part of a church, would see itself as the Gathered Church, a community of 'Saints' against the world, or the other churches. This can be most clearly observed in the development of the Methodist movement, which developed rebellious tendencies after the death of its great founder in 1791. As early as 1797 the Methodist New Connexion set up its own chapels; it produced a hymn book in 1798 and another in 1804. Both of them contained hymns to supplement Wesley's 1780 *Collection*. Another group, the Independent Methodists, was instituted in 1807; another, the Bible Christians, dates from 1816. The latter produced a supplement to Wesley's book in 1820, and *A Collection of Hymns for the Use of the People called Arminian Bible Christians* in 1824.

The most spectacular of the separating movements was Primitive Methodism. Beginning in 1807 at Mow Cop (a hill outside Stoke-on-Trent), they held 'Camp Meetings', inspired by the American Great Awakenings and the visits of the weird but charismatic evangelist Lorenzo Dow, especially his visit of 1805. The music of their hymns is unrecorded, but it is thought that they used 'ranter tunes', popular music from street ballads and folk songs. Climbing the hill, followed by singing, praying, and preaching, led to frenzied scenes of conversion and commitment, which were reflected in their hymns: 'Camp meetings with success are crown'd' is the opening line of a hymn by one of the founders, Hugh Bourne (1772–1852). Another, William Sanders (1799–1882?), wrote 'Prayer for the saving presence of Him who favoured the camp-meetings of the wilderness':

> Encamped here, to thee we bend, –
> To thee, who art the sinner's Friend,
>   We pour our fervent prayer: –
> We do not worship thee alone
> In temples made of brick or stone,
>   But in the open air.

The Primitive Methodists placed considerable emphasis on meeting in the open air, and were suspicious of the use of musical instruments: 'great caution should be used...and none but decidedly pious persons should, on any account, be allowed to play on any musical instrument, in the congregation during the time of worship'.[22] They were not unmindful of their heritage, and their books, after their first *General Collection of Hymns and Spiritual Songs* (1809), had a good representation of Isaac Watts, Charles Wesley, and the Anglican evangelicals. But their own hymns had a fervent energy that must have been very powerful. The finest of them, which was in use until fairly recent times in Methodist books, and is still found in the *Song Book of the Salvation Army* (1986), was probably by Sanders and Bourne jointly ('W.S. & H.B.' in the 1824 book). It began with free grace:

> Hark! the gospel news is sounding,
>   Christ hath suffered on the tree;
> Streams of mercy are abounding;
>   Grace for all is rich and free:
>   Now, poor sinner,
>   Look to him who died for thee.

The streams of mercy give way to the hill on which the Primitive Methodists first worshipped, and the streams become a fountain:

> O escape to yonder mountain,
>   Now begin to watch and pray;
> Christ invites you to the fountain,
>   Come, and wash your sins away;
>   Do not tarry,
>   Come to Jesus while you may.

The fountain then becomes a river, flowing from the side of the crucified Christ:

> Grace is flowing like a river;
>   Millions there have been supplied;
> Still it flows as fresh as ever
>   From the Saviour's wounded side;
>   None need perish
>   All may live, for Christ hath died.

Finally, the sinner, through grace, is given the hope of heaven, as the streams and the fountain and the river all give way to the magnificence of 'the full ocean':

> Christ alone shall be our portion;
>   Soon we hope to meet above,
> Then we'll bathe in the full ocean
>   Of the great Redeemer's love;
>   All his fullness,
>   We shall then for ever prove.

---

[22] Preface to the *Large Hymn Book, for the use of the Primitive Methodists*, edited by Hugh Bourne (Bemersley, 1824), n.p.

The gradual crescendo of this hymn, and the power of its imagery, suggest that the emotional excitement that was latent in much eighteenth-century Dissenting hymnody was beginning to emerge as a force that found its full voice later in the nineteenth century with gospel hymnody and the revivals of Dwight L. Moody and Ira D. Sankey; and in the twentieth century with the Pentecostal and Charismatic churches.

All this was very different from the culture of the traditional Baptist and Congregationalist Churches, or from the rational and intellectual beliefs that were beginning to attract many Dissenters, particularly Presbyterians. By the time of the 1828 repeal of the Test and Corporation Acts, orthodox Dissent was beginning to become respectable: a little later, in 1859, George Eliot contrasted early Methodists, who endured privations and hardship, with 'that modern type which reads quarterly reviews and attends in chapels with pillared porticos' (*Adam Bede*, chapter 3). Dissent had become settled, and Dissenters prosperous, because they were hard-working and honest. Their hymn books express a thoughtful Dissent rather than an emotionally charged experience. Thus the Unitarians published a major hymnal in 1795, *A Collection of Hymns for Public and Private Worship*, in which many of Isaac Watts's hymns were altered to fit their non-Trinitarianism, even as their predecessors had altered the liturgy. Other denominations published standard, solid books. The Baptist John Haddon printed *A New Selection of Hymns* in 1828 (the profits were to go to the widows and orphans of Baptist ministers or missionaries). The Wesleyans published their definitive edition of *A Collection of Hymns* in 1831, incorporating a series of supplements that had been made to the 1780 book (it lasted until 1876). For the Independents, Josiah Conder's *The Congregational Hymn Book* of 1836 marked a new beginning that was also an end: the beginning of the Congregational Church of the nineteenth century, and the end of a period in which Dissenters and their hymnody had enriched the religious life of Britain with hymns that in English have never been equalled.

SELECT BIBLIOGRAPHY

Aalders, Cynthia Y., *To Express the Ineffable: The Hymns and Spirituality of Anne Steele* (Milton Keynes, 2008).
Baker, Frank, *Representative Verse of Charles Wesley* (London, 1962).
Binfield, Clyde, *So Down to Prayers: Studies in English Nonconformity, 1780–1920* (London, 1977).
Davie, Donald, *A Gathered Church: The Literature of the English Dissenting Interest, 1700–1930* (London, 1978).
Davies, Horton, *Worship and Theology in England from Watts and Wesley to Maurice, 1690–1850* (Princeton, NJ, 1961).
Dyer, George, *Memoirs of the Life and Writings of Robert Robinson* (London, 1796).

Escott, Harry, *Isaac Watts, Hymnographer: A Study of the Beginnings, Development and Philosophy of the English Hymn* (London, 1962).
Kimbrough, S. T., Jnr, *The Lyrical Theology of Charles Wesley* (Eugene, OR, 2011).
Lord, Fred Townley, *Achievement: A Short History of the Baptist Missionary Society, 1792-1942* (London, 1942).
Lovett, Richard, *The History of the London Missionary Society, 1795-1895* (London, 1899).
Manning, Bernard L., *The Hymns of Wesley and Watts: Five Informal Papers* (London, 1942).
Nuttall, Geoffrey F., ed., *Calendar of the Correspondence of Philip Doddridge, DD (1702-51)* (London, 1979).
Rivers, Isabel, *Reason, Grace, and Sentiment: A Study of the Language of Religion and Ethics in England, 1660-1780*, 2 vols. (Cambridge, 1991-2000).
Rivers, Isabel and Wykes, David, eds, *Dissenting Praise: Religious Dissent and the Hymn in England and Wales* (Oxford, 2011).
Vaughn, James Berry, 'Public Worship and Practical Theology in the Work of Benjamin Keach (1640-1704)' (PhD Thesis, St Andrews, 1977).
Watson, J. R., *The English Hymn: A Critical and Historical Study* (Oxford, 1997).
Watts, Michael R., *The Dissenters: From the Reformation to the French Revolution* (Oxford, 1978).
Young, Carlton R., *Music of the Heart: John and Charles Wesley on Music and Musicians* (Carol Stream, IL, 1995).

18

Dissent and Education

Mark Burden

EDUCATION AND THE LAW

The origins of eighteenth-century Dissenting education may be glimpsed in the turbulent years of the Civil War and Commonwealth (1642–60), which saw an outpouring of educational reforms, both in pamphlets and in practice.[1] During this time, Puritan-backed committees packed the universities and schools with sympathetic tutors in a manner analogous to the replacement of the sequestered clergy by Presbyterian and Congregational ministers. Following the Restoration the situation reversed, as Puritan educators were ejected from their positions in large numbers to make way for returning clergymen and the new wave of Anglican apologists. Many Puritan university tutors were unseated by the Act for the Confirming and Restoring of Ministers (1660) which enshrined the rights of the sequestered clergy, but the greatest blow to the Puritans' educational fortunes was the Act of Uniformity (1662), which required all university tutors and grammar school teachers to subscribe to the articles of the Church of England in order to be licensed. Thereafter, nonconformist educators teaching in schools or tutoring academical subjects ran the risk of prosecution. Public sentiment towards Dissenters' schools reached a state of near fever-pitch in the years between the Popish Plot and Monmouth's rebellion, a period in which Dissenting students were often accused (with varying degrees of accuracy) of inciting seditious, rebellious, and revolutionary activity.[2]

---

[1] John Philip Morgan, *Godly Learning* (Cambridge, 1986); Richard L. Greaves, *The Puritan Revolution and Educational Thought* (New Brunswick, 1969). I would like to thank Michèle Cohen, Mary Clare Martin, and Isabel Rivers for their comments on an earlier draft of this chapter.

[2] Mark Burden, 'Academical Learning in the Dissenters' Private Academies, 1660–1720', unpublished PhD thesis (University of London, 2012), pp. 44–101.

The Toleration Act (1689) was a further disappointment to Dissenting educators. It left the law relating to grammar schools unchanged from the Act of Uniformity, and it did not include any measures to define or to safeguard the higher education academies run by Dissenters which had emerged since the late 1660s. Nevertheless, although it was still possible to prosecute Dissenting schoolmasters and academy tutors during William III's reign, there were fewer citations in the ecclesiastical courts; outcomes might include a fine, a fairly amicable audience with the local bishop, or a collapse in the prosecution's case.[3] The general situation for Dissenting tutors deteriorated during the reign of Queen Anne following complaints about Dissenting schoolmasters raised at Canterbury convocation in 1702, and hostile comments published in the prefaces to Clarendon's *History of the Rebellion*. Tutors with a particularly public profile were once again accused of indoctrinating students with 'seditious and antimonarchical principles', a claim which found expression and agency in the rabble-rousing words of Samuel Wesley that Dissenting educators promulgated 'KING-KILLING DOCTRINES'.[4] Meanwhile the Oxford cleric Henry Sacheverell was preaching incendiary sermons against the Dissenters' '*Schismatical Universities*' which—he claimed—poisoned students with principles of '*Atheism, Deism, Tritheism, Socinianism*'.[5] The hostile atmosphere reached its nadir with the passage of the Schism Act (1714, repealed 1719); this statute repeated the requirement of the Act of Uniformity that every schoolmaster or private tutor should subscribe to a declaration to conform to Anglican liturgy, and formally extended the requirement to any person working as a tutor in a 'seminary' or teaching reading, scholastic, or academical literature.[6]

Although the Schism Act proved to be a short-lived and rather blunt instrument for controlling Dissenting education, it was not completely toothless, causing several Dissenting schools and academies to close permanently or intermittently in the period 1714–20. The usual narrative claims that proceedings against Dissenting educators then rapidly declined, coming to a halt following the failed prosecution of Philip Doddridge in 1733. This version of events is not entirely accurate: representations between 1732 and 1791 to the

---

[3] Burden, 'Academical Learning', pp. 102–43 surveys the primary sources.

[4] Gloucestershire Archives GDR B4/1/1056; Samuel Wesley, *A Letter from a Country Divine to his Friend in London* (London, 1703), pp. 1–7.

[5] Henry Sacheverell, *The Nature and Mischief of Prejudice and Partiality Stated* (London, 1704), pp. 53–5, and *The Perils of False Brethren* (London, 1709), p. 25.

[6] David L. Wykes, 'Religious Dissent, the Church, and the Repeal of the Occasional Conformity and Schism Acts, 1714–19', in Robert D. Cornwall and William Gibson, eds, *Religion, Politics and Dissent, 1660–1832* (Aldershot, 2010); James E. Bradley, 'Nonconformist Schools, the Schism Act, and the Limits of Toleration in England's Confessional State', in Jordan J. Ballor, David Sytsma, and Jason Zuidema, eds, *Church and School in Early Modern Protestantism* (Leiden, 2013), pp. 597–612; Daniel Defoe, *A Brief Survey of the Legal Liberties of the Dissenters* (London, 1714), pp. 19–24.

powerful committee of the Dissenting Deputies, set up to campaign for the repeal of the Test and Corporation Acts, reveal that Dissenting schoolmasters were targeted across the eighteenth century, and that the Birmingham riots of 1791 were far from an isolated outbreak of intolerance. The committee, which provided legal and practical advice to Dissenters facing prosecution, intervened in numerous cases involving the attempted closure of Dissenting schools.[7] It also campaigned to protect the education of the children of poor Dissenters, arguing for their right to be admitted to charity schools without prejudice or enforced subscription.[8]

There were minor legal victories for Dissenting educators in the later decades of the eighteenth century. These included the Dissenters' Relief Act (1779), which protected schoolmasters from prosecution if they were prepared to subscribe to a declaration against Popery, and the addition of clause 19 to the Seditious Meetings Act (1795), by which (in the words of the Dissenting Deputies) 'all doubt respecting its possible operation on Dissenting Tutors & Schoolmasters was removed'.[9] However, despite the repeal of the Test and Corporation Acts (1828) and a failed University Admission Bill (1834), it was not until the middle of the nineteenth century that the universities at Oxford (1854) and Cambridge (1856) abolished mandatory subscription to Church of England articles at graduation. Meanwhile, of major significance for the Dissenters' higher education colleges was the establishment of the University of London (1836), through which degree-awarding powers were conferred to prominent Dissenting institutions in the 1840s and 1850s. This process paved the way for the abolition of religious tests by the Universities Test Act (1871), which in turn enabled the eventual acceptance and chartering of Dissenting colleges at Oxford and Cambridge in the twentieth century.[10]

CHARITY SCHOOLS, GRAMMAR SCHOOLS, AND SUNDAY SCHOOLS

The commitment of Dissenters of the middling sort to charity schools across the eighteenth century has rarely been appreciated, although their endeavours in this area matched their achievements in educating their own more privileged children, and were on a considerably larger scale. Many would have

---

[7] Examples include schools at Pontypool (1740), Leicestershire (1742), Suffolk (1748), Henley (1749), Maldon (1757), Haverfordwest (1762), Cheltenham (1764), Rutland (1775), Durham (1777), Kirkby Woodhouse (1777), Bassingbourn (1778), and Framlingham (1785).
[8] London Metropolitan Archives (hereafter LMA) CLC/181/MS03083/1-2.
[9] LMA CLC/181/MS03083/3, p. 91.
[10] Michael Twaddle, 'The Oxford and Cambridge Admissions Controversy of 1834', *British Journal of Educational Studies*, 14, 3 (1966), pp. 45–58.

assented to Doddridge's private observation that he would rather 'do good to the least & poorest Children than be admired & extolled by the [nobl]est & great[est]'.[11] The purpose of schools for poor children was elegantly summarized by a subscription proposal from the Dissenters at Denton in 1778: 'teaching children to read that they may better learn and know the word of God, which is able to make them wise unto Salvation thro' Faith that is in Jesus'.[12] The committee of subscribers to the Weigh House charity school put it more bluntly: they were helping to combat the 'deplorable ignorance almost universally discovered amongst the children of the lower class of people'.[13] One of the earliest of the Dissenters' charity schools was opened in 1687 in Gravel Lane, Southwark, with forty scholars, later increased to fifty; its aims were to teach its pupils to read Scripture, to instruct them in the Westminster Assembly's catechism, to supervise their attendance at Sunday worship, to oversee their morals, and to enable them 'to write and Cypher so far as to qualify them for an honest Trade'.[14] Following the accession of George I, and despite the unwelcome intervention of the Schism Act, fundraising sermons to the Gravel Lane school were delivered and printed annually from 1714 by the great and the good of the Dissenting ministry, while a new charity school meeting at the Baptist chapel in Horsley Down was begun in the same year by 'several Protestant Dissenters of different Denominations', and also grew swiftly to cater for fifty boys.[15]

The suggestion that private schools in general, and London charity schools in particular, were becoming an almost exclusively Tory preoccupation can thus be rejected.[16] Printed episcopal visitation queries, such as those for Hereford diocese in 1719, still felt the need to include questions such as the following: 'Doth every Person that keepeth a School in your Parish, come to Church himself, and cause his Scholars also to come at the time of Divine Service? Doth he instruct them in the Church Catechism?' The answer from Leominster parish was typical of those from towns where there was a notable Dissenting interest: 'there is a Master of an English School & others y^t teach English about ye Town y^t do not come to Church they profess themselves Dissenters'.[17] Some sense of the vitality of Dissenting schools may be gauged from the relatively complete surviving set of returns for Winchester diocese in 1725, which included parts of London. The return for Lambeth, an area known to harbour substantial numbers of Dissenters, included a note that

---

[11] Dr Williams's Library (hereafter DWL) NCL L1/1/45.
[12] Norfolk Record Office FC 37/1. [13] LMA CLC/228; DWL 38.380.
[14] Daniel Neal, *A Sermon preach'd for the Benefit of the Charity-school in Gravel-lane, Southwark* (London, 1723), pp. 7–14, 29.
[15] *A Brief Account of the Charity School, at Horsly-Down, Southwark* (London, 1781), p. 1.
[16] Craig Rose, '"Seminarys of Faction and Rebellion": Jacobites, Whigs and the London Charity Schools, 1716–1724', *Historical Journal*, 34, 4 (1991), pp. 831–55.
[17] Herefordshire Archives and Records Centre HD5/15/77, pp. 6–7.

'a dissenter teaches school at Stockwell, and preaches on Sundays to a small congregation'; the return for St Olave's in nearby Southwark was even more precise: 'John Seager, the master of another charity school in Unicorn Yard, Tuly Street, takes Care of 50 boys of Protestants of every Denomination mostly Anabaptists', while 'Mrs Secell near the Artillery Ground takes care of twenty five Girls of Protestants of every Denomination'. But perhaps the most striking feature of the Winchester returns were those for Wandsworth, which included a description of a 'Nursery of Quakers whose Master is one John Kuwidt', and which admitted 'Twelve Boarders and about Thirty Day Scholars'; meanwhile, another Quaker, John Savory, ran a school in the same parish with 'about Forty Day Scholars'. Both schools reputedly taught their scholars to 'Write, Read, and cast Accompts', while an usher (in both cases another Quaker) instructed them in grammar learning. In the same parish were 'less considerable Schools taught by Women' named Harris, Savory, Dowsom, Stubington, and Hanwell, 'most of whom are [also] Quakers'.[18]

The growth in Dissenting charity schools was not limited to London. Seventeenth-century Puritan and nonconformist initiatives to extend the provision of free schools in Wales were furthered by the initiation of subscription schools in the eighteenth century: at Llanwenarth in 1721, for instance, subscribers agreed to twenty-one rules to ensure that the children at the Dissenting charity school were 'freely instructed in Reading Writing Arithmetick, &... the Principles of Religion... according to their Capacities'.[19] An important early bequest in the north of England founded the Leonard Chamberlain Trust (from 1716), which provided schoolmasters in association with the Bowl Alley Lane chapel in Kingston-upon-Hull, before expanding to other educational projects.[20] In Norwich, two charity schools for reading and writing were set up by the Calvert Street Presbyterians, supported from 1709 by the Joanna Scott Foundation and supplementary bequests.[21] The Sudbury charity school in Suffolk (1723), administered by trustees including the local Presbyterian minister, provided for the schooling of ten children in the town 'whose parents shall be most unable and uncapable to put them to School to learn to read well in the Bible or old Testament', without 'any Distinction to be made between the Children of Dissenters and the children of Persons of the Church of England'.[22] At the charity school at New Meeting, Kidderminster (1758), a master and mistress were employed to teach reading, writing, and accounts to the boys, and reading and sewing to the girls.[23]

---

[18] Hampshire Archives and Local Studies 21M65 B4/1/3.
[19] National Library of Wales 410B, pp. 215–22.
[20] Hull History Centre C/DSCL.   [21] Norfolk Record Office FC 122/1-3.
[22] Suffolk Record Office (Bury) FK3 501/11/1; FK3 501/5/33.
[23] Worcestershire Archive and Archaeology Service b250.6 BA7589.

In marked contrast to their charity schools were those establishments set up by leading Dissenters in order to educate their own children in grammar learning. One of the best known of these is John Aikin's school at Kibworth, the pupils of which included Thomas Belsham (1757–8), Newcome Cappe (1748–9), Thomas Cogan (1747/8–50), Doddridge's son Philip (until 1749), John Gardner's son Philip (1742), Thomas Robins (until 1750), and John Simpson (1754–8).[24] Across the century, middle-class Dissenters expected their sons to develop proficiency in Latin, Greek, Hebrew, and modern languages, and this usually extended to the reading of secular literature. By the age of 12, Philip Doddridge Jnr could read Homer 'very prettily', could manage Horace and Cicero 'with ease & pleasure' and could render a passage of Racine into English 'with very little preparation'.[25] A report written by John Collett Ryland at his Northampton school in 1764 implied that one of his 11-year-old pupils had read Pope's verse translations of the *Iliad* and *Odyssey*, Horace and Virgil in Latin, the whole of the Greek New Testament, the Book of Genesis in Hebrew, and Fénelon's *Télémaque* in French.[26] Aikin himself was educated at a Dissenting school in St Albans, where he was taught by a man who, according to later reports, had 'once been upon the stage, and was fond of exercising his boys in theatrical declamation'.[27]

Despite these efforts to inculcate the principles of a polite and classical education, there was a widespread perception by the middle of the eighteenth century that the structures, personnel, and funding for teaching grammar learning to intelligent and pious Dissenting children remained deficient. In 1749, Doddridge wrote of the continuing need 'to assist promising Young Persons in getting Grammar Learning before they come to an Academy, on promise of engaging in the Ministry'. By the following year Doddridge had raised between £60 and £80 in subscriptions in and about London for a project to extend the provision of grammar learning by and for Dissenters, and he continued to support the scheme throughout his life.[28] It is less frequently noted that Doddridge's plan was only one of a number of projects to develop links between the Dissenters' grammar schools and their higher education academies. For example, James Watson's school at Mount Sorrel served to prepare pupils for entrance into John Jennings's academy in the early 1720s,

---

[24] David L. Wykes, 'The Revd John Aikin Senior: Kibworth School and Warrington Academy', in Felicity James and Ian Inkster, eds, *Religious Dissent and the Aikin–Barbauld Circle 1740–1860* (Cambridge, 2012), pp. 28–51; DWL NCL L1/1/35; G. F. Nuttall, ed., *Calendar of the Correspondence of Philip Doddridge DD* (London, 1979), pp. 154–6 (hereafter *Doddridge Correspondence*).

[25] DWL NCL L1/10/84.

[26] John Rippon, *The Gentle Dismission of Saints from Earth to Heaven* (London, 1792), p. 42 Timothy Whelan, 'John Ryland at School', *Baptist Quarterly*, 40, 2 (2003), pp. 90–116.

[27] V. F., 'A Historical Account of the Warrington Academy', *Monthly Repository*, 8 (1813) pp. 161–72.

[28] *Doddridge Correspondence*, pp. 306, 337, 339, 352, 357.

whereas Doddridge's academy took pupils from Samuel Clarke's school in St Albans and Thomas Lee's school at East Farndon (where he was assisted by Aikin).[29] Another solution was proposed by the minister Samuel Wilton and his colleagues: they would contribute towards the expenses of a few pious young men in a short course of studies, sufficient to qualify them for serving congregations that 'did not require ministers of profound learning'; one tutor chosen for the scheme was Robert Gentleman, whose efforts were criticized by the influential minister Job Orton on account of the presumed deficiency of the education provided.[30]

Presbyterian and Congregational educational tracts aimed at the young included catechisms, sermons, school textbooks, philosophical writings about children's learning, and literary works, including poetry.[31] Many of these texts reached sympathetic audiences beyond the confines of middle-class Dissenting circles. Isaac Watts's *Essay towards the Encouragement of Charity Schools* (1728) earned the approbation of the future archbishop of Canterbury Thomas Secker in 1743, while Watts's *Psalms of David* (1718) and *Hymns and Spiritual Songs* (1707), published in numerous formats, became stalwarts of Church of England and Dissenting schools across the eighteenth and nineteenth centuries.[32] Doddridge's *Sermons on the Religious Education of Children* (1732), *Sermons to Young Persons* (1735), and *Principles of the Christian Religion expressed in Plain and Easy Verse* (1743) all went through multiple editions.[33] Also influential were Doddridge's corrections to the manuscript of David Fordyce's *Dialogues on Education* (1745), a work published in London (1745), Belfast (1753), Cork (1755), and Glasgow (1768).[34] Among the most adventurous of the educational writings of Anna Laetitia Barbauld were her *Lessons for Children* (1779) and *Hymns in Prose for Children* (1781), both of which were frequently reprinted and repackaged. John Aikin's *The Calendar of Nature* (1784) had an international appeal among children and adults of both sexes, while his *Evenings at Home* (1792), co-written with Barbauld, helped to extend the boundaries of informal education, a strategy which became an increasing preoccupation of eighteenth-century publishers.[35] Other Dissenting women became well-known authors of conversational children's books on natural history, a notable

---

[29] DWL NCL L1/8/144, L1/10/35; *Doddridge Correspondence*, pp. 4, 10, 21, 46, 48, 54, 67–8.

[30] Walter Wilson, *The History and Antiquities of Dissenting Churches and Meeting Houses*, 4 vols. (London, 1810–14), IV, p. 191.

[31] See Ian Green, *The Christian's ABC* (Oxford, 1996) and the same author's *Humanism and Protestantism in Early Modern English Education* (Farnham, 2009).

[32] *Doddridge Correspondence*, pp. 185, 317.

[33] DWL NCL L1/1/45; NCL L1/10/59.

[34] DWL NCL L1/4/64–5, L1/5/171, L1/10/29, L1/10/63; *Doddridge Correspondence*, pp. 178, 185–6, 193.

[35] Stephen Daniels and Paul Elliott, '"Outline Maps of Knowledge": John Aikin's Geographical Imagination', in James and Inkster, eds, *Religious Dissent*, pp. 94–125.

example being the Quaker Priscilla Wakefield, author of *Mental Improvement* (1794) and *An Introduction to Botany* (1796). The Baptist John Ash's *Easiest Introduction to Dr Lowth's English Grammar* (1766) was a work used widely by Dissenting and Church of England schoolmasters and mistresses. More ambitious altogether was David Williams's *Treatise on Education* (1774), comparing the educational methods of Milton, Locke, Rousseau, and Helvétius; this was only one of a number of philosophical 'projects of reformation' delineated in print by Williams, including *The Philosopher* (1771), *Illustrations of Maxims and Principles of Education* (1783), *Lectures on Education* (1789), and *Lessons to a Young Prince* (1790).

Quakers' interest in education sprang directly from George Fox's early enthusiasm for developing a network of Friends' schools.[36] By the 1670s Quakers were running grammar schools in and around several major towns and cities, including London, Bristol, and Dublin, and plans were afoot (later aborted) for Thomas Lawson to set up a school for languages and botany. The type of education advocated by Quakers varied, but at least some seem to have particularly endorsed practical subjects: William Penn wished his children to learn 'useful knowledge', including mathematics and agriculture, and the early eighteenth-century Quaker school in Sidcot taught arithmetic and merchants' accounts as well as Cicero and the Latin Bible.[37] John Bellers's *Proposals for Raising a Colledge of Industry of All Usefull Trades and Husbandry* (1695), endorsed by William Penn, Robert Barclay, and Thomas Ellwood, led to the lease of a workhouse at Clerkenwell in 1702. The workhouse children moved to a new house on the Islington Road in 1786, and the institution continued into the twenty-first century as Walden School.[38] Nevertheless, not all Quaker educational projects went unhindered: the threat of prosecution in 1705 against Richard Claridge, a Quaker grammar school master who opened his doors to all children of the parish, was a more typical consequence of the hostility faced by Quaker schoolmasters from elements of 'the *High-Church-Party*' in the early eighteenth century.[39]

Quakers opened many of their most prominent and long-lasting schools during the period 1770–1828, including the Ulster Provincial School (1774), Ackworth School (1779), Trinity Lane Girls' School, York (1785), Newtown

---

[36] Michael Quane, 'Quaker Schools in Dublin', *The Journal of the Royal Society of Antiquaries of Ireland*, 94 (1964), pp. 47–68.

[37] William C. Braithwaite, *The Second Period of Quakerism*, 2nd edn (Cambridge, 1961), pp. 525–32; for an account of the role later played by Quaker women in promoting scientific literacy, see Camilla Leach, 'Religion and Rationality: Quaker Women and Science Education 1790–1850', *History of Education*, 35, 1 (2006), pp. 69–90.

[38] David W. Bolam, *Unbroken Community* (Cambridge, 1952), p. 55; Essex Record Office D/Q 49.

[39] *High-Church Antipathy to Protestant Liberty* (London, 1705); David L. Wykes, 'Quaker Schoolmasters, Toleration and the Law, 1689–1714', *Journal of Religious History*, 21, 2 (1997), pp. 178–92.

School, Waterford (1798), Sidcot School (1808), and Bootham School (1823). Of these institutions, the history of Ackworth is best documented, although early descriptions survive of several other Quaker schools from the period. For example, in 1774 at the Quaker school in Kendal, George Bewley taught Latin, Greek, French, merchants' accounts, algebra, and arithmetic to the boys, while George Raw taught English, writing, and common accounts to the girls; meanwhile two ushers taught English grammar, reading, writing, and cyphering. One student was studying Latin works by Florus, Virgil, Horace, Cicero, and Juvenal, the Greek New Testament and Homer, and French works by Chambaud, Fénelon, and Lesage; other authors read at the school included Ward and Cordery (grammar), Guthrie (geography), Rollin (history), and Euclid (geometry). The equipment consisted of a reflecting telescope, air pump, microscope, theodolite, quadrant, and a pair of globes, and the school hours were 8.00–12.00 and 13.00–17.00, with two fifteen-minute breaks a day.[40] By the early nineteenth century, the Quaker boarding school at Compton near Sherborne (opened 1759) was taking between twelve and fourteen boys, aged 12 or younger, for forty guineas per annum, to learn Latin, Greek, and English grammar, arithmetic, book-keeping, geography, 'useful' mathematics, experimental philosophy, and (for an extra fee) French and drawing. The school's equipment included a library, globes, an electrical machine, and an air pump.[41] Like other denominations, Quakers sought to combine pastoral care and high educational standards with their own distinctive brands of piety and ethics: Joseph Sams's Darlington school (opened 1810) purposed to provide 'a religious, guarded, and liberal education' in 'Reading, Spelling, English Grammar, Writing, Arithmetic, Mathematics, Geography, History, the Elements of Astronomy, and the use of the Globes' for five guineas per annum, with Latin and Greek for three guineas, and French and Drawing for four guineas each.[42]

The early history of Ackworth School provides a case study in the financial management of Dissenting schools and the problems they faced. The school opened in 1779 on the eighty-four-acre site of a former foundling hospital, but the estate swiftly trebled in size to about 242 acres. The children were admitted between the ages of 9 and 14 and by 1831 the fee was held at £10, although the school's costs per pupil were estimated to be £18.[43] The school was funded through annual subscriptions, legacies, and annuities. Subscriptions came from Quaker meetings across the country, with yearly contributions often

---

[40] Quaker Library TEMP 32/9/3-4.

[41] It attracted Quakers from across the south of England, especially Bristol: Quaker Library TEMP 32/9/1-2, pp. 5–8.

[42] Quaker Library VOL S 25. The mathematics course at the Rochester academy attended by Quaker Joshua Green in 1825 required students to absorb definitions, propositions, rules, exercises, and proofs relating to compound interest, single and double fellowship, loss and gain, barter, and exchange: Quaker Library BOX T3/4.

[43] *Ackworth School Catalogue* (London, 1831), 'Advertisement'.

exceeding £50 from Yorkshire, Lancashire, Durham, Norfolk, Warwickshire, Bristol, Surrey, and the London meetings at Devonshire House and Gracechurch Street. According to early printed reports of the school (1783–1829), the largest costs were for house expenses, clothing, and salaries and servants' wages. The school's finances were dependent upon wider economic forces. Across the troublesome 1790s, house expenses actually fell from £2,007 9s. ½d. (1791) to £1,871 4s. 6¼d. (1793), before rising steeply to £2,410 4s. 1d. (1795); by 1814 they had risen to £4,103 1s. 11¼d. before falling back to £2,567 17s. 8d. (1824) and £2,828 7s. 0d. (1829). The 1796 report lamented that the previous year's expenses had been 'unavoidably increased by the dearness of provisions', and in 1800 it was noted that 'the expenditure still exceeds the income, notwithstanding... the advance of the price of admission'. By 1814 a worrying 'deficiency' of income was explained by 'Donations and Legacies... considerably below the usual average' and 'an advance in the price of most of the necessaries of life' over the past seven years. By contrast, the healthier finances for 1824 were attributed to 'the continued low price of provisions', although this advantage was not expected to continue. Costs for clothing the children ranged from £702 (1783) to £1,054 (1800), while total payment for salaries and wages to the school remained more stable, fluctuating between £577 (1783) and £664 (1829), even though the number of staff employed rose from forty to fifty-eight.[44]

Children were admitted to Ackworth following an application made to a school agent, who then completed a printed recommendation and provided a remittance equivalent to one year's school fees; the children underwent a medical examination, and might be vaccinated, although these precautions did not prevent some serious outbreaks of life-threatening diseases at the school.[45] From its early days, Ackworth employed a housekeeper, nurse, cook, baker, brewer, and gardener, at least six maids, five tailors, two mantua makers, a linen repairer, and three shoemakers; by 1829 the staff also included seven day labourers, two husbandmen, and a houseman. By 1831 the school employed nine schoolteachers and nine apprentices to teach up to 300 children reading, spelling, writing, arithmetic, English grammar, and geography; the girls also learnt sewing and knitting, while some of the boys studied farming, gardening, 'the more useful parts' of mathematics, and Latin.[46] Pupils were taught the elements of spelling, punctuation, and grammar through weekly dictation exercises, which were to be corrected, written as fair copy, and memorized, in order to 'prove useful maxims to you through life'.[47] Practical exercises in

[44] Staffordshire Record Office D3159/2/84.
[45] Staffordshire Record Office D3159/2/85.
[46] Staffordshire Record Office D3159/2/84.
[47] Quaker Library BOX R2/10. The Ackworth writing method was to 'Sit in an easy, upright posture; rest only on the left Arm, & hold the right at liberty', and turn the pen 'lightly': Quaker Library BOX G1/5/1.

arithmetic involved various imperial measurements for money, weight, and time, as well as measures for wine, ale, beer, and cloth.[48] Ackworth sewing samplers often included fancy work such as embroidery and were ornately patterned, if not brightly coloured; they were distinguished by a penchant for octagonal medallions, often inscribing the name of the school, the maker, and the date.[49]

Smaller in scale than Ackworth was the school opened by the Methodist John Wesley in the coal-mining district of Kingswood near Bristol (1748). In its early years, Kingswood catered for up to fifty male boarders, admitted between the ages of 6 and 12, and was intended to form their minds 'to wisdom and holiness, by instilling the principles of true religion, speculative and practical, and training them up in the ancient way, that they might be rational, Scriptural Christians'.[50] The school had an unusual daily timetable: the pupils rose at four a.m. and went to bed at eight p.m. Wesley's plans for the school included an ambitious and probably unrealized curriculum of 'reading, writing, arithmetic, English, French, Latin, Greek, Hebrew, history, geography, chronology, rhetoric, logic, ethics, geometry, algebra, physics, music'; among the texts certainly studied were works by Claude Fleury, William Cave, Mathurin Cordier, John Bunyan, Jean-Baptiste Saint-Jure, Thomas Haliburton, and William Law.[51] Wesley could be deeply critical of the 'corrupted' and 'destructive' principles of other eighteenth-century schools, not least when their teachers and committees chose books which he felt were deficient in sense, style, or standard.[52] One of his greatest educational achievements was the publication of many dozens of educational texts and tracts, some of which were specifically aimed at children and students to remedy the shortcomings of the existing literature.[53]

The widespread organization and patronage of Sunday Schools by Methodists across the period 1780 to 1830 is well documented,[54] although it is not always appreciated that Presbyterians, Congregationalists, Baptists, and Unitarians

---

[48] Quaker Library BOX G1/5/2.

[49] I am grateful to Bridget Long and Rosanne Waine for these points.

[50] *The Works of the Reverend John Wesley, A.M.*, ed. John Emory, 7 vols. (London, 1831), VII, p. 339; the phrase was also noted by Robert Southey, *The Life of Wesley*, 2nd edn, 2 vols. (London, 1820), II, p. 158.

[51] A. H. L. Hastling, W. Addington Willis, and W. P. Workman, *The History of Kingswood School* (London, 1888), pp. 13–33.

[52] *Works*, ed. Emory, vii, p. 337.

[53] Isabel Rivers, 'John Wesley as Editor and Publisher', in Randy L. Maddox and Jason E. Vickers, eds, *The Cambridge Companion to John Wesley* (Cambridge, 2010), pp. 144–59; Joseph Stubenrauch, *The Evangelical Age of Ingenuity in Industrial Britain* (Oxford, 2016), pp. 100–31.

[54] David N. Hempton, 'Wesleyan Methodism and Educational Politics in Early Nineteenth-Century England', *History of Education*, 8, 3 (1979), pp. 207–21.

were also among the earliest founders of Sunday Schools.⁵⁵ The main differences between Dissenting and Anglican Sunday Schools were that the former oversaw pupils' attendance at chapel rather than the parish church, and (in the case of non-Methodist schools) used versions of the Westminster Assembly's catechism rather than the prayer book. However, in their central aims and modus operandi there were considerable similarities between Sunday Schools of all denominations, and the earliest Dissenting efforts in this field claimed direct descent from the work of Robert Raikes, the Anglican founder of the Sunday Schools of Gloucestershire. The Sunday Schools of Yorkshire and Lancashire grew out of correspondence between Raikes and the Dissenter Richard Townley of Belfield, and the movement spread to Newcastle at the instigation of William Turner, minister of the Hanover Square chapel, who was also suitably effusive about Raikes's achievements.⁵⁶ In London, the Hoxton Academy Sunday School was opened by James Kemp on 14 October 1784, again in direct emulation of Raikes's Gloucestershire model.⁵⁷ Unlike boarding schools such as Kibworth, Ackworth and Kingswood, Sunday Schools were designed primarily to educate poor children in the immediate vicinity of the chapel, and surviving attendance registers tend to reinforce the view that most children were of a labouring or artisanal background, and lived locally.⁵⁸

The speedy dissemination and growth of Sunday Schools have sometimes led to inflated claims for their role in the development of universal education in an industrial age, but there is no doubting their contribution to rising literacy rates in the early nineteenth century.⁵⁹ The basic plan of the Raikes-inspired Sunday Schools was to teach pupils to read by starting with the alphabet, then learning two-letter words, and gradually increasing the length of the words until they were ready to study the chosen catechism and the Bible; like charity schools, many Sunday Schools also taught writing, although fewer children learned this skill, and less time was devoted to it.⁶⁰ Depending on the size of the school, the number of staff, and (later) the number of monitors, this

---

⁵⁵ Surviving minute books from early Dissenting Sunday Schools are widespread and have never been effectively surveyed; the manuscript volumes perused for this essay include Berkshire Record Office D/N11/7/1/1, D/N33/7/1/1; Centre for Buckinghamshire Studies NB/16/7; Kent History and Library Centre R/N1/6; Leicestershire, Leicester and Rutland Record Office 15D64, 15D66; LMA CLC/182/MS5118, N/C/64/19; Staffordshire Record Office D1114/1, D1174/3/3/8, D1183/1/2, D7005/24/3/1; Suffolk Record Office (Bury) FK3502/53; Sussex History Centre 2615/1/7 Tyne & Wear Archives C.NC66/78, C.NC66/80, C.NC104/2-4; Wiltshire and Swindon History Centre 2194/27.

⁵⁶ A. P. Wadsworth, 'The First Manchester Sunday Schools', *Bulletin of the John Rylands Library* 33, 2 (1951), pp. 299–326; William Turner, *Sunday Schools Recommended* (Newcastle, 1786).

⁵⁷ William Harris, *Advice and Encouragement to Sunday School Teachers* (London, 1819).

⁵⁸ Staffordshire Record Office D1114/2; LMA CLC/182/MS5118; Thomas W. Laqueur, *Religion and Respectability* (London, 1976).

⁵⁹ K. D. M. Snell, 'The Sunday-School Movement in England and Wales', *Past & Present*, 164, 1 (1999), pp. 122–68.

⁶⁰ Tyne & Wear Archives C.NC66/78.

programme might be delivered across any number of classes. By 1800, the Methodist Sunday School in Leek catered for 200 scholars divided into fourteen classes; the Dissenters' Sunday School in Bury, by contrast, c.1805, had only six classes.[61] Aside from editions of the Westminster Assembly's catechism, the core books used differed little from those in Anglican Sunday Schools, and included Bibles, New Testaments, spelling books, specially compiled hymn books, and one of a number of books bearing the title *Reading Made Easy*.[62] However, instruction in literacy was always tantamount to fostering a literary culture. Some schools, such as the Hanover Square School, gave children in the advanced classes access to a 'Library of useful Books'.[63] Sunday School teachers and committee members, as well as the Auxiliary Christian Instruction Societies of the nineteenth century, all recognized that their schools offered 'an excellent opportunity for the distrubotion [*sic.*] of religious Tracts'.[64] Books were frequently awarded as prizes, using a quite complicated system of awarding tickets for good attendance, good attainment, and good behaviour. At the Edmonton and Tottenham Sunday School, over twenty different titles were awarded as prizes in 1828.[65] At the Baptist Sunday School in Princes Risborough, prizes included copies of the New Testament, Campbell's *Picture of Human Life*, and (for the higher classes), a set of 'Anecdotes & short stories'; a method was also developed of 'rewarding the Children by Tickets Picture Cards & small Magazines'.[66]

The advent of the monitorial system led to an increased diversity of voluntary schooling, and although coverage remained patchy the standards of monitorial schools were not necessarily as low or the discipline as tyrannical as has sometimes been suggested.[67] Joseph Lancaster, a Quaker, developed his notion of using children as school monitors in the late eighteenth century, at around the same time that the Madras system was being popularized in Church of England schools by Andrew Bell. In Lancasterian schools, pupils in the senior classes were appointed 'monitors', recording attendance and assisting learning in the junior classes.[68] Lancaster's messianic zeal for the improvement of educational provision, driven by his constant hope that 'under all this Rubbish and Ruin there may be Diamonds in the rough', echoes the peripatetic peregrinations of the early Quaker prophets, including

---

[61] Suffolk Record Office (Bury) FK3502/53.
[62] Staffordshire Record Office D1114/1.
[63] Tyne & Wear Archives C.NC66/78; Surrey History Centre 2615/1/7; see also Francis Westley, *A Catalogue of Sunday-School Publications* (London, c.1814).
[64] Centre for Buckinghamshire Studies NC 18/3/3; LMA N/C/19/10.
[65] LMA N/C/64/19 and CLC/228.   [66] Centre for Buckinghamshire Studies NB/16/7.
[67] Paul Sedra, 'Exposure to the Eyes of God', *Paedagogica Historica*, 47, 3 (2011), pp. 263–81; Mary Clare Martin, 'Church, School and Locality', *Paedagogica Historica*, 49, 1 (2013), pp. 70–81.
[68] Kent History and Library Centre R/N1/6/1; Derbyshire Record Office D3839.

Fox himself.[69] His single-mindedness and profligacy as he toured the country to give public lectures on his method meant that he required constant financial assistance from his wealthy and enthusiastic supporters, and in 1808 a small group of them came together to aid his endeavours and relieve his debts.[70] The result of this meeting was the formation of the Lancasterian Institution, known from 1814 as the British and Foreign School Society (the Dissenting equivalent of the Anglican-controlled National Society of 1811); its aims were to provide education, procure employment, and furnish clothing for poor children, as well as to encourage the use of vaccines for inoculation. The Society also oversaw the operations of a sizeable printing office in Borough Road, a project which Lancaster initially hoped would help to offset his debts through the provision of prospectuses, educational literature, and spelling books, but which was also badly managed. Of greater long-term significance were the Society's decisions to use the Borough Road address as a base to train teachers in Lancaster's methods, to become actively involved in the provision of teachers in Ireland, and to oversee the expansion of Lancaster's programme to other countries in Europe, North America, Asia, and Africa.[71] Through the pursuit of these projects, the Society became one of the most powerful educational bodies of the early nineteenth century, finally clearing its major debts in 1829.[72]

DISSENTING ACADEMIES AND COLLEGES

The earliest of the Dissenters' networks of higher education in the 1660s and 1670s were not ministerial academies so much as private arrangements by which puritan gentlemen could send their sons to an ejected minister for instruction in philosophy and classical literature.[73] This avoided the perceived double hazard of moral contamination and subscription to church articles attendant upon university matriculation, while providing nonconformist tutors with a reasonable, if fluctuating, income. Following the first ordinations of Dissenting ministers in the 1670s, these tutorial arrangements were increasingly viewed by Presbyterians and Congregationalists as instrumental for the production of an educated ministry. In several cases they quickly outgrew their original function and developed into fully fledged private academies, now catering for the children of Dissenters from the mercantile as well as the

---

[69] Brunel University BFSS 'Letters of Joseph Lancaster', No. 6.
[70] Brunel University BFSS /1/1/1/1/1. See the annual printed reports, also held at Brunel University Archives.
[71] Brunel University BFSS 1/1/1/1/2-4.   [72] Brunel University BFSS 1/2, folder 3.
[73] William Hamilton, *The Life and Character of James Bonnel Esq* (Dublin, 1703), pp 11–12.

professional and landed classes. The best surviving evidence of this process comes from Richard Frankland's academy in Kendal, which opened with only a small handful of students in 1670, before growing to over thirty students in the early 1690s.[74] Meanwhile, gifted and imaginative tutors, such as Charles Morton of Newington Green, began composing their own systems of philosophy from the 1670s onwards, in Morton's case extending to brief manuscript works of logic, natural philosophy, ethics, pneumatology, and even heraldry.[75] These texts were frequently modelled on useful printed works by Franco Burgersdijk, Adriaan Heereboord, Robert Sanderson, and other well-established European philosophers, although they might also incorporate fairly recent scientific observations and theories by Robert Boyle and Henry More among others. Some tutors, such as Theophilus Gale and Samuel Cradock, had their scholarly works printed, while others, including Thomas Doolittle, chose to publish practical writings, and kept their academic works in manuscript.[76]

Before 1690, the funding of nonconformist tutors and students was dependent on the patronage of wealthy individuals, most notably Philip Wharton, or bequests and endowments, such as the money left by Gale and distributed by John Owen to needy students in London.[77] In the 1690s, it became easier for Dissenters to collect and distribute funding centrally, and after an ill-fated attempt at running a Common Fund in the early 1690s, a Presbyterian Fund Board and a Congregational Fund Board had both emerged by 1695.[78] In the early years of its existence, the Presbyterian Fund Board spread its net widely and sponsored students at a large number of academies; the most important of these were Frankland's academy, and those of John Woodhouse (Sheriffhales, Shropshire), Matthew Warren (Taunton), Samuel Jones (Brynllywarch), James Owen (Shrewsbury), John Ker (Bishop's Hall, Bethnal Green), and Joshua Oldfield (briefly at Coventry, then moving to Hoxton Square). Several of these academies came to national prominence during the print controversies over Dissenting education in the early eighteenth century. The intellectual eclecticism of Ker's academy was defended by Samuel Palmer in 1703 in an attempt to counter Wesley's claims that the academies fostered sedition and heresy, while in the same year Owen published a fulsome defence

---

[74] Francis Nicolson and Ernest Axon, *The Older Nonconformity in Kendal* (Kendal, 1915), pp. 532–612.
[75] Wellcome Library 3635–8.
[76] Dewey D. Wallace, *Shapers of English Calvinism, 1660–1714* (Oxford, 2011), pp. 87–119; J. William Black, *Reformed Pastors* (Carlisle, 2004), pp. 241–54; Mark Burden, *A Biographical Dictionary of Tutors at the Dissenters' Private Academies, 1660–1729* (London, 2013), pp. 12–55, 123–31, 140–52, 195–222, 381–94.
[77] Samuel Wesley, *A Letter from a Country Divine to his Friend in London* (London, 1703), pp. 4–8.
[78] DWL OD67–8, OD401.

of the Dissenters' right to convene private academies.[79] Owen's early death in 1706 gave rise to the first detailed description of an academy to appear in print: his brother Charles Owen's hagiographical account painted James as a deeply learned, kind, and moderate man, whose teaching was a natural accompaniment to his ministry.[80]

Analysis of the education provided by the early Congregational Fund Board academies has suffered from an anachronistic view that their teaching provided a rearguard action against the softening of Calvinist principles. In truth, the texts and methods used by Thomas Goodwin (Pinner: son of the Commonwealth president of Magdalen College, Oxford) and Isaac Chauncey (Moorfields: son of Charles Chauncey, tutor at Harvard) are entirely unknown. Timothy Jollie's academy (Attercliffe) has been unduly denigrated on account of the hostile comments of Thomas Secker (who dismissed Jollie's language skills) and Joseph Mottershead (who bewailed the lack of mathematical instruction): other early commentators, such as John Barker, provided more balanced assessments.[81] The reputation of Rice Price (Tyn-ton) still requires rehabilitation from its excoriation by biographers of his son Richard Price, who rejected his father's theology and educational methods.[82] A more positive assessment is possible of John Langston (Ipswich), who began his teaching career as a schoolmaster in London, publishing two poetry digests, one in Latin and the other in Greek.[83] The breadth of reading of James Forbes (Gloucester) may be ascertained from the survival of a large number of his books at the Thomas Fisher Library, Toronto. Thomas Rowe's teaching can be described using his manuscript systems of logic and pneumatology, as well as two separate guides to theological reading, one of which belonged to his pupil Isaac Watts. Rowe's philosophy was a compote of ideas from the Dutch Aristotelians, the Port-Royal Cartesian logic, and the writings of Gale, his mentor; for their private studies, his pupils were encouraged to read a wide array of Episcopalian, Lutheran, Calvinist, and Protestant Dissenting works of practical piety and theological commentary.[84]

Among the early crises undergone by the academies, some were triggered externally by the prosecution of tutors, but others were self-inflicted, such as the divisive squabbles between the largely Presbyterian and Baxterian

---

[79] Samuel Palmer, *A Defence of the Dissenters Education in their Private Academies* (London 1703); James Owen, *Moderation a Virtue* (1703).

[80] Charles Owen, *Some Account of the Life and Writings of the Late Pious and Learned Mr. James Owen* (London, 1709).

[81] Nicholas Saunderson, *The Elements of Algebra*, 2 vols. (Cambridge, 1740), II, p. iii; Lambeth Palace Library 2598 fos. 4–5; John Barker, *A Sermon Occasioned by the Death of the Reverend Benjamin Grosvenor, D.D.* (London, 1758), pp. 27–8.

[82] William Morgan, *Memoirs of the Life of the Rev. Richard Price* (London, 1815), pp. 3–8.

[83] John Langston, *Lusus poeticus Latino-Anglicanus* (London, 1675), and *Encheiridion poietikon* (London, 1679).

[84] Bristol Baptist College Library G95/Zc4.

defenders of Daniel Williams and the largely Congregational and Calvinist defenders of Isaac Chauncey in the early 1690s.[85] In the late 1710s another major disagreement surfaced at the Exeter academy over the nature of the Trinity, with the Presbyterian tutor Joseph Hallett, his ministerial colleague James Peirce, and his students all being accused of harbouring Arian beliefs. When Hallett and his students refused to subscribe to an agreed form of words on the Trinity, the Exeter academy was closed; meanwhile the controversy spread to London, where at a meeting at Salters' Hall leading Dissenting tutors and ministers were split evenly between 'subscribers' and 'non-subscribers'.[86] While the primary issue at stake at Exeter and Salters' Hall was subscription, there is good evidence that the surface debate barely masked the considerable theological disagreements between the participants, and far from invigorating the academy movement, it initially threatened to undermine much of its energy and creativity. In November 1725, the Presbyterian Fund Board named the three academies at Carmarthen, Taunton, and Findern as the only institutions to which 'all the Students who for the future shall be Encourag'd by this fund shall be plac'd'. The Board now formalized the requirements that students were to be examined on Cicero, the Greek and Hebrew Testaments, and science, as well as their ability to draw up a thesis on a Latin question, and to compose a sermon on a practical subject.[87] Surviving manuscript systems of learning from Taunton and Findern suggest that these academies were prioritized on account of their openness to new scientific ideas and their rational theological principles.[88] These institutions fostered the acquisition of polite learning, and one of the Taunton tutors, Henry Grove, had a significant career as a moralist and essayist.[89]

Retrospectively, it is easy to view the opening of Philip Doddridge's Northampton academy in 1729 as an important landmark in Dissenting education. Doddridge's lectures on 'Pneumatology, Ethicks and Divinity', and 'Preaching' were among the most widely used works in the eighteenth-century academies, but they were only two of an enormous array of manuscript texts which he composed, compiled, and edited.[90] Nevertheless, Doddridge himself conceded that many of his ideas, texts, and methods were derived from the writings of his own gifted tutor, Joseph Jennings, tutor at Kibworth,[91] and

[85] DWL OD67, OD68, OD401; Isaac Chauncey, *Neonomianism Unmask'd* (London, 1692); Daniel Williams, *Gospel-truth Stated and Vindicated* (London, 1692).
[86] Mark Burden, 'Theology and Education', *Southern History*, 36 (2014), pp. 130–48.
[87] DWL OD69, p. 50.
[88] Derby Local Studies Library 3368; Wellcome Library 3636; Harris Manchester College Oxford Grove 1; Huntingdon Library, Pasadena, CA, HM46326; Congregational Library 1h.1–3, 1h.10–11.
[89] Alan P. F Sell, *Testimony and Tradition* (Aldershot, 2005), pp. 91–118.
[90] Tessa Whitehouse, *The Textual Culture of English Protestant Dissent 1720–1800* (Oxford, 2015), pp. 22–121.
[91] Isabel Rivers, *The Defence of Truth through the Knowledge of Error* (London, 2003); Tessa Whitehouse, ed., *Dissenting Education and the Legacy of John Jennings*, 2nd edn (London, 2011).

there are other signs of the growing confidence of Dissenting scholarship in the years before he opened his academy. An analysis of the large number of surviving manuscripts from the Presbyterian Samuel Jones's academy at Gloucester and Tewkesbury in the 1710s points to the influence of the Dutch scholars Jakob Gronow, Hermann Wits, Jakob Voorbroek, and Huig de Groot, alongside the growing importance of non-Aristotelian subjects, such as Jewish antiquities, natural law, geography, and biblical criticism.[92] At a pioneering Congregational academy in Moorfields (1712–44), John Eames, a Fellow of the Royal Society, taught ethics, natural philosophy (including anthropology), and mathematics, while the Congregational minister Thomas Ridgley lectured in Jewish antiquities and compiled a system of divinity which he revised for publication. Eames's works of mechanics and anthropology, together with the systems of natural philosophy drawn up by Charles Morton (Newington Green), Robert Darch (Taunton), and Ebenezer Latham (Findern), serve as a reminder of the vitality of Dissenting pedagogy prior to the foundation of Doddridge's academy, although the notion that the academies harboured any major scientific achievements prior to the 1770s must be treated with considerable scepticism.[93]

The eighteenth century also saw the gradual expansion of Baptist higher education. The first significant bequest for the establishment of a Baptist academy was made by Edward Terrill of Bristol in 1679, although there is no evidence that the Bristol Baptist academy operated before the tenure of Bernard Foskett (*fl.*1720–58). From its early years, ministerial students at the academy were supported by the Particular Baptist Fund in London; from 1770 a small number of students were also funded by the Bristol Education Society. A diary of subjects and texts intended for study by John Collett Ryland in 1744 includes philological texts by Cordery, Pufendorf, Marck, and Buchanan, scientific and philosophical works by Watts, Gordon, Martin, and Locke, and Calvinist theological works by Vincent and Ridgley; many of the same texts appear in the annual reports of the Education Society students in the early 1770s.[94] The Particular Baptists also expanded their academical provision in the north of England through the labours of John Fawcett, who provided ministerial and lay education at Wainsgate, Brearley Hall, and Ewood Hall; in 1787 he collaborated with Samuel Medley of Liverpool to form the Lancashire and Yorkshire Association, and he was instrumental in the re-establishment of the Northern Educational Society in 1804, which

---

[92] Tessa Whitehouse, 'Intellectual and Textual Entrêpots', *English Studies*, 92, 5 (2011) pp. 562–75.

[93] David A. Reid, 'A Science for Polite Society', *History of Universities*, 21, 2 (2006) pp. 117–58; Burden, *Biographical Dictionary*, pp. 152–60, 348–55, 436–41.

[94] Bristol Baptist College Library B/01/1770; Regent's Park College Oxford 'Ryland Diaries' 1 and D/PBF 3/1–6.

oversaw the establishment of the Baptists' Horton Academy (1806–59).[95] Of equal importance was the Baptist Academical Institution at Stepney (1810–56), sponsored by the Particular Baptist Fund, which was initially designed to serve the interest of Calvinist Baptists only, although in practice it became more inclusive. In 1840 the college was granted degree-awarding powers by the University of London, after which the course was lengthened to five years.[96] The General Baptist Education Society fared less well, despite its attempts from 1795 to fund the ministerial students of John Evans of Islington. Unfortunately, Evans was more used to teaching grammar subjects, and offered little more than studies in English, Latin, Greek, Scriptural history, and portions of Doddridge's lectures on 'Pneumatology, Ethics and Divinity'. Following complaints from students, Evans resigned in 1819 and was replaced by James Gilchrist, under whose tenure the course expanded from two years to three.[97]

The narrative of late eighteenth-century Unitarian educational achievement has been so widespread that few historians have stopped to think about the problems faced by Warrington Academy, New College Hackney, and New College Manchester, all of which were strictly speaking nondenominational institutions, and all of which were chronically short of money for much of their existence.[98] Warrington Academy (1757–86) has received an incomparably positive reception on account of its employment of some of the leading lights of rational dissent, including Joseph Priestley, John Seddon, and John Aikin, although the content of their teaching has rarely been sensitively explored.[99] Among the most interesting documents to survive from the academy are the annual descriptions of the two courses, designed to appeal to ministerial students (three years), and those designed for 'a Life of publick Business, or Commerce' (five years). In practice, there was very considerable overlap between the two curricula, with both groups studying languages and mathematics in the first year, natural philosophy in the second, and moral philosophy in the third; however, the formal divinity instruction for lay students consisted only of a third-year course in 'Christian evidences', whereas ministerial students studied theological subjects for a further two years,

---

[95] John Fawcett Jnr, *An Account of the Life, Ministry and writings of the late Rev. John Fawcett, D.D.* (London, 1818); Peter Shepherd, *The Making of a Northern Baptist College* (Manchester, 2004); David Bebbington, 'The Baptist Colleges in the Mid-Nineteenth Century', *Baptist Quarterly*, 46, 2 (2015), pp. 49–68.

[96] R. E. Cooper, *From Stepney to St Giles': The Story of Regent's Park College, 1810–1960* (London, 1960).

[97] *The Proceedings of the General Assembly of General Baptist Churches* (London, 1843); *Christian Reformer*, 17 (1861), p. 316.

[98] David A. Reid, 'Education as a Philanthropic Enterprise', *History of Education*, 39, 3 (2010), pp. 299–317.

[99] Herbert McLachlan, *Warrington Academy: Its History and Influence* (Manchester, 1943); a new and more balanced account of the intellectual history of the academy is badly needed.

including preaching and pastoral care.[100] After the collapse of Warrington, the hopes of Arians and Unitarians were invested heavily in New College, Hackney (opened 1786), which was fortunate enough to employ Joseph Priestley (history and natural philosophy), Thomas Belsham (theology), and Abraham Rees (who taught mathematics through algebra and mechanics). Unfortunately, the overambitious capital costs of the academy, combined with its declining numbers and growing accusations of seditious activity, forced it to close in 1796.[101] The early years of New College, Manchester (1786), the sister academy to Hackney, were also fraught with difficulties, as the committee failed to raise adequate subscriptions, suffered a fall in student numbers, and went through ten tutors in its seventeen-year existence.[102] The two tutors who left the greatest impression on the operation of the academy were Thomas Barnes (1786–98), who taught theological subjects, law, and commerce, and the scientist John Dalton (1793–1800), both members of the Manchester Society for Literature and Philosophy.[103] In 1803 the college moved to York and for the period 1803–40 is best described as Manchester College, York; for much of this period, students were tutored in grammar and classics by the gifted pioneer of German historical criticism John Kenrick (1788–1877), in a philosophy and science course mirroring the Cambridge curriculum by William Turner (1809–28), and in theology by the principal Charles Wellbeloved (1803–40), in whose house the academy was resident.[104] Although it was criticized for devoting insufficient attention to practical preaching skills, the college was able to offset its early debts due to a growth in subscriptions and endowments, coupled with its reputation for high academic standards in languages and science.[105]

Historians' focus on the educational achievements of Unitarians and their supporters has masked the vitality of the Congregational academies in the later eighteenth century. In part, this growth came as a response to the decline of the 'liberal' Presbyterian-controlled academies. It is no coincidence that the Congregational Fund Board's Western Academy opened at Ottery St Mary in 1752, just as the Presbyterian academy at Taunton was facing closure. Its first tutor, John Lavington, used Marck's *Christianae theologiae medulla* to

---

[100] *A Report of the Progress that has been made in the Establishment of the Academy in Warrington* (Warrington, 1758). Both courses underwent various modifications across the academy's thirty-year history.
[101] Stephen Burley, *Hazlitt the Dissenter* (Basingstoke, 2014), pp. 49–90.
[102] David L. Wykes, 'Sons and Subscribers: Lay Support and the College 1786–1840', in Barbara Smith, ed., *Truth, Liberty, Religion* (Oxford, 1986), pp. 31–77.
[103] Jean Raymond and John Pickstone, 'The Natural Sciences and the Learning of English Unitarians', in Smith, ed., *Truth, Liberty, Religion*, pp. 127–64.
[104] Ruth Watts, 'Manchester College and Education 1786–1853', in Smith, ed., *Truth, Liberty, Religion*, pp. 79–110.
[105] Harris Manchester College Oxford M.N.C. Misc. 1, 4, 62–9, 87, 89, 93, 97.

emphasize the importance of the Trinity, election, and God's decrees, in obvious contrast to the Arian tendencies of Richard Price's friend Thomas Amory, the Presbyterian tutor at Taunton.[106] In other areas of the curriculum, however, the Western Academy, which later moved to Bridport (1765), Taunton (1780), Axminster (1796), and Exeter (1829), borrowed pre-existing texts and methods from other Dissenting intellectuals, teaching Watts's introductions to logic, geography, and astronomy, and Thomas Gibbons's guide to rhetoric.[107] Gibbons was a tutor at the Mile End Academy (1754), which later moved to Homerton (1769), and was controlled until 1817 by the Calvinist-leaning King's Head Society.[108] Homerton's most eminent early tutor was John Pye Smith, under whose tenure the college was given the power in 1840 to award University of London degrees.[109] Meanwhile, through the work of Edward Hitchin (London) and James Scott (Yorkshire), the Northern Education Society was formed in 1756, which oversaw the work of an academy at Heckmondwike (1756) and its successors at Northowram (1783) and Rotherham (1795–1888).[110] An entirely separate academy, begun by William Roby at Mosley Street chapel in Manchester in 1803, migrated to Leaf Square (1811–13) and Blackburn (1816–43) before returning to Manchester (1843) and enjoying a long history as the Lancashire Independent College, otherwise known as the Northern Congregational College.[111]

The growing self-confidence of late eighteenth-century Congregationalism and Unitarianism put further pressure on the Presbyterian-controlled academies. After the Congregational Fund Board withdrew its support and created the Abergavenny Academy (1757), the Carmarthen Academy was run by Presbyterians, although it has been suggested that its students largely went on to serve Congregational churches in the nineteenth century.[112] In 1771 the academy became embroiled in controversy after its tutor, Jenkin Jenkins, opposed Calvinist demands for subscription to orthodox doctrine, and thereafter the academy's size and reputation declined, forcing its temporary closure in 1794.[113] However, after a successful relaunch in 1795 the number of students and the expected standards rose, leading to stricter entrance criteria

---

[106] DWL WES.5-7; Inga Jones and David L. Wykes, 'Western Academy (1752–1845)', *Dissenting Academies Online: Database and Encyclopedia* (Dr Williams's Centre for Dissenting Studies, 2011–17), http://dissacad.english.qmul.ac.uk/sample1.php?contid=9&detail=academies&parameter=showarticles&acadid=5 (last accessed 13 January 2017).

[107] DWL L54/4/71. [108] DWL MS NCL/105-12.

[109] John Medway, *Memoirs of the Life and Writings of John Pye Smith* (London, 1853).

[110] Simon N. Dixon, 'James Scott's Academy, Heckmondwike (1756–1783)', *Dissenting Academies Online*, http://dissacad.english.qmul.ac.uk/sample1.php?parameter=academyretrieve&alpha=69 (last accessed 13 January 2017).

[111] Elaine Kaye, *For the Work of Ministry* (Edinburgh, 1999).

[112] DWL OD72-3; Michael R. Watts, *The Dissenters: Volume III: The Crisis and Conscience of Nonconformity* (Oxford, 2015), p. 191.

[113] *A Vindication of the Conduct of the Associated Ministers in Wales* (Carmarthen, 1771).

in 1827, a new course of study in 1828, and affiliation with the University of London in 1842.[114] Although the earliest Methodist higher education academy was the Wesleyan Theological Institution at Hoxton (1834), Wesley had previously drawn up an ambitious scheme of academical learning for the use of advanced students at Kingswood. This plan, which is often overlooked, included the study of Latin, Greek, Hebrew, French, Spanheim, Pufendorf, Euclid, Newton, Mosheim, Hume, Milton, Watts, Locke, and Malebranche among others. The extent to which Wesley's scheme was implemented has never been established, although Wesley's stated preference for students to proceed to a university rather than to remain at Kingswood was dinted after the expulsion of six Methodist students from St Edmund Hall, Oxford in 1768.[115]

Another energetic evangelical whose endeavours led to the creation of Dissenting schools and academies was Selina Hastings, whose association with the Calvinist Methodist George Whitefield contributed to the establishment of the Countess of Huntingdon's College, Trevecka (1768–91) and its successor, Cheshunt College (1792–1967), which later merged with Westminster College, Cambridge.[116] Trevecka College's first tutors included Joseph Benson, the former schoolmaster of Kingswood, who was one of a number of men later dismissed by Hastings on account of their refusal to renounce Wesley's Arminianism.[117] From 1771 she funded and supervised the operations of the college herself, focusing on training preachers rather than inculcating academical subjects. By contrast, academic standards at the Congregational-sponsored English Evangelical Academy at Mile End and Hoxton (1778) and its successor, Highbury College (1826) were high, including attendance at lectures in moral and mental philosophy from the University of London, and the study of the Bible in Latin, Greek, and Syriac.[118] Although they had been a significant element of instruction at many of the Dissenters' academies since the 1680s, skills in preaching and catechizing were to be seen as increasingly important following the establishment of the Particular Baptist Missionary Society (1794), the evangelical London Missionary Society (1795), and the Unitarian Fund (1806), and an important Congregational college which pioneered the education of missionaries was David Bogue's academy in Gosport (1777–1826).[119] The practical support offered to young ministers

---

[114] Noel Gibbard and Isabel Rivers, 'Carmarthen Academy, later Presbyterian College, Carmarthen (1795–1963)', *Dissenting Academies Online*, http://dissacad.english.qmul.ac.uk/sample1.php?parameter=academyretrieve&alpha=206 (last accessed 13 January 2017).

[115] Hastling, Willis, and Workman, *History of Kingswood*, 65–73.

[116] Alan Harding, *The Countess of Huntingdon's Connexion* (Oxford, 2003); Edwin Welch, ed., *Cheshunt College: The Early Years* (Linton, 1990).

[117] Stephen Orchard, *Cheshunt College* (Saffron Walden, 1968), p. 20.

[118] John Stoughton, *Recollections of a Long Life* (London, 1894), pp. 16–22.

[119] Christopher A. Daily, 'From Gosport to Canton: A New Approach to the Beginnings of Protestant Missions in China', unpublished PhD thesis (University of London, 2010).

by these organizations, combined with the training of teachers in the Lancasterian method by the British and Foreign School Society, helped to ensure the global reach of Dissenting education in the nineteenth century.[120]

THE REPUTATION AND INFLUENCE OF DISSENTING EDUCATION

The perceived divisiveness of Dissenting education has always been largely a question of its relationship to wider social and political structures. The origins of the terms of debate lie in the competing claims of later Stuart political discourse. While High Church controversialists accused Dissenting students of playing a leading role in Monmouth's Rebellion, the 1689 revolution, and the Whig ministry which followed, discussions of political radicalism and heterodoxy were almost entirely absent from Dissenters' own descriptions of their educational achievements in the early eighteenth century. In 1714, the publication of the High Churchman John Walker's extensive historical researches into the educational intolerance of the Commonwealth regime led to renewed accusations of hypocrisy against those Dissenting schoolmasters who complained of legal restrictions;[121] his antagonist, the Presbyterian memorialist Edmund Calamy, responded by presenting Dissenting tutors as paragons of moderation, quietly engaging in private teaching in the face of establishment intolerance.[122] In recent years, Calamy's interpretation of the work of his friends and colleagues has gained ground among historians broadly sympathetic to the aims of Dissenting educators. However, these scholars often pay insufficient attention to Calamy's construction of the concept of 'moderation', a self-consciously Baxterian discourse that now threatens to mask the economic, political, and social relations which helped to propel early Dissenting education through its many periods of externally and internally induced difficulty.

Dissenters have often viewed their eighteenth-century schools and academies as the pinnacle of their intellectual and social achievement, whereas their detractors have assessed Dissenting academic achievement as minimal and have sharply criticized their institutions for spreading religious separatism and political sedition. For example, the presumed radicalism of later eighteenth-century

---

[120] Brunel University BFSS/2/6/1-3.
[121] John Walker, *An Attempt towards recovering an Account of the Numbers and Sufferings of the Clergy* (London, 1714).
[122] Edmund Calamy, *A Continuation of the Account of the Ministers, Lecturers, Masters and Fellows of Colleges, and Schoolmasters, who were Ejected and Silenced after the Restoration in 1660*, 2 vols. (London, 1727), I, pp. 177-211; II, pp. 731-5.

Dissenting schools and colleges has often been appropriated by later commentators wishing to present them as engines of middle-class social reform, religious toleration, and educational liberalism.[123] There is some truth in these claims: Dissenting institutions were both shaped by and served as a motor of political and legal changes, while several prominent tutors and students at the late eighteenth- and nineteenth-century liberal academies campaigned for social reforms, including the abolition of slavery.[124] However, the presence of these issues should not blind us to the centrality of moral and theological principles, as well as practices, in eighteenth-century student dissertations and periodicals.[125]

Since Irene Parker's path-breaking account in 1914 of the relationship of Dissenting scholarship to the 'classical' and 'modern' learning of the eighteenth century,[126] Dissenting education has been analysed and appropriated by historians of dissent, education, literature, and literacy,[127] but much work remains to be undertaken on the surviving manuscript materials. Some strands of Dissenting education, such as the London charity and Sunday Schools, the Northampton–Daventry academy tradition, and the Warrington–Manchester–York colleges, are very well documented in contemporary manuscripts, although the simple fact of preservation should not lead to inflated perceptions of these archives' educational importance, influence, and legacy.[128] Unfortunately, the manuscript records of many other institutions are almost entirely lost, a situation which has caused interpretive problems ever since the very earliest memorials of Dissenting education were undertaken in the late eighteenth century.[129] The most promising means for deepening our knowledge of Dissenting education in the near future looks set to be the close study of manuscript notebooks compiled by tutors and students, but to produce any balanced assessment of these texts it will always be necessary to keep in view the wider picture of Dissenting educational achievements and limitations across the period.

---

[123] John Seed, 'Gentleman Dissenters: The Social and Political Meanings of Rational Dissent in the 1770s and 1780s', *Historical Journal*, 28, 2 (1985), pp. 299–325, provides a useful intervention in this debate; see also Ruth Watts, *Gender, Power, and the Unitarians in England, 1760–1860*, 2nd edn (Oxford, 2013), pp. 33–76.

[124] G. M. Ditchfield, 'Manchester College and Anti-Slavery', in Smith, ed., *Truth, Liberty, Religion*, pp. 185–224.

[125] DWL 69-8-11; NCL L11-12.

[126] Irene Parker, *Dissenting Academies in England* (Cambridge, 1914).

[127] Some of the crucial early interventions included Herbert McLachlan, *English Education under the Test Acts* (Manchester, 1931); Oliver M. Griffiths, *Religion and Learning* (Cambridge 1935); Mary Gladwys Jones, *The Charity School Movement* (Cambridge, 1938); and Nicholas Hans, *New Trends in Education in the Eighteenth Century* (London, 1951).

[128] The main manuscripts are held at LMA, DWL, and Harris Manchester College Oxford respectively.

[129] DWL 24.59; Birmingham University Library XMS 281; Burden, 'Academical Learning', pp. 10–43.

SELECT BIBLIOGRAPHY

Burden, Mark, *A Biographical Dictionary of Tutors at the Dissenters' Private Academies, 1660–1729* (London, 2013), http://www.qmulreligionandliterature.co.uk/online-publications/a-biographical-dictionary/.

Burley, Stephen, *Hazlitt the Dissenter* (Basingstoke, 2014).

Greaves, Richard L., *The Puritan Revolution and Educational Thought* (New Brunswick, 1969).

Green, Ian, *Humanism and Protestantism in Early Modern English Education* (Farnham, 2009).

James, Felicity and Inkster, Ian, eds, *Religious Dissent and the Aikin–Barbauld Circle 1740–1860* (Cambridge, 2012).

Jones, Mary Gladwys, *The Charity School Movement* (Cambridge, 1938).

McLachlan, Herbert, *English Education under the Test Acts* (Manchester, 1931).

Morgan, John Philip, *Godly Learning* (Cambridge, 1986).

Nuttall, Geoffrey F., ed., *Calendar of the Correspondence of Philip Doddridge DD* (London, 1979).

Parker, Irene, *Nonconformist Academies in England* (Cambridge, 1914).

Rivers, Isabel and David Wykes et al., *Dissenting Academies Online* (London, 2011–17), http://www.qmulreligionandliterature.co.uk/research/the-dissenting-academies-project/dissenting-academies-online/.

Rivers, Isabel and Wykes, David, eds, *Joseph Priestley: Scientist, Philosopher, and Theologian* (Oxford, 2008).

Smith, Barbara, ed., *Truth, Liberty, Religion* (Oxford, 1986).

Whitehouse, Tessa, *The Textual Culture of English Protestant Dissent 1720–1800* (Oxford, 2015).

19

The Material Culture of Dissent

Meeting Houses, Chapels, and Churches in England and America, 1600–1830

Carl Lounsbury

In the century and a half between the Act of Toleration in 1689 and the disestablishment of the Congregational Church in the state of Massachusetts in 1833, Dissenting houses of worship rose from tentative beginnings to become an integral presence in Britain and America. At the end of the seventeenth century in backstreet meeting places that looked like cottages and in small clapboard buildings raised in timbered clearings in New World settlements, individual congregations of Presbyterians, Congregationalists, Baptists, Quakers, and other groups took their first steps in forging a new heterogeneous religious landscape, one that proclaimed the materiality of Nonconformity. For the most part these were modest, often austere buildings whose compact form reflected their primacy as places of preaching rather than venues for elaborate ceremonies and ritual processions. They lacked towers and the soaring pointed apertures traditionally associated with Anglican churches, and their centralized plan and simple wooden fittings arranged around a tall pulpit or elders' bench signalled a demonstrable break with the old forms and image of public worship.

By the 1830s, Dissenting meeting houses had become so commonplace in England and indistinguishable in America that it was hard to imagine a time without them.[1] Success also marked the beginning of their decline as a distinctive type. The social standing and wealth achieved by a number of nonconformist congregations heralded the adaptation of architectural features

---

[1] On the growth in the number of Dissenting meeting houses in England and Wales from the early eighteenth century to the middle of the nineteenth century see, Michael R. Watts, *The Dissenters: From the Reformation to the French Revolution* (Oxford, 1978), p. 269; *Census of Great Britain, 1851; Religious Worship in England and Wales: Abridged from the official Report Made by Horace Mann* (London, 1854), pp. 2, 79–80.

previously considered alien to the material expression of Nonconformity. In England, nonconformist chapels could never displace the familiar presence and scale of thousands of historical Anglican churches, but large, new chapels increasingly reflected the self-confidence of their members. They stood prominently 'exposed to the street, instead of being buried like [old] meeting houses behind shops and houses'.[2] In America, the Quakers and some Baptists rejected innovation and retained their characteristic meeting-house forms, but steeples, axial plans, stained glass, and bold ornamentation would begin to bring chapel architecture much closer to the design aesthetics formerly associated with liturgical houses of worship. Many congregations in both countries embraced a generic building form marked by an embellished gable-fronted entrance that led into a rectangular body, which made it nearly impossible to determine the confessional identity of the worshippers from the exterior.[3]

Yet, that blending of forms was short-lived and would be reversed in the 1840s with the emergence of the Ecclesiology movement in the Anglican Church, whose advocates looked backward to medieval Gothic architecture for inspiration in church design and sought liturgical innovation through new ceremonies associated with the pre-reformed church.[4] For three-quarters of a century, the power of these ideas shaped new construction and the restoration of thousands of medieval churches so thoroughly that the liturgical perspective of the Ecclesiologists long influenced scholarly and popular perceptions, which accentuated the polarity between Anglican churches and Dissenting meeting houses following the Toleration Act. In truth, the architectural dichotomy was seldom that rigid in the long eighteenth century.

REFORMED THEOLOGY AND THE ARCHITECTURAL SETTING OF WORSHIP

The material culture of dissent had its origins in the Reformation. The impact of the new religion on ecclesiastical architecture was profound. Reformers rejected the subdivision of the medieval church with its many altars, which emphasized the sacrificial nature of the Catholic Mass. They abolished the doctrine of purgatory with its concomitant investment in the spiritual welfare

---

[2] *The Gentleman's Magazine*, 100 (June, 1830), p. 541.

[3] Carl Lounsbury, 'God is in the Details: The Transformation of Ecclesiastical Architecture in Early Nineteenth-Century America', in Carl Lounsbury, *Essays in Early American Architectural History* (Charlottesville, VA, 2011), pp. 177–94; Terry Friedman, *The Eighteenth-Century Church in Britain* (London, 2011), pp. 450–65.

[4] Nigel Yates, *Buildings, Faith, and Worship: The Liturgical Arrangements of Anglican Churches 1600–1900* (Oxford, 1990), pp. 128–34.

of the dead at side altars where priests had said requiem masses. What the new religion demanded was a Church devoted to the living, accessible to everyone, and a changed relationship between priest and congregation. By stripping the altars and destroying idolatrous images, Protestants cleansed them of the most egregious features and practices associated with the old faith, but differed vociferously among themselves on how far to take those reforms.

Through the early seventeenth century, the Anglican Church was strongly Calvinist in theology, but its members differed over the implications of those principles when it came to the nature and structure of worship and its associated ceremonies. More conservative churchmen such as Archbishop William Laud wished to retain many of the old ways in order to celebrate the 'beauties of holiness' in divine worship. The Puritan wing of the Church, however, argued that the Church needed to be purged of all of its medieval 'abuses'. Its members asserted that 'Scripture is not a partiall, but a perfect rule of Faith', traditions were 'simply evill', and that churches 'ought to bee reformed, freed, and cleared' of unwarranted trappings and ceremonies unsanctioned by biblical authority.[5]

For English Protestants, the centrepiece of worship was hearing a minister expound the Word of God. Preaching became the principal focus of the service and the auditory experience of reformed worship required seating around a centrally placed pulpit. Hundreds of surviving Elizabethan and Jacobean pulpits and reading desks in parish churches across England testify to the newfound presence of preaching, prayer, and readings from the Bible, made clear by the words, 'Faith is by Hearing', inscribed on the 1613 pulpit canopy at St Michael's Church in Lyme Regis.

Like Calvinists in other countries, English Puritans diminished the significance of the Holy Communion as a sacramental celebration, interpreting it more as a commemorative meal. This meant that the traditional pre-reformed position of the altar at the east end of the chancel had no symbolic importance that needed to be treated with particular reverence. This undermined the obligation to maintain or enhance in any architectural fashion the liturgical significance of the east end or even orient new buildings in the old prescribed manner. Where convenient, many Puritan congregations emphasized this fact by setting the communion table in the body of the church near the pulpit. In redefining the nature and place of worship, they effectively abandoned the chancel, and in so doing, established one of the chief characteristics of a nonconformist place of worship—a single room focused on the pulpit.

Dissenters with strong Calvinist views embraced aesthetic sensibilities that looked warily on the excessive adornment of churches. This stemmed from

---

[5] William Ames, *The Marrow of Sacred Divinity Drawne Out of the Holy Scriptures* (London, 1639), p. 150; Henry Jacob, *Reasons Taken Out of Gods Word and the Best Humane Testimonies Proving a Necessitie of Reforming Our Churches in England* (London, 1604), p. 16.

their profound aversion to ascribing spiritual attributes to material objects or places. They believed in God's omnipresence, which meant that a place of worship was no more holy than a dwelling, barn, or grove. That perspective countered the conservative Anglican idea of God's special presence in a church that required appropriate adoration. Since God was disassociated with a particular place, Puritans considered a church not as a building, but a gathering of true believers. They began to call their places of worship 'meeting houses' in an effort to divert attention from the physical place to the spiritual activities that were the true core of the church.[6]

Calvinists and Quakers avoided what they regarded to be the decorative exuberance associated with ceremonial worship. They abhorred the Catholic veneration of images as blasphemous and dismissed ostentation as a distraction to the true nature of worship. They deemed crosses an anathema, a sign of popish superstition. Unlike their English counterparts, Puritans in New England shunned 'round-topped windows and the corresponding form of doors, vestibules, and entrances', considering them tainted by their association with 'prelatical houses of worship'.[7] The Quaker George Fox dismissed established churches as irrelevant 'steeple houses' and castigated one particular Yorkshire church for its superfluous ornament, decrying 'the painted Beast has a painted House'.[8]

The ecclesiastical landscape in colonial America and, to a significant degree, England as well, could be measured by incremental gradations in embellishments ranging between Anglican ceremonial ostentation at one end and Baptist and Quaker asceticism at the other. Protestant denominations worked within this sliding scale of ornamentation consonant with their theological principles. The decorative restraint of Dissenting meeting houses marked them as a recognizable building type setting them apart from their Anglican counterparts.

THE PURITAN AUDITORY CHURCH

Long before the Act of Uniformity in 1662 turned the Puritan wing of the Church of England into disenfranchised Dissenters along with the Separatists,

---

[6] For Puritan arguments for the use of the term, which first gained broad currency in New England in the 1630s, see Isaac Chauncy, *The Divine Institution of Congregational Churches* (London, 1697), p. 2; Cotton Mather, *Ratio Disciplinae Fratrum Nov-Anglorum* (Boston, MA, 1726).

[7] Quoted in Gretchen Buggeln, *Temples of Grace: The Material Transformation of Connecticut's Churches, 1790–1840* (Lebanon, NH, 2003), p. 111.

[8] *A Journal or Historical Account of the Life, Travels, Sufferings, Christian Experiences, and Labour of Love in the Work of the Ministry of that Ancient, Eminent, and Faithful Servant of Jesus Christ, George Fox* (London, 1709), p. 124.

Quakers, and other groups that emerged from the turbulence of the 1640s and 1650s, reformed theology had made an impact on English church architecture. Langley Chapel, a small medieval chapel of ease located in the remote Shropshire countryside, was substantially repaired in 1601 and its early seventeenth-century fittings illustrate how Puritans responded to these new ideas. The stone chapel never had a chancel but consists of one large room. The congregation sat on a series of east-facing benches on either side of a central aisle at the west end of the chapel. The north and south benches give way to a pair of gentry pews near the centre. Next to them are a large reading desk on the north wall and a smaller pulpit across the aisle. There is no chancel screen separating the interior into two spaces and the placement of the table several feet out from the east wall reflects Puritan practices. Parishioners took communion seated at two rows of benches arranged along the north, east, and south walls, which enclosed three sides of the large wooden table.

Langley's small rectangular plan remained a popular form for Puritans even when freed from the restraint of conservative churchmen during the Commonwealth. A few meeting houses built during this time are hardly distinguishable from traditional small Anglican chapels of ease and the absence of a structurally separate chancel is often the only exterior indication that they might have been built by congregations that took exception to prayer book worship. Such is the case of Bramhope Chapel located a few miles north-west of Leeds in Yorkshire. It is a long, low stone building with a single roofline erected in 1649 by the local lord of the manor with Puritan inclinations. The six-bay front wall has two doorways at the second and fifth bays. A small pulpit window slightly east of centre lights the pulpit on the opposite wall. The long rectangular room is lined with seventeenth-century pews on either side of the central aisle, which terminates at the east gable end with a five-light window. The communion table stands below it.[9] If this arrangement is original, then there is little here that marks the chapel architecturally as Puritan except the absence of a chancel screen. Equally ambiguous is Guyhirn Chapel erected in Cambridgeshire in 1660 at the very end of the Puritan Commonwealth. It was unconsecrated for many years and what little is known of its early history suggests that its minister and congregation retained their Puritan practices well into the 1680s. A 44- by 24-foot brick building with flat-headed windows similar to those at Bramhope, the chapel has a single doorway in the west corner of the long south wall. The present fittings are old but not original.[10] A single window just east of centre suggests that the pulpit may have been located in this position. If so, then benches

---

[9] Christopher Stell, *Nonconformist Chapels and Meeting-Houses in the North of England* (London, 1994), pp. 239–41.
[10] Brian Payne, *Guyhirn Chapel* (London, 2006), pp. 2–6.

may well have been arranged around it. Small rectangular chapels such as Bramhope and Guyhirn demonstrate the ease with which small auditories could be arranged to accommodate either prayer book or Dissenting worship.

Scholarly attention devoted to the extreme positions of Laudians and Puritans has overshadowed substantial areas of agreement about church planning within the Anglican Church. Precursors to the Dissenting meeting-house form appeared before the Act of Toleration, but have long been unrecognized. Some of the largest auditory churches were constructed in London and its eastern suburbs between the 1630s and 1650s by Anglicans of moderate Calvinist leanings. As Peter Guillery has demonstrated, they were the work of men who found themselves between Laudian ceremonialists and Puritan zealots on the reform spectrum.[11] They built churches that were squarish in plan with shallow or unarticulated chancels and centrally positioned pulpits. A few were small brick chapels of ease erected at modest expense while others were large parish churches intended to supply demand in growing Thames-side communities such as Poplar and Shadwell. Most have disappeared and their stories have been overshadowed by the monumental effort to rebuild London's city churches in the classical style by Christopher Wren and others following the Great Fire in 1666. The design pedigree of these chapels has also suffered because of the absence of well-known architects associated with them. Their squat proportions, multiple parapet gables, and mongrel style, which often combined Tuscan columns and entablatures, round- and flat-headed windows with Gothic tracery, and an eclectic set of decorative details, make it difficult to place them in the standard stylistic narrative of the period.

Guillery cites Broadway Chapel, erected in Westminster in 1635–9, the surviving Poplar Chapel, begun in 1642 but not completed until the following decade, and Shadwell Chapel erected in 1656–7, as three of the most important models for subsequent church design, influencing not only the work of Wren and others after the fire, but providing, perhaps, the pattern for what later churches with non-separating congregations led by prominent Calvinist ministers may have looked like had such individuals not been driven from the Church of England with the Act of Uniformity. The arrangement of each church was nearly identical. They had centrally planned interiors with two rows of columns of the Tuscan order that supported the valleys of the triple M-shaped roofs. They also had a slight projection in the centre of both long walls. At Broadway and Poplar, it defined a cross-vault that intersects with a central east–west vault. Doorways located at each end of the two long walls provided access into the buildings. Unfortunately, little is known about the

---

[11] Peter Guillery, 'Suburban Models, or Calvinism and Continuity in London's Seventeenth-Century Church Architecture', *Architectural History*, 48 (2003), p. 70.

original layout of the pulpit, communion table, and seating, though a 1711 survey reveals that the pulpit was located just east of the central crossing in these churches.[12] The overall dimensions of these chapels were similar. Poplar Chapel measures 90 feet by 60 feet, forming a 1 to 1.5 ratio of width to length, which accentuated the centralizing principle of an auditory though it retained a strong east–west axis. This proportion matches that later advocated by Christopher Wren for the ideal auditory church. They are also consonant with the range of most Anglican churches (outside of Virginia) and other denominational meeting houses erected in America in the eighteenth century.[13]

EUROPEAN MODELS

Another source of English nonconformist architecture derived from European models. Looking north of the border to Scotland or across the channel to the Netherlands and France, English Puritans encountered Calvinist principles fully realized in centralized room churches. Beginning in the late sixteenth century, Reformed Scots, Huguenot, and Dutch builders experimented with geometric shapes—square, rectangle, cruciform, T, polygon, and elongated polygon—to create a large open space that contained a prominently placed pulpit located against or slightly out from one of the walls.[14] Many interiors had substantial columns or posts to support broad roof spans or carry vaulted or domed ceilings. These room churches were lined with benches, chairs, and pews. Some had tiered gallery seating that repeated the ground-floor arrangement. In Dutch churches, women generally sat in the centre of the room on chairs and benches facing the pulpit and men took their places on banks of benches or pews arranged around the perimeter of the room and in galleries. For communion, participants took their place at long narrow tables and benches set up in a wide aisle near the pulpit.[15]

---

[12] Guillery, 'Suburban Models', pp. 72–6.
[13] Based on the limit of how far a minister's voice could be heard by his congregation, Wren recommended that the ideal new 'church should be at least 60 Feet broad, and 90 Feet long' Lydia Soo, ed., *Wren's 'Tracts' on Architecture and Other Writings* (Cambridge 1998) pp. 115–16.
[14] Per Gustav Hamberg, *Temples for Protestants: Studies in the Architectural Milieu of the Early Reformed Church and the Lutheran Church* (Gothenburg, 2002); C. A. van Swigchem, T. Brouwer, and W. van Os, *Een Huis voor het Woord: Het Protestantse Kerkinterieur in Nederland tot 1900* (Zeist, 1984).
[15] William Brereton, *Travels in Holland, the United Provinces, England, Scotland, and Ireland, 1634–35* (London, 1844), p. 110.

Variations appeared in style, materials, and workmanship in these Calvinist preaching boxes. The massive square plan of the church at Burntisland, Fife (1592) is an early but improbable prototype unlike the long rectangular plans typical of later Scottish churches. The low, one-storey stepped gabled roof of the now ruinous Durness Parish Church at Balnakiel (1619) is more characteristic of the profile and elongated proportions of many reformed churches in Scotland, which were later replicated in America by Scots and Ulster Presbyterians who settled in Pennsylvania and the Southern backcountry. This form contrasts to the soaring proportions of the Greek cross-plan of the church at Renswoude, Utrecht (1639) and the octagonal Marekirk, Leiden (1639), both of which terminate in domes.[16] As Keith Sprunger has observed, 'in spite of claiming inspiration from Scripture for their architecture', English and New England Puritans 'found brick-and-mortar examples' in early seventeenth-century Dutch Reformed Churches that were 'compatible with their theology'.[17]

NEW ENGLAND EXPERIMENTS

The centralized plans of Dutch churches and the auditory principles inherent in Calvinism shaped the design of early New England meeting houses built on the heels of the Great Migration of English Separatists and Puritans to New England from 1620 to the early 1640s. These colonists faced few of the legal and cultural impediments encountered at home. Rather than an embattled minority, Separatists in the Plymouth colony (the Pilgrims who had been in exile in Holland) and non-separating Puritans in Massachusetts Bay and Connecticut formed gathered churches in state-supported ecclesiastical polities. In these Puritan Commonwealths, coffers enriched by taxes gathered from a relatively thickly settled population within narrowly drawn town boundaries allowed leaders to build meeting houses that quickly moved from modest endeavours to sizeable structures with English-framed walls and roofs covered with clapboards. However, as Peter Benes has documented, more than half of the first- and second-generation meeting houses were small rectangular structures. Dedham settlers erected a daubed and thatched 36- by 20-foot building in 1638.[18] The plan and arrangement of the apertures are

---

[16] Andrew Spicer, *Calvinist Churches in Early Modern Europe* (Manchester, 2007), pp. 72, 146.
[17] Keith Sprunger, 'Puritan Church Architecture and Worship in a Dutch Context', *Church History*, 66 (March 1997), p. 49.
[18] Peter Benes, *Meetinghouses of Early New England* (Amherst, MA, 2012), pp. 290–1.

unknown, but the proportions and materials scarcely differentiated the meeting house from surrounding buildings.

Many towns erected meeting houses whose footprints were square or near square, ranging from 20 feet by 20 feet to as large as 66 feet by 60 feet. One of the earliest, the 1639 meeting house in New Haven, Connecticut, was 50 feet by 50 feet while the 1651 structure erected in Cambridge, Massachusetts, measured 40 feet by 40 feet and had a steep 'four-square roof' that formed a flat platform at the apex, which was crowned by a wooden bell turret.[19] The verticality of the steeply pitched roof appears to have been inspired by contemporary Dutch churches.

Of the more than 300 meeting houses erected in New England by the end of the first decade of the eighteenth century, only one survives, Old Ship meeting house, erected in Hingham, Massachusetts, in 1681. Though altered and enlarged twice in the eighteenth century, evidence of its early plan and finish survives. The original building measured 55 feet by 45 feet whose structural bays are defined by large chamfered posts. The two-storey meeting house was covered by a high hip roof lit by cross gables and topped by a turret. With no ceiling, worshippers peered into an open roof consisting of three kingpost trusses with curved braces, which support the turret platform. The plan of the meeting house consisted of a pulpit on the longer back wall with the main, double-door entrance opposite in the centre of the front wall and a door in each of the two side walls. Two tiers of eight-foot wide by four-foot tall casement windows lit the building. The doors, windows, and other trim were painted a reddish brown, but much of the woodwork remained unfinished.[20] The pulpit was surrounded on three sides by galleries and the benches on both levels were arranged in three directions to face the pulpit.

The Hingham plan represents the full maturation of a type most commonly associated with nonconformist meeting houses. With long-wall entrances opening into pulpit-centred rooms often enclosed on three sides by galleries, the form was flexible, used by large urban congregations as well as smaller rural ones. The 'four-square' form of the early New England meeting houses gave way in the following century to gable-roof buildings such as the meeting house in Amesbury, Massachusetts (1785), which were more rectangular in plan (Figs 19.1 and 19.2). The form spread across New England, but was not peculiar to the region as it was the choice of many different denominations throughout colonial America. It also became one of the most common types in England.

---

[19] Ibid., pp. 289–99.
[20] Brian Powell and Andrea Gilmore, 'Old Ship Meeting House, First Parish, Hingham Massachusetts: Historic Structure Report', unpublished report, Dedham, 2007; author's field notes, 4 November 2006.

Fig. 19.1 Rocky Hill meeting house, Amesbury, Massachusetts, 1785: exterior.
© Carl Lounsbury.

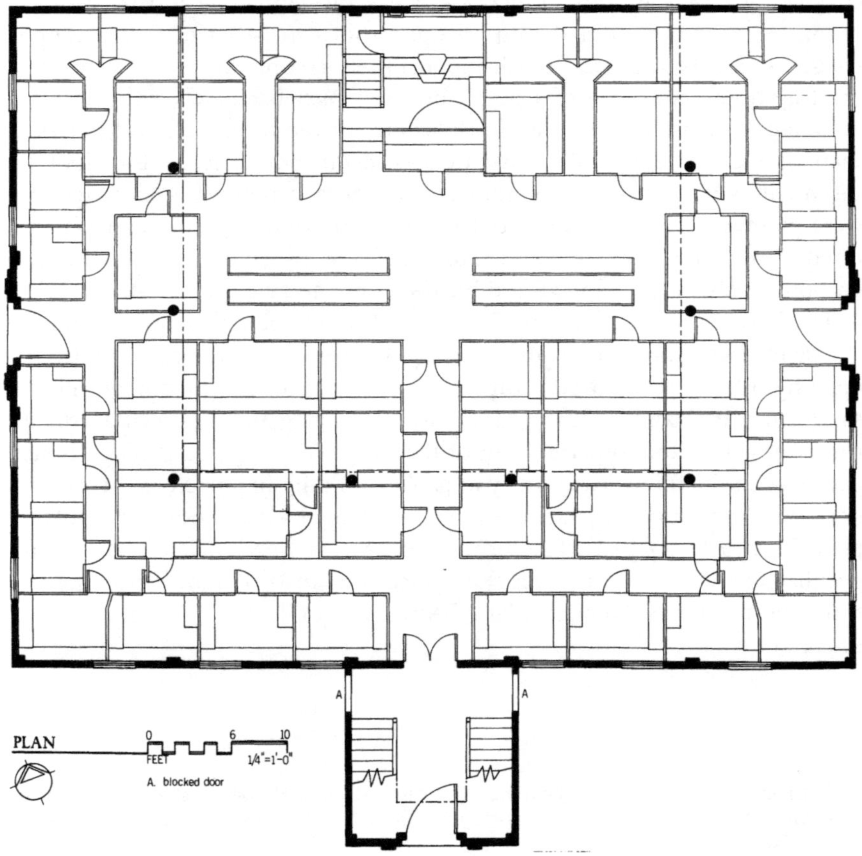

Fig. 19.2 Rocky Hill meeting house, Amesbury, Massachusetts, 1785: plan.
© Carl Lounsbury.

ENGLISH MEETING HOUSES

The Act of Uniformity (1662) turned a sizeable segment of the English population into Dissenters and placed great restrictions on their ability to worship openly. Those hundreds of ministers who could not accept the terms of the act chose to resign 'their livings rather than genuflect before the ghost of Archbishop Laud'.[21] The most common practice of these Dissenting congregations was to meet in private houses, rented halls, and even barns. Few wanted to invest in buildings that might be closed and even destroyed when local magistrates chose to enforce penal codes prohibiting public worship. Quakers bore the brunt of many such destructive acts in the 1660s.[22] Others managed to survive despite waves of persecution, especially small chapels erected on rural estates protected by sympathetic landowners or new and refurbished buildings in towns where large numbers refused to conform and officials turned a blind eye such as at Great Yarmouth where in 1669 'Independents have fitted up a place for public meetings with seats for the people and desk for the parson, where at least 1000 meet'.[23]

In London, Dissenters erected some meeting houses only a few years after their prohibition and took advantage of Charles II's Declaration of Indulgence in 1672 to build additional ones.[24] What little is known about these structures suggests that at least some corresponded to the New England meeting-house model. In Monkwell Street, the Presbyterians raised a large substantial brick building that was square in plan and had three deep galleries.[25] Large pews filled the ground floor around the central pulpit. The building was situated under a gateway and was said to be 'invisible from the street' and 'admirably adapted for the purposes of concealment'.[26] Another Presbyterian congregation led by Samuel Annesley erected a two-storey brick meeting house at Little St Helen's, Bishopsgate Street, in 1672. The building survived the withdrawal of the declaration the following year and remained unmolested for the next two decades in part because it blended in with the surroundings, looking more like a series of houses with dormers and multiple doors than a public meeting hall (Fig. 19.3). In fact, part of the meeting house was given over to domestic use. The interior was fitted with a three-sided gallery that enclosed the pulpit, which stood against the front wall. Only a pair of large arched and mullioned windows, which lit the pulpit, suggested something other than a residence from the outside.

---

[21] Watts, *The Dissenters*, p. 219.   [22] Ibid., pp. 222–45.
[23] J. E. Clowes, *Chronicles of the Old Congregational Church at Great Yarmouth, 1642–1858* (Great Yarmouth, 1906), p. 36.
[24] Walter Wilson, *The History and Antiquities of Dissenting Churches and Meeting Houses in London, Westminster, and Southwark*, 4 vols. (London, 1808–10), I, pp. 363–4.
[25] John Strype, John Hughes, and Kevin White, *A Complete History of England: With the Lives of all the Kings and Queens Thereof*, 3 vols. (London, 1706), III, p. 282.
[26] Wilson, *The History and Antiquities of Dissenting Churches and Meeting Houses*, III, pp. 185–6.

Fig. 19.3 Annesley's meeting house, Little St Helen's, Bishopsgate Street, London, 1672. © Carl Lounsbury. Demolished in 1799. Based on John Thomas Smith, *Antiquities of London*, 1800.

The link between the Puritan chapels of the Commonwealth and Dissenting meeting houses of the late seventeenth century can be traced in the peripatetic ministry of Matthew Mead. He had been the first preacher at Shadwell Chapel in the late 1650s and after being ejected from his living spent time in the mid-1660s in Holland. He became pastor of a Dissenting congregation in Stepney in 1671 and three years later its members erected a two-storey brick meeting house set back from the street behind a brick wall.[27] The building was a deep squarish rectangle six bays wide and four deep. Like other early meeting houses, the double tier of windows was domestic in appearance. With doors in the second and fifth bays on the front facade and three off-set dormers in the low M-roof, the building blended in with its domestic neighbours (Fig. 19.4).

---

[27] Edmund Calamy and Samuel Palmer, *The Nonconformist's Memorial*, 3 vols., 2nd edn (London, 1802), II, p. 461.

Fig. 19.4 Stepney meeting house, London, 1674.
© Trustees of Dr Williams's Library, London. Demolished in 1863. View from 1783 when the Rev. Samuel Brewer occupied the pulpit.

Apparently, it was built in such a manner that it could be converted into dwelling houses if the meeting was suppressed, and the wrecking of the building's fittings in 1682 by soldiers demonstrated just how precarious these early meeting houses were.[28] The building survived the calamity and with Toleration in 1689, it was improved by the construction of a three-sided gallery and pews. Tradition holds that the four round posts used to support the galleries and M-roof were given by the Dutch government in appreciation of Mead's preaching in Utrecht.[29]

The Toleration Act (1689) freed Dissenters from the restrictions and subterfuge of the previous three decades and many congregations seized the opportunity to build. Some proceeded cautiously either because of limited resources or uncertainty about the staying power of the act. Keach's Baptist meeting house (1695), a small brick structure built on a back lot in Winslow, Buckinghamshire, could be mistaken for a work building rather than a place of worship. The cottage-style form with a long-wall doorway and small windows consists of a single 23- by 15-foot room that originally had a pulpit on the back wall.[30]

Other congregations built more confidently without fear of official or mob violence, though a few spasmodic riots in some cities reminded Dissenters that

---

[28] T. F. T. Baker, ed., *A History of the County of Middlesex: Volume 11, Early Stepney with Bethnal Green* (Oxford, 1998), pp. 82–3.
[29] *The Christian's Penny Magazine* (No. 75), 9 November 1833, pp. 353–4.
[30] Christopher Stell, *Nonconformist Chapels and Meeting-Houses in Central England* (London, 1986), pp. 27–9.

their position in English society could still be threatened.[31] Even so, the progress of reshaping the religious landscape moved forward, especially in areas where dissent had flourished previously in large industrial towns and in places where the parochial system was weak.[32] Prosperous congregations erected architecturally ambitious meeting houses in many urban areas. In 1693, an Independent congregation in Norwich built a two-storey brick, 69- by 49-foot meeting house whose front facade had rubbed pilasters crowned with stone Corinthian capitals. Presbyterians undertook an equally impressive meeting house in 1711 in Bury St Edmunds. The front facade of the 50- by 48-foot, two-storey building is a virtuoso display of rubbed and gauged brickwork in the central Doric frontispiece, the two oversized windows flanking it with their rubbed arches and carved stone keystones, and a rubbed oval window with keystones in the four quadrants set between the top of the doorway and the molded cornice, which is capped by a panelled parapet (Figs 19.5 and 19.6). Although the ground-floor pews have been removed, much of the early

Fig. 19.5 Presbyterian meeting house, Bury St Edmunds, Suffolk, 1711: exterior.
© Carl Lounsbury.

[31] Watts, *The Dissenters*, pp. 264, 487.　　[32] Ibid., pp. 267–89.

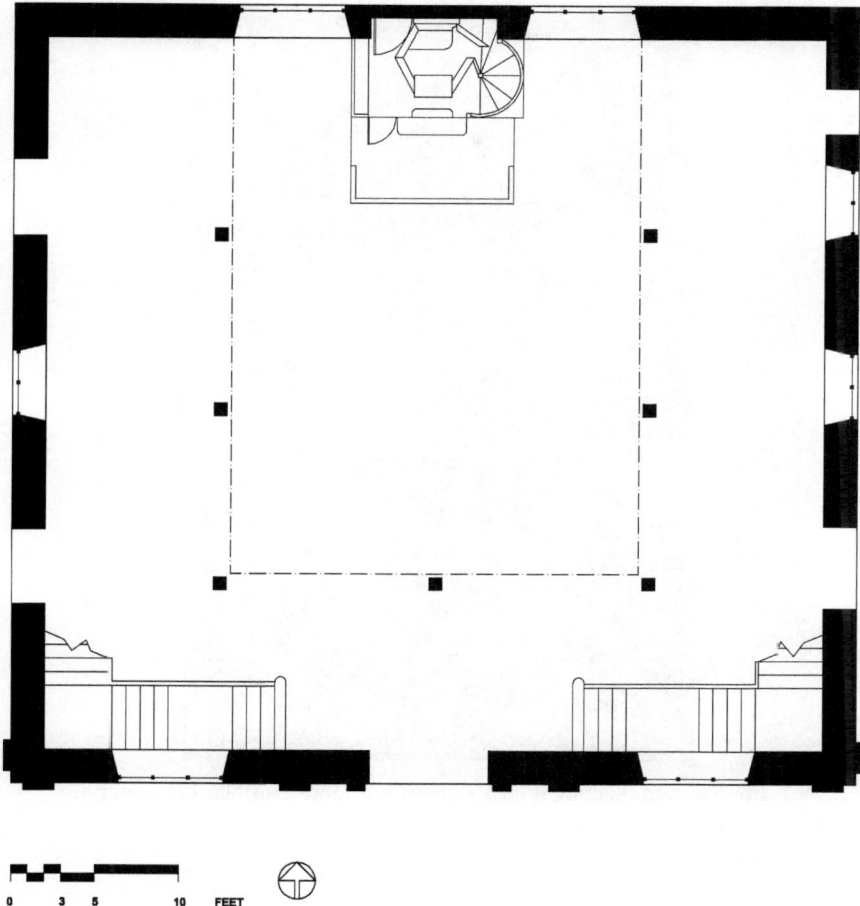

Fig. 19.6 Presbyterian meeting house, Bury St Edmunds, Suffolk, 1711: plan.
© Carl Lounsbury.

woodwork survives including the tall pulpit (Fig. 19.7) with its canopy flanked by two large windows on the back wall opposite the entrance and a three-sided gallery and benches built against the side and front walls. A large post in the centre of the room rises to the flat ceiling and with the gallery posts supports the valley framing of the M-roof.[33]

---

[33] Many English meeting houses have one or two large freestanding posts in the centre of the building that rise uninterrupted to the ceiling to support the roof framing. This is an English feature rarely used in America where most meeting houses had taller hipped or gable roofs rather than low M-roofs. In New England, carpenters occasionally provided additional support to the roof with exposed angle braces that ran from the wall posts to tie beams.

Fig. 19.7 Presbyterian meeting house, Bury St Edmunds, Suffolk, 1711: pulpit.
© Carl Lounsbury.

The interior of the Presbyterian meeting house in Bury St Edmunds would have been very familiar to contemporary American visitors. The scale of the room, the placement and shape of the pulpit and canopy, the turned columns and curve of the pulpit stair, the moulded breastwork of the galleries, the bench supports in the gallery seating, and the mouldings of the door and window architraves appeared throughout the Anglo-American world. Its ornamentation represents the upper level of workmanship seldom matched in other eighteenth-century English and American meeting houses, though its plan could be found in all but the most humble structures. There are variations in the plan: many have large arched windows flanking the pulpit on the entrance wall instead of the back wall; some have gable-end wall entrances in addition to a long-wall doorway; still others have no galleries.

In addition to the meeting-house plan, English congregations tried other arrangements. A few experimented with geometric shapes made popular in the Netherlands and early New England. Presbyterians built a cruciform chapel in St Saviourgate, York, in 1692–3. Next to the Old Meeting House in Norwich, Presbyterians erected in 1754 an elegant 64-foot-wide octagonal chapel with galleries around all sides supported by Corinthian capitals. John Wesley admired the form and recommended it to his followers. In Yorkshire, Methodists erected octagonal meeting houses at Yarm in 1748 and Heptonstall in 1764, both of which were much more modest in finish and about two-thirds the size of the Norwich chapel.[34]

Friends' meeting houses were arranged differently on the inside though there was little on the exterior that set them apart from other denominations. Quakers organized their congregations in a hierarchical fashion from local meetings to national gatherings. The smallest meeting house had a single room and looked like a small cottage.[35] The 27- by 21-foot brick meeting house erected in Wallingford, Oxfordshire, in 1724 has a doorway and window on the front long wall, and it is only the elders' or facing bench at one end of the room, reserved for those men and women who had recognized abilities of 'speaking the truth' during worship, that indicates its Quaker affiliation.[36]

Preparative, monthly, and quarterly meetings commonly had two meeting spaces: a large meeting room where men and women met for worship and a smaller space partitioned off at one end for women's business meetings. This arrangement appears at Jordans in Buckinghamshire (1688), a brick meeting house, which has a door in the long wall, which opens into the larger room with the elders' bench at one end at right angles to the entrance. Following the service, women left this main room and gathered in the smaller one at the opposite end of the building where they would discuss business matters. The men remained in the large room for their own business meetings. The women's end of the meeting house is divided into two storeys with two tiers of windows. There is a heated room below and another room above, which in other meeting houses was sometimes used to accommodate travelling Friends or a schoolroom.[37]

---

[34] Stell, *Nonconformist Chapels and Meeting-Houses in the North of England*, pp. 185–6, 225, 272–3; Christopher Stell, *Nonconformist Chapels and Meeting-Houses in Eastern England* (London, 2002), pp. 260–1.
[35] David Butler, 'Quaker Meeting Houses in America and England: Impressions and Comparisons', *Quaker History*, 79 (Fall 1990), p. 94.
[36] David Butler, *The Quaker Meeting Houses of Britain*, 2 vols. (London, 1999), I, p. 19.
[37] Butler, *The Quaker Meeting Houses of Britain*, I, pp. 25–6; II, pp. 787–9.

CHURCH AND MEETING HOUSE IN COLONIAL AMERICA

American Dissenters began in circumstances substantially different from their confessional brethren in England. By 1700 colonists from New Hampshire to South Carolina had established about 400 individual congregations among eight different denominations.[38] This amalgam of denominations on the American continent turned into a complex tapestry of confessions in the eighteenth century as a steady wave of immigration brought English, Welsh, and Irish Quakers, Scots and Ulster Presbyterians, German-speaking Anabaptists, Moravians, Catholics, Reformed, and Lutherans to new colonies and to older settled regions such as New England and the Chesapeake. As one bewildered German Lutheran who arrived in Pennsylvania in 1750 observed, 'there exist so many varieties of doctrines and sects that it is impossible to name them all'.[39] No matter where these various groups settled, church building patterns were similar. Seaports and cities such as Newport, New York, Philadelphia, and Charleston were filled with churches and meeting houses of many different denominations competing against one another to build well-appointed places of worship. In many regions, the countryside was a mixture of ethnic groups and denominations. The absence of state support for most of these groups meant that each individual congregation was primarily responsible for the construction of its own place of worship, though there was some support from co-religionists and Old World sources.[40] Most early churches and meeting houses were small, perishable wooden structures, which were replaced by more durable ones when frontier settlements turned into stable and prosperous farming communities. Except for Catholic and Quaker congregations, nearly all of these were auditories often arranged in meeting-house fashion with a central pulpit and galleries clustered around it.

An important exception to this pattern was Anglican Virginia where the standard form of the colony's parish churches from first settlement in 1607 until the disestablishment of the church in the 1780s was an elongated rectangle whose length was at least twice its width.[41] The nave and chancel were incorporated beneath a single unbroken wall and roofline. The principal entrance was in the west gable end and there was a secondary door in one of

---

[38] Edwin Gausted and Philip Barlow, *New Historical Atlas of Religion in America* (New York, 2001), p. 7.

[39] Gottlieb Mittelberger, *Journey to Pennsylvania*, ed. Oscar Handlin and John Clive (Cambridge, MA, 1960), p. 21.

[40] For a study of church building in Pennsylvania and New Jersey, see Carl Lounsbury, '"Building is a Heavy Burden": The Legacy of Eighteenth-Century Church Building in the Middle Atlantic Colonies', in *Essays in Early American Architectural History*, pp. 154–76.

[41] Carl Lounsbury, 'Anglican Church Design in the Chesapeake: English Inheritances and Regional Interpretations', in *Essays in Early American Architectural History*, pp. 127–31.

the side walls of the chancel near the east end. Pews and benches flanked a central aisle and the pulpit and reading desk were located against one of the walls near the east end where the communion table was surrounded by an altar rail. Newport Parish Church (c.1682) in Isle of Wight County, is the earliest surviving example of this traditional form in Virginia, which as Nigel Yates has observed, had its origins in the late sixteenth century in smaller English parish churches, but it seldom appeared in America outside Britain's oldest Anglican colony.[42]

The Anglican foothold was far more tenuous in other colonies, even in ones where it became state-supported, such as the Carolinas and Maryland at the beginning of the eighteenth century, despite concerted opposition from newly denominated Dissenters. Access to public money enabled Anglican vestries in these colonies to build solid frame and brick churches of squarish proportions with long-wall entrances and sometimes with short articulated chancels. St James, Goose Creek, (1707–19), one of the first parish churches erected in the South Carolina low country, is squarish in plan with three doors opening into the sanctuary from the middle of the west, north, and south walls, which are lit by arched windows with stuccoed cherub heads as keystones. Additional iconography included a stuccoed bas-relief over the west door of a pelican plucking her breast to feed her young and the royal arms of George I over the east-end altar. Despite these decorative expressions of Anglican faith, loyalty to the Crown, and the prayer book liturgy, St James and other churches did not deter some Nonconformists from taking seats in them on Sundays, especially 'when their own Ministers did not preach'.[43] Another minister in South Carolina noted that 'my auditory is usually a mixt multitude (some Presbyterians, some Independents, some Anabaptists, besides those of our own communion'.[44]

Dissenters from the Anglican Church in Maryland consisted primarily of Catholics and Quakers. The earliest Catholic churches seldom aspired to anything more than small rectangular chapels with few flourishes. The one exception was in St Mary's City, the colony's first capital, where Jesuit priests in the late 1660s directed the construction of a 54- by 29-foot brick church with two small projecting transepts. Quaker meeting houses and a few Anglican chapels appeared in the late seventeenth century. Nearly all of these buildings, except the St Mary's chapel and the well-finished and solidly framed Third Haven meeting house (1682) built by the Quakers in Talbot County, were 'plain country buildings' or 'clapboard houses' no more than 20 feet by 40 feet in size, of little workmanship, erected 'after the manner of a tobacco

---

[42] Yates, *Buildings, Faith, and Worship*, pp. 68–71.
[43] Letter from Rev. Samuel Thomas, St James, Goose Creek, Parish, 21 December 1705, Lambeth Palace Library, London, SPG Papers, Vol. XVII.
[44] Ibid., Vol. XVI, Letter from Rev. William Dun, St Paul's, Stono, Parish, 27 April 1707.

house'.⁴⁵ At the end of the century, Catholics lost many of their privileges when the colony's Anglican faction managed to establish the Church of England. Symbolic of the Protestant ascendancy, the St Mary's chapel was dismantled.

These new Anglican churches in Maryland matched the scale, proportion (1 to 1.5 ratio of width to length), and plan of their South Carolina counterparts. Most retained their liturgical orientation with communion tables railed in at the east end with the pulpit somewhere nearby or in the centre of the long wall as at St Anne's (1763–5) in Anne Arundel County. In some cases the differences between Anglican auditory and meeting-house plans were negligible. Emmanuel Church (1768) built in Chestertown on the Eastern Shore is a two-storey brick structure that measures 61 feet by 40 feet and originally had its main entrance in the centre of the front long wall. A central aisle led from the door to the pulpit located directly opposite it. The altar was positioned in front of the pulpit instead of at the liturgical east end like most churches. There were two secondary gable entrances with a transverse aisle running through the building. Galleries surrounded the pulpit on three sides. Except for the prayer book liturgy, there was nothing architecturally about the plan of the building to indicate its denominational affiliation. It could have been mistaken for one of the large boxy Presbyterian meeting houses erected three score miles to the north-east across the Delaware Bay in southern New Jersey.

Elsewhere in the Protestant patchwork of colonial America, the meeting-house plan predominated. Dutch Calvinists in New York and New Jersey replicated a few of the geometric meeting-house forms that had developed in the Netherlands, though the octagonal and square churches in Bergen (1680), New Utrecht (1700), Hackensack (1728), and other places were far smaller than their Dutch counterparts. Dutch and German Reformed and Lutheran churches built in the Hudson and Mohawk Valleys were squarish rectangles with long-wall entrances, three-sided galleries, and pulpits in the centre of the back wall. The stone Palatine Lutheran church (1770) is 50 feet by 40 feet with large arched windows and reflects the scale of the first generation of permanent churches on the frontier.

The denominational mixture was just as pronounced in Delaware. The Anglican Society for the Propagation of the Gospel in Foreign Parts (SPG) missionary George Ross observed in 1727 that 'there are seven Meeting Houses used by Dissenters, besides a Lutheran Congregation, within the limits of what I call my Parish, 4 Presbyterians who are generally Scotch-Irish; one Anabaptist being Welsh … two Quakers-mingling of English and Irish'.⁴⁶ The

---

⁴⁵ William Stevens Perry, ed., *Historical Collections Relating to the American Colonial Church*, 5 vols. (Hartford, 1871–8), *Maryland*, IV, pp. 21–3.

⁴⁶ Ibid., *Delaware*, V, p. 46.

strong competition for souls in the Delaware Valley in the early eighteenth century produced something of a building competition among the Anglicans, Presbyterians, and Quakers to win the allegiance of this assortment of colonists. Ross had arrived in the old Dutch town of New Castle in 1704 to take up his duties in his sprawling parish. He immediately oversaw the construction of his parish church on the central green, liturgically sited so that it was skewed to the town grid. The 50- by 30-foot brick building contained a doorway in the west gable end with the principal entrance in the centre of the south long wall. The pulpit stood opposite it on the north wall.

No sooner had Ross and his vestry finished their work in 1708 than the Presbyterians erected 'a very spacious meetinghouse in the very face of their church' across the town green.[47] The new brick meeting house was similar in scale and form to its neighbour with the principal doorway in the centre of the long front wall flanked by an arched window on either side. The plan of the meeting house followed that of the church with the pulpit located in the centre of the long back wall, although the Presbyterians took communion in the centre aisle at tables and benches instead of around a communion table at the east end of the church as the Anglicans did. In New Castle, the most obvious architectural markers that set churches apart from meeting houses had dissolved. Elsewhere, traces of those Old World distinctions remained through the colonial period, but would soon play themselves out.

Settlement in Pennsylvania spread progressively outward from Philadelphia and eventually stretched more than a hundred miles west and north with many German and Ulster immigrants moving southward into the backcountry of Maryland, Virginia, and North Carolina. Congregations of Lutherans, Reformed, Presbyterians, and Moravians often started with small log buildings, the American equivalent of the cottage form used by Dissenters in England. Many of these temporary places of worship had roughly hewn log walls with a central doorway cut out in the centre of the long wall. A late surviving example is Shellsburg meeting house, a 30- by 25-foot union church built jointly in 1806 by German Reform and Lutheran congregations in Bedford County, Pennsylvania, two hundred miles west of Philadelphia. A central door in the long front wall opens into the meeting house, which has a pulpit opposite it and galleries on three sides.

Over time, buildings such as these were replaced by stone, brick, and frame buildings as congregations grew and became more prosperous. Invariably, they had meeting house plans. Rocky Spring meeting house in Franklin County was built in 1794 by a Presbyterian congregation composed of descendants of Ulster families who had immigrated into the Cumberland Valley in the 1730s.[48] With

---

[47] Ibid., *Delaware*, V, p. 9.

[48] S. Wylie and A. Nevin Pomeroy, *A History of the Rocky Spring Church* (Chambersburg, 1895), pp. 13, 20, 26.

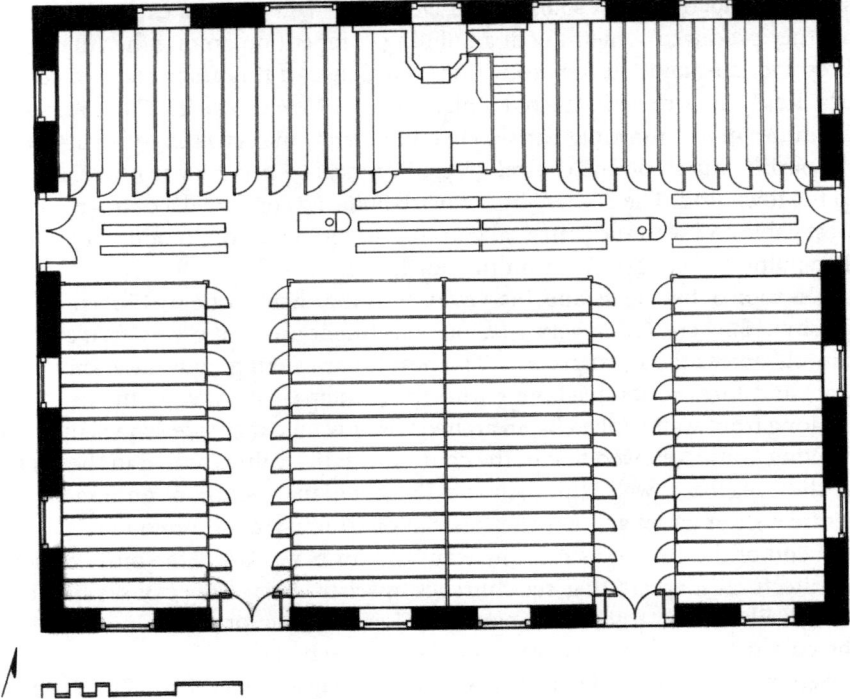

Fig. 19.8 Rocky Spring Presbyterian meeting house, Franklin Co., Pennsylvania, 1794: plan.

© Carl Lounsbury.

arched apertures in the brick walls, the church is 60 feet by 48 feet with two entrances on its long front wall and offset doorways in each gable end. The interior is well preserved with whitewashed walls and arched ceiling. There are no galleries but the full complement of unpainted boxed pews is arranged on three sides of the tall panelled pulpit, which stands in the centre of the back wall. The wide transverse aisle that runs in front of it is where members of the congregations sat down on benches on either side of a narrow communion table to celebrate the sacrament in the reformed manner (Fig. 19.8).

As in England, a large number of Quaker meeting houses dating from the 1690s through to the 1820s survive, especially in William Penn's former colony and in southern New Jersey. The first buildings varied in plan, but generally shared the English pattern of a single large meeting room for a mixed ensemble of worshippers with a small room or separate building to which women retired to hold their business meetings. This arrangement is still evident in parts of New England. The 1704 Saylesville meeting house in

Lincoln, Rhode Island, a 49- by 39-foot two-storey frame building, had a smaller one-storey heated room added to one gable end in the middle of the eighteenth century for women's meetings. However, by the late colonial period, this asymmetrical arrangement of Quaker meeting houses in America was superseded by one where women and men sat separately for worship and for business in their own rooms that were set side by side and divided by wooden shuttered partitions that would be opened for service and closed for business meetings, a practice that did not develop in Britain.

The 1768 Buckingham Monthly meeting house north of Philadelphia was the first structure designed to accommodate meeting spaces for men and women in a balanced, double symmetrical composition. Instead of one central doorway flanked by a window on either side, the new plan doubled the old formula with two entrances on the long wall, each leading into one of the two equal-sized rooms, which is divided by a retractable partition (Figs 19.9 and 19.10). Once developed in the Delaware Valley, the form spread throughout most of America and became the standard plan well into the nineteenth century. Older meeting houses were enlarged and renovated to create the dual symmetry of the Buckingham plan, which reflected the equality of men and women in worship and discipline.

Fig. 19.9 Buckingham Friends meeting house, Buckingham Co., Pennsylvania, 1768: exterior.
© Carl Lounsbury.

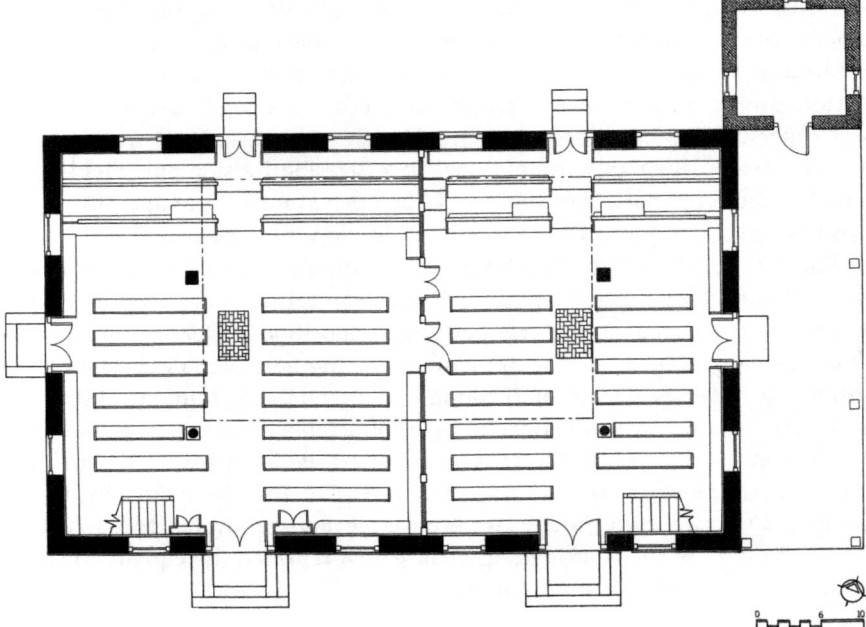

Fig. 19.10 Buckingham Friends meeting house, Buckingham Co., Pennsylvania, 1768: plan.
© Carl Lounsbury.

THE AXIAL PLAN

The long-wall meeting-house plan preferred by a large segment of nonconformist congregations in England and America since the late seventeenth century began to be displaced in the second half of the eighteenth century by one that re-oriented the front facade ninety degrees and reconfigured the seating pattern of its worshippers. Nonconformists and Anglicans devised buildings whose principal entrance was located on the shorter gable-end wall. The pulpit stood at the other end of the long axis. Long before the Ecclesiology movement discouraged such an arrangement in Anglican churches, the communion table in the new plan was located just below or, in some cases, behind the pulpit, as at St George's, Portsea, Hampshire (1753), and Trinity, Brooklyn, Connecticut (1771).[49] This shift eliminated the dual liturgical centres that had marked many churches that were otherwise arranged like meeting houses. With the single orientation, the sacramental

---

[49] Yates, *Buildings, Faith, and Worship*, p. 87; Frederick Kelly, *Early Connecticut Meetinghouses*, 2 vols. (New York, 1948), I, pp. 45–51.

and preaching focus came together. Instead of benches and box pews with seats oriented in two or three directions as in the old plan, long slip pews were arranged in a linear fashion with rows divided by wide aisles. Nearly all seats faced the pulpit. Upstairs, the three-sided arrangement of the meeting-house plan shifted a quarter turn so that there were two long side galleries and a short gallery at the back of the sanctuary.

The axial plan appealed to nonconformists in England and America since the pulpit remained the central focus as in meeting-house plans, but with the added advantage that more congregants had an unobstructed view of the minister. This became increasingly important among evangelical congregations where new preaching styles made seeing as important as hearing.[50] In England, George's meeting house (1760), a two-storey brick structure erected by Presbyterians in Exeter, has an axial plan with the entrance located in the centre of one of the shorter walls that face the street (Fig. 19.11). Two aisles flanked by forward-facing pews lead to the pulpit at the opposite end.[51]

Fig. 19.11 George's Presbyterian meeting house, Exeter, Devon, 1760.
© Carl Lounsbury.

---

[50] Lounsbury, 'God is in the Details', pp. 187–91.
[51] Christopher Stell, *Nonconformist Chapels and Meeting-Houses in South-West England* (London, 1991), pp. 79–81.

In America, the plan appears in New York City at the Brick Presbyterian meeting house (1767), which may have been influenced by the design of the nearby St George's Anglican Chapel erected fifteen years earlier. From the city the plan spread to northern New Jersey and Long Island following the Revolution and into New England by the late 1780s. From the 1790s through to the 1830s, hundreds of old meeting-house plans throughout America as well as England were altered to conform to the new plan. Long-wall entrances were blocked, new doorways cut, and pews and galleries turned to face the new pulpit positioned on the short wall opposite the new entrance. The German Lutheran Church in Dutchess County, New York (1786) was re-oriented in this fashion in 1824, a pattern that was repeated in the United States among all denominations including the Episcopalians.[52] In New England, some towns literally turned their old meeting houses by building new foundations and physically rotating their buildings ninety degrees. By the end of the eighteenth century, these temple-fronted meeting houses began to take on a more decorative appearance with columns, pediments, towers, and spires, inspired by designs developed by Christopher Wren and James Gibbs.

Nearly two centuries after factions in the Church of England bitterly disputed the material manifestations and practices of Protestant worship, the descendants of those English Puritans who chose exile in New England managed to meld the Anglican ceremonialists' penchant for display and ornamentation with the Nonconformists' emphasis on the pre-eminence of the auditory preaching box in building forms that found favour among a wide array of denominations on both sides of the Atlantic. The architectural convergence between Nonconformity and the Established Church was never complete and would diverge again when the allure of the medieval past led Anglicans to embrace Gothic forms. The lifting of restrictions on Catholics in England and the disestablishment of Congregationalism in New England appeared at a time when the material culture of most Protestant denominations momentarily found a common ground.

SELECT BIBLIOGRAPHY

Benes, Peter, *Meetinghouses of Early New England* (Amherst, MA, 2012).
Buggeln, Gretchen, *Temples of Grace: The Material Transformation of Connecticut's Churches, 1790–1840* (Lebanon, NH, 2003).
Butler, David, 'Quaker Meeting Houses in America and England: Impressions and Comparisons', *Quaker History*, 79, 2 (1990), pp. 93–104.
Butler, David, *The Quaker Meeting Houses of Britain*, 2 vols. (London, 1999).

---

[52] Lounsbury, 'God is in the Details', pp. 183–7.

Guillery, Peter, 'Suburban Models, or Calvinism and Continuity in London's Seventeenth-Century Church Architecture', *Architectural History*, 48 (2003), pp. 69–106.
Hamberg, Per Gustav, *Temples for Protestants: Studies in the Architectural Milieu of the Early Reformed Church and the Lutheran Church* (Gothenburg, 2002).
Kelly, Frederick, *Early Connecticut Meetinghouses*, 2 vols. (New York, 1948).
Lounsbury, Carl, 'Anglican Church Design in the Chesapeake: English Inheritances and Regional Interpretations', in Carl Lounsbury, *Essays in Early American Architectural History: A View from the Chesapeake* (Charlottesville, VA, 2011), pp. 127–42
Lounsbury, Carl, '"Building is a Heavy Burden": The Legacy of Eighteenth-Century Church Building in the Middle Atlantic Colonies', in Carl Lounsbury, *Essays in Early American Architectural History: A View from the Chesapeake* (Charlottesville, VA, 2011), pp. 154–76.
Lounsbury, Carl, 'God is in the Details: The Transformation of Ecclesiastical Architecture in Early Nineteenth-Century America', in Carl Lounsbury, *Essays in Early American Architectural History: A View from the Chesapeake* (Charlottesville, VA, 2011), pp. 177–94.
Spicer, Andrew, *Calvinist Churches in Early Modern Europe* (Manchester, 2007).
Sprunger, Keith, 'Puritan Church Architecture and Worship in a Dutch Context', *Church History*, 66, 1 (1997), pp. 36–53.
Stell, Christopher, *Nonconformist Chapels and Meeting-Houses in Central England* (London, 1986).
Stell, Christopher, *Nonconformist Chapels and Meeting-Houses in Eastern England* (London, 2002).
Stell, Christopher, *Nonconformist Chapels and Meeting-Houses in the North of England* (London, 1994).
Stell, Christopher, *Nonconformist Chapels and Meeting-Houses in South-West England* (London, 1991).
Van Swigchem, C. A., Brouwer, T., and van Os, W., *Een Huis voor het Woord: Het Protestantse Kerkinterieur in Nederland tot 1900* (Zeist, 1984).
Watts, Michael, *The Dissenters: From the Reformation to the French Revolution* (Oxford, 1978).
Yates, Nigel, *Buildings, Faith and Worship: The Liturgical Arrangements of Anglican Churches 1600–1900* (Oxford, 1990).

20

Dissenting Print Culture

Tessa Whitehouse

Religious works were the largest category of printed books during the long eighteenth century and Dissenting authors were disproportionately active contributors to that body of material.[1] But the nature of a distinctively Dissenting print culture is difficult to define. Significant connections across protestant traditions within and beyond the Church of England and within and beyond the borders of the British Isles were developed and maintained throughout the period. Partly because of supportive communication that helped to sustain anglophone protestant traditions of print across denominational divides, religious writing was produced in many different contexts making it difficult to generalize about the qualities or circumstances of Dissenting print culture. Printed objects gained their meaning within a broader culture of piety, communication, and politics and cannot easily be detached from those settings. Preaching events, domestic conversation, and academic lectures are just three kinds of activity that gave rise to enduring printed matter but originated in unique moments of face-to-face communication. Print was the instrument by which Dissenters refashioned such social circumstances into educative, devotional, and doctrinal materials for wide readerships.

This chapter will explore not only the particular books that emerged in and from Dissenting culture but also the kinds of activity that contributed to the print culture of Dissent in a period when restrictions on Dissenting religious practices had been eased by the 1689 religious settlement and when the lapse of 14 Charles II c. 33 ('the Licensing Act') in 1695 meant it was no longer possible to censor works prior to publication. It will survey the principal forms of printed writing produced by and for Dissenters in the period in terms of materiality and genre, taking works

---

[1] Ian Green and Kate Peters, 'Religious Publishing in England 1640–1695', in John Barnard and D. F. McKenzie, eds, *The Cambridge History of the Book in Britain: Volume IV, 1557–1695* (Cambridge, 2002), pp. 67–93, esp. p. 67 and p. 77. Isabel Rivers, 'Religious Publishing', in Michael F. Suarez, S.J. and Michael L. Turner, eds, *The Cambridge History of the Book in Britain: Volume V, 1695–1830* (Cambridge, 2009), pp. 579–600, p. 580.

based on Scripture, life-narratives, and serial publication as three central topics. Booksellers, authors, and editors were, of course, all significant producers of print but the ways in which they worked depended on the religious tradition within which particular individuals operated and the priorities animating such work in particular places at a given time. The shifting identity of Methodism from a society within the Church of England to a group of denominations outside it and the continuities and changes in its attendant publishing programme is one significant example of this development, while the tightly controlled circuits of Quaker book production and distribution provide evidence of an alternative model for the management of denominational print culture.[2]

The discussion of Dissenting print culture that follows focuses on printed books.[3] But what is meant by the term 'religious book' and what did such works typically contain? Ian Green has emphasized the clergy's tendency to prefer theological, liturgical, or pastoral works to belle lettres and topical pieces.[4] Published religious books were, according to Isabel Rivers, divided by contemporary writers into three categories: doctrinal, controversial, and practical, and '[n]o one doubted that the last category was the most important'.[5] It was this third category that was most likely to be read by the laity as well as the clergy, though this was not a tendency unique to Dissenters. As Green has noted, 'if we devote more attention to the kind of didactic and edifying works which sold steadily for decades, we find regular overlaps in aims, content, and technique, and little evidence of a clear divide along party lines'.[6] However, Andrew Cambers has argued for 'the special importance of collective, social and public reading to the godly', emphasizing how communal and familial reading *practices* (if not particular books) characterized puritan culture into the eighteenth century.[7] In these terms, the way books were used as much as their content created a distinctive print culture for Nonconformists.

FORMS AND FORMATS

Bibles and genres derived from Scripture such as commentaries, catechisms, primers, prayers, psalms, sermons, expositors, and harmonies represent, when

---

[2] Brett C. McInelly, *Textual Warfare and the Making of Methodism* (Oxford, 2014), ch. 1 and J. William Frost, 'Quaker Books in Colonial Pennsylvania', *Quaker History*, 80, 1 (1991), pp. 1-25.

[3] Though single-sheet textual and pictorial pieces also served the ends of dissenting religion, their survival is rare.

[4] Ian Green, *Print and Protestantism in Early Modern England* (Oxford, 2000), p. 31.

[5] Isabel Rivers, 'Dissenting and Methodist Books of Practical Divinity', in Isabel Rivers, ed., *Books and their Readers in Eighteenth-Century England* (Leicester, 1982), pp. 127-64 (p. 127).

[6] Green, *Print and Protestantism*, p. 7.

[7] Andrew Cambers, *Godly Reading: Print, Manuscript and Puritanism in England, 1580-1720* (Cambridge, 2010), p. 76 and ch. 3.

taken together, the dominant category of printed matter in the period. The Dissenting contribution to this body of work is remarkably substantial given the small number of Dissenters in the population as a whole.[8] That circumstance came about in part because of the significance of print in securing the primacy of the spiritual and civil establishment. Uncomfortable with the forms of worship sanctioned by the Book of Common Prayer, Dissenters provided alternative manuals for piety and guides to scriptural interpretation at all price points. Rather than acquiesce in the dominance of the Authorized Version of the Bible (which was produced by Royal patent) as the sole permitted translation, they found ways to provide their own translations of both Old and New Testaments, often in the form of expensive, carefully produced expositors in folio or crown quarto such as Matthew Henry's *Exposition of all the books of the Old and New Testament* (1708–10), Philip Doddridge's *Family Expositor* (1739–56), and John Guyse's *Practical Exposition* (1739–52). The fact that these works went through several editions during this period despite their great expense to publishers and purchasers indicates that they served a need among readers who could pay for the costly volumes, though, as Doddridge's *Family Expositor* clearly shows both in terms of the subscription-gathering campaign that partly financed the publication and from epistolary evidence for the reception of the work, the readership for such works was not anticipated to be Dissenters alone.[9]

In addition to these reactive impulses related to the print culture of the Established Church, key principles of Dissenting belief contributed to the proliferation of printed matter. The centrality of individual experiences of grace animated not only the profusion of expositors and commentaries designed to ensure that Scripture was comprehensible to all Christians, but also the production of the myriad pamphlets, chapbooks, and other small-format volumes at the other end of the scale in terms of price and format to learned tomes. Devotional narratives in duodecimo were as familiar to readers as practical works presenting good methods of prayer, meditation, and general conduct. For example, John Bunyan's *Pilgrim's Progress* was widely distributed as a chapbook both within the British Isles and across the expanding international missionary field for free, subsidized by wealthier Christians who

---

[8] N. H. Keeble, *The Literary Culture of Nonconformity in the Later Seventeenth Century* (Leicester, 1987), 128–9.

[9] Alan Everitt, 'Streams of Sensibility: Philip Doddridge of Northampton and the Evangelical Tradition', in *Landscape and Community in England* (London and Ronceverte, 1985), pp. 209–46; Isabel Rivers, 'Philip Doddridge's New Testament: *The Family Expositor* (1739–56)', in Hannibal Hamlin and Norman W. Jones, eds, *The King James Bible After Four Hundred Years: Literary, Linguistic, and Cultural Influences* (Cambridge, 2010), pp. 124–45; Tessa Whitehouse, '*The Family Expositor*, the Doddridge Circle and the Booksellers', *The Library*, 7th ser., 11 (2010), pp. 321–44; Rivers, 'Religious Publishing', p. 588.

purchased copies in large quantities.¹⁰ Throughout the period, writers and editors commented on the desirability of small volumes. Philip Doddridge had hoped to publish an abridgement of *The Family Expositor* 'in neat pocket volumes... for the sake of the poor'. Though he died before he could do this, his example influenced his editor and former student Job Orton who produced the abridgement and adopted a small format when publishing his own sermons, telling a friend, 'I love little books, that may easily be carried in the pocket.'¹¹

Like these Congregationalist ministers, John Wesley made small books function as physically and intellectually accessible guides to religion. The series of fifty practical works he abridged to form *A Christian Library* reduced titles that had originally been far longer to fit within 350 duodecimo pages. Wesley's series included works by Roman Catholics, Scottish Episcopalians, Nonconformists, and members of various groups within the Established Church.¹² Originally intended for itinerant preachers and produced by a clergyman of the Church of England, the series was republished between 1819 and 1827, when Methodism was no longer within the Established Church. Works of divinity produced by men from a range of religious traditions were thereby available in an inexpensive Methodist version for nineteenth-century members of a church that had separated from the establishment.

Two genres whose experiential capacities and functions meant they were important to Dissenting culture and which had a significant presence in print publications of all formats were poetry and life writing. The latter encompassed letters, biographies, and conversion narratives. Deathbed scenes were especially popular in published life writing by and for all Dissenting groups. A typical narrative that concentrates on the final days of an individual is to be found in the unique surviving copy in the British Library. Melicent Sills, aged only twenty-three and stricken with consumption, provided a fine example of Christian assurance to her assembled friends and subsequent readers of this tract. She experienced 'joys' and 'raptures' rather than fear; recited appropriate hymns, and '[s]eeing some weep, she said, "weep not for me, I love a death bed"'.¹³ In her town of Chesham, the Particular Baptist minister was also the local stationer. James Sleap both converted Sills and published the narrative of her death as a twenty-four-page duodecimo pamphlet. Local publishing endeavours such as this provided particular congregations with bespoke printed material in genres and forms that imitated bigger projects and national trends.

---

¹⁰ Isabel Hofmeyr, *The Portable Bunyan: A Transnational History of The Pilgrim's Progress* (Princeton, NJ, 2004), chs 1–3.
¹¹ Philip Doddridge to Job Orton, May 1751 and Job Orton in a letter to Samuel Clark 26 December 1762. Both in Job Orton, *Letters to Dissenting Ministers*, 2 vols. (London, 1806), I, p. 89
¹² Rivers, 'Dissenting and Methodist Books', pp. 153–4.
¹³ [Anon.], *A Brief Narrative of the Experience and Dying Sayings of Melicent Sills, of Chesham, Bucks, Taken Chiefly from her Husband's Notes* (Chesham, 1800), pp. 8–10.

Substantial and enduring collections of similar material presented in formats far larger and at prices far greater than Sills's account include the Congregationalist Richard Burnham's *Pious Memorials*, an anthology of the final hours of godly individuals including Burnham himself, for it was published posthumously. This work was first published in 1753 in octavo, went through several reprints including a quarto version and was extended by George Burder (also a Congregationalist) in 1820. The first edition was relatively expensive at 5s. The range in price for works of Christian biography from a few pence to many shillings suggests that biographical examples appealed to wealthy audiences who read them for their own edification as well as subsidizing the production of individual life narratives through tract society publishing programmes. Deathbed accounts were a staple of the *Arminian Magazine* and the *Methodist Magazine* and in this context, a body of exemplary practice for emulation was built up gradually, issue by issue, in the later part of the eighteenth century and into the nineteenth.

The most systematic dissemination of deathbed piety was the long-running Quaker serial *Piety Promoted* (1701–1829) which had reached its ninth part by 1796. 'Production of each volume was a collective enterprise', notes J. William Frost, comprising several stages: the local Monthly Meeting commissioned someone who had been present at the deathbed to write a narrative account which was then sent on to London to be read at the Yearly Meeting.[14] The account might then be included in the next issue of *Piety Promoted*, a duodecimo publication whose parts (some of which were translated into French and Latin) regularly went into multiple editions. The cumulatively and collectively produced work had a long life and broad reach. A three-volume collected edition of the first eight parts was published in 1789 and an abridged selection in one volume came out in 1797. These late-century collected editions of narratives that had been produced throughout the century indicates a wide readership especially when taken in conjunction with the translated versions.

Funeral sermons often included an account of the deceased's life and published versions of these sermons could, like William Tong's for Elizabeth Bury (1720), include extracts of diaries. Bury's diary, the letter from a friend of Sill's appended to the narrative of her final days, and the frequent references to hymns in deathbed accounts all point to the enriching crossings between manuscript and print that took place throughout this period. Active scribal communities and ongoing oral encounters not only provided material for print but also recorded the use of print in particular settings. The converse was the case with hymns: printed hymn collections were central to public worship, and prefatory treatises of hymnody explained and justified the

---

[14] Frost, 'Quaker Books in Colonial Pennsylvania', p. 18, n. 18.

practice which, by the eighteenth century, had been accepted by all Dissenting denominations (except Quakers).

Hymns also played a part in domestic religious life and the textual representation thereof, particularly around the deathbed. The hymns of Watts in particular, along with those of Doddridge and Charles Wesley, were deathbed staples across the Dissenting traditions but there is also evidence that denominational and familial ties guided the selection of hymns. Annajane Blatch read from John Rippon's collection of hymns for Baptist worship with her parents during her long final illness in 1809. The hymns of Anne Steele were a particular favourite in the Blatch household, perhaps because Steele was kin as well as being a fellow-Baptist.[15] But this personal connection does not account for Steele's enormous popularity in print elsewhere. Julia Griffin has calculated that substantial numbers of her hymns were included in five distinct collections between 1787 and 1808, with as many as 102 to be found in *A Collection of Hymns and Psalms, For Public and Private Worship* (1795) edited by the Presbyterians Andrew Kippis and Abraham Rees.[16] This underscores the significance of anthologies and compilations in Dissenting print culture, as in literary culture more broadly. Such collections (be they verse or prose) were an important channel for the circulation of writing by women. In the case of Steele, her work circulated far more widely thanks to its place in hymn collections than it did through the stand-alone volumes of her works issued in 1760, 1780, and 1808.

PRODUCING PRINT

The role of booksellers in the production and dissemination of printed material was absolutely central in this period but the significance of religious commitment to a bookseller's output has not been systematically analysed as yet. A handful of important Dissenting booksellers has been studied individually, including the Sowle family, Richard Hett father and son, John Clark and Richard Ford, Martha Gurney, and Joseph Johnson.[17] Some generalizations based on this research indicate that few consistent conclusions are possible.

---

[15] Jane Attwater's diary, in Timothy Whelan, general ed., *Nonconformist Women Writers 1720–1840*, 8 vols. (London, 2011), VIII, pp. 266–7.

[16] Julia B. Griffin, 'Introduction to Anne Steele', in *Nonconformist Women Writers*, vol. I, ed. Timothy Whelan and Julia B. Griffin, pp. 10–12.

[17] Rivers, 'Religious Publishing', pp. 581–3; Helen Braithwaite, *Romanticism, Publishing and Dissent: Joseph Johnson and the Cause of Liberty* (Basingstoke, 2012); Paula McDowell, *The Women of Grub Street: Press, Politics, and Gender in the London Literary Marketplace 1678–1730* (Oxford, 1998), ch. 3.

The monopoly a religious publisher could have on the output of printed works from a particular group is striking in the case of the Sowle business for Quakers and Wesleyan printing at the Foundery (*sic*) in City Road in Wesley's lifetime and afterwards. In other cases, the range of publishing a particular bookseller might undertake beyond their own denomination and beyond straightforwardly 'religious' subject-matter is remarkable. Joseph Johnson published works written by Dissenters across many genres including poetry by Anna Letitia Barbauld and Mary Scott, novels such as Thomas Amory's *The Life of John Buncle* (1763) and Mary Hays's *The Victim of Prejudice* (1799) and sermons (practical, doctrinal, and controversial) by orthodox ministers as well as the Unitarians he is often associated with such as John Disney, William Enfield, Richard Price, and Joseph Priestley. He also published materials by evangelical Anglicans including more than a dozen works by Sarah Trimmer, showing that though today he is most strongly associated with radical politics, Johnson was responsible for educational and devotional staples, and retained this side of his business through the 1790s and beyond.

In the early years of his career, Joseph Johnson collaborated with the Dissenter James Buckland, a significant figure in the London book trade who was committed to the wide dissemination of Dissenting printed matter. Buckland did not exclusively publish works written by Dissenters, but a survey of his output shows that a very high proportion of the books he published were by Dissenting writers addressing religious topics. Orthodox writers made up the bulk of his list (including Thomas Gibbons, Job Orton, and Samuel Palmer) though popular writers with more complicated reputations such as Isaac Watts and Elizabeth Rowe were among his best sellers, and heterodox Dissenters like Robert Robinson, Thomas Belsham, and Henry Grove also appeared under Buckland's imprint. He frequently worked with other Dissenting booksellers (John Ward and James Waugh for example) and acted as the London distributor for works printed regionally such as Caleb Evans's works published in Bristol.

Regional publishing of Dissenting authors was a growing business, in line with the development of regional publishing generally in the period. Joshua Eddowes of Shrewsbury was an active bookseller and printer in two languages: English and Welsh. His output includes Doddridge's *Hymns*, Job Orton's biography of Doddridge, editions of works by Matthew Henry and abridgements of Richard Baxter by Benjamin Fawcett. Like Buckland, he published a range of other materials but his output is striking for the preponderance of orthodox Dissenting authors. Eddowes supported local literary sociability by subscribing to books written by Dissenters in order to donate them. The subscription list to Elizabeth Harrison's *Miscellanies* (1756) shows he took three copies of the collection of prose, verse, and letters on devotional and moral subjects; one for himself, and one each for the 'Reading Society' and the 'Ladies Reading Society'.

Between 1751 and 1773, Eddowes published eleven works in Welsh, including Baxter's *Call to the Unconverted*, Bunyan's *Pilgrim's Progress*, Matthew Henry's *A Church in the House* and Job Orton's *Three Sermons on Eternity*. In doing this, he was continuing the tradition of Shrewsbury as an English centre for Welsh-language publishing and, specifically, was building on a market for Welsh-language Dissenting-oriented printed material that had been developing since the seventeenth century. The Welsh Trust (1674–84) predates the period covered by the present volume but it was a significant antecedent to later tract societies in Wales and elsewhere. Notably, it was supported by Anglicans and Dissenters though its leaders were ejected ministers and the books it sponsored and translated (such as Bunyan's *Pilgrim's Progress*) were largely written by Nonconformists. One major project was a new edition of the Bible in Welsh, of which 7,000 were to be sold and a further 1,000 to be freely distributed to poor families. Through the foundation of schools the Welsh Trust contributed to the spread of education that fed a growing appetite for Welsh-language printed material in the century that followed.[18] Other early efforts in regional Welsh-language publishing were organized by Nonconformists animated by religious commitments who invited Samuel and Felix Farley from Bristol to Pontypool in 1740, where they printed Welsh translations of George Whitefield's sermons, a Baptist catechism, and hymn books.[19]

Other countries in the British Isles had religious publishing systems that were less abundantly nourished by the dissenting culture of England. Scotland had its own book business, and its own church establishment. While there was some crossover of ideas and texts in the two areas of university education and religious revival, the number of writers, publishers, and readers actively involved was small and the demographic rather circumscribed. In the field of university philosophy, students and tutors in the Scottish universities and English Dissenting academies learned something of one another's work through lectures and set texts.[20] There was also exchange between English Dissenters and Scottish ministers in publishing and distributing evangelical texts of practical religion, particularly the work of Henry Scougal which was much admired by English Dissenters.[21] Gaelic publishing was a small industry but an overwhelmingly religious one animated principally by evangelical

---

[18] Rheinallt Llwyd, 'Printing and Publishing in the Seventeenth Century', in Philip Henry Jones and Eiluned Rees, eds, *A Nation and its Books: A History of the Book in Wales* (Aberystwyth, 1998) pp. 93–103 (pp. 100–1), and Philip Henry Jones, 'Wales', in *The Cambridge History of the Book in Britain: Volume IV*, pp. 719–34.

[19] Rees, 'The Welsh Book Trade from 1718 to 1820', in *A Nation and its Books*, p. 124.

[20] Paul Wood, *The Aberdeen Enlightenment: The Arts Curriculum in the Eighteenth Century* (Aberdeen, 1993).

[21] Isabel Rivers, 'Scougal's *The life of God in the soul of man*: The Fortunes of a Book 1673–1830', in Ruth Savage, ed., *Philosophy and Religion in Enlightenment Britain: New Case Studies* (Oxford, 2012), pp. 29–55 (esp. section III).

endeavours in the Highlands which supported the spread of scriptural knowledge and translation of works such as Baxter's *Call to the Unconverted* and Joseph Alleine's *Alarm to the Unconverted*.[22] In Ireland the proportion of the Protestant population that dissented from the Established Church was small, and does not appear to have supported its own print culture.

American booksellers imported English books, particularly religious 'steady sellers', from London (and, as the century went on, from Dublin) but did not start to print Dissenters' works on their own account in significant numbers for many decades.[23] In fact, the inverse was the case. The print culture of British Dissent (particularly in England, and especially in London) supported and promoted American evangelical writers such as David Brainerd and Jonathan Edwards.[24] The publication of journals, letters, and testimonies served to disseminate news of religious projects from around the world and bring scattered experiences and communities together. But it was not only specifically religious works by British Dissenters that were popular in America, as the example of Isaac Watts shows. Watts's hymns were phenomenally successful, but also remarkably persistent were his educational writings, particularly when edited for American audiences.[25]

In London publications, the lists of books for sale appended to volumes Dissenters published reveal something of the way they balanced the ideological and commercial elements of their businesses. Richard Hett and James Buckland marketed Dissenting print culture in terms of a specific group of writers that would interest readers with an appetite for practical and literary but not controversial works. A new book would come with a complete list of the other works by that author, for example Philip Doddridge's sermon *The Necessity of a General Reformation* (1740) included details of the eleven works by Doddridge already published, including ones originally anonymous, and *The Rise and Progress of Religion in the Soul* (1740) ended with four pages of advertisements: two detailing nineteen works by Doddridge and two listing twelve works by other authors published by James Waugh across all categories of religious writing: sermons and practical works by John Mason, Nathaniel Lardner's historical and controversial work *The Credibility of Gospel History*, and various other funeral sermons and practical texts including a family prayer book.

---

[22] Ann Matheson, 'Religion', in Stephen W. Brown and Warren McDougall, eds, *The Edinburgh History of the Book in Scotland, Volume II: Enlightenment and Expansion* (Edinburgh, 2012), pp. 459–70 (pp. 467–8).

[23] Hugh Amory and David D. Hall, 'Afterword', in *A History of the Book in America, Volume I: The Colonial Book in the Atlantic World*, 2nd edn (Cambridge, 2007), pp. 477–85 (p. 483) and Appendix 1, graph 9 (pp. 517–18).

[24] Philip Doddridge, ed., *The Journal of David Brainerd* (London, 1748).

[25] Joseph Emerson, *Questions and Supplement, to Watts On the Improvement of the Mind* (Boston, MA, 1831).

In the Doddridge lists, over four-fifths of the books are sermons, and another indicator of the strong correlation between Dissenting booksellers and Dissenting authors comes from sermon publication generally. Jennifer Farooq has found that while the 'concentration of the publication of sermons by a few booksellers' was a trend in general, it was 'even more pronounced for Dissenting sermons, for over 63 per cent of these sermons were printed by just ten booksellers'.[26] Given the dominance of sermons in the printed book market (and not only the religious book market), this is a remarkable concentration of print activity in the shops of a handful of booksellers who shared a religious identity with their authors.

The active female printers and booksellers in this period belonging to Dissenting communities predominantly produced religious, historical, and biographical works related to their own traditions. The Quaker Tace Sowle had a very long career as the leading printer and distributor of Friends books from 1691 to her death in 1749. Her biographer Paula McDowell has identified the three principle categories of her business as 'landmark works in the history of Quakerism' including major and collected works of George Fox, Margaret Askew Fell Fox, and William Penn and William Sewell's history of Quakers; Quaker women's writings ('the single largest category of women's writings in this period'), and 'virtually all routine business printing for the Quakers'[27] This last category included the 1,000 copies of the *Yearly Meeting Epistle*, indicating the scale as well as variety of Sowle's output. She was responsible for the local, national, and international distribution of Quaker works to American and Caribbean colonies and to continental Europe.

Sowle took over her parents' printing business at her father's death though her mother Jane Sowle continued to be identified on imprints for several years. Mary Fenner was another woman who operated a successful book business, though in her case the details of her career are scarcely known. In the early 1740s, she was in partnership with John Wilson, who sold Dissenters' works (including Daniel Williams's *Practical Discourses*) from the Turk's Head in Gracechurch Street. Wilson died in 1741 and between 1742 and 1744, Mary Fenner was identified as the bookseller with the formulation 'printed and sold by' on over forty practical and controversial books by orthodox Dissenting ministers including Caleb Fleming, Henry Grove, Philip Doddridge, David Jennings, Obadiah Hughes, Samuel Bourn, and Nathaniel Lardner. Even though her name ceased to appear on imprints following her marriage to James Waugh in 1744, her shop (the Turk's Head in Gracechurch Street and later in Lombard Street) continued to be the site for selling Dissenting books

---

[26] Jennifer Farooq, *Preaching in Eighteenth-Century London* (Woodbridge, 2013), p. 76.
[27] Paula McDowell, 'Sowle, Tace (1666–1749)', *Oxford Dictionary of National Biography*, Oxford University Press, 2004; online edn, Jan. 2008 [http://www.oxforddnb.com/view/article/67077, accessed 21 Sept. 2015].

and there is strong evidence that she continued to work as a printer. Delays to the publication of the third volume of *The Family Expositor* caused her financial loss, according to Doddridge, even though it was her husband who was named as the bookseller on the volume's title page.[28] In 1748, it was she who had authority to commission a fifth edition of his *Rise and Progress of Religion in the Soul* and this raises the question of whether the books advertised as being sold by James Waugh in the 1740 edition of the same work were in fact commissioned, printed, and distributed at his wife's command.[29] Doddridge was a personal friend, and his correspondence conveys a strong sense of her continuing significance. He often stayed with the Waughs when in London (on one occasion reporting that Mrs Waugh had hosted an evening's entertainment for him) and was a guest at her home during July 1751, his final visit to London before his death.[30] Though admittedly these are social markers rather than evidence of business decisions, it is nevertheless striking that a centre of production for moderate Dissenters' books at the midpoint of the eighteenth century was sustained by a woman with strong social religious commitments as well as trade expertise.

The Particular Baptist Martha Gurney was another female printer with a long career in the London book trade. Between 1772 and 1813 her name appeared on 130 titles as printer, bookseller, or both. She played a significant role in the abolitionist movement and according to Timothy Whelan 'was one of London's leading Dissenting printers and sellers of radical political pamphlets and abolitionist tracts. In fact, she was the *only* woman bookseller/printer engaged in such activities at that time.'[31] He calculates that between 1788 and 1802 Gurney printed and/or sold thirty-six radical pamphlets, fourteen of which strongly attacked the slave trade. Her publishing work championed the Dissenting principle of liberty in other respects too. John Gurney, her brother, was a parliamentary stenographer and through this connection she printed thirty-one trials between 1774 and 1806 including the state trials of Thomas Paine and Thomas Hardy. And yet Gurney continued to pursue more traditional bookselling too. Her nephew's reminiscences highlight the wide range of her trade interests for he describes her as a seller of 'old Divinity and Bibles'.[32] This insight into the life of Gurney's bookshop vividly creates a sense of the second-hand book trade coexisting with the production of new works.

---

[28] Doddridge to Mercy Doddridge, 11 July 1747, in G. F. Nuttall, ed., *A Calendar of the Correspondence of Philip Doddridge* (London, 1979), letter 1252.

[29] Doddridge to Mercy Doddridge, 30 July 1748, in Nuttall, *Calendar*, letter 1373.

[30] Philip Doddridge to Mercy Doddridge, Aug. 1747, 4 and 6 July 1751, in Nuttall, *Calendar*, letters 1265, 1760, and 1762.

[31] Timothy Whelan, 'Martha Gurney and William Fox: London Baptists and Radical Politics, 1791–94', in John Briggs, ed., *Pulpit and People: Studies in 18th Century Baptist Life and Thought* (Milton Keynes, 2009), pp. 165–201 (pp. 170–1).

[32] W. B. Gurney, 'Reminiscences', quoted in Whelan, 'Martha Gurney and William Fox', p. 170.

The idea of orthodox practical divinity and large format Bibles being shelved in proximity to inexpensive polemical works engaging in current political debates underscores the points that Dissenting culture was nourished by books of all types and that certain prices and formats did not necessarily entail circumscribed groups of readers. Biblical and devotional works served to strengthen the piety and understanding of readers, while principles of conscience were expressed and invoked through controversial works. Both sorts of books connected readers with a developing tradition of Dissenting literature from the seventeenth century to the present.

The lives and work of these women illustrate three major patterns by which print trade work served Dissenting religious life. It is significant that all three women were printers as well as booksellers in a period when, according to many interpretations, the financial and distribution power of print lay principally with booksellers rather than printers, who were increasingly seen as technical service providers. Sowle, Fenner, and Gurney all used their printing expertise to produce works that served the religious, social, and political interests of their particular Dissenting communities in ways that indicate financial success was not always the primary goal. Gurney, for instance, used her power as both producer and distributor of William Fox's *Address to the People of Great Britain* (1791) to announce the number of copies printed so far and to reduce the price as demand increased. Whelan has calculated that 'by the twenty-sixth edition she would have printed 130,000 copies'.[33]

Writing about religious publishing, Ian Green has claimed that 'most of the shortest and cheapest works of all in the seventeenth century were issued by publishers seeking to make a quick buck' and even for more expensive works 'a clear majority [of booksellers] probably came down on the side of profit' rather than sincerity.[34] This may be true in some cases, but the longstanding relationships between Dissenting booksellers and authors attested publicly by title pages and the printed lists of books for sale that were often included at the ends of volumes, and the personal warmth expressed in letters addressed to booksellers or written from their homes, tell a more complex story of personal religious commitments and business decisions being mutually constitutive on the part of booksellers and of authors.

Dissenting authors were predominantly men rather than women and ministers rather than the laity. Indeed, as the authors and titles discussed so far in this chapter signal, it was orthodox ministers writing within the traditions and structures of the Three Denominations who provided booksellers with their steady sellers. Writers such as Richard Baxter, Matthew Henry, Isaac Watts, and Philip Doddridge were significant figures in the print culture of Dissent

---

[33] Timothy Whelan, 'William Fox, Martha Gurney, and Radical Discourse of the 1790s', *Eighteenth-Century Studies*, 42, 3 (2009), p. 402.
[34] Green, *Print and Protestantism*, p. 11 and p. 24.

not only in terms of their own published works but also through their personal example and teaching about how books should be used. This information appeared in their writings (published in their lifetimes and posthumously) and in biographies of them.

Women were far more often imagined as the audience for or subject of printed materials than named as the producers of them. They appeared as exemplars of godly living through the deathbed scenes described above and in biographies (usually edited by men) such as the popular biography of the North American Quaker Hannah Hill. Those who were authors in their own right tended to be poets and imaginative writers from ministerial circles within the Three Denominations. Elizabeth Rowe, Anne Steele, and Anna Letitia Barbauld are the best known. In the later part of the period, the writings of some seventeenth-century Puritan women were published for the first time, such as Agnes Beaumont's *Narrative* (written c.1674, published 1760 in the 1s. collection edited by Samuel James entitled *An Abstract of the Gracious Dealings of God with Several Eminent Christians*), and Lucy Hutchinson's biography of her husband and autobiographical fragment (written c.1664–8, published 1806 as *Memoirs of the Col. Hutchinson*). The success of the latter was presented by its editor as evidence of 'that sound and unvitiated state of the Moral Sense in British Society' but not connected to a distinctively Dissenting culture.[35]

A significant dynamic that characterized the print culture of Dissent throughout this period that had existed since the first century of Reformed printing but increased throughout the eighteenth century and into the nineteenth was the editing by Dissenters of the works of their puritan and nonconformist forebears. Lucy Hutchinson's descendant was the editor of her mid-seventeenth-century work that he retitled *Memoirs of Colonel Hutchinson* but this is a rare instance of such editorial work being undertaken for a woman writer. It was much more common for Dissenting ministers to reissue (often in abridged form) the works of admired male forebears, such as Benjamin Fawcett's abridgements of Richard Baxter in the 1750s and 1760s, Job Orton's edition of Matthew Henry's biography of his father, Philip Henry (1765), and Samuel Palmer's new version of Edmund Calamy's directory of ejected ministers (based on Richard Baxter's *Reliquiae Baxterianae* (1696)) which Palmer called *The Nonconformist's Memorial* (1775). All these works served to sustain the traditions of Nonconformity by making its writing and principles available to new audiences.

An important way in which customers contributed to the production of books was through subscription publishing. Although the practice of asking purchasers to give their financial contribution early in the publication process (to cover the cost of printing) rather than at the end of it once the book was in

---

[35] Julius Hutchinson, 'Advertisement', in *Memoirs of the Life of Colonel Hutchinson*, 2nd edn (London, 1808), p. v.

the shops was widely used to finance book publication in the eighteenth century, it has been claimed that Dissenters had an especially strong cultural disposition towards the practice. Indeed, N. H. Keeble has argued that subscription publication was developed intensively within seventeenth-century nonconformist groups because of their closely bound communities, and was necessary because of the legal restrictions they faced. The subscriber lists for Doddridge's *Family Expositor* in the 1730s, 1740s, and 1750s support this contention, for though the work achieved a wide base of support in geographic, social, and religious terms, it was personally sustained Dissenting networks that generated the bulk of the subscribers.[36] It was not just ministerial works that were financed in this way. The example of Elizabeth Harrison's *Miscellanies* described above shows that the practice continued, and was extended to the works of the laity, in the second half of the eighteenth century. Subscription publishing had a long and productive history for Dissenters.

Subscription characterized a wide range of cultural and religious endeavours in this period, from infirmaries to charity schools to missionary societies. There were strong connections between charitable associations and the production and distribution of print across the British Isles and further afield. The work of the Welsh Trust at the end of the seventeenth century is an early example of this and the tradition was continued throughout the eighteenth and nineteenth centuries. Free provision of Bibles and devotional materials in local languages was, ever since John Eliot's work translating the Bible, the psalms, and other pieces into Algonquian in the mid-seventeenth century, a central task of subscriber-funded missionary endeavour. Over time, such work became formalized.

The December 1819 issue of the *Methodist Magazine* contains a full section of 'Missionary Intelligence' and is typical of publications in the period in this respect. Extensive extracts from 'the last report of the Colombo Bible Society' provide fascinating detail about the process of translation, production, and distribution (including difficulties with style and need for a glossary) of 'the means of acquaintance with the truths of religion' in Sri Lanka. It comments on the (unsuccessful) practice of circulating 200 advance copies of the gospels of Matthew and Mark to see if they are comprehensible and accurate, and describes the work of the press, which 'continues still under the skilful and active management of the Wesleyan Missionaries', and whose output in the preceding year has included 'the glossary to the Cingalese translation of the New Testament'. But productivity is not restricted to Bibles alone: '2,000 copies of Green's Principles of Religion, with a preface in Cingalese and English'; '2,000 copies of... "The Folly of Idolatry exposed from the Scriptures", in Cingalese and English'; '2,000 Discourses and 2,000 Sermons of our

---

[36] Keeble, *The Literary Culture of Nonconformity*, p. 130; Tessa Whitehouse, *The Textual Culture of English Protestant Dissent, 1720–1800* (Oxford, 2015), pp. 181–2.

Saviour upon the Mount, in Tamul and English' have also been produced.[37] The scale of the publication programme and the range of languages—which included Portuguese—was matched in ambition by technical aims such as establishing a type foundry on the island so that the missionaries were not reliant on Sinhalese and Tamil type imported from Calcutta. The conjunction of literacy and religious knowledge that was fundamental to reformed Christianity generated large quantities of printed materials that were often produced through collective fund-raising and voluntary work by non-professionals and did not have commercial aims.

CONSUMING PRINT

Printed materials that reflected, debated, and created Dissenting culture were consumed in a wide variety of settings. Many of the most highly valued forms and sites of reading can be characterized as educational: schools, academies, and homes (particularly family prayers, though private devotion also had an educative purpose). Learning from pulpit teaching by listening to sermons as they were preached, perhaps taking notes of them, and reading published versions of sermons away from the meeting house were longstanding cultural practices that persisted throughout this period and affirmed the meeting house as a site for learning as well as for worship.

As well as fulfilling these receptive roles, Dissenting congregations could actively request the production of print. For example, Jonathan Edwards's *A Faithful Narrative of the Surprizing Work of God* (1737) was published in order to communicate news about edifying and extraordinary instances of religious awakening that began among a small community in Massachusetts and spread through the local area. The news reached Britain via the Boston minister Benjamin Colman, who sent the abstract of Edwards's letter to him which had been published at the end of a volume of sermons to his correspondent Isaac Watts. Watts and his fellow Congregationalist minister John Guyse originally thought the account should be published in Boston, and sent £5 each for this purpose but, perhaps proving the difficulties of religious publishing in America at that time, it was eventually printed in London.[38]

---

[37] *Methodist Magazine*, 62 (1819), pp. 949–51.

[38] Jonathan Edwards, *A Faithful Narrative of the Surprizing work of God... In a Letter to the Revd. Dr. Benjamin Colman* (London, 1737), C. C. Goen, ed., *The Works of Jonathan Edwards, IV: The Great Awakening* (New Haven, 1972; repr. 2009), pp. 32–46; Susan O'Brien, 'Eighteenth-Century Publishing Networks in the First Years of Transatlantic Evangelicalism', in Mark A. Noll, David W. Bebbington, and George A. Rawlyk, eds, *Evangelicalism: Comparative Studies of Popular Protestantism in North America, the British Isles, and Beyond 1700–1900* (Oxford, 1994), pp. 38–57; Whitehouse, *Textual Culture*, pp. 156–61.

This edition had a preface by the two English ministers which highlighted the positive global benefits, to clergy and laity, that such examples could have. The preface specifically presented the publication as a response to the wishes of the laity, recounting how Guyse's congregation in London had heard an epistolary account of the occurrences read out at a meeting and wanted more information. Though ordained ministers directed the flow of religious news, Dissenting print culture was animated by the interests and preferences of the laity and presented as being intended to serve the godly of all stations and backgrounds.

Nevertheless, students for the ministry were a particular target for guidance about the uses of print. In *The Christian Directory* (1674; reprinted as volume one of the *Practical Works* of 1707), Baxter provided lists of books suitable for family reading and for students of different degrees of poverty.[39] Students were also addressed in Philip Doddridge's *Course of Lectures* (1763) which gave detailed lists of references to arguments on both sides of so many philosophical, ethical, and theological questions that its nineteenth-century editors declared it 'the most complete syllabus of controversial theology, in the largest sense of the word, ever published in the English language'.[40] At £4 10s. and 16s. respectively, it is unlikely that many students would have been able to afford either the folio *Practical Works* in four volumes or *A Course of Lectures* in crown quarto when the books were new, but they would have been able to consult copies owned by the tutor or in the academy library.[41] Doddridge's correspondence, first published in 1789 and in a fuller five-volume edition between 1802 and 1805, contained evidence of his own reading practices as a student and young minister that readers could emulate. His guidance about reading in the *Course of Lectures* and *Lectures on Preaching* (first extracted in denominational magazines and published in full in 1804) made it clear that heterodox texts and authors should only be encountered once a certain level of knowledge and wide reading had been reached.

Reading lists made by individual students demonstrate a clear focus on practical works. In the case of Thomas Blackmore (a student at Daventry academy in the 1760s) sermons by Dissenting ministers and nonconformist writers formed the bulk of this scheme of reading. The first year is focused on works encouraging self-knowledge and personal piety and the second year on religious practice. In the third year writers from the Established Church are introduced, bolstered by Doddridge's own sermons. The final two years of practical reading cover advanced doctrinal matters, including John Owen's

---

[39] Richard Baxter, *Christian Directory* in *Practical Works*, 4 vols. (London, 1707), I, pp. 454–5 and 717–22.

[40] Edward Williams, 'Advertisement', in E. Williams and E. Parsons, eds, *The Works of the Rev. P. Doddridge, D.D.*, 10 vols. (Leeds, 1802–5), IV, 281–2.

[41] See Edward Arber, ed., *Term Catalogues, 1668–1709 A.D.*, 3 vols. (London, 1903–6), III, 500; *London Chronicle*, 28 April 1763.

sermons on indwelling sin, mortification, grace, and temptation which acquainted students with puritan perspectives from the previous century and more recent works directed towards ministerial comportment such as John Jennings's *Two Discourses* (1723) on evangelical preaching.[42]

Surviving catalogues and loans registers of Dissenting academy libraries give a sense of how students accessed the works recommended to them by tutors. For example, five different editions of Jennings's *Two Discourses* were held in academy libraries at Manchester, York, Airedale, Homerton, Northampton, London, and Bristol from the 1730s through to the mid-nineteenth century. Copies of the 1668 edition of John Owen's *Of the Mortification of Sin in Believers* were being borrowed in 1816 at Homerton, having been in the library since 1793 or earlier. The work remained in the library at Manchester College (both in Manchester and in York) until at least the middle of the nineteenth century. While it is not always possible to ascertain how (or whether) these copies were used, the survival of puritan and nonconformist books in academy libraries marks these out as physical depositories that served the perpetuation of Dissenting traditions of reading and scholarship and therefore as significant sites in the construction of a nonconformist culture that valued its own history as well as its future.[43]

Evidence for the acquisition and circulation of books beyond educational and ministerial settings is much harder to find. It is, however, possible to examine the ways in which those who controlled printed material sought to direct its consumption. The work of tract societies is very informative in this regard. Potential rather than actual readers, people who had not chosen to purchase religious books (including ones written by Dissenters) but might be encouraged to read them, and those whose station in life was deemed to make them particularly vulnerable to worldly dangers, were the anticipated audiences for the publications sponsored by tract societies, which proliferated in this period.

These societies were founded to produce and distribute religious materials on a large scale. Though the earliest (including the Society for Promoting Christian Knowledge (SPCK) founded in 1698) were strongly associated with the Church of England, many others were cross-denominational, including the Society for Promoting Religious Knowledge Among the Poor (founded in 1750 by a group of Dissenters) and the Religious Tract Society (founded 1799).[44] They all had a common commitment to the non-commercial distribution of religious works in small formats. Though Bibles and psalms were the priority of

---

[42] Thomas Blackmore, Castle Hill Church Northampton, Blackmore MSS. vol. V, pp. 15–16, 18, 20–4.

[43] The Virtual Library System of *Dissenting Academies Online* is freely accessible at http://vls.english.qmul.ac.uk/.

[44] Isabel Rivers, 'The First Evangelical Tract Society', *Historical Journal*, 50 (2007), pp. 1–22.

all these societies, as with the Sri Lankan Methodists, a vast library of practical, devotional, and biographical materials were published under the auspices of various tract societies. An 1803 publication lists the sixty-seven tracts issued since the Religious Tract Society's foundation including a number of titles addressed to children: *To a Youth* (which commences with an image and description of Doddridge learning Bible stories from chimney tiles borrowed from Orton's biography), *To a Youth at School, To a Child, A Present to the Children of Sunday Schools*, and Watts's *Divine Songs*. Other groups particularly targeted by tracts were prostitutes (*To the Unfortunate Female* and *The Penitent Prostitute*), drunks, soldiers, and sailors, and the poor and afflicted. The price was 1*d*. each, or 5*s*. 6*d*. per hundred.[45] The low price for such materials was central to the societies' operation. Indeed, the work of tract societies demonstrates that the equation of small size with cheapness and consequent widespread circulation noted above was not only appreciated by individual writers but also characterized all manner of publishing movements in this period when 'improvement' was a watchword and activism was characteristic of evangelical ministers and laypeople.

CONCLUSION

As this chapter has noted, authors and titles suggest that the principal Dissenting authors were overwhelmingly male and ministerial. Dissenting consumers of print were in theory more demographically balanced, for women and children are clearly addressed by many writers but rarely or never wrote books of their own. Though scholarship into records of reading and personal piety (including letters and diaries) has found evidence of active reading, there is more research to be done to uncover and analyse the lay experience of print culture. There has been a tendency to follow ministerial patterns of authorship, editorship, and distribution partly because the materials are more readily available and partly, perhaps, because a great deal of the significant work on the print culture of dissent has been produced by men (and particularly ministers) working within modern-day successors to Dissenting traditions.

It is significant that in this period consumers of print became its producers through the proliferation of magazines. This was not a uniquely religious (let alone Dissenting) phenomenon but the capacity for readers to become contributors was enthusiastically promoted by magazines ranging from titles with deliberately broad appeal such as the *Evangelical Magazine* to those with more

---

[45] [Anon.], *An Account of the Origin and Progress of the London Religious Tract Society* (London, 1803), pp. 40–1.

closely defined audiences such as the *Methodist Magazine* or the *Protestant Dissenter's Magazine* and, in the nineteenth century, denominationally specific titles such as the *Congregational Magazine*. Those activities were welcomed in terms of the promotion of Dissenting culture through print. Significant too is the large-scale development of non-commercial publishing models (enabled by Tract Society membership, for example, and subscription publishing) which were also not the exclusive preserve of Dissenting readers, writers, and book producers. Indeed, Dissenting print culture in this period is remarkable for the energy and imagination with which it adopted innovations, fashions, and tricks of the commercial print trade and repurposed them for evangelical and community-building ends.

SELECT BIBLIOGRAPHY

Amory, Hugh and Hall, David D., eds, *A History of the Book in America, Volume I: The Colonial Book in the Atlantic World*, 2nd edn (Cambridge, 2007).

Cambers, Andrew, *Godly Reading: Print, Manuscript and Puritanism in England, 1580–1720* (Cambridge, 2010).

Frost, William, 'Quaker Books in Colonial Pennsylvania', *Quaker History*, 80, 1 (1991), pp. 1–23.

Green, Ian, *Print and Protestantism in Early Modern England* (Oxford, 2000).

Hofmeyr, Isabel, *The Portable Bunyan: A Transnational History of The Pilgrim's Progress* (Princeton, NJ, 2004).

Keeble, N. H., *The Literary Culture of Nonconformity in the Later Seventeenth Century* (Leicester, 1987).

McDowell, Paula, *The Women of Grub Street: Press, Politics, and Gender in the London Literary Marketplace, 1678–1730* (Oxford, 1998).

McInelly, Brett C., *Textual Warfare and the Making of Methodism* (Oxford, 2014).

Rivers, Isabel, 'Dissenting and Methodist Books of Practical Divinity', in Rivers, Isabel, ed., *Books and their Readers in Eighteenth-Century England* (Leicester, 1982), pp. 127–64.

Rivers, Isabel, 'Religious Publishing', in Suarez, Michael F. and Turner, Michael L., eds, *The Cambridge History of the Book in Britain: Volume V, 1695–1830* (Cambridge, 2009), pp. 579–600.

Whitehouse, Tessa, '*The Family Expositor*, the Doddridge Circle and the Booksellers', *The Library*, 7th ser., 11 (2010), pp. 321–44.

Whitehouse, Tessa, *The Textual Culture of English Protestant Dissent 1720–1800* (Oxford, 2015).

Index

Abernethy, John 126, 348
Abolition Society *see* Society for Effecting the Abolition of the Slave Trade
Abolitionism 3, 93–5, 111, 217–18, 284–301
Abney, Thomas 34–5
Acts of Parliament
  Affirmation (1696) 77, 80–2, 277
  Affirmation (1714) 153
  Indemnity 278
  Irish Indemnity 125
  Irish Popery (1704) 273
  Occasional Conformity (1711) 38, 274
  Marriage (1753) 58
  Sacramental Test (1828) 280
  Schism (1714) 38, 124, 274, 387
  Settlement (1701) 272–4
  Slave Limitation or Dolben (1788) 292–3
  Test and Corporation (1673 and 1661) 7, 30, 52, 58, 181, 243, 273, 275, 277–8, 287, 289, 298, 388
  Toleration (1689) 5, 6, 7, 14, 23, 30, 47, 58, 77, 101, 160, 189, 195, 270, 275, 306, 308, 387, 423
  Toleration (1712) 143
  Uniformity (1662) 163–4, 270, 386, 414
  Union (1707) 4, 123, 279
  Universities Test (1871) 388
Addison, Joseph 358
Aikin, John 288, 391, 404
Alison, Francis 128–9
Allard, William 26
Allen, Richard 209, 217
Allen, William 92, 97
Alline, Henry 208, 215
American Bible Society 216
American Revolution xviii, 110, 133, 145, 184, 200, 209, 213, 219, 338
American Sunday School Union 216
Amory, Thomas 444
Anderson, James 337, 343
Anne, queen 35, 38, 124, 143, 272–4, 387
Annesley, Samuel 1, 364, 421
Annesley, Elizabeth 364
Antinomianism 19–20, 31, 105
Anti-popery 127–8, 131, 133, 341
Arianism 11, 21, 26, 58, 127, 167, 173, 204, 234, 317, 354
Arminianism 19, 21, 100, 142, 172–3, 230, 234, 324–5

Asbury, Francis 209, 210, 211, 217
Ash, John 72, 365, 369–70, 393
Ashwood, John 17
Ashworth, Caleb 322
Aspland, Robert 14, 26
Avery, Benjamin 278

Backus, Isaac 194, 196, 198
Bangorian Controversy 126, 276, 319
Baptist Missionary Society xvii, 55, 73–5, 244, 245, 248, 254, 259, 379
Baptists xv, xvi, xvii, 5, 6, 13, 14, 30, 48, 54–76, 102, 104, 105, 108, 119, 120, 122, 131, 152, 156–8, 161–2, 166, 169–71, 172, 181, 200, 201, 202, 211, 213, 214, 216, 217, 218, 220, 226, 238, 245, 246, 247, 249, 250, 251, 253, 254, 271, 278, 289, 290, 295, 308, 316, 317, 321, 323, 325, 326, 328, 329, 349, 365, 382, 384, 389, 390, 396, 403–4, 411, 414, 428, 429, 443, 445
  Covenants and 56–7
  Ecclesiology of 55, 56–7
  Evangelical Revival and 66–9
  Identity of 58–60
  In colonial USA 183–99
  Mission and 55, 244, 245, 248, 254, 259
  Numerical strength 60–6
  Scotch 155
  Social structure of 55–6
  In Scotland 156–8
  In USA 207–9
  Welsh 162, 169–71
Barbauld, Anna Letitia 288, 370, 392, 444, 450
Barclay, John 154–5
Barclay, Robert 81, 307, 393
Barker, John 27
Barnard, Hannah 88
Barrington, John Shute 265–6
Baxter, Richard xvi, 19, 24, 100, 287, 306–7, 308, 311–12, 315, 444–5, 449, 450, 452
Bayley, Lewis 59
Beaufoy, Henry 288, 293
Beaumont, Agnes 450
Beddome, Benjamin 72, 73, 366–7, 370
Bedford, Peter 97
Belsham, Thomas 14, 391, 405, 444
Bennett, James 13, 271
Benson, Joseph 113, 293

Bereans 155
Bevan, Bridget 178
Beveridge, William 106
Bezenet, Anthony 94–5, 111, 290
Bible Society 45
Bingham, John 100
Black, William 211
Blackburne, Francis 288, 321
Blackstone, William 25
BMS *see* Baptist Missionary Society
Boddington, George 35
Bogue, David 13, 156, 251–2, 255, 271, 407
Book of Common Prayer (1662) xviii, 25, 109, 143, 340, 440
Booth, Abraham 62, 317, 326
Bourn, Samuel 23, 25, 27, 447
Bourne, Hugh 229
Boyle, Robert 42
Boyne, Battle of 120
Boyse, Joseph 339
Bradburn, Samuel 295
Bradbury, Thomas 274–5
Bragge, Robert 349, 352, 354, 356
Brainerd, David 245, 446
Bright, Henry 38
Brine, John 60, 63, 326
British and Foreign School Society 399
Brontë, Charlotte 240
Brooksbank, John 15
Brougham, Henry 297
Browne, Simon 359, 360
Bruich, Ivor 79
Buckland, James 444
Bugg, Francis 88
Bull, William 48
Bunting, Jabez 259
Bunyan, John xxi, 59, 316, 368, 440, 445
Burder, George 370–1, 442
Burke, Edmund xviii, 321
Burnham, Richard 442

Caffyn, Matthew 60
Calamy, Edmund (1671–1732) 17, 20, 23, 24, 27, 265–6, 309, 342, 408
Calvinism 19, 22, 31, 60–1, 100, 142, 170, 172, 215, 230, 266, 291, 307–8, 310, 321, 323–6, 328, 341, 356, 413
Cambuslang Wark 150, 151, 235
Cameron, Richard 141–2
Campbell, Thomas 137
Canada 200, 202
Cane Ridge 206
Carey, William 64, 74–5, 238, 243–4, 247, 251, 325–6, 379
Carpenter, Mary 300
Caryl, Joseph 35

Caryl, Sarah 35
Catholics 30, 188–9, 190, 192, 270–1, 341, 441
Cennick, John 131, 233, 375
Chandler, Samuel 24–5
Channing, John 40
Channing, William Ellery 203
Chalmers, Thomas 238
Charity Schools 4, 336–7, 388–90
Charles, Thomas 176, 238
Chauncy, Charles 203, 401
Chauncy, Isaac 37, 41, 401, 402
Cheshire classis 16, 289
Cheshunt College 48, 407
Church Missionary Society (CMS) 246, 253
Church of England xviii, xx, 44, 99, 160, 184, 200, 210, 264–5, 279, 285, 307, 329, 356, 357, 360–1, 438
 And Comprehension 31
 Porous boundaries with Dissent 18, 33, 185–6
Church of Ireland 123, 264–5
Church of Scotland 128, 139–40, 145–9, 245, 264–5
Church rates 77, 287
Claridge, Richard 79
Clark, John 443
Clarke, John 191, 196
Clarke, Samuel (1675–1729), Anglican clergyman 21–3, 319
Clarke, Samuel (1684–1750), Dissenting minister 39
Clarkson, Thomas 92, 284, 291
Clayton, John 47
Clegg, James 15, 18, 21
Clowes, William 228
Coke, Thomas 209, 210, 253, 256–9
Collier, Thomas 59
Comenius, Jan 34
Common Fund (1690) 15, 17, 32, 35
Compton Census (1676) 33, 161
Conder, James 43
Conder, John 43
Conder, Richard 42
Confessional state 120, 129, 265, 266, 288
Congregationalism xvi, xix, 11, 14, 16, 17, 18, 24, 28, 30–53, 108, 113, 119, 122, 137, 152, 154, 158, 161, 162, 169, 171, 181, 200, 245, 247, 251, 278, 289, 290, 308, 316, 319, 321, 323, 325, 328, 349, 362, 421, 429
 Denominational boundaries 30–1, 49, 161, 305–6
 Doctrine of 36–9
 Emergence of 30–2
 Fund Board 19, 36, 37, 166–7, 305, 400, 405
 In colonial USA 4, 36, 183–99

Intellectual and social impact 42-3
Old and New Light split 193-4
Old Scottish Independents 154-5
Size and development 32-6
Spirituality and revival in 43-7
In USA 201-4
Welsh 161-2
Congregational Union of England and Wales (1831) 30, 50
Connecticut 190, 202
Conscience, liberty of 183-4, 196-8
Conyers, Richard 369
Cooke, John 333-6, 340
Cottle, Joseph 47
Cotton, Thomas 40
Coward, William 37, 40
Coward Trust 37-8
Cotton, John 187
Countess of Huntingdon's Connexion 47, 49, 230, 253-4, 295
Crisp, Tobias 19-20
Cropper, James 298, 300
Cruttenden, Robert 44
Cumming, John 335

Dale, David 154
Defoe, Daniel 34-5, 339
Delaware 188
Dickinson, John 197
Disney, John 14, 444
Dissenting Academies 4, 19, 21, 37, 165-8, 173, 305, 399-408, 445, 452
    Abergavenny 326, 406
    Attercliffe 401
    Bristol 69-70, 73, 247, 321, 349, 403
    Brynllywarch 166, 400
    Carmarthen 166, 173, 402, 406
    Chancefield 167, 177
    Clerkenwell Green 37
    Daventry 322, 453
    Deptford 37
    Exeter 319, 402
    Findern 402
    Gosport 407
    Hoxton 48, 49
    Kendal 400
    Kibworth 40
    Llwyn-llwyd 177
    Mile End 70, 345
    Moorfields 37, 43, 401, 403
    Morton's, Newington Green 1, 400, 403
    Newport Pagnell 48, 49
    Northampton 40, 151, 288, 308-9, 402, 453
    Rotherham 51, 326
    Taunton 342, 400, 402
    Trefeca/Trevecca 47, 48, 230, 407

Trosnant 166
Warrington 288, 322, 404
Dissenting Deputies 13, 58, 277-82, 289, 296-7, 297-8, 388
Dissenting Ministers, General Body of (London) 24, 274, 278, 289, 293, 297
Doddridge, Philip 32, 39-43, 63, 247, 287, 308-9, 312, 316, 340, 346-7, 356, 368-9, 377, 389, 392, 440-1, 443, 444, 446, 447-8, 449, 452
Dow, Lorenzo 137, 228, 382
Drennan, Thomas 128
Drennan, William 134
Drysdale, A. H. 11
Dunlop, Samuel 126
Dutton, Anne 60, 63, 66
Dwight, Timothy 203, 238-9

Eames, John 37, 43, 403
East India Company 248, 249-50
Eddowes, Joshua 444-5
Edwards, Jonathan 22, 151, 204, 227, 230, 238, 247, 309, 323-5, 327, 446, 452
Education 70-1, 96-7, 164-5, 178-9, 386-410
Edwin, Humphrey 273-4
Ellwood, Thomas 393
Emans, Peter 345-6, 356
Embury, Philip 132
Emlyn, Thomas 342-3
Enfield, William 370
Enlightenment 3-4, 120, 126-32, 183-4, 361
Entwhistle, Joseph 227
Erskine, Ebenezer 145-9, 234
Erskine, John 150
Erskine, Ralph 145-9
Estlin, John Prior 288
Evangelical revival 43-7, 55, 61, 66-9, 126-32, 155-7, 168-72, 180, 192-6, 204, 225-42, 243
    Interconnectedness of 225-9
    In Scotland 233-6
    In Wales 236-8
Evans, Caleb 70, 72, 111, 338, 365, 369-70, 444
Evans, Christmas 72, 75, 171, 178
Evans, Hugh 69
Evans, John 12, 339
Exeter Assembly 16, 17, 18, 37, 275-6, 319

Family Expositor 40, 312, 440, 441, 448, 451
Fanch, James 65
Farmer, Hugh 40
Fawcett, Benjamin 27-8
Fawcett, John 67, 68, 70, 74
Fenner, Mary 447-9

Field, Henry 43
Finch, Daniel, earl of Nottingham 270, 275
Finney, Charles Grandison 213, 228–9
Fleming, Caleb 447
Fletcher, John 113, 232
Foskett, Bernard 69, 403
Foskett, Edward 321
Foster, James 341, 342
Ford, Richard 443
Fothergill, Thomas 97
Fox, Charles James 280, 281
Fox, George 81, 88, 93, 393, 414, 447
Fox, John 23
Fox, William 449
Frankland, Richard 400
Freeman, James 203
French Revolution 13, 47, 134, 155, 157, 238, 243, 249, 280, 293, 296, 301, 321, 323, 328, 337, 338
Freylinghuysen, Theodore 229–30
Friends *see* Quakers
Fry, Elizabeth xxi, 86–7, 97
Fryer, John 339
Fuller, Andrew 61, 64, 73, 74, 238, 245, 247, 255, 296, 323, 325–6
Fuller, Stephen 296

Gadsby, William 317
Gainsborough, Humphrey 43
Garrettson, Freeborn 211, 215
General (Arminian) Baptists 54, 55, 58, 59, 63, 308, 321
George I 274, 276, 389
George III 280, 281
George, David 211, 218
Georgia 185, 204, 229, 230–1, 371
Gill, John 60, 317, 326
Gillespie, Thomas 151
Glas, John 153–4
Glasites 66, 153–4
God, doctrine of 317–23
Goodwin, John 100
Grammar Schools 391–6
Grantham, Thomas 59
Greatheed, Samuel 49
Greenshields, James 143
Griffiths, Vavasor 166, 167
Grimshaw, William 68
Grove, Henry 342, 402, 444, 447
Gunston, Mary 35
Gurney, Martha 443, 448–9
Guyse, John 440, 452

Haldane, James 156, 234, 239, 255
Haldane, Robert 156, 234, 239, 255
Hall, Joseph 92

Hall, Robert 74, 309–10
Hallett, Joseph 37, 319, 402
Halliday, Samuel 126
Hamilton, Archibald 15
Happy Union (1691) 17, 28, 35
Hardy, Thomas 448
Harley, Robert 34
Harris, George 26
Harris, Howel 66, 168–72, 174, 177, 226, 228, 230–1, 233, 237, 323
Harris, William 341
Harrison, Elizabeth 444, 451
Hastings, Selina, countess of Huntingdon 45–7, 67, 102, 230, 295, 375
Hartopp, John 37–8
Haweis, Thomas 49, 215, 253
Hays, Mary 444
Heck, Barbara 132
Henry, Matthew 27, 312–14, 315, 317, 320, 440, 444–5, 449
Henry, Patrick 195–6
Henry, Philip 18
Heywood, Samuel 13, 28
Hicks, Elias 213
Hill, Hannah 450
Hill, Rowland 137, 381
Hoadley, Benjamin 276
Holden, Samuel 278
Hopkins, Samuel 203
Horne, Melvill[e] 249, 251
Horsley, John 15
Horsley, Samuel 294
Howe, John 17, 34–5
Howe, William 111
Hughes, Stephen 161–2, 164
Hume, David 230, 315
Hunt, Jeremiah 38
Huntingdon, Selina countess of *see* Hastings, Selina, countess of Huntingdon
Hussey, Joseph 1, 2, 7, 306
Hutcheson, Francis 128–9, 134
Hutchinson, Anne 186
Hutchinson, Lucy 450
Hymnody 3, 72, 108, 358–85, 442–3

Independents *see* Congregationalism
Ireland 271
    Dissent in 119–38
    Numerical strength 120–2

James II 38, 119–20, 139–40, 189, 269–70, 272
James, Thomas 15
Jebb, John 288
Jefferson, Thomas 196, 197–8
Jennings, John 40, 454
Jews 188, 192, 254

Johnson, Joseph 443–4
Jollie, Timothy 401
Jones, Griffith 167, 171, 178, 233, 236–7

Keach, Benjamin 57, 79, 359–60
Keen, Robert 48
Keighly, Sarah 322
Kelsall, John 83
Kempis, Thomas à 106, 107
Kenrick, Samuel 294–5
Kentucky 206
Kiffin, William 59
King, Boston 211
Kinghorn, Joseph 62
King's Head Society 37, 406
Kippis, Andrew 443
Kirkpatrick, James 124
Knibb, William 285, 297
Knollys, Hanserd 59
Knox, John 234

Lacey, John 68
Lancaster, Joseph 398–9
Lardner, Nathaniel 314–15, 320, 321, 446, 447
Law, William 105, 232
Leile, George 218
Leslie, Charles 78
Letsome, Sampson 333–6, 340
Lightfoot, John 311
Lindsey, Theophilus 63, 203, 321, 444
Livingstone, David 154
LMS *see* London Missionary Society
Lobb, Stephen 20
Locke, John 41–2, 183–4, 269, 308–9, 318, 324, 342
London Confession of Faith (1689) 56
London Missionary Society xvii, 49, 50, 51–2, 244, 245, 247–8, 251–3, 254, 255, 379
Losh, James 285, 300
Luther, Martin 31, 310

M'Crie, Thomas 11
McBride, John 124
McCracken, Alexander 124
McCulloch, William 235–6
McDowell, Benjamin 127, 131
MacMillan, James 141
Madan, Martin 369
Maine 202, 207
Makemie, Francis 190
Martin, William 130
Mary, queen 35, 38, 140, 189, 272
Maryland 185, 188
Massachusetts xix, 186, 190, 202, 203, 266
Maurice, Henry 161
Mayhew, Jonathan 203

Meeting Houses 2, 411–37
  Axial plans 434–6
  Colonial American 428–33
  English 421–7
  European models for 417–18
  New England experiments with 418–20
  Puritan Auditory Church and 414–17
  Reformed theology and architectural setting 412–14
Meidel, Christopher 79
Menzies, John 18
Merrick, James 370
Methodism xvii, xviii, xix, 5, 12, 13, 40, 44, 45, 49, 55, 66, 67, 68, 72, 99–115, 131–2, 137, 149, 158, 163, 168–72, 174, 175, 176–81, 200, 201, 206, 207, 213, 214, 216, 217, 218, 219, 220, 225–6, 228, 229, 230, 231, 232, 233, 239, 240–1, 246, 251, 253, 254, 285, 290, 294, 295, 296, 323, 329, 334, 349, 364, 376, 377, 378, 382, 383, 384, 396–8, 407, 427, 439, 441, 455
  American Revolutionary war and 110–12
  Hymns of 371–5
  In Ireland 131–2
  Mission and 102–4, 256–60
  Model deeds 109
  Nature of 104
  Organization of 107–12
  Printing 110
  Relationship with other Dissenters 100–2
  In Scotland 149–51
  Separation from Church of England 112–14
  Theology of 104–7
  In USA 209–12
  In Wales 168–72, 176–81, 230
Miles, John 162
Milton, John 36
Mission 3, 243–60, 378–9, 451
  In Bengal 246, 248
  In Cape Colony 229, 250
  In Ceylon 229
  In China 250
  In Greenland 229
  In Java 250
  In Sierra Leone 250, 256
  In Sumatra 250
  In Surinam 229
  In Tahiti 250, 254
  In West Indies 229, 244
Missionary Societies 243–60
  In USA 216, 246
Molther, Philip 231
Molther, William 106
Montgomery, James 379–81
Monthly Repository 26

Moore, John 63
Moravians 106, 131, 226, 231, 244, 371, 379
Morris, Joseph 343
Morton, Charles 1, 400

Nairn, Thomas 141
Nayler, James 88
Neal, Daniel 282, 355
Neville, Grey 38
New Connexion General Baptists 67, 70, 317, 326, 329
New Connexion Methodists 114
New Hampshire 202, 208
New Jersey 188, 213, 229
New York 185, 204, 213
Newton, Isaac 42, 43, 309
Newton, John 68–9, 71, 228, 239, 371, 377
Nicholson, Elizabeth 287
North Carolina 185, 188, 213
Nott, Henry 254

Occasional conformity 18, 34, 273–4
Ohio 208
Old Dissent xvi, xvii, 5, 13, 40, 61, 66, 70, 72, 73, 172, 180, 200, 209, 285, 323, 328, 329, 334, 337, 349, 351, 449
Oldmixon, John 282
Orton, Job 368, 392, 444–5, 450
Ousley, Gideon 137
Owen, John 38, 41
Owen, Robert 154

Paine, Thomas 448
Palmer, Samuel 450
Parliament
  Dublin 120, 271
  Edinburgh 140
  London 264–82, 289–301
Parsons, Samuel 37
Particular (Calvinistic) Baptists 54, 55, 56, 58, 59, 63, 111, 226, 243, 247, 290, 295, 296, 308, 316, 317, 321, 338, 448
  Particular Baptist Fund 65, 305, 403
Particular Baptist Society for the Propagation of the Gospel Amongst the Heathen *see* Baptist Missionary Society
Patronage, disputes over 2, 146–8
Patton, Isaac 130
Peckard, Peter 291
Peel, Robert 281
Peirce, James 24, 275–6, 319–20, 337, 402
Penn, William 81, 88, 188, 191, 393, 447
Pennsylvania 188, 192, 197, 204, 213, 291, 323
Peace campaigns 299–300
Perkins, William 59, 71
Petitioning 292–3

Phillips, James 291
Pietism 3
Pitt, William, the younger 280, 281, 292
Powell, John 170
Powell, Vavasor 161
Protestant Dissenting Deputies *see* Dissenting Deputies
Preaching
  Field 108, 141
  Lay 108
Presbyterianism xvi, xvii–xix, 2, 4–6, 11–28, 30, 31, 34, 35, 36, 37, 44, 48, 50, 58, 107, 108, 161, 166, 183, 184, 185, 187, 200, 202, 208, 209, 213, 214, 215, 217, 218–20, 229, 233, 246, 251, 252, 253, 256, 264, 270, 271, 273, 278, 289, 306, 308, 311, 319–20, 323, 329, 335, 337, 346, 370, 384, 386, 392, 396, 401, 405, 411, 418, 421, 424, 427, 428–31
  Anti-Burghers 129, 148, 157–8
  Burghers 129, 148, 157–8
  Cameronians 141–2
  Covenanters 130, 139
  Denominational boundaries 14, 18, 49, 161, 305–6
  Fund Board 14, 19, 35, 166–7, 305, 400, 402
  In Colonial USA 183–99
  Irish 120–1, 123–4, 126–32, 132–7, 276
  Laity 26–8
  New Light 127, 130
  Numerical strength 12–13
  Old Light 127, 130
  Relief Church 151–2
  Scottish 139–59, 276
  Secessions 28, 130, 145–9
  Theology of 19–26
  In USA 204–7
  Welsh 161–2
Price, Richard 21–2, 111, 167, 291, 309, 321, 338, 444
Priestley, Joseph 14, 22–3, 25–6, 33, 42, 204, 291, 293, 294, 309, 322–3, 404, 444
Primitive Methodists 228–9, 382–3
Print culture 4, 110, 163–4, 332–6, 438–56
Provoost, Samuel 203
Pugh, Phylip 162, 169–70

Quakers xvi, 5, 6–7, 77–98, 107, 108, 119, 120, 121, 122, 123, 152–3, 155, 158, 162–3, 264, 268, 271, 277–8, 289, 290, 291, 292, 299, 306, 307, 312, 329, 330, 334, 347, 350, 390, 393–6, 398, 411, 412, 414, 421, 427, 428, 429, 430, 431, 433, 439, 442, 443, 444, 447
  Anti-slavery campaigns and 93–5, 289–92
  Business and respectability 89–90

Denominational status 88–9
In colonial USA 183–99
Internal discipline of 82–7
In Ireland 120–2
London Yearly Meeting 79, 84, 289, 290
Meeting for Sufferings 81, 277
Oaths and Affirmation crisis 80–2
Pacifism of 77, 91–3
Schism and 87–9
In Scotland 152–3
Toleration and 78–80
In USA 212–13
In Wales 162–3

Randel, Benjamin 208
Rankin, Thomas 210
Rastrick, John 16, 19
Rational Dissent 13, 28
Rees, Abraham 443
Religious Tract Society 454–5
Remington, Mary 44
Renwick, James 141
Revivalism 3, 225–42 *see also* Evangelical Revival
Revivalist (Separate) Baptists 207–8
Reynolds, Thomas 17
Rhode Island 188, 191
Richardson, John 133
Riddell, John 124
Ridgley, Thomas 37
Rippon, John 69, 215, 370, 443
Robinson, Robert 62, 67, 293, 444
Roman Catholicism *see* Catholics
Rose, Samuel de la 27
Rowe, Elizabeth 41, 364–5, 444, 450
Rowe, Thomas 364, 401
Rowland, Daniel 168–72, 176, 178, 226, 228, 237, 326
Russell, Lord John 280, 281
Ryland, Frances Barrett 71
Ryland, John Snr 62, 64, 69, 71, 391, 403
Ryland, John Jnr 62, 64, 71, 74, 238, 249, 325, 326, 349, 379

Sacheverell, Henry 387
Sacraments 315–17
Saffrey, John 75
Sagar, Joshua 349
St John, Henry, Viscount Bolingbroke 230
Salters' Hall debates (1719) 14, 23, 28, 36, 58, 276, 309, 318–19, 329
Sandeman, Robert 154
Sandemanians 154, 188
Savage, Samuel 16
Savoy Declaration (1658) 23, 31, 308
Schools 452

Ackworth 96, 393–6
Bootham 394
Kibworth 391–3
Kingswood 396
Sidcot 96, 394
Wigton 96
Scotland xv, xix, 2, 139–59, 233–6, 255–6, 266
Scott, John, Lord Eldon 280
Scott, Mary 444
Scottish Episcopalians 142–5, 441
Scougal, Henry 335, 445
Scriptural interpretation 3, 293, 307, 310–15, 439–40
Seabury, Samuel 145, 203
Second Great Awakening 213–19, 238–9
Sermons 3, 72, 332–57, 438, 447
Seward, William 67
Sharp, Granville 284
Shaw, Ferdinando 337
Shower, John 350, 356
Sills, Melicent 441–2
Simson, John 145
Skepp, John 60
Slavery 217–18, 284–301
Sleap, James 441
Smeathman, Henry 42
Smith, John 297
Smith, John Pye 327, 406
Smith, Thomas Southwood 14
Smith, William 280, 297
Socinianism 11, 21, 58, 204, 268, 308, 317–18, 354
Society for Effecting the Abolition of the Slave Trade 291–2
Society for Promoting Religious Knowledge among the Poor 454
Society for Propagating the Gospel at Home 156
Society for Promoting Christian Knowledge (SPCK) 5, 164, 243–4, 245, 454
Society for the Propagation of the Gospel in Foreign Parts (SPG) 215, 243–4, 258, 430
Society in Scotland for Promoting Christian Knowledge (SSPCK) 245
Sola Scriptura 310–15
South Carolina 185, 188, 204
Sowle, Jane 443, 447–8
Sowle, Tace 443, 447–8, 449
Spangenberg, August Gottlieb 108
Steadman, William 72, 75
Steele, Anne 64, 72, 365–6, 370, 377, 443, 450
Stennett, Joseph 359–60, 370
Stennett, Samuel 72–3, 339, 370

Sterne, Laurence 288
Stogdon, Hubert 22, 319
Stone, Barton 206
Sturge, Joseph 300
Subscription controversies 6, 263-4
Sunday Schools 178-9, 381, 396-8
Sutcliff, John 64, 74, 238, 247-8, 325
Swertner, John 375
Swift, Jonathan 33-4, 125

Taylor, Abraham 37
Taylor, Dan 67, 70, 73, 326
Taylor, Jeremy 106, 232
Taylor, John 22, 23, 27
Tenison, Thomas 78
Tennent, Gilbert 194, 229, 230
Theology 19-26, 104-7, 305-31, 341-2
Thirty-Nine Articles xviii, 14, 23, 25, 31, 46, 101, 109, 126, 270-1, 279, 305
Thomas, John 75
Thomas, Micah 70
Thompson, John 38
Thomson, Andrew 293
Thornton, Henry 296
Thoyras, Paul de Rapin de 282
Tisdall, William 124
Tithes 6, 77, 83, 122, 124, 133, 189, 277, 287, 289
Toleration 183-99, 263-82
Tomkins, Martin 23
Tone, Theobald Wolfe 135
Toplady, Augustus 232, 369, 377
Tories 124-5, 272-4
Towers, Joseph 336-7, 346, 354, 356
Towgood, Micaiah 25
Towgood, Stephen 17
Townshend, Charles, second Viscount 275
Trimmer, Sarah 444
Trinder, Martha 71
Turner, Daniel 62, 65, 370

Unitarianism 6, 11, 32, 36, 63, 173-4, 247, 264, 309, 329-30, 343, 356, 384
    Fund Board 26
    In USA 201-4

Virginia 184-5, 188, 208
Virginia Statute (1786) 196, 198, 291
Virginia Company 184

Wake, William 106
Wakefield, Gilbert 14
Wakefield, Priscilla 393
Wales 5, 160-82, 236-8, 390, 444-5
Wallin, Benjamin 370
Walpole, Robert 275, 277, 292
Ware, Henry 203

Watts, Isaac 32, 38, 39-43, 247, 309, 316, 320, 359, 362-4, 369, 376, 383, 392, 401, 443, 444, 446, 449, 452
Waugh, Alexander 252-3, 255
Waugh, James 444, 446, 447-8
Wedgwood, Josiah 291
Welsh Calvinistic Methodists 174, 176-81, 226, 230
Welsh Trust 164, 445, 451
Wesley, Charles 5, 44, 99, 104, 108, 111, 114, 174, 228, 229-31, 323, 364, 371-5, 383, 443
Wesley, John 5, 22, 44, 45, 99-115, 132, 149-50, 174-5, 209, 225-6, 228, 229-31, 235-6, 239, 257-8, 323, 364, 371-5, 441
Wesley, Samuel 364, 387
Wesley, Susanna 364
Wesleyan Methodism 55, 68, 99-115, 174, 181, 211, 239, 256-9, 290, 334
Wesleyan Methodist Missionary Society 246, 256-9
West, Daniel 48
Westminster Confession (1646) 19, 23, 31, 126, 140, 142, 205, 308
Whigs 125, 272-4
Whiston, William 319-20
White, Esther 194
Whitefield, George 40, 44, 45, 55, 67, 101, 108, 111, 131, 149-50, 174, 201, 209, 228, 229-31, 232, 234-5, 295, 323, 349, 375, 445
Whitehead, George 81, 88
Whitty, Thomas 38
Widows Fund 59
Wilberforce, William 94, 228, 239, 284, 286, 287
Wilkinson, Moses 211
William III 1-2, 38, 81, 120, 140, 189, 243, 269-70, 272, 281, 337, 387
Williams, Daniel 19-20, 26, 402
Williams, David 170
Williams, Edward 326-7
Williams, Helena Maria 294
Williams, Joseph 27, 40
Williams, Moses 165
Williams, Roger 186
Williams, William, Pantycelyn 172-3, 176-7, 238
Wilson, James 133
Wilson, Joshua 45, 49-50
Wilson, Thomas 44, 45, 49
Witherspoon, John 128, 205
Woolman, John 94, 290
Woolston, Thomas 341
Wright, Richard 26

Zinzendorf, Nicholas count of 106, 229, 247